Charles Henry Anderson

**A Digest of the Principles and Practice of Common Law**

conveyancing, equity, bankrupty, and criminal law. Vol. 1

Charles Henry Anderson

**A Digest of the Principles and Practice of Common Law**
*conveyancing, equity, bankrupty, and criminal law. Vol. 1*

ISBN/EAN: 9783337123383

Printed in Europe, USA, Canada, Australia, Japan

Cover: Foto ©Suzi / pixelio.de

More available books at **www.hansebooks.com**

# A DIGEST

OF THE PRINCIPLES AND PRACTICE OF

# COMMON LAW, CONVEYANCING,

# EQUITY, BANKRUPTCY

AND

# CRIMINAL LAW.

BY

CHARLES HENRY ANDERSON, Esq.,

OF THE INNER TEMPLE, BARRISTER AT LAW;
LECTURER AND READER IN COMMON LAW TO THE INCORPORATED LAW SOCIETY;
INNS OF COURT EXHIBITIONER, AND SENIOR JULY EXHIBITIONER.

VOL. I.

LONDON:
STEVENS AND SONS,
Law Booksellers and Publishers,
26, BELL-YARD, LINCOLNS INN.

1867.

# PREFACE.

The First Volume of this work (published November, 1865) has met with such success, that I have been induced to publish a Second Volume, including the whole of the Questions and Answers on Bankruptcy and the Criminal Law to this date. An Addenda to the First Volume, including many new Questions and the legal alterations of last Session, brings that also to the present time. In the preparation of the Bankruptcy Answers and the Index to the Second Volume, I have received most valuable assistance from my friend, Mr. JOHN SCOTT.

CHARLES H. ANDERSON.

7, KING'S BENCH WALK,
    *Michaelmas Term*, 1867.

# CONTENTS OF VOL. I.

A DIGEST OF ALL THE EXAMINATION QUESTIONS AND ANSWERS IN THE COMMON LAW.

|  | PAGE |
|---|---|
| I. Nature of the Jurisprudence administered by, and the distinctive jurisdictions of, the Common Law Tribunals | 1 |
| II. The Right of Personal Liberty | 3 |
| III. Actions, their Nature, Forms, and Characteristics | 3 |
| IV. The Law of Contracts | 7 |
| V. Bills of Exchange, Promissory Notes, and Bankers' Cheques | 21 |
| VI. Landlord and Tenant | 27 |
| VII. The Law of Torts or Private Wrongs | 30 |
| VIII. The Attorney and his Client | 35 |
| IX. The three considerations preliminary to bringing an action:— | |
|     (1) The Statutes of Limitation or Repose | 37 |
|     (2) The proper Parties to an Action | 39 |
|     (3) The Notice required before Action | 44 |
| X. Tender before Action | 44 |
| XI. The Citation of the Defendant | 45 |
| XII. The Defendant's Appearance | 50 |
| XIII. Affidavits | 51 |
| XIV. The Arrest of the Defendant on Mesne Process and the Law of Bail | 56 |
| XV. The Venue or Locus in quo | 56 |
| XVI. The Pleadings or Contending Statements of the Litigants | 56 |
| XVII. Collateral Proceedings, Orders, and Rules | 69 |
| XVIII. Evidence—Notices to inspect and admit, and to produce—Witnesses—Verbal Proofs—Documental Testimony | 72 |
| XIX. Consequences of a Plaintiff neglecting to proceed | 81 |
| XX. Notice of Trial and Computation of Time | 82 |
| XXI. The Trial at Nisi Prius, with its Incidents | 83 |
| XXII. Trial before the Under-Sheriff | 86 |
| XXIII. New Trial—Arrest of Judgment—Judgment *Non obstante veredicto*—Error | 86 |
| XXIV. Judgment and its Registration | 89 |
| XXV. Expensæ Litis | 94 |
| XXVI. The Writs of Execution | 103 |
| XXVII. Steps in an Action | 109 |
| XXVIII. The Mixed Action of Ejectment | 110 |
| XXIX. Action for Mesne Profits | 114 |
| XXX. Redress of private Wrong by the injured Party himself taking a Distress | 114 |

## CONTENTS

|  |  | PAGE |
|---|---|---|
| XXXI. | The Tort Action of Replevin | 118 |
| XXXII. | The Practice under a Warrant of Attorney, Cognovit Actionem, or a Judge's Order for Judgment | 120 |
| XXXIII. | Arbitration and Award | 123 |
| XXXIV. | The Interpleader Act (1 & 2 Wm. IV., c. 58) | 125 |
| XXXV. | Contempt of Court | 126 |
| XXXVI. | Outlawry | 127 |
| XXXVII. | The Inferior Tribunals | 128 |
| XXXVIII. | Highways | 131 |

### A DIGEST OF ALL THE EXAMINATION QUESTIONS AND ANSWERS IN CONVEYANCING.

|  |  | |
|---|---|---|
| I. | Introductory | 132 |
| II. | Classification of Things | 132 |
| III. | The Tenures | 134 |
| IV. | Quantity of Estate | 135 |
| V. | Quality of Estate | 148 |
| VI. | Tangible and Non-tangible Property | 153 |
| VII. | Copyholds | 157 |
| VIII. | Uses, Trusts, and Powers | 161 |
| IX. | Terms and their Merger | 170 |
| X. | Personalty in Suspense | 172 |
| XI. | The Evidence of ownership | 174 |
| XII. | Baron and Feme | 175 |
| XIII. | Infancy | 182 |
| XIV. | Settlements | 182 |
| XV. | Artificial Persons | 190 |
| XVI. | Bankrupt-Owner | 190 |
| XVII. | Landlord and Tenant, and the Law of Leases | 190 |
| XVIII. | Fructus Industriales | 199 |
| XIX. | Pledges securing Loans | 200 |
| XX. | Vendor and Vendee | 210 |
| XXI. | Judgments as they affect Realty | 226 |
| XXII. | The Essentials of Deeds | 228 |
| XXIII. | Alienation by act inter vivos | 231 |
| XXIV. | Registration and Enrolment of Deeds, etc. | 239 |
| XXV. | Posthumous destination of Property | 241 |
| XXVI. | Trustees | 254 |
| XXVII. | Executors and Administration | 255 |
| XXVIII. | Intestacy, and its consequences | 258 |
| XXIX. | Assets and Debts | 264 |

### A DIGEST OF ALL THE EXAMINATION QUESTIONS AND ANSWERS IN EQUITY.

|  |  | |
|---|---|---|
| I. | Nature and Object matter of Equity Jurisprudence | 266 |
| II. | The Equity Fora, their Judges and Officers | 272 |
| III. | The Statutory Jurisdiction | 274 |

## CONTENTS.

|  |  | PAGE |
|---|---|---|
| IV. | The Specially-Delegated Jurisdiction | 278 |
| V. | The Equity or Extraordinary Jurisdiction. | |
| | (I.) As it is Assistant or Auxiliary:— | |
| | (a) Discovery | 279 |
| | (b) Preservation of Testimony | 281 |
| | (c) Restraining Common Law Judgments | 282 |
| | (II.) As it is Concurrent:— | |
| | (a) Fraud | 282 |
| | (b) Prevention of Fraud | 287 |
| | (c) Accident and mistake with the doctrine of Cy près or Approximation | 293 |
| | (d) Account | 296 |
| | (e) Delivery of specific Chattels | 297 |
| | (f) Specific Performance of Contracts | 297 |
| | (III.) As it is Exclusive:— | |
| | (a) Trusts and the Administration of Assets | 306 |
| | (b) Infancy | 326 |
| | (c) The Equitable Rights of Wives | 329 |
| | (d) Legal and Equitable Mortgages | 334 |
| | (e) Partition | 339 |
| | (f) Charities or Public Trusts | 339 |
| VI. | Notices | 340 |
| VII. | Retainer and Commencement of Litigation | 342 |
| VIII. | Appearance | 355 |
| IX. | The Defence | 357 |
| | § 1. Answer | 358 |
| | § 2. Demurrer | 362 |
| | § 3. Plea | 363 |
| | § 4. Disclaimer | 365 |
| X. | Amendment of Bills | 365 |
| XI. | Equitable Bail in aid of the concurrent Jurisdiction of Equity | 367 |
| XII. | Nemo debet bis vexari pro eâdem causâ | 368 |
| XIII. | Receivers | 368 |
| XIV. | Replication | 369 |
| XV. | Dismissing Suits | 370 |
| XVI. | Evidence | 372 |
| XVII. | Setting down Causes | 379 |
| XVIII. | The Hearing | 380 |
| XIX. | Legal Rights, Doubtful Facts, and Damages | 382 |
| XX. | Motion for Decree, Decrees, and their Enforcement | 383 |
| XXI. | Appeals | 386 |
| XXII. | Funds in Court, Stock, etc. | 388 |
| XXIII. | Costs | 391 |
| XXIV. | Business at Chambers | 394 |
| XXV. | Motions and Petitions | 399 |
| XXVI. | Contumacy | 401 |
| XXVII. | Miscellaneous and General | 401 |

### APPENDIX.

Directions to be observed before and at the Final Examination . . 405

# CONTENTS OF VOL. II.

### A DIGEST OF ALL THE EXAMINATION QUESTIONS AND ANSWERS IN BANKRUPTCY.

|  | PAGE |
|---|---|
| I. The Bankruptcy Laws | 1 |
| II. The Court, their Jurisdiction, Officers, and Procedure | 2 |
| III. Persons liable to be made Bankrupt:— | |
|    (a) Generally | 5 |
|    (b) As Traders only | 7 |
| IV. The Acts of Bankruptcy | 9 |
| V. Proceedings relating to Adjudication in Bankruptcy:— | |
|    (a) Petitioning Creditors | 13 |
|    (b) Proceedings by Petition | 16 |
|    (c) Trader Debtor Summons | 20 |
|    (d) Judgment Debtor Summons | 21 |
|    (e) The Adjudication and its Incidents | 21 |
|    (f) Showing cause against, appealing from, annulling, and superseding Adjudication | 22 |
| VI. Effect of the Adjudication:— | |
|    (a) On the Property of the Bankrupt | 24 |
|    (b) On Persons having Dealings with the Bankrupt | 29 |
| VII. Administering the Estate:— | |
|    (a) Assignees and their Duties | 38 |
|    (b) Proof of Debts | 43 |
|    (c) As to Creditors having Security or Priority | 49 |
|    (d) Dividends | 52 |
|    (e) Joint and Separate Estate | 53 |
| VIII. The Bankrupt; his Rights, Duties, Liabilities, and Discharge | 54 |
| IX. Proceedings incidental to Bankruptcy:— | |
|    (a) Generally | 62 |
|    (b) Of Change from Bankruptcy to Arrangement | 64 |
| X. Trust Deeds, Deeds of Assignment, Composition, and Inspectorship | 65 |

### A DIGEST OF ALL THE EXAMINATION QUESTIONS AND ANSWERS IN THE CRIMINAL LAW.

|  | |
|---|---|
| I. Preliminary | 68 |
| II. Crimes and their Natures. | |
|    (a) Generally | 69 |
|    (b) Treason | 72 |
|    (c) Homicide | 74 |

## CONTENTS.

|   |   | PAGE |
|---|---|---|
| (d) Burglary | | 77 |
| (e) Larceny, Embezzlement, and obtaining Money under False Pretences | | 79 |
| (f) Arson and other Injuries to Property | | 91 |
| (g) Piracy | | 92 |
| (h) Bigamy | | 93 |
| (i) Forgery | | 93 |
| (j) Perjury | | 95 |
| (k) Conspiracy | | 97 |
| (l) Libel and Slander | | 98 |
| (m) Miscellaneous Offences | | 99 |
| III. Criminal Responsibility | | 104 |
| IV. Kinds and Degrees of Offenders | | 106 |
| V. Criminal Procedure. | | |
| (a) Courts and their Jurisdiction | | 107 |
| (b) Summary Jurisdiction of Justices | | 112 |
| (c) Arrest | | 119 |
| (d) Preliminary Enquiry and Committal | | 120 |
| (e) Indictment | | 122 |
| (f) Venue | | 125 |
| (g) Evidence | | 126 |
| (h) Trial and Conviction | | 137 |
| (i) Appeal | | 143 |
| (j) Punishment | | 147 |
| (k) Incidental Procedure | | 152 |
| VI. Civil Jurisdiction of Justices of the Peace. | | |
| (a) Poor Laws | | 156 |
| (b) Highways | | 159 |
| (c) Bastards | | 161 |
| (d) Landlord and Tenant | | 162 |
| (e) Master and Servant | | 162 |
| (f) Licenses | | 163 |
| (g) Church Rates | | 163 |
| VII. The Office of the Coroner | | 163 |

# ERRATA ET ADDENDA

(*Comprising New Questions asked since the publication of this Volume, also Questions on the Acts of* 30 & 31 *Vic.*)

───◆───

## COMMON LAW.

*Page* 1, No. 2, *for* 8 & 9 Vic., c. 106, *read* 8 & 9 Vic., c. 109.

*Page* 2. Q. What are the duties of the masters of the Superior Courts?

A. They are to tax bills of costs, preside at references, draw up rules, examine witnesses under a judge's order, pursuant to 1 Wm. IV., c. 22, s. 4, and under the 46th and other sections of the C. L. P. Act 1854. By 30 & 31 Vic., c. 68, power is given to the judges to make rules empowering the masters to transact at Chambers business which the judges themselves now dispose of. The order of the master is subject to appeal to the judge. The masters, also, frequently have referred to them cases of attornies charged with mal-practice, in order to report to the Court thereon. One of their number usually presides at the examination of articled clerks.

*Page* 13. Q. In what cases is an agent liable on contracts entered into for a principal, and what is the meaning of a *del credere* agent?

A. As a rule, an agent is not liable upon any agreement into which he enters merely in his representative capacity; but whenever an agent enters personally into a contract, or pledges his own credit by concealing his principal, or otherwise, this gives the other party a right of action against him. And whenever he enters in his own name into an agreement in writing, he cannot relieve himself from this liability even by showing that at the time such agreement was made the other contracting party knew that he was only an agent. An agent is also personally liable whenever he knowingly exceeds his authority, provided that his want of authority be not known to the person with whom he deals; also, if he fraudulently misrepresents his authority; also, where he contracts under seal in his own name. A *del credere* agent is one who acts for a higher reward than is usually given, and becomes responsible to his principal for the solvency of the vendee, or, in other words, he guarantees in every case of sale the due payment of the price of the goods sold. Chit. Cont., 193—210.

*Page* 13. *Q.* If a guarantee is given to several persons who are not themselves interested in the subject-matter of the guarantee, who must be the parties to sue on the guarantee?
*A.* As a general rule, the parties interested only can sue upon a guarantee. In other words, the parties from whom the consideration moves must be plaintiffs. Thus, if A gives a guarantee to B and C, for a debt due to them by D, in consideration that B and C will forbear to sue D, the consideration is the inconvenience B and C are put to by forbearing to proceed. A benefit is also conferred upon D by an act moving from B to C. They must, therefore, sue; any other parties would be strangers to the consideration. From this it will be obvious that a guarantee given to persons not interested would be useless, excepting in the case of principal and agent. For if the guarantee were given to agents, the principal, if disclosed, could sue, or if undisclosed, the principal or the agents might sue. Also, if a guarantee is given to one partner, the whole firm may sue upon it, if there be evidence that it was given for the benefit of all. This, too, is on the principle of agency. Chit. Cont., 53; Bullen & Leake, 198; Sm. Merc. Law, 155.

*Page* 13, No. 32, *for* 14 *read* 4.

*Page* 14. *Q.* If an agent agrees to act for a firm in partnership for a term of years, is the contract dissolved by the death of one of the partners during the term?
*A.* The partnership is dissolved by the death of one of the firm, therefore the authority of the agent also determines. Chit. Cont., 237, 195.

*Page* 18, No. 59, *for* money lost *read* money lent.

*Page* 19. *Q.* Is a contract of hiring and service between master and servant dissolved by the death of master?
*A.* As a general rule, by the death of the master the servant is discharged, the contract being one of a personal nature. Wms. Exors., 644.

*Page* 19, No. 63, *for* Midsummer, 1864, *read* Midsummer, 1854.

*Lien.*

*Page* 19. *Q.* Has the agister of cattle any right of lien on the cattle agisted? State the reason.
*A.* He has no lien. The reason is that a lien only exists in cases where an individual has bestowed labour and skill in the alteration and improvement of the properties of the subject delivered to him. This is not the case in an agistment. The term is probably little known to north countrymen. It is analogous to a cattle gate. Sm. Merc. Law, 559.

# ERRATA ET ADDENDA.

*Page* 19. *Q.* Is a workman who detains a chattel in exercise of his right of lien, entitled to charge warehouse rent for keeping the chattel?
*A.* He has no such right. The lien merely extends to his claim for work. *Somes* v. *The British Empire Shipping Company*, 30 L. J., Q. B., 229.

## Bills of Exchange.

*Page* 23. *Q.* A sues B for a debt simply. B pleads a bill of exchange given in payment which A has lost. What course should you advise A to pursue?
*A.* If the bill is not negotiable, the defendant must show by his plea that it is still running. *Price* v. *Price*, 16 M. & W., 232. If it be still running, the plaintiff cannot recover on the consideration, as by taking the bill he in effect gives credit until it is due; and he should, therefore, discontinue; but if it was overdue at the commencement of the action, he may recover on either the bill or the consideration. If the bill is shown to have been negotiable, that fact is an answer to the declaration on the consideration; but the plaintiff may reply that the bill had never been indorsed away; and was overdue at the commencement of the action, or he might get leave to amend his declaration by adding a count on the bill; and by C. L. P. Act 1854, the defendant could be restrained from setting up the loss of the bill, provided a proper indemnity was given. It is assumed that the bill had not been negotiated.

*Page* 23, *No.* 12, *line* 1 *of Answer, for* 18 and Vic. *read* 18 & 19 Vic.

*Page* 29, *No.* 13, *for* 14 & 15 Vic., c. 23, *read* 14 & 15 Vic., c. 25.

## Torts.

*Page* 35. *Q.* What was decided in the "Six Carpenters' Case"?
*A.* It was decided, that if a man abuse an authority given him by the law, he becomes a trespasser *ab initio*. Thus, if one enters an inn for refreshment, and then carries away goods of the landlord, he may be treated and sued as a trespasser, although his original entry was legal. The hardship this doctrine created, in the case of distress for rent, led to 11 Geo. II., c. 19, s. 19, which enacts that, where a distress is made for rent due, and any irregularity is afterwards done by the party distraining, he shall not be liable as a trespasser, but merely for special damage occasioned by the wrongful act. 1 Sm. L. C., 128.

*Page* 35. *Q.* In an action for an injury caused by the bite of a savage dog, what may the defendant put the plaintiff to prove in support of his action?
*A.* The plaintiff must prove what is termed a *scienter*. In other words, it must appear that the dog had savage propensities, to the knowledge of the owner. The declaration must also allege this *scienter*, or it will be demurrable. *Stiles* v. *Cardiff Steam Navigation*, 33 L. J., Q. B., 310.

*Page* 54, *No.* 11, *line* 2 *of Answer, for* bail below *read* bail above.

*Page* 57, *No.* 6, *line* 5 *of Answer, for* defendant *read* plaintiff.

*Page* 61, *No.* 26, *line* 2 *of Answer, for* declaration *read* pleas.

*Page* 62, *No.* 34, *for* C. L. P. Act 1852, *read* C. L. P. Act 1860.

*Pleadings.*

*Page* 64. *Q.* Can a feme covert, sued alone, appear by attorney; and if she succeeds on a plea of coverture, to what costs is she entitled?

*A.* She must appear in person, as she cannot appoint an attorney. It is doubtful whether she is entitled to costs out of pocket only or to costs generally. In the Queen's Bench, she is entitled only to the former. 2 Chitty's Archbold, 1243.

*Page* 67, *No.* 62, *line* 1 *of Answer, for* defendant *read* plaintiff.

*Page* 68, *No.* 69, *for* C. L. P. Act 1852, *read* C. L. P. Act 1854.

*Collateral Proceedings.*

*Page* 70. *Q.* When particulars of demand are endorsed on the writ, can any other particulars be delivered with the declaration?

*A.* No other particulars need be delivered without order of the Court or a Judge. And it seems that a delivery of particulars without such an order would be irregular. C. L. P. Act 1852, s. 25; Chitty's Archbold, 1437.

*Page* 70. *Q.* Under what circumstances can a defendant obtain an order for particulars in an action of trespass, and how?

*A.* An order may be obtained if an affidavit be produced, showing that the defendant does not know for what the plaintiff is proceeding. Also other special circumstances will do to ground the application  The application is by summons to a Judge, or to the Court by rule. Ibid., 1440.

*New Trial, etc.*

*Page* 86. *Q.* If points of law are reserved at *nisi prius*, state the usual steps by which they are subsequently disposed of.

*A.* The party in whose favour the points are reserved should move the Court, sitting in banc, to enter the verdict or nonsuit in his favour, pursuant to leave reserved. A rule *nisi* is obtained, and then made absolute, or discharged on argument before the full Court. The Judge's notes taken at the trial should be in Court, for which purpose application should be made to the Judge's clerk. Chitty's Archbold, 1517.

*Page* 86. By 30 & 31 Vic., c. 142, a writ of trial is abolished.

## Judgment.

*Page* 89. *Q.* What is the effect of the plaintiff, in an action *ex contractu* against several defendants, entering a *nolle prosequi* as to one of the defendants?

*A.* The other defendants will be released, unless the one against whom the *nolle prosequi* is entered has pleaded a plea which goes to his *personal discharge*, such as bankruptcy. The plaintiff will have to pay the costs to the defendants or defendant. Chitty's Archbold, 1500.

## Costs.

*Page* 100. *Q.* What is the rule as to costs, where a plaintiff in a Superior Court recovers not exceeding £20 on contract, or not exceeding £10 on tort?

*A.* He will get no costs in either case, unless the Judge certify on the record that there was sufficient reason for bringing such action in a Superior Court, or unless the Court, or a Judge at Chambers, shall by rule or order allow such costs. This enactment applies to verdicts, judgments by default, or on demurrer. 30 & 31 Vic., c. 142, s. 5.

*Page* 100. *Q.* Upon what scale will the above costs be taxed?

*A.* In the action on contract, the costs will be taxed on the lower scale, unless the Judge certify on the *postea* that the cause was proper to be tried before him, and not before the Judge of an Inferior Court ("Directions to the Masters," H. T., 1853). In actions of tort, there is no lower scale.

*Page* 101. *Q.* What is the rule as to costs, when money is paid into Court in respect of any particular sum or cause of action, and is accepted by the plaintiff in satisfaction, there being issues in respect of other causes of action?

*A.* The plaintiff, when the costs are taxed, is entitled to the costs of the cause in respect of that part of the claim so satisfied up to the time the money is taken out, whatever may be the result of the other issues. If the defendant succeed in defeating the residue of the claim, he will be entitled to the costs of the cause in respect of such defence, commencing at "Instructions for Plea," Rule 12; H. T., 1853. If the plaintiff chooses, he may enter a *nolle prosequi* as to the other issues, upon which the defendant would be entitled to costs. 2 Chitty's Archbold, 1501, 11th ed.

*Page* 103. *Q.* What length of notice at Common Law of taxing costs is required?

*A.* One day's notice of taxation is necessary. A copy of the bill and affidavit of increase must accompany the notice. Rule 59; H. T., 1853.

*Page* 103. *Q.* What is the effect, as regards recovery of costs, as against client and adverse party respectively, of the attorney omitting to take out his certificate?

*A.* By the joint operation of 37 Geo. III., c. 90, and 6 & 7 Vic., c. 73, an attorney is disabled from recovering his fees for business done while he is without a proper certificate to practise, and he is liable to a penalty of £50, and has no lien for such business. But the fact of an attorney being uncertificated does not deprive the client of his right to costs against the opposite party to the extent of advances made by the client, where they have been made in ignorance of his attorney being uncertificated; where, however, the client has made no advances, the want of a certificate is a good defence by the opposite party. The objection to the want of a certificate must be taken at the taxation, it cannot be made a distinct ground for setting aside the taxation. *Fullalove* v. *Parker*, 31 L. J., C. P., 239.

### Execution.

*Page* 105. *Q.* How long do writs of execution remain in force after issuing?
*A.* One year; and if renewed, one year from renewal. C. L. P. Act 1852, s. 54.

### Replevin.

*Page* 119. *Q.* In a replevin suit in the County Court, can any other cause of action be joined in the summons?
*A.* No other cause of action can be joined in the same summons.

### Bills of Sale.

*Page* 122. *Q.* Is it necessary to renew the registration of a bill of sale which has once been duly registered under the Bill of Sale Act; and, if so, how often should such registration be renewed?
*A.* The registration of a bill of sale, registered under the "Bill of Sale Act 1854," must, during the subsistence of the security, be renewed once in every period of five years, commencing from the day of registration. 29 & 30 Vic., c. 96, s. 4.

### County Courts.

*Page* 128. *Q.* A, having obtained a County Court judgment against B for an amount exceeding £20, finds that B has no goods within the jurisdiction of the County Court, but has goods beyond such jurisdiction, how can he satisfy his judgment out of such last-mentioned goods?
*A.* On application to a Judge of a Superior Court, a writ of *certiorari* may be obtained to remove the judgment of the County Court into one of the Superior Courts, and when removed, execution may be issued thereon. 19 & 20 Vic., c. 108, s. 49. Also a

warrant of execution issued from the County Court in which judgment was recovered, may be transmitted to be executed in the jurisdiction of the Court in which the goods may be. 9 & 10 Vic., c. 95, s. 104; *infra,* 119.

*Page* 128. *Q.* Out of what County Court may a summons now issue, and is leave ever necessary?

*A.* A plaint may be entered in the County Court within the district of which the defendant, or one of the defendants, shall dwell or carry on business at the time of action brought, or by leave of the Judge or registrar where the defendant dwelt or carried on business at any time within six months, or in the district of which the cause of action or suit wholly or in part arose. 30 & 31 Vic., c. 142, s. 1.

*Page* 128. *Q.* In what case may a Judge of a Superior Court order a cause to be tried in a County Court?

*A.* In actions of contract not exceeding £50, or where the amount, though it originally exceeded £50, is reduced by payment, or admitted set-off, to not exceeding £50. To obtain the order, the defendant must apply by summons within eight days after service of the writ. The costs up to the removal are regulated by the scale of the Superior Court, but afterwards by that of the County Court. 30 & 31 Vic., c. 142, s. 7.

*Page* 128. *Q.* Does the power of the Judge extend to actions of tort?

*A.* By the same act, section 10, actions for malicious prosecution, illegal arrest, illegal distress, assault, false imprisonment, libel, slander, seduction, or other action of tort, may be ordered to be tried in the County Court. No order, however, will be made if the defendant makes an affidavit that the plaintiff has no visible means of paying the costs of the defendant, and the plaintiff thereupon, pursuant to order, gives security for costs; *or* if the plaintiff satisfy the Judge that he has a cause of an action fit to be prosecuted in the Superior Court.

*Page* 128. *Q.* Has the jurisdiction of the County Court been recently extended?

*A.* Yes; independently of the preceding answers, actions of ejectment, where neither the value of the lands, nor the rent payable, exceeds £20 per annum, may be brought in the County Court of the district where the lands are situate. Also with a similar limit as to value, actions where the title to corporeal or incorporeal hereditaments come in question, may be brought in the County Court. But the defendant may, within one month from the service of process, apply to a Judge to have the action tried in a Superior Court, on the ground that the property is of greater value. 30 & 31 Vic., c. 142, s. 12.

*Page* 128. *Q.* Is an appeal allowed in the above cases?

*A.* An appeal is allowed in cases of ejectment, and where the title to land is in question. Also, with leave of the Judge, an appeal is allowed in all actions in which an appeal is not now allowed, if he think it reasonable and proper. 30 & 31 Vic., c. 142, s. 13.

*Page* 131. *Q.* Has any amendment recently been made in 28 & 29 Vic., c. 99? (*infra*, 131).

*A.* By 30 & 31 Vic., c. 142, s. 8, provision is made for the removal from the Court of Chancery to the County Court of proceedings which might have been commenced therein. Also the jurisdiction of the County Court as to specific performance is extended to all suits for specific performance of, or for the reforming, delivering up, or cancelling any agreement for the sale, purchase, or lease of any property, where, in the case of a purchase, the purchase-money does not exceed £500, or, in case of a lease, the value of the property does not exceed that sum (section 9, re-enacting clause 4 of sec. 1 of 28 & 29 Vic., c. 99). Also by section 24 of 30 & 31 Vic., c. 142, trustees may pay trust moneys into the County Court where the same do not exceed £500, in a similar manner to the proceedings under 10 & 11 Vic., c. 96. If money is paid in, it is to be invested in the Post Office Savings' Bank of the town where the County Court is held.

## CONVEYANCING.

### *Real Property.*

*Page* 134. *Q.* When lands adjoin a river, to whom does the soil of the river presumptively belong, and does it make any difference whether the river be a tidal one or no?

*A.* Where lands adjoin a river the soil of one-half of the river to the middle of the stream is presumed to belong to the owner of the adjoining lands. But if it be a tidal river, the soil up to high water mark appears presumptively to belong to the Crown. Wms. R. P., 294.

### *Estates Tail.*

*Page* 142. *Q.* If a tenant in fee simple contracts to make a conveyance, and dies before it is made, equity will enforce the contract against his heir. Is there a like equity as to the contract of a tenant in tail? Give a reason for your answer.

*A.* The heir is not bound; the reason being that 3 & 4 Wm. IV., c. 74, s. 40, enacts to this effect, in analogy to the Common Law rule on the subject. This rule arose from the fact that the heir was not bound by his ancestor's contracts, inasmuch as the heir did not inherit from the ancestor, but from the donor of the estate tail. Shelford's R. P. Stats., 364.

### *Incorporeal Hereditaments.*

*Page* 154. *Q.* On appointment of a fit clerk to a living, state generally what forms must be gone through in case of an advowson presentative and of an advowson donative?

*A.* In the case of the advowson presentative, the patron presents the fit clerk, whom the Bishop is bound to institute to the benefice. Institution is an investiture of the spiritual part of the benefice. He is then inducted into the living, which is commonly called "being read in." It is performed by a mandate from the Bishop to the Archdeacon. Corporeal possession is given to the clerk, by holding the ring of the door or tolling the bell. In the case of the donative the patron's deed is alone sufficient. Wms. R. P., 305.

*Page* 154. *Q.* What are the obligations and rights of a lay rector with reference to the chancel of the parish church?
*A.* He is bound to keep the chancel in repair. He cannot make a grant of it. He is not entitled, as of right, to make a vault or affix tablets in the chancel without leave of the ordinary. His rights are that he has the freehold in him, and is entitled to have the chief seat in it. In a lesser chancel he is entitled to all the seats, and can maintain trespass against others, because these lesser chancels were created for the sole use of the noblemen to whom they belonged. His rights are, therefore, more limited with regard to the ordinary chancel, as the use of this belongs to the parishioners for the celebration of the Holy Communion and the solemnization of marriage. 1 Steph. Clergy Law, 230.

*Page* 155. *Q.* If the vendor of land is entitled to a tithe rent-charge, issuing out of the land, and then executes a conveyance of the land with its rights, members, and appurtenances, what is the operations of the conveyance on the tithe rent-charge, and state the reason for your answer?
*A.* A conveyance of the land with its appurtenances, without mentioning the tithes, will leave the tithes in the hands of the conveying party. This is because the tithes exist as distinct from the land. Wm's. R. P., 321.

*Page* 155. *Q.* What will be the effect as regards merger of subjecting a tithe rent-charge by a settlement to the same limitations as the land out of which it issues, and is any one who may be entitled under such settlement able to control such effect?
*A.* The effect of such a limitation would not be to merge the tithe rent-charge in the land, but any person seized in possession of an estate in fee-simple, or fee-tail, or for life, of the rent-charge, and the land may, by deed or declaration under his hand and seal, and to be confirmed under the seal of the Commissioners, merge the title in the freehold and inheritance of the land. 6 & 7 Wm. IV., c. 71, s. 71; 1 & 2 Vic., c. 64, s. 3.

## Uses, Trusts, and Perpetuities.

*Page* 162. Q. How is a condition for taking and using the name and arms of a settlor enforced?

A. This may be done by way of shifting use. Thus to A and his heirs to the use of B and his heirs, but if B refuse or neglect, within a given time to assume the name and bear the arms of the settlor, to the use of C and his heirs. Wms. R. P., 270, 7th ed.

*Page* 167. Q. Does the law against perpetuities prohibit the breaking up of an estate in fee-simple into several estates in fee-tail, to take effect one after another, and if not, why not?

A. The rule against perpetuities is considered not to apply to limitations after an estate-tail, the reason being, that as the tenant in tail may bar all subsequent estates, the event on which the executory limitation is to arise will not affect its validity. Wms. R. P., 295, 7th ed.

## Husband and Wife.

*Page* 176. Q. If jewels or other personal chattels are given to the separate use of a married woman, but without naming a trustee, and the husband receives possession of them, is the wife protected on any, and if any, what principle?

A. The husband will be regarded as a trustee for the wife upon the principle that a trust will never be allowed to fail for want of a trustee. He may, therefore, be restrained from disposing of her separate estate the possession of which he acquires. See the notes to *Hulme* v. *Tenant*, 1 L. C. Eq., 394.

*Page* 180. Q. A power of jointuring an intended wife, exerciseable only by an appointor from time to time in receipt of the rents of a settled estate, is exercised by one entitled to receive the rents, but not actually in receipt of them. Will equity in any, and what, circumstances uphold the jointure against the estate?

A. The Court will uphold the jointure against the appointor when he actually comes into receipt of the rents. It would, also, be good against other parties deriving their title from the appointor, for the consideration for the jointure is valuable. The wife is, therefore, a purchaser for value. Sugd. on Powers, 552.

*Page* 182, No. 1, *for* 32 Hen. VIII., c. 34, *read* 12 Car. II., c. 24.

*Page* 189. Q. Who is entitled to prepare a marriage settlement, and by whom are the expenses borne?

A. The solicitors of the lady are entitled to prepare the settlement both of the husband's property and her own, but he has the privilege of paying the costs. *Helps* v. *Clayton*, 34 L. J., C. P., 1.

## Leases.

*Page* 190. *Q.* Can a parol lease be granted for any period of the right of sporting over an estate?
*A.* A right of sporting being an incorporeal right, can only be demised by deed for however short a period. The principle which requires a deed does not depend upon the quality or amount of the interest granted, but on the nature of the subject matter. Such a right, therefore, can no more be created for years, or even days, without a deed than in fee-simple. A parol licence to shoot without the privilege of carrying away the game would be so far good that the sportsman could not be treated as a trespasser until the licence was revoked, which it might be at any time. To an indifferent shot such a privilege would be a secondary consideration, but a true sportsman would prefer carrying away his game. Such a right is a profit *a prendre*, and must be created by deed. *Wood v. Leadbitter,* 14 L. J., Ex., 161. Taylor on Evidence, 838, 4th ed.

*Page* 193. *Q.* Does a lessor usually enter into any covenant on a lease? And if so, why?
*A.* The lessor usually covenants for quiet enjoyment. The word "demise" no doubt raises an implied covenant for quiet enjoyment, but this implied covenant does not extend beyond the life of the lessor, or beyond his estate and interest. The covenant being founded on privity of estate, determines with that privity. The lessee, therefore, should have an express covenant. So should the lessor, because the implied covenant is an absolute one. Lewis, Conv., 359.

*Page* 194. *Q.* Why do we insert in a lease two distinct clauses for payment of rent, the reservation or "yielding and paying" clause, and the covenant to pay? State the several functions of these two clauses.
*A.* The function of the first clause is to make the rent certain in amount so to enable the lessor to distrain. The second clause is to enable the lessor to sue in covenant for the rent, the only common law remedy being by distress. The covenant also binds the lessee after an assignment by him, whereas, in the absence of it, the lessor's remedy would, as against him, cease on assignment, because the implied covenant which the reddendum creates is dependent upon privity of estate. Coote, L. & T., 494.

*Page* 194. *Q.* How does the rent that is reserved in a lease differ from a rent-charge?
*A.* They differ, in that a tenure exists between a lessor and lessee by virtue of which he could at common law distrain for the rent. The owner of a rent-charge could not do this, he having merely a rent seck; but now he may do so by virtue of 4 Geo. II., c. 28, s. 5. In the case of the lease also a grant of the reversion passed

the rent with it; but it was otherwise in the case of a rent-charge. Wms. R. P., 228, 306.

## Mortgages.

*Page* 202. Q. State the essential points to be observed in framing a power of sale in a mortgage in fee.

A. Care should be taken to give the power to the mortgagee, his executors, administrators, and assigns, and in the case of a mortgage to several, to the survivors and survivor of them. The personal representatives being entitled to the debt, they are the proper persons to exercise the power. This frame also prevents difficulty arising, owing to the heir of the mortgagee being an infant. If the word "assigns" is omitted, an assignee cannot exercise the power. The power should also be drawn so as to be exerciseable after default, to prevent a purchaser from the mortgagee requiring the concurrence of the mortgagor. It should be provided that the notice may be given to the mortgagor or his heir, or one of his real or personal representatives, or left at his residence, instead of its being given to the "mortgagor, his heirs or assigns." The latter would include all subsequent incumbrancers. Provision should be made that the purchaser need make no enquiry as to notice. 1 Prid. Prec., 319.

*Page* 208. Q. On a contemplated re-conveyance of mortgaged estates, would you allow such re-conveyance to be endorsed on the mortgage deed, if not, why?

A. If acting for the mortgagee, I should object, because the solicitor of the mortgagor is entitled to prepare the re-conveyance and engross it. In order to do the latter, he would require the mortgage deed, which my client should not part with until the money is paid. It is, however, the common practice to endorse the re-conveyance, and a form for that purpose is given in all precedents.

## Vendor and Vendee.

*Page* 213. Q. What is the rule as to a vendor employing one or more persons to bid for him at a sale by auction, where a right to bid is not by the conditions expressly reserved to the vendor? Does this rule vary at law and in equity?

A. If the conditions contained the provision that the highest bidder should be the purchaser, the Courts of Law held that it was a fraud on the vendor to employ a bidder. In equity, a different rule was said to prevail, and it was generally stated that one puffer might be employed, but not more than one was allowed in equity (*Mortimer* v. *Bell*, 1 Law Rep., Ch. Ap. 10). Now, by stat. 30 & 31 Vic., c. 48, sales invalid at law are also invalid in equity; and the conditions must state whether the sale is without reserve, and if so, the employment of a puffer is unlawful; but where the seller reserves leave to bid by the conditions, he may employ one person to bid on his behalf. Secs. 1—6.

*Page* 216. *Q.* Is a vendor bound to disclose to a purchaser a latent defect in the title?
*A.* Yes, he is bound to do so, otherwise he cannot compel the purchaser to accept the title when such latent defect is discovered. *Edwards* v. *Wickwar*, 1 Law Rep., Eq. 69.

*Page* 216, *No.* 25, *line* 4 *of Answer, for* 26 & 27 Vic., c. 67, *read* 25 & 26 Vic., c. 67.

*Page* 221. *Q.* If A contracts to sell land to B, and upon investigation of the title it is found doubtful, can B compel A to complete the sale, either with or without giving an indemnity?
*A.* He may compel completion without indemnity, if he chooses to take the risk; but the Court will not compel a vendor to give an indemnity. Sugden's Vendors, 306, 14th ed.

### Alienation of Freeholds.

*Page* 239. *Q.* A gives land for building thereon the church of a new parish, to be constituted under the Church Building Acts. To whom is the site to be conveyed, and state precisely the proceedings relating to the conveyance?
*A.* The site is to be conveyed to the Ecclesiastical Commissioners, and it will not be valid unless the assent of the Commissioners is testified by their seal. The conveyance is a simple deed-poll by way of grant to the Commissioners and their successors, for the purposes of the various Church Buildings Acts, which are far too numerous to mention. The powers of the Church Building Commissioners are transferred to the Ecclesiastical Commissioners by 19 & 20 Vic., c. 55.

*Page* 239. *Q.* A gives land for building thereon a school, to be in union with the National Society for Promoting the Education of the Poor according to the Principles of the Church of England, who promise a grant towards the building. To whom is the conveyance to be made, and state generally its form and mode of proceeding?
*A.* The grant may be made to one or more corporations, aggregate or sole, or to trustees, or to the ministers and churchwardens and overseers. It is in form a deed-poll, and provides for the inspection of the school, and that it is to be in union with the National Society; also that the religious instruction is to be managed by the minister of the parish, and all other matters by a committee. The schoolmaster to be a member of the Church of England. Application should be made to the Education Committee, who provide a printed form. One witness only is requisite to the conveyance, and the death of the grantor within twelve months from the execution will not render it void. Enrolment in Chancery is necessary.
5 Davidson's Precedents, 1024; Wms. R. P., 71.

## Wills.

*Page* 244. *Q.* What is the construction of the words "die without issue" in a devise or bequest of real or personal estate?

*A.* In a will, dated before 1st January, 1838, these words import an indefinite failure of issue; therefore, if real and personal estate were given to A, and if he die without issue, to B in fee, A would take an estate tail in the real estate, with remainder to B in fee, and the whole interest in the personalty would belong to A absolutely. Since this date, the words mean a failure of issue at the death of A; therefore, he would take the fee of the real estate and the whole interest of the personalty, but defeasible as to both by his dying without leaving issue living at his death. B, therefore, is entitled to an executory devise or bequest, which A cannot defeat. Hayes & Jarm., 110.

*Page* 244. *Q.* Devise to B after the death of A, does A take any and what estate?

*A.* If B is the heir of the testator, A will take an estate for life by implication; but if B is a stranger, no estate will pass to A by implication. 1 Jarm., 497.

*Page* 245. *Q.* In the case of a will coming within the operation of the New Wills Act, 1 Vic., c. 26, and containing a residuary devise, how will void accumulations, if directed to be made out of real estate, pass?

*A.* If the accumulations are of the rents of land, they would pass to the residuary devisee, as forming part of the residue. If the accumulations are of the income of personalty, they would pass to the residuary legatee. 1 Jarm., 292.

## Intestacy.

*Page* 258. *Q.* Suppose a testator to have devised all his land away from his eldest son, and to have declared by his will that his eldest son should not be his heir, would this declaration have any, and if any, what effect? Give a reason for your answer.

*A.* The devise would be good, but the declaration would have no effect, the maxim being *solus Deus hæredem facere, potest non homo.* Wms. R. P., 62, 7th ed.

*Page* 258. *Q.* An owner in fee of land dies intestate, leaving a son A and a daughter B by his first wife, and a son C by his second wife. A dies intestate and unmarried, who, then, is entitled to the land, and why?

*A.* I assume that the deceased intestate was the purchaser. A takes by descent from his father, and on his death, intestate and unmarried, the descent will have to be traced from the father, whose heir is, therefore, C, the son of the second wife. Had A been the purchaser, his sister by the whole blood, B, would have taken in preference to his brother of the half-blood. 3 & 4 Wm. IV., c. 106.

*Page* 258. *Q.* A and B (each being an only child) become separately possessed of land in fee-simple, A as heir of his mother, and B under his mother's will. A and B both die intestate, each leaving a brother of his father and a brother of his mother surviving him. To whom will the lands of A and B respectively go?

*A.* The lands of A will go to the brother of his mother, because descent is traced from her, she being, I presume, the last purchaser. The brother of her husband cannot inherit, being no blood relation. The lands of B will go to his father's brother, inasmuch as, taking under the devise, B is the purchaser. It is a rule that the paternal ancestors and their issue are preferred to the maternal.

*Page* 264. *Q.* If A, having expended £2,000 in the purchase of a business for one of his two sons, dies intestate, leaving a widow and his two sons, and personal property of the value of £10,000, how much will the widow and two sons be entitled to receive?

*A.* The £2,000 advanced to purchase the business is an advancement to the son, and comes within the provisions of 22 & 23 Car. II., c. 10, enacting that a son advanced by his father, shall abate in his distributive share to the extent of the sum so advanced. In respect of an advance of personal estate, it is immaterial whether the son advanced is the heir-at-law or not. Therefore the £10,000 will be divided—£4,000 to the widow, £4,000 to the son not advanced, and £2,000 to the son for whom the business was purchased. 2 Wms. Exors., 1388, 6th ed.

### *Partnership.*

*Page* 265. *Q.* State shortly the usual clauses introduced in a partnership deed between merchants.

*A.* They are—as to the duration of the partnership, the title of the firm, specifying the place of business, the capital, as to advances by partners bearing interest, as to payment of rent, salaries, etc., as to the profits, as to keeping books, partners to give up their whole time and to be faithful, not to deal with the capital, or to lend money, or compound debts, or enter into bonds without the consent of all. Annual accounts to be kept, after which the profits to be divided; a reserved fund to be set apart out of the profits, power to each partner to draw out monthly sums for personal expenses; powers to determine the partnership if no profits; accounts to be taken on dissolution or death; power to one to expel the other in certain events. Arbitration Clause; 2 Prid. Prec., 496.

---

## EQUITY.

### *Statutory Jurisdiction ; Winding up.*

*Page* 274. *Q.* Describe briefly the jurisdiction of Courts of Equity in winding up a joint-stock company, and state under what authority the jurisdiction arises.

*A.* By virtue of 25 & 26 Vic., c. 89, the Court has jurisdiction in certain events to make an order for winding up the affairs of a company. It will appoint official liquidators, whose duty it is to get in the estate, and do all acts necessary for the winding up. The Court has jurisdiction to settle a list of contributories, and it finally disposes of the assets amongst the various classes of claimants. It may also stay proceedings by injunction.

*Page* 274. *Q.* In what event may a joint-stock company, registered under the Companies Act 1862, be wound up by the Court?
*A.* 1. Whenever the company has passed a special resolution requiring the company to be wound up by the Court; 2, whenever the company does not commence its business within a year from its incorporation, or suspends its business for the space of a whole year; 3, whenever the members are reduced in number to less than seven; 4, whenever the company is unable to pay its debts; 5, whenever the Court is of opinion that it is just and equitable that the company should be wound up.

*Page* 274. *Q.* How and upon what notice is the order for winding up such a company obtained?
*A.* A petition is presented for the winding up intituled in "the Companies Act 1862." It must be advertised seven clear days before the hearing in the *London Gazette* and two London or country papers. The petition must be served at the registered office of the company. G. O., 11 Nov., 1862.

*Lunatics.*

*Page* 278. *Q.* Can a man, under any circumstances, be found a lunatic without personal inspection by the jury?
*A.* He may be found a lunatic on an enquiry before a commissioner in lunacy without a jury, but even if there is a jury he need not be examined, if the presiding judge so direct. 25 & 26 Vic., c. 86, s. 6. Also, if the lunatic is out of the jurisdiction, he cannot be examined. Ibid.

*Page* 278. *Q.* If parties fail in establishing the lunacy, do the costs of the inquiry in any case fall on the alleged lunatic?
*A.* They may be ordered to be paid out of the lunatic's estate by the Lord Chancellor. 25 & 26 Vic., c. 86, s. 11.

*Page* 278. *Q.* To whom is the term "*non compos mentis*" applicable?
*A.* The term includes all persons who are not of sound memory and understanding. Such are idiots or natural fools, imbeciles, and persons who are unable to take care of their own affairs, arising from mania or dementia; the members of this latter class are chiefly termed lunatics, though the term "lunatic" was formerly applied to those persons affected by the moon. Wharton's Lexicon, 438.

*Fraud respecting Deeds and Contracts.*

*Page* 285. *Q.* In the case of a voluntary gift by deed *inter vivos*, upon whom, if the gift be afterwards challenged by the donor, will the burden of proof fall, and what must be shown to set the gift aside? State the rule.

*A.* A voluntary gift by deed *inter vivos* may be set aside at the instance of the donor, if obtained by fraud, surprise, or undue influence, and, in the case of fiduciary relation between the donor and donee, undue influence may be inferred from the manifest improvidence of the gift. The rule as to proof is, that wherever one person obtains by voluntary donation a large pecuniary benefit of another, the burthen of proving that the transaction was righteous falls on the person taking the benefit. 2 L. C. Eq., 488.

*Page* 285. *Q.* And between what relations does the rule apply, and against whom principally does the Court of Chancery seek to protect the owner of the property?

*A.* The above rule as to proof applies whether or not the parties stand in fiduciary relations. The Court in these cases principally extends its protection to donors between whom and the donee the relations of child and parent, ward and guardian, client and attorney, *cestui que trust* and trustee exist. *Hunter* v. *Atkins*, 3 My. & K., 113.

*Injunctions.*

*Page* 288. *Q.* State briefly the principles on which the interference of the Court of Equity by injunction rests. And under what circumstances a party originally entitled to this form of protection may forfeit his title to it. In exercising its jurisdiction by injunction, does the Court merely prohibit mischief, or can it also give compensation in respect of past mischief?

*A.* The Court will stay proceedings at law upon the principle that under certain circumstances other Courts may be used as instruments of injustice. Special injunctions are granted on the principle of preventing irreparable injuries to individuals or great public injury. The Court considers that if the wrongful act is allowed to proceed, damages at law will be inadequate. The Court will not interfere where the plaintiff has been guilty of laches. He must apply quickly. The Court, in addition to the injunction, may give compensation. 21 & 22 Vic., c. 27.

*Page* 288. *Q.* Will the Court grant an injunction to restrain a public nuisance; and, if so, at whose suit: and is it in all cases necessary to show that the party applying for the injunction had sustained some special or particular damage?

*A.* It will interfere by information at the suit of the Attorney-General. The Court will, however, interfere at the suit of a private individual, but he must show that he suffers some special or particular damage. *Sottau* v. *De Held.* 2 Sim. (N.S.), 133.

*Mistake.*

Page 294. Q. If, after a deed has been executed by all the parties, and acted upon, it is discovered that it is in some respects inconsistent with the real agreement, can either party obtain relief; and, if so, how, and is it necessary to establish fraud or unfair conduct?
A. If a deed contains something inconsistent with the intention of the parties, and inserted by mistake, other than a mistake in law, the deed may be rectified at the instance of any person interested under it, except as against a party having an equity equal to that of the plaintiff. The relief may be obtained by bill. It is unnecessary to establish fraud or unfair conduct. Thus, when a solicitor is instructed to settle property to the separate use of the intended wife, but omits doing so, the settlement will be corrected. *Rooke* v. *Lord Kensington*, 2 K. & J., 753.

Page 294. Q. In cases of mistake in a written instrument, does it make any difference in the relief granted, whether the defendant is one of the parties to the deed, or is his heir or devisee, or a purchaser from him, with or without notice of the mistake?
A. Take the case of rectifying a written instrument on the ground of mistake. The instrument will be corrected as against the parties to it or their heirs or devisees, as the latter take the estate of the deceased subject to all its equities, of which mistake is one. A purchaser, however, from the party himself, or from his heir or devisee, without notice, will not be affected by the mistake. 2 Spence, 195.

*Specific Performance.*

Page 302. Q. Where the consideration in a contract for a purchase is an annuity for the life of the vendor, and the vendor dies before completion, will the Court enforce it?
A. The Court, in this case, will enforce the contract. After it is entered into, the land is treated as the purchaser's, and the consideration as the vendor's, therefore the loss will fall upon the latter. The vendor agrees to sell for a contingent price, and those who represent him cannot complain that the contingency has turned out unfavourably. *Mortimer* v. *Capper*, 1 Bro. C. C., 156.

Page 309, *No.* 9, *line* 6 *of Answer*, *for* B's share *read* C's share, and line 7, read D for B.

*Trustees.*

Page 311. Q. If a trustee allows his agent to apply his trust fund in a manner constituting a breach of trust, of which the agent is aware, can the *cestui que trust* proceed in Chancery both against the trustee and his agent, or against either of them, at his option?

*A.* As a general rule, the Court would not allow the *cestui que trust* to proceed both against the trustee and the agent. He might proceed against the trustee, and if he turned out to be insolvent, he could then proceed against the agent where he has participated in the breach of trust. As a rule agents are only accountable to their employers, the trustees; but it is otherwise where they have fraudulently mixed themselves up with the breach of trust, as is mentioned in the question. *Fyler* v. *Fyler*, 3 Beav., 550; *Bodenham* v. *Hoskyns*, 2 De. G., M. & G., 903; Lewin on Trusts, 416.

*Page* 311. *Q.* Is a trustee liable under any, and what, circumstances for loss of the trust fund by the fraudulent act of his solicitor?

*A.* The trustee would be liable if he improperly allowed the solicitor to get possession of the fund. Thus, where trustees execute a conveyance, and sign a receipt endorsed, and leave the deed in the hands of their solicitor, who completes the sale and receives the purchase-money, and misapplies it, they will be personally liable. *Ghost* v. *Waller*, 9 Beav., 497.

*Page* 313. *Q.* What are the rights of a lessor against the executor or administrator and estate of a deceased lessee, in respect of the ordinary rent and covenants contained in the lease after assignment thereof by the executor or administrator to a purchaser?

*A.* If the executor or administrator of a deceased lessee, liable as such to the rents and covenants contained in a lease, shall have satisfied all subsisting liabilities, and set apart a sufficient sum to answer any future claims agreed to be laid out on the property in respect of any fixed or ascertained sum, and shall have assigned the property, he may distribute the personal estate. But the lessor may follow the assets into the hands of the distributees. Wms. R. P., 373; 22 & 23 Vic., c. 35.

*Page* 314. *Q.* Trustees under a settlement of real estate have power to sell with consent of the tenant for life; the tenant for life incumbers his life estate, can he consent to a sale?

*A.* If the settlement contains an actual or implied engagement that the alienee or incumbrancer shall enjoy the property in specie, the consenting power cannot be exercised as against the incumbrancer without his concurrence, because no one can derogate from his own grant. But, if the settlement contain an actual or implied recognition of the liability of the property to conversion during the existence of the life estate, the consenting power is in equity unaffected. At law an absolute alienation by the tenant for life appears to destroy the consenting power. Dart, 47, 3rd ed.

*Page* 318, *No.* 54, *line* 1 *of Answer, for* B *read* A.

## Administration.

*Page* 324. *Q.* In the ordinary administration of an estate in Chancery, in what class are voluntary deeds of gifts or bonds payable, before or after legacies, or *pari passu* with them? Give the reason for your answer.

*A.* A voluntary deed of gift, executed *inter vivos*, unless void under 13 Elizabeth, c. 5, will be effectual to prevent the property passing under it from being assets applicable to the debts of the donor upon his decease. Debts created thereby, and by voluntary bonds, are payable after the simple contract debts and before the legacies. The reason is that the voluntary creditors are entitled to rank as creditors, and, consequently, before legatees, but, as between them and the creditors for value, they are postponed in case of deficiency of assets. *Lomas* v. *Wright*, 3 L. J., Ch., 68.

## Mortgages.

*Page* 336. *Q.* If a mortgage contains a covenant for the insurance of the buildings on the premises, and the mortgagor fails to perform that covenant, has the mortgagee, in the absence of any provision for the purpose in the deed, any power to effect an insurance, and to recover the amount with or without interest?

*A.* The mortgagee has power to insure the premises and add the premiums paid for such insurance to the principal at the same rate of interest. This power is conferred by 23 & 24 Vic., c. 145, but the provisions of the act may be negatived by express declaration, and only apply to deeds executed since the act came into force. 28th August, 1860.

*Page* 336. *Q.* Blackacre, of the value of £10,000, and Whiteacre, of £5,000, are mortgaged to A to secure £7,500; B has a second mortgage on Blackacre alone to secure £5,000. Will a Court of Equity aid B to compel A to realise his security in part against Whiteacre, and how?

*A.* Yes, the Court will assist B by compelling A to resort to that estate out of which he (B) is not entitled to receive payment (Whiteacre), and to exhaust that, before he will be permitted to receive anything out of that estate to which B only can resort (Blackacre). This is a good illustration of the doctrine of marshalling securities. 2 L. C. Eq., 79.

*Page* 336, *No.* 12, *line* 2 *of Answer, for* C *read* B.

*Page* 339. *Q.* Is the assignee of a chose in action bound by all the equities to which it was liable in the hands of the assignor, and why?

*A.* The assignee of a chose in action, although without notice, in general takes it subject to all the equities which subsist against the assignor. Thus, the assignee of a satisfied bond has no claim on the obligor. *Turton* v. *Benson*, 1 P. Wms., 497. But the general rule may be varied, if the parties, otherwise entitled to the equities, have misled the assignee or been guilty of laches. And the case of a bill of exchange, indorsed for value, is an exception. L. C. Eq., 677-8.

### Commencement of Suits.

*Page* 343. Q. Can a private individual institute a suit against a corporation to compel the performance of a public trust or for exceeding the powers of their Act; or who is able to take such proceedings?

A. The proceedings being to compel the performance of a public trust, should be taken by information at the instance of the Attorney or Solicitor General, the private individual being named as a relator. If the private individual is himself interested in the trust, as where a shoemaker proceeds to compel the performance of a trust in favour of himself and other shoemakers, the proceeding is termed an information and bill.

*Page* 359, No. 8, *line* 2 *of Question, insert* not *after* of.

*Page* 361, No. 26, *line* 4 *of Answer, for* plaintiff *read* defendant.

*Page* 368, No. 7, *line* 3 *of Answer, for* defendant *read* plaintiff.

### Evidence.

*Page* 373. Q. Within what period must a subpœna be served, and does the same rule apply to all subpœnas?

A. A subpœna in general must be served within twelve weeks after the teste. One to hear judgment before return, ten days at least. Times of Equity, 4.

*Page* 377. Q. Give a form for the admission of documents in a suit between the plaintiff and the defendant.

A. In Chancery:—
Between A B, Plaintiff
and
C D., Defendant.

We, the undersigned, Messrs. ———, Solicitors for the above-named plaintiff, and Messrs. ———, Solicitors for the above-named defendant, do hereby, on behalf of the parties for whom we severally and respectively act as such Solicitors respectively, mutually each for the benefit of the other, agree upon the following admissions, and that the same may be used and read as evidence upon the hearing and for all the purposes of this cause, save and except all just cause of exception to the admissibility of the same. (Here specify the documents).

*Page* 377. Q. What must be done to enable you to use, in

support of a motion, an affidavit filed before the date of the notice; and what, to use one filed after the date, and why?

*A.* Notice must be given of the intention to read the affidavit, filed before the date of the notice of motion, and a list of those filed at the time of the notice must be given at the foot of the notice. In the case of an affidavit filed (by plaintiff), after the notice, leave of the court must be obtained before it can be read. The reason for this is that the plaintiff must verify his case in the first instance. But the defendant may file affidavits within fourteen days after notice of motion, and if there is any new matter to answer, the plaintiff may file affidavits in reply within seven days of the fourteen. Consol. Ord., 23, r. 8.

*Motion for Decree.*

*Page* 383. *Q.* Give the form of notice of motion for a decree.
*A.* In Chancery :—

Between A B, Plaintiff
and
C D, Defendant.

Take notice that this Honorable Court will be moved before The Right Hon. the Master of the Rolls on the     day of     , or as soon after as counsel may be heard, by Mr.     , Counsel for the plaintiff, that [*recite prayer of bill*] or that the plaintiff may have such further or other relief as the nature of the case may require. Dated this     day of     Yours, &c., X Y, Plaintiff's Solicitor. No.     Lincoln's Inn Fields. To Mr.     , Defendant's Solicitor. List of Evidence.

*Page* 387. No. 7, *line* 3 *of Answer, for* defendant *read* plaintiff.

*Fund in Court.*

*Page* 390. *Q.* What are the investments prescribed by the Lands Clauses Consolidation Act for the purchase money of the land of a party under disability, and how is it dealt with in the meantime?

*A.* They are—The purchase or redemption of the land-tax, or the discharge of incumbrances. The purchase of other land, to be settled to the same uses. If paid in respect of buildings, to be applied in replacing them. The money may be paid to any party becoming absolutely entitled. In the meantime, the money is to be invested in Consols or in Government or Real Securities. 8 Vic., c. 18, ss. 69, 70.

*Costs.*

*Page* 392. *Q.* On what amount is the lower scale of costs chargeable, and give the form of certificate for the application of it?

*A.* In suits where the amount recovered or sum in question is under £1,000. Form of Certificate—"I hereby certify that, to the best of my judgment and belief, the lower scale of fees of Court is applicable to this case. Dated, etc. A B, Solicitor for ———." Morgan's Costs, 402.

*Page* 394. *No.* 16, *for* 27 & 28 Vic., c. 127, *read* 23 & 24 Vic., c. 127.

### *Proceedings at Chambers.*

*Page* 395. *Q.* In what respects is an administration summons less effectual than a bill for the administration of the estate and effects of a deceased person?

*A.* In proceeding by summons the real estate cannot be dealt with, unless the whole of it is devised in trust for sale. Also, a wilful default of the executors cannot be charged upon summons, and generally a bill should be resorted to in cases which involve special complications.

*Page* 396. *Q.* Within what period is a decree directing accounts and enquiries to be brought into the Judges' Chambers? and in case of default by the party entitled to prosecute the same, can any other party take steps to prosecute the decree?

*A.* It must be brought in within ten days after the decree shall have been passed and entered. In default, any party to the cause or matter may bring in the same, and may prosecute them, unless otherwise ordered. Consol. Ord., 35, r. 22.

*Page* 399. *Q.* On a sale of property by the Court, when will the biddings be re-opened, and when should the application be made?

*A.* As to the former rule, see *infra*, 399. Now, the highest *bond fide* bidder, provided he bids a sum equal to or higher than the reserve price (if any), shall be declared the purchaser, unless the Court or Judge shall, on the ground of fraud or improper conduct in the management of the sale, upon the application of any person interested in the land (before the Chief Clerk's certificate of the sale is binding), either open the biddings, holding such bidder bound by his bidding, or discharge him from being the purchaser, and order the land to be resold. 30 & 31 Vic., c. 48, s. 7.

# A DIGEST

OF ALL THE

# EXAMINATION QUESTIONS AND ANSWERS
# IN THE COMMON LAW.

---

I.—*Nature of the jurisprudence administered by, and the distinctive jurisdictions of, the Common Law Tribunals.*

1. *Q.* Give some explanation of the phrase:—"Common and Statute Law."

*A.* The Common Law includes those principles, usages, and rules of action applicable to the government and security of person and property, which do not rest for their authority upon any express or positive declaration of the Legislature, but depend upon immemorial usage and custom; many of the usages and customs are as old as the primitive Britons, others having been, from time to time, introduced by the Romans, the Picts, the Saxons, the Danes, and the Normans. It is usually called the *lex non scripta*, in contradistinction to the *lex scripta*, which is the Statute Law enacted, from time to time, by Parliament. 1 Step Com. 41-84.

2. *Q.* State some of the leading Acts of Parliament relating to the Common Law, passed during the present reign.

*A.* The following may be mentioned:—1 and 2 Vic. c. 110, as to arrests, etc.; 6 and 7 Vic., c. 85, Evidence; c. 96, Libels; 8 and 9 Vic., c. 109, Gaming; c. 113, Evidence; 9 and 10 Vic., c. 93, Death from Negligence; c. 95, County Courts; 11 and 12 Vic., c. 42, 43, 44, Summary Convictions; 13 and 14 Vic., c. 61, County Courts; 14 and 15 Vic., c. 25, Landlord and Tenant; c. 52, Absconding Debtors; c. 99, Evidence; the Common Law Procedure Acts of 1852, 1854, and 1856; 16 and 17 Vic., c. 83, Evidence; 17 and 18 Vic., c. 31, Railway and Canal Traffic; c. 36, Bills of Sale; 18 and 19 Vic., c. 67, Bills of Exchange; 19 and 20 Vic., c. 97, Mercantile Law Amendment; Wharton's Articled Clerks' Manual, xxix, 9th edition, by Anderson; Notes on "Reading for Honours;" The Legal Examiner, Nos. I—X.

3. *Q.* Supposing a Statute passed repealing a former Act and such Statute becomes itself repealed, does the former Act revive?

*A.* No, unless words be added for that purpose.—13 and 14 Vict. c. 21, s. 5. Formerly it was otherwise.

4. *Q.* What are the Superior Courts of Common Law at Westminster, and what is their separate and concurrent jurisdiction ?

*A.* The Courts of Queen's Bench, Common Pleas, and Exchequer of Pleas. The Court of Queen's Bench has separate jurisdiction in criminal matters. It exercises control over inferior jurisdictions; superintends all civil Corporations, and commands magistrates to do their duty where there is no other remedy. The Court of Common Pleas has separate jurisdiction in real actions; appeals from revising Barristers' Courts ; applications under "The Railway and Canal Traffic Act," 17 and 18 Vic., c. 31, 51; acknowledgments of deeds by married women; registration of judgments, writs of execution, lis pendens, crown debts, and annuities. The Court of Exchequer of Pleas has separate jurisdiction in revenue matters. All the Courts have jurisdiction in personal actions; also by 20 and 21 Vic., c. 43, they can hear appeals from the decisions of justices.—Step. Com. 3, 402-413.

5. *Q.* What are the limits of the jurisdiction of Her Majesty's Superior Courts of Common Law at Westminster ?

*A.* The territorial jurisdiction of the Courts is confined to England and Wales, and the town of Berwick-upon-Tweed. That is, any judgment obtained in such Courts can only be enforced within these limits. They, however, as mentioned below, constantly entertain matters which have occurred in other countries, transitory in their nature. Also a writ of *habeas corpus* may be issued to the Colonies; but, since 25 and 26 Vic., c. 20, such a writ is not to issue if the colony has a competent Court of its own. *John Anderson's* case. 30 L. J. Q. B., 129 ; Broom's Coms., 45, 3rd ed.

6. *Q.* What is a Court Baron, and what a Court Leet ?

*A.* See *infra*, conveyancing "Copyholds."

7. *Q.* What general powers, previously exercised by Courts of Equity, were given to the Common Law Courts by "The Common Law Procedure Act, 1854.?"

*A.* They are powers to grant injunctions ; to grant a mandamus to enforce a public duty in which the Plaintiff is interested, s. 68, *Benson* v. *Paull,* 2 Jur., N.S., 425 ; power in detinue to order the specific delivery up of chattels, s. 78 ; power to a Defendant to set up equitable defences, ss. 83, 86. *Wodehouse* v. *Farebrother,* 5 E. and B. 277 ; lastly, the Common Law Courts may prevent the loss of a bill of exchange or other negociable instrument from being set up, s. 87. The above will be found treated more in detail *infra*. It must be remembered that though equitable jurisdiction is given to the Common Law Courts, the Courts of Equity still retain their former powers. Per Lord Eldon in *Kemp* v. *Pryor,* 7 Ves. 237.

8. *Q.* Mention some of the alterations in the law made by "The Mercantile Law Amendment Act, 1856 " ?

*A.* They are as follows :—That writs of execution against goods of a debtor are not to bind them against a *bond fide* purchaser for value, without notice of the writ being issued and unexecuted, unless actually seized before the sale ; that in suing on contracts to deliver specific goods, their specific delivery may be ordered ; the consideration for a guarantee need not appear on the face of it; if guarantee given to or by a firm, or single person trading under the name of a firm, it is to cease on change of firm; a surety, on discharging his liabilities, to be entitled to the assignment of all securities held by the creditor; the acceptance of a bill to be in writing; absence beyond coat of Plaintiff in certain cases to be no disability to his suing; if one joint debtor is in the Kingdom, the period of limitation is to run as to him, though the other is out of it, and he may be sued on his return although judgment recovered against the former; acknowledgment to revive a debt statute-barred may be signed by an agent; part-payment by one co-contractor not to prevent certain statutes of limitation running in favour of another.

II.—*The Right of Personal Liberty.*

1. *Q.* State a few of the Acts of Parliament securing the personal liberty of the subject, and in whose reign were they passed.

*A.* First in order of date and importance is Magna Charta, passed in the reign of King John, confirmed in the reign of Henry III.; the Petition of Right, 3 Car. I., c. 1; the statutes of 16 Car. I., c. 10, and 31 Car. II., c. 2, as to the writ of *habeas corpus*; the Bill of Rights, 1 Wm. and M., St. 2, c. 2; the Act of Settlement, 12 and 13 Wm. III., c. 2. As to the provisions of the above, see "Hallam's Middle Ages," c. 8, and "Hallam's Constitutional History."

2. *Q.* What is the personal security acquired by "The *Habeas Corpus* Act," and what is the mode of obtaining the writ?

*A.* It entitles a person imprisoned to shew cause against the legality of such imprisonment. The Act, however, is merely considered as declaratory of the Common Law in this respect. 3 Hallam's Const. Hist. 12. The writ is obtained on motion by counsel to the Court of Queen's Bench or Common Pleas, or from a judge in vacation by summons at Chambers, excepting in cases of treason or felony expressed in the warrant. 4 Bl. Coms. by Kerr, 144.

III.—*Actions, their Nature, Forms and Characteristics.*

1. *Q.* What is an action?

*A.* It is the form of proceeding pointed out by law for the recovery of one's due, or the lawful demand of one's right. Wharton's Law Lexicon.

2. *Q.* Actions are divided into real, personal and mixed:—what actions are real, what personal, and what mixed?

*A.* Real actions are those relating to real property, but they have now ceased to exist as real actions; for by the Common Law Procedure Act of 1860, s. 26., the action of writ of right of dower, dower, and *quare impedit*, are to be commenced by writ of Summons issuing out of the Common Pleas. Upon the writ is to be endorsed a notice that the plaintiff intends to declare in dower or for free-bench or in *quare impedit* as the case may be.

Personal actions include those brought for the specific recovery of goods and chattels, or for damages for breach of contract, or wrongs done to the person or property. They are divided into actions *ex contractu* and actions *ex delicto*.

Ejectment is termed a mixed action, it is brought for the recovery of the possession of land. Broom's Coms. 117, 3rd ed.

3. *Q.* What are the principal causes of action at Common Law?

*A.* They are injuries to real or personal property, or to the person, accompanied with immediate violence, as trespass *quare clausum fregit*, assault, &c. Similar injuries not accompanied with immediate violence, as slander, (Case). The question of the right to certain goods, (Trover). The recovery of specific goods, (Detinue). The wrongful taking of goods, (Replevin). Damages for breach of contract by deed, (Covenant). Also for breach of a simple contract, (Assumpsit). See further *infra*.

4. *Q.* In adjudicating upon causes of action which have arisen abroad, by what laws and practice are the laws of this country governed?

*A.* In actions on a contract the rule is, that the law of the country where it is made (*lex loci contractus*) is to be considered in expounding the contract. *De la Vega* v. *Vianna*, 1 B. and Ad., 284. An exception to this is admitted when the parties at the time of making the contract had a view to a different kingdom. For example, a bill payable in France though drawn in England is governed by the law of France, and in suing on it in this country it is sufficient to prove a notice of dishonour, according to the law of France. *Rothschild* v. *Currie*, 1 Q. B., 43. With regard to torts the maxim is also *locus regit actum*. The above rules do not, however, apply to the *practical conduct* of the suit, and, therefore, the time and mode of proceeding must be regulated according to the law of the country. That is, the *lex loci fori*, in which the action was brought shall prevail. It should be remembered that only these causes of action accruing abroad can be brought here which are transitory in their nature. Chitty, Jun., on Contracts, 90; *Mostyn* v. *Fabrigas*, Cowp. 161; 1 Sm. L.C., 607.

5. *Q.* What is an action of *Assumpsit*?

*A.* It is one brought to recover damages for an injury, sustained by the non-performance of a parol agreement. Formerly it was considered an action on the case, but this was otherwise decided in *Slades' Case*, 4 Rep. 94a. The amount recovered is the damage suffered by the plaintiff; for instance, in an action for the non-delivery of goods, the plaintiff recovers the difference between the price agreed for, and that which goods of a similar quality bore when the goods ought to have been delivered. Selwyn's Nisi Prius, tit. *Assumpsit*.

6. *Q.* What are the principal actions at Common Law arising upon contract, their respective incidents and comparative advantages?

*A.* They are, *assumpsit, debt, covenant, account, detinue,* and *scire facias.* As to Assumpsit see previous answer. Debt is brought for the recovery of a sum certain upon simple contract, bond, or other specialty, or record, or upon a statute, or for rent in arrear. *Covenant* is brought to recover damages for the breach of a covenant, express or implied between two or more in a deed indented or deed poll. If the damages are liquidated it lies concurrently with debt. The party suing must be named in the deed, and if it is *inter partes* he must be a party, excepting in certain cases, such as those coming within 8 and 9 Vic., c. 106, s. 5. *Account,* brought to compel the rendering of an account, is now superseded by bill in Equity. *Detinue,* is brought by a plaintiff having property in goods, wrongfully detained by another. He seeks to recover the goods in specie, or on failure thereof the value, also damages for their detention. *Scire Facias,* is brought to enforce a record, but it is now to a great extent superseded by writ of revivor. The advantages of debt over assumpsit and covenant are that it may be brought either on simple contract or specialty, whereas assumpsit only lies on simple contracts, and covenant on specialty only. Covenant and debt on a deed have an advantage in that twenty years is allowed to sue, six years only being allowed for assumpsit and detinue. Wharton's Articled Clerks' Manual, 9th ed., by Anderson, 38. Selwyn's Nisi Prius, the various titles of the actions. Broom's Coms. 117, 3rd ed.

7. *Q.* Does an action of debt lie on a deed under seal containing a covenant for payment of a sum certain, with interest on a given day that has expired; or to recover principal and interest on a mortgage deed, or for rent upon a lease under seal, or upon a bond, for the faithful conduct of a person; or must the plaintiff declare in covenant?

*A.* Debt or covenant may be brought upon the covenant, the sum being certain and ascertained. So, also, in the case of the mortgage debt, for if there is no covenant to pay in the deed the common money count will lie. Bullen and Leake, 196. Debt may also be brought for the rent. 11 Geo. II., c. 19, s. 14. Woodfall, 656. In suing upon the bond, debt may also be brought, and breaches would be assigned under 8 and 9 Wm. III., c. 11.

8. *Q.* Suppose A is indebted to B £100 for goods sold and delivered, in what form or forms of action can B recover the debt?

*A.* He may sue in debt or assumpsit. Selwyn's Nisi Prius, tit. *Assumpsit* and *Debt.*

9. *Q.* In case of the deed made between A and C containing a covenant by C to pay to A monies for the use of B, which of the two, A or B is the proper person to sue C for the breach of covenant?

*A.* In this case A only can sue, the rule being that in deeds *inter partes,* the action must be brought by the parties only. If the instrument were a deed poll, B could have sued, being named in it. *White* v. *Hancock,* 2. C and B, 830. 8 and 9 Vic., c. 106, s. 5 does not apply to this question, the covenant not being respecting tenements and hereditaments.

10. *Q.* What is an action of trover?

*A.* It is an action upon the case at the suit of anyone who has an absolute or special property in goods, for the recovery of the value of them. The defendant is supposed to have obtained possession of the goods by lawful means, and to have afterwards converted them to his own use. The requisites are—1. An absolute or special property in the goods; 2. Right of possession in the plaintiff; 3. That the goods are of a personal nature; 4. Conversion by the defendant. Selwyn's Nisi Prius, tit. *Trover.*

11. *Q.* What is the difference between detinue and trover?

*A.* Detinue differs from trover as described in the previous answer, in that it is an action *ex contractu,* and brought to recover the goods in specie or the value, and also damages for the detention. A verdict in trover has the effect of vesting the property in the goods in the defendant, which is not the case in detinue. Ibid. tit. Detinue.

12. *Q.* Can an action be supported on a lost bond or deed where the loss can be accounted for, and the once existence of the original proved?

*A.* Yes, *profert* and *oyer* being now unnecessary. 15 and 16 Vic., c. 76, s. 55.

13. *Q.* Is a civil action maintainable in any case in which the cause of the action constitutes an indictable offence?

*A.* As a general rule a civil action is maintainable for a wrong, although it may constitute an indictable offence. In cases of felony (except in cases where 9 and 10 Vic., c. 93, s. 1 applies), public justice must first be satisfied by indictment before the action is brought, but in a misdemeanour, such as assault, battery, or libel, an action may be brought without first prosecuting. As to felony it is of course seldom worth while bringing an action after conviction, the goods of the felon being forfeited to the crown. Broom's Maxims, 209. 4th ed.

14. *Q.* What action must be brought for—1. A libel or slander? 2. A nuisance (as carrying on an unwholsome trade)? 3. Seduction? 4. Non-payment of a Bill of Exchange or Promissory Note? 5. The recovery of possession of a house? 6. The recovery of calls on shares?

*A.* 1. Trespass on the case. 2. The like. 3. Trespass for the direct injury, or case for the consequential. 4. Assumpsit. Also debt where there is privity of contract, as between drawer and acceptor. 5. Ejectment. 6. Debt. Bullen and Leake's Precedents, 119. Selwyn's Nisi Prius, the various titles.

15. *Q.* How is a contract by matter of record to be enforced, and by what evidence must it be supported?

*A.* It may be enforced by action of debt. In some instances by *Scire Facias.* If a judgment, it may also be enforced by execution, as to which see *infra.* It may be proved by an official copy of the record, except when *nul tiel record* is pleaded, when the original must be produced. Roscoe's Evidence, 3.

16. *Q.* How are contracts under seal to be enforced, and what are the requisites of proof?

*A.* They may be enforced by action of debt, in case the sum due is ascertained, or covenant. Also by bill in equity, where an adequate remedy cannot be had at law, as for an injunction to restrain defendant carrying on a trade in defiance of a covenant not to do so. This writ may now be had at law in certain cases. It is necessary to prove that the deed was duly signed, sealed, and delivered by the defendant.

17. *Q.* State the forms of action founded on tort, and what is the gist of each action?

*A.* They are—Trespass. Trespass on the case. Trover. Replevin. Trespass lies for a direct injury to the person or goods, accompanied by immediate violence. Case lies where the injury is not immediate but consequential. For example—If A throw a log of wood into the street, and in its transit it strike B, his remedy is trespass; but if the log, having lodged on the ground, B tumbles over it and is injured, his remedy is case. *Scott v. Shepherd*, 1 Sm. L.C. 399. As to trover see *supra*. Replevin lies for the recovery of damages occasioned by the wrongful taking of chattels It is usually brought for a wrongful distress. Selwyn's Nisi Prius tit. Replevin.

18. *Q.* What is the difference between an action of trespass and replevin?

*A.* (See previous answer).

19. *Q.* What causes of action can be joined in the same suit? A applies to B for a debt due from B and C, partners, and in C's absence is assaulted by B. Can A join these two causes of action?

*A.* All excepting replevin and ejectments may be joined, of whatever kind, if by and against the same parties, and in the same rights. A cannot join the two causes of action, the trespass being against B, but the debt against B and C. C. L. P., Act 1852, s. 41.

20. *Q.* The plaintiff has claims against the same person on a deed, for a trespass, and for a libel, and also on a cause of action on which he must sue as executor. Can any and which of these causes of action be joined in the same action?

*A.* The causes of action on the deed, for the trespass, and for a libel, may be joined, being between the same parties and in the same rights. But the cause of action by the plaintiff as executor cannot, being in a different right from the others, viz., that of the deceased. In practice, however, separate actions would be brought. C. L. P., Act 1852, s. 41.

IV.—*The Law of Contracts.*

1. *Q.* How many descriptions of contracts are there, and what is an executory contract?

*A.* Contracts are, of record, by specialty, and simple contracts. An executory contract is one not completed at the time of making, as to build a ship by a certain time. Chitty on Contracts, 2.

2. *Q.* State some of the maxims by which contracts are expounded.

*A.* The following may be mentioned:—The construction shall be liberal and favourable, and according to the intention of the parties; the popular meaning of the words is to be adopted; the whole contract is to be considered; the *lex loci contractus* shall prevail in expounding the contract, but the *lex loci fori* in suing on it; a deed or other instrument is to be taken most strongly against the grantor or contractor; the agreement of the parties overrules the law. Chitty on Contracts, 70—96.

3. *Q.* What is the difference between a simple contract and a specialty debt? and has one any priority over the other, in the respective events of the bankruptcy or death leaving an insolvent estate of the debtor?

*A.* A simple contract differs from a specialty, in that it requires a valuable consideration to support it; it need not, excepting in certain cases, be in writing; it is not an estoppel; it is merged by a specialty; the period of limitation to it is six years, but that of a specialty is twenty; it is not binding on the heir of the debtor, which a specialty is if the heir is specially named therein, but only as to lands descended; it may be enforced by the *common* counts, but a specialty must be declared on specially. The specialty debt has priority, in the event of the debtor's decease, whether insolvent or not, excepting where the assets are equitable (see *infra*, Equity). If the estate is administered under 3 and 4 Wm. IV., c. 104, the specialty creditors, in which the heirs are bound, alone have priority. In bankruptcy they have no priority, as specialties, but certain debts have priority over others in various cases. See 28 and 29 Vic., c. 86, s. 5. Chitty on Contracts, 2—8.

4. *Q.* State the requisites of a contract not under seal; and also some of the most prominent rules by which contracts not under seal are to be construed.

*A.* It requires the reciprocal or mutual assent of two or more persons; a valuable consideration; something to be done or omitted, the object of the contract; competent parties to contract; a legal object; and in some cases it must be in writing. For the rules of construction see *supra*, No. 2. Chitty on Contracts, 8.

5. *Q.* Will a moral obligation be sufficient to support an express promise, where no legal liability has ever existed?

*A.* No, the consideration must be valuable. *Eastwood* v. *Kenyon*, 11 A. and E., 452.

6. *Q.* What is the meaning of the term "*nudum pactum*"?

*A.* It signifies a bare promise from which no cause of action arises. It is a promise for which there is no consideration. Thus, if A promises to pay B £100, the promise cannot be enforced, there being no consideration moving from the promisee. See the next answer.

7. *Q.* Define a consideration.

*A.* It is some benefit or advantage to the promisor (defendant), or some detriment, labour, or inconvenience sustained by the promisee (plaintiff), however small the benefit or inconvenience may be, if such act is performed, or such inconvenience suffered, by the plaintiff, with the consent, either express or implied, of the defendant. Selwyn's N. P., 41. Broom's Maxims, 718, 4th ed.

8. *Q.* Name the contracts required to be in writing by the 4th section of the Statute of Frauds.

*A.* They are the following :—1. To charge an *executor* or *administrator*, on any special promise, to answer damages out of his own estate; 2. to charge the defendant on a promise to answer for the debt, default, or miscarriage of another person; 3. to charge any person upon any *agreement* made upon *consideration of marriage;* 4. or upon any contract for the sale of lands, tenements, or hereditaments, or any interest in or concerning them; or 5. upon any agreement not to be performed within a year from the making thereof. The writing must be signed by the party to be charged, or some one by him lawfully authorised. 29 Car. II., c. 3, s. 4. See also next answer as to sale of goods.

9. *Q.* What circumstances will render a contract for the sale of goods for the price of £10 or upwards valid, if no memorandum in writing of the bargain be made and signed by the parties?

*A.* The buyer must either accept part of the goods sold, and actually receive the same; or give something in earnest to bind the bargain, or in part payment. 29 Car. II. c. 3, s. 17.

10. *Q.* Can money won by a wager be recovered in an action at law?

*A.* No, not since 8 and 9 Vic., c. 109. At common law the action would lie. *Good* v. *Elliott*, 3 T. R., 693.

11. *Q.* What transactions are void against creditors, within the meaning of the statutes of Elizabeth, as to fraudulent gifts and conveyances of land or chattels?

*A.* All deeds, when made with an express intent to defraud creditors, even though made for valuable consideration, except as regards a *bond fide* purchaser without notice, are void against them; so also are all conveyances and assignments of real or personal property by the debtor, he being at the time or immediately after insolvent. Possession of the goods after the sale is *prima facie* evidence of fraud. 13 Eliz., c. 5; Smith's Real and Personal Property, 773; see also *Twynne's Case* and Notes, 1 Sm. L. C., 1.

12. *Q.* To what nature of property do these statutes apply, realty or personalty?

*A.* The statute as to creditors (13 Eliz., c. 5) applies to real and personal property; 27 Eliz., c. 4, is doubtless the other statute referred to, but this statute has no application to creditors, but merely to purchasers; it applies to real property only, including chattels, real and copyholds. Smith's Real and Personal Property, 776.

13. *Q.* What is a bond? Describe a common money bond.

*A.* It is an acknowledgment in writing, and under seal, of an obligation by one party (termed the obligor) to do some act on behalf of another party (the obligee). A money bond is for the payment of a sum of money at a certain time, or on the happening of a certain event. It usually provides for the payment of double the sum due as a penalty for the non-performance of the condition. No more can however be recovered than the debt actually due, with interest and costs. Wharton's Law Lexicon, "Bond."

14. Q. When the Statute of Frauds requires an agreement to be in writing, is it necessary that the consideration should appear on the agreement, or may it be supplied by parol evidence?

A. The consideration must appear on the face of the agreement, and cannot be supplied by parol evidence, excepting in the case of guarantees by virtue of 19 and 20 Vic., c. 97, s. 3.; *Wain* v. *Warlters*, 5 East. 10; 2 Sm. L. C. 208.

15. Q. Can you question the legality of the consideration to a contract under seal?

A. Yes, the consideration may be shown to be illegal by parol evidence. This is an exception to the rule against admitting parol evidence to contradict or add to a written contract. *Collins* v. *Blantern*, 2 Wils. 347; 1 Sm. L. C., 310.

16. Q. What is an estoppel? Give examples.

A. It is where a man is concluded by some act of his, from denying or offering evidence to controvert it. It occurs by matter of *record*, by *deed*, or in *pais*. Thus, if a judgment is entered up against a man, he cannot deny anything appearing on the record. So also a party to a deed is taken to have admitted the statements contained in the deed. *The Duchess of Kingston's case*, 2 Sm. L. C., 643. Estoppel in *pais* occurs where a man wilfully causes another to believe the existence of a certain state of things, and induces him to act on that belief, so as to alter his former position, the former is estopped from averring a different state of things. Thus where the owner of goods in the hands of A. leads the sheriff in executing a writ against A. to believe that the goods are not his but A.'s, the owner is estopped from afterwards denying it. *Pickard* v. *Sears*, 6 A. & E., 469.

17. Q. When is a person liable as executor *de son tort*?

A. Intermeddling with the goods of the deceased, will constitute a person executor *de son tort*. Thus, killing the cattle, giving away or selling the goods, demanding the debts of the deceased, will suffice; but locking up the goods for preservation, directing the funeral, and other similar acts of necessity, will not make a stranger doing these and other acts of necessity, an executor *de son tort*. Wms. Exors, 225.

18. Q. Can an infant enforce a contract made with him?

A. Yes, he may, although it cannot be enforced against him. The reason for this want of mutuality is, that were it otherwise, his incapacity would be detrimental to him, instead of beneficial. Chitty on Contracts, 148.

19. Q. Can any other party to a contract, except an infant, take advantage of the infancy to defend an action on the contract?

*A.* See the previous answer.

20. *Q.* How can a debt contracted during infancy, and not recoverable on that ground, be made binding on the party after he comes of age?

*A.* It will be binding on him if he ratify the debt after coming of age, either by making a new promise, or by doing some act which clearly shows that he means to ratify the transaction. The promise to pay any debt, or the ratification of any promise or simple contract, must be in writing, and signed by the party to be charged. 9 Geo. IV., c. 14, s. 5. Signature by an agent is not sufficient. *Hyde* v. *Johnson*, 3 Scott, 289; Chitty on Contracts, 145—148.

21. *Q.* Is a father liable under any circumstances, for debts incurred by an infant son?

*A.* A father is not liable to pay debts contracted by his child, even for necessaries, unless he gives his child express or implied authority to pledge his credit, or himself orders the goods. The liability of the father will therefore depend on the circumstances of each particular case. His liabilities for necessaries is usually implied when the infant is living under the parental roof, and the father has made no other provision for the child's support. Chitty on Contracts, 144.

22. *Q.* Can a minor be sued on a breach of promise of marriage? And give your reasons.

*A.* No, he cannot be sued, marriage not being considered a necessary. The infant can, however, sue upon such a contract.—Ibid. 148.

23. *Q.* Is an infant liable on his warranty of a horse sold by him, if the horse is unsound?

*A.* The infant is not liable in such a case. *Howlett* v. *Haswell*, 4 Camp., 118.

24. *Q.* Is an infant liable for any debts? And if so, what debts? Does it make any difference if he is residing under the parental roof or not?

*A.* An infant is liable for reasonable necessaries supplied to him, either for ready money or on credit, such as meat, drink, apparel, lodgings, and medicine. Anything also is considered a necessary, if proper for the infant's age, state, and degree, as the livery of a servant to an infant captain in the army, regimentals sold to him as member of a volunteer corps. *Coates* v. *Wilson*, 5 Esp. 152; Chitty on Contracts, 137. As mentioned above, the parent would probably be liable if the infant was residing under his roof.

25. *Q.* When is a husband liable for the debts of his wife, contracted during coverture, and in what cases is he not liable? Does it matter if the husband is an infant?

*A.* The husband is liable on any contracts of his wife made with his assent, either express or implied; when living together, she has an implied authority to order necessaries for herself and the household. This liability may, however, be rebutted, if he disapproved of her conduct, or if the tradesman gave credit exclusively to the wife; also, where the husband expressly warns a tradesman not to trust his wife. After a separation by mutual consent, the husband is similarly liable, unless he pays her a sufficient sum for support, or she has funds of her own, or is able to support herself. If he wrongfully turns her away, he is liable to support her, and cannot by notice limit his liability. If the separation occurs by her misconduct, the husband is not liable. *Manby* v. *Scott*, 1 Sid. 109; *Montague* v. *Benedict*, 3 B. and C., 630; *Seaton* v. *Benedict*, 5 Bing. 28, 2 Sm. L. C., 408. If the husband is an infant, he is liable for necessaries supplied to the wife by his authority. Chitty on Contracts, 137.

26. *Q.* Is a husband liable for the debts of his deceased wife, such debts having been incurred before marriage?

*A.* The husband's liability on such debts ceases on the wife's death, unless he take out administration for the purpose of getting in some of her *choses in action*. He may then be sued in his capacity of administrator. Chitty on Contracts, 151.

27. *Q.* What rights, as to property, have been conferred by recent legislation upon wives deserted by their husbands, and how may they be secured?

*A.* If a married woman is deserted by her husband she may apply to a justice or metropolitan police magistrate, or to the Divorce Court, or to the Judge Ordinary, for an order to protect any money or property she may acquire by her own lawful industry, and property which she may become possessed of after such desertion, against her husband or his creditors. As to such property, whether possessed of it beneficially or not, she will be considered a Feme Sole. 20 and 21 Vic., c. 85, s. 21; 21 and 22 Vict. c. 108 ss. 6—10.

28. *Q.* When a husband wrongfully turns away his wife, is he liable for necessaries supplied to her after due notice in the newspapers that he will not be liable?

*A.* The husband's liability is not affected by the notice, even if the notice is particular. Ibid. 163.

29. *Q.* Upon what principle does the liability of a husband for his wife's contracts rest; and in what cases may a wife be regarded as the general agent of her husband?

*A.* The husband's liability rests upon the supposition that the wife contracts as his agent and by his authority. As to when the wife is regarded as his agent see *supra*, No. 25.

30. *Q.* Is there any and what restriction to a husband's liability for the debts of his wife contracted before marriage?

*A.* His liability is restricted to the coverture (see *supra*).

31. *Q.* If a man marry a woman to whom he is indebted, and to whom he has given a security for the debt, what becomes of the debt and the security; and how can this be prevented?

*A.* The debt becomes released, and the security is gone at law. But it may be kept alive in equity if by a settlement of the debt or otherwise it appeared to be the intention of the parties that it should be kept alive. Equity disregards the rule that the husband and wife are one person. Story's Eq., s. 1370.

**32.** *Q.* What is the nature of a guarantee? Is it affected by the Statute of Frauds?

*A.* It is a promise by one party to be responsible for the performance of some act by another, which act such other person is bound to perform. By the Statute of Frauds, s. 4, such a promise must be in writing.

**33.** *Q.* In a guarantee on behalf of a third person, must any consideration be stated?

*A.* The statement of a consideration is now rendered unnecessary by virtue of 19 and 20 Vic., c. 97, s. 3. This enactment does not, however, dispense with the necessity for a consideration.

**34.** *Q.* You are consulted as to the liability of a party upon a guarantee. In advising upon this, to what particular points would your attention be directed?

*A.* I should ascertain if it was in writing and signed by my client or his agent lawfully authorised; if it was barred by the Statute of Limitations; if the creditor had done any act to release my client as mentioned in the next answer; also, if there was a valuable consideration. And a stamp upon it as an agreement. *Glover* v. *Halkett*, 2, Ex. 487.

**35.** *Q.* Give an instance of how a surety for the payment of a debt due from a third party can be discharged from his liability by the conduct of the creditor?

*A.* He may be discharged by the failure of an intended co-surety to execute, if he himself executed on the faith of the co-surety joining. By the creditor conniving at the principal's default. By the creditor omitting to perform certain conditions; by his laches, as if the creditor accept payment in country bank notes which are not paid. *Guardians of the Lichfield Union* v. *Green*, 1 H. and N. 884. By the creditor discharging the principal. Also any alteration of the terms of the contract *as between the creditor and the principal* without the assent of the surety will discharge him. Chitty on Contracts, 477—485.

**36.** *Q.* What liability does a factor incur by the receipt of a *del credere* commission?

*A.* He renders himself responsible to his principal for the solvency of the person with whom he deals. For doing so, he receives a higher commission. *Morris* v. *Cleasby*, 4 M. and S. 474.

**37.** *Q.* What authority does an agent require to execute a deed for a principal, so as to bind the principal?

*A.* He must be authorised by deed. Chitty on Contracts, 193.

**38.** *Q.* Under what circumstances is a principal bound by the acts of a sub-agent?

*A.* As a general rule the principal is liable for acts done not only by his immediate agent, but also for those done by others employed by that agent. But the relationship of master and servant must be established between the sub-agent and the principal. Thus, the principal is liable for the acts of workmen employed by his farm bailiff; but it is otherwise where the agent exercises an independent calling in the execution of which calling he employs others. Therefore a railway company are not liable for the negligence of a workman in the employ of a contractor who has agreed to make a portion of their line. *Reedie* v. *London and North Western Railway Company*, 4 Exch. 244. Addison on Torts, 342.

39. *Q.* If A be authorised to make a valuation of goods, is such valuation valid if made by A's clerk?

*A.* In this case A is employed as an agent to make a valuation, and as such he cannot delegate his authority. Still the valuation would be valid if the principal assented to it, or if it was the custom of the trade amongst valuers for valuations to be made by their clerks. Broom's Maxims, 755.

40. *Q.* A factor in this country buys for a merchant abroad, can the factor be sued in this country? On what principle do the courts proceed?

*A.* In this case the presumption is, that credit is given to the British buyer, and not to the foreigner. This may, however, be rebutted, and the agent's liability will depend on the intention of the parties to be collected from the terms of the contract or explained by custom or usage. *Green* v. *Kopke*, 18 C.B. 549. *Mahoney* v. *Kekulé*, 14 C.B. 390.

41. *Q.* State the general rule regulating the liability of partners for the acts of each other.

*A.* It is, that the act or contract of one partner with reference to and in the ordinary course and management of the partnership, business, and affairs, is in point of law the act or contract of the whole firm and binding on them, even although it violate some private arrangement between the partners. Thus a Solicitor cannot bind his co-partners by drawing a bill of exchange, but a Merchant could do so. Chitty on Contracts, 228.

42. *Q.* Can one partner maintain an action against another to recover a share of money received on account of the firm?

*A.* As a general rule he cannot sue him for money received for the use of the firm, but it is otherwise if the defendant have entered into a covenant to account. One partner may also sue the other for a balance found to be due to one of them. See the next answer.

43. *Q.* A and B are partners in trade, A improperly uses the partnership name by making a promissory note in the name of the firm, B is compelled to pay the note. Has B any and what remedy against A?

*A.* As a general rule partners cannot sue one another at law, but the above is an exception, and B may recover the money from A as money paid to his use. *Cross* v. *Cheshire*, 7 Exch. 43.

44. *Q.* State the conditions of profit and loss necessary to constitute a partnership as between the members of the firm, and to create liability as to third persons.

*A.* As between the members of the firm an agreement to share in the profits and losses, however unequal the shares may be, will constitute a partnership, unless it clearly appears that such agreement should not have such an effect as if there is an express stipulation to the contrary. *Waugh* v. *Carver*, 1 Sm. L. C., 818—844. As regards third parties, a man will be liable as a partner if he allows his name to be used, although he does not participate in the profit and loss. As to third parties, moreover, it has been considered that a participation in the profits makes the party receiving such profits liable for the debts, although he is not an ostensible partner. Upon this subject it is now provided, that the advance of money to a trader, upon contract that the lender shall receive a rate of interest varying with the profits, or shall receive a share of the profits, shall not constitute the lender a partner; nor shall a contract to remunerate a servant or agent, by a share in the profits, render him liable as a partner, or give him the rights of one. No widow or child of a deceased partner receiving, by way of annuity, a portion of the profits, shall be liable as a partner; nor shall the vendor of a goodwill be deemed a partner of the vendee, by reason of his receiving, by way of annuity, a portion of the profits of the business. In the event of a bankruptcy, the lender and vendor of the goodwill are to be postponed to other creditors. 28 and 29 Vic., c. 86.

45. *Q.* How should a person proceed for the recovery of damages, who has delivered goods to a common carrier to carry and deliver, but which have not reached their destination?

*A.* He may either sue the carrier in assumpsit for the breach of contract, or in case for the breach of the duty to carry safely and deliver, which the law imposes on carriers. Trover may be brought if the goods are delivered to the wrong person, but not for merely losing the goods. Bullen and Leake, 101, 2nd Ed. Selwyn's Nisi Prius, 460, 12th ed.

46. *Q.* A orders goods of B to be sent by a carrier C, who receives, but loses the goods. A refuses to pay for them. What remedy have the parties, and against whom?

*A.* In this case A is liable to be sued by B for the price of the goods, in assumpsit or debt; as the delivery by B to the carrier is a delivery to A (subject to B's right to stop *in transitu*), he having directed them to be *sent by a carrier*. From the time of delivery the goods are at the risk of A, and this would be so even if B were to pay the carrier. From this it also follows that A is the party to sue the carrier, in case for the loss of the goods, assuming the loss to have arisen through his negligence. *Coombes v. The Bristol and Exeter Railway Company*, 27 L. J. Ex. 269. Selwyn's Nisi Prius, 456.

47. *Q.* State the instances, if any, in which a carrier is not liable for the loss of goods intrusted to him, and for what losses is a common carrier liable?

*A.* He is not liable if the plaintiff have contributed to the loss of the goods, or if the loss arose from the act of God or the Queen's enemies. A common carrier by land is not liable for any loss or injury to any gold or silver coin, gold or silver in a manufactured or unmanufactured state, precious stones, jewellery, watches, clocks, notes, bills, title deeds, pictures, glass, etc., contained in any parcel, where the value exceeds the sum of £10, unless at the time of the delivery to the carrier their value and nature be declared, and an agreement made to pay the extra charge for them. But the carrier must have a notification of such increased charge affixed in legible characters, in some public and conspicuous part of his office. He must also, if required, give a receipt for the extra charge. 1 Wm. IV., c. 68. The act, however, does not protect the carrier from loss arising from the felonious acts of his servants; nor does it prevent the parties entering into a special contract. Such a contract, however, with regard to railway and canal companies, must be just and reasonable. 17 and 18 Vic., c. 31. As to this see *McManus* v. *The Lancashire and Yorkshire Railway Company*, 4 H. and N., 327. 28 L. J. Ex., 353. *Peek* v. *the North Staffordshire Railway Company*, 10 H. of L. 473, 32 L. J., Q. B. 241.

48. *Q.* The property of a traveller at an inn is stolen by some person unknown, without any imputation of connivance or neglect in the landlord or his servants. Is the landlord liable to make good the loss?

*A.* His liability would depend upon circumstances. The general rule is, that an innkeeper is liable for such a loss, if it occurred while the guest is making use of the inn, through the negligence of himself or his servants, unless the theft was by enemies of the Queen, the guest's servant, or friend, or was caused by his own gross negligence. His liability is now limited to £30, unless the goods or property consist of a horse or other live animal, or their gear, or a carriage. This limited liability does not, however, exist—1. Where the loss has occurred through the wilful act, default, or neglect of the innkeeper or his servants. 2. Where the goods have been deposited with the innkeeper expressly for safe custody. 26 and 27 Vic., c. 41, s. 1. He may require the goods to be deposited in a box, but cannot have the benefit of the act, unless a plain copy of the first section was posted in a conspicuous part of the hall or entrance, when the goods were brought in; nor if he refuse to take the goods on deposit. Sects. 2, 3, 4. Calye's Case, 1 Sm. L.C., 102—110.

49. *Q.* Where a traveller is preparing to depart from an inn without paying his bill, may the landlord detain either his person or baggage until payment?

*A.* He cannot detain his person, or take off his clothes, *Simbolf* v. *Alford*, 3 M. and W., but he may detain his baggage. Selwyn's Nisi Prius, 1362.

50. *Q.* A traveller on his journey stops at an inn, and desires to put up for the night; the landlord, although he has room in his house, refuses to receive him. Is, or is not, the landlord warranted in so doing; and, if not, has the traveller any, and what remedy, against the landlord for such refusal?

*A.* The landlord is bound to receive the traveller, unless he be drunk or disorderly, or have an infectious disease, provided he tender or be willing to pay for his board and lodging. The landlord is liable to an action on the case, and to an indictment for a misdemeanour. Woolrych's Criminal Law, 1306.

51. *Q.* What is the law as to the liability of innkeepers; and what is the leading case?

*A.* See *Supra.* The leading case is Calye's Case, *Supra.*

52. *Q.* In an action on the warranty of a horse, would an implied warranty be sufficient upon which to maintain an action? Does a sound price amount to a warranty?

*A.* There is no implied warranty in such a case to maintain an action upon, an implied warranty only existing in cases where a tradesman, knowing for what purpose goods are wanted, sells them to answer that purpose. It is also implied by the custom of some trades. Chitty on Contracts, 409, 410. A sound price does not amount to a warranty.

53. *Q.* Must the warranty of a horse be in writing?

*A.* There is no necessity for a written warranty, but it is always better to have one, for the purpose of proof. Probably nothing is more difficult to sustain than that there was a warranty, dealers in horses being proverbially obstinate upon the point. If, however, the contract is reduced into writing, the warranty must be embodied in it, otherwise proof of it cannot be given. Chitty on Contracts, 413.

54. *Q.* What remedies has the vendee of a warranted chattel on breach of warranty? And is a warranty made subsequent to the sale void or not? Give the reasons for your answer.

*A.* He has four courses open to him, viz:—1. He may in certain cases refuse to accept the article. 2. He may rescind the contract as soon as the unsoundness or defect is discovered, and return or tender the chattel; but if the sale is of a specific chattel, tendering or returning it is no defence to an action for the price. 3. He may accept it, and bring a cross action on the warranty, or he may sue in tort for the fraud. 4. He may, without bringing a cross action, use the breach of warranty in reduction of damages, when sued for the price. If made subsequent to the sale the warranty would fail for want of consideration. Selwyn's Nisi Prius, 655. Bullen and Leake, 289.

55. *Q.* Is a contract for the sale of a horse for £10 or more affected by the Statute of Frauds; and, if so, must the consideration be expressed in the written agreement?

*A.* Yes, such a sale comes within the provisions of sec. 17, as to which see the next answer; and if in writing the consideration must be expressed.

56. *Q.* What are the requisites of the Statute of Frauds (29 Car. II., c. 3) as to a sale of goods of the value of £10 or upwards, and how has the same been extended by Lord Tenterden's Act (9 Geo. IV., c. 14, s. 7)?

*A.* The buyer must accept part of the goods sold, and actually receive the same, *or* give something in earnest to bind the bargain, or in part payment, *or*, thirdly, there must be a memorandum or note in writing of the bargain signed by the parties charged, or their agents lawfully authorised (s. 17). The latter act extends the provisions of the former to executory contracts, *i.e.*, goods intended to be delivered at a future time, or not made when the bargain was entered into.

57. *Q.* To maintain an action for the price of goods sold, but not delivered, is it necessary that the contract should be in writing? And if it is necessary under some circumstances only, state under what circumstances.

*A.* No, if there has been part payment, part delivery, or something given to bind the bargain; and this whether they be of the value of £10 or not.

58. *Q.* Can an action be maintained on a verbal contract for a year's service, to commence from a day subsequent to the making of the contract; and would it be different if the year were to commence from the making of the contract?

*A.* No, the contract must be in writing, under 29 Car. II., c. 3, s. 4, as it cannot be performed within a year from the making. *Bracegirdle* v. *Heald*, 1 B. and Ald. 722. But if the hiring were to commence from the date of the contract it would be otherwise.

59. *Q.* A lends B £20 to be paid on a certain day; B after the day is past enters into a contract with A under seal to pay the amount. Can A sue B for money lent?

*A.* The contract under seal has the effect of merging the simple contract to pay, which first existed. A, therefore, must sue on the specialty, and the common count for money lent would be improper. The form of action would be debt or covenant. Chitty on Contracts, 7.

60. *Q.* What is meant by the term privity of contract?

*A.* Privity of contract means "a connection or bond of union existing between parties in relation to some particular transaction." If there is no privity an action will not lie, because the parties are strangers to each other, *quoad* the subject matter in dispute. Thus, if B the country attorney of A, sends a sum of money to his London agent to be paid to C on account of A, and the agent promise B to pay the money as directed, but afterwards on the application of C refuse to pay it, A cannot sue the agent for money had and received because there is no privity between the town agent and the country client. *Cobb* v. *Beeke*, 6 Q. B. 930. So, also, if I give money to my servant to pay a tradesman, the latter cannot sue the servant for the money. Per Parke J. in *Baron* v. *Husband*, 4 B. and Ad. 611. Broom's Coms., 316, 3rd ed. As to privity of contract connected with estate, see *infra*, "Conveyancing."

61. *Q.* Describe the nature of a *chose en action*. Give an instance of a *chose en action* reduced into possession by a husband.

*A.* It is a *chose* which the person entitled to has not the possession of, but which he must take proceedings to recover. Such are debts, legacies, etc. If A owed B a *feme sole* £50 and B were to marry C, the latter to reduce the debt into possession must sue for and recover judgment, or actually receive the money. Chitty on Contracts, 150.

62. *Q.* A gentleman is in the habit of sending his servant to a shop and receiving goods on credit, the servant misapplies some of

the goods to his own use; has the seller a remedy for the value of the goods so misapplied, against the master? The same servant also obtains goods on credit, in his master's name, of a tradesman who has never before had dealings with the master, and takes the goods to his own use; can the tradesman recover the value against such master?

*A.* In the first case put the tradesman can sue the master, if on supplying the goods he trusted the master. Under such circumstances the servant is considered to be authorised to pledge the master's credit. No such authority is, however, presumed in the second case, the master having never before dealt with the tradesman, and it was the duty of the latter to enquire if the order was given by the master's authority. *Hiscox* v. *Greenwood*, 4 Esp. N. P. C. 174. Selwyn's Nisi Prius, 1117.

63. *Q.* A servant's wages are payable quarterly, and have been paid to Lady-day, 1854. Between Lady-day and Midsummer, 1854, namely, on the 1st May, the servant misconducts himself, and for such misconduct is turned away by his master without warning. Is the servant entitled, *pro ratâ*, to wages from Lady-day to May?

*A.* He is not entitled to the wages, the master being justified in discharging him for acts of misconduct, *e.g.* being absent when wanted, sleeping from home at night without leave. *Turner* v. *Mason*, 14 M. and W. 112. *Same* v. *Robinson*, 2 Sm. L. C. 37.

64. *Q.* What is the law as to the payment of the debts of relations and third parties?

*A.* Apart from the natural disinclination to pay, no one is *prima facie* bound to pay the debts of third parties or relations. But a man may make himself liable to do so if he give a guarantee. As to which see *supra*, No. 34.

65. *Q.* What is a lien, and how is it created? How does a general lien differ from a particular lien?

*A.* It is the right of retaining the possession of a chattel from the owner until a certain claim upon it is satisfied. A *general* lien is the right to detain a chattel until payment be made, not only for the particular articles, but for any balance that may be due on a general account in the same line of business; thus attorneys have a general lien on all papers in their hands belonging to their clients for their general costs. A *particular* lien is given to every person to whom a chattel has been delivered for the purpose of bestowing his labour upon it. In such case he may withhold the chattel until the price of his labour is paid. Thus a tailor is not bound to deliver clothes which he has made until the price for making them be paid; but, he cannot retain other goods for the price. 2 Steph. Coms. 82.

66. *Q.* What steps are necessary to render a bill of sale available against creditors of the person who gives the bill of sale?

*A.* Possession of the goods should be given to the person advancing his money, or the requirements of 17 and 18 Vic. c. 36 should be complied with, which enacts: That every bill of sale of personal chattels, and every schedule, or inventory thereto annexed, or therein referred to, or a true copy thereof, and of every attestation of the execution thereof must, with an affidavit of the time of giving the bill of sale, and a description of residence and occupation of the person making or giving it, and of every attesting-witness to it, be filed in the Court of Queen's Bench within twenty-one days after the giving the bill of sale. Any defeasance or condition must also be written on the same paper or parchment as the bill of sale. In case a copy is filed the original must be produced duly stamped. The Legal Examiner, 138.

67. *Q.* What is the general Common Law rule as to interest on a debt in the absence of any express stipulation to pay it?

*A.* It is, that there is no implied contract on the part of the debtor to pay interest on the debt, although it be of a fixed amount, and have been frequently demanded, excepting in the cases of bills of exchange and promissory notes, overdue bonds, money payable on an account stated, money payable under an award. This rule is modified by 3 and 4 Wm. IV., c. 42, s. 28, which see and consider; also next question.

68. *Q.* Is there any mode in which a creditor for goods sold and delivered can make his debt carry interest?

*A.* No; but he may make a demand of the debt in writing, containing a notice that interest will henceforth be claimed. If the debt is payable by virtue of a *written instrument* at *a certain time*, the demand and notice is unnecessary. On proof of the written instrument or demand and notice, the jury may in their *discretion* give interest. 3 and 4 Wm. IV., c. 42, s. 28.

69. *Q.* How is the liability to pay interest on simple contract debts affected by the Statute 3 and 4 Wm. IV., c. 42.

*A.* See the previous answer.

70. *Q.* What is the effect of a release given to one of two or more joint and several debtors?

*A.* It has the effect of releasing all the debtors, unless it is expressly provided that it is only to extend to the one. Chitty on Contracts, 693.

71. *Q.* Explain briefly the terms, "charter-party," "bill of lading," "general average," and "particular average."

*A.* The term "charter-party" is applied to an agreement in writing, sometimes under seal, by which a shipowner agrees to let his ship to a merchant for the carriage of goods on a specified voyage or for a certain time, the merchant agreeing to pay freight for the carriage.

A "bill of lading" is a memorandum signed by masters of ships, in their capacity of carriers, acknowledging the receipt of merchants' goods.

"General average" is the contribution which the owners of the cargo and ship make to reimburse one of themselves who has suffered a loss for the general safety, as if a mast is cut away in a storm and the ship is saved in consequence.

"Particular average" arises where any damage is done to the cargo or vessel by accident or otherwise, such as the loss of an anchor or cable; the turning sour of wine. In these cases, the loss rests where it falls, *i.e.*, the owner of the damaged goods bears the loss and gets no general contribution from the others. Maude and Pollock's Merchant Shipping. (It is difficult to see why the latter is called "average" at all.)

72. *Q.* How is the property in a British ship transferred from the vendor to the purchaser?

*A.* It is transferred by bill of sale containing a description of the vessel, and executed in the presence of, and attested by, one or more witnesses. The transferee must make a declaration in conformity with "The Merchant Shipping Act, 1854," which, with the bill of sale, must be produced to the registrar of the port where the ship is registered, who will register the transferee as owner. Maude and Pollock, 91.

73. *Q.* What is meant by "stoppage *in transitu*," and how is the right lost?

*A.* It is the right which the consignor of goods has of stopping them *in transitu*, if unpaid for, upon the insolvency of the consignee. It is lost by the determination of the *transitus*, as where the goods are delivered to the consignee, or in any other way he takes possession of them. It is also lost by the consignee transferring the bill of lading to a third person *bonâ fide* and for value. *Lickbarrow* v. *Mason*, 1 Sm. L. C. 681. *Birkley* v. *Presgrave*, L. C. Mercantile Law, 74.

V.—*Bills of Exchange, Promissory Notes, and Bankers' Cheques.*

1. *Q.* Can a person lawfully receive more than £5 per cent. interest; and, if so, on what security?

*A.* He may now on any security. This question was asked before the repeal of the usury laws. 17 and 18 Vic., c. 90.

2. *Q.* Define a bill of exchange, and state the parties to it. Which of them is primarily liable; and how is this liability affected by the bill being accepted for accommodation?

*A.* It is a written order or request signed but not sealed, by one person to another, for the payment of a sum of money at a specified time, unconditionally. The person making the request is termed the drawer; the person to whom it is made, the drawee, and after acceptance by him, the acceptor; the person in whose favour it is made, the payee. The acceptor is primarily liable, that is, when the bill falls due it must be presented for payment to the acceptor, or the other parties cannot be sued. If the acceptance is for accommodation, the acceptor can only be sued by a *bonâ fide* holder for value, not by the drawer. Smith's Manual of Common Law, 192.

3. *Q.* Define a promissory note.

*A.* It is a written engagement by one person to pay another therein named, absolutely and unconditionally, a certain sum of money at a time specified therein. The person who makes the note is called the maker, and the person to whom it is payable the payee. Chitty on Bills, 1.

4. *Q.* State in what particulars bills of exchange and promissory notes differ from other simple contracts.

*A.* Bills and notes require all the essentials of a simple contract, but differ from them in that in suing on them it is unnecessary to prove consideration until the want of it is shown. They must always be in writing. An infant cannot bind himself by them for necessaries. Interest is recoverable on them though not specially stipulated for. They are assignable at law. The consideration need not appear on the face of them. They must be for the payment of money only. They must be stamped. Chitty, jun., on Contracts, c. 1.

5. *Q.* What is the liability incurred by an indorser?

*A.* He is considered a surety for the previous parties to the bill, and is liable as such to be sued by a *bond fide* holder for value, in default of acceptance or payment by the drawee. He contracts that if the drawee do not at maturity pay the bill, he, the indorser, will, on receiving due notice of dishonour. *Suse* v. *Pomp.*, 30 L. J. C. P. 75. Byles on Bills, 139, 8th ed.

6. *Q.* Is there any difference in the extent of the liability of an acceptor of a bill of exchange, as between himself and third parties, and as between himself and the drawer?

*A.* As before mentioned if the acceptance is for the accommodation of the drawer, the acceptor cannot be sued by him; but he is liable, at the suit of a *bond fide* holder, for value, whether such holder took the bill before or after maturity. *Supra.*

7. *Q.* A client brings an overdue bill of exchange to his attorney: give a detailed account of the steps that must be taken to enforce payment, and suggest any difficulties occurring to you that may arise as to its recovery, also some of the different ways in which the client might be holder of the bill.

*A.* The bill must first be presented for payment, and if a foreign bill its dishonor should be protested. Assuming the client to be the payee, he should give notice of dishonor to the drawer. Before suing, the attorney should consider whether the bill was barred by the Statute; whether properly stamped; whether there was a valuable consideration; whether it was unconditional and for the payment of money at a specified time; whether the proposed defendants were persons capable of binding themselves by such an instrument, *i.e.*, not infants, lunatics, etc.; whether the debt had been released by his client. Should none of these objections appear, a writ may be issued under "The Bills of Exchange Act, 1855," (as to which, see *infra*, No. 18,) or if the bill is six months overdue, an ordinary specially endorsed writ must be resorted to. As to the proceedings in the action, see *infra*, No. 18. The client might, instead of being the payee, be the indorsee.

8. *Q.* By whom can a bill of exchange be accepted; what constitutes such acceptance; and what is the difference between an inland and a foreign bill?

BILLS, NOTES, AND CHEQUES. 23

*A.* By all persons labouring under no disability, general or partial. Thus infants and married women are wholly incapacitated from accepting bills. Also corporations, agents, and partners, under certain circumstances. An engagement in writing to pay, by the drawee, upon the bill signed by him or some duly authorised agent constitutes an acceptance. 19 and 20 Vic., c. 97., s. 6. A foreign bill is one drawn by a person abroad upon a person in England, or *vice versa,* it must be protested when dishonoured; this is not necessary in the case of an inland bill. The stamp duty is different. Also in suing on a foreign bill the contract is expounded according to the law of the country where the bill is payable, but in an inland bill by the *lex loci contractus.* Chitty on Contracts, 89.

9. *Q.* In an action on a bill of exchange, how can the plaintiff prevent the defendant from setting up the loss of the instrument?

*A.* By applying to the Court or Judge for an order that the loss shall not be set up. The plaintiff must give an indemnity against the claims of any other person upon the bill. 17 and 18 Vic., c. 125, s. 87.

10. *Q.* What steps are necesssary to enable a holder of a bill of exchange to sue the acceptor?

*A.* The bill must be presented for payment to the acceptor at his usual residence or place of business. If the bill is a foreign one the non-payment must be protested.

11. *Q.* To which parties to a bill of exchange or promissory note must a notice of dishonour be given, if it be wished to hold them liable?

*A.* It should be given to the drawer for the purpose of enabling him to draw his effects out of the hands of the acceptor. Also to any previous indorser whom the holder intends to sue. Notice to the acceptor of the bill or maker of the note is of course unnecessary. Selwyn's Nisi Prius, 399.

12. *Q.* The holder of a bill of exchange has a right to sue the drawer, acceptor, and indorser of it; can he do so by means of one writ, or is he bound to issue three separate writs?

*A.* In suing under 18 and Vic., c. 67, he may sue them in one writ or separately at his option. A holder is, however, not bound to proceed under this act, but he may issue separate writs. In cases not coming within this act separate writs *must* be issued. Thus, if the bill was six months overdue one writ will not suffice.

13. *Q.* What is the meaning of a bill of exchange accepted *per pro.?* And what is the consequence if this be done without authority?

*A.* It is an acceptance by an agent of a bill of exchange in the name of his principal, and is notice that the party so accepting professes to act under an authority. It imposes on the indorsee the duty of ascertaining that the party so accepting is acting in accordance with the terms of such authority, *Alexander* v. *Mackenzie,* P. O., 6, C. B., 766. If there be no authority, the party accepting *per pro.* is personally liable to be sued on his implied warranty that he had authority as agent to contract. *Polhill* v. *Walter,* 3 B. and Ad., 114; *Collin* v. *Wright,* 26 L. J. (Q. B.) 147. He cannot, however, be sued upon the bill. Chitty on Bills, 28. 10th ed.

14. *Q.* If the acceptor of a bill of exchange refuse payment of it when due, is any and what step necessary before you can sue the drawer or indorser?
*A.* Notice of dishonour should be given as mentioned, *supra*.

15. *Q.* Within what time ought notice of the dishonour of an inland bill, accepted for value, be given to the drawer and indorser by the holder?
*A.* Where the holder and the party to whom notice is given live at different places, it is sufficient if the notice is sent off on the day next after the day of dishonour, or if the post does not depart the next day, then by the next post day. *Williams* v. *Smith*, 2 B. and Ald., 496. Where both parties live in the same town, or where they live in London, notice must be given in time to be received in the course of the day following the day of dishonour. Byles on Bills, 263, 8th ed.

16. *Q.* When a bill of exchange is payable to bearer can a person who is holder for value sue upon it, whether the party from whom it was taken had a title to it or not?
*A.* Yes, he can sue, provided he had no notice of the want of title, but took it *bona fide* and for valuable consideration. *Clarke* v. *Shee*, Cowp. 197. See also the notes to *Miller* v. *Race*, 1 Sm. L. C. 450, 5th ed.

17. *Q.* In an action brought under 18 and 19 Vic., c. 67, against the acceptor of a bill of exchange who has not paid the bill when due, can the defendant appear and plead as in other actions; and, if not, what steps must he take to enable him to do so?
*A.* No, leave to appear must be first obtained as mentioned in the next answer.

18. *Q.* State shortly the principal provisions of the summary procedure on Bills of Exchange Act (1855).
*A.* They are to enable a holder of bills, notes, and cheques, to sue on them within six months of their being payable, by means of a writ requiring the defendant to appear within twelve days after the service of the writ inclusive of the day of service, but to do this, he must first obtain leave from a Judge. The application must be supported by an affidavit showing a defence on the merits, or that it is reasonable, that he should be allowed to appear. Payment into court of the sum indorsed on the writ will have a similar effect. If no leave obtained, plaintiff may sign judgment and issue execution on the expiration of the twelve days. See *infra* "Appearance," No. 7.

19. *Q.* What is the proper mode of suing on a bill of exchange or promissory note with respect to indorsing the writ under the above act?
*A.* The indorsement consists of a copy of the bill or note and all indorsements upon it. A claim for the principal and interest. Also for the costs of noting. A notice that judgment will be signed and execution issued, and that leave to appear may be obtained at Judges' Chambers. Reg. Gen., Nov. 1855.

20. *Q.* Where several actions are brought on a bill of exchange

or promissory note, upon what terms can the acceptor of the bill of exchange, or the maker of the promissory note, stay the proceedings?

A. Upon the terms of paying the costs in that action only. Reg. Gen. H. T., 1853.

21. Q. State the ordinary evidence to support an action by an indorsee of a bill of exchange against the acceptor, where everything necessary to be proved is put in issue.

A. The plaintiff must first prove the bill by producing it; he must then prove the acceptance of the bill by the defendant by giving proof of his handwriting. The acceptance once proved admits the drawing. He must then prove the indorsement, and if it be special it must appear that the indorsee is the person described in it. If the instrument is payable to bearer or indorsed in blank, no subsequent indorsement need be proved. It will be unnecessary to prove consideration unless the defendant makes out a *prima facie* case against him by shewing that the bill was obtained by undue means, as by fraud. Presentment need not be proved. Byles on Bills, 109, 410, 8th ed.; Chitty on Bills, 413, 10th ed.

22. Q. In an action upon a bill of exchange by drawer against acceptor, and the defendant pleads payment only, has the plaintiff anything and what to prove?

A. This plea would entitle the defendant to begin, therefore the plaintiff would have nothing to prove. But he should be prepared with evidence to disprove that adduced by the defendant. Smith's Action at Law, 142, 6th ed.

23. Q. What evidence can be adduced against an endorser in an action on a bill of exchange?

A. The defendant would probably traverse the indorsement and the plaintiff would have to prove the genuineness of defendant's signature, the fact of the delivery to the plaintiff, and that the delivery was not for temporary purpose. Various other defences might be set up which would add to the proof of the plaintiff. Chitty on Bills, 282, 10th ed.

24. Q. State the evidence necessary to support an action upon a bill of exchange by a second or subsequent indorsee against a drawer, where everything is required to be proved.

A. Prove the drawing of the bill by the defendant the indorser's signature; a due presentment for payment, and the dishonour; lastly, prove notice of dishonour. Byles on Bills, 411.

25. Q. In an action upon a bill of exchange, brought by an indorsee against the acceptor, where the bill is drawn payable to the drawer's own order, and by him endorsed to the plaintiff, what evidence is necessary to enable the plaintiff to obtain a verdict, supposing the defendant to plead only that he did not accept the bill?

A. Produce the bill and prove the defendant's handwriting as having accepted the bill. This will admit the drawing of it, but it will be further necessary to prove the indorsement by the drawer, as the acceptance does not admit this. *Bosanquet* v. *Anderson*, 6 Esp. 43.

26. *Q.* How is the debt affected in law when the payee of a promissory note dies leaving the maker of the note his executor?

*A.* The debt is considered to be gone, as the debt is at law looked upon merely as a right to bring an action, and the executor cannot sue himself. The rule is otherwise in equity. See *infra*, Williams on Executors, 1128.

27. *Q.* Are notes or bills, given to secure money lost at play at unlawful games, altogether void, or may they be enforced under any, and if any, what circumstances?

*A.* They are not void, but are deemed to be given for an *illegal* consideration. 5 and 6 Wm. IV., c. 41. The effect of this enactment is to render such securities good in the hands of a *bond fide* holder. *Hay* v. *Ayling*, 20 L. J. Q. B., 171.

28. *Q.* Define a promissory note?

*A.* It is an unconditional promise in writing to pay to A or order, or to A or bearer, a sum of money, either at sight, or at a certain time after sight, or after date, or on demand. Selwyn's Nisi Prius, 425.

29. *Q.* A promissory note is made payable to a woman before her marriage. She afterwards marries, and the husband dies leaving her surviving. Can she bring an action upon the note?

*A.* If the husband has not reduced the chose en action into possession, by recovering it, the right to sue will survive to the wife, and if not barred by the statute she can bring her action.

30. *Q.* A promissory note is made payable to a husband and wife, and the husband dies before it is paid, his wife surviving him. Can she maintain an action upon the note?

*A.* She may sue upon the note, as upon the husband's death all the choses en action upon which the wife might have sued jointly with him, survive to her, whether they accrued before or during the coverture. Lush's Practice, 45, 3rd edit.

31. *Q.* Define a cheque.

*A.* It is a written order by a customer on his banker, directing him to pay a sum of money to a certain person, to his order, or to bearer, or on demand.

32. *Q.* A takes a cheque of B on his bankers, and cannot, without some inconvenience, present it for payment until some days after; and, when he does so, finds that the bankers have stopped payment in the meantime. Can he recover the amount afterwards against B?

*A.* No, he cannot; the draft should be presented within a reasonable time, otherwise A must bear the loss in the event of the failure of the bank. If the bank does not fail, presentment within six years will be good as against the drawer. *Robinson* v. *Hawksford*, 9 Q. B., 52; *Laws* v. *Rand*, 3 C. B., N. S., 442.

33. *Q.* What is the legal effect of "crossing" a cheque with the name of a banking firm? Is the banker upon whom the cheque is drawn at liberty to disregard the crossing?

*A.* The effect of the crossing is to prevent its being cashed excepting through the medium of a banker; that is, if A gives a crossed cheque to B, the latter cannot get it cashed over the counter, but must pay it into his own banking account, and his banker will get the money from A's banker. If the banker disregards the crossing, and pays the cheque over the counter to a person not entitled to it, he is responsible to his customer, unless indeed the crossing has been so skilfully erased as not to be apparent. 21 and 22 Vic., c. 79.

## VI.—*Landlord and Tenant.*

1. *Q.* Is it necessary that a notice to quit should in all cases be in writing?
*A.* Unless specially agreed that a written notice is to be given, or for the purpose of recovering double value under 4 Geo. II. c. 28, the notice need not be in writing. Chitty on Contracts, 322.
2. *Q.* What notice to quit should be given by or to a tenant who holds under a yearly, monthly, or weekly tenancy?
*A.* By a yearly tenant, half a year's notice should be given; but a monthly or weekly letting of apartments will cease at the end of the term without any notice to quit, unless there be some local custom or stipulation to the contrary. If there is such a custom, the notice would be a month or a week. Woodfall, 291, 8th ed.
3. *Q.* Does a half-year's notice to quit refer to any particular period of the tenancy?
*A.* It should refer to the end of the current year of the tenancy. Thus, if a tenancy commenced on January 1st, 1864, the notice should refer to January 1st, 1865. *Ibid*, 322; Stephs. Coms. 1, 298.
4. *Q.* What are the quarter-days of the year? If a tenancy from year to year commence at Lady-day, 1857, when would it be determinable?
*A.* They are: Lady-day (25th March), Midsummer-day (24th June), Michaelmas-day (29th September), Christmas-day (25th December). This tenancy would be determinable at Lady-day, 1858, by half a year's notice.
5. *Q.* If a house and stables are let from year to year under one letting, can the landlord give a valid notice to quit the stables only?
*A.* No; a notice to quit part of premises which have been let together is bad. *Doe* and *Dodd* v. *Archer*, 14 East. 245.
6. *Q.* A notice to quit being given by a landlord to his tenant, what liability does the tenant incur by holding over?
*A.* If a demand of possession was made, and the notice was in writing, he must pay at the rate of double the yearly value for the time he holds over. 4 Geo. II., c. 28. He is also liable to be ejected.
7. *Q.* Receipt for half a year's rent to Christmas last; does it prove payment of the rent to the previous Midsummer?
*A.* Such receipt is *prima facie* evidence that previous rent has been paid, but it may be rebutted on proof to the contrary. Woodfall's L. and T., 698.

8. *Q.* An occupier of two houses under two different landlords, one at a rent certain, the other without any agreement for any specific sum: have the two landlords the like remedy for rent, or how does it differ?

*A.* In the former case the landlord may distrain, the rent being certain; he may also bring an action of debt. In the latter, an action for use and occupation would be the remedy, if the occupation was not by virtue of a deed. 11 Geo. II., c. 19, s. 14. If there was a deed, the remedy would be covenant. Selwyn's Nisi Prius, 1380.

9. *Q.* A grants a lease to B for 21 years, at the rent of £100 *per annum*; at the end of three years B assigns the remainder of the term to C, subject to the rent; after this assignment, rent becomes due to A, who, not being able to obtain payment from C, calls upon B to pay; B objects that he has assigned to C: is B liable to pay the rent?

*A.* The liability of the lessee remains during the whole of the term, notwithstanding an assignment by him. This liability is in consequence of the privity of contract created by the lease. B is, therefore, liable to pay the rent and may be sued on this covenant. Woodfall's L. and T., 104.

10. *Q.* Is a tenant liable to pay the rent of premises accidentally destroyed by fire, under any and what circumstances?

*A.* If the tenancy is created by deed and there is a covenant to pay rent, without excepting the event of destruction by fire, the tenant is still liable to be sued. So also if the letting is not by deed. Use and occupation will also lie. Selwyn's Nisi Prius, 495. 1386.

11. *Q.* Must a lease for seven years be in writing, and what is the limit of time for which a parol lease may be legally made?

*A.* Yes, by virtue of 29 Car. II, c. 3, s. 1. A parol lease not exceeding three years from the making, and on which not less than two thirds of the full improved value is reserved, is legal. Ibid., s. 2.

12. *Q.* If an original lessee in a lease covenant to insure against fire, but omit to do so, and he by covenant is bound to uphold, and the premises be burned down, he having assigned his term, and the assignee will not reinstate the premises, are the original lessee and assignee liable to do so, or which of them?

*A.* The lessee would be bound to reinstate them, owing to the privity of contract existing between himself and the lessor, to repair and uphold. The assignee would also be liable, the covenant to repair being one running with the land. The case would be otherwise if, as is usual, damage by fire were excepted from the covenant to repair. Woodfall, 465.

13. *Q.* What fixtures may a tenant remove, and when must such removal be made?

*A.* He may remove articles erected for the purposes of trade or manufacture, such as cider mills, vats, steam engines; also things put up for ornament or domestic use, as book cases, grates, hangings.

Their removal must be without causing any material injury to the estate. Fixtures erected for the purpose of trade and agriculture mixed, or agriculture alone, are removable by virtue of 14 and 15 Vic., c. 26, if put up with the consent in writing of the landlord. One month's notice of removal must be given, and the landlord has the option to purchase the fixtures. The removal must be made during the tenancy. *Elwes* v. *Mawe*. 2 Sm. L. C. 141. Selwyn's Nisi Prius, 1343.

14. *Q.* What constitutes a waiver of a proviso of re-entry?

*A.* Generally the doing of any act acknowledging the continuance of the tenancy, knowing that a forfeiture has taken place, is a waiver. Such acts are, distraining for rent accrued due after the forfeiture or accepting payment of it. Woodfall's L. and T., 283.

15. *Q.* If a landlord let a house on an agreement, and the tenant run away, leaving no sufficient property on the premises to pay the rent, how is the landlord to obtain possession so as to put an end to the agreement? And how would the case be altered by the tenant secreting himself on the premises, and shutting them up?

*A.* The landlord should request two justices to attend and view the premises. The justices should affix a notice, on a conspicuous part of the premises, that (at the distance of fourteen days at least) they will return and take a second view, at which view, if the tenant do not appear and pay the rent, or there is not sufficient distress on the premises, the justices will give the landlord possession. 11 Geo. II., c. 19, s. 16. If the tenant were to secrete himself on the premises, they would not be "deserted" within the above Act, and the landlord could not proceed under it, but must take the ordinary remedy by ejectment. The rent must be at a rack rent, or three fourths of the yearly value, and must be in arrear half a year. See the cases collected by Woodfall, 886.

16. *Q.* What repairs or dilapidations is a tenant from year to year liable to make good in respect of a messuage or land so let to him?

*A.* He is liable to make tenantable repairs, such as putting in windows or doors broken by him, and other injuries arising from his voluntary negligence; but he is not liable to make substantial and lasting, or general repairs, as the putting on a roof. Woodfall's L. and T., 405. Chitty on Contracts, 307.

17. *Q.* If a landlord let a house by parol for three years, and nothing is mentioned as to repairs, state what repairs each party would be liable to, and what would be dilapidations on the part of the tenant.

*A.* The landlord would not be under any liability to repair, as there is no implied covenant by him to do so; but there is an implied contract by the tenant to use the buildings in a tenantable manner and to do ordinary repairs for keeping them in this state. The cases on this latter point are, however, doubtful. See Woodfall's L. and T., 116. Dilapidation by the tenant would be pulling down walls, breaking windows, etc., allowing the house to go out of repair (*sed quare*).

18. *Q.* Is a landlord or incoming tenant, and which, liable at the expiration of a lease to pay the outgoing tenant in respect of manure, crops, etc., who holds under a lease, and what will be the difference if he be only a tenant at will?

*A.* It is almost a universal custom to allow the outgoing tenant for his away-going crop, and generally also for manure, unless the lease negative the custom. Where the right exists, the tenant may avail himself of it against the new tenant, or, if no new tenant, against the landlord. Woodfall's L. and T., 565. In the case of a tenancy at will being determined suddenly by the landlord, he would also be entitled to his away-going crop. Ibid., 178.

19. *Q.* In what cases can the Common Law Courts relieve tenants from forfeiture in actions of ejectment under "The Common Law Procedure Act, 1860"?

*A.* 1. In the case of ejectment being brought for a forfeiture for non-payment of rent; 2. In case of forfeiture for non-insuring pursuant to a covenant where no loss or damage by fire has happened, and the breach has, in the opinion of the Court, been committed through accident, or mistake, or otherwise, without fraud or gross negligence, and there is an insurance on foot at the time of the application, in conformity to the covenant. 23 and 24 Vic., c. 126, ss. 1, 2; 22 & 23 Vic., c. 35, s. 4.

20. *Q.* A house is let to a tenant for one year certain from 1st January, 1860, and so on from year to year, as long as both parties please. What is the earliest day on which this tenancy can be determined?

*A.* The tenancy cannot be determined until the 31st December, 1861, as half a year's notice must be given *to end* at the period of the year, when the tenancy commenced. The first year being *certain*, no notice could determine it, and, therefore, the tenancy must continue another year. *Denn* v. *Cartwright*, 4 East. 32; but see *Thompson* v. *Maberly*, 4 Camp., 28.

## VII.—*The Law of Torts or Private Wrongs.*

1. *Q.* Is an infant liable for torts committed by him?

*A.* Yes, he is liable, if the torts are unconnected with contract, such as for an assault, battery, or the like. But if the tort arise out of contract, he cannot be sued. Thus, where an infant obtained goods, not necessaries, by fraudulently misrepresenting that he was of full age, he was held not to be liable, as if it was otherwise he would lose the protection of his infancy. *Bartlett* v. *Wells*, 1 B. and S., 836. A similar principle applies to married women. *Liverpool Loan Association* v. *Fairhurst*, 9 Ex. 422.

2. *Q.* An orphan of tender years has had his leg broken by wilful negligence: can he bring an action for the injury? if so, how and what action?

*A.* The infant may sue by guardian or *prochein amy*, appointed by a judge on petition. If the injury was caused by some direct act, as negligently dropping a log of wood on the infant in the street, the action would be trespass. But if it arose consequentially on the wrongful act, the action would be trespass on the case; as if the log of wood being dropped, and the infant, while walking along, was to tumble over it, and break his leg. *Scott* v. *Shepherd*, 1 Sm. L. C. 399.

3. *Q.* A father and his child, aged ten, receive injuries by a collision on a railway. State by whom an action must be brought for compensation for these injuries, and whether it must be by one or more actions.

*A.* The father should bring one action as to the injury to himself, and a separate one should be brought by the child, suing by guardian or *prochein amy*. There is no objection to the father being such guardian or next friend, but still separate actions must be brought, the claims being in different rights. Addison on Wrongs, 819, 2nd ed.

4. *Q.* What is the difference between slander and libel?

*A.* The chief distinction is, that slander is the malicious defamation of a person by words; libel is the same by writing, pictures, statues, etc. Many words, though not actionable if spoken, are so if written. Thus, to call a man a swindler, is not actionable (unless spoken in reference to his trade or business), but to write this of him would be actionable. The reason of this is the more lasting effect which anything written must have. The remedy for a libel also differs, in that it is indictable as well as actionable. The period of limitation, too, is six years, in cases of libel, but two years in those of slander. Selwyn's Nisi Prius, 1,049—1,252.

5. *Q.* For what damages are hundredors liable, and what are the necessary steps to be taken before a writ is issued, and against whom should it issue?

*A.* Hundredors are now only liable for damages done by rioters *feloniously*. If the damage exceed £30, an action may be brought within three calendar months. Prior to bringing the action the plaintiff, or his servant, having the care of the property injured, shall, within seven days after the commission of the offence, go before some near resident justice, and state on oath the names of the offenders, and submit to an examination, and enter into a recognizance to prosecute. The process is the same as in ordinary cases; it is directed to "the men inhabiting within the hundred of         , in the county of         ," or other like district generally, and not against any individuals by name. The writ is served on the high constable, or on any one of the high constables of the hundred (15 and 16 Vic., c. 76, s. 16). If the damage done does not exceed £30, no action can be brought, but the proceeding is summary before justices at a special petty session (7 & 8 Geo. IV., c. 31). 2 Chitty's Archbold, 1187.

6. *Q.* In actions of libel or slander, what is the meaning of the communication being privileged? Give some instances of privileged communications.

*A.* It means some communication which, under ordinary circumstances, would be actionable, yet, being made *bonâ fide* upon some subject matter, in which the party communicating has an *interest*, or in reference to which he has a *duty*, is privileged from being actionable, if made to a person having a corresponding interest or duty. Such are communications between solicitor and client; the character of a servant. This privilege is, however, no defence, if express malice can be shown. Selwyn's Nisi Prius, 1,053—4.

7. *Q.* A B, in the presence of a witness, makes a representation concerning the character of a third party, upon which credit is given to the latter; such representation proving false, can an action be successfully maintained against A B?

*A.* He cannot be sued, unless the representation were in writing, and signed by him. 9 Geo. IV., c. 14, s. 6. It must also be shown that A B knew the representation to be untrue, and that it was made with an intention to obtain credit for the third party. Selwyn's Nisi Prius, 645.

8. *Q.* A man commits an assault in the street, and in so doing breaks, unintentionally, a square of valuable plate-glass in a shop window; another slips down accidentally, and does the like. Has the owner of the glass a remedy at law against both or either of the persons? State briefly the ground upon which your answer is founded.

*A.* In the first case, the owner of the glass may sue the wrong doer for the damage, the reason being that he must be compensated for the damage, even although it was caused unintentionally, and whether in the doing of a lawful or unlawful act. In this case the act was unlawful. In the case of the man slipping down, no action would lie if the accident was inevitable, or if it was occasioned by the shopkeeper's negligence. This must be decided by the actual facts of the case. It must, however, be borne in mind, that to constitute a right of action for an injury to the property of another, the intent of the person causing damage is wholly immaterial. Broom's Coms., 674, 3rd ed.

9. *Q.* A commits on assault upon B, and before action brought B dies. Can B's executors or administrators sue A for the recovery of damages for the assault?

*A.* No, the action does not survive, unless the death ensued from the assault. See next answer.

10. *Q.* Define the maxim *Actio Personalis Moritur cum Persond*; and state if there are any, and what exceptions?

*A.* This maxim embodies the ancient rule of the Common Law, that actions *ex-delicto* do not survive either for or against the representatives of a deceased person. The maxim does not embrace actions *ex contractu*. Various exceptions to the rule have been introduced by statute, and executors may now maintain ejectment, *quare impedit, trover or replevin*, the conversion or taking having been in the testator's lifetime. An executor may also sue a sheriff in case, for a false return to a *fi. fa.* made in the lifetime of the testator; also for injuries to the real estate of the deceased committed in his lifetime, the injury having been committed within six

## TORTS. DEATH FROM NEGLIGENCE.

calendar months before the death, and the action brought within one year from the death. 4 Ed. III., c. 7; 3 and 4 Wm. IV., c. 42. Also by 9 and 10 Vic., c. 93, an action is maintainable against a person who by his wrongful act has occasioned the death of another. The personal representatives of a deceased may also be sued for any wrong committed to another in respect of his property real or personal. 3 and 4 Wm. IV., c. 42, s. 2.

11. *Q.* A party is injured while travelling by railway. State a case in which he has a remedy, and one where he has not any against the company.

*A.* If the injury arises from the negligence of the company, as from the too frequent running of trains, the bad construction of their lines, etc., he has a remedy. But should the injury have arisen from his own want of care, they would not be liable, as in such a case he is the author of his own wrong. Selwyn's Nisi Prius, 446. See also *infra,* No. 17.

12. *Q.* In case of injury to a person, from which death ensues, is there any mode by which compensation can be sought, and by what means, and by whom, and against whom must it be brought?

*A.* An action to recover damages may be brought by the executor or administrator of the deceased, for the benefit of his or her, wife, husband, parent (the term "parent" includes father and mother, grandfather and grandmother, and stepfather and stepmother), and child ("child," includes son and daughter, and grandson and granddaughter, and stepson and stepdaughter). The action is to be brought against the person who would have been liable, had death not ensued, that is, usually the party causing the injury, and must be brought within twelve calendar months after the death. 9 and 10 Vic., c. 93. By a recent statute, if there be no personal representative, or if there be one and he does not bring the action within six months after the death, the action may be brought by the persons beneficially interested. Also, if money is paid into court, it may be paid in in one sum, without regard to its division into shares, and if the jury think it sufficient, the defendant is entitled to a verdict. 27 and 28 Vic., c. 95.

13. *Q.* If I start game in my own land, have I a right to follow it into the land of my neighbour?

*A.* You have no such right at common law, and, therefore, are a trespasser, and liable as such to be sued. Stephs. Coms. 2, 22. You would also be liable to be prosecuted as a trespasser in pursuit of game, under 1 and 2 Wm. IV., c. 32. If, however, you were to flush a pheasant on your own land, and it flew over the boundary fence, after which you fired at it and killed it, and then went and picked it up, you could not be prosecuted, under s. 30 of the above act. It would be otherwise if you had only wounded the bird. *Kenyon* v. *Hart,* 34 L. J. M. C., 87.

14. *Q.* When is a master answerable for damage done by his servant, and when not, and how may his liability be altered by the fact of the injured party being also his servant?

*A.* The master is liable for damage caused by the negligence or unskilfulness of the servant whilst acting in his master's employ. As where the servants of a carman ran over a boy in the street and maimed him by negligence. But if the servant commits a *wilful* trespass without the direction or assent of his master the servant only is liable. As where a servant of the defendant wilfully drove defendant's carriage against the plaintiff's. The defendant was not present, nor had he in any manner directed or assented to his servant's act. Held, that he was not liable. *M'Manus* v. *Crickett*, 1 East, 106. But see *Limpus* v. *The London General Omnibus Company*, 32 L. J. Ex. 34. The master is not liable if the damage is done to a fellow servant; provided the servants had one common employment and were not exposed to unreasonable risks, and the master had selected proper servants, and had not acquiesced in the negligence. Selwyn's Nisi Prius, 1119.

15. *Q.* Whilst A is riding in his carriage, his coachman in driving knocks a man down, and injures him. Upon another occasion, when A is not in his carriage, his coachman does a similar thing. Can the party injured bring an action of trespass against A in both, or either, and which of, these cases?

*A.* As mentioned in the previous answer, if the act was *wilful* the master would not be liable if absent (*sed quære* if he were present). If the act was not done wilfully but arose through negligence or unskilfulness, and the servant was doing his master's work, the master would be liable whether present or not. If the master was in the carriage the form of action would be " Trespass"; if not, it would be " Case." Ibid.

16. *Q.* In case of injury to a person on the Queen's highway by job horses on a yearly hiring not driven by the job-master's servant, who is liable for it, and to what extent?

*A.* If the injury arose from the negligence or unskilfulness of the driver the hirer of the horses would be liable, he having supplied the driver and having control over him. Selwyn's Nisi Prius, 1122.

17. *Q.* In what way is a stage-coach proprietor liable to a passenger travelling by his coach, for hurt or injury? and does the same liability extend to common carriers, whether by land or water, or railway? And how, and against whom, should he seek redress?

*A.* He is liable for an injury arising from the negligence or misconduct of the driver, or from the bad construction of his coach, even if the defect be out of sight and is not discoverable on ordinary examination. *Sharp* v. *Grey*, 9 Bing. 457. All common carriers *of passengers* are in like manner bound to provide for their safety, so far as human care and foresight can go. Redress should be sought against the carrier with whom the contract to carry is entered into. A carrier of passengers therefore is not an insurer of his passengers as a carrier of goods is of the goods, *supra*. Selwyn's Nisi Prius. Contracts No. 46, " Carriers."

18. *Q.* If A sues for damage, arising from the negligent conduct of B, how far may his right to recover be affected by his own want of care?

*A.* If the negligence of A has been such that it has contributed to and caused the accident, notwithstanding the negligence of B, no action will lie. But *any* negligence will not prevent him recovering, as in the great *Donkey Case* of *Davies* v. *Mann,* 10 M. and W., 546. There the plaintiff had improperly left an ass fettered on the highway, and it was held that he was entitled to recover against the defendant who negligently drove against it. It was considered that the defendant by the exercise of ordinary care and skill need not have run into the ass, therefore the plaintiff's negligence in allowing it to go hoppled could not be said to have been the proximate cause of loss. *Tuff* v. *Warman,* 27 L. J. C. P., 332. See the notes to *Ashby* v. *White,* 1 Sm. L. C., 252.

19. *Q.* State some of the nuisances affecting dwelling-houses and lands, for which an action will lie.

*A.* They are: Building a house so as to hang over the land of another, whereby rain falls upon it. The erection of a swine stye, lime-kiln, privy, smith's forge, tobacco mill, tallow furnace, so near the house of another as to render it unfit for habitation. Carrying on an offensive trade. Blocking up ancient lights. Diverting water courses. Blocking up or obstructing ways. Disturbing the enjoyment of a pew annexed to a house in the parish. Selwyn's Nisi Prius, "Nuisance."

20. *Q.* May the owner of a horse, which has been stolen from him, retake it in any, and what, place?

*A.* In such a case the horse may be taken wherever he is found, even if in a private stable. 3 Steph. Coms., 253. If not feloniously stolen he can only be taken on a common, in a fair, or at a public inn. Broom's Maxims, 274.

21. *Q.* How should a person proceed for damages against a wilful trespasser, when they would not amount to £5?

*A.* He should lay an information before a justice of the peace who will thereon issue a summons to the offender. The justice has power to commit to prison for a term not exceeding two months, or else to impose a penalty not exceeding £5, which will be paid to the party aggrieved by way of compensation, 25 and 26 Vic,. c. 97, s. 52.

22. *Q.* What is the difference between liquidated and unliquidated damages? Give instances of actions in which each species of damages is recoverable.

*Q.* The former consists of a certain fixed and ascertained sum, such as £20 for goods sold. The latter is damage, the amount of which is unascertained and uncertain. As if A assaults B, the damage done to B is unliquidated. After the verdict of the jury it becomes liquidated. So in an action for the price of goods at a certain rate, the damages are liquidated. Chitty on Contracts, 765.

VIII.—*The Attorney and his Client.*

1. *Q.* An attorney, at Christmas, delivers bills to five clients. One for borrowing £1000 on mortgage; another, for de-

fending an action for a libel; a third, for filing a bill in equity, to compel the completion of a purchase; a fourth, for defending a client charged with an assault, at the sessions; and a fifth, for preparing a marriage settlement. Are any, and which, of these bills liable to be taxed? and if the bills are delivered on the 1st of January, and not paid, when can the attorney commence an action to recover them? If the attorney had died, and the bills were delivered by his executor, would that make any difference as to the taxation?

*A.* All the bills might be taxed upon an order being obtained for that purpose, under 6 and 7 Vic., c. 73, s. 37, and it would make no difference if the attorney were dead. The bills may be sued for on the 2nd of February following. See *infra.* Pulling on Attorneys, 336.

2 *Q.* What must be done by an attorney before commencing an action to recover his costs?

*A.* He must, one calendar month before suing, deliver or send to the client his bill of fees, charges, and disbursements, signed by himself, or enclosed with a letter from him referring to the bill. 7 and 8 Vic., c. 73.

3. *Q.* Has an attorney any lien upon a judgment, and, if so, of what nature?

*A.* He has a lien for his costs upon a judgment recovered by his client, in a cause in which he was employed. In its nature, however, it is merely a right to ask the equitable interference of the Court, which may order the judgment to stand as security for his costs. 1 Chitty's Archbold, 136, 11th ed. The Court has now power to make the costs a charge upon the property recovered in the action. 23 and 24 Vic., c. 127, s. 28.

4. *Q.* Is there any and what difference between the lien of a country attorney and that of his town-agent, as to costs due from a client?

*A.* The country attorney has a general lien against his client; but the lien of the town-agent is limited to his charges in the particular matter, in respect of which the papers upon which he claims a lien come into his hands. An agent, moreover, has no lien upon a judgment or money recovered in a cause as the principal attorney has. 1 Chitty's Archbold, 154, 11th ed.

5. *Q.* Assuming an attorney for a plaintiff or defendant by negligence or unskilfulness so to misconduct his client's cause, that it is lost. Has such client any remedy by action against his attorney; and, if so, in what form of action must he sue him; and has he an election of more than one form of action?

*A.* The client may sue the attorney in this case. He may either frame his count upon contract or in tort, for the breach of duty imposed upon him. *Fray* v. *Voules,* 1 E. and E., 839. The tort is said to flow from the breach of contract. Attorneys impliedly undertake to discharge their duty with reasonable skill and integrity. The omission of this, to the damage of their client, is a tortious act, for which case may be brought; it is also a breach of contract. Carriers, surgeons, engineers, and others, are in a similar position to attorneys in this respect. *Brown* v. *Boorman*. 11 Cl. and F., 44; Broom's Coms., 663, 3rd ed.

6. *Q.* When an attorney has carried on a cause to a certain point, can he stay it unless his client furnishes him with money; or how must he proceed?

*A.* He should request the client to supply him with funds necessary to carry on the cause. If upon this the client do not supply him, the attorney may refuse to proceed. 1 Chitty's Archbold, 90, 11th ed.

7. *Q.* Can a party change his attorney during an action, and, if so, are there any conditions imposed on such party?

*A.* He may do so upon obtaining an order from a judge for the purpose. The client must pay the taxed costs of the attorney before the change can be effected, and he must be served with the order. Under special circumstances the order will be refused. Ibid., 90.

IX.—*The Three Considerations preliminary to bringing an Action.*
(1.) *The Statutes of Limitation or Repose.*

1. *Q.* Within what time must an action of debt on simple contract, or on a specialty, or trespass to the person, or slander, be brought, except in cases of disability? Is the time of limitation governed by the Statute or Common Law?

*A.* Debt on simple contract, six years; on specialty, twenty years; trespass to the person, four years; slander, if the words are actionable *per se*, two years; if by reason of special damage, six years. Each of the periods is reckoned from the time the cause of action arose. The time is governed by 21 James I., c. 16, and 3 and 4 Wm. IV., c. 42.

2. *Q.* In respect of a lease under seal, how long does the liability of a lessee last, and within what time may an action of covenant be brought?

*A.* It continues the whole term for which the lease is granted. Covenant must be brought within twenty years after the cause of action accrued. 3 and 4 Wm IV., c. 42, s. 3.

3. *Q.* In what cases of disability may actions be brought after the disability ceases?

*A.* If when the cause of action accrued the plaintiff was an infant, or married woman, or *non compos*, the same period of limitation is allowed after such disability ceases. Formerly absence beyond seas, or imprisonment of the plaintiff came in the same category, but are no longer a disability. 19 and 20 Vic., c. 97, s. 10.

4. *Q.* When there are several parties who are entitled jointly to sue in an action of contract, and one of them is abroad, does the Statute run against the others?

*A.* The Statute runs as against those in the Kingdom though some are abroad. *Perry* v. *Jackson*, 4 T. R., 516. The rule is now the same with regard to defendants, some of whom are abroad. 19 and 20 Vic., c. 97, s. 11.

5. *Q.* Suppose a debt to be incurred by a party resident in this

country, and some months after the debtor leave the country and reside abroad, when would the Statute of Limitations begin to run?

*A.* It would begin to run the moment the creditor had a right to sue for the debt, which would be directly it was incurred, unless suspended by a condition, or the money was to be paid at a future time. In such cases the Statute would run from the happening of the event or the expiration of the time. The Statute once having begun to run, the debtor's going beyond seas would not stop it. Broom's Maxims, 810.

6. *Q.* When a party is beyond seas at the time when a cause of action accrues to him, is he entitled to any, and what, further time for commencing his action beyond the period prescribed by the Statute of Limitations?

*A.* No; not now. See *supra*, No. 3.

7. *Q.* What is required to take a debt out of the Statute of Limitations?

*A.* A debt statute-barred may be revived by an express promise to pay, or an admission or an acknowledgment of the debt in terms so distinct as that a promise to pay on request may be inferred. Such promise or admission must be in writing and signed by the party chargeable, or his duly authorised agent. 9 Geo. IV., c. 14, s. 1; 19 and 20 Vic., c. 97. s. 13. The debt may also be revived by part payment of the debt or interest. Chitty on Contracts, 744.

8. *Q.* If a creditor has two distinct debts owing to him from the same debtor, one of which is barred by the Statute of Limitations; under what circumstances, if any, may he apply money paid by such debtor in satisfaction of the debt so barred?

*A.* He may do so when the debtor in making a general payment on account, does not specify to which debt he intends the payment to be applied. It is the right of the party paying money to appropriate it, but in default, the payee may do so, and he would naturally apply it to the debt which is statute-barred. If neither party appropriate the payment, the law applies it to the first debt in order of date. *Devaynes* v. *Noble, Clayton's Case*, 1, L. C. Merc. Law, 1.

9. *Q.* What is necessary to prevent the Statute of Limitations running against a debt where a defendant has not been served with a copy of a writ?

*A.* The writ should be renewed within six months from its date. This is effected by making out a *præcipe* and having the writ re-sealed at the Master's office. 15 and 16 Vic., c. 76, s. 11.

10. *Q.* Is the Statute of Limitations a good answer to an action of *assumpsit* on a bill of exchange more than six years old, on which bill the interest has been paid within six years?

*A.* No, the payment of the interest would take the debt out of the statute. Chitty, 746.

11. *Q.* If a defendant plead the Statute of Limitations to an action of debt or *assumpsit*, will a verbal promise suffice to prevent

the operation of the statute; or with what evidence must a plaintiff be prepared?

A. No, the promise must be in writing. See *supra*, No. 7.

12. Q. In an action against two or more joint contractors, to recover a debt which is barred by the statute, evidence of an acknowledgment by one of them can be given: will this revive the debt against the other joint contractors?

A. The acknowledgment of one will not suffice. 9 Geo. IV., c. 14. Neither will part payment by one. 19 and 20 Vic., c. 97. s. 14.

13. Q. Does the Statute of Limitations apply where a debtor was abroad when the cause of action accrued, and who has not returned to this country; and, if not, within what time may the action be commenced?

A. The plaintiff has the full period for bringing the action of debt after the defendant's return. 4 and 5 Anne, c. 16, s. 19; 3 and 4 Wm. IV., c. 42, s. 4.

14. Q. Can a defendant take advantage of the statute who has been the whole period out of the country?

A. No. See previous answer.

15. Q. When a person has a lien on goods or title-deeds as a security for his debt, and such debt is afterwards barred by the Statute of Limitations: does the lien continue, or is it determined?

A. In this case the remedy merely is barred, the debt is not extinguished, therefore the lien continues. *Higgins* v. *Scott*, 2 B. and Ad., 413, 414. It should be borne in mind that the Statute of Limitations with regard to land and other real property has not this effect, the right being extinguished also. 3 and 4 Wm. IV., c. 27. s. 34.

(2.) *The proper Parties to an Action.*

1. Q. What person cannot bring actions in their own names?

A. An infant cannot prosecute an action, but must sue by guardian or *prochein amy*. The writ is, however, issued in the infants name. Married women, also, should sue jointly with their husbands. Lunatics sue by their committee. Bankrupts cannot sue in their own names for causes of action passing to the assignees. Outlaws cannot sue until their outlawry is reversed. Chitty's Archbold, 12, 30 *et seq.*

2. Q. What are the exceptions to the general capacity to sue enjoyed by all persons in England? and is a right to sue accruing in foreign parts taken away by a residence abroad of him to whom it accrues?

A. They are the following: persons of non-sane mind; infants; married women; alien enemies; outlaws and persons convicted of felony; bankrupts. The right to sue in our courts would, in general be taken away by residence abroad of the claimant for the period allowed by the law of this country for bringing the action. 19 and 20 Vic., c. 97, s. 9. This act is supposed to include foreigners and British subjects abroad at the time of the cause of action accruing. If the cause of action was *local*, the claimant could not sue here at all, and his remedy would depend upon the *lex loci*. If the cause of action is *transitory*, the *lex loci fori* in which the remedy is sought must prevail, as to the time of limitation. If, therefore, the remedy is barred in this country, it does not follow that it may not be still enforced in a foreign one. Chitty on Contracts, 90.

3. *Q.* How can an infant bring an action?

*A.* The process is sued out in the name of the infant; but, before declaration a guardian or *prochein amy* should be appointed. The appointment is made by rule drawn up, either on the attendance of the parties at Chambers before a judge who will grant a fiat to the Master to draw up the rule, or on petition signed by the infant, directed to the Chief Justice of the Court, praying to be admitted to sue by *prochein amy* or guardian. At the foot of the petition a consent is written signed by the *prochein amy*. The fiat for the rule is granted on the petition. Ibid., 1231.

4. *Q.* If an infant be sued, how can he appear and defend?

*A.* He can appear and defend by guardian only, who is appointed as mentioned in the previous answer. Ib., 1234.

5. *Q.* When an infant plaintiff is nonsuited, or has a verdict against him, who is liable to pay the costs?

*A.* In the former case either the guardian or *prochien amy* are liable; but, an infant defendant is liable personally. The guardian is not liable. Ibid., 1235.

6. *Q.* Can a married woman maintain an action alone, under any circumstances?

*A.* She may when judicially separated. 20 and 21 Vic., c. 85, s. 7. When her husband is *civiliter mortuus*, as when a convicted felon. If he is an alien enemy. If he has been abroad and unheard of for seven years, as then he will be presumed to be dead. If she has obtained a protection order under 20 and 21 Vic., c. 85, s. 21.

7. *Q.* In what cases must you join husband and wife in an action?

*A.* In actions on contracts entered into by the wife *dum sola*; also where she sues as executrix he must join. Also, in actions brought in respect of a personal wrong to the wife, and in actions to recover land belonging to her, or for waste committed on them. Selwyn's Nisi Prius, 344. The Legal Examiner, 162.

8. *Q.* Where a person wishes to recover a debt contracted by a woman before marriage, but who has since married, who is or are the proper party or parties to be made defendant or defendants?

*A.* The husband and wife should be sued jointly. Ibid., 351.

9. *Q.* In the case of a seduction, who is the party to bring the action, and what action must be brought?

*A.* The action must be brought by the person who has lost the services of the girl, that is the parent or her master. It may be brought either in tresspass for the direct injury, or in case for the consequential damages. *Chamberlain* v. *Hazlewood*, 5 M. and W. 515.

10. *Q.* What is the foundation of the action at the suit of a parent for the seduction of his daughter?

*A.* It is his loss of her services, and evidence must be given of her acts of service. The slightest will be sufficient, such as milking the cows. Selwyn's Nisi Prius, 1125.

11. *Q.* A and B, partners, bring an action for a client C When the cause is at issue, A dies, B continues the action, and fails. C afterwards refuses to pay the costs incurred. Who should sue C for the costs?

*A.* The action should be brought by the surviving partner. The contract was made with A and B, but on the death of A it survives to B, who may alone sue.

12. *Q.* If A give a bond to B for £100, and B assign the bond to C, and C bring an action to recover the amount: in whose name should the action be brought? and state the reason for your answer.

*A.* The action should be brought in the name of B, the bond debt being a *chose en action* and not assignable at law. This rule of the common law was made to prevent the increase of litigation, but is rendered quite nugatory for that purpose. If C was the king he might sue in his own name. 2 Steph.'s Coms., 45,-6.

13. *Q.* A effects a policy of assurance upon his own life, and then assigns it to trustees. After A's death it being necessary to sue at law for the amount of the policy, in whose name must the action be brought? Will it make any difference if notice of assignment be given to the assurance office?

*A.* The policy being a *chose en action*, the money due must be sued for in the names of A's representatives. As to this point notice to the office is immaterial, but such notice will have the important effect of taking the policy out of the "order and disposition" of A within the meaning of the bankrupt laws, and will make the title of the trustees good against the assignees. Selwyn's Nisi Prius, 286.

14. *Q.* If there be two joint obligors in a bond, and one of them die, against whom should the action be brought?

*A.* Against the surviving obligor, as the liability survives exclusively to him, and the estate of the deceased debtor is discharged both at law and in equity. It would be otherwise if the bond was joint and several. Williams' Pers. Prop., 283, 5th ed.

15. *Q.* A testator dies, having a right of action for money due to him upon bond, and also a right of action for slander or libel: can his executors maintain an action in respect of both or either, and which, of the above rights of action of their testator?

*A.* They can sue on the bond, but not in respect of the slander or libel, as to these the maxim *Actio personalis moritur cum persona* applies. See *supra*, p. 32, No. 10.

16. *Q.* A dies, and by his will appoints B and C to be his executors—they prove his will; B afterwards dies, leaving C him

surviving. C, the surviving executor, then dies intestate, and D becomes administrator of his effects. Debts due to A remain outstanding, and for recovery of them actions become necessary. Can such actions be maintained by D, or who is the proper party to bring them?

A. The actions cannot be brought by D, as he does not represent A. But administration *de bonis non* must be taken out to A by his next of kin, and such administrator is the proper party to sue. Cootes' Probate Practice, 132.

17. Q. In an action against executors for a debt due by their testator, which of the executors should be joined as defendants?

A. Those only need be joined who have proved the will and administered to the deceased. Chitty's Archbold, 1217.

18. Q. If a joint promise is made by A and B to C, who are all dead, leaving executors, who are the parties to sue and be sued?

A. The executors of C would sue the executors of the survivors of A and B. For the promise being a joint one by A and B the liability on it would survive. Lush's Practice, 26.

19. Q. How must a corporation aggregate sue or defend?

A. In either case by attorney appointed under its common seal. Chitty's Archbold, 1135, 1136.

20. Q. For any debt due to a bankrupt previously to his bankruptcy (in which debt he is personally interested), who should sue?

A. The assignees should sue, as all his choses en action vest in them on adjudication, and they alone can sue. 12 and 13 Vic., c. 106, s. 141. Lush's Practice, 48.

21. Q. At common law, when a deed is made *inter partes*, can a person beneficially interested in the covenant, but who is not a party to the deed, maintain an action on the deed?

A. As a general rule no one but a party to a deed *inter partes* can sue on it. There are, however, exceptions, as in the case of an assignee of a lease suing on a covenant running with the land. Also the heir may sue on a covenant relating to realty which does not determine on the death of his ancestor. Spencer's Case, 5 Co. 16; 1 Smith's L. C. 43. Certain exceptions have also been made by statute, for by 32 Henry VIII., c. 34., the assignee of a reversion may sue on a covenant in a lease affecting the thing demised. Also by 8 and 9 Vic., c. 106, s. 5, an estate in lands and the benefit of a condition or covenant respecting any tenements or hereditaments may be taken, although the taker be not named a party. It should be borne in mind that the above rule does not apply to deeds poll, upon which any one may sue if named or designated therein. *Sunderland Marine Insurance Company* v. *Kearney*, 16 Q. B. 925; Chitty on Contracts, 54.

22. Q. In the case of a deed made between A and C containing a covenant by C to pay to A moneys for the use of B, which of the two A or B is the proper person to sue C for the breach of covenant?

A. Here A should sue. See the previous answer.

23. Q. If a contract be made between agents or factors for

their respective undisclosed principals, who can sue and be sued; and does it make any difference whether the contract is or is not under seal?

*A.* The agents themselves may sue, or their respective principals may come forward and sue. The principals have no such right if the agents contracted for them personally *under seal*. Chitty on Contracts, 206; *Addison* v. *Gandessequi,* and *Paterson* v. *same,* 2 Sm. L. C. 295, 302.

24. *Q.* A sells goods to B in his own name when he is really selling as agent for C. Can C sue B for their price? How is C affected by the existence of a cross debt due by A to B?

*A.* The principal C may come forward and sue, but B the buyer if unaware of any principal is entitled to stand in the same position as against C as he was with regard to A, and therefore may avail himself of the same defence to an action for the price at the suit of C, as he could have done if sued by A the apparent principal. If, therefore, the debt alluded to be one which could be set off by B against A, he (B) has the same right of set-off against C. (As to what debts can be set off, see *supra*). *George* v. *Glagett,* 2 Sm. L. C. 106; Chitty on Contracts, 206.

25. *Q.* If a parol contract be made between A on the part of C and for his benefit, and B, in whose name must an action be brought to enforce the contract against B; and would it make any difference if the contract were in writing, but not under seal?

*A.* If A disclosed the agency C only could sue, but if *contra*, as mentioned above (No. 23), either A or C could sue. The contract being in writing but not under seal would make no difference. Lush's Practice, 15, 3rd ed.

26. *Q.* Who is the proper party to sue on a contract, the party with whom it is made or the party from whom the consideration moves. For instance, if a contract be made between agents for their respective principals who can sue and be sued?

*A.* The party from whom the consideration moves should sue, see *supra.* Contracts, No. 7. As to the agent suing, see the previous answers.

27. *Q.* Who is usually the right party to bring an action and to be sued on a bill of lading?

*A.* The action should be brought by the party to whom the goods are to be delivered according to its terms. An indorsee of the bill may also sue on it. 18 and 19 Vic., c. 111, s. 1. The carrier is the party to be sued. Chitty on Contracts, 450.

28. *Q.* As a general rule, should an action against a carrier for the loss of goods be brought in the names of the consignor or consignee? and give an instance of an exception to the rule.

*A.* As a general rule, the action should be brought by the person in whom the property of the goods is vested, as upon him the loss falls. If the consignee orders the goods to be sent by a carrier, the delivery to him operates as a delivery to the purchaser, and the whole property (subject to the sight of *stoppage in transitu* by the consignor) vests in the consignee. He must therefore sue. This is so, even though no particular carrier be named by the consignee. Or, even if the carrier be paid by the consignor. If the consignee have given no order for the sending, delivery to the carrier is not delivery to the consignee, and in such a case the goods are sent at the risk of the consignor, who must therefore sue the carrier for the loss. *Coombes* v. *Bristol and Exeter Railway Company*, 27 L. J. Ex., 269. Selwyn's Nisi Prius, 456

(3.) *The Notice required before Action.*

1. *Q.* What is the first step an attorney should take when instructed to bring an action?
*A.* He should write a letter for payment, and, if necessary, give notice of action. If no notice is requisite, he should, if satisfaction is not given, issue a writ of summons.

2. *Q.* Is it necessary, in any and what cases, previously to the commencement of an action, to give notice to the opposite party, in order to complete the cause of action ? If any notice be necessary, state the consequences of the plaintiff failing, upon the trial, to prove the service of a notice.
*A.* Notice is necessary to persons secondarily liable on bills of exchange and promissory notes, when the acceptor or maker does not pay. In such cases, notice should be sent at latest by the post of the day following the day of dishonour when the defendant lives in the country, if he lives in the same town, notice should be sent on the same day. Before suing a Justice in respect of any judicial act done by him, one month's notice must be given. Also, before suing a surveyor of highways, or a contractor employed by a board of health, and in various other cases under local and personal acts notice is necessary. Where notice is required *one calendar month's notice* is sufficient. 5 and 6 Vic., c. 97. If the plaintiff fail to prove the proper notice having been given, he will be nonsuited. Chitty's Archbold, 129. *Supra* 24, No 15.

3. *Q.* What should be done before commencing an action of trover?
*A.* The question probably alludes to the demand sometimes made of the delivery of goods in order to prove the conversion. If the defendant was in possession of the goods and refuse to deliver them up on demand, such refusal will be considered a conversion. Selwyn's Nisi Prius, 1348.

4. *Q.* In an action against a constable, who has acted under a warrant, what demand must be made?
*A.* A *demand in writing* of the perusal and copy of the warrant signed by the plaintiff or his attorney. If within six days the warrant is produced, the plaintiff must make the justice who made the warrant a co-defendant. 24 Geo. II., c. 44, s. 6.

X.—*Tender before Action.*

1. *Q.* What are the requisites to constitute a valid tender, and what is the effect of a tender before action?
*A.* The money must be produced or its production dispensed with.

The tender must be unconditional, and be made to the creditor or his agent. It must be of the full amount due which must be paid in current undefaced coin. Gold is a good tender to any amount, silver up to 40s. Bank of England' Notes above £5, except at the Bank and its branches. Copper up to sixpence. The effect of a tender before action is to bar any claim for subsequent damages or interest, for not paying or for detaining the debt. It entitles the defendant to judgment for his costs. It also admits the contract in respect of which the money is tendered. Chitty on Contracts, 710.

2. *Q.* Will a tender be good, if clogged with any, and what, conditions?

*A.* No, it must be unconditional. Thus a tender of a sum of money "if the plaintiff," who claimed a larger sum, "would accept it as the whole balance due" is not a legal tender. Ibid. 715.

3. *Q.* Where a defendant before the action has made a tender sufficient, as he considers, to cover the demand, what is the mode of proceeding; and will the plaintiff receive or pay costs, if he do not recover more than the amount tendered?

*A.* He must pay the amount tendered into court and plead the tender. The plaintiff will have to pay the defendant's costs, and his own also. Chitty's Archbold, 1351.

4. *Q.* If a tender be made and refused before action, what steps should be taken to prevent the party availing himself of it by plea in any action to be afterwards commenced?

*A.* If after the tender the plaintiff has the right by the terms of the contract to make a demand of payment and he make such demand and the defendant refuse to pay, the plea of tender will be of no avail. Chitty on Contracts, 717.

### XI. *The Citation of the Defendant.*

1. *Q.* What is the form of the commencement of an action?

*A.* Actions in the Superior Courts are commenced by writ of summons. C. L. P. Act, 1852, s. 2.

2. *Q.* What are the different writs for commencing actions, and under what circumstances are they respectively applicable?

*A* They are—Against defendant within jurisdiction, with or without a special indorsement. Against a British subject out of the jurisdiction. Against a Foreigner out of the jurisdiction. Against a defendant under the Bills of Exchange Act, 1855. Against a trader, member of Parliament under 12 and 13 Vic., c. 106, s. 77. A writ in ejectment to recover possession of land. Smith's Action at Law, 58.

3. *Q.* What is the meaning of suing *in formâ pauperis?* and what is requisite to be allowed to do so?

*A.* It means a plaintiff suing without paying any fees either to the officers of the court or to his counsel or attorney. The requisites of suing thus are — To lay a case before counsel and obtain his opinion that there is good cause of action. The plaintiff or his attorney must then swear by affidavit that the case contains a true statement of the facts. Also, the plaintiff must swear that he is not worth £5, except his wearing apparel, and the matter in question in the cause. Upon this affidavit and opinion application is made by motion or petition to be allowed to sue *in formâ pauperis*, and to have a counsel and attorney assigned. Chitty's Archbold, 1277. A defendant cannot be allowed to sue *in formâ pauperis* in a civil action. *Anon* Barnes, 328.

4. *Q.* What are the rules affecting actions by paupers?

*A.* In addition to the foregoing it is ordered, that no fees shall be payable by a pauper, in consequence of his obtaining a verdict for £5. Also, that where he omits to proceed to trial, pursuant to notice, he may be called upon by rule to show cause why he should not pay costs, though he has not been dispaupered, and why all further proceedings should not be stayed until the costs be paid. Rules H. T., 1853, 121, 122.

*Q.* 5. By what process are personal actions commenced in the Queen's Bench, Common Pleas, and Exchequer; and is there any difference in either of the courts in the process against private persons and others having the privilege of peerage or of parliament?

*A.* By writ of summons. There is no difference with regard to Peers and Members of Parliament, excepting in suing the latter when a trader, under 8 and 9 Vic., c. 106.

6. *Q.* What is the course of proceeding under "The Common Law Procedure Act, 1852," in actions against British subjects resident abroad?

*A.* The practice is to issue a writ in the form specially provided for such a purpose in Schedule A, to the "Common Law Procedure Act, 1852." Upon satisfying a judge that there is a cause of action, arising within the jurisdiction, and that the writ was personally served, or it came to defendant's knowledge, or he is evading service, the judge will from time to time give the plaintiff liberty to proceed. The plaintiff must prove the amount of his claim either before a Jury or a Master. C. L. P. Act, 1852, s. 18. The enactment excepts a defendant residing in Scotland or Ireland.

7. *Q.* How long does a writ of summons remain in force, and how may it be continued; and on what days, and at what hours, and where, can it be served?

*A.* It remains in force for six calendar months from its date; within which period it must be served, unless renewed for additional period of six months. C. L. P. Act, 1852, s. 11. It may be served on any day except Sunday, at any hour, and in any county. Chitty Archbold, 196.

8. *Q.* How many defendants may be included in one writ?

*A.* There is no limit as to number, provided they are defendants in the same action. C. L. P. Act, 1852, s. 4. This enactment does not apply to cases under the "Bills of Exchange Act, 1855," as mentioned, *supra*, Bills and Notes, No. 12.

9. *Q.* On what day must a writ of summons be dated? and in whose name must it be tested?

*A.* It must bear date on the day of its issue, and be tested in the name of the Lord Chief Justice or Lord Chief Baron of the Court, or in case of vacancy in these offices, in the name of the Senior Puisne Judge of the same Court. C. L. P. Act, 1852, s. 5.

10. *Q.* If the names of several defendants have been inserted in the same writ, can you afterwards proceed against any or either of them separately, for any different cause of action?

*A.* Yes, the fact of suing a man for one cause of action cannot affect his liability for another.

11. *Q.* In what cases is personal service of process dispensed with?

*A.* If the plaintiff can make it appear to a judge that the defendant is evading personal service, or the writ has come to his knowledge. Under such circumstances, if it appears that reasonable efforts have been made to effect personal service, an order may be obtained from the Court or a judge to proceed in default of appearance. The usual practice is to make three or more calls, sometimes two may be sufficient, but there is no very strict rule upon the point, it being for the judge to consider what are reasonable efforts, or if the writ has come to defendant's knowledge. The facts must be shown on affidavit. Day's Practice, 11. The Legal Examiner, 135, 192.

12. *Q.* An affidavit in support of such order, as mentioned in the preceding answer, stated that the attorney had made two appointments at the defendant's club, that he had left the writ with the porter; and that the defendant had written acknowledging the receipt of the writ. Is this sufficient? State your reasons.

*A.* This has been held to be insufficient, because it did not show that any efforts had been made to discover the defendant's residence. *Davis* v. *Westmacott,* 7 C. B., N. S., 829; 29 L. J. C. P., 150.

13. *Q.* If there be more than one defendant in a writ, must each defendant be served before the plaintiff can take a further step?

*A.* Each defendant must be served, except in the case of husband and wife, when service on the husband will suffice for both. There is, however, nothing to prevent a plaintiff declaring against those who have been served, subject, in an action *ex contractu*, to a plea in abatement as to others within the jurisdiction. It would, however, be better to serve the others first or obtain an order against them for substituted service, as no proceedings by way of *non pros* can in the mean time be taken by the defendants. Lush's Practice, 372, 3rd ed.

14. *Q.* If several defendants are partners, is it necessary to serve each of them with a copy of the writ of summons?

*A.* They must each be served. See the preceding answer.

15. *Q.* In case of a writ of summons issued against a corporation aggregate, how is service to be effected?

*A.* It may be served on the mayor or other head officer, or on the town clerk, clerk, treasuror, or secretary. C. L. P. Act, 1852, s. 16.

16. *Q.* Where several defendants live in different counties, can they all be served with copies of one writ of summons?

*A.* Yes, one writ will be sufficient, as mentioned above; under such circumstances, however, concurrent writs are frequently issued.

17. *Q.* What indorsements must a writ of summons bear upon it? Does the omission of any such indorsements make the writ void?

*A.* 1. It must be endorsed with the name and place of abode of the attorney and agent, if any, or plaintiff if he sues in person. 2. If issued for the payment of any debt, the amount thereof and costs, and it must be stated that on payment within four days to the plaintiff or his attorney, further proceedings will be stayed. An indorsement *must* also be made within three days at least after service, of the day of the month and week of the service thereof. The omission of any of the requisite indorsements renders the writ irregular, and the defendant may set the service aside. The plaintiff is usually allowed to amend on payment of costs. Chitty's Archbold, 189.

18. *Q.* In what cases may a special indorsement of the particulars of the plaintiff's claim be made on a writ of summons, and what is the consequence of an omission to make such indorsement should the defendant not appear, having been served with the writ?

*A.* In cases where the claim is for a debt or liquidated demand in money, with or without interest, arising upon a contract, express or implied, as on a bill of exchange, or on a bond or statute, or on a guarantee, whether under seal or not. If in the cases where a special indorsement could have been made, it is omitted, the plaintiff cannot sign final judgment in default of appearance without first filing a declaration with a notice to plead in eight days in addition to the ordinary affidavit or order. He may sign judgment for default of plea, but is not entitled to the costs of the declaration and notice to plead. C. L. P. Act, 1852, ss. 25, 28.

19. *Q.* Is any further indorsement necessary upon a specially indorsed writ than the particulars of demand?

*A.* Yes, in addition to particulars of the claim and also to the indorsement mentioned *supra,* No. 17, the plaintiff must indorse a notice, that if a defendant served with the writ within the jurisdiction of the Court do not appear, according to the exigency thereof, the plaintiff will be at liberty to sign final judgment for any sum not exceeding the sum above claimed (with interest at the rate specified), and the sum of £ (above £20, town, £3 8s.; country, £4; under £20, town, £2 14s.; country, including mileage, £3 2s.), or such sum as may be allowed on taxation for costs and issue, execution at the *expiration* of eight days from the last day for appearance. If the action is for less than £20 a further notice should be endorsed, that if judgment is signed for default of appearance, the plaintiff will without summons apply to a judge for his costs of suit, unless before such judgment the defendant gives notice that he intends to oppose such application. R. E. T., 1857. 1 Chitty's Archbold, 195, 11th ed.

20. *Q.* Within what time after service of a writ of summons must the memorandum of service be indorsed; and what is the consequence of omitting such indorsement?

*A.* As above-mentioned, it must be made within three days after service. If not made proceedings in default of appearance cannot be taken, as in the affidavit of service it must be sworn that the indorsement was made pursuant to the statute. C. L. P. Act, 1852, s. 15.

21. *Q.* In cases where a defendant cannot be arrested, or is out of the kingdom, state the best mode to proceed against him.

*A.* A writ should be issued against him for service out of the jurisdiction. The cause of action must have accrued within the jurisdiction. If a British subject and he reside in Scotland or Ireland he must be sued in the courts of those countries, but a foreigner if there, may be sued out of these courts. C. L. P. Act, 1852, ss. 18, 19. As to a Scotch plaintiff suing an English defendant, see *L. & N.-W. Ry.* v. *Lindsay*, 3 McQueen's H. L. Rep., 99

22. *Q.* In a writ of summons, would it be a sufficient description if the defendant were described as "A B, of the city of London"; and what description is required by the statute?

*A.* This description would be insufficient. *Cotton* v. *Sawyer*, 10 M. and W., 328. The statute requires a description of defendant's residence or supposed residence. It has been decided that a reasonable degree of certainty will suffice as " Tufton-street, in the County of Middlesex," *Cooper* v. *Wheal*, 4 Dowl., 281. The number of the house, or the parish need not be stated Chitty's Archbold, 184.

23. *Q.* State some of the alterations made by "The Common Law Procedure Act, 1852," as to writs of summons.

*A.* It abolished the necessity of stating in the writ the nature or subject matter of the action. It abolished alias and pluries writs. It provided for renewing writs as mentioned, *supra*. It introduced proceedings in default of appearance in lieu of issuing a distringas to compel an appearance.

24. *Q.* What is meant by a concurrent writ? what is the object of it? and is there any limited time within which it must be issued?

*A.* It means a duplicate writ having the same force as the original, and issues in cases where there are several defendants in different parts of the country, or where it is not exactly known where the defendant is. In such cases the original is sent to one place for service, and the concurrent writs to other places. Concurrent writs must be issued within six months from the issuing the original. C. L. P. Act, 1852, s. 9.

25. *Q.* In the event of its being necessary to issue a concurrent writ of summons, can a writ for service in England be issued and marked as a concurrent writ with one for service in France?

*A.* Yes, or *vice versâ*. C. L. P. Act, 1852, s. 22.

26. *Q.* What was the object sought to be attained by the provision in "The Common Law Procedure Act, 1852," as to the renewal of a writ of summons?

*A.* It was to keep the debt alive and prevent the operation of the Statutes of Limitation, in case a defendant could not be served with process. C. L. P. Act, 1852, s. 11.

27. *Q.* Where the defendant pays the debt and the amount of the costs indorsed on the writ, but objects to the costs as being excessive, what is his remedy?

*A.* He may have the costs taxed, and if more than one-sixth is disallowed the plaintiff's attorney will have to pay the costs of taxation. Chitty's Archbold, 192.

28. *Q.* If a person contract a debt in England, and then goes to France, and resides there, is there any, and what, remedy for the creditor?

*A.* As mentioned *supra* No. 21, he may be sued. To enable the plaintiff to proceed in such a case he must obtain leave from a Judge to do so. This may be obtained on showing on affidavit, 1. That there is a cause of action which arose within the jurisdiction, or in respect of a breach of contract made within the jurisdiction; 2. That the writ was personally served, or that reasonable efforts were made to effect service, and that the writ had come to defendant's knowledge; 3. That the defendant wilfully neglects to appear, and is living out of the jurisdiction to defeat and delay his creditors. 15 and 16 Vic., c. 76, s. 18.

29. *Q.* In what case can you proceed with an action against a foreigner resident abroad?

*A.* In similar cases to those mentioned in the preceding answer, and the procedure is similar, excepting that a notice of the writ is served instead of a copy, and the affidavit of service should specify the service of the "notice" instead of the "copy." Day's Practice, 24.

### XII.—*The Defendant's Appearance.*

1. *Q.* What should a person, after having been served with a copy of a writ, do, if he have a defence to the action?

*A.* He should instruct his attorney to defend it, giving him full instructions. The attorney would appear. Or the defendant might enter an appearance in person.

2. *Q.* When must a defendant appear to an action?

*A.* Within the time limited by the writ, which, in ordinary writs of summons, is eight days from service, inclusive of the day of service. To a writ under the Bills of Exchange Act, twelve days also inclusive. To a writ of ejectment, sixteen days, not inclusive. In proceedings under s. 217 of C. L. P. Act, 1852, ten days. By Trader, Member of Parliament, when sued under 12 and 13 Vic., c. 106, one month. If no proceedings are taken in default an appearance may be entered any time before judgment by default. Chitty's Archbold, 216.

3. *Q.* When an attorney who has given an undertaking to enter an appearance has not appeared, in pursuance of his undertaking, what will be the consequence?
*A.* In such a case proceedings cannot be taken in default of appearance, but the writ will have to be reserved. The attorney is liable to attachment. Rules H. T., 1853, 3.

4. *Q.* If a *feme covert* be sued alone, how must she appear, and why so?
*A.* She should appear in person, because she cannot appoint an attorney. Chitty's Archbold, 1242.

5. *Q.* In case the defendant, in an action for debt, refuse to appear, can a plaintiff sign final judgment for the whole amount claimed?
*A.* Yes, he may do so if the writ is specially indorsed as mentioned, *supra*, p. 48, No. 19.

6. *Q.* Where a defendant appears in person and gives a false address, what course should the plaintiff take?
*A.* He should apply to the court or a judge on affidavit showing the address to be false, upon which he can obtain an order to stick up the proceedings in the Master's office without further service. " C. L. P. Act, 1852, s. 30. As to where no address is given, or where that given is not within three miles of the General Post Office, see R. H. T., 1853, 166.

7. *Q.* When a writ is issued under 18 and 19 Vic., c. 67, within what time and in what manner must the defendant appear to it?
*A.* The defendant must appear within twelve days of service inclusive of the day of service. Leave to appear must first be obtained, either on the defendant paying the sum indorsed in the writ into court, or upon affidavit showing a legal or equitable defence, or such facts as would make it incumbent on the holder to prove consideration or such other facts as the judge may deem sufficient to support the application. s. 2.

## XIII.—*Affidavits.*

1. *Q.* Before and after action brought, how must affidavits be entitled?
*A.* Before action, the affidavit should be entitled in the court in which the affidavit is intended to be used. After action, in the court in which the cause is, and also with the title of the cause, namely, the plaintiff's and defendant's christian and surname. Chitty's Archbold, 1,600.

2. *Q.* If a person who is required by a party to a cause to make an affidavit, refuse to do so, by what mode may he be compelled to give evidence, as to the matter concerning which he has refused to make an affidavit?
*A.* An order may be obtained to have him examined on oath before a judge or master concerning the matter in question. C.L.P. Act, 1854, s. 481.

3. *Q.* Has any, and what alteration been recently made as to

the form of affidavits? and if the alteration be not adopted, in what way will the costs be affected?

A. They must be expressed in the first person, and be divided into paragraphs, and each paragraph must be numbered consecutively, otherwise no costs will be allowed for any affidavit. R. M. V., 1854, 2.

4. Q. Needs an affidavit to hold to bail be entitled as well in the cause as the court?

A. If sworn after the issuing of the writ, the affidavit should be entitled both in the cause and court; but if before, the title of the court to which the application is to be made will suffice. Chitty's Archbold, 737.

5. Q. Will an affidavit not containing any description of the deponent, or his residence, be good?

A. No; both must be accurately stated. R. G. H. T., 1853, r. 138.

6. Q. What is required to be sworn in an affidavit of merits?

A. This nature of affidavit is required, in order to set aside a judgment, and the deponent must swear that he has "a good defence to this action upon the merits." Chitty's Archbold, 979.

7. Q. By whom may an affidavit of increase be made?

A. It must be made by the person who has made the payments sworn to have been made to the witnesses, counsel, etc. The attorney often makes it, but more frequently his managing clerk.

8. Q. How are affidavits sworn in the country?

A. They are sworn to by the deponent, either in court or before a judge at chambers, or before a commissioner duly empowered to take affidavits. Chitty's Archbold, 1,613.

9. Q. What are the requisites of a *jurat* to an affidavit?

A. It should state the day of the month and year of its being sworn, also the place and county, if sworn before a commissioner. If more deponents than one, the names of the deponents should also be inserted. The words "Before me" must be inserted if sworn before a commissioner, and it must be signed by the judge or commissioner before whom sworn. Lastly, there must be no interlineation or erasure in the *jurat*. If the deponent is an illiterate person, it must be stated in the *jurat* by the commissioner or judge that the affidavit was read, in his presence, to the party making the same, and that such party seemed to understand it, and also that such party wrote his or her signature or mark in the presence of the judge or commissioner. R. G. H. T., 1853, r. 141. Chitty's Archbold, 1,610.

10. Q. If there are two or more deponents in an affidavit, and the names of all are not mentioned in the *jurat*, or if the *jurat* omit to state the day on which the affidavit was sworn, what will be the consequence?

A. The affidavit cannot be read, as when there are two or more deponents, the names of all must be inserted in the *jurat*; so also the date must be inserted. Chitty's Archbold, 1,612.

11. Q. When may an affidavit sworn before a judge of one of

the superior courts be received in another court to which such judge does not belong?

A. It may be so used when entitled of the court in which it is to be used. R. G. H. T., 1853, r. 144.

12. Q. May an affidavit in a cause be used in court, or before a judge (not being an affidavit to hold to bail), be sworn before the attorney in the cause, or his clerk, each of them being a commissioner authorised to take affidavits in the country?

A. The affidavit, if so sworn, is not receivable in the cause. R. G. H. T., 1853, r. 143. See also rule 142, to the same effect as to an affidavit of service.

XIV.—*The Arrest of the Defendant on Mesne Process, and the Law of Bail.*

1. Q. There is an act for the abolition of arrest except in certain cases; do you understand that the power of arrest at the commencement of an action is entirely taken away, or is there any excepted case?

A. The act alluded to is 1 and 2 Vic., c. 110, and it entirely abolishes the writ of *capias* as a means of commencing an action. The excepted case alluded to is in proceeding against a prisoner for debt, under s. 85 of the act, but this section is now repealed by the Bankruptcy Act, 1861.

2. Q. Are any persons privileged from arrest; and if so, who are they? Distinguish between those temporarily and those permanently privileged.

A. The following persons are permanently privileged:—The Royal family, peers and peeresses, the judges of the superior courts. Those temporarily privileged are:—Servants of the King or Queen regnant, members of the House of Commons and of Convocation, beneficed clergymen, foreign ambassadors, and their servants, barristers, attorneys and officers of the courts, coronors, parties to suits, and witnesses, bankrupts, married women, members of corporations and hundredors, seamen of the Royal Navy, soldiers and marines, persons already arrested for the same cause or action. Chitty's Archbold, 716.

3. Q. Can a clergyman be arrested on civil process whilst performing divine service on any other day than Sunday, or in going to or returning from the performance thereof?

A. Such an arrest is illegal, and the person effecting it is guilty of a misdemeanor, punishable by imprisonment, for any term not exceeding two years, with or without hard labour. 24 and 25 Vic., c. 100, s. 36.

4. Q. A debtor being about to quit England, it is wished to hold him to bail; what proceedings must be taken?

A. A writ of summons must be issued, and an affidavit made by the plaintiff, or some one else, showing, to the satisfaction of a judge of the superior courts, that the plaintiff has a cause of action to the amount of £20, or upwards (debt or damages unliquidated will do), and that there is cause to believe the defendant is about to quit England, unless forthwith apprehended. If this affidavit satisfies the judge, he will make an order directing the defendant to be held to bail. Upon this order a writ of *capias* may be issued, directed to the sheriff. The writ is lodged with the sheriff, who makes the arrest. This must be done within one month from the date of the order. When arrested, the defendant gives bail to the sheriff. Chitty's Archbold, 737.

5. *Q.* What is the first step in order to arrest a defendant?
*A.* (See preceding answer).

6. *Q.* When a writ of *capias* is granted by a judge for the arrest of a defendant, is such writ the commencement of the action? If not, how is the action begun?
*A.* The action is commenced by writ of summons, whereas, before 1 and 2 Vic., c. 110, the *capias* was the commencement.

7. *Q.* Can a defendant be arrested on a *capias* issued under an order to hold to bail, although he have already been served with a copy of a writ of summons in the action, and have entered an appearance according to the exigency of such writ?
*A.* The arrest may be made at any stage of the proceedings before final judgment. 1 and 2 Vic., c. 110, s. 5.

8. *Q.* What steps would you take before you proceed to hold a defendant to bail in an action of trover?
*A.* They would be the same as those mentioned, *supra*, No. 4.

9. *Q.* What means has a defendant arrested of getting out of custody?
*A.* A defendant when arrested has several courses open to him for the purpose of getting out of custody. They are, giving bail to the sheriff, or depositing with him the sum sworn to be due together with £10 for costs, escape or rescue, and application to a judge for discharge owing to some informality in the proceedings, privilege from arrest, etc. Smith's Action at Law, 308.

10. *Q.* Who are bail below, and bail above?
*A.* Bail below is the security given to the sheriff by the defendant and one or two sureties for the sum indorsed on the writ. It is in the form of a bond, conditioned to put in special bail within the time (eight days) mentioned in the writ. These special bail are the bail above, and they undertake that if the defendant is condemned in the action that he shall satisfy the debt and costs or render himself to custody. They must be two persons at least. Chitty's Archbold, 818.

11. *Q.* Can an attorney or his clerk be bail in an action under any, and what, circumstances?
*A.* There is no objection to their being bail below; but, if put in as bail below, the bail may be treated as a nullity and judgment signed by the plaintiff. R. G. H. T., 1853, r. 94.

12. *Q.* State some of the most common objections to the sufficiency of bail above.
*A.* The following may be mentioned:—That they are not housekeepers or freeholders. That they are not worth double the sum

indorsed on the writ. That they are privileged from arrest. That they have been previously rejected as bail. That they are hired to be bail. That they are attorneys or clerks of attorneys. That they are sheriffs officers. 2 Chitty's Archbold, 838.

13. *Q.* In an action on a bill of exchange by the endorsee against the acceptor, is the drawer competent to become bail; and is the acceptor of a bill of exchange competent to justify as bail in an action against the drawer?

*A.* The drawer is competent to become bail and the acceptor to justify in the above cases.

14. *Q.* What is a bail-bond, and when may it be sued upon?

*A.* The bail-bond is the security given to the sheriff as mentioned above, and it may be sued on if special bail is not put in within the eight days, or the defendant is rendered to custody. Chitty's Archbold, 818.

15. *Q.* In what cases will the court direct the bail-bond to stand as a security?

*A.* Since 1 and 2 Vic., c. 110, it seems not to be the practice to direct the bond to stand as security. Chitty's Archbold, 814.

16. *Q.* By what mode other than a bail-bond can a defendant be released from custody?

*A.* See *supra* No. 9.

17. *Q.* How are bail above put in when the defendant resides in the country?

*A.* It is taken before a commissioner appointed to take the recognisances, also before a judge of assize on circuit. It must then be transmitted to London and filed. A notice of the filing is then served on plaintiff's attorney, until which notice is given bail will not be considered put in. Chitty's Archbold, 850.

18. *Q.* If bail be desirous of getting discharged from their liability, what means have they of doing so?

*A.* They may render their principal to custody. Ibid, 861.

19. *Q.* What, if any, is the difference between the liability of bail in proceedings in error, and of bail above, *i.e.* bail to the action, or special bail?

*A.* Bail in error are bound to prosecute the proceedings, and pay (if judgment affirmed or proceedings discontinued) the debt and costs of all the proceedings; whereas special bail do not contract to prosecute the proceedings, but to pay the debt and costs, or render defendant to custody. Chitty's Archbold, 565.

20. *Q.* When are bail discharged from their liability by the acts of the plaintiff?

*A.* They are discharged if the plaintiff give time to the principal without the consent of the bail. As if subsequently to the bail being given the principal gives a cognovit by virtue of which he is to have further time. Ibid, 872.

21. *Q.* What additional powers for the benefit of creditors are given by "The Absconding Debtor's Arrest Act, 1851"?

*A.* This Act enables a creditor to obtain a warrant from a country commissioner of bankruptcy or a county court judge (except in

London and Middlesex) on an affidavit similar to that used for obtaining a *capias* (*supra*, No. 4). Upon this warrant defendant may be arrested, within seven days, by the messenger, or bailiff. The warrant may be obtained before action commenced, but a *copius* must be obtained within seven days of the date of the warrant. The object of this enactment is to avoid the delay which arises in instructing the London agent and obtaining the *copias*.

### XV.—*The Venue or Locus in Quo.*

1. *Q.* What is the meaning of the word "venue;" and what are the rules to be observed respecting it?

*A.* The word signifies the place from which the jury are to come to try a cause. It should always be laid by the plaintiff in the county where the witnesses reside and the cause can be most conveniently tried, or where "local" in the county where the cause of action arose.

2. *Q.* What is the difference between a local action and a transitory action? Name a few of the principal actions of each sort.

*A.* An action is said to be local when the cause of action could only have happened in some particular place, as for trespass to land, obstructing a right of way, etc. It is transitory when independent of locality, in the sense above used, as an action for trover or slander, either of which injuries might have been caused anywhere.

3. *Q.* What is the maxim of law that applies to transitory actions?

*A.* It is "*contractus est nullius loci*," indicating that a cause of action arising upon a contract is transitory in its nature. *Mostyn* v. *Fabrigas*, 1 Sm. L. C , 607.

4. *Q.* In an action against a justice of the peace, where must the venue be laid?

*A.* In the county where the act complained of was committed. 11 and 12 Vic., c. 44, s. 10.

5. *Q.* In order to change a venue, what is it now necessary to obtain?

*A.* A venue may be changed by consent of the parties, or by order of a judge, or the court. To obtain such an order, the plaintiff must shew on affidavit very strong grounds, as the courts are averse to allowing a plaintiff to change his own venue. A defendant can obtain the order more easily, such as by showing the cause of action to have arisen in another county, or by the witnesses residing in another county. Chitty's Archbold, 1,344.

6. *Q.* What is the proper venue in an action of ejectment?

*A.* See *infra* "ejectment," No. 14.

### XVI.—*The Pleadings or Contending Statements of the Litigants.*

1. *Q.* What are the names of the different pleadings in an action? and are they the same in all actions, or what are the differences?

*A.* They are :— 1. Declaration of the plaintiff. 2. Plea of the defendant. 3. Replication of the plaintiff. 4. Rejoinder of defendant. 5. Surrejoinder of plaintiff. 6. Rebutter of defendant. 7. Surrebutter of plaintiff. The pleadings seldom go so far as this, but may do so, and even further, but then have no particular names. A demurrer is also a pleading, and so is a joinder in demurrer. In replevin the plea is called an avowry, or cognizance, and the replication a plea in bar. In ejectment there are no pleadings. Smith's Action at Law; Chitty's Archbold.

2. *Q.* When a defendant has been served with process, what is the next step in the cause on the plaintiff's part, and what must be the state of the parties?

*A.* He should search for appearance, after which, if entered, he should deliver a declaration, which is a statement of his cause of action, written on draft paper, with a notice to plead indorsed upon the back of it. The parties should be all before the Court, otherwise the plaintiff may have to abandon his proceedings against some of the defendants, or he may have to amend on a plea in abatement on notice of objection to parties being put in. "Judgment," etc., No. 6.

3. *Q.* If a defendant have been taken on a writ of *capias*, can you declare against him upon that writ alone, or how otherwise?

*A.* Yes; if an appearance is entered a declaration may be delivered.

4. In what cases must the declaration be filed, and in what cases delivered?

*A.* Declaration is always delivered, excepting in the case of judgment being signed in default of appearance upon a writ not specially indorsed. In such a case, in addition to an affidavit of service, copy writ, or order to proceed, a declaration with notice to plead thereon must be filed at the Master's office, and, in default of plea, judgment may be signed. C. L. P. Act, 1852, s. 28.

5. *Q.* A defendant quits and altogether gives up his place of residence, after service of a copy of writ of summons, but before the plaintiff has declared. How do you proceed in the action?

*A.* The question assumes an appearance to be entered by defendant in person giving an address at which proceedings are to be left. This he is bound to do, or the appearance will not be received by the officer. On it appearing to a Judge that the address was illusory or fictitious he would on the application of the plaintiff give him an order to proceed by affixing the proceedings in the master's office. C. L. P. Act, 1832, s. 30.

6. *Q.* When is a plaintiff obliged to declare; and if he omit to declare, what steps can the defendant take to get rid of the action?

*A.* He must declare within the term next ensuing the term or vacation in which the appearance is entered. If he do not declare within this time (not having obtained further time), the defendant may give him notice to declare in four days, otherwise judgment. If this notice is not given the ~~defendant~~ has a year from the service of the writ to declare in. Chitty's Archbold, 222.

7. *Q.* How soon after the service of a copy of the writ of summons is the cause out of court, if the plaintiff do not declare?

*A.* At the expiration of one year from service of the writ. C. L. P. Act, 1852, s. 58.

8. *Q.* Can a plaintiff join more than one cause of action in the same suit? State some of the causes usually joined.

*A.* He may join any causes of action except replevin and ejectment, provided they be by and against the same parties and in the same rights. C. L. P. Act, 1852, s. 41. Debt, assumpsit, and covenant are frequently joined. So also are trespass, case, and trover. Separate trials may be ordered, see *supra*.

9. *Q.* Is any, and what, permission necessary before a plaintiff can include several counts in his declaration? and what is the rule as to several pleas by a defendant? In actions of trespass, can you have more than one count for acts committed at the same time and place?

*A.* No permission need be obtained; but if the counts are on the same cause of action, they may be struck out on the application of the party objecting; but on such application the court or a judge may allow such counts or pleas as are proper to determine the question in controversy. R. G. T. T., 1853, rr. 1, 2, 3.

10. *Q.* What are the most common grounds for setting aside a declaration for irregularity?

*A.* They are,—that the venue is omitted, that the declaration is by one plaintiff only, but the writ is by two or more, that the plaintiff is out of court owing to a year having elapsed from service, that the writ has never been served, etc.

11. *Q.* Where a Christian name in a declaration varies from that in a writ of summons, within what time must the objection be taken?

*A* This is an irregularity, and should be objected to within the time for pleading. *Kitchen* v. *Brooks*, 5 M. and W., 522. The general rule is, that applications of this nature should be made within a reasonable time, and before a fresh step has been taken by the party applying with knowledge of the irregularity. R. G. H. T., 1853, r. 135.

12. *Q.* If there be any defect in the validity of a pleading, in what shape is it met; and is the proceeding available to either party?

*A.* If the defect be merely an irregularity as mentioned in the preceding questions, Nos. 10 and 11, it may be set aside. If framed to embarrass or prejudice a fair trial application may be made to strike out or amend the pleading. If the pleading is bad in substance as not disclosing in the face of it a good cause of action or defence, it is demurrable. These proceedings are available to either party. Chitty's Archbold, 235, et. seq.

13. *Q.* Several actions are brought against different defendants for the same cause of action. Is there any way of avoiding the expense of defending more than one action?

*A.* In one or two cases the court has made an order consolidating the actions (*i.e.*, making them all abide the event of one), as in suing underwriters on the same policy of assurance. Generally, however, the rule has been refused where, as in this case, the parties in the actions are not the same. Chitty's Archbold, 1347.

14. Q. State some of the usual defences to an action, and the mode of making them by plea or otherwise.

A. This question which is very general may be answered from various answers in this chapter. See especially *infra*, Nos. 26, 30.

15. Q. State briefly the difference between a plea in bar and a plea in abatement. Can the latter be pleaded when the defendant is under terms to plead issuably?

A. They differ in that the former is a substantial answer to the action, either by traversing the declaration or confessing and avoiding it; whereas a plea in abatement merely abates the particular writ or declaration by pointing out that they are improperly framed, without impugning the right of action. Thus the non-joinder of a co-defendant may be pleaded in abatement. A plea in abatement is not an issuable plea. *Shepeter* v. *Durant*, 14 C. B., 582. Stephens on Pleading, 44.

16. Q. Within what time must a defendant, who resides in England, plead?

A. He must plead in abatement within four days exclusive, after delivering or filing the declaration. Chitty's Archbold, 901. The time for pleading in bar is eight days from delivering or filing notice to plead. C. L. P. Act, 1852, s. 63.

17. Q. What is meant by *traversing*? and what by *confessing and avoiding*? Give instances of each.

A. By a traverse is meant a plea which denies facts stated in the declaration material to the cause of action; as to a count for goods sold and delivered, " never indebted" would be a traverse. A plea which confesses and avoids on the other hand admits the facts stated in the declaration, but shows some new matter which avoids their legal effect. As to the count above-mentioned, "Infancy" would be a plea in confession and avoidance. Bullen and Leake on Pleading, 375.

18. Q. What effect has the plea of *non est factum* in actions on specialties and covenants?

A. It puts in issue that the defendant executed the deed alleged in the declaration; any variance therefore between the deed as alleged in the declaration, and as proved in evidence, may be taken advantage of under the plea. Thus to a deed pleaded as a release, *non est factum* puts in issue not only its execution, but also its effect as a release. *North* v. *Wakefield*, 13 Q. B., 536. Bullen and Leake, 403.

19. Q. Is the general issue—*non assumpsit*—a good plea in an action of debt on a bond?

A. No, such plea is applicable only to actions in simple contract. Ib. 401.

20. Q. In an action in a warranty will a plea traversing the agreement alledged in the declaration operate as a denial of the fact of the sale and of the warranty, and of the breach, and what is the effect of it?

*A.* Such a plea will only operate as a denial in fact of the express contract alleged. Therefore in the case put the plea of traverse will deny the effect of the sale and warranty having been given, but not of the breach. R. G. T. T., 1853, r. 6.

21. *Q.* What is the effect of the plea of *non assumpsit* to a declaration on a policy of assurance containing averments of the plaintiff's interest and of the loss?

*A.* The plea will operate as a denial of the subscription to the alleged policy by the defendant, but not of the interest of the plaintiff or of the loss. These must be specially traversed. Pl. Rules, T. T., 1853, r. 6.

22. *Q.* What is put in issue by the plea of never indebted first to an *indebitatus* count for goods sold and delivered? secondly, to a count for goods bargained and sold; under the plea, can payment be set up?

*A.* The plea puts in issue the sale and delivery, and the bargain and sale respectively. It has been decided that under the plea the following defences may be given: — Sale on credit; Sale with warranty with which the goods did not agree; that the goods were worthless; deficiency in quantity. Bullen and Leake, 399. Payment must be specially pleaded. R. G. T. T., 1853, r. 8.

23. *Q.* What does the plea of "not guilty" operate as a denial of in actions of tort?

*A.* It is a denial of the breach of duty or wrongful act alleged to have been committed by the defendant. Thus to a declaration for a libel it is a denial of the publication of the alleged libel, and also of meaning ascribed to it in the declaration. Steph. on Pleading, 155, R. G. T. T., 1853, rr. 19, 20.

24. *Q.* A declaration is delivered containing only the following count:—That the plaintiff, on the 1st January, 1863, by his bill of exchange, now overdue, directed to the defendant, required the defendant to pay to the plaintiff £100 two months after date, and the defendant accepted the same bill, but did not pay the same. Defendant pleads never indebted. Is the plea good?

*A.* The plea is inadmissable, some matter of fact should be traversed specially as the drawing or making of the bill. R. G. T. T., 1853, r. 7.

25. *Q.* Define a common count. A agrees with B to construct an engine for him according to the terms of a special contract. B delivers the engine in accordance with the contract. What form of count is to be adopted in an action for the recovery of the price?

*A.* A common count is one frequently used in suing on a simple contract. Actions for debt on simple contract being of such frequent occurrence, convenience has adopted certain short forms to be used in such cases, the particulars of the debt being shown by the evidence at the trial. The following is a common count:— "Money payable by the defendant to the plaintiff for goods sold and delivered by the plaintiff to the defendant. A common count will be sufficient in the case put, unless the contract was under seal, in which event the contract must be sued on specially." Bullen and Leake, 29.

26. *Q.* State some of the defences which must be specially pleaded. Can illegality be given in evidence under a plea that the parties did not agree as alleged? Debt for goods bargained and sold; defence that the price of the goods exceeds £10, there was no note in writing, and that the defendant did not accept them, or pay anything for them. Under what form of plea can a defendant raise this defence?

*A.* All matters in confession and avoidance must be specially pleaded, *i.e.*, the facts must be set out in the declaration. Such are infancy, coverture, payment, release, illegality of consideration. The illegality must be specially pleaded. R. G. T. T., 1853, r. 8. The Statute of Frauds need not be specially pleaded, but may be given in evidence under the general issue, that plea throwing on the plaintiff the burden of proving a contract in fact. Bullen and Leake, 1403.

27. *Q.* When it is intended to give special matter in evidence by virtue of an Act of Parliament under the plea of the general issue, what does the pleading rule on the subject require?

*A.* It is necessary that the defendant should insert in the margin of the plea "By statute," together with the year of the reign, chapter, and section of the act on which he relies, specifying whether the act is public or otherwise. R. G. T. T., 1853, r. 21.

28. *Q.* May payment be given in evidence in reduction of damages, or must it in all cases be pleaded, and why?

*A.* It must be specially pleaded. (See No. 26 *supra*).

29. *Q.* When a defendant is sued for a debt which he has tendered, what act must accompany the plea of tender to render it good?

*A.* The money tendered must be paid into court, and the receipt of the officer for the money written in the margin of the plea. Chitty's Archbold, 1362.

30. *Q.* What pleas may be pleaded together without leave?

*A.* They are—a plea denying any contract or debt alleged in the declaration; a plea of tender as to part, the Statutes of Limitation, set-off, bankruptcy of the defendant, discharge under an insolvent act, *plene administravit*, *plene administravit præter*, infancy, coverture, payment, accord and satisfaction, release, not guilty, a denial that the property, an injury to which is complained of, is the plaintiff's leave and license, *son assault demesne*. C. L. P. Act, 1852, s. 84.

31. *Q.* In case of a plea in abatement on the ground of the non-joinder of a necessary party, which is an essential accompaniment of such plea in ordinary cases, and what is the effect of its absence?

*A.* The plea should be accompanied by an affidavit verifying it. If this is omitted the plaintiff may treat the plea as a nullity, and sign judgment, or may get it set aside for irregularity. Chitty's Archbold, 903.

32. *Q.* To a declaration in contract against a single defendant,

he pleads in abatement the non-joinder of another co-contractor, what course should the plaintiff pursue in order to proceed against both? If in such a case it turns out that the defendant originally sued is liable, but that the added defendant is not liable as a contractor, to what judgment will the plaintiff be entitled, and how are the costs of the added defendant, and of the plea in abatement and amendment, to be paid?

*A.* The plaintiff should (if the plea is well founded) amend his writ, and serve it on the person thus added as defendant, and declare *de novo*. The plaintiff in the case put would be entitled to judgment against the defendant, who appears to be liable, and the defendant who is not liable is entitled to judgment against the plaintiff for his costs. The plaintiff is allowed such costs, together with the costs of the plea in abatement and amendment, as costs in the cause against the original defendant who pleaded the plea. C. L. P. Act, 1852, s 39.

33. *Q.* What is the consequence of the non-joinder of persons as plaintiffs? 1. Where the defendant gives a notice of objecting to such non-joinder? 2. Where he does not give such a notice?

*A.* The notice of objection being given before time of pleading, the plaintiff must amend the writ and other proceedings before plea, by adding the name of the person non-joined, on payment of the costs of amendment. If he do not so amend such non-joinder will prove fatal at the trial, as it is submitted the C. L. P. Act, 1860, s. 19, does not apply to the case of non-joinder. If no such notice be given, the defect may be amended, either before or at the trial, under C. L. P. Act, 1852, ss. 34, 35.

34. *Q.* What is the consequence of joining too many plaintiffs in an action upon a contract?

*A.* It is not now fatal as formerly, as in the event of mis-joinder judgment may be entered in favour of such of the plaintiffs as the court adjudges entitled to recover. C. L. P. Act, 1852, s. 19.

35. *Q.* In an action by two plaintiffs, one of whom is improperly joined, can the defendant, under a plea of set-off, avail himself of a debt due from both plaintiffs, or either, or which of them alone?

*A.* Yes, he may prove that all the parties named as plaintiffs are indebted to him, notwithstanding that one or more of them is or are improperly joined C. L. P. Act, 1860, s. 20.

36. *Q.* What is a new assignment?

*A.* It is a proceeding rendered necessary by the defendant applying his defence to a matter different from that which the plaintiff is really suing for. Thus, if the plaintiff has been twice assaulted by the defendant, one of which is justifiable, and the other not so, and the plaintiff sues for the latter, the defendant, from anything which appears on the declaration, may infer that the plaintiff sues for the former, and he pleads *son assault demesne*. The plaintiff, thereupon, must assign as his cause of action the second assault. This is termed a new assignment. Step. Pl., 187, 5th ed.

THE PLEADINGS. DEMURRERS. 63

37. *Q.* What is the difference between pleading and demurring?

*A.* Pleading and demurring are terms used to indicate two distinct methods of defence. A plea is a denial of the declaration, or a confession and avoidance of it, or some material part, in point of fact, and differs from a demurrer, in that the latter is a defence to the declaration, or a subsequent pleading, upon some error in law apparent upon the face of such pleading. A demurrer admits the facts, but denies that they are sufficient in law, thus raising an issue for the decision of the court in banc; whereas, a plea raises a question of fact to be tried before a jury. Replications, rejoinders, etc., are also pleadings. The *Legal Examiner*, 192.

38. *Q.* Give an example of a declaration which would be demurrable.

*A.* Supposing that I go upon a visit to a friend, and whilst there sustain bodily injury, in consequence of the delapidated condition of his premises, without default on his part. If I sue him, stating these facts in my declaration, he might demur. I have no cause of action, for when a guest accepts an invitation, he becomes, to all intents and purposes, one of the family; and, therefore, cannot complain. It is upon the same principle that a master is not liable for injuries done to a fellow-servant. *Southcote* v. *Stanley*, 25. L. J. Ex., 339.

39. *Q.* Is the signature of counsel necessary to a joinder in demurrer?

*A.* Counsel's signature is not necessary.

40. *Q.* When either party demurs to his adversary's pleading, and they join in demurrer, what course is to be taken to dispose of the issue in law?

*A.* A demurrer book, consisting of copies of the material parts of the pleadings, is made up by the plaintiff. The demurrer is set down for argument. Four days before the day appointed, the plaintiff delivers two copies of the book and points of argument to the chief and senior puisne judge, and the defendant two copies to the next senior judges. In default of either, the other party may deliver, the next day, the copies omitted to be delivered. Counsel are instructed, and when the case is reached in the special paper, it is argued by one counsel on each side. Judgment is then given.

41. *Q.* A defendant demurs to part of a declaration, and plead issuably to the remainder. What course must the plaintiff take, and how is the action to be continued?

*A.* As to the demurrer, he should join in demurrer, and proceed as mentioned in the previous answer. He will join issue on the plea, and proceed to trial in the ordinary way. Frequently the decision of the issue in law puts an end to the case; the plaintiff should, therefore, before proceeding to trial, consider the necessity of it. Chitty's Archbold, 912.

42. *Q.* Can a defendant demur specially to a declaration? How can he object to a declaration on the ground that it discloses no cause of action?

*A.* Special demurrers, that is, those objecting to defects of the pleading in point of form, are abolished; but a defendant can demur generally to the substance of the pleading, and this is usually done when it discloses no cause of action. C. L. P. Act, 1852, ss. 50, 51.

43. *Q.* Can the defendant plead the bankruptcy of the plaintiff as a bar to the action, as a matter of course?

*A.* If a plaintiff in an action which his assignees might maintain for the benefit of his creditors, becomes bankrupt, such bankruptcy cannot be pleaded in bar, unless the assignees decline to continue it, and give security for costs. A judge's order is obtained, giving them a certain time to elect; after this time has expired without their electing, the defendant may, within eight days, plead the bankruptcy. C. L. P. Act, 1852, s. 142. After the bankruptcy of the defendant he may plead his order of discharge.

44. *Q.* Where a plea is clearly false and tricky, is the plaintiff bound to demur?

*A.* In such a case the plaintiff should not demur, but apply to a judge to strike out the plea. Day's C. L. P. Acts, 48.

45. *Q.* How far is payment into court to the *indebitatus* counts an admission of the cause of action? Is there any difference in the effect of paying money into court where the declaration sets out a special contract?

*A.* To an *indebitatus* count it is an admission of a debt upon the consideration stated in the declaration to the amount paid in, but no more; so that the plaintiff is bound to prove a further debt in order to recover a greater amount. *Stevenson* v. *Corporation of Berwick,* 1 Q. B., 154. To a count on a special contract the payment admits all the material allegations in the declaration which the plaintiff might be compelled to prove in order to recover the money paid in, it, therefore, would admit the contract and the breach. Bullen and Leake, 562.

46. *Q.* Where an executor is sued for a debt owing by his testator, and he pleads *plene administravit,* or *plene administravit præter* only, and the plaintiff cannot disprove the plea, but there is other personal estate to be received, what course should the plaintiff take?

*A.* The plaintiff may take issue upon these pleas and proceed to trial, or he may confess them, and, as to the former, pray judgment of assets *in futuro,* or upon the latter take judgment presently of assets come to hand, and of assets *in futuro* for the residue of his debt left unliquidated. To the first-named plea he may, also, take judgment of assets *quando.* Chitty's Archbold, 1219.

47. *Q.* John Wilson sues Amelia Henderson for £20, due to him for goods sold and delivered. Amelia appears, and pleads coverture as an answer to the action. Can she appear and plead by an attorney, or must she appear and plead in person? and if the latter, state the reason why.

*A.* She must appear and plead in person, for she cannot appoint an attorney. Ibid., 1242.

PAYMENT INTO COURT. SET-OFF. 65

*Q*. 48. A has an action brought against him by B, a carpenter, for, say, £250. A considers the charges exorbitant, and proposes through his attorney to pay B, £170 and his costs then incurred. B declines it. This is at an early stage of the cause—say after writ served, or after declaration and before plea. Is there any mode by which A can pay, or offer to pay, that amount to B, so as to prevent his being liable to further costs, provided B, does not succeed in recovering more than £170 ?

*A*. He may pay the £170 into court and plead the tender. He may also take out a summons to stay all further proceedings, on payment of £170 and costs up to that time, to be taxed. If the plaintiff go on for more than is paid into court, or refuse the sum mentioned in the summons, he will get no costs for the proceedings subsequent, and probably will have to pay the subsequent costs of the defendant, Chitty's Archbold, 1368.

49. *Q*. In what cases may money be paid into court ?

*A*. It may be paid in in all actions except actions for assault and battery, false imprisonment, libel, slander, malicious arrest or prosecution, and debauching plaintiff's daughter or servant. C. L. P. Act, 1852, s. 70. In an action against a newspaper or other publication for libel, money may now be paid into court by the defendant. 6 and 7 Vic., c. 96, s. 2.

50. *Q*. In what actions must leave be obtained for payment of money into court ?

*A*. Leave is necessary when one of several defendants pays in money; also, when paid in actions on money bonds and in detinue. C. L. P. Act, 1852, s. 72 ; C. L. P. Act, 1860, s. 25.

51. *Q*. An order for the particulars of the plaintiff's demand is obtained, with a stay of proceedings in the meanwhile, pending the time allowed for pleading: what time has the defendant to plead after those particulars are delivered?

*A*. If not otherwise provided for in the order, the defendant will have the same time after the delivery of the particulars as he had on the day the summons was made attendable at Chambers. R. G. H. T., 1853, r. 21. From the question the order itself seems specially to provide for a stay of proceedings; the time to plead would, therefore, I think, be regulated by the date of such order and not by the rule of court, above-mentioned.

52. *Q*. When a defendant is under the usual terms of *"pleading issuably, rejoining gratis*, and taking *short notice of trial,"* what is understood by these phrases respectively ?

*A*. "Pleading issuably," means pleading a plea which puts the merits of the cause at issue, either on the facts or the law of the case. "Rejoining gratis," indicates that a rejoinder must be delivered within four days of replication, without a notice being given to rejoin. Taking "short notice of trial," means that the plaintiff, if he has not time to give long notice (ten days), may give short notice, or four days. The above terms are usually introduced into an order, giving time to plead as a condition for

F

the allowance of time. Chitty's Archbold, 246; Bullen and Leake, 378.

53. Q. If a defendant be under terms to plead issuably, and he plead a plea which is not issuable, what course should the plaintiff adopt?

A. He should sign judgment, as for default of plea, if the time for pleading has expired. And this, though there be other pleas which are issuable; as one non-issuable plea vitiates the whole. Chitty's Archbold, 249.

54. Q. What is a set-off, and give instances in which cross demands may and may not be set off against each other?

A. It is a cross claim which a defendant has a right of setting off against the plaintiff's demand. Such right did not exist at Common Law, but is given by statute. 2 Geo., 2, c. 22. The debts sued for and to be set off, must be mutual and liquidated. It cannot, therefore, be pleaded to an action for breach of covenant for quiet enjoyment. Nor will liability under a guarantee be sufficient, but it would be otherwise if money had been actually paid by defendant under a guarantee. Money due on a judgment may be set off, unless plaintiff had been taken in execution on it. Chitty on Contracts, 756.

55. Q. What is the law as to set-off, where an undisclosed principal sues on a contract made by his agent?

A. It is that the debtor has the same right of set-off against the undisclosed principal as he had against the agent for any debts due by the agent to him. Chitty on Contracts, 206.

56. Q. When a plaintiff has employed an agent in the sale of goods, for the price of which he is suing, under what circumstances is the defendant entitled to the benefit of a set-off which he has against the agent?

A. See the previous answer.

57. Q. Is it compulsory on a defendant to set off his claim against the plaintiff's demand in an action brought by the plaintiff? or can he bring his action for the amount of the set-off?

A. It is not compulsory, and the defendant may pay the plaintiff the whole of his claim and then bring a cross action for his debt. Also, if the set-off exceed the plaintiff's demand, an action will lie for the surplus. Chitty on Contracts, 753.

58. Q. One Anderson owes Baldwin and Crompton £100. Baldwin and Crompton bring an action against him to recover it. Baldwin alone owes Anderson £100. Can Anderson set off this £100 due to him from Baldwin as an answer to Baldwin and Crompton's action against him? If not, why not?

A. He cannot, because the debts are not *mutual*, but due in different rights. Ibid., 761.

59. Q. How is advantage to be taken of a cause of defence arising after plea and before verdict, and how, and in what manner, should the defendant proceed; and what is the plea called?

A. The defence should be pleaded within eight days after the matter arose accompanied by an affidavit verifying its truth, and that it arose within eight days of its being pleaded. It is called a plea *puis darrein continuance*. It may be pleaded in vacation and at Nisi Prius. Chitty's Archbold, 907.

60. *Q.* If a plaintiff discontinue his action after such a plea, will he have to pay costs? and if any, what costs?

*A.* Excepting in the case of the plea being pleaded by one or more of several defendants, the plaintiff on confessing the plea is entitled to the costs of the cause up to the time of pleading the plea. He, therefore, has not to pay them. R. G. T. T., 1853, r. 23.

61. *Q.* If a defendant sued by two joint plaintiffs, pleads that after action brought one of them released him, is this a good defence against both? and in what manner can the plaintiffs obtain their costs in such a case?

*A.* The release of one joint creditor of a debt or claim to damages is a good defence to the action, even though made after action brought, unless the party giving the release had no interest in the action. This would be the case if the plaintiffs sued as trustees for creditors or if a husband, separated from his wife, released a debt due from a third person to which she was beneficially entitled. In such cases the Court will set aside the plea, and order the release to be cancelled, so also if there is fraud. If the release is unobjectionable it would probably be pleaded *puis darrein continuance* in which case the plaintiffs would be at liberty to confess the plea and would be entitled to the costs of the cause up to the time of pleading it. Chitty on Contracts, 691. R. G. T. T. 1853. r. 23.

62. *Q.* If the plaintiff fail to carry on an action after plea, has the defendant any, and what, means of forcing him on?

*A.* He may give the defendant notice to reply in four days, otherwise judgment. If no replication is delivered pursuant to the notice, judgment may be signed. Chitty's Archbold, 1467.

63. *Q.* When a defendant has pleaded, what is the next proceeding on the plaintiff's part?

*A.* He may reply or demur to the pleas, or (by leave) do both. Usually the replication is a simple joinder of issue; but, occasionally, it sets out facts specially.

64. *Q.* When the plaintiff replies without joining issue, what is the defendant's next pleading called?

*A.* A rejoinder, taking issue on the replication, or pleading to it specially, or he may demur to the replication, or he may, by leave, plead and demur together. C. L. P. Act, 1852, s. 180.

65. *Q.* Before what hour must service of pleadings, notices, summonses, etc., be made? and what is the consequence, if made after that hour?

*A.* They should be served before seven o'clock p.m., except on Saturdays, when they must be served before two o'clock p.m. If made after seven, on any day except Saturday, they are deemed to be served the following day, and if after two p.m. on Saturdays, on the Monday following. Chitty's Archbold, 163.

66. *Q.* Describe an issue.

*A.* An issue is some point of dispute either as to the law or facts in an action. As if A sues B for an assault and B pleads "not guilty," an issue of fact is raised as to whether B assaulted A. Again, if A were to sue B for an assault committed by C, and to state the facts in his declaration, B would demur, and thus raise the issue of law, as to his liability for the torts committed by C. There may be several issues raised in a cause in this way. It is usually come to after plea or demurrer. The term *issue* is also applied to the copy of the pleadings after issue joined, which is delivered to the defendant by the plaintiff, and usually indorsed with notice of trial. Stephens on Pleading, 50.

67. *Q.* How are issues in fact and in law respectively disposed of?

*A.* The former are decided by a jury, or a judge without a jury, at Nisi Prius; the latter by the full court sitting in banc on hearing the question argued. See *supra*, No. 40.

68. *Q.* What is a feigned issue? in what cases is it resorted to? and by what authority is it framed?

*A.* It is an issue which is framed for the purpose of trying some disputed question of fact, which may arise in a suit and cannot be raised in the ordinary course above mentioned. Thus, on a motion founded on affidavits, the court sometimes is not satisfied with the proof of a certain fact by affidavit and directs a feigned issue to ascertain the truth. This proceeding is also frequently adopted to settle disputed claims to goods arising on interpleader summonses. An order or rule must be obtained to the issue, after which it is drawn by the person named as plaintiff in the order and agreed to by the defendant. Notice of trial is then given, and the trial proceeds in the ordinary way. Feigned issues are now regulated by 8 and 9 Vic., c. 109. Chitty's Archbold, 891.

69. *Q.* Can an injunction be obtained at common law, and how?

*A.* It may be obtained in cases of breach of contract, or other injury, where the party injured is entitled to bring and has brought an action. The writ is obtained by indorsing a notice of intended claim on his writ, and inserting such claim in the declaration. The writ is granted after the verdict, or if the cause is decided on demurrer, it is given when judgment is given. It may also be obtained at any stage of the proceedings by application to a judge or the court. C. L. P. Act, 1852, ss. 79, 82.

70. *Q.* From what court does a writ of mandamus issue, and how is it obtained?

*A.* There are now three writs of mandamus, viz., 1. the prerogative writ, which issues to enforce the performance of public duties, as to compel an arbitrator to proceed. This writ issues out of the Court of Queen's Bench, and is obtained on a motion to the court. 2. A mandamus to examine witnesses in India, under 1 Wm. IV, c. 22, 3, obtained by application to a judge or any of the superior Courts. 3. A mandamus under 17 and 18 Vic., c. 125, to compel the defendant to fulfil any duty in the fulfilment of which the plaintiff is personally interested. This does not extend to the performance of a contract, *Benson* v. *Paul*, 25 L. J. Q. B., 274, but only to a public duty, such as the compelling a company to register the plaintiff as a shareholder. *Norris* v. *The Irish Land Company*, 27 L. J. Q. B., 115. It may be obtained from any of the superior courts, in a manner similar to that above mentioned with regard to an injunction. 17 and 18 Vic., c. 125, ss. 68—77.

### XVII.—*Collateral Proceedings, Orders, and Rules.*

1. *Q.* What is meant by interlocutory proceedings? Describe some of the proceedings in an action termed "interlocutory;" and how are questions thereon decided?

*A.* They are proceedings in an action which occur before its final termination and do not conclude the cause. Such are summonses, rules, judgments for unliquidated damages, writs of inquiry, writs of trial. Wharton's Law Lexicon, 472.

2. *Q.* What is a *stet processus*, and its effect?

*A.* It is an order of court, the effect of which is to stay proceedings in a cause. It cannot be made without consent of the parties. But, practically, the court may compel the parties to consent by refusing to give them assistance. 2 Lush's Practice, 893.

3. *Q.* How would proceedings be affected by the death of the plaintiff—1. After declaration, and after issue joined? 2. After trial and before judgment? 3. After judgment and before execution? and what must be done in consequence?

*A.* 1. In the event of the plaintiff's death before trial, his legal representative may proceed with the action, first entering a suggestion of the death, and of his being the legal representative. C. L. P. Act, 1852, s. 135. 2. If death happens after trial and before judgment, the death cannot be alleged as error if judgment be entered within two terms after verdict. The judgment is entered for the deceased party, as if he were living, but before execution can be issued the judgment must be revived in the name of the representatives. 3. If the plaintiff die after final judgment, it must be revived by his personal representatives against the defendant, before execution can be issued. This may be done by writ of revivor or suggestion. Ibid, s. 139; Chitty's Archbold, 1115.

4. *Q.* How do you proceed in the case of the death of a sole or surviving plaintiff?

*A.* If the cause of action survives to the personal representative, I should proceed as mentioned in the preceding answer. If it does not survive, no proceedings can be taken, as the suit abates. Ibid.

5. *Q.* Point out any defects or irregularities in the proceedings which would entitle a defendant to apply to set them aside.

*A.* The following may be mentioned:—Service of an informal writ. Proceeding in default of appearance, when the writ has been improperly served, where the time to appear has not expired, or where an appearance has been entered. On account of objections to the declaration mentioned, *supra*, p. 58, No. 10. Going to trial without giving notice of trial. Signing judgment in default of plea before the time to plead has expired, etc., etc. Chitty's Archbold, 1457.

6. *Q.* Within what time must application be made to a court or judge to set aside any proceedings for irregularity? and what act of the party applying debars him from relief?

*A.* It must be made within a reasonable time, and not after the party applying has taken a fresh step with knowledge of the irregularity. R. G. H. T., 1853, r. 135.

7. *Q.* Where a summons is applied for to set aside proceedings for irregularity, what must be stated therein?

*A.* The several objections intended to be insisted on. R. G. H. T., 1853, r. 136.

8. *Q.* State the distinction between an irregularity in practice and a nullity.

*A.* The chief distinction is, that the former can be waived by the opposite party taking a subsequent proceeding, but a nullity cannot be thus set up. Those proceedings are treated as nullities which transgress the practice of the court, not merely in their details (which are irregularities), but in their substance. Thus, to serve a writ on a Sunday without a date would be an irregularity and also a nullity, but to serve it on a Monday without a date would be merely an irregularity. See Chitty's Archbold, 1458.

9. *Q.* When a declaration does not disclose the particulars of the plaintiff's demand in actions of *assumpsit* or debt, how are they to be obtained, and can they be obtained before appearance?

*A.* A defendant may apply by summons to a judge for an order for the delivery of particulars of demand, and such application may be made before appearance. Chitty's Archbold, 1439.

10. *Q.* Is a party taking out a summons before a judge entitled to an order on its return, or must he take any further step?

*A.* If the opposite party attends the summons he may consent, or the summons must be attended before the judge who will decide the case. If the party summoned do not attend, the party taking it out must make an affidavit of its service and of attendance at chambers for half an hour. Upon this affidavit the order will be drawn up. Ibid, 1592.

11. *Q.* An order for three days' time to plead is dated on a Friday: on what day may the plaintiff sign judgment in default of a plea?

*A.* On the Tuesday following, the time being counted exclusive of the Friday, and inclusive of the third day. R. G. H. T., 1853, r. 174.

12. *Q.* After a judge's order for time to plead, further time is required: within what time should the summons for it be served and returnable in order to prevent a judgment by default?

*A.* The summons should be served the day before the last day for pleading, and should be returnable the day following. This will give time to obtain and serve an order on the last day. It frequently happens in practice that the summons has been forgotten until the last day for pleading. The course adopted in such a case to avoid judgment by default is to obtain from the judge a summons returnable the next morning at Westminster, at 10.30 a.m. This enables the applicant to obtain an order before the judgment office is open at 11 a m.

13. *Q.* If a party, after having been served with a judge's order, neglect to obey it, what steps should be taken?

*A.* The order should be made a rule of court, by motion, in term time. The rule is absolute in the first instance, A copy of the rule being served personally and the original produced, an attachment may be moved for against the party, or if the rule is for payment of money, execution may be issued upon it. Chitty's Archbold, 1595, 1 and 2 Vic., c. 110, s. 18.

14. *Q.* Upon service of a rule or order, must the original be always shown?

*A.* It is not necessary to show an original order on the service of a copy. But with regard to a rule the original must be shown, otherwise it cannot be enforced by attachment. Chitty's Archbold, 1702.

15. *Q.* When personal service of a rule is not required, will putting it under the door of the chambers of defendant's attorney or place of business, or into the letter box, be sufficient, or what is further required to make it good? if a rule nisi is improperly served, can it ever be made absolute?

*A.* Such service will not suffice unless there is a notice requesting papers, etc., to be so left, or unless it has been ascertained by enquiry that it has been received, and belief as to its receipt can be sworn to. 1 Chitty's Archbold, 164. The irregularity in the service will be waived by the party moving to enlarge the rule or showing cause against it. Ibid., 1569.

16. *Q.* What is necessary to enable a party to include in his execution the costs of making an order a rule of court?

*A.* An affidavit must be made and filed that the order has been served on the party, his attorney or agent, and disobeyed. R. G. H. T., 1853, r. 159.

17. *Q.* In a case where a rule is obtained to show cause why proceedings should not be set aside for irregularity with costs, and the rule is discharged generally, without any express direction as to costs, what becomes of them?

*A.* The rule is understood to be discharged with costs. Practice Rules, 1853, H. T., r. 137.

18. *Q.* State the usual matters referred by the court or a judge to one of the masters?

*A.* They are frequently directed to ascertain the amount of damages upon a judgment by default, where the amount is substantially a matter of calculation. C. L. P. Act, 1852, s. 94. Also to examine witnesses orally before the trial, C. L. P. Act, 1854, s. 46. Also a witness who refuses to make an affidavit. s. 48. Also if a party does not sufficiently answer interrogatories, s. 53. He is also frequently directed to review his taxation of costs. Also if a motion is made to strike an attorney off the rolls for malpractice, the case is frequently referred to the master to report thereon to the court, and upon his report the court act.

## XVIII.—*Evidence.*

*Notices to inspect and admit, and to produce—Witnesses—Verbal Proofs—Documental Testimony.*

1. *Q.* Into what divisions is evidence usually classed? are there any degrees of secondary evidence? Give an instance to illustrate your answer.

*A.* Evidence is divided into direct and circumstantial. Direct evidence is that which directly proves a fact, which is the subject of inquiry, as if A swears that he saw B trespassing on C's close. But if he swore that he saw B coming from the direction of C's close, such evidence might be presumptive of the fact of B's trespass. Direct evidence is subdivided into primary and secondary. Primary is the highest kind of evidence, as the production of a deed, and the proof of it is primary evidence of its contents. But a copy would only be secondary evidence, and can only be tendered when the deed is lost or the opposite party refuses to produce it. There are no degrees of secondary evidence. By this is meant, that in the case above-mentioned of the deed being lost, parol evidence of its contents could be given, although it could be proved that the party giving the evidence had a copy or a counterpart in his possession. Taylor on Evidence, 489

2. *Q.* What alterations in the law of evidence have been made by recent statutes?

*A.* No objection can be taken to a witness on account of his being interested in the suit or of having committed a crime, 6 and 7 Vic., c. 85. Certified copies of bye-laws of a corporation and other official documents to be received in evidence without proof of the seal, 8 and 9 Vic., c. 113. Parties to suits are competent witnesses, excepting in actions for breach of promise of marriage, or proceedings in consequence of adultery, or in criminal cases, 14 and 15 Vic., c. 99. Also husbands and wives are made competent witnesses against one another, but they are not bound to disclose communications made during the marriage. Criminal proceedings and proceedings instituted in consequence of adultery are excepted, 16 and 17 Vic., c. 83. But now in proceedings to dissolve a marriage on the ground of cruelty and adultery, or cruelty and desertion, the husband and wife may give evidence as to the desertion and cruelty, 22 and 23 Vic., c. 61, s. 6. Important provisions as to evidence are also contained in 17 and 18 Vic., c. 125; as to the proving a deed by an attesting witness; also as to discrediting a witness, etc.

3. *Q.* A plaintiff or defendant, prior to the trial of a cause, wishes to ascertain facts which he believes to be in the knowledge of the opposite party: what proceedings should he adopt to do so?

*A.* He should obtain leave from a judge to deliver interrogatories upon the facts he wishes to have discovery. The application for the order must be supported by an affidavit of the applicant and his attorney or agent that material benefit will be derived from the discovery sought for, that there is a good cause of action or defence on the merits, and if the application is by the defendant, that it is not made for the purposes of delay. A copy of the proposed interrogatories should be served with the summons. C. L. P. Act, 1852, s. 51. Chitty's Archbold, 1412.

4. *Q.* If a document in your possession is to be produced at a trial, should the expense of taking a witness to prove it be incurred, or is there any way of avoiding that expense?

*A.* I should give to the opposite party a notice to admit the document in question, saving all just exceptions to its admissability. Should he attend at the hour named in the notice, and inspect and afterwards admit its execution, I should make an affidavit of such admission, the production of which at the trial would enable me to put in the document without further proof. If the party refuse to admit and the judge do not certify at the trial that such refusal was reasonable, he will have to pay the costs of proof whatever the result of the cause may be. C. L. P. Act, 1852, s. 117. Chitty's Archbold, 319.

5. *Q.* Does the rule of court, which requires a notice to admit written documents to be adduced in evidence, apply to all documents, or to such only as are in the party's possession?

*A.* It applies to all documents that a party means to produce in evidence though not within his possession, or in his control, or if it is out of the kingdom. Chitty's Archbold, 320.

6. *Q.* Within what time must a party called upon by notice to admit documents either admit or refuse to admit?

*A.* The notice to admit specifies certain hours for inspection of the documents, and the party has forty-eight hours from the last hour named for inspection, to make the admission. This time may be extended by order. Chitty's Forms, 141.

7. *Q.* If the defendant wish to inspect a deed or document in the possession of the plaintiff, what course is to be adopted? and what course was it necessary to adopt previously to the recent alteration of the law in this respect?

*Q.* In such a case the defendant should apply to the court or a judge for an order to inspect and take a copy of the document. The document must appear to relate to the action. 14 & 15 Vic., c. 99, s. 6. Before this act the court, under its equitable jurisdiction, would frequently make such an order; but, it was usually necessary to resort to Equity. Power to compel *discovery* of documents at law is given by C. L. P. Act, 1854, s. 50.

8. *Q.* If your client has an unstamped written agreement and it is doubtful if it requires a stamp, and it has to be used as evidence at a trial at *Nisi Prius*, what advice would you give your client as to stamping it, and what is the latest time it could be stamped?

*A.* I should consider whether the time for stamping it without paying a penalty (fourteen days from its execution) would expire before the trial. If it would do so I should at once stamp it with an agreement stamp. If the time for stamping had expired I should wait until the trial, and if the judge ruled that it required a stamp I should pay the officer of the court, the duty and penalty and a fee of £1, after which payment it could be read in evidence. On production (at my leisure) of the receipt of the officer for the duty, &c., to the Commissioners of Inland Revenue I could get the stamp impressed. C. L. P. Act, 1854, ss. 28, 29.

9. *Q.* If a party to a cause call a witness to prove the execution of any written instrument, without first requiring the admission of its due execution, what will be the consequence of such omission?

*A.* He will be disallowed the costs of proof unless not giving the notice was a saving of expense in the opinion of the taxing master. C. L. P. Act, 1852, s. 117.

10. *Q.* Where a verdict has been set aside, and a new trial ordered, and previously to the first trial the usual notice to inspect and admit documents was given, and an admission made; is it necessary to give fresh notice, and to obtain a fresh admission of the same documents upon the second trial?

*A.* No; an admission once made will hold good for a subsequent trial. Chitty's Archbold, 322.

11. *Q.* If a deed or document required for the purpose of the cause be in the possession of the adverse party, what is the usual course to be pursued, with a view to its production; or if not produced, to be enabled to give secondary evidence of its contents?

*A.* I should give notice to produce the document at the trial. I should be prepared at the trial with an affidavit of the service of the notice. If the document was not produced I could, on production of my affidavit and proof of the document being in the opposite parties possession, put in secondary evidence. The notice once given will extend to subsequent trials. Chitty's Archbold, 322. In the case of *Lomer* v. *The Itchin Bridge and Road Company of Southampton*, tried at the Croydon Summer Assizes, 1865, August 10th, brought to recover damages for injury to the plaintiff whilst getting out of one of the defendants ferry-boats, the defendant gave notice to produce the plaintiff's crinoline, their defence being that it was the cause of the accident, and it was produced in court accordingly.—*Times*, August 11th, 1865.

12. *Q.* A deed of gift and a will are both executed by the same person and attested by the same witnesses. Is there any, and what, difference in the necessary mode of proving the execution of the two instruments?

*A.* The deed might be proved by verifying the hand writing of the parties by the oath of persons, not necessarily witnesses to its execution. But the will being an instrument which by law requires attestation for its validity, (7 Wm. IV. & 1 Vic., c. 26.) can be proved only by the oath of one of the witnesses to it, unless, indeed, the absence of the witness is accounted for, and his signature proved, or unless the will proves itself by age or proper custody. C. L. P. Act, 1854, s. 26.

13. *Q.* With what exceptions may the parties or their wives be examined as witnesses in their own causes?

*A.* As mentioned above, parties to suits and their husbands and wives are generally competent witnesses. The exceptions are in actions for breach of promise of marriage and criminal cases. And, as to husband and wife, communications made during marriage are privileged as between one another. Their evidence is also inadmissable in proceedings instituted in consequence of adultery (16 & 17 Vic., c. 83.), subject to an exception in the case of a wife petitioning in the Divorce Court for dissolution of marriage on the ground of her husband's adultery coupled with cruelty or desertion. In either of these cases both husband and wife are competent and compellable to give evidence of or relating to such cruelty or desertion .22 & 23 Vic., c. 61, s. 6.

14. *Q.* If a witness refuse to attend voluntarily, how are you to proceed?

*A.* I should serve him with a writ of *subpœna* summoning him to attend.

15. *Q.* How many witnesses may be included in a common *subpœna?*

*A.* The names of four may be inserted. Chitty's Archbold, 349.

16. *Q.* Is it necessary to serve a witness with a copy of a *subpœna* personally, or will it be sufficient to leave it at his dwelling-house?

*A.* The writ must be served personally and the original produced. His expenses should also be tendered, or if he resides within the weekly bills of mortality and the cause is a town one, payment of one shilling will suffice. Ibid., 350.

17. *Q.* What is necessary to be done in case a witness is in custody?

*A.* If his evidence is required on a trial application should be made to a judge of one of the superior's courts for a writ of *habeas corpus ad testificandum.* The application must be supported by an affidavit stating that he is a material witness and willing to attend. If the application is granted the writ is engrossed and endorsed by the judge, after which the master of the court seals it. It is then delivered to the officer having the custody of the witness. Ibid., 354.

18. *Q.* What is a *subpœna duces tecum?*

*A.* It differs from an ordinary *subpœna ad test* in that it requires the witness to bring with him some document which he has in his possession. The particulars of the document are set out in the *subpœna.* Ibid., 353.

19. *Q.* What proceedings can be taken against witnesses for non-attendance upon a *subpœna?*

*A.* He may be proceeded against by motion for attachment for contempt of court. He may also be sued under the provisions of 5 Eliz., c. 9., for such damages as the court in banc may award. Or, he may be sued at Common Law in case for damages actually sustained owing to his non-attendance. Ibid., 357.

20. *Q.* If a witness in a cause be about to sail on a distant voyage, is it advisable to detain him here till the trial, or is there any other way of obtaining his testimony?

*A.* His detention may be avoided by obtaining an order from the court or a judge to have him examined upon oath before the trial, upon interrogatories or *vivâ voce*. His examination being taken he may set sail, and should he not return before the trial his evidence may be read. A similar course may be adopted if the witness is ill. *Brown* v. *Mollett*, 24 L. J. (C. P.), 213. Chitty's Archbold, 330.

21. *Q.* When a judge grants an order to examine witnesses in a cause, and they afterwards appear at the trial, and are examined, what becomes of the costs of the commission?

*A.* The costs of the commission will be borne by the party obtaining it. They will only be costs in the cause if the evidence taken on the commission is read at the trial. See 1 Chitty's Archbold, 345.

22. *Q.* Where a material witness in a cause is resident at Calcutta, what different modes may be adopted to obtain his evidence?

*A.* His evidence may either be obtained by commission to commissioners to take his evidence in the ordinary manner, or by mandamus directed to the Chief Justice and Judges of the Supreme Court of Judicature, to examine the witness. The examination being taken, it will be returned to the court in this country out of which the mandamus issued. 13 Geo. III., c. 63, s. 44; 1 Wm. IV., c. 22, s. 4. Chitty's Archbold, 337—344.

23. *Q.* A brings an action on a policy of insurance; his principal witnesses reside at Bordeaux and Dublin, and refuse to come over to be examined. Can the plaintiff enforce their attendance, or how can he obtain their testimony?

*A.* The attendance of the witnesses living at Bordeaux cannot be enforced, either here or on a commission issued to Bordeaux, and if they persist in their refusal he must do without their testimony. The Irish witnesses may, however, be compelled to attend, upon an order obtained from the court here, or a judge thereof. If they disobey the order, application must be made to the Irish courts to compel them to come. 17 & 18 Vic., c. 34. As mentioned below, No. 42, their attendance may also be enforced on a commission. Taylor on Ev., 1071, 4th ed.

24. *Q.* What evidence is necessary for a plaintiff on the trial of an undefended action for goods sold and delivered, plea the general issue; or on the execution of a writ of inquiry in a like action?

*A.* The plaintiff will have to prove the sale and delivery of the goods to the defendant, as ordered by him, at the price sued for; upon this evidence he will be entitled to a verdict. If judgment has been signed by default, the sale and delivery is admitted, but evidence of value must be given on the writ of inquiry. Such a case would not now occur, as the writ would be specially indorsed, and the judgment would be final. Taylor on Evidence, 81, 4th ed.

25. *Q.* Has a copyhold-tenant of a manor a right to an unqualified inspection of the court-rolls and books of the manor? and, if so, before or pending action?

*A.* He is not entitled to an unqualified order for inspection, but he may inspect and take copies of such parts of the rolls as relate to his own title, privilege, or interest; and this whether an action be pending or not. An order to compel the lord to allow such inspection is absolute in the first instance. Ibid, 1271.

26. *Q.* Can parol evidence be in any case received to explain, or alter, or contradict an agreement in writing?

*A.* Parol evidence cannot be given to alter or contradict an agreement in writing. It is, however, admissable to explain it in the following cases. Where there is a latent ambiguity, *i.e.*, one not patent on the face of the contract, but ascertained by extrinsic facts. Thus, a contract to sell "the manor of A," the party having two manors of that name may be explained, because the ambiguity is ascertained by parol evidence, and it is only fair to explain it by the same medium. But if it was a contract to sell "one of my manors of A," the ambiguity would be patent, and the same reasoning would not apply. Parol evidence is also allowed to explain custom and usage, and to defeat a contract on the ground of *illegality, duress,* or *fraud.* Chitty on Contracts, 97—107; Broom's Maxims, 551.

27. *Q.* In what cases is it necessary to call an *attesting* witness, in order to prove a document? What alteration has been recently made in the law on this subject?

*A.* It is now only necessary to call an attesting witness, when attestation is necessary to the validity of the instrument. 17 & 18 Vic., c. 125, s. 26. Before this act it was necessary to call one, at least, of the witnesses. Taylor on Evidence, 1540, 4th ed. See the next answer.

28. *Q.* What written instruments now require an attesting witness to make them valid?

*A.* The following may be mentioned:—Instruments under powers requiring attestation; wills; warrants of attorney; cognovits and satisfaction pieces; conveyances to charitable uses under the Mortmain Act; bills of sale of British ships; bargains and sales enrolled for exchanging charity lands; certificates of searches and memorials; and some copies of enrolments granted by the registrars of deeds and wills in Yorkshire and Middlesex. See further Taylor on Evidence, 1541.

29. *Q.* In an action upon a deed, where its execution is required to be proved, and the attesting witness is dead, how is the plaintiff to prove such execution?

*A.* If the deed does not prove itself by age and proper custody, and requires attestation for its validity, proof of the handwriting of the witness must be given. If it do not require attestation, proof of the handwriting of the party executing it will suffice. Ibid., 1542.

30. *Q.* After what period does a deed or will prove itself, without calling a witness?

*A.* After it is thirty years old, and comes from the proper custody, the deed is evidence without proof. It is sufficient if it is produced by persons whose possession of it may be reasonably accounted for, though their custody is not strictly the proper one.

Notwithstanding age and custody, if there is any erasure or interlineation on the document it ought to be proved. Selwyn's Nisi Prius, 580.

31. *Q.* A plaintiff brings an action of covenant to enforce payment from the defendant of £100 and interest, which the defendant, by an indenture between the plaintiff of the one part, and the defendant of the other part, covenanted to pay, and which is overdue. Defendant pleads that the indenture is not his deed. What evidence must the plaintiff give at the trial, so as to entitle him to a verdict? Can the defendant go into evidence that the deed was obtained by fraud, or that the consideration money was not paid?

*A.* The plea alluded to of "*non est factum*," merely puts in issue the execution of the deed in point of fact only. The plaintiff must, therefore, prove the signing, sealing, and delivery of the covenant. If the defendant wishes to go into evidence of fraud, it must be specially pleaded. Want of consideration would be no defence. Taylor on Evidence, 300, 4th ed.

32. *Q.* In an action for libel, as, for instance, a libel published in a newspaper, state generally what are the leading points that require to be proved.

*A.* The plaintiff must prove the publication of the libel by the defendants. This is usually done by calling a witness who bought the paper. That the person alluded to by the defendant was the plaintiff. Where the words are uncertain in the meaning, as calling the plaintiff "a lame duck," the intended meaning of the words must be proved. This meaning is stated in the declaration, and called the *innuendo*. Such proof is not necessary if the words are actionable *per se*, without reference to particular circumstances. As if the plaintiff is called a *swindler*. If special damage is alleged, it must be proved, unless the words are actionable, *per se*. The plaintiff may also put in evidence other defamatory matter, showing the animus of the defendant. The proprietorship of a newspaper is proved by a certified copy of the declaration, delivered at the office of Inland Revenue, pursuant to 6 & 7 Wm. IV., c. 76, under the hand of one of the commissioners. Taylor on Evidence, 1355, 4th ed.

33. *Q.* State the evidence to be adduced on the trial of an action of trover.

*A.* The plaintiff must prove—1. Property and right of possession in himself in the goods in question. 2. The nature and value of the goods. 3. A conversion. A demand and refusal of the goods is generally evidence of the conversion. Selwyn's N. P., 1372, 12th ed.

34. *Q.* What is the necessary evidence to support an action on an attorney's bill, when the pleas are "never indebted," and " no signed bill delivered"?

*A.* The plaintiff should prove the retainer by the defendant, which, if in writing, must be produced. If no writing, the evidence of any one present, or the plaintiff's admission, would suffice. Also that the work and disbursements charged for were respectively done and laid out. This would be proved by the attorney or his clerks. Also that a bill signed, or inclosed in, or accompanied by a letter signed and referring to it, was delivered, sent to, or left with the defendant, at his dwelling house or last place of abode, one month before the action commenced. The party who delivered it will be the proper witness to prove this. Chitty's Archbold, 129.

35. *Q.* May an answer in Chancery be used in evidence at Nisi Prius against the party making it?

*A.* The answer is evidence, but the whole of it must be read. The party against whom it is read may also have the bill read, on the ground that the bill and answer form a kind of conversation, both sides of which should appear. Taylor on Evidence, 627, 4th ed.

36. *Q.* On a plea of *nul tiel record*, how is a record in the same court to be proved, and how is a record of another court to be proved?

*A.* If of the same court, the party having to produce the record must bespeak it of the clerk of the court, who has it in his custody, and desire it to be delivered to the master and brought into court on the day appointed by a notice previously given to produce it. It is then proved by its production. If the record is of another court, it is proved by production of a transcript or exemplification in open court. If the record is of an inferior court, a writ of certiorari is sued either out of the court in which the action is pending or out of Chancery. If the record is of a superior court, as in an action in the Common Pleas, if the record be one of the Queen's Bench, a certiorari must be issued out of the Petty Bag Office of Chancery to the Lord Chief Justice of the Queen's Bench returnable in Chancery. Upon the record being certified into that Court, an exemplification of it will be sent by writ of mittimus, sued out of the Petty Bag Office to the Common Pleas. If the action is in the Queen's Bench and the record in the Common Pleas or Exchequer, the proceedings may be by certiorari out of Chancery and mittimus thereon, or by certiorari direct. Chitty's Archbold, 928.

37. *Q.* Assuming it to be necessary in an action brought to give evidence of letters-patent under the great seal, and the probate of a will, in what mode are such proofs to be established?

*A.* Letters-patent may be proved by production of the originals under the great seal, or by exemplification under the great seal, or by examined copies. The probate may be proved by producing it, when due notice will be taken of the seal. Also production of the Act Book or registry from the Court of Probate, containing an entry that the will has been proved and probate granted, or a certified or examined copy of such book will suffice. As to proving the will itself, see *infra* "ejectment," No. 18. Taylor on Evidence, 1334, 4th ed.

38. *Q.* What is the distinction between the admissibility and the credibility of a witness?

*A.* A witness is spoken of as being admissible when there is no objection to his being examined in a cause. In consequence of changes in the law of evidence above mentioned few persons are inadmissible; still there are some cases. For example, the parties to an action for breach of promise of marriage are inadmissible as witnesses. 14 & 15 Vic., c. 99. The credibility of a witness, however, is first raised when his admissibility is admitted. When giving his evidence, it is the interest of the party calling him to show that what he says is to be relied on. The cross-examining counsel, on the contrary, endeavours to shake the weight of his testimony by showing him to be a man of bad character, or that he has, on another occasion, made statements contrary to his present evidence. It is for the judge to decide on the admissibility of a witness, but his credibility is a question for the jury to consider.

39. Q. If a witness, *subpœnaed* to attend the assizes, is arrested on civil process on his way to the assizes, what course should he pursue to be released?

A. He should apply at once to the court, or a judge out of which the process issued, or even he may apply to another court, or judge of it, for release from custody. Upon hearing the application, and it appearing that the witness was going to attend under a subpœna, he will be released. Chitty's Archbold, 781.

40. Q. In what cases can entries in the writing of a deceased person be given in evidence, to prove the facts stated in them?

A. Such entries are admissable as evidence, when they are within the knowledge and against the interest of the deceased, *i.e.*, entries whereby he charges himself, or discharges another upon whom he would otherwise have had a claim. Thus, the entry by a man midwife, who had delivered a woman of a child, of having done so on a certain day, and received his fee, was held to be evidence of the child's age. *Higham* v. *Ridgway*, 10 East, 109. So also entries made in the course of business, by a deceased who had no interest to mis-state what had happened, are admissable. Thus, an entry by a drayman (since deceased), of having delivered beer to the Earl of Torrington was held evidence of the delivery. *Price* v. *Earl of Torrington*, 1 Sm. L. C., 5th ed., 277. Entries in a family Bible as to the birth of members of the family, are also evidence of such facts.

41. Q. Give instances where the statements of persons not upon oath are admissable as evidence of the facts stated.

A. See the previous answer.

42. Q. How is the attendance of witnesses enforced on commissions?

A. If the commission is directed to be executed in Scotland or Ireland, a written notice should be served upon the witness to attend the commission, signed by the commissioner. If he do not attend, application may be made to one of the superior courts of law in that part of the kingdom, or to a judge for an order compelling the witness to attend. 6 & 7 Vic., c. 82, s. 5. If the commission is executed in a foreign country, there is no means of compelling the attendance of a witness. As to compelling the attendance of witnesses before arbitrators, see *infra*, "Arbitration and Award."

XIX.—*Consequences of a Plaintiff neglecting to proceed.*

1. *Q.* A defendant is served with a writ of summons, and the plaintiff proceeds no further. What steps must the defendant take, and when, to enable him to terminate the action?

*A.* After the defendant has appeared he must wait until the expiration of the term next after the appearance, whether he appeared in term or vacation. He may then give the plaintiff a notice to declare in four days otherwise judgment, at the expiration of which time, if no declaration delivered or time obtained, he may sign judgment and tax his costs. Chitty's Archbold, 222.

2. *Q.* What are the proceedings under "The Common Law Procedure Act. 1852," in lieu of judgment as in case of a nonsuit? If a plaintiff, after issue joined, neglect to go on to trial, how may the defendant proceed?

*A.* In town causes, where issue is joined in any term, or the vacation before it, and the plaintiff does not proceed to trial during or before the following term or vacation, the defendant may give twenty days' notice to the plaintiff, to try the cause at the sittings next after the expiration of the notice. In country causes, if issue joined in, or in the vacation before Hilary or Trinity Term, and the plaintiff neglects to try the issues at, or before the *second* assizes following such term; or, if issue joined in Easter or Michaelmas Term, and there be a similar neglect to try the issues at, or before the *first* assizes following such term, the defendant may give a similar notice for the assizes. If plaintiff do not act on such notice, the defendant may suggest the plaintiff's failure to proceed, and sign judgment for his costs. C. L. P. Act, 1862, s. 101. He may also give the plaintiff notice of trial and carry down the record himself for trial by *proviso*.

3. *Q.* Which are the issuable and which are the non-issuable terms?

*A.* For country causes Hilary and Trinity Terms are the issuable terms, as in them the country issues are made up for the ensuing assizes. All the terms are issuable with regard to town causes. Wharton's Law Lexicon, 478.

4. *Q.* When a plaintiff has proceeded to trial, and obtained a verdict, which is afterwards set aside, and a new trial directed, and the plaintiff does not give fresh notice, what steps can the defendant take to terminate the cause?

*A.* In such a case it seems the defendant cannot compel the plaintiff to proceed as mentioned above (No. 2), but he may take the case down by *proviso*. He would give notice of trial to the plaintiff, enter the record, and proceed in the ordinary way to trial. Chitty's Archbold, 1488, 1480.

5. *Q.* Where a cause has been taken to trial, and made a *remanet* so as to prevent a defendant signing judgment for his costs, what steps can the defendant take in order to put an end to the cause?

*A.* If the cause is a country one the defendant cannot compel the plaintiff to go to trial under the circumstances mentioned, but he may try the cause by *proviso*. It is, however, otherwise with regard to town causes. In such causes, the defendant may proceed as mentioned above (No. 2), or he may try by *proviso*. Chitty's Archbold, 1487.

6. *Q.* Where a plaintiff neglects to try his cause within the time given after the defendant's notice, can he take any course to prevent the defendant signing judgment for his costs?

*A.* The plaintiff may apply to the court or a judge to have the time for proceeding to trial extended. Any trifling excuse will be ground for the order, if it does not appear that the object is delay. Thus the absence of a material witness will suffice. Chitty's Archbold, 1492.

7. *Q.* If no steps have been taken in a cause for one year from the last proceeding, what is the course to be taken by the party wishing to proceed?

*A.* He must give one calendar month's notice to the opposite party of his intention to proceed. R. G. H. T., 1853, r. 176.

8. *Q.* Is a summons without an order or a notice of trial, a proceeding, although countermanded?

*A.* A summons without an order is not a proceeding, but a notice of trial, although countermanded is one. Ibid.

## XX.—*Notice of Trial and Computation of Time.*

1. *Q.* What distance from London makes a country cause?

*A.* There is no particular limit as to distance; but, in practice, if there is an agent at or near the place of the defendant's residence, the cause would be considered a country cause, and the writ sent to him for service. Thus, Kingston is within easy distance of London; but if the defendant lived there a plaintiff would be entitled to treat the cause as "country," and so get more costs on judgment by default. In transitory actions the plaintiff may lay his venue in town or the country at his option, subject to it being changed as mentioned below.

2. *Q.* How many days' notice of trial is necessary; and how are the days calculated? and is there any difference between town and country causes?

*A.* Ten days' notice of trial is in all cases necessary, unless otherwise ordered, excepting when the defendant is under terms to take short notice. Short notice is four days. The days are calculated exclusively of the day on which the notice is given, but inclusively of the commission or sittings day. Thus if the commission day is July 11th notice of trial must be given on the 1st July, short notice on the 7th July. There is no difference between a town and country cause. Chitty's Archbold, 312.

3. *Q.* What number of days is sufficient countermand of full, and short, notice of trial respectively? What is the effect of such notice on the costs of a cause, and what is the effect of such a notice given after the proper time?

*A.* Four days is notice of countermand of notice of trial, and two days of short notice of trial. If the notice is given in due time no liability will be incurred by the plaintiff as to costs; but if after, the plaintiff will have to pay the costs of the defendant incurred subsequently to the time when the notice ought to have been given. Ibid., 317.

4. *Q.* Where a defendant is under terms to take short notice of trial for particular sittings, is the plaintiff at liberty to give short notice of trial for any subsequent sittings?
*A.* No, the order binding him to take short notice for particular sittings does not bind him for any other sittings. Ibid., 313.

5. *Q.* If a cause be made a *remanet*, is a new notice of trial necessary, either in town or country?
*A.* In a town cause no new notice of trial is necessary, and tho cause will appear in the list for the ensuing sittings. At the assizes, however, there are no remanets, strictly so called, as a cause if not reached has to be re-entered and fresh notice of trial given. Ibid., 312.

6. *Q.* How is time computed upon the rules of practice in the course of a cause? If a party have four days to do any given act from the first of the month, when does the time expire?
*A.* When any particular number of days not expressed to be clear days, as prescribed by the rules of the court, they are reckoned exclusively of the first day, and inclusively of the last day. Therefore, the time expires in the case mentioned on the fifth of the month. If, however, it were "four clear days" the party would have all the sixth day to do the act in. The last day, also, is always reckoned exclusively when it falls on a Sunday, Christmas-day, Good Friday, or public fast or thanksgiving. Chitty's Archbold, 159.

### XXI.—*The Trial at Nisi Prius with its Incidents.*

1. *Q.* What is the derivation and meaning of the phrase "*nisi prius,*" as applied to the courts holden for the trial of causes in the superior courts of Westminster Hall? What is the business at *nisi prius* exclusively confined to?
*A.* It is a term which is applied to the sittings of the superior courts for the purpose of trying issues of fact; and arose in consequence of the writ of *Venire*, summoning the jurors to Westminster on a certain day, unless before (*nisi prius*) that day the judges came into the country to try the cause in question. It should be remembered that, originally, actions were formerly triable only in the court in which they were brought. That is at Westminster. Magna Charta, however, provided that the assizes of novel disseisin and mort ancestor should be tried in their proper counties instead of at Westminster. This provision was by 13 Edw. I., st. 1, c. 30, extended to all other actions. The trials before the justices sent to try the issues are as valid as if tried in the court itself. 14 Edw. III., c. 16. Thus it arises that when any of the judges

sit alone for the trial of issues in any county and in the City of London, such sittings are termed sittings at "*nisi prius*." The business is exclusively confined to the trial of civil actions; criminal cases are in the country tried at the same time, but the judges when trying criminal cases, do so under commissions of oyer and terminer and general gaol delivery. 4 Steph. Coms., 393, 5th ed.

2. *Q.* Distinguish between the proper functions of a judge and jury in the trial of a cause — which should decide matters of law — which matters of fact — and which united matters of law and fact?

*A.* The duty of a judge at a trial at *nisi prius* is threefold: 1. He must decide all questions respecting the admissibility of evidence. 2. He must instruct the jury as to the rules of law by which the evidence when admitted is to be weighed; lastly, he must explain and enforce the general principles of law applicable to the point at issue. The jury must decide the facts left to them by the judge. Mixed questions of law and fact are to be decided by the judge. Thus in an action for malicious prosecution "probable cause" is for the judge so soon as the jury have ascertained whether the circumstances upon which probable cause is founded existed. Taylor on Evidence, 32 *et seq.*

3. *Q.* If a cause be tried by a special jury obtained by the plaintiff or defendant, and the party who obtained it succeed in getting a verdict, but the judge omit to certify that it was a proper cause to be so tried; on whom will the costs of the special jury fall?

*A.* They will fall upon the party obtaining the special jury; he ought to have obtained a certificate immediately after the verdict on the back of the record. Chitty's Archbold, 515.

4. *Q.* Is there any, and what, difference between a plaintiff being nonsuited, and the defendant obtaining a verdict in actions of debt, *assumpsit*, or covenant?

*A.* If nonsuited the plaintiff may bring the cause on again, either in another shape or when better prepared with evidence; but after verdict and judgment the plaintiff is barred from suing the defendant for the same cause of action. For this reason a plaintiff frequently elects to be nonsuited. This course is open to him in other actions besides those mentioned in the question. Chitty's Archbold, 445.

5. *Q.* What is a nonsuit, and in what respect is it more beneficial than a verdict for the defendant?

*A.* It is a proceeding by which judgment is entered against the plaintiff, in consequence of his not following up his action to its conclusion when the cause comes on for trial. For the plaintiff it is more beneficial to be nonsuited, as he may bring a fresh action for the same cause when better prepared for success. A verdict for the defendant is, however, more beneficial to the latter as after it he cannot be further harassed. Chitty's Archbold, 409, 9th ed.

6. *Q.* Can a plaintiff be nonsuited without his consent, and if he cannot, what should he do to prevent it? and in what respect is his situation better by a nonsuit than a verdict for the defendant?

*A.* Suffering a nonsuit being entirely a voluntary act of the plaintiff he cannot be nonsuited against his will. In general, however, when a judge directs a nonsuit to be entered the plaintiff's counsel submits to it, as it would be generally useless to go to the jury when the judge will direct them to find for the defendant. If the ruling of the judge is erroneous a new trial will be ordered by the court. Ibid. Smith's Action at Law, 150, 8th ed.

7. *Q*. What is the form of a voluntary nonsuit?

*A*. There is no form used at the trial. The nonsuit is marked by the associate on the back of the *nisi prius* record. The postea states "that the jury having considered what verdict they should give and the plaintiff being solemnly called on, came not, nor does he further prosecute his suit against the defendant. Chitty's Forms, 245, 9th ed.

8. *Q*. Where a cause goes to trial, and a juror is withdrawn, does it prevent the plaintiff from bringing another action for the same cause?

*A*. Yes; at least, if the plaintiff afterwards proceeds, an order may be obtained to stay the proceedings. This order should be obtained promptly, as if the defendant allows the cause to go to trial he cannot then object. Chitty's Archbold, 407, 9th ed.

9. *Q*. Has the discharging the jury a similar effect?

*A*. No, if the jury is discharged by consent, the suit may be brought on again for trial. Ibid.

10. *Q*. How did 9 Geo. IV. c. 15 (commonly called Lord Tenterden's Act) affect amendments on the record? and how has the same been further extended by 3 & 4 Wm. IV. c. 42, s. 23, and 15 & 16 Vic. c. 76 s. 222?

*A*. The first-named act allowed amendments to be made in certain cases, but its provisions and also those of 3 & 4 Wm. IV. c. 42, on the same subject are now superseded by 15 and 16 Vic. c. 76, s. 222. This act empowers the court or a judge to amend all defects and proceedings, whether there is any thing in writing to amend by or not, and whether the defect or error be that of the party applying to amend or not, upon such terms, as to costs, as the court thinks fit, and all amendments for the purpose of deciding the real question in controversy shall be so made. This provision has been liberally construed. But in an action against a husband for a debt of his wife *dum sola*, the court would not allow the wife to be made a party by way of amendment. *Garrard* v. *Giubilei*, 31 L. J. C. P., 131.

11. *Q*. How is a verdict enforced?

*A*. See *infra* "execution," p. 103, No. 1.

12. *Q*. What is the origin and meaning of the word Postea?

*A*. It is a word applied to the return of the judge of what took place at the trial. It is indorsed upon the back of the *nisi prius* record, and is so called because it gives the history of the proceedings after the conclusion of the pleadings, which are stated in the record itself. Therefore, it begins "afterwards on the     day of    , at Westminster Hall, in the county of Middlesex, before, &c." Chitty's Archbold, 467.

## XXII.—*Trial before the Under-Sheriff.*

1. *Q.* What is a writ of trial, and a writ of inquiry respectively?

*A.* The former is a writ issued to the sheriff or judge of any civil court of record in the county to try a cause commenced in the superior court, and in which an issue of fact is raised, the amount in dispute being under £20, and no difficult question of law or fact being involved. The writ is obtained by order from a judge, and on its return with the finding of the jury judgment is signed forthwith and execution issued, unless the sheriff suspend the judgment to give time, to move for a new trial. Chitty's Archbold, 415. A writ of inquiry is issued to ascertain the amount of damages upon an interlocutory judgment signed in the superior court, where the damages are not *substantially a matter of calculation*; as in this case, a reference to the master is the proper course. It issues without order, and, on its receipt, the sheriff summonses a jury who assess the amount, which is returned to the court above, and final judgment may be signed at the expiration of four days from the return. Ibid, 982—995.

## XXIII.—*New Trial—Arrest of Judgment—Judgment non obstante veredicto—Error.*

1. *Q.* When must application be made for a new trial?

*A.* If the trial takes place in vacation, the rule must be moved for the first four days of the ensuing term, unless entered in a list of postponed motions by leave of the court. If tried in term, the motion must be made before the expiration of four days from the day of trial, and if after the trial there is not four days of the term unexpired, the motion must still be made within the term. R. G. 50, H. T. 1853.

2. *Q.* If a cause be tried at the last sittings in term, what time has the party against whom there is a verdict to move for a new trial?

*A.* See previous answer.

3. *Q.* Within what time can a motion for a new trial be made after a writ of inquiry, or when a cause is tried before the sheriff?

*A.* Application may be made to set aside the inquisition on a writ of inquiry within four days after the return of the writ, or at any time before final judgment is signed. If the writ is executed in vacation, application should be made to a judge or the sheriff to stay proceedings until the next term. After a writ of trial has been executed, a new trial should be moved for within four days after the return of the writ, if in term. In other cases within the same time as is limited for a like motion in ordinary cases. *Supra,* No. 1. Chitty's Archbold, 993, 428.

4. *Q.* State some of the cases in which the courts will grant a new trial; and in actions for debts what is the amount recovered under which a motion for a new trial is prohibited? and what is the rule on writs of trial before the under-sheriff? and within what period must the application be made in the latter case?

*A.* A new trial may be obtained on the following grounds—

NEW TRIALS. ARREST OF JUDGMENT. 87

Wrongful admission, or rejection of evidence; misdirection of the judge; on account of the judge improperly nonsuiting the plaintiff; improperly discharging the jury; if the judge allows the wrong party to begin; if a jury-man is sworn on the jury by a wrong surname; where the jury are interested in the question in dispute; if the verdict is perverse; where verdict against evidence; where the damages are excessive or too small; where the jury misconduct themselves, as during the trial sleeping at the defendant's house; surprise; misconduct of witnesses; where no notice of trial has been given. The amount in dispute must generally be £20 to induce the court to interfere; but this rule does not apply where the verdict has been obtained by fraud, or there has been misdirection, or the judge has received improper or excluded proper evidence, or some particular question of right is involved. In the case of trial before the sheriff the limited sum is £5. If the writ of trial is returned in term, the motion must be made within four days after the return, or before the end, of the term, if four days are not unexpired. If returned in vacation, the motion must be made the first four days of the ensuing term. Chitty's Archbold, 428.

5. *Q*. If evidence, legally inadmissible, be received on a trial, what remedy has the party injured thereby?

*A*. If in the event of the evidence not having been admitted the result of the trial might have been different, the court will grant a new trial. The evidence must have been objected to by counsel. A bill of exceptions might also be tendered. Ibid, 1506.

6. *Q*. When, as a general rule, are new trials granted upon payment of costs only, and when without costs?

*A*. In those cases where the granting a new trial is matter of discretion, as on the ground of the damages being excessive or too small, the misbehaviour of the jury, etc., the court will sometimes impose payment of costs of the first trial. The court will grant the rule without costs where the new trial is a matter of right, as where plaintiff submits to an erroneous nonsuit, or misdirection of the judge. Ibid, 1528.

7. *Q*. At what period must a motion be made in arrest of judgment, or for judgment *non obstante veredicto?*

*A*. Within a similar time to a motion for a new trial mentioned *supra* No. 1, namely within four days of trial if tried in term; if in vacation, within the first four days of the ensuing term.

8. *Q*. What is a judgment *non obstante veredicto*, and upon what grounds may it be obtained?

*A*. It is a judgment which is, in some cases, given by the court for the plaintiff, when a verdict has been already found for the defendant at the trial. It can only be obtained when, on a retrospective examination of the record, the cause of action stands confessed by the defendant. Thus, if to a count for trespass infancy was pleaded and issue was joined on the plea, and a verdict found for the defendant upon the issue, the plaintiff could obtain judgment notwithstanding the verdict. The plea is no answer to the action and ought to have been demurred to. Upon the face of the record, therefore, the cause of action is confessed by the defendant, and the law is against him. Stephens on Principles of Pleading, 88.

9. *Q.* What is a motion in arrest of judgment, and on what grounds may it be made?

*A.* It is a motion by an unsuccessful defendant to arrest the judgment on the ground that there is some error on the face of the record which vitiates the proceedings. It is a proceeding the reverse of that mentioned in the previous answer, and might be made where a count in the declaration is bad in substance and ought to have been demurred to. Chitty's Archbold, 1542.

10. *Q.* To what tribunals successively do appeals lie from the Court of Queen's Bench, Common Pleas, and Exchequer?

*A.* From each of these courts there is an appeal to the Court of Exchequer Chamber, composed of those judges of the superior courts from which the appeal is not made. The House of Lords is the next and ultimate court of appeal. Chitty's Archbold, 3.

11. *Q.* Is there any limit as to the time for bringing error upon a judgment, and what is it? and are there any exceptions to the limit?

*A.* Error must be brought within six years from the date of the judgment, excepting in cases where the party at the time he is entitled to bring error is an infant, *feme covert, non compos mentis*, or beyond seas, when a further period of six years is allowed after the disability ceases. C. L. P. Act, 1852, ss. 146, 147.

12. *Q.* By "The Common Law Procedure Act, 1854," in what cases are new powers given for obtaining the opinion of a court of error?

*A.* Under this act there is an appeal from a judgment on a special case, unless the parties agree to the contrary, which privilege did not formerly exist. There is also an appeal as mentioned in the next answer, on motion for a new trial, and to enter a verdict or nonsuit. C. L. P. Act, 1854, ss. 32—34.

13. *Q.* Where a rule for a new trial or to enter a verdict is either made absolute or discharged, in what cases can the party against whom the rule is made appeal?

*A.* In the case of the new trial, if the rule is refused or granted, and then discharged or made absolute, there is an appeal where the motion for a new trial is on the ground of misdirection, provided one of the judges dissent from the rule being refused, made absolute, or discharged, or if the court allow an appeal. With regard to the rule to enter a verdict, if it is refused or granted, and then discharged or made absolute, the party decided against may appeal. Notice of appeal must be given in writing, to the opposite party, within four days of the decision complained of. C. L. P. Act, 1852, ss. 34—37.

14. *Q.* The Common Law Procedure Act of 1854 speaks of a garnishee. To whom is this term applied?

*A.* It is applied to the party who is ordered to pay to an unsatisfied judgment creditor a debt owing by him to the judgment debtor. The order is called an order for attachment, and is obtained on application to a judge, the judgment debtor being first orally examined before a master, or some other person appointed, as to the debts due to him. An order is obtained for the garnishee to appear and show cause why he should not pay the debt. If he disputes his liability, the plaintiff may proceed against him by writ; if he does not dispute it, execution may be levied against him on non-payment. C. L. P. Act, 1854, ss. 60—67.

## XXIV.—*Judgment and its Registration.*

1. *Q.* Explain the difference between a verdict and a judgment.

*A.* A verdict differs from a judgment in that it is the decision of the jury, upon the issues of fact raised by the pleadings for their decision, whereas, a judgment is the decision of the court upon the law of the case. A verdict is either general or special. The former is given *vivâ voce* by the jury; thus we find for the plaintiff (or defendant) damages ———. A special verdict is given as to certain facts proved at the trial, to which the court in banc will apply the law, and direct the verdict to be entered according to their decision. Chitty's Archbold, 448.

2. *Q.* State the different kinds of judgment.

*A.* Judgments are either interlocutory or final, and are of the following kinds : — on nonsuit, *non pros, retraxit, nolle prosequi* discontinuance, *stet processus,* by default, judgment on demurrer, in ejectment, on plea in abatement, in error, against executors or administrators, of assets *quando acciderint, non obstante veredicto,* upon *nul tiel record,* and after verdict. Chitty's Archbold, "Judgment."

3. *Q.* Are all judgments by default final?

*A.* No; for if judgment be signed for default of appearance on a writ where unliquidated damages are sought, the judgment is interlocutory.

4. *Q.* When and by whom may a judgment of *non pros* be signed?

*A.* It may be signed by a defendant for his costs when the plaintiff declines proceeding in the action, after the time limited for his taking any step has expired, and notice has been given him to proceed. Thus, supposing a plaintiff does not declare within the term ensuing the vacation or term in which the appearance was entered, the defendant may give a four days' notice to declare otherwise judgment. On the expiration of the four days judgment may be signed. Smith's Action at Law, 92.

5. *Q.* What is the difference between an interlocutory and a final judgment?

*A.* A judgment is considered interlocutory when some further act remains to be done before the plaintiff can avail himself of it as a means of satisfying his claim, or if obtained by the defendant before he can consider himself freed from the suit. Thus, if a plaintiff signs judgment for default of appearance, when the writ is issued for unliquidated damages, the damages must be assessed by a master or sheriff before the proceedings can be completed, and then final judgment can be signed. If the writ had been, or might have been, specially indorsed, the judgment by default will be final in the first instance, and not interlocutory. Chitty's Archbold, 970.

6. *Q.* In what manner and within what time may judgment be signed for non-appearance to a writ specially indorsed; and where one of two defendants upon whom such a writ has been served appears, and the other does not, how may the plaintiff proceed?

*A.* The plaintiff may, on the expiration of eight days from the service of the writ, and no appearance having been entered, file an affidavit of personal service, and of the due endorsement of service having been made, or a judge's order, giving leave to proceed as if personal service had been effected, and a copy of the writ, and sign judgment. Supposing, therefore, writ served May 1st, judgment might be signed on the 9th May. If one defendant appears, but the other does not, the plaintiff may sign judgment against the one not appearing, and before declaration against the other issue execution thereon. This execution will be deemed an abandonment of the action against the other. Instead, however, of pursuing this course, the plaintiff may declare against the appearing defendant suggesting the judgment against the other, and on the trial the jury will assess the damages against the defendants. C. L. P. Act, 1852, s. 33.

7. *Q.* In actions upon contracts, either express or implied, where some of the defendants let judgment go by default, and others plead, and upon trial a verdict is found for one or all the defendants who pleaded, would the jury proceed to assess damages against the defendants who suffered judgment by default, or what would be the result?

*A.* The judgment by default in such a case would be inoperative, and damages could not be assessed against the defendant who has not appeared. 2 Chitty's Archbold, 937, 11th ed. *Morgan* v. *Edwards*, 6 Taunt., 398.

8. *Q.* What penalty is incurred upon signing judgment for want of a plea, where the writ of summons has not been specially indorsed, when the defendant is within the jurisdiction, and the claim is for a liquidated demand?

*A.* In such a case the plaintiff will not be entitled to more costs than if he had made a special indorsement. Therefore, he will be disallowed his declaration and notice to plead. Chitty's Archbold, 973.

9. *Q.* Is a writ of inquiry necessary now in all cases where the defendant has suffered judgment by default for an unliquidated demand?

*A.* No; the damages may be in certain cases ascertained by the master, as mentioned in the next answer.

10. *Q.* In what sort of actions is it referred to the master to inquire the amount of damages, and what steps are to be taken to obtain such inquiry?

*A.* A reference to the master to assess the damages may be had when they are substantially a matter of calculation. After interlocutory judgment signed, a summons must be taken out to refer the case supported by affidavit, giving particulars of the action, and stating that judgment has been signed. Attend the summons, and if order made draw it up, and obtain an appointment from the master to proceed with the reference. Serve the order and appointment. Issue subpœnas to your witnesses, and attend with them at the time appointed. On the amount of damages being ascertained, tax the costs and sign final judgment. The opposite party also attends the reference if he chooses. Chitty's Archbold, 985.

11. *Q.* Suppose an action of debt on a money bond to secure one sum payable at one time, and a similar action to recover a sum payable by instalments, and a similar action for non-performance of covenants, or for breach of covenant, for the faithful conduct of a party, and a judgment by default obtained in each action, is there any, and what, difference in the steps to be taken by the plaintiff before he can issue execution?

*A.* In the action on the money bond to secure a gross sum, the judgment is final, and the plaintiff may issue execution at once for the whole penalty. In such a case, the defendant, to avoid such a result, should have paid into court the principal, interest, and costs actually due under 4 & 5 Anne, c. 16, s. 13. The judgments signed in the other cases mentioned would, however, only be interlocutory, as they are within 8 & 9 Wm. III., c. 11. The plaintiff must assign any breaches which have occurred, and get the damages for such breaches assessed by a jury, before a judge of assize, or the sheriff. The judgment has to be entered on the roll, and the breaches suggested on it, and the jury assess the damages as in ordinary cases. The interlocutory judgment stands for the full penalty as security for future breaches, but final judgment is signed, and execution issued, for the amount found by the jury, and costs. Chitty's Archbold, 996.

12. *Q.* Where a plaintiff or defendant has obtained a verdict, or a plaintiff has been nonsuited, within what time may judgment be signed and execution issued, unless otherwise ordered? and what power has the judge in such case?

*A.* Judgment may be signed, and execution issued, fourteen days after the verdict or nonsuit, unless a judge or the court shall order execution to be expedited or stayed. This latter a judge has power to do, if he shall think the circumstances require it. As if a party is making away with his goods, or if there is ground for a new trial, and the cause is tried in vacation. Chitty's Archbold, 412; C. L. P. Act, 1852, s. 120.

13. *Q.* Can the judges amend defects in records after judgment given? If so, how must it be done?

*A.* They may amend defects where there has been some mistake in recording the verdict or judgment, the mistake being compared with the judge's notes of the trial. An order must be obtained from the judge who tried the cause, and served on the opposite party. On production of the order the officer of the court will amend the record. Chitty's Archbold, 464.

14. *Q.* Is there any difference in the proceedings after a verdict on a feigned issue and a real issue as to enforcing the decision?

*A.* Yes; in the case of a verdict on a feigned issue, for instance an interpleader, judgment cannot be signed and execution issued as in ordinary cases, but a rule of court must be obtained on motion for payment of the costs and the amount in dispute. (The latter, however, is generally paid into court.) Whatever sum the rule directs to be paid may be recovered by execution. Application for an order for costs should first be made at Chambers, and, on the order being made, it may be made a rule of court. 2 Lush's Practice, 781, 3rd ed.

15. *Q.* How do you, and after what time must you proceed to revive a judgment?

*A.* A judgment may be revived by writ of revivor or by entering a suggestion on the record of the fact which has rendered revival necessary. This suggestion is entered by leave obtained on rule or summons. If the order is refused a writ of revivor may nevertheless be issued. C. L. P. Act, 1852, ss. 129, 130. After the expiration of six years, from the recovery of the judgment, it must be revived. If under ten years old the writ of revivor issues without order; above ten and under fifteen years old, a rule of court or judge's order is necessary; over fifteen and under twenty years old, a rule to show cause. Ibid, s. 134.

16. *Q.* If a *feme sole* plaintiff or defendant marry after judgment and before execution, what must be done in order to execute the judgment?

*A.* In either of the above cases, before the judgment can be executed, proceedings to revive must be taken, either by the husband or wife, or against them. The proceedings to revive may be either by *scire facias*, under the 132nd section of C. L. P. Act, 1852, or by writ of revivor or suggestion, under the 129th and subsequent section of the Act. Chitty's Archbold, 1120—1122; Smith's Action at Law, 8th ed., 293.

17. *Q.* What proceedings would you take in order to enforce a judgment against the heirs, executors, or administrators of a defendant?

*A.* With regard to proceedings against the heir, he must be sued by writ under 11 Geo. IV. & 1 Wm. IV., c. 47, and the action proceeds to trial as in ordinary cases. As to the executors and administrators, proceedings may be taken by writ of revivor or suggestion, as mentioned above, No. 15, or they may be sued in debt on the judgment. Chitty's Archbold, 1225.

18. *Q.* Judgment against two defendants, and one dies. What is necessary to enable the plaintiff to take out execution, and against whom?

*A.* If one defendant die after judgment, and within six years, a *fi fa* or *ca sa* may be sued out without reviving the judgment. This should be executed against the survivor only, as the judgment survives as to the personalty and only binds the goods of the survivor. If it be wished to proceed against the lands of the deceased, which remain bound, as well of those of the survivor, a writ of revivor must be issued or proceedings may be taken by *scire facias*. After the judgment is revived, a writ of elegit may be issued against the lands of the survivor and of the deceased in the hands of the heir. 1 Chitty's Archbold, 676, 11th ed.

19. *Q.* Where a judgment remains unsatisfied, when is a suggestion or writ of revivor necessary, before the judgment can be enforced by execution?

*A.* A suggestion or writ of revivor is necessary, after six years from date of judgment, on the death of either plaintiff or defendant, on the marriage of a *feme sole*, plaintiff or defendant, and on the bankruptcy of plaintiff or defendant. Chitty's Archbold, 1112.

20. *Q.* When a plaintiff has obtained a judgment against a defendant in the character of executor or administrator, in respect of future assets when they may come into such defendant's hand, and such assets are afterwards received, what steps should the plaintiff take in order to make such assets available to satisfy the judgment?

*A.* A writ of *scire facias* must be issued against the executor or administrator before execution can be had. This writ issues out of the court in which the judgment was obtained, and the proceedings upon the writ are analogous to those on a writ of revivor under the Procedure Act of 1852. That is, the writ must be served like a writ of summons; an appearance must be entered by notice in writing to the opposite party, in eight days from service declaration is delivered, then plea, and the case goes to trial as in ordinary cases. If no appearance, judgment by default may be signed. C. L. P. Act, 1854, s. 91. Chitty's Archbold, 1126.

21. *Q.* When two or more persons are joined as plaintiffs in an action, and one of them only has a right to recover, state what course may now be adopted in respect of judgment and costs.

*A.* Judgment may be given in favor of the plaintiff whom the court shall adjudge entitled to recover, and the defendant will be entitled to his costs occasioned by improperly joining the party in whose favour judgment is not given, unless the court otherwise order. C. L. P. Act, 1860, s. 19.

22. *Q.* If either plaintiff or defendant die after interlocutory and before final judgment, will the action abate, or how must it be proceeded with to final judgment?

*A.* The action does not abate, but may, if the cause of action survive to or against the personal representatives, be revived by or against such personal representatives, by writ of revivor, in a special form given by "The Procedure Act, 1852," calling on the opposite party to show cause why the damages should not be assessed. If no cause is shown, a writ of inquiry is issued to the sheriff, or the amount referred to the master. When the damages are assessed, final judgment may be signed. C. L. P. Act, 1852, s. 140.

23. *Q.* In what cases is registration of a judgment necessary, and what advantages attend the doing so, and how should the same be registered?

*A.* Registration is necessary, in order to affect by the judgment purchasers, mortgagees, and creditors of the judgment debtor, and it must be done even though a purchaser should have express notice of the judgment. The judgment must be registered every five years. 1 & 2 Vic., c. 110; 2 & 3 Vic., c. 11; 18 & 19 Vic., c. 15. Judgments entered up after the 23rd July, 1860, are not to affect any land as to a *bond fide* purchaser for value or a mortgagee (whether such purchaser or mortgagee have notice or not of the judgment), unless a writ of execution of such judgment shall be issued and registered before the conveyance or mortgage, and the execution must be put in force within three months of the registering. 23 & 24 Vic., c. 38. This act was intended to place judgments as to freeholds and copyholds on the same footing as against leaseholds of the debtor; these latter, like all chattels, not being bound as against a purchaser until seizure. (Morgan's Chancery Acts, 296, Note A). The act, however, did not completely effect this object, therefore by 27 & 28 Vic., c. 112, it was enacted that judgments entered up after 29th July, 1864, shall not affect land of whatever tenure until such land shall have been actually delivered in execution by virtue of a writ of elegit or other lawful authority, s. 1. The act also provides for registration of such writ in the debtor's name and not in that of the creditor, as carelessly provided by 23 & 24 Vic., c. 38. Registration of a judgment is also necessary to entitle the creditor to his position of preference over other creditors against heirs, executors, or administrators in the administration of their ancestor's, testator's, or intestate's estates. 23 & 24 Vic., c. 38, s. 3. The method of effecting the registration is to fill up a printed form with the date, amount, and parties' names, and leave this at the office of registration in Sergeant's Inn, Chancery Lane, paying the fee of 5s. (see further as to registration, *infra*, "Conveyancing").

24. *Q.* Can government stock, funds, or annuities of a judgment debtor be made chargeable with the amount of the judgment debt?

*A.* Such property, if standing in the name of the debtor or any one in trust for him, may be charged by obtaining a judge's order that it shall be charged with the payment of the amount. This gives the creditor the same remedies as if the charge had been made by the debtor himself, but no proceedings are to be taken until the expiration of six calendar months from the date of the order. Notice of the order has in the meantime the effect of a distringas. 1 & 2 Vic., c. 110, ss. 14, 15; 3 & 4 Vic., c. 82.

### XXV.—*Expensæ Litis.*

1. *Q.* What were double costs?

*A.* They were estimated by first allowing the prevailing party single costs, including the expenses of witnesses, counsels' fees, &c., and then allowing him one-half of the amount of the single costs.

They were abolished by 5 & 6 Vic., c. 27, s. 6; the party instead receiving ordinary costs.

2. *Q.* In what cases and how can a party to the action obtain security for costs?

*A.* Security may be obtained in those cases where the plaintiff *permanently* resides anywhere out of the jurisdiction of the court, whether suing in an individual or representative capacity, and whether for his own benefit or that of another. But security will not be required where the residence out of the jurisdiction is of a temporary nature, as in the case of sailors constantly returning to this country; nor will it be required from naval and military officers or others in the public service; nor from Peers or foreign ambassadors or their servants. But foreign potentates are not exempt. The application is made by summons to a judge at chambers, which should not be taken out until appearance entered, and in ordinary cases the application must be before issue joined. R. 22., H. T., 1853. If the defendant is not apprised of the ground for the order until after issue joined he should apply promptly and not take any fresh step. But taking a fresh step before issue joined does not waive his right. In ejectment, also, where a plaintiff having failed in one action brings another, security will be ordered. Chitty's Archbold, 1402.

3. *Q.* If a plaintiff be a foreigner, or reside out of the jurisdiction of the court, has a defendant any, and what, mode of obtaining or securing the payment of his costs should the plaintiff fail? and can he obtain this in any stage of the cause?

*A.* (See preceding answer).

4. *Q.* When are executors or administrators personally liable to pay the costs of an action brought by or against them?

*A.* Executors and administrators when plaintiffs are now on the same footing, with regard to costs, as other plaintiffs, unless the court otherwise order. 3 & 4 Wm. IV., c. 42, s. 31. The court will interfere where there has been fraud or mis-representation by the defendant, by means of which the verdict was lost. Also, if it appear that the plaintiff acted *bonâ fide* and under the advice of counsel, and that due diligence was used. In actions against executors or administrators if the judgment is that the costs be levied *de bonis testatoris*, the defendant is not personally liable to pay them. But, if they are directed to be levied *de bonis testatoris*, and if those insufficient then of the defendant's own goods; he is personally liable for the costs the assets are not sufficient to satisfy. Gray on Costs, 229—230.

5. *Q.* What is an affidavit of increase, and what does it contain?

*A.* It is an affidavit which is made by the attorney of the party, taxing his costs, verifying certain charges and payments charged in the bill, and which do not appear on the face of the proceedings. The disbursements sworn to generally are counsels' fees, payments to witnesses, service of *subpœnas*, length of attendance at the trial, court fees, &c. The master is not justified in allowing these unless sworn to. Chitty's Archbold, 508. As to the party to make the affidavit, see *Supra* "Affidavits," p. 52, No. 7.

6. *Q.* What is the present practice as to costs on cross issues, and what must be sworn in the affidavit of increase on those found for the plaintiff, and those for the defendant, to get the expenses of their respective witnesses allowed?

*A.* If the plaintiff succeed on a material issue which entitles him to recover his debt or damages or part of them, he will be entitled to the general costs of the cause. These include (except where no material issue of fact is found for him) all the costs excepting those of such part of the pleadings, brief, and counsels' fees, and of such of the witnesses and other expenses as are applicable only to the issues on which he has failed. These the defendant will be entitled to deduct from the plaintiff's costs. If, however, the defendant succeed upon an issue, where the defence raised goes to the whole cause of action, the above position will be reversed; as, if to a count for libel, not guilty and justification are pleaded and the defendant succeed in the general issue, the plaintiff on the justification, the defendant gets the general costs of the cause. The affidavit of increase of the party obtaining the general costs of the cause must show that his witnesses related either wholly or partially to the issue or issues he succeeded on. The opposite party must show that the evidence of the witnesses he claims for exclusively related to the issue on which he succeeds. C. L. P. Act, 1852, s. 81; R. G. H. T, 1853, r. 62. By this rule, however, even the party entitled to the general costs of the cause is not entitled to the costs of the *trial* unless it is a material issue of *fact* as distinguished from one of *law*, which entitles him to such general costs. (See *Infra*, No. 8.) Chitty's Archbold, 49.

7. *Q.* On the trial of a cause, the defendant succeeds upon one of several issues which *goes* to the whole cause of action, and the plaintiff on the other issues, which party is entitled to the *postea*?

*A.* The defendant is entitled to the *postea*. It is always accorded to the party who substantially succeeds at the trial. Chitty's Archbold, 467.

8. *Q.* A plaintiff demurs to one of several pleas, which the court holds good as affording an answer to the action. The plaintiff goes to trial on the other issues and succeeds. To what costs is each party respectively entitled?

*A.* In this case the defendant succeeds on a material issue of law by pleading a plea which is an answer to the action, and this entitles him to the costs of the *cause;* he does not, however, get the costs of the *trial*, such as witnesses, etc., not having, also, succeeded on a material issue of *fact*, pursuant to R., 62; H. T., 1853. These latter the plaintiff will be entitled to under the same rule.

9. *Q.* When some issues are found for the plaintiff and others for the defendant, is the allowance for witnesses taxed to the party having the general costs upon the same principle as to the other party?

*A.* See *supra*, No. 6.

10. *Q.* In an action of trespass, or a special action on the case, where the defendant pleads the general issue, and also a special plea of justification to the whole declaration, and a verdict for the plaintiff on the general issue without damages, and for the defendant on the special plea; to what costs is the plaintiff entitled?

*A.* The plaintiff is only entitled to the costs of such part of the pleadings, counsels' fees, and witnesses, as he can show were incurred exclusively in proving the issue on which he succeeds. Chitty's Archbold, 501 (*Supra,* No. 6).

11. *Q.* An action is brought by a pauper, to which three pleas are pleaded, and three issues joined; the defendant recovers a verdict on two issues, being the material issues, but the plaintiff recovers on one issue, though to a certain extent an immaterial one; who will be entitled to the costs?

*A.* In this case the defendant will be entitled to no costs, the plaintiff being a pauper; nor will the plaintiff either, unless by order of the court or a judge. Chitty's Archbold, 1279.

12. *Q.* How did the 3 & 4 Vic., c. 24, affect actions of trespass or trespass on the case?

*A.* It enacted that if the plaintiff in either of these actions recover in a superior court or palatine court less than 40s. damages, he will be entitled to no costs whatever, unless the judge who tried the cause immediately afterwards (*i.e.*, within a reasonable time after the trial) certify, on the back of the record, or writ of trial, or enquiry, that the action was really brought to try a right besides the mere right to recover damages for the trespass or grievance, *or* (not and) that the trespass or grievance was wilful and malicious. 3 & 4 Vic., c. 24, s. 2. Chitty's Archbold, 471.

13. *Q.* When a married woman is sued as a *feme sole,* and she pleads her coverture, and a verdict is found for her, is she entitled to any and what costs?

*A.* It is the better opinion that in this case she is entitled only to her costs out of pocket. *Findlay* v. *Farquharson,* 3 C. B., 347. This is also the rule where a party, not an attorney, sues or defends in person. Marshall on Costs, 236, 2nd ed.

14. *Q.* What sum is it necessary to recover for damages in actions for slander or libel to entitle the plaintiff to costs of increase?

*A.* With regard to libel and slander, 40s. damages must be obtained to entitle the plaintiff to his costs. 3 & 4 Vic., c. 24.

15. *Q.* Supposing a plaintiff not entitled to costs, where the damages recovered by verdict do not amount to 40s., in the forms of action stated in the last preceding question: is there any and what application necessary, so as to entitle a plaintiff to the costs of the action? and how, to whom, and when should such application be made?

*A.* Supposing only 30s. damages to be recovered in libel and slander, a certificate under 3 & 4 Vic., c. 24, must be obtained, as mentioned *supra,* No. 12, both being actions of trespass on the case. The effect, however, of the certificate in the action of slander, would only be to give the plaintiff as much costs as damages, viz., 30s., or whatever the sum might be. But in the action for libel he would get his full costs. This is in pursuance of 21 James I., c. 16, s. 6. But this act only applies to slanderous words actionable *per se;* such are, words charging a man with an indictable crime, or with *having* (not "*having had*") a contagious disorder. Words actionable only by reason of special damage, such as abusing the plaintiff's title to land, whereby he is prevented selling it, etc., are, therefore, as in libel, exclusively governed as to costs by 3 & 4 Vic., c. 24. Selwyn's Nisi Prius, 1259; Chitty's Archbold, 474.

16. *Q.* If one of several defendants, who defended jointly, obtain a verdict, will he now, as formerly, be restricted to 40s. only for his costs, or in what proportion will he be entitled?

*A.* He will be entitled to an aliquot portion of the joint costs of the defence, unless the master thinks some smaller portion ought to be allowed. Thus, if there are two defendants, he will have half the costs, if three, one-third. In addition to this, he may occasionally be entitled to separate costs. Chitty's Archbold, 496. The judge may deprive such defendant of his costs by certifying that there was reasonable cause for making him a defendant. 3 & 4 Wm. IV., c. 42, s. 32.

17. *Q.* A sues B and C in trespass, verdict is against B, and for C; what costs is A entitled to? and is C entitled to any costs?

*A.* If A recovers 40s. damages, and the judge does not certify to deprive him, under 23 & 24 Vic., c. 126, s. 34, he will, on obtaining a certificate that the cause was proper to be brought in the superior court, be entitled to his full costs against B. Such costs, however, will not include extra costs incurred in making C a party, for to these C would be entitled, as mentioned *supra*, No. 16, unless the judge certify that there was reasonable ground for making C a party. If A does not recover 40s., he must also get a certificate under 3 and 4 Vic., c. 24; *supra*, No. 12. Chitty's Archbold, 496.

18. *Q.* What alteration has recently been made in the law with reference to costs in actions for alleged wrongs, in which less than £5 are recovered? If a plaintiff in an action in a superior court for an alleged wrong recover less than £5, can he, independently of the County Court Acts, be deprived of costs in any, and what, manner?

*A.* In actions for an alleged wrong, if the plaintiff do not recover £5, he may be deprived of his costs by the judge certifying immediately after the trial, on the back of the record, writ of trial, or enquiry—(1) that the action was not really brought to try a right besides the mere right to recover damages; (2) that the trespass or grievance was not wilful and malicious; (3) that the action was not fit to be brought. The conjunctive "and" is here used, therefore the judge must certify all three. *Gooding* v. *Britnell*, 31 L. J. C. P., 5. Actions of *detinue* are not within the act. *Danby* v. *Lamb*, 31 L. J. C. P., 17; 23 & 24 Vic., c. 126, s. 84.

19. *Q.* Suppose a juror to be withdrawn by consent on the trial

of a cause without any terms as to the costs, what is the result as to the costs of the trial, and the expenses of the witnesses?
*A.* Each party pays his own costs. Chitty's Archbold, 407.

20. *Q.* On a judgment *non obstante veredicto*, is either party entitled to costs?
*A.* The defendant is entitled to the costs of the trial of any issues of fact rendered abortive by the judgment *non obstante*; that is, the unsuccessful party gets the costs, and may set them off against the costs recovered by the plaintiff, a punishment to the plaintiff for not demurring, and thus preventing the cost of trial. On a motion in arrest of judgment, the plaintiff is similarly entitled to costs. C. L. P. Act, 1852, s. 145.

21. *Q.* Where a new trial is granted on the ground of the verdict being against evidence, what is the rule as to the costs of the first trial? Does this rule apply where there has been more than two trials?
*A.* The costs of the first trial would abide the event of the second, which signifies that if the party who succeeded on the first trial succeeded on the second also, he would get the costs of both trials, otherwise each party would pay their own costs of the first trial. This rule as to the costs of the first trial equally applies to where there have been three trials, and the party who succeeded on the first succeeded on the last also. The costs of the second trial would, in such a case, depend on the terms of the rule granting the third trial. C. L. P. Act, 1854, s. 44; Chitty's Archbold, 1530.

22. *Q.* Suppose a trial had, and a rule for a new trial afterwards made absolute, and such rule be silent as to costs; what is the result as to the costs of the trial already had, and the motion for the new trial? Is there any rule of court on this subject? if there be, state it, or its effect.
*A.* In the case put the costs of the first trial will not be allowed to the successful party, though he succeed on the second, unless the rule is granted on the ground of the verdict being against evidence, in which case they abide the event. C. L. P. Act, 1854, s. 44. The costs of the rule will be costs in the cause. The rule of court referred to is R. G. H. T., 1853, r. 54.

23. *Q.* A new trial is obtained in a cause, where the plaintiff had a verdict "the costs to abide the event." The verdict upon the second trial is given for the defendant: to what costs is he entitled?
*A.* He will be entitled to the costs of the cause, and of the second trial. The costs of the first trial will be borne by each party. *Supra*, No. 21.

24. *Q.* If you indorse a writ for a sum under £20, and you recover on a trial at nisi prius, or on a judge's order, above that sum, on what scale are the costs allowed?
*A.* The costs will be allowed on the higher scale. The higher scale means that the allowance for attendances, etc., would be greater than under the lower scale. Thus, the charge for a letter

under the lower scale is 2s., but under the higher 3s. 6d. Chitty's Archbold, 517.

25. *Q.* To what cases does the lower scale of costs apply in actions in the superior courts?

*A.* It applies to actions on contracts in the superior courts, other than cases wherein on account of the nature of the action no writ of trial can be issued (such are actions on contract for unliquidated damages) where less than £20 exclusive of costs is recovered. The judge trying the cause may, however, certify that the cause was one proper to be tried before him and not before a sheriff, which certificate will entitle the party to costs on the higher scale. Directions to the Taxing Master, 1853.

26. *Q.* Writ specially indorsed. Debt under £20. Defendant allows judgment to go by default. How does the plaintiff get his costs?

*A.* The plaintiff may, in pursuance of a notice to that effect in the writ, apply *ex parte* to a judge at chambers for a certificate for costs which is obtained as of course. If the notice of application is not endorsed an order may be obtained on it appearing that a plaint could not have been entered in the county court, that there was sufficient reason for bringing the action in the superior court, or that there was concurrent jurisdiction between the superior court and county court. Chitty's Archbold, 479.

27. *Q.* If a plaintiff in a superior court prove a debt exceeding £20, but the defendant proves a cross debt, by which the balance due to the plaintiff is reduced below £20, can the plaintiff recover his costs without a certificate under the County Courts Acts?

*A.* The plaintiff will require the judge's certificate to give costs as he does not "recover" in the action above £20. Ibid., 478.

28. *Q.* When a plaintiff in a superior court recovers less than £20 on contract, are there any cases in which he can recover his costs without a certificate or judge's order?

*A.* A certificate is not required in an action for breach of promise of marriage. If less than £20 was paid into court, and taken out in full satisfaction, it has been decided that no certificate is necessary. *Chambers* v. *Wiles*, 24 L. J., Q. B. 257. But this case is overruled by *Parr* v. *Lillicrap*, 11 W. R., 94.

29. *Q.* How are the costs adjusted in an action in which the plaintiff seeks to recover £100, which the defendant reduces to £50 by succeeding to the extent of £50 on a plea of set-off, and the plaintiff gets a verdict of £50 accordingly?

*A.* Set-off being a distributive plea, the defendant will be entitled to a verdict as to £50. This will entitle him to costs incurred exclusively in respect of such plea of set-off. The plaintiff will get the general costs of the cause and trial. See *supra*, No. 6.

30. *Q.* Where a summons is taken out before or after declaration to stay proceedings on payment of a certain sum, with costs, and the judge refuses to make an order because the plaintiff claims a larger sum, the action proceeds, and, upon the defendant pleading,

he pays the sum offered into court, and the plaintiff (without any circumstance to justify his refusal of the sum when offered by the summons) takes the sum out of court, and replies that the money is accepted in full discharge of the action, and applies to have his costs taxed: what costs is such a plaintiff entitled thereto?

*A.* The plaintiff will only be entitled to costs up to the time of the summons to stay proceedings, as he might have avoided the expense of the subsequent proceedings by consenting to an order on the summons. Chitty's Archbold, 1366.

31. *Q.* Is the defendant entitled to any, and what, costs under the circumstances stated in the last question?

*A.* As a general rule the defendant would be entitled to his costs incurred subsequently to the plaintiff's refusal. The fact of the plaintiff going on and then taking the sum previously offered in satisfaction is *primâ facie* evidence of oppressive and vexatious conduct of the plaintiff. If, however, it appeared that the plaintiff had reasonable grounds for such refusal, or acted under a mistake, such presumption would be rebutted, and the plaintiff, instead of paying, would get his whole costs. Ibid., 1369.

32. *Q.* In what cases is a plaintiff not entitled to costs?

*A.* He is not entitled to costs if in actions of tort he recovers less than 40s. damages, or in actions of contract less than £20, without a certificate of a judge as mentioned; Nos. 12, 14, 15, 24, 25. In actions on a judgment also he gets no costs without a certificate. 43 Geo. III., c. 46, s. 4. Pauper plaintiffs are not entitled to costs without order. R. G., 28, T. T., 1853. In certain actions against justices a plaintiff gets no costs. 11 & 12 Vic., c. 44, s. 4. A common informer is not entitled to costs unless expressly given by the statute under which he sues. Chitty's Archbold, 470. If the verdict is for the defendant on all the issues the plaintiff gets no costs. Also on judgment *non obstante veredicto*, as mentioned above, No. 20.

33. *Q.* In what cases may the judge certify to give the plaintiff costs? and when and how must the certificate be given?

*A.* The judge must certify in the cases mentioned in the previous answer, and Nos. 36, 37. The certificate may be given within a reasonable time after the trial. But it is usual and better to apply for it at once, when the circumstances of the case are fresh upon the judge's mind. If this is not done, application is usually made by summons at chambers. The certificate should of course be obtained before taxation. Chitty's Archbold, 484, 11th ed.

34. *Q.* What is the rule as to costs (excluding the County Court Acts) where the plaintiff recovers or takes out of court a sum not exceeding £20, in actions on contracts?

*A.* In such actions, without reference to the County Court Acts, the plaintiff would, by virtue of the Statute of Gloucester, 6 Ed. I., c. 1, get his costs, even if he recovered under 40s. But, under 43 Eliz., c. 6, s. 2, the judge may certify to deprive him of costs if the verdict be for less than 40s. Chitty's Archbold, 484.

35. *Q.* If a plaintiff commence an action in covenant, debt, detinue, or *assumpsit*, in any of the superior courts of record, and

shall not recover a sum exceeding £20, or obtain a certificate from the judge at the trial, is any step necessary under 13 & 14 Vic., c. 61, to deprive him of his costs?

*A.* None whatever. (See next answers).

36. *Q.* Can such a plaintiff take any step to obtain his costs, and what would be sufficient grounds to support his application?

*A.* The plaintiff must, except in an action for breach of promise of marriage, apply to the judge to certify on the back of the record that the cause of action was one for which a plaint could not have been entered in the county court, *or* that there was sufficient reason for bringing the action in the superior court. As to where a plaint could not be entered, see *infra* "The Inferior Tribunals," No. 4. A "sufficient reason" would be where, if the action was brought in the county court, execution could not be had on it; as suing members of a joint-stock company. An order may also be obtained where there is concurrent jurisdiction with the county and superior courts (see post, p. 129, No. 6). Also if the plaint has been removed by certiorari. 15 & 16 Vic., c. 54, s. 4. These provisions apply also to actions of trespass trover, or case, where not exceeding £5 is recovered.

37. *Q.* Does it make any difference if the defendant suffer judgment by default, or when an order to stay is granted?

*A.* In actions where the writ is specially indorsed, a notice should be indorsed, that if judgment be signed for default of appearance, the plaintiff will, without summons, apply for his costs to a judge, unless before such judgment the defendant gives notice to the plaintiff or his attorney that he means to oppose. If the defendant does give notice of opposition, or if the notice is not endorsed on the writ, the plaintiff applies by summons, and the judge will allow the costs as mentioned, No. 36, *supra.* The order to stay would no doubt be granted on payment of costs by defendant. Chitty's Archbold, 1363.

38. *Q.* To a declaration claiming £100 defendant pleads, 1st, except as to £30, never indebted; 2nd, as to £30, payment of £30 into court in satisfaction. Plaintiff joins issue on the first plea, and takes the £30 out of court in satisfaction of so much of his claim. At the trial the plaintiff fails to prove any debt due to him beyond £30. How should the *postea* be entered; and to what costs will each party be entitled?

*A.* The *postea* should state that the jury find the sum paid into court sufficient, and as to the residue of the claim verdict for defendant. The plaintiff will get the costs up to the time the £30 is taken out of court. The defendant will be entitled to the costs of the cause after this time, beginning with "Instructions for plea." R. G., 12, H. T., 1853.

39. *Q.* What costs are usually allowed under a rule for costs of the day?

*A.* Costs of the day include resealing of subpœnas, the subpœnaing of witnesses and payments to them if proper, refreshers to counsel, also if another consultation is necessary, the consultation fee and attendance thereat. The costs of taxation are of course included. Marshall on Costs, 125.

40. *Q.* In *scire facias*, if a plaintiff obtain judgment by default or otherwise, is he entitled to costs? and if so, does the right accrue at common law, or is it given by statute?

*A.* The plaintiff is entitled to costs in cases of judgment by default, or otherwise, by virtue of 3 and 4 Wm., c. 42, s. 34. See also C. L. P. Act, 1852, s. 132.

41. *Q.* Make out a plaintiff's bill of costs on a judgment by default, with a judge's order to proceed as if personal service had been effected, on both scales.

| | (Above £20) | (Under £20) |
|---|---|---|
| *A.* | £ s. d. | £ s. d. |
| Letter for payment | 0 3 6 | 0 2 0 |
| Instructions to sue | 0 6 8 | 0 3 4 |
| Writ and paid fee | 0 12 6 | 0 10 0 |
| Special indorsement | 0 5 0 | 0 2 6 |
| Attendances endeavouring to effect service (three are usually allowed) | 1 1 0 | 0 10 6 |
| Copy Writ and leaving same | 0 5 0 | 0 4 0 |
| Searching appearance, and paid | 0 3 10 | 0 3 10 |
| Drawing and engrossing special affidavit of the circumstances to obtain an order for leave to proceed, and of non-appearance, fo. 10, and copy writ | 0 14 4 | 0 14 4 |
| Paid oath | 0 1 0 | 0 1 0 |
| Attending judge for order and paid | 0 11 8 | 0 8 4 |
| Paid filing affidavit | 0 1 0 | 0 1 0 |
| Copy and service of order | 0 6 0 | 0 6 0 |
| Close copy order | 0 1 0 | 0 1 0 |
| Copy to keep | 0 1 0 | 0 1 0 |
| Paid filing | 0 2 0 | 0 2 0 |
| Copy writ to file | 0 1 0 | 0 1 0 |
| Paid filing | 0 2 0 | 0 2 0 |
| Drawing judgment | 0 3 4 | 0 3 4 |
| Entering proceedings on paper | 0 4 0 | 0 3 0 |
| Attending to sign | 0 3 4 | 0 3 4 |
| Paid | 0 5 0 | 0 5 0 |
| Bill of costs and copy | 0 6 0 | 0 6 0 |
| Attending taxing | 0 6 8 | 0 3 4 |
| Paid | 0 2 0 | 0 2 0 |
| Letters, &c. | 0 5 0 | 0 3 0 |

It is impossible to give any fixed amount for a bill of this nature. The costs allowed for substituted service depend on the circumstances of each case. These should be set out in the bill, that the master may be able to form an opinion. He will, however, consider any explanation given to him at the time of taxation. See further Le Riche's Costs, 46.

## XXVI.—*The Writs of Execution.*

1. *Q.* By what means can a judgment of the superior courts be enforced?

*A.* It may be enforced at Common Law by execution, by attachment of debts due to the debtor, and by action upon the judgment.

In Equity by filing a bill for sale; also by a summary application for a sale under 27 & 28 Vic., c. 112, s. 4.

2. *Q.* What are the different kinds of execution upon a judgment?

*A.* Upon a final judgment on contract, or for tort, a *fieri facias, capias ad satisfaciendum,* or *elegit,* may be issued. Upon a judgment in ejectment a writ of possession (*habere facias possessionem*) is issued. In an action for detinue, or for the breach of contract for the non-delivery of goods, the judgment may be enforced by *fi. fa.* and distringas. C. L. P. Act, 1854, s. 78; 19 & 20 Vict., c. 97, s. 2. A judgment on behalf of the Crown is enforced by writ of extent. If the defendant is a beneficed clergyman, a writ of *sequestrari facias* is issued to the bishop. *Levari facias* is superseded by *elegit.* Chitty's Archbold, 1273.

3. *Q.* What property can be taken under the above writs respectively?

*A.* Under a *fi. fa.* the sheriff may take the personal chattels, leaseholds, growing crops, and certain fixtures of the debtor. Under a *ca. sa.* the debtor's person only can be taken. Under an *elegit,* the goods and lands of the debtor. Under a *habere facias,* the lands recovered in ejectment. In *detinue,* the goods detained. Under an *extent,* the body, lands and goods of the debtor. Under a *sequestrari facias,* the rents, tithes and profits of the benefice, and other ecclesiastical goods of the defendant. Chitty's Archbold, 1273, and various titles.

4. *Q.* Is there any property which cannot be taken in execution?

*A.* The wearing apparel and bedding of a judgment debtor or his family, and the tools and implements of his trade, not exceeding £5 in value, cannot be seized. 8 & 9 Vic., c. 127, s. 8. The goods of strangers cannot be taken, unless indeed the real owner led the sheriff to believe that the goods belonged to the debtor. In such a case the real owner would be estopped from afterwards saying the goods were his. *Pickard* v. *Sears,* 6, A. & E., 469. Goods in the actual use and possession of the debtor, such as money in his pocket, also goods in the possession of the debtor upon which he has a lien. Fixtures which the tenant cannot remove. Animals *feræ naturæ* are also privileged. Oxen and beasts of the plough cannot be taken under an elegit. The goods of a bankrupt debtor are also privileged, unless there has been a seizure and sale before adjudication. *Edwards* v. *Scarsbrook,* 11, W. R. 33. Chitty's Archbold, 635.

5. *Q.* What are writs of *fi. fa.* and *ca. sa.,* and whence are these names derived? Can they be used together, and can the latter be always resorted to?

*A.* A writ of *fi. fa.* is used upon a judgment for the purpose of satisfying it out of the debtor's goods and is directed to the sheriff of the county to cause to be made (*fieri facias*) the debt. A *ca. sa.* is also issued to the sheriff directing him to take the defendant's body to satisfy (*capias ad satisfaciendum*) the debt. Wharton's Law

Lexicon, 367, 147. They can be issued together, but only one must be executed. If the *ca. sa.* is executed, no *fi. fa.* can afterwards issue or be executed. If a *fi. fa* is executed and a levy made, such writ must be returned before the *ca. sa.* can be executed. Chitty's Archbold, 687.

A *ca. sa.* can only be resorted to by plaintiff in an action for the recovery of a debt exceeding £20, exclusive of costs. In an action of tort, however, the amount is unimportant. A defendant also can, in all cases, adopt it to recover costs. The writ does not lie against members of the Royal family and their servants, peers or peeresses, members of Parliament, corporations or hundredors, executors or administrators for debts of the testator or intestate, heirs for debt upon land descended, bankrupts having protection, debtors having executed a deed of arrangement under 23 & 24 Vict., c. 134. The writ cannot be executed after lands of the debtor have been taken under an *elegit*, unless indeed the plaintiff has been evicted. Chitty's Archbold, 678, 682.

6. *Q.* Can a plaintiff issue a *fieri facias* after a *capias ad satisfaciendum* had been executed?

*A.* As a general rule, such writ would be irregular. But, if the defendant die in prison, escape from it, or is discharged by privilege of Parliament, the plaintiff may issue a *fi. fa.* See *infra*, No. 19.

7. *Q.* A levy having been made under a *fi. fa.*, in what cases and when can another writ of execution issue on the same judgment?

*A.* If the whole of the debt has not been levied, another writ of *fi. fa.* may issue for the residue. Also if the debt is above £20, a writ of *ca. sa.* may issue. Also a writ of elegit, to take the defendant's land, may issue at the option of the plaintiff. Whatever writ he adopts, the original *fi. fa.* must be returned by the sheriff, and the levy under it recited in the second writ. No writ can issue after six years from the date of the judgment without revivor. 1 Chitty's Archbold, 594.

8. *Q.* When can execution be issued upon a verdict?

*A.* Whether the verdict be obtained in or out of term, execution may be issued in fourteen days after the verdict, unless a judge orders execution to issue at an earlier or later period. C. L. P. Act, 1852, s. 120; R. G. H. T., 1853, r. 55.

9. *Q.* When can execution be issued on a judgment by default?

*A.* If the writ is specially indorsed, execution may be issued at the expiration of eight days from the last day for appearance. C. L. P. Act, 1852, s. 27. If appearance entered, but no plea, execution may be issued directly judgment is signed. If the judgment is signed under "The Bills of Exchange Act," execution may issue at once. If the judgment by default is in ejectment, execution may also issue at once. In the event of the judgment by default being interlocutory, no execution can of course be issued until final judgment is obtained.

10. *Q.* How does the remedy for costs under a judgment differ from the remedy for costs under a rule?

*A.* If judgment is signed and the costs are taxed, they may be recovered by the ordinary writs of execution *fi. fa., ca. sa.,* or *elegit.* Also an action may be brought upon the judgment. If the costs are payable by rule of court, their payment may be enforced by attachment, or by execution in the ordinary way under 1 & 2 Vic., c. 110, ss. 18, 19, which Act makes the proceedings upon rules analogous to those upon judgments. 2 Chitty's Archbold, 1583. See the next answer.

11. *Q.* What is the proper course to be adopted with respect to executions founded upon orders which are made rules of court, to give the party an opportunity of being heard?

*A.* The order must be made a rule of court on motion, against which cause may be shown. If the rule when made orders the payment of a specific sum of money, execution may issue at once without leave. If, however, this is not the case, a rule must be obtained calling upon the party to show cause why he should not pay the money. Upon this rule being made absolute, execution may issue at once. For example, if the order was an order of reference and the award directed the payment of a sum of money, the order of reference must first be made a rule of court, and then a second rule to pay the money obtained. Chitty's Archbold, 1583.

12. *Q.* The venue in a cause being laid in the county of Surrey, and the plaintiff having obtained final judgment against the defendant, and being desirous of issuing an execution against the defendant's effects in Norfolk, can he or can he not issue a *fi. fa.* at once into the latter county, although the venue in the action be laid in Surrey?

*A.* He may issue a *fi. fa.* directed to the sheriff of Norfolk or any other county he may choose at his option. C. L. P. Act, 1852, s. 121.

13. *Q.* Suppose a plaintiff recovers a verdict against two joint defendants, should he issue execution against each defendant for a half; or, if he issue execution against one for the whole, would the other be thereby entirely exonerated? or could he be compelled to contribute, and, if so, how? and would it be the same if the action be in tort?

*A.* The execution must be issued against the two, but it may be executed against either at the option of the plaintiff. The plaintiff usually directs the sheriff to levy on the man who is most likely to pay. If one pays the whole, he may in actions on contract obtain contribution from his joint defendant. It is, however, otherwise in actions against joint tortfeasors, between whom there is no contribution, for *ex turpi causâ non oritur actio. Merryweather* v. *Nixan,* 2 Sm. L. C., 456. Contribution in the case of the joint debtor would be compelled by action of assumpsit or by bill in equity. *Dering* v. *Earl of Winchelsea,* 1 L. C. Eq., 78.

14. *Q.* Did the 1 & 2 Vic., c. 110, make any alteration as to executions after judgment obtained?

*A.* This act extended the power of the sheriff considerably by enabling him to seize money or bank-notes, cheques, bills of exchange, bonds and other securities, belonging to the debtor. Such securities may be sued on in the name of the sheriff, the plaintiff giving an indemnity. By the same Act also the whole of a debtor's land may be extended under an elegit, instead of one half, as formerly. The copyholds may be taken. Also lands over which the debtor has an uncontrolled power of appointment for his own benefit. Also trust estates. As to charging orders on stock, see *supra*, No. 24. p. 94.

15. *Q.* How should writs of execution be endorsed?

*A.* Writs of *fi. fa.* and *ca. sa.* are endorsed with the name and place of abode or business of the attorney and agent (if any). A direction to the sheriff as to the amount of debt, interest, and costs to be levied for or satisfied, also to recover his own fees and poundage. The occupation and residence of the defendant is also usually endorsed, but this is not necessary. Writs of possession have no indorsement excepting the attorney's name, &c. Chitty's Archbold, 602.

16. *Q.* When a judgment has been recovered against the registered officer of a joint-stock company, can it be enforced against the individuals forming the company, and by what means?

*A.* Before execution can be issued on a judgment obtained against a public officer, leave must be obtained on motion to the court in which the judgment is recovered. Notice of the motion must be given to such shareholder. In other cases where it is sought to make shareholders liable the proceedings should be by *scire facias* on the judgment. Chitty's Archbold, 1172, 1135.

17. *Q.* A is indebted to B £15. B sues A and recovers final judgment for £15 debt, and £27 costs. Has B his election to issue execution against the goods and effects, or against the body of A, or is he limited to one only of such remedies; and, if so, to which?

*A.* B can only issue a *fi. fa.*, the debt recovered not being £20 exclusive of costs. If, however, the judge trying the cause be of opinion that the debt was contracted under false pretences, or with a fraudulent intent, or without a reasonable probability of paying it, or that the debtor has made any gift or removal of his property to defraud his creditors, such judge may order the defendant to be arrested upon the judgment. 7 & 8 Vic. c. 96, s. 59.

18. *Q.* If a debtor in execution escape from the custody of the sheriff, or other person having his lawful custody, what remedy has the creditor?

*A.* As against the debtor, the plaintiff's remedy is not affected by the escape, he may, therefore, sue out another *ca. sa.*, or any other execution against him. As against the sheriff, the creditor has a right of action on the case to recover damages for the escape, or he may proceed against him by attachment. Chitty's Archbold, 693.

19. *Q.* Supposing a defendant to die while in custody in execution upon a judgment debt, what is the effect? Is the debt gone, or does it continue?

*A.* The death of the defendant in custody has no effect upon the debt. It still exists, and the plaintiff may proceed against the deceased's lands and goods. 21 James I., c. 24.

20. *Q.* Supposing the person of a defendant to be in execution for a judgment debt, and that, with the plaintiff's consent he is let out of prison on a promise to return into custody. What is the effect of his so being let out of prison upon the debt, and may he be re-taken?

*A.* The effect of such a release would be to extinguish the debt, and all remedies for it, and the defendant cannot be re-taken. This is so even although the defendant agree to be again arrested. Chitty's Archbold, 696.

21. *Q.* In the case of a joint debt due from A and B, and both of them are in custody, in execution upon a judgment recovered for such debt and the plaintiff discharges A out of prison, does or does not the discharge of A affect the debt as regards B, and how?

*A.* In this case B will be entitled to his discharge; the release of one joint debtor being a release of all. Ibid., 696.

22. *Q.* Is there any mode by which a judgment-creditor can attach any debts due to the judgment-debtor, and how?

*A.* The creditor may obtain an order from the court or a judge for the examination of the debtor as to what debts are owing to him. An order may also be obtained attaching any such debts. The third party is called the garnishee, and an order may be obtained for him to show cause why he should not pay the debt to the judgment creditor. If the garnishee does not appear or pay the debt a judge will order execution to issue against him. If he disputes his liability the creditor may sue the garnishee. C. L. P. Act, 1854, ss. 60, 67.

23. *Q.* Goods of A B are in the house of C D, against whom there is a distress for rent of the house, and also a writ of *fieri facias*. Can the goods be taken and sold either under the distress or writ?

*A.* Under a distress for rent the goods may be taken and sold, provided the goods in question were not delivered to C D in the course of his trade or business to be manufactured or worked upon, or were placed there with the leave and license of the landlord. The sheriff under a *fi. fa.* cannot take such goods, unless, indeed, A B were to make him believe the goods actually belonged to C D. Addison on Torts, 444; *Pickard* v. *Sears*, 6, A. & E., 469.

24. *Q.* What is the consequence if a sheriff remove goods seized by him under an execution, after notice that rent is due to the landlord?

*A.* The sheriff will be liable to an action on the case at the suit of the landlord, or he may be proceeded against by motion to the superior court. It is the duty of the sheriff when making an execution to pay the landlord one year's rent before removal of the goods. 8 Anne, c. 14, s. 1. Chitty's Archbold, 639.

25. *Q.* What property can be seized under a writ of *elegit*, and how is it executed?

*A.* As mentioned above, the lands and goods of the debtor can be extended under a writ of *elegit.* The practical proceedings are to issue the writ and lodge it with the sheriff's agent. Upon this being done the sheriff will summon a jury, whose duty it is to find what lands and goods defendant has in the bailiwick. To enable them to do this the plaintiff must be prepared with evidence proving possession by defendant. This proceeding is *ex parte.* The inquisition or finding of the jury is prepared by the sheriff, and sealed by the sheriff and jurymen. The inquisition is then returned by the sheriff and filed with the writ of *elegit* in the court out of which it issued. Absolute possession of the property can only be obtained by ejectment founded on the inquisition. The goods are delivered to the creditor at the price set upon them by the jury. Chitty's Archbold, 670.

26. *Q.* What is a sequestration, and to what property does it apply? If a beneficed clergyman incur debts, is there any, and what, mode of obtaining payment out of the proceeds of his living?

*A.* A sequestration is process which issues against a defendant who is a beneficed clergyman directing the Bishop to sequestrate the rents and profits and glebe lands of the benefice and other ecclesiastical property belonging to the defendant. A judgment must be obtained before the writ can issue. Sequestration may be effected either by *fi. fa. de bonis ecclesiasticis* or by writ of *sequestrari facias.* A sequestrator is appointed to get in the profits and pay them in satisfaction of the debt. Provision must be made out of such profits for the proper performance of the services of the church. Ibid., 1272.

27. *Q.* Where it is desired to charge in execution a person already in the Queen's prison, what is now the proper course to be pursued?

*A.* A judge's order may be obtained on affidavit that judgment has been signed and not satisfied. Service of this order on the keeper of the prison has the effect of a detainer. C. L. P. Act, 1852, s. 127. If the debtor is in the custody of the sheriff only, a *ca. sa.* must be delivered to the sheriff. Owen v. Owen, 2 B. & Ad., 805.

## XXVII.—*Various Steps in an Action.*

1. *Q.* Describe shortly the several steps in a common action at law, not involving anything special.

*A.* After receiving instructions from his client to sue, the attorney should fill up and issue a writ of summons, which, if the claim is for a liquidated demand in money, should be specially endorsed. A copy of the writ should be served personally upon the defendant, or an order for substituted service obtained. An affidavit of service and of the endorsement of service having been made upon the writ, or the order for substituted service, should then be filed at the master's office, if upon search no appearance is found. Final judgment is then signed. If, however, the action is for unliquidated damages, or the writ has not been specially endorsed, a declaration and notice to plead must be filed, and judgment signed, on the expiration of eight days from the filing. The defendant may appear within eight days of service, after which the plaintiff must declare, and give notice to plead in eight days, otherwise judgment. The defendant must then plead, the plaintiff delivers replication and makes up the issue. This latter consists of a copy of the pleadings from the commencement. Upon the issue notice of trial is indorsed. The issue is engrossed on parchment, and then forms the nisi prius record. This is filed with the associate. *Subpœnas* are issued and served; the briefs prepared, counsel retained. The cause is then tried before a judge, and a special or common jury, at nisi prius. Judgment may be signed and execution issued fourteen days after verdict, unless expedited or delayed by order.

### XXVIII.—*The Mixed Action of Ejectment.*

1. *Q.* What is the proper remedy at common law to recover lands?

*A.* The remedy is by action of ejectment; also by entry on the lands. A widow also obtains the lands out of which she is dowable by action of dower or writ of right of dower. Also in certain cases the possession of lands may be given by justices of the peace, under the Small Tenements Act, 1 & 2 Vic., c. 74, *infra* "Conveyancing." Steph. Com. 3, 513.

2. *Q.* What is an action of ejectment? Is there any alteration recently in the process of ejectment? and, if so, state it.

*A.* Ejectment is brought to recover possession of lands. Formerly a similar remedy was obtained by action of *ejectio firmæ*, commenced without writ, by declaration. Now, however, ejectment is commenced by writ directed to the parties in possession. Selwyn's Nisi Prius, 692. 15 & 16 Vic., c. 76, ss. 168—221.

3. *Q.* In what case is an action of ejectment brought?

*A.* It is usually brought by the real owner of property against a wrongful holder, to recover possession of the land; by mortgagee against mortgagor; and by a landlord against a tenant for a similar purpose. Chitty's Archbold, 1005, *et seq.*

4. *Q.* Is an equitable title sufficient to found this action?

*A.* An equitable title is not sufficient. The plaintiff must be clothed with the legal right to possession at the time of issuing the writ. Selwyn's Nisi Prius, 695.

5. *Q.* Within what time may an action of ejectment be brought?

*A.* In ordinary cases for the recovery of land the action must be brought within twenty years from the time when the right to possession accrued, unless at such time the party entitled is under the disability of infancy, coverture (if a woman), idiotcy, lunacy, unsoundness of mind, or absence beyond seas. In such cases, the action may be brought within ten years after the disability ceases, provided it be within forty years from the time the right accrued.

3 & 4 Wm. IV., c. 27. A mortgagee may bring ejectment within twenty years of his right having accrued, and also within twenty years from the last payment on account of principal or interest, though more than twenty years has expired from the time of the right having accrued. 3 & 4 Wm. IV., c. 27; 7 Wm. IV., & 1 Vic., c. 28. A spiritual or eleemosynary corporation sole must sue within the period during which two persons have held the office or benefice in respect whereof the land is claimed in succession, and six years after the appointment of a third person, if such periods together make up sixty years; if not, then within sixty years. 3 & 4 Wm. IV., c. 27. Steph. Com. 3, c. 9.

6. *Q.* Who should be named as a plaintiff in a writ of ejectment? and to whom by name should the writ be addressed?

*A.* The plaintiffs should be the persons legally interested in the land, and the defendants should be the tenants actually in possession of the premises. C. L. P. Act, 1852, ss. 168, 169.

7. *Q.* Must the service of the first proceeding in ejectment be upon the premises, or are there any exceptions?

*A.* The service need not necessarily be on the premises. The writ may be served on the tenant in possession anywhere. As to service on his wife, see next question. Selwyn's Nisi Prius, 724.

8. *Q.* Can a writ in ejectment be served on the wife of the tenant under any and what circumstances?

*A.* Service on the wife is effectual if made on the premises, or even anywhere off the premises, if at the residence of the husband. In such cases, the court presumes the husband and wife to be living together, and that the husband has notice. Selwyn's Nisi Prius, 724.

9. *Q.* When the tenant cannot be met with, may a writ in ejectment be served on any one of the family, without anything further being done?

*A.* As to service on the wife see previous answer. Service on a servant, child, or niece of the tenant will be good if made on the premises, and the tenant afterwards himself acknowledge such service. Such service will also be sufficient without an acknowledgement, if it appear that defendant resides abroad, or evades service. Selwyn's Nisi Prius, 724; Chitty's Archbold, 1015.

10. *Q.* How many days has a defendant to appear in ejectment?

*A.* He has sixteen days from the service of the writ to appear in. Thus, if writ is served January 2, 1865, the appearance must be entered on the 18th January, 1865. C. L. P. Act, 1852, s. 169. If the ejectment be brought by a landlord against his tenant, when the tenancy expires in or after Hilary or Trinity terms, the time for appearance is ten days from service. Ibid., s. 217.

11. *Q.* What is the mode by which a defendant in ejectment may, if he think proper, limit his defence to part of the premises sought to be recovered?

*A.* He may limit his defence by notice to the plaintiff's attorney (if no attorney it is filed at the master's office) within four days after appearance. The notice must describe the part defended for, with reasonable certainty, and be signed by the party appearing, or his attorney. If no such notice is given, the appearance will be deemed for the whole. C. L. P. Act, 1852, s. 174.

12. *Q.* If a tenant be served with a writ in ejectment, and the landlord, devisee, or mortgagee, wish to defend, is he allowed to do so, and if so, how does he obtain leave to do so?

*A.* Such parties may appear and defend on obtaining leave from the court or a judge to do so. The order is obtained by rule or summons, supported by affidavit, showing the applicant's title, and that they are in possession, either by themselves or their tenants. C. L. P. Act, 1852, s. 172; Chitty's Archbold, 1020.

13. *Q.* Under what statutory obligation is a tenant, on whom a writ in ejectment has been served, to give notice thereof to his landlord?

*A.* The tenant must forthwith give notice of the writ to his landlord, or his bailiff, or receiver, otherwise he will forfeit the value of three years' improved or rack rent of the premises he holds to the person of whom he holds, recoverable by action at law. C. L. P. Act, 1852, s. 209.

14. *Q.* In an action of ejectment, where must the venue be laid?

*A.* The venue is a local one and, therefore, must be laid in the county where the land in question is situate. Broom's Com., 164, 3rd ed.

15. *Q.* In ejectment, when can the plaintiff be nonsuited?

*A.* If the claimant does not appear at the trial, but the defendant does, the claimant shall be nonsuited. The defendant will be entitled to his costs. C. L. P. Act, 1852, s. 183.

16. *Q.* What are the steps to be taken in an action of ejectment before the cause is at issue?

*A.* After service of the writ and the defendant has appeared, the issue must be made up and delivered with notice of trial. There are no pleadings in ejectment. Chitty's Archbold, 1028.

17. *Q* What constitutes the issue in an action of ejectment?

*A.* The issue consists of a copy of the writ, a statement that an appearance has been entered, with its date, and the notice limiting the defence (if any). It concludes with — "Therefore, let a jury come," &c. The issue ought not to be delivered until the expiration of four days from the appearance, the defendant having this time to give a notice limiting his defence. See No. 11. Chitty's Archbold, 1028.

18. *Q.* In an action of ejectment for freehold land, how is a will affecting the title proved?

*A.* If the will has already been proved in solemn form and the parties interested in the real estate have been cited in the Court of Probate to see proceedings, the probate or a copy thereof stamped with the seal of Her Majesty's Court of Probate *is conclusive evidence of the validity and contents of the will* in all courts and in all suits respecting real estate. Also, even if the will *has not been proved in solemn form,* a party wishing to give the will in evidence as to real estate, may give to the opposite party ten days' notice that he intends at the trial to give the probate or a copy thereof in evidence. Such probate, however, will not be evidence if such opposite party, within four days after the receipt of the notice, give a counter notice that he disputes the validity of the devise. 20 & 21 Vic., c. 77, ss. 61—64. If the will is not proved as above-mentioned, or the notice is not given, or being given, a counter notice is given, strict proof of all the requirements of the Wills Act having been complied with will be necessary. A witness must be called or his absence accounted for, so as to let in secondary evidence, such as proof of the handwriting of the testator and witnesses. If the will is thirty years old and comes from the proper custody, it proves itself on production. Taylor on Evidence, 131, 1544.

19. *Q.* Where judgment in ejectment is signed for want of appearance, is the claimant entitled to costs?

*A.* In judgment by default the plaintiff to obtain his costs must bring an action for mesne profits, when he can recover them as damages. If, however, the judgment is signed after verdict the plaintiff gets his costs. C. L. P. Act, 1852, s. 185. Chitty's Archbold, 1027.

20. *Q.* A grants a lease to B, who sub-lets to C; to whom does A give notice to quit, previous to bringing an action of ejectment? How shall the notice be served?

*A.* He should give the notice to B the lessee, and not to C the sub-tenant whom the landlord need not recognise. Service, however, of this notice would be sufficient if made upon C the tenant in possession. The notice may, also, be sent by post to the lessee or be left at his usual place of abode. Woodfall, 304.

21. *Q.* When a plaintiff has recovered a verdict in ejectment, how does he recover possession?

*A.* He signs judgment and issues a writ of *habere facias possionem* to the sheriff directing him to deliver possession of the premises. This the sheriff will do, and in doing so may even break open doors, &c. Judgment may be signed, and execution issued by order of the judge or court who tried the cause, at any time within the fifth day in term after the verdict. If no such order is made judgment may be signed and execution issued on the fifth day in term after the verdict, or *after the expiration of* ("within" in the Act) fourteen days after such verdict, whichever shall first happen. C. L. P. Act, 1852, s. 185.

22. *Q.* Can the unsuccessful part in ejectment re-try the same question as often as he pleases without leave of the court?

*A.* If a plaintiff is unsuccessful at the trial a verdict being found for the defendant, he is not precluded from bringing another action to recover the same premises. Such plaintiff may, however, be compelled, on the application of the defendant after appearance, to give security for costs. The proceedings, also, may be stayed until the costs of the first action are paid. The reason for ejectment being an exception to the maxim *nemo debet bis vexari pro una et eadem causa* is that a plaintiff may have a title to land at one time, though not at another. Also, there being no pleadings in the action the judgment cannot operate as an estoppel. Broom's Maxims, 306.

23. *Q.* Where judgment in ejectment is signed for want of appearance, is the claimant entitled to costs?

*A.* He is not entitled to costs upon the judgment, but he may recover them as part of the damages in an action for *mesne* profits. See *infra*.

## XXIX.—*Action for Mesne Profits.*

1. *Q.* At whose suit must an action for mesne profits be brought, and against whom?

*A.* The action must be brought by the plaintiff in a previous action of ejectment, and against the defendant against whom the judgment is entered. It may, also, be brought against any person found in possession prior to the judgment. Chitty's Archbold, 1068.

2. *Q.* What is the plaintiff entitled to recover in such an action?

*A.* He may recover the amount of rent and annual value of the premises during the time of defendant's occupation, and any extra damages the jury may give for his trouble, &c. He may, also, recover as damages the costs of the action of ejectment. Ibid., 1069. If defendant plead the statute of limitations the plaintiff cannot recover more than six years' profits. Selwyn's Nisi Prius, 762.

## XXX.—*Redress of Private Wrong by the injured Party himself taking a Distress.*

1. *Q.* What is a distress and what are distresses usually taken for?

*A.* A distress is a taking without legal process, of a personal chattel from the possession of a wrong-doer into the hands of a party grieved, as a pledge for redressing an injury, the performance of a duty, or the satisfaction of a demand. Distresses are usually taken for non-payment of rent, for damage done by cattle, or for the non-performance of some duty, as, for not shearing the sheep of the lessor. Wharton's Law Lexicon, 288.

2. *Q.* What things may be distrained for rent?

*A.* As a general rule, all chattels and personal effects found upon the premises may be distrained, whether they belong to the tenant or a stranger, unless indeed the goods of such stranger are upon the premises *ex necessitate* to be worked upon in the ordinary course of trade, or are in the possession of the owner. Growing crops and corn are also distrainable. 2 W. & M., c. 5, s. 3; 11 Geo. II., c. 19, ss. 8, 9. Also under the latter act goods fraudulently removed off the premises to avoid distress may be distrained. Woodfall, 377, 8th ed.

3. *Q.* What things are by law privileged from distress for rent?

*A.* The following things are absolutely privileged from distress:— 1. Tenants' fixtures annexed to the freehold by nails or permanent fastenings, but it is otherwise if the fastening is temporary, as by a bolt. 2. Things delivered to a person exercising a public trade to be worked in the way of his trade. 3. Perishable articles, such as milk, fruit, etc., also money, unless in a sealed bag. 4. Things in actual use. This is to prevent a breach of the peace. 5. Animals *feræ naturæ*, such as grouse, partridges, deer, when wild, etc. 6. Things in the custody of the law, such as property taken, damage feasant, or in execution by the sheriff. The following are *conditionally* privileged—that is, they cannot be taken if there are other goods not privileged at all:—1. Beasts of the plough, and instruments of husbandry. But these do not include unbroken colts, steers, and heifers. *Keen* v. *Priest*, 4 H. & N. 236. 2. The instrument of a man's trade or profession. 3. Beasts which improve the land, as sheep. Goods also of a stranger placed on the land with express or implied assent of the landlord are privileged. *Simpson* v. *Hartopp*, 1 Sm. L. C., 368—380.

4. *Q.* At what time of the day on which it is due must rent be paid, in order to prevent proceedings?

*A.* The rent must be paid before sunset on the day it is due, otherwise the landlord may distrain the following day. If, however, the tenant tender the rent before the distress is made it is in time, as after the tender the distress is wrongful. *Bennett* v. *Bayes*, 29 L. J. Ex., 224. Addison on Wrongs, 440.

5. *Q.* Can an outer, or any and what other door be broken, in order to make a distress?

*A.* The outer door of a dwelling-house, or even of an out-house or barn not connected with the dwelling-house, cannot be broken open in making a distress. But lifting up the latch in the ordinary way and walking in is not a breaking open. *Ryan* v. *Shilcock*, 21 L. J. Ex., 55. An outer door may be broken if the bailiff is forcibly ejected, having entered the house. So also an inner door may be broken open when the bailiff has entered the house. If the distress is at the suit of the Crown an outer door may be broken open. Also if goods are fraudulently removed off the premises to avoid a distress the landlord may within thirty days of removal follow them, and if they are locked up may break open the door in the day time. The assistance of the constable or peace officer of the place must be first called in, and in the case of a dwelling-house oath must be made before a justice of a reasonable ground to suspect that the goods are in the house. 11 Geo. II., c. 19, s. 17. *Semayne's* Case, 1 Sm. L. C., 85, and the Notes.

6. *Q.* What is the proper course to be observed in making a distress?

*A.* It should be made by the landlord or his authorised bailiff upon the premises, out of which the rent issued, except where goods removed as mentioned in the preceding answer, and excepting at the suit of the Crown. The seizure must be between sunrise and sunset. After seizure an inventory of the goods must be made and served, with a notice of the amount of rent due and things distrained, on the tenant or premises. This is called impounding the goods. If after receipt of the notice the tenant does not replevy for five days or pay the rent, the goods should be appraised by two appraisers sworn in the presence of the sheriff or constable. This done, they may be sold for the best price, the rent and expenses of sale paid, and the balance, if any, handed to the sheriff or constable for the owner's use. 2 Wm. & Mary, c. 5, s. 1. Addison on Wrongs, 453—459.

7. *Q.* When a landlord distrains for rent, after what time can he proceed to sell the goods distrained?
*A.* (See previous answer).

8. *Q.* Must a bailiff have a written authority to distrain?
*A.* The authority need not necessarily be in writing, but it is the practice to give a written authority and is highly expedient. Woodfall, 393, 8th ed.

9. *Q.* Are the goods of a lodger liable to be taken under a distress on his landlord, and if so, has he any remedy, and what, against his landlord?
*A.* The lodger's goods may be distrained, unless at the time they were in the actual possession of such lodger. He may sue the landlord in case founded upon the implied contract to indemnify the tenant against the consequences of a distress. Woodfall, 543, 8th ed.

10. *Q.* Can goods belonging to a third party be seized under a distress for rent, and under what limitations? Does the same principle extend to a seizure under a writ of *fi. fa.*?
*A.* With regard to distress for rent, the goods of a third party may be seized if in possession of the tenant on the demised premises. But it is otherwise if the goods are in the possession of the stranger. Thus the carriage and horses of a morning visitor standing at the door of the tenant's dwelling-house are privileged. Nor can the goods be taken if placed on the premises by permission of the landlord, or to be manufactured or worked upon, or property of guests at an inn. Under a *fi. fa.* the goods of a stranger cannot be taken unless indeed the owner were to lead the sheriff to believe that the goods were the defendant's. In such a case he would be estopped from saying they were his. *Pickard* v. *Sears*, 6 Ad. & E., 469. Also *Freeman* v. *Cooke*, 2 Exch. Rep., 662.

11. *Q.* What do you understand by the expression—"cattle *levant* and *couchant*"?
*A.* It is a term applied to cattle of a stranger, which have strayed upon the lands owing to their being improperly fenced, indicating that before being distrained they must have been on the land long enough to lay down and rise up again to feed. This is held to be for a period of one night at least. After the period the law presumes that the owner may have notice as to whether his cattle have strayed, and it is his own negligence for not taking them away. If,

however, the lessor or his tenant were bound to repair the fences and did not, and thereby the cattle escaped into their grounds without the negligence or default of the owner, the cattle cannot be distrained for rent, even though they have been *levant* and *couchant*, until actual notice is given to the owner to remove them and he do not do so. If the cattle themselves break the fences they are distrainable for rent immediately, without being *levant* and *couchant*. 3 Bl. Coms., by Kerr, 8.

12. *Q*. In what cases may cattle be impounded? and if impounded for an excessive sum, what are the remedies? and against the party impounding, or the pound-keeper?

*A*. Whenever animals are trespassing on lands, the owner of the land may impound them until paid compensation for the trespass. But the landowner must not have been guilty of negligence in not repairing his fences, by means of which want of repair the cattle entered. *Singleton* v. *Williamson*, 7 H. & N., 410. The animals may be taken in the night time. Cattle, dogs, etc., may be distrained damage feasant, but not animals under the control or use of the owner. Cattle taken by distress for rent may also be impounded, and for this purpose the landlord may turn any part of the premises into a pound *pro hâc vice*. 11 Geo. II., c. 19. The landlord subjects himself to an action in the case if he makes an excessive distress. The pound-keeper is not liable. Woodfall, 748, 8th ed.

13. *Q*. Where a landlord grants a mortgage, and afterwards lets the premises by lease or at will, can the mortgagee distrain for rent if the tenant have not attorned to him, or what remedy has he against the tenant? and would the remedy be the same, if a lease of the premises had been granted before the mortgage? and, if not, what would be the difference?

*A*. 1. If the lease is granted by the mortgagor alone after the mortgage, the mortgagee cannot by giving notice of the mortgage to the tenant make him his tenant and entitle himself to receive the rents. *Evans* v. *Elliot*, 9 A. & E., 342. At one time the contrary was held. *Pope* v. *Biggs*, 9 B. & C. Nor will attornment by the tenant make any difference. The mortgagee may, however, eject the tenant without notice to quit. *Keech* v. *Hall*, 1 Sm. L. C., 505. A new tenancy may also be created, by virtue of which the mortgagee could distrain for rent due under it. 2. If the lease is prior to the mortgage, the mortgagee may, after giving notice of the mortgage to the tenant, distrain for the rent in arrear at the time of the notice, as well as for that which accrues afterwards. This point was decided in the leading case of *Moss* v. *Gallimore*, 1 Sm. L. C., 542.

14. *Q*. Is the summary remedy of a landlord for rent suspended, if he take a note, or bill, or bond; and what proceeding can he take?

*A*. The rent being of a higher nature than the securities mentioned, the remedy by distress is not suspended; unless, indeed, judgment be obtained on the bond, or it be proved that the landlord, at the time he accepted the security, bound himself not to distrain, or, unless it be proved that the security has been paid by tenant to landlord. Addison on Torts, 440.

15. *Q.* Under the Tithe Commutation Act. (6 & 7 Wm. IV., c. 71), to whom is the tithe-owner to apply, in the first instance, for his rent-charge? and if not duly paid, what course must he pursue to enforce payment, and against whom?

*A.* His remedy is by distress and entry on the lands charged. If the rent-charge is not paid for twenty-one days after ten days' notice, distress may be made in the ordinary way, to recover the rent-charge, and 2s. 6d. for the notice. The notice may be sent by post to the tenant in possession. 23 & 24 Vic., c. 93, ss. 29, 30. If the rent-charge is in arrear forty days, and there is no sufficient distress on the premises, any judge of the courts of record at Westminster may, upon affidavit of the fact, order a writ to be issued, directed to the sheriff of the county in which the lands are situate, requiring him to summon a jury to assess the arrears of rent-charge remaining unpaid. A copy of the writ, with notice of the time and place of execution, is then served ten days before its execution. After the writ is executed, the owner of the rent-charge may, by writ of possession, obtain possession of the lands. If the rent-charge does not exceed £10, summary proceedings may be taken for its payment, before a justice of the peace. Only two years' arrears can be recovered in any case. 6 & 7 Wm. IV., c. 71, s. 82; Cripp's Church & Clergy, 392, 4th ed.

16. *Q.* What is the remedy for an unlawful distress?

*A.* If the goods have been wrongfully taken, the remedy is by replevin. If the landlord has distrained when no rent is in arrear, the remedy is by action, to recover double the value of the chattels distrained, under 2 Wm. & Mary, sess. 1, c. 5, s. 5. If the distress is for more rent than is due, and the tenant has tendered the amount due before distress, the remedy would be either by replevin or an action for trespass, or for the wrongful seizure and conversion of the things distrained. If the tender is made after distress, an action of *detinue* would lie. If a second distress is made, when enough might have been taken under the first, trover may be brought for the goods taken under the second. For the wrongful seizure of goods which are privileged, trespass, as well as case may be brought. Addison on Wrongs, 467.

## XXXI.—*The Tort Action of Replevin.*

1. *Q.* In what cases is replevin made? Define replevin, and state the nature of the action. How is it carried on in the County Court, and how in the court above?

*A.* It is made when goods have been wrongfully taken, and consists in a return of the goods so taken to the party from whom they were taken, until the lawfulness of the taking is decided. In the County Court a plaint is entered by the person whose goods are taken, and a bond is entered into to prosecute an action within one month, and return the goods if a return be adjudged. The replevin is then granted by the registrar. The suit is then commenced, is tried before the court, who decides the question, and orders accordingly. In the superior court the preliminary proceedings are, as above mentioned, the conditions of the bond being to commence the action in the superior court within one week, and unless judgment be obtained thereon, by default to prove before the court that the replevisor had good ground for believing either that the title to some corporeal or incorporeal hereditament, or to some toll, market, fair, or franchise, was in question, or that the rent or damage exceeded £20. The writ is then issued, and the cause is conducted to trial like an ordinary action, the pleadings being somewhat different, as mentioned below, No. 5. Chitty's Archbold, 1074; Smith's Action at Law, 360.

2. *Q.* By whom are replevins now granted; and in what court may an action of replevin be commenced?

*A.* The registrar of the County Court of the district where the goods are taken grants replevins in all cases. 19 & 20 Vic., c. 108, ss. 63, 64; C. L. P. Act, 1860, s. 22. The action may be commenced in the County Court, or in a superior court, where the plaintiff can prove the facts above mentioned (No. 1).

3. *Q.* What is the first writ in an action of replevin called?

*A.* It has now no distinctive name as formerly, but the action is commenced by ordinary writ of summons in the superior court, and by summons in the County Court. 19 & 20 Vic., c. 108, ss. 66, 67.

4. *Q.* How would you proceed to remove an action of replevin into the superior courts?

*A.* I should make an affidavit that I had good ground for believing the title to some corporeal or incorporeal hereditament, or to some toll, market, fair, or franchise, was in question, or that the rent or damage exceeds £20. I should take out a summons at judges' chambers for a *certiorari* to issue, serve it on the registrar of the County Court and the plaintiff; attend the summons and read my affidavit, and obtain an order. The order I should draw up and serve on the parties summoned. Obtain an appointment to settle the bond with the master. When settled, get it signed by the defendant and sureties, file it and issue the writ of *certiorari* upon the order. Serve the writ on the judge of the County Court, whose duty it is to return it to the court above. Chitty's Archbold, 1088.

5. *Q.* Name the various pleadings in an action of replevin.

*A.* They are—1. Declaration by plaintiff. 2. Avowry or cognisance by defendant. 3. Plea in bar by plaintiff. 4. Replication by defendant. They may be continued as in ordinary actions. A demurrer may also be delivered. Ibid., 1077.

6. *Q.* What is the meaning of the term "avowry"?

*A.* The term signifies that the defendant in replevin avows the taking of the goods, as alleged in the declaration, justly, as a distress for rent due. If the goods were taken by a bailiff, the justification of the taking by him is called a cognisance. Bullen and Leake's Precedents, 655.

7. *Q.* Is a defendant in replevin in a different character from a defendant in any other action? and, if so, explain the difference.

*A.* The defendant in replevin is really the plaintiff; for, if B distrains on A for rent in arrear, and A replevies and sues B, it is the interest of B the defendant to succeed and get his rent. Whereas, A is interested in a contrary direction, not to pay it. Hence it is that in replevin the defendant has frequently to compel the plaintiff to proceed by giving him notice to plead in bar, etc., otherwise judgment. Also either party may make up the issue, and give notice of trial. The defendant may also make up the record, and enter the cause for trial. Chitty's Archbold, 1082.

### XXXII.—*The Practice under a Warrant of Attorney, cognovit actionem, or a Judge's Order for Judgment.*

1. *Q.* If a party borrow money upon personal security, or for a temporary purpose, where no mortgage is given, is there any security at common law which can be taken?

*A.* The borrower may take a bill of exchange or promissory note; also a warrant of attorney or *cognovit*.

2. *Q.* What is the difference between a warrant of attorney and a *cognovit actionem*?

*A.* In effect, a warrant of attorney is very similar to a *cognovit actionem*. The former is an authority in writing to one or several attorneys to appear and accept a declaration, and confess judgment, without a writ being first issued, against the person giving the warrant. He is also authorised to release errors on the judgment. A *cognovit actionem*, on the contrary, is entitled in an action, a writ having been first issued, but it need not have been served. It consists of a confession by the defendant in person that he has no defence, and that in the event of default of payment on a certain day named, the plaintiff may sign judgment and issue execution. The defendant also undertakes not to proceed in error on the judgment. A *cognovit* need not be by deed, but a warrant of attorney, if it contain a release of errors, must. A *cognovit* is almost entirely superseded in practice by a judge's order to stay proceedings. Chitty's Archbold, 930—938; 2 Lush's Practice, 801—818, 3rd ed.

3. *Q.* When does a *cognovit* require to be stamped?

*A.* If the *cognovit* contain the terms of an agreement to the amount of £5 it must be stamped with a stamp of sixpence, as an agreement. Ibid., 932.

4. *Q.* Can an infant execute a *cognovit*, or warrant of attorney?

*A.* A *cognovit*, or warrant of attorney, by an infant, is not binding on him, even if it is for necessaries. Chitty on Contracts, 142.

5. *Q.* Where an infant joins an adult in a warrant of attorney, is it wholly void, or to what extent?

*A.* The warrant will only be void against the infant. It may be enforced against others who are *sui juris*. Ibid, 143.

6. *Q.* When a party is about to execute a warrant of attorney, or *cognovit*, what is the course of proceeding?

*A.* They must be executed:—1. In the presence of an attorney of one of the superior courts. 2. The attorney must be present on behalf of the person who executes. 3. The attorney must be expressly named by and attend at the request of the person who executes. 4. The attorney should inform the person about to execute of the nature and effect of the warrant, or *cognovit*, before it is executed. 5. The attorney should subscribe his name as witness to the instrument, and in the *attestation* declare himself to be the attorney for the person executing, and state that he subscribes as such attorney. 1 & 2 Vic., c. 110, s. 9. The warrant, or *cognovit*, if given by a trader in order to be valid as against assignees in bankruptcy, must also be filed with an affidavit of execution, in the Court of Queen's Bench, within twenty-one days next after the execution. A copy may be filed instead of the original. 12 & 13 Vic., c. 106, s. 136; 3 Geo. IV., c. 39.

7. *Q.* Give the form of attestation to a warrant of attorney.

*A.* "Signed, sealed, and delivered, by the above named C D, in my presence, and I declare myself to be attorney for the said C D, and that I subscribe my name as such his attorney." Chitty's Forms, 487.

8. *Q.* A defendant being in custody when he executes a *cognovit*, or warrant of attorney, is any and what additional form necessary?

*A.* At the present time no other formality is necessary in such a case than is required by 1 & 2 Vic., c. 110, in ordinary cases.

9. *Q.* A warrant of attorney, dated 21st July, 1841, authorized judgment to be entered up "as of Trinity term last, Michaelmas term next, or of any subsequent term." Judgment was signed in August, 1841. Was this judgment regular?

*A.* The judgment was regular. This was so decided in *Jarvis* v. *South*, 13 M. & W., 152. Also in *Alcock* v. *Sutcliffe*, 4 D. & L., 612 a similar point was decided chiefly upon the ground that the words "as of" did not necessarily mean "in."

10. *Q.* What is the advantage of filing a warrant of attorney, or *cognovit*, under the Statute, and within what time must it be filed?

*A.* The advantage of filing the warrant of attorney, or *cognovit*, in the Court of Queen's Bench, is to make it good, as against the assignees of a *trader* in bankruptcy. If the filing is omitted, the security is still good against the debtor himself. Notwithstanding the filing, a warrant of attorney, given within two months of the filing of the petition for adjudication, and being for an antecedent debt or money demand; and a *cognovit*, if made in an action commenced by collusion with the bankrupt and not adversely, and if given before the commencement of an action, will be bad against the assignees, the bankrupt being at the time unable to meet his engagements. The warrant, or *cognovit*, must be filed within twenty-one days after execution, and if there is any defeasance or condition it must be written on the same paper as the *cognovit*, or warrant. 12 & 13 Vic., c. 106, ss. 135, 136; Selwyn's Nisi Prius, 308, 309.

11. *Q.* What is required to enter judgment on a warrant of attorney above one and under ten years old?

*A.* Leave must be obtained by order of a judge *ex parte*. If the warrant is ten years old or more, there must be a summons to show cause. R. G. H. T., 1853, r. 26.

12. *Q.* A warrant of attorney to confess a judgment for £1,000 having been given by two parties jointly (and not jointly and severally), one of them dies before judgment entered up, can the party to whom the warrant of attorney was given enter up judgment against the survivor?

*A.* On the death of one judgment cannot be entered up against the survivor, unless indeed it was expressly stipulated in the warrant, that it should be done. Chitty's Archbold, 947.

13. *Q.* Where a judge's order is made by consent given by any trader-defendant, in any personal action authorizing judgment to be entered up and execution issued, what is necessary to be done with such order, so as to prevent the same, and the proceedings under it, from becoming null and void?

*A.* The order, or a copy, with an affidavit of the time of the consent being given, and a description of the residence and occupation of the defendant, must be filed in the Court of Queen's Bench within twenty-one days of its date, otherwise it will be void against the assignees in bankruptcy of the trader, but not against the trader himself. Whether filed or not, it is, however, bad as against the assignees, in the same manner as a *cognovit* (*supra*, No. 10), if made in contemplation of bankruptcy. 12 & 13 Vic., c. 106, ss. 135, 136, 137; Selwyn's Nisi Prius, 311.

14. *Q.* How is a security effected upon chattels?

*A.* Possession of the goods should be given to the person advancing his money, or the requirements of 17 & 18 Vic., c. 36, should be complied with, which enacts:—That every bill of sale of personal chattels, and every schedule, or inventory thereto annexed, or therein referred to, or a true copy thereof, and of every attestation of the execution thereof must, with an affidavit of the time of giving the bill of sale, and a description of the residence and occupation of the person making, or giving it, and of every attesting-witness to it, be filed, in the court of Queen's Bench, within twenty-one days after giving the bill of sale. Any defeasance or condition must also be written on the same paper or parchment as the bill of sale. In case a copy is filed, the original must be produced duly stamped. Chattels real are not within the Act.

15. *Q.* What are the necessary facts to be sworn to in an affidavit filed with a bill of sale pursuant to 17 & 18 Vic., c. 36?

*A.* The deponent must depose to the date when the bill of sale was made or given, and also give a description of the residence and occupation of the person making or giving the bill of sale, or, in case the same is given by any person under or in the execution of any process, then a description of the residence and occupation of the person against whom such process shall have issued. Also of the residence and occupation of every attesting witness. Great care must be observed in describing the occupation of the attesting witness (if any). The description of an attorney or his clerk as "gentleman" is insufficient. *Tuton* v. *Sanoner*, 27 L. J. Ex. 293; 1 Chitty's Archbold, 659.

## XXXIII.—*Arbitration and Award.*

1. *Q.* What are the modes of submitting a question to arbitration?

*A.* Reference to arbitration, of all matters in difference between the parties, may be made by mutual agreement, or by order of a judge at *nisi prius*, by consent of the parties. The cause only may be referred compulsorily by the court in banc, on a rule, or a judge at chambers on summons. C. L. P. Act, 1854, s. 3. *Robson* v. *Lees*, 6 H. & N., 258; 30 L. J., Ex., 235. Also by a judge when trying issues of fact under sect. 1 of the C. L. P. Act, 1854. Day's Procedure Acts, 189, 197.

2. *Q.* To what tribunals and under what authority may an action involving matters of account, which cannot conveniently be tried by a jury, be referred?

*A.* Such matters may be decided by a judge in a summary way, or he may order a reference to an arbitrator appointed by the parties, or to an officer of the court. Formerly a reference could be made to a county court, judge in country causes, but this cannot now be done. 21 & 22 Vic., c. 74, s. 5; C. L. P. Act, 1854, s. 3.

3. *Q.* A brings an action against B for the recovery of a disputed debt; after the action is brought, the cause is referred to an arbitrator by a judge's order; before the award is made, A wishes to revoke the arbitrator's authority. Is he at liberty to do so of his own will, or must he have any, and what, leave?

*A.* To revoke the arbitrator's authority, he must have leave of the court in which the order was made or of a judge. 3 & 4 Wm. IV., c. 42, s. 39.

4. *Q.* How are you to enforce the attendance of witnesses before arbitrators?

*A.* I should obtain an order from a judge at chambers or the court, for the attendance of the witnesses. Such order should be served upon the witnesses a reasonable time before the time of meeting. The order is obtained on production of the submission and appointment of meeting by the arbitrator. 3 & 4 Wm. IV., c. 42, s. 40; Chitty's Archbold, 1639.

5. *Q.* What are the usual grounds for setting aside an award?

*A.* They are, that the conduct of the arbitrator has been corrupt or irregular; when the award is not final; when it is uncertain; when the arbitrator has exceeded his authority; when one of the parties has deceived the arbitrator or his opponent; also, on the ground of surprise, and new matter having been discovered. Russell on Arbitration, 656 *et seq.*, 3rd ed.

6. *Q.* What is the time for setting aside an award?

*A.* If the award is under a reference by consent of all matters in difference, the application must be made before the last day of the next term after publication of the award. If the cause *only* is referred at nisi prius the arbitrator is in the position of the jury, and the motion should be made within the first four days of the ensuing term, if award made in vacation, if in term within four days after the award, similar to a new trial. If the reference is compulsory the application must be made within the first seven days of the term next following the publication, whether made in vacation or term. Chitty's Archbold, 1675. C. L. P. Act, 1854, s. 9.

7. Q. How may an award be set aside?

A. The agreement of submission or order must be made a rule of court, which is a matter of course. Counsel should then be instructed to move for a rule to show cause why the award should not be set aside. An affidavit of the facts should accompany his instructions. If a rule nisi is granted it is served, and on a day fixed cause is shown against it, and the rule either made absolute or discharged. Chitty's Archbold, 1677.

8. Q. What power has an arbitrator over the costs of the reference or of an action referred to arbitration?

A. In the absence of stipulation the arbitrator has no power over the costs of the reference or the award, therefore, each party must bear his own expenses of the reference, and is liable to half the costs of the award. He has, however, an implied authority to adjudicate respecting the costs of an action referred to him, but not of the reference or award. Russell on Arbitration, 358, 3rd ed.

9. Q. Where a cause is tried at *nisi prius*, and referred to an arbitrator, without power being reserved to him to certify as to the cause being proper to be tried before a judge of the superior courts, and he awards a sum less than £20 due to the plaintiff, can the arbitrator, notwithstanding, give any directions so as to entitle the plaintiff to have the costs taxed upon the higher scale?

A. The arbitrator may give a certificate for costs on the higher scale, which may form the ground of an application to the judge before whom the cause was brought on for trial for his certificate. But the arbitrator's certificate will of itself be of no effect unless he has special authority to certify. Ibid., 382.

10. Q. Where all matters in difference *not in a cause* are referred to arbitration, the costs of the reference to abide the event, and the arbitrator finds partly in favour of each party, can either of them have the costs of the reference?

A. In this case the arbitrator has no power over the costs, and each party will have to pay their own costs of the reference, and this, although there be a substantial balance in favour of one. *Gribble* v. *Buchanan*, 26, L. J. C. P., 24.

11. Q. Must the successful party under an award wait until the time for setting aside the award has expired before he can tax his costs?

A. He may tax his costs before such period has elapsed. R. G. H. T., 1853, r. 170.

12. *Q.* What are the means of enforcing an award, when there is no cause pending, and the submission contains a clause that it shall not be made a rule of court?

*A.* Such an award can only be enforced by action, as the provision that the submission shall not be made a rule of court precludes its being so made and enforced by attachment. The action might be assumpsit or debt if the submission is not under seal, or by debt or covenant when it is by deed. Russell on Arbitration, 505, 3rd ed.

13. *Q.* What are the proceedings to enforce an award, whether it directs the payment of money or not?

*A.* An award may generally be enforced by action upon it, by attachment, and if for the payment of a sum of money, also by execution. Also if a verdict has been taken at Nisi Prius, judgment may, in some cases, be signed and execution issued on the judgment. The submission must first be made a rule of court. If, however, it is expressly provided by the submission, as in the preceding answer, that it shall not be made a rule of court, it cannot be made a rule, and the remedy on the award is only by action. Every submission, in writing, may be made a rule of court, unless the contrary be shown by the instrument. 17 & 18 Vic., c. 125, s. 17. In proceeding by attachment a copy of the rule making the submission a rule of court, together with the award must be served personally on the party to perform the award, and a demand made of performance. An affidavit is made of the service and the rule for attachment moved for. In proceedings by execution similar proceedings are taken, and a rule ordering payment moved for. The proceedings in an action are as in ordinary actions. Chitty's Archbold, 1681.

## XXXIV.—*Interpleader.*

1. *Q.* What is the meaning of an interpleader?

*A.* An interpleader occurs when two parties claim from a third something in which that third person has no interest, and does not know to whom it belongs. Under such circumstances the Court of Chancery compelled the claimants to plead *inter se*, and granted an injunction against proceedings at law against the plaintiff. This beneficial equitable jurisdiction was given to the Courts of Common Law by 1 & 2 Wm. IV., c. 58, and they have concurrent jurisdiction with the Court of Chancery.

2. *Q.* If a person was sued for money or goods, also claimed of him by a third party, what course should you advise on his behalf?

*A.* I should recommend him to interplead at law, or file a bill of interpleader in Equity. The latter is frequently the more preferable course to adopt.

3. *Q.* In what cases where there are adverse claims, may a defendant apply for protection under the "Interpleader Act"?

*A.* He may apply where he is sued in assumpsit, debt, detinue or trover. 1 & 2 Wm. IV., c. 68, s. 1.

4. *Q.* How does he apply, and at what period should he do so?

*A.* He may apply to the court or a judge by rule or summons, usually the latter, for an order compelling the claimant to interplead. The application must be supported by an affidavit that defendant claims no interest in the subject matter of the suit, but that the right thereto is claimed or supposed to belong to some third party who has sued or is expected to sue for the same, and that the defendant does not collude with such third party, but is ready to bring into court, or pay, or dispose of the subject matter as may be ordered. Upon this affidavit an order will be made, even where the claims have not a common origin, 23 & 24 Vic., c. 126, s. 12, (as to what is a common origin see *Maynell* v. *Angell*, 11 W. R., 122). The time for making the application is after declaration and before plea. 1 & 2 Wm. IV., c. 58.

5. *Q.* What are the proceedings on an Interpleader?

*A.* The defendant moves for a rule or takes out a summons. This he serves on the claimants, makes his affidavit, attends to support the rule or summons. Obtains the order, draws it up, and serves it. If the claimant does not appear on the rule or summons, the court may bar his claim. The order will direct an issue to be tried, and specifies which claimant is to be plaintiff and which to be defendant. It also provides for the disposition of the subject matter pending the dispute. The plaintiff prepares the issue, and defendant approves it. There are no pleadings, the issue raising the question to be decided. When engrossed on parchment the issue forms the Nisi Prius record. The cause then proceeds like an ordinary cause to trial. The costs are applied for after verdict, at chambers. Instead of making an order the judge may, if the amount is small, at the request of either party, decide the case himself. Also if the facts are not in dispute he may decide any point of law, or order a special case to be stated. C. L. P. Act, 1860, ss. 1—18, & notes by Day.

6. *Q.* What are the cases in which the courts grant a rule of interpleader at the instance of the sheriff?

*A.* The sheriff may interplead when the goods seized by him under an execution are claimed by persons other than the parties against whom the execution is issued. He may apply although no action has been commenced against him, and provided the claim is made *bond fide.* 1 & 2 Wm. IV., c. 58, s. 6.

## XXXV.—*Contempt of Court.*

1. *Q.* What are the proceedings in cases of contempt?

*A.* The proper course is to move the court for an attachment against the offending party. See *infra.*

2. *Q.* What is the nature of a writ of attachment?

*A.* It is a process from a court of record awarded by the judges at their discretion on a bare suggestion, or on their own knowledge, against a person guilty of a contempt, who is punishable in a summary manner. Wharton's Law Lexicon, 89.

3. *Q.* When an attachment is issued against the sheriff, to whom is it addressed?

*A.* It is addressed to the coroner for execution, and if the coroner is also attached it is directed to elisors, two persons appointed by the court to execute the writ. Chitty's Archbold, 1708.

4. *Q.* In what cases may an attachment be obtained?

*A.* It will issue against attorneys or officers of the court for misbehaviour; against sheriffs and coroners for not executing a writ or executing it oppressively; against judges of inferior courts, justices of the peace, gaolers, etc., for oppression or misconduct; against suitors fraudulently perverting the course of justice; against a witness for not attending a trial in pursuance of a subpœna; against a party for disobeying a rule or order of the court. Chitty's Archbold, 1700.

5. *Q.* What service is necessary to enable a party to obtain an attachment?

*A.* Service of the rule must be made personally upon the party sought to be attached. Such service will not be dispensed with, except under special circumstances. Ibid., 1707.

6. *Q.* In what two cases are rules for attachments absolute in the first instance?

*A.* 1. For non-payment of costs on a master's allocatur. 2. Against a sheriff for not obeying a rule to return a writ, or to bring in the body. R. G. H. T., 1853, r. 168.

## XXXVI.—*Outlawry.*

1. *Q.* In what cases may a plaintiff outlaw a defendant; and how must he proceed?

*A.* A defendant in civil causes against whom final judgment has been recovered, and the debt has not been paid and the defendant cannot be arrested, may be outlawed. A *ca. sa.* is first sued out to the sheriff, *non est inventus* is returned to it, and then an *exigi facias* must be sued out. This writ is delivered to the sheriff, who executes it by calling on the defendant to appear at five successive county courts in the country, or in London at five hustings. If he does not appear on any of these occasions a return is made by the sheriff of the fact; and upon this, judgment of outlawry may be signed. Outlawry to compel appearance is now abolished by the C. L. P. Act, 1852, s. 24. Chitty's Archbold, 1295.

2. *Q.* What are the disabilities of a defendant under outlawry, and how must he regain his rights?

*A.* Upon outlawry the defendant forfeits at once to the Crown, his personal chattels, property, debts, and choses in action, and his real chattels and the profits of his land upon office found. He cannot sue in his own name, but may sue *in autre droit*, as executor, &c. He cannot appear in any court excepting to reverse his outlawry. He may, however, be sued. He cannot contract. He may obtain the removal of his outlawry by the Queen's pardon, or by reversing it either by application to the court or a judge at chambers, or by proceedings in error. Chitty's Archbold, 1295.

## XXXVII.—*The Inferior Tribunals.*

1. *Q.* Describe the different modes by which causes are removed from inferior courts.

*A.* Plaints may be removed by writ of *certiorari*, which may be obtained on *ex parte* application to a judge or the court. Plaints may also be removed by order of a judge of a superior court, if a removal appears expedient, upon such terms as to costs, and giving security as he may think fit. 9 & 10 Vic., c. 95, s. 90; 19 & 20 Vic., c. 108, s. 38. Practically, also, a plaint may be removed by the defendant giving notice of his objecting to the jurisdiction of the county court. This he may do where the plaintiff claims more than £20 on contract or £5 for a tort. The defendant must give security to be approved of by the registrar for the amount claimed and the costs of the trial in one of the superior courts, not exceeding in the whole £150. 19 & 20 Vic., c. 108, s. 39.

2. *Q.* In order to remove an action from an inferior court of record to a superior court, by what process is it effected?

*A.* See the previous answer.

3. *Q.* Are the county courts modern introductions, or are they of any antiquity? How far back does their antiquity extend? and name one or more writers by whom they are mentioned.

*A.* The county courts are exceedingly ancient, having been instituted by Alfred the Great. This jurisdiction extended to both ecclesiastical and civil matters, the bishop and the earl, or sheriff sitting in the same county court with equal jurisdiction, until the reign of William the Conqueror, when its ecclesiastical jurisdiction was taken away. The court was held once in every four weeks, and was presided over by the earl or sheriff. The suitors, that is the freemen or landholders, were the judges, the sheriff sitting merely in a ministerial capacity to pronounce the judgment of the suitors and execute it. It was the principal court of civil business until the reign of Henry II., when justices of assize were appointed. From that time its jurisdiction fell into disuse, until its sole business was what it still retains, namely, the proclamation of outlawries, and holding elections of knights of the shire and coroners. It was not a court of record. The county courts are mentioned by Bracton, Britton, Author of Fleta, Finch, and Blount. Pollock and Nicol, Introduction, 5th ed. The Articled Clerks' Manual, 56, by Anderson.

4. *Q.* State generally the jurisdiction of the modern county courts.

*A.* They have jurisdiction in all personal actions, where the debt or damage claimed is not more than £50, whether on balance of account or otherwise; but not (except by agreement) in an action in which the title to any corporeal or incorporeal hereditament, or to any toll, market, fair, or franchise, is in question, nor in any case in which the validity to any devise, bequest, or limitation, under any will or settlement may be disputed, nor in any action for malicious prosecution, libel, slander, seduction, or breach of promise of marriage. Possession of lands may be obtained where the rent does not exceed £50. They have also jurisdiction to determine differences in friendly societies. 18 & 19 Vic., c. 63. In Bankruptcy. 24 & 25 Vic., c. 134. Also to issue a warrant under the absconding debtor's arrest act. 14 & 15 Vic., c. 52. In cases of charities, the incomes of which do not exceed £30. 16 & 17 Vic., c. 137. Under the Probate Act to prove a will where the personalty is under £200 and the realty under £300. 20 & 21 Vic., c. 77. A county court judge may take the acknowledgment of a married woman under 3 & 4 Wm. IV. c. 74; 19 & 20 Vic., c. 108, ss. 26, 73. The court may also give damages for the piracy of copyright. 21 & 22 Vic., c. 70. Also penalties under the Alkali Act, 26 & 27 Vic., c. 124, are recoverable in the county court. The Articled Clerks' Manual by Anderson, 60.

5. *Q.* What is the name of the form of commencing an action in the county courts, as distinguished from that in use in the superior courts?

*A.* In the county courts actions are commenced by plaint instead of writ of summons. The plaintiff, in all cases where he seeks to recover over 40s., delivers as many copies of the particulars of demand to the registrar as there are defendants and an additional copy to be filed. The copies are signed by the plaintiff or his agent. Upon this the registrar gives the plaintiff a plaint note and issues a summons to the defendant, which is served by the bailiff ten clear days before the hearing. Ibid., 57.

6. *Q.* In what cases have the superior courts concurrent jurisdiction with the county courts in actions respecting contracts and torts?

*A.* They have concurrent jurisdiction in actions of contract and tort up to £50, excepting in the cases above mentioned (No. 4) where the county has no jurisdiction at all. If, however, the plaintiff's claim for debt does not exceed £20, or for tort £5, and he sues in the superior court, he will, except in the cases mentioned, *infra*, No. 7, get no costs. The term "concurrent" is often applied to these latter cases. Ibid., 57.

7. *Q.* Under what circumstances may a party sue and get his costs in the superior court for a debt recoverable in the small debts court?

*A.* He may do so in actions of contract where he recovers over £20, or in tort over £5. Also under those sums where the plaintiff dwells more than twenty miles from the defendant, or where the cause of action did not arise wholly or in some material point within the jurisdiction of the court within which the defendant dwells or carries on his business at the time of action brought, or where any officer of the county court is a party (except in respect of any claim to any goods and chattels taken in execution of the process of the court or the proceeds or the value thereof). Also where the judge certifies that there was sufficient reason for bringing the action in the superior court. Chitty's Archbold, 479.

8. *Q.* State the cases in which you are compelled to sue under the small debts county court acts, and how and where the suit must be brought: and where must the respective parties be residing at the time.

*A.* There is no actual compulsion in suing in the county court; but, as above mentioned, if the county court is not resorted to the plaintiff is liable to lose his costs. The suit is commenced by plaint, as mentioned, *supra* No. 5. It should be entered at the court in the district of which the defendant or one of them dwells or carries on business, or by leave of the court in that of the district in which he shall have dwelt or carried on his business at some time within six calendar months next before the entry of the plaint, or by leave of the court or registrar where the cause of action arose. 9 & 10 Vic., c. 95, s. 60; 19 & 20 Vic., c. 108, s. 15. If the plaintiff dwells or carries on his business within one of the metropolitan districts, and the defendant dwells in one of the districts, the summons may issue in the plaintiff's or defendant's district. 19 & 20 Vic., c. 108, s. 18.

9. *Q.* Will any privilege protect a person from being sued in the small debts court; and would the same privilege allow the party to sue in the superior court for a debt that might be recovered in the petty court?

*A.* The privilege referred to is that of an attorney of being sued in the court of which he is an attorney. This privilege, however, does not extend to the county courts in which he may be sued. 12 & 13 Vic., c. 101, s. 18.

10. *Q.* Can a party prosecute a plaint in a county court upon a judgment recovered in one of the superior courts for a debt less than £50.

*A.* He cannot now do so. 19 & 20 Vic., c. 108, s. 27.

11. *Q.* Suppose a judge of a county court should have exceeded his jurisdiction, by trying a cause which he ought not to have tried, what steps can be taken against him?

*A.* The defendant should apply to a judge of any of the superior courts on summons, or to the court by motion for a writ of prohibition. The application should be supported by affidavit. The writ, when obtained, should be lodged with the registrar, and will be a stay of the proceedings. Indeed a summons or rule nisi will have this effect if so provided in the summons or rule. The judge is not answerable personally unless he directs an act to be done when he has no jurisdiction, in which case he would be liable in trespass. *Houlden* v. *Smith*, 19, L. J. Q. B., 170. Pollock and Nicol, 197, 5th ed.

12. *Q.* Is there any appeal from decisions in the county courts, and in what cases, and what is the practice in county court appeals?

*A.* Either party may in any cause above £20 appeal against the direction of the court in point of law, or upon the admission or rejection of any evidence, to any of the superior courts at Westminster, or to two or more of their judges sitting out of term as a court of appeal. Ten days' notice of the appeal must be given to the opposite party, and security must be given for the costs of the appeal and for the amount of the judgment, if the appellant be the defendant, if the appeal be dismissed. There is no appeal if the parties previously agree, in writing, that the decision of the judge shall be final. The appeal is in the form of a case agreed to by both parties. It is signed by the judge, and within three days after signature transmitted to the master's office of the court in which the appeal is to be brought, and notice of such transmission given to the successful party. Pollock and Nicol, 184.

13. *Q.* Has any equitable jurisdiction been recently conferred upon the county courts. If so, what is it?

*A.* The county court has now jurisdiction : 1. To administer a deceased person's real or personal estate at the suit of creditors, legatees, devisees, heirs-at-law, or next of kin, where it does not exceed in value £500. 2. In suits for the execution of trusts of property of a like value. 3. In foreclosure or redemption suits where the mortgage money does not exceed £500. 4. In suits for specific performance where the purchase money does not exceed this sum. 5. In proceedings under the trustee relief acts where the trust fund does not exceed this sum. 6. In proceedings relating to the maintenance or advancement of infants where the property of the infant does not exceed £500. 7. In suits for the dissolution of partnerships where the property and credits do not exceed the above sum. 8. In proceedings for orders in the nature of injunctions for granting relief in aid of the above, or for stay of proceedings at law to recover any debt proveable under an administration order. 28 & 29 Vic., c. 99, s. 1.

## XXXVIII.—*Highways.*

1. *Q.* How are highways to be stopped up, diverted, or turned?

*A.* The stopping up or diversion having been deemed expedient by the vestry, the chairman must direct the surveyor to apply to two justices to view the highway. If, upon a view, it appears expedient to divert or stop up or turn the highway, and the owner of the land through which the highway is to go consents, notice of the intention so to do is to be affixed on the *locus in quo* and advertised in the newspapers. The certificate of the justices that they have had the view, and that the proposed alteration is convenient, is then obtained, on proof of the notices having been given and on production of a plan and the consent of the landowner. The certificate is transmitted to the Clerk of the Peace and confirmed at the next Quarter Sessions. 5 & 6 Wm. IV., c. 50, ss. 84, 85.

# A. DIGEST

OF ALL THE

# EXAMINATION QUESTIONS AND ANSWERS

# IN CONVEYANCING.

## I.—*Introductory.*

1. *Q.* What was the origin of conveyancing?
*A.* Conveyancing had its origin at the time when the transfer of lands from subject to subject was introduced. In the early ages of this country, mere occupation of land conferred a title to it, but this was abandoned when the occupier thought fit to change his habitation. Subsequently, however, a more permanent right of ownership was claimed and recognised, until at length the country was parcelled out between different owners, who may now, almost at their pleasure, transfer their rights from one to another. This transfer is effected by individuals termed "conveyancers," who employ "conveyances" to effect their object. To the equity tribunals we are chiefly indebted for our present conveyancing jurisprudence, those courts, after the introduction of uses, having possessed an almost complete monopoly of the subject.

## II.—*Classification of Things.*

1. *Q.* Define the several kinds of property according to the English law, and the distinction in transferring each.
*A.* They are, things real and things personal. The former comprise things immoveable, such as lands, and the rights and profits issuing out of them. Things personal comprise personal goods, such as furniture, money, and other moveable property. A third division may also be mentioned, viz., mixed property, which partakes of the character of both of the two former classes. Such are estates at will and sufferance. As to the mode of transfer, see *infra*, XXIII. Steph. Com. 1, 172; the Articled Clerks' Manual, by Anderson, 100.

2. *Q.* What word as applied to real property is the most comprehensive?
*A.* The word "hereditament," as it includes not only lands and tenements, but whatsoever may be inherited. Thus, an heirloom which by custom descends to the heir, is a hereditament. Hereditaments are either corporeal or incorporeal. See *infra*, 1 Steph. Com., 175.

3. *Q.* What is the distinction between real and personal property? and to whom do they respectively devolve on the death of an intestate owner?

*A.* In addition to the nature of the property just mentioned, there are other distinctions. Thus, upon the death of the owner intestate, the realty descends to his heir, or escheats to the lord or the Crown, whereas the personalty goes to the next-of-kin, according to their degrees of relationship to the deceased, or is forfeited to the Crown. Again, personalty cannot be entailed, nor is it within the Statute of Uses; neither can it be the subject of tenure. See *infra,* "Intestacy."

4. *Q.* What are chattels real, and chattels personal?

*A.* Chattels real come within the class of property just mentioned as partaking partly of realty and personalty. They are estates in land, but estates of a personal nature, and cannot be recognised as freeholds. Thus, estates at will, by sufferance and for years, are chattels real. Like other personalty they devolve upon the next-of-kin. As to chattels personal see No. 1. 1 Steph. Com., 288.

5. *Q.* When is realty considered personalty, and *è converso?*

*A.* This anomaly exists by virtue of a direction to convert the realty into personalty, or *vice versâ,* for certain specified purposes. From the moment that the direction operates, a notional conversion of the property takes place, and the rights of the parties interested must be considered and adjusted as if the property were actually converted. The doctrine is an equitable one. (See the subject more fully discussed *infra* "Equity," "Specific performance," and the authorities there cited. Many of the points there mentioned would be properly included in this answer). As to partnership property, see the next answer.

6. *Q.* If real estate be purchased with partnership funds, is it real or personal estate, in any and what respect?

*A.* Such property is considered in equity as personal estate; that is, the court considers that in every agreement of partnership there is an implied agreement to sell the property upon the termination of the partnership, the produce to be equally divided between the partners, according to their shares in the concern; or if dead, between their personal representatives. This is upon the maxim, *jus accrescendi inter mercatores locum non habet.* The courts of law, although they recognise this rule with regard to personal property of the partnership in possession, do not extend it to choses in action, and land. Therefore, the legal estate in the real estate devolves upon the surviving partner, who is considered in equity as a trustee for the representatives of the one deceased. *Darby* v. *Darby,* 25 L. J. Ch., 371; Wms. Pers. Prop., 279.

7. *Q.* If land be conveyed, do the buildings thereon, and mines and minerals thereunder, pass? State the maxim, or legal *dictum,* as quoted by Blackstone.

*A.* They do pass without being specially mentioned. The maxim referred to is *Cujus est solum ejus est usque ad cœlum.* 1 Steph. Com., 174.

8. *Q.* If a pool, lake, or piece of water be granted, what passes by such grant? What words should be used to assure the freehold of the land itself to a purchaser?

*A.* By the use of the word "pool" the water and land upon which it stands will pass; but by the grant of the lake or piece of water the grantee will only obtain the privilege of fishing. The proper words to assure the freehold of the land are—"I grant unto and to the use of A and his heirs all that eleven acres of land situate at Kensington, in the county of Middlesex, now covered with water, called the river Serpentine." Steph. Com. 1, 173, Co. Litt. 5 *b.*

9. *Q.* In whom is the ownership of the sea-shore below high-water mark vested, as a general rule, and what exceptions may there be to such rule?

*A.* The sea-shore, between the medium high and low-water mark, is presumptively vested in the Crown. A subject may, however, claim under a grant from the Crown, or by a local custom. Also if the sea gradually recedes, the rights of the Crown below the original high-water mark are transferred to the owner of the adjoining land. So also if the sea washes up sand and earth, these, termed alluvion, though originally belonging to the Crown, become vested in the adjoining owner. *Rex* v. *Lord Yarborough*, 3 B & C., 9; Steph. Com. 1, 457.

### III.—*The Tenures.*

1. *Q.* By what tenures may property be held?

*A.* At the present day land may be held by the tenures of free and common socage; copyhold; the honorary services of *grand serjeanty; petit serjeanty,* and *frankalmoign.* The other feudal tenures which formerly existed were abolished by 12 Car. II., c. 24. A lease for years may also be considered as a tenure of property. Wms. R. P., 105.

2. *Q.* Of what tenure will an allotment under an inclosure act, made in respect of copyhold-estate, be, supposing the act to be silent in this respect?

*A.* The allotment will be of the same tenure as the land alloted, not as that in respect of which it is allotted. Thus, if the land allotted is freehold it will remain as such in the hands of the copyholder. This was so decided before 2 Wm. IV., c. 45, giving copyholders a right to vote. Accordingly, when a contrary effect is desired, the act expressly provides that land allotted in respect of copyholds shall be deemed copyhold; 8 & 9 Vic., c. 118, s. 94; 1 Scriven on Copyhold, 557, 4th ed.

3. *Q.* Explain the tenure of gavelkind, and state where it prevails.

*A.* It is a species of socage tenure by virtue of which, upon the death of the owner of land intestate, the estate descends to all his sons, and in default of sons to his collateral male relations equally. It is peculiar, also, in that the tenant may at fifteen convey the land by feoffment. Also, that the land does not escheat on conviction for murder. The husband has curtesy out of a moiety only of his wife's lands, and his estate ceases on his second marriage, but the right attaches without issue being born. The widow has dower out of half the lands, but her estate ceases on marriage or unchastity. The tenure is almost exclusively confined to Kent. Williams R. P., 116.

4. *Q.* What is the tenure of borough-English?

*A.* This, also, is a species of socage tenure which prevails in certain boroughs and localities. By virtue of it land descends to the youngest son instead of the eldest, upon the death of the owner intestate. It does not extend to collaterals, unless by special custom to admit the youngest brother. Ibid., 118.

5. *Q.* State what tenures you are aware of, by which lands less than freehold are held.

*A.* The estates less than freehold by which lands are held are estates for years, at will and by sufferance. 1 Steph. Com., 288.

## IV.—*Quantity of Estate.*

1. *Q.* State the division of estates with reference to their quantity of interest.

*A.* They may be divided into:—1. Fees or inheritable freeholds. Such are, fee simple absolute, fee tail, and fee qualified or base. 2. Life or uninheritable freeholds. Such are, for the life of the tenant, for the life or lives of others, tenancy in tail after possibility of issue extinct, by the curtesy of England, in dower. 3. Non-freeholds or chattels real. Such are, for years, from year to year, at will, on sufferance and by elegit. The Articled Clerk's Manual, 101. *Rouse's Case. Richardson* v. *Langridge,* 1 L. C. Conv., 1—26.

2. *Q.* Mention the different senses in which the terms "estate" and "freehold" are used in connection with real property.

*A.* The word "estate" is used with regard to the quantity of interest (see previous answer). Secondly, with regard to the time of its enjoyment, whether in possession, reversion, or remainder. Thirdly, with regard to the number and connection of the tenants. An estate may, also, be legal or equitable. The term "freehold" is used to designate an interest in land of inheritance, or one not of inheritance, which formerly required a feoffment and livery of seisin for its transfer, 1 Steph. Com., 235.

3. *Q.* Give the different kinds or classes of estates in lands, tenements, and hereditaments; state which of them arise by operation of law, and which by the acts of the parties.

*A.* See *supra,* Nos. 1 & 2. Those arising by operation of law are estates in reversion, tenancy in tail after possibility of issue extinct, by curtesy, and in dower. The others arise by acts of the parties.

4. *Q.* What are the words of limitation properly to be used in a deed in creating each respective class?

*A.* "Grant, unto and to the use of A, his heirs and assigns for ever." (Fee simple.) "Unto and to the use of A, and the heirs of his body lawfully begotten." (Fee tail.) "Unto and to the use of A, and his heirs, tenants of the Manor of Dale." (Base fee.) A conditional fee at the common law is now an estate tail. "Unto and to the use of A for his natural life, or for the life of B," (for life and *pur autre vie*), "to A his executors, administrators and assigns, for the term of twenty-one years, or to A from year to year" (for years and year to year). It is needless to add that this question has no application to those estates arising by operation of law, mentioned in the previous answer.

5. *Q.* Give an instance of a freehold estate of inheritance, and one not of inheritance.

*A.* A freehold of inheritance is an estate in fee simple (the largest estate of freehold), or fee tail. One not of inheritance, is an estate for life (the smallest estate of freehold), or *pur autre vie.* 1 Steph. Com., 234.

6. *Q.* What is an estate upon condition? Give an instance.

*A.* It is an estate which depends upon some condition being fulfilled, the performance or non-performance of which will cause the estate to vest or be divested. If an estate is granted to A for life, and upon payment of a certain sum he shall have the fee, the latter is an estate upon condition. 1 Steph. Com., 305. See the next answer.

7. *Q.* What is a fee simple estate, and when a condition is annexed to the grant of a fee simple estate, what is the result of a breach of the condition—1st, when it is precedent; 2nd, when it is subsequent?

*A.* It is an estate which, upon the death of the owner, descends to his heirs general, that is both lineal and collateral, male or female. The owner has an absolute power of disposition over it, *inter vivos,* or by will. If the condition is precedent and there is a breach the estate will not vest in the person intended to take the estate. But, if it is subsequent it will vest in him, but will be divested on the breach of condition.

8. *Q.* In what three kinds of hereditaments may a person have a fee simple?

*A.* This question was asked inadvertently. Upon enquiry at the examination, the question was explained by the examiner to mean: What three kinds of estates in fee simple may a person have in hereditaments? The answer, therefore, is—1. Fee simple absolute. 2. Fee simple qualified or base. 3. Fee simple conditional. See *supra.* 1 Steph. Com., 243.

9. *Q.* What are proper words for creating an estate in fee simple, by deed or will, and mention some of the expressions which, prior to the "Wills Act," conferred the fee simple?

*A.* In a deed the proper words are, "Grant unto and to the use of the said A, his heirs and assigns for ever." If the conveyance is to a corporation the word "successors" should be substituted for "heirs." A devise "to A," simply, without words of limitation is sufficient to pass the fee, assuming the testator has such an estate and no contrary intention appears. 7 Wm. IV., & 1 Vic., c. 26, s. 28. Before this act a fee simple was conferred by a devise to A in *fee simple*, or *for ever*, or by a devise of all the testators' *estate*, or *property*, and various other expressions indicating an intention to pass the fee. Wms. R. P., 195.

10. *Q.* A enfeoffs to B and his assigns for ever. Livery of seisin is duly made. What estate does B take by the feoffment?

*A.* He will only take an estate for life, the word "heirs" being necessary to confer the fee. Wms. R. P., 131.

11. *Q.* Can an estate in fee simple be conferred *inter vivos*, without the use of the word "heirs"?

*A.* By virtue of the doctrine of constructive conversion an estate in fee simple is in equity conferred upon the purchaser of an estate, so soon as the contract is signed, even though the word in question is not inserted. So, also, by bargain and sale enrolled the fee may be passed without the word "heirs." This is, however, doubtful. Also in conveyances to corporations the word "successors" will suffice. Watkins' Conv., 143.

12. *Q.* Give a definition (as nearly as possible in the words of Littleton) of a tenant in fee simple.

*A.* See *supra*, No. 7.

13. *Q.* What is the rule in Shelley's case, and where is such rule to be found?

*A.* The rule is, that when the ancestor by any gift or conveyance takes an estate of freehold, and in the same gift or conveyance an estate is limited either mediately or immediately to his heirs in fee or in tail, in such cases "the heirs" are words of limitation of the estate and not of purchase. By virtue of it, therefore, an estate in fee or in tail will vest in the ancestor, and, upon his death, the heirs, unless the estate has been disposed of, will take by descent, and not as independent purchasers. The case is reported. 1 Coke, 93, b, decided, 23 Eliz., L. C. Conv., 507.

14. *Q.* Land is devised by will or limited by deed to A for life, remainder to his right heirs; state what estate A takes; and mention the rule of law which governs the construction of such limitation.

*A.* By virtue of the rule just mentioned, A will take an estate in fee. Had it not been for the rule, A would only have had a life estate, and the heirs a contingent remainder.

15. *Q.* What is an estate tail? and what statute originated it?

*A.* It is an estate which upon the death of the owner descends to his lineal heirs, and, unlike a fee simple, not to his collateral heirs. It is limited to the heirs of a man's body. These words formerly created a conditional fee; that is, the fee was conditional upon the donee having heirs of his body. When he had issue born he could at once alien the lands, the condition being complied with. To prevent this the statute *de donis conditionalibus*, 13 Edw. I., c. 1, was passed, enacting that the estate should no longer be aliened on issue being born, but that it should devolve *per formam doni* to the heirs of the donee's body. From the descent being thus strictly confined to the heirs of the body, the estate has since been termed an estate tail, or an estate cut down (*tailler*) to particular heirs. Wms. R. P., 41.

16. *Q.* What constitutes an estate in tail general, and what in tail special?

*A.* An estate in tail general is one limited to the heirs of a man's body without mentioning particular heirs. Thus, "to A and the heirs of his body" confers an estate tail general. An estate tail special is one limited to the heirs of a man's body by a particular wife. Thus, to A and the heirs of his body on Mary, his now wife to be begotten, confers an estate tail special. 1 Steph. Com., 249.

17. *Q.* Define an estate in tail male general, and an estate in male special.

*A.* They are estates similar to those mentioned in the preceding answer, excepting that the word "male" would be inserted after the word "heirs," the effect of which is that no females could inherit under the entail, and in default of sons the estates would revert to the donor. Ibid.

18. *Q.* If land be given to a man and the heirs male of his body, and he has issue only a daughter, who has issue a son, and dies, and then the donee dies, what is the effect as to the estate given?

*A.* The estate will revert to the donor, as the estate could only descend to an heir male of the donee. The son of the daughter is not such an heir. Ibid.

19. *Q.* Can personal property be entailed?

*A.* Personal property not being within the statute *de donis* cannot be entailed. It may, however, be limited to trustees upon trusts similar to limitations in tail of lands, and this course is frequently adopted in practice. Wms. Pers. Prop., 242.

20. *Q.* What would be the effect of a devise or gift of a leasehold for years by words which would create an estate-tail if the estate were a freehold?

*A.* Its effect would be to vest the absolute interest in the devisee or donee. This is in consequence of the rule just mentioned, that personalty cannot be entailed. Fearne, Cont. Rem., 461.

21. *Q.* What is a tenancy in tail in remainder, and an estate-tail in possession? and what is the meaning of the term "possession"?

*A.* An estate tail in remainder is one which awaits the termination of some preceding estate before the tenant comes into possession of the estate. Thus if land is limited to A for life remainder to his first and other sons in tail. The first son during the life of his father is a tenant in remainder. But the moment that A dies, the son comes into possession of the estate. Possession means the actual enjoyment of the property as distinguished from the present or future right to the occupation. 1 Steph. Com., 318.

22. *Q.* State the date and title of the Act of Parliament under which an estate tail can now be barred?

*A.* The act referred to is 3 & 4 Wm. IV., c. 74, passed 28th August, 1833, and entitled "An Act for the Abolition of Fines and Recoveries, and for the Substitution of more Simple Modes of Assurance."

23. *Q.* What was the mode by which an estate tail could be barred before such act?

*A.* It might be barred by suffering a recovery, also by levying a fine. The proceeding by recovery was effected by the lands being conveyed to a stranger called the tenant to the *præcipe.* Against him an action was brought in the Court of Common Pleas. Upon this the defendant called upon the tenant in tail to warrant his title, called vouching him to warranty. The tenant in tail then vouched the crier of the court to warranty. The demandant then went out of court to confer with the crier, and the latter never returning judgment was entered for the demandant against the tenant in tail, and the tenant in tail had a judgment to recover lands of equal value from the crier. The judgment against the tenant in tail had the effect of vesting the lands in the demandant freed from the remainders and reversions, and the demandant being a friend of the tenant in tail, or frequently a purchaser from him, disposed of the lands as desired, or held them beneficially. The bar by fine was also effected by fictitious proceedings, but it differed materially from a recovery in that it only barred the issue of the tenant in tail. Wms. R. P., 44.

24. *Q.* What are the principal enactments of the 3 & 4 Wm. IV., c. 74, commonly called the Fines and Recoveries Act?

*A.* They are, the abolition of fines, and recoveries, and the making provision for the more simple method of barring estates tail mentioned *infra.* The act also provides for the case of a tenant in tail becoming bankrupt, and for the disposition of real property by married women.

25. *Q.* How is an estate tail to be barred by the tenant in tail in possession?

*A.* He may bar the entail by a deed executed by him, and enrolled in the court of chancery within six calendar months after its execution. The deed is a simple conveyance to a stranger to the intent that the entail be barred. The stranger is, of course, a mere nominal party. 3 & 4 Wm. IV., c. 74.

26. *Q.* If the tenant in tail is not in possession, but in remainder, how is the same object to be effected?

*A.* In this case the consent of the protector of the settlement would be necessary if there was one. If the tenant for life took his estate under the same instrument as the tenant in tail, he would be the protector, and must consent by the same or a separate deed, executed before or at the time of the execution of the disentailing deed. The separate deed must also be enrolled. 3 & 4 Wm. IV., c. 74.

27. *Q.* Who is the protector of the settlement, and what would be the effect of his consent being withheld to the barring of an entail?

*A.* The protector is the owner of an estate for years determinable on the dropping of a life or lives, or any greater estate (not being an estate for years) prior to the estate tail, and subsisting under the same settlement. The settlor may also appoint, by the settlement by which the lands are entailed, any number of persons *in esse* not exceeding three and not being aliens, to be protectors in lieu of the owner of the prior estate. The effect of the protector's consent being withheld would be to create a base fee, as to which see *infra,* No. 46. 3 & 4 Wm. IV., c. 74, ss. 22—32.

28. *Q.* In case the person who would otherwise be protector is a lunatic, idiot, or of unsound mind, who is then the protector?

*A.* The Lord Chancellor, or Lord Keeper, or Lords Commissioners of the Great Seal for the time being, or other the persons entrusted with the custody of lunatics, is the protector in such a case. 3 & 4 Wm. IV., c. 74, s. 33.

29. *Q.* Who was the protector before A. D. 1834?

*A.* The owner of the preceding estate of freehold was then the protector. His consent was necessary to convey the legal estate to the tenant to the *præcipe* against whom the action was brought. 1 Steph. Com., 579.

30. *Q.* When a married woman is "protector of the settlement," how is her consent given, in order to bar the entail?

*A.* If the married woman is protector by virtue of an estate not settled to her separate use, she and her husband are deemed the protector. If, however, the estate is settled to her separate use, she alone is the protector. 3 & 4 Wm. IV., c. 74, s. 24.

31. *Q.* Where money is settled upon trust to be invested in real estate, and to which A (a married woman) is entitled for life, and B (a tenant in tail) is entitled in remainder—in what way should a transfer of their interests in the money be effected?

*A.* The estate tail should be barred by a disentailing assurance executed by B with the consent of A and her husband; this being done, the whole interest may be disposed of by A and her husband and B. Without, however, barring the entail, A and her husband may together by deed dispose of her life interest, she being privately examined, in pursuance of 3 & 4 Wm. IV., c. 74. If the money was settled to the separate use of A, she could make this disposition alone.

32. *Q.* A person previously to 31st December, 1833, devised lands to the use of A, B and C, their heirs and assigns, in trust for C, for his life, with remainder to his children as tenants in common in tail, remainder over; remainder to A, B, and C, as tenants in common. Who is the protector of the settlement?

*A.* The trustees A, B, and C, are the protectors, because before the act they would have been the proper parties to create the tenant to the *præcipe,* and the devise being dated before the 31st December, 1833, they are now to be considered the protectors. 3 & 4 Wm. IV., c. 74, s. 31. Shelford's Real Prop. Stats , 355.

33. *Q.* A is tenant for life, B is tenant in tail in remainder; A sells his life interest to C. Who are the necessary parties to the

instrument, by which B may acquire an estate in fee-simple in remainder, and what estate can B alone acquire?

*A.* If A and B take their estates under the same settlement, A is the protector and, therefore, B must convey to a third person to bar the entail with the concurrence of A. The sale to C has no effect upon the protectorship of A, the office being purely personal. Alone, B could only create a base fee. 3 & 4 Wm. IV., c. 74, s. 22.

34. *Q.* Land is devised to a son A for life, remainder to a daughter B for life, remainder to the heirs of the body of A. A has one son (his heir apparent, of course) and several daughters. A wishes to make the land go to his daughters. How can he do it without the consent of his son?

*A.* He may alone bar the entail under 3 & 4 Wm. IV., c. 74, by deed enrolled in Chancery within six months of execution. The devise vests in A an estate tail in possession subject to B's life estate, therefore the consent of A's son is unnecessary. When the entail is barred, A can settle the estate upon his daughters.

35. *Q.* Estate settled to A for life, remainder to B for life, remainder to the heirs of the body of B, remainders over; can B by any and what means bar the entail in the lifetime of A?

*A.* Here A is tenant for life. B, if the remainder to the heirs of his body is by the instrument creating his life estate, is tenant in tail in remainder, under the rule in Shelley's case. That this is so is assumed by the enquiry as to his barring the entail. As such tenant in tail, he can, if of full age, bar his issue and the reversions and remainders over by any deed of conveyance executed by him with the concurrence of A to the same deed, or given by a separate one executed before or at the time of the disentailing deed—assuming A to take his life estate by virtue of the same instrument as that under which B takes the entail. If this is not so there is no protector, and the entail may be barred by B alone. The deed in each case being enrolled in Chancery within six months of execution. If A is protector and refuses his consent, B may alone bar his issue and create a base fee by deed enrolled. 3 & 4 Wm. IV., c. 74.

36. *Q.* A is tenant for life, and B tenant in tail of an estate, and B has agreed to sell the fee simple to C: by what assurance and under what authority can the fee simple estate be assured to C?

*A.* The assurance would be a conveyance by way of disentailing deed to which A as protector should consent. The authority for this is 3 & 4 Wm. IV., c. 74. See also *supra*.

37. *Q.* Land is by deed limited to the use of A for life, with remainder to B in fee. B dies, having by another instrument, namely, by his will, devised the land (subject to A's life estate) to C in tail, with remainder over. A is still living; C is desirous of barring his estate tail. State whether there is any protector of the settlement whose consent is necessary in order to enable C to bar the estate tail.

*A.* There is no protector in this case, as A, the owner of the estate previous to that in tail of C, takes his interest under a different instrument to that creating C's estate. C may, therefore, alone bar the entail. 3 & 4 Wm. IV., c. 74, s. 22.

38. *Q.* Within what period must a disentailing deed be enrolled, and where? and what is the effect of omitting such enrolment within the specified time? and is any reference to the statute, or to the purpose for which the deed is made, necessary in a disentailing assurance?

*A.* It must be enrolled in chancery within six calendar months of its execution. If the property disentailed is copyhold the enrolment need not be made in chancery, but must be upon the court rolls of the Manor within a similar time. *Honeywood* v. *Forster*, 30 Beav., 1. The deed will be inoperative if the enrolment is omitted. No reference to the statute is necessary in the deed, but the purpose for which it is made is always stated in the deed, though not actually necessary. 2 Prideaux's Precedents, 431.

39. *Q.* Prior to the 3 & 4 Wm. IV., c. 74, if a tenant in tail, with the immediate remainder or reversion in fee to himself, levied a fine, he created what was called a base fee, which immediately merged in the reversion, and became subject to any charges affecting the latter, the title to which he was also in future obliged to show. What difference in this respect has been made by the above statute, both as respects past and future cases?

*A.* The base fee now no longer merges in the reversion, but it becomes enlarged into a fee simple. This removes the inconvenience mentioned in the question. The act applies to the unison of the two estates at the time it passed, and since. 3 & 4 Wm. IV., c. 74, s. 39.

40. *Q.* How was a base fee acquired previous to the 28th August, 1833? How since that time can a base fee be acquired by a tenant in tail in remainder?

*A.* It was acquired by the tenant in tail levying a fine with proclamations, which had the effect of barring his issue only, and not the remainders and reversions. Now, a similar estate may be created, by a tenant in tail barring it without the consent of the protector. 1 Steph. Com., 574.

41. *Q.* If real property be limited to A for life, with remainder to B for life, with remainder to the right heirs of the body of A, with remainder to the right heirs of B, what estates do A and B respectively take?

*A.* If the various limitations are by the same instrument, A takes a life estate in possession, with an estate tail on the termination of B's life estates. B takes a life estate in remainder, with an estate in fee simple in remainder, after the determination of A's estate tail. Shelley's Case, L. C. Conv., 507, *supra*, No. 13.

42. *Q.* A, a minor, is tenant in tail in possession of a landed estate, consisting partly of freeholds, partly of copyholds, and partly of leaseholds, for terms of years held by trustees upon trusts to correspond with the uses of the freeholds. On A attaining twenty-one, what must be done in order to make him absolute owner of the different classes of property?

*A.* The estate tail in the freeholds must be barred, as mentioned *supra*. With regard to the copyholds, they must be barred by surrender, unless the estate in them is an equitable one, when they may be barred by deed or surrender. With regard to the leaseholds, as they cannot be entailed, no bar will be necessary, but A may call upon the trustees to vest the legal interest in him as absolute beneficial owner. 3 & 4 Wm. IV., c. 74, s. 50.

43. *Q.* If lands are conveyed to A and the *heir* of his body, what estate or interest does A take? does he take an estate for life, an estate tail, or an estate in fee simple?

*A.* If the limitation is in a deed, the better opinion seems to be that A will only take an estate for life. Co. Litt., 8 b. In a will, however, he would take the fee, even independently of the provisions of 1 Vic., c. 26, s. 28. Notes to *Taltarum's* and *Seymor's* Cases; L. C. Conv., 628.

44. *Q.* What is the difference between an estate in fee simple and an estate in tail?

*A.* The distinctions between these estates are, that the fee simple confers upon the owner the free right of alienation, but not so the fee tail. Also upon the death of the owner, the fee simple descends to the lineal and collateral heirs, the fee tail to the lineal only. The former may also be devised by will, but the latter cannot. See *supra*, and authorities cited.

45. *Q.* Can a tenant in tail make a lease which will bind any, and what, persons after his decease? State the authority for your answer.

*A.* By barring the entail a tenant in tail may grant a lease for any period. Without, however, taking this course, he may grant leases binding on his issue, and the reversioners, and remainderman, for any term not exceeding twenty-one years, to commence from the date of the lease, or from any time not exceeding twelve calendar months from the date, a rack rent, or not less than five-sixths of a rack rent being reserved. 3 & 4 Wm. IV., c. 74.

46. *Q.* Define a base fee, and illustrate your answer by an example.

*A.* It is a fee simple estate which has a qualification annexed to it, upon the determination of which the estate determines. Thus, "to A and his heirs, *tenants of the manor of Dale*" is a base fee, the estate determining when the heirs of A cease to be tenants of Dale. The term is, however, usually applied to the estate created by a tenant in tail barring the entail without the consent of the protector. Thus, if land is conveyed to A for life remainder by the same instrument to C and the heirs of his body, C during the life of A, and without his consent, may create a base fee by barring the entail. He merely bars his issue. Steph. Com. 1, 244. 3 & 4 Wm. IV., c. 74, s. 1.

47. *Q.* How does a fee simple differ from a base fee?

*A.* See the previous answer.

48. *Q.* A and B are man and wife but have no child; land is limited to the heirs of A's body by B. During the life of B, or

after her death, can A by any and what means acquire an estate in fee simple in the lands?

*A.* A has an estate in tail special, and during the life of his wife B, may by deed executed with the consent of the protector, if any, and enrolled in chancery within six calendar months of execution, bar the entail, and create a fee simple estate. Should this not be done before B dies, A will become tenant in tail after possibility of issue extinct, and as such cannot bar the entail. Wms. R. P., 52; *The Legal Examiner*, 277.

49. *Q.* Explain the term "tenant in tail after possibility of issue extinct," and the nature of the estate?

*A.* The expression is applied to the estate which a tenant in special tail has upon the decease of his wife without issue, as in the previous question. The estate in its nature partakes of the peculiarities of an estate tail, in that the tenant is not impeachable for waste, and it resembles a life estate in that the tenant holds only for his life, and the entail cannot be barred. Wms. R. P., 52.

50. *Q.* At what time is a possibility of issue extinct in law?

*A.* The law considers issue possible even though the parties be each of them a century old; therefore, possibility of it is not extinct until death. Co. Litt., 28 a.

51. *Q.* Conveyance of fee simple estates to A, and the heirs of his body by B his wife. B dies without issue, leaving A surviving: what, after B's death, is the nature of A's estate, and how can he acquire the fee simple?

*A.* As to the nature of A's estate see the previous answers. He cannot acquire the fee, except by purchasing the reversion.

52. *Q.* If a tenant in tail, in possession, or remainder, pays off an incumbrance, is such incumbrance deemed to be extinguished? and in what way would you proceed, to keep alive the charge, in favour of the tenant, in whose case it would be otherwise extinguished?

*A.* The payment by the tenant in tail in possession will be deemed to be for the benefit of the estate, which he can at any moment convert into a fee simple. But it is otherwise with regard to the tenant in remainder, who, under ordinary circumstances, has no such power, and the payment by him will be deemed to be for his own benefit. Upon his death, therefore, his personal representatives would have a claim for the money advanced. In the case of the tenant in possession, I should, upon his paying off the debt, assign it to a trustee, so as to keep it alive, and prevent the operation of the presumption of equity above mentioned. Story, s. 486.

53. *Q.* What are estates for life, and the general tenures of them?

*A.* They are estates which are determinable upon the death of the tenant, or of some other person. In their nature they are freeholds, and their different kinds are, estates for one's own life, and for the life of another. Tenancy in tail after possibility of issue extinct. An estate by the curtesy of England, and an estate in dower. 1 Steph. Com., 260.

## ESTATES FOR LIFE.

**54. Q.** Define an estate for life, and by what means may it be destroyed?

*A.* See the previous answer. It may be destroyed by forfeiture, or surrender, or merger, or in the case of an estate during widowhood, by the marriage of the tenant. Also the death of the tenant puts an end to his estate. Also if tenant by the curtesy or in dower of gavelkind lands marry, the estate will determine. See *supra,* and authorities cited.

**55. Q.** What are the usual powers of a tenant for life over his estate?

*A.* He is entitled to the possession of the estate, and to receive the rents, issues, and profits during his life, or he may sell such rights to a stranger. He may hunt, fish, and shoot upon the property; he may cut timber for fuel and repairs; he may also cut turf and work mines already opened; he may grant leases, as mentioned *infra,* No. 57; he must not commit waste by opening mines, nor allow the mansion to go out of repair. *Lewis Bowles's Case,* L. C. Conv., 27; 1 Steph. Com., 262.

**56. Q.** Under what circumstances is a tenant for life entitled to cut timber for his own benefit?

*A.* If the estate is limited to him "without impeachment of waste," he may cut timber in a husbandlike manner, and sell it; but he must not cut down a whole wood, or timber for ornament, or shelter. For these acts, together with defacing the family mansion, he would still be impeachable in equity. Hence it is termed equitable waste. *Garth* v. *Cotton,* 1 L. C. Eq., 559, and the notes.

**57. Q.** What power has a tenant for life to grant leases binding upon expectant owners of the estate?

*A.* By common law he can only make a lease determinable on his own death, but now by statute tenants for life taking under settlements, executed since 1st November, 1856, are empowered to grant leases for twenty-one years, unless it is provided to the contrary. The principal mansion, house, and demesnes cannot, however, be leased, the lease must take effect in possession, the best rent must be reserved without fine, the demise must be by deed, the tenant must be impeachable of waste, there must be a covenant for payment of the rent, and such other usual and proper covenants as the lessor thinks fit; also, a condition of re-entry on non-payment of rent for a period not less than twenty-eight days, and a counterpart must be executed, the execution of the lease by the lessor being deemed sufficient evidence of the execution of the counterpart. 19 & 20 Vic., c. 120, s. 32. As to the tenant's power to grant leases by the authority of the Court of Chancery. See *infra,* "Equity," "The Statutory Jurisdiction."

**58. Q.** What is the effect of a lease by tenant for life as to the interests of any parties entitled to any charge or incumbrance affecting the estate out of which the lease takes effect?

*A.* Such a lease has no effect upon the incumbrancers, unless they

L

concur. Therefore, a lessee should be careful to obtain the concurrence of the mortgagee. 19 & 20 Vic., c. 120, s. 41.

59. Q. What are the principal rules which regulate the apportionment of rents as between a tenant for life and a remainder-man?

A. The executors of the tenant for life are now entitled to a proportionate part of the rent according to the time that elapses between the last period for payment and the death of the tenant for life. But, such amount is to be recovered from the remainder-man and not from the tenant. The tenant of course pays his rent to the remainderman. 4 & 5 Wm. IV., c. 22.

60. Q. Is a tenant for life bound to pay off incumbrances, or to keep down the interest? And if a tenant for life discharge incumbrances, what is the consequence?

A. He is not bound to pay off incumbrances, but he is bound to keep down the interest, so far as the rents of the estate extend. If he does pay off the incumbrances it will be considered that he does so for his own benefit, and will, therefore, have a charge upon the property to the extent of the money paid off. It is not presumed that a tenant for life, having only a limited interest, would expend money for the benefit of the estate. *Lewis Bowles's Case*, L. C. Conv., 82.

61. Q. Can a tenant for life by any and what means create a permanent charge on the estate for improvements upon it?

A. By leave from the Court of Chancery he may raise money for the purpose of draining the lands, or for warping, irrigation or embankments, and for necessary buildings, and charge it on the inheritance. The money to be re-paid by equal annual instalments, not less than twelve or more than eighteen in number; or in case of buildings, by equal annual instalments, not less than fifteen or more than twenty-five in number. 8 & 9 Vic., c. 56. The tenant for life may, however, apply to the Inclosure Commissioners for leave to make improvements to the land, by draining, irrigating, embanking, enclosing lands and re-dividing fields, re-claiming land, making roads, clearing the land, erecting cottages, farm-houses and other buildings, planting for shelter, constructing engine-houses, &c. The money for these improvements is to be charged on the land, and repaid by an annual rent charge, to be fixed by a provisional order. A memorial of the order of the commissioners creating the rent charge is to be registered in the Land Registry Office. 27 & 28 Vic., c. 114. The provisions of this act will, probably, supersede former acts on the subject. It has, indeed, repealed the "Private Money Drainage Act, 1849." 12 & 13 Vic., c. 100.

62. Q. What is a special occupancy?

A. It is an estate which accrues to the heir of a tenant *pur autre vie*, on the death of his ancestor, the estate having been limited to the ancestor (A) and his heirs for the life of another (B). The heir is entitled to enjoy the estate for the residue of the life of the *cestui que vie*. He takes it, however, subject to the debts of his ancestor. Wms. R. P., 20.

63. *Q.* What are estates less than freehold? Define a chattel real.

*A.* They are those interests in land which are of a personal nature, and which, unlike freehold, were not conveyed by livery of seisin. They are termed chattels real, because they partake of the nature of chattels, and also of real estate. They devolve upon the personal representatives of the deceased owner, and are not within the statutes, *De donis*, 13 Edw. I., c. 1; Uses, 27, Henry VIII., c. 10, or 17 & 18 Vic., c. 113; *Soloman* v. *Soloman*, 12 W. R., 540. They are, however, within 27 Eliz. c. 4. Notes to *Ellison* v. *Ellison*, 1 L. C. Eq., 233.

64. *Q.* By what means may an estate for years be destroyed, and how is such an estate transferred to a purchaser?

*A.* It may be destroyed by surrender of the term to the lessor or by a release of the reversion to the tenant, in which cases the term becomes merged. Upon the sale of such an estate, the usual form of conveyance is by assignment, which must be in writing and by deed. 29 Car. II., c. 3; 8 & 9 Vic., c. 106.

65. *Q.* What is the difference between a lease for the life of the lessee; a lease for 99 years, if the lessee shall so long live; a lease to A for 99 years; and a lease to A for 99 years, if B shall so long live?

*A.* A lease for the life of the lessee is an estate of freehold. A lease for 99 years, if the lessee shall so long live, is a chattel real, determinable on the death of the lessee. So also is the lease to A for 99 years, if B shall so long live, and the lease for 99 years.

66. *Q.* Of what estates, comprised in the preceding question, have the owners a disposing power by will of their several interests?

*A.* The only estates disposable by the will of the owner are the two leases vested in A, the interest in the others determines upon the owner's decease, namely the lessee.

67. *Q.* Which is the more valuable in quality, an estate for life which may terminate to-morrow, or for an absolute term of 1,000 years? Is the owner of both estates entitled to exercise full proprietary rights, or in what respect is he limited in each case?

*A.* The estate for life is in quality more valuable than the chattel real, the former being a freehold. As to the proprietary rights of a tenant for life, see *supra* Nos. 55—58. The right of a lessee as to botes, estovers, and waste, are similar to those of a tenant for life, though it is doubtful if he is liable in the absence of stipulation for permissive waste. 1 Steph. Com., 293.

68. *Q.* Can a lessee for 999 years grant a lease for life? Give a reason for your answer.

*A.* The lessee for years cannot grant an estate for life as the interest of the former is, technically speaking, less than an estate for life. See preceding answer.

69. *Q.* Is there any, and if any what, distinction between a tenancy from year to year, and a tenancy at will?

*A.* These tenancies differ in that the latter is determinable at the will of either party, whereas to determine a yearly tenancy a formal notice must be given. Also upon the decease of a tenant from year to year, the residue of his term devolves upon his personal representatives; but the death of a tenant at will determines the tenancy. Moreover, a tenant at will cannot assign, as such an act determines the tenancy; but it is otherwise with a tenant from year to year. *Richardson* v. *Langridge*. Notes L. C. Conv. 97—105.

70. *Q.* What is an *interesse termini*, and is it assignable?

*A.* It is that interest which a lessee for years has after the lease has been granted to him, and before entry upon the premises and taking possession. It is in fact the right of entry by virtue of the lease. The lessee cannot, however, bring trespass before entry, but he may assign his *interesse termini* to a purchaser. 1 Steph. Com., 293.

71. *Q.* What is an estate at sufferance?

*A.* It is an estate which arises in consequences of a tenant holding over after his tenancy has determined. Thus, if a lessee for years continues in possession after his tenancy has expired, he will be a tenant at the sufferance of his landlord. Such tenancies are frequently converted into tenancies from year to year upon the terms of the old lease. 1 Steph. Com., 299.

72. *Q.* What are the remedies of reversioners for the recovery of possession from tenants at sufferance?

*A.* The premises may be recovered by ejectment or by entry upon the lands, if such entry can be effected peaceably. Also if the term expired has not exceeded seven years, or the rent £20 per annum, possession may be obtained by summary procedure before two justices in petty sessions, who will issue a warrant for possession. 1 & 2 Vic., c. 74.

## V.—*Quality of Estate.*

1. *Q.* What are the several kinds of estates with regard to the time of their enjoyment?

*A.* They are:—1. Estates in possession; 2. Estates in reversion; 3. Estates in remainder. As to their peculiarities, see *infra*. 1 Steph. Com., 318.

2. *Q.* Explain the phrase, "particular estate."

*A.* This term is applied to that estate which the owner of lands creates by granting an interest in them of less duration than he possesses. Thus, if a tenant in fee simple grants a lease, the term is a particular estate, being a part, or *particula*, of the whole. Wms. R. P., 216.

3. *Q.* Define a reversion.

*A.* It is that estate which the grantor has after the creation of a particular estate, as mentioned in the previous answer. It comes into existence by operation of law and determines as soon as the particular estate ceases to exist, being then converted into an estate in possession. Ibid, 217.

4. *Q.* What is a remainder, and what are the different species?

*A.* It is an estate in lands which is created by the grantor of a particular estate, at the same time granting another estate out of the same lands, to come into possession when the particular estate determines. It arises, therefore, by express grant and unlike a reversion, which is by operation of law. Remainders are of three kinds :—1. Vested. 2. Contingent. 3. Cross. As to their peculiarities, see *infra*. Ibid, 217.

5. *Q.* What is a vested remainder?

*A.* It is a remainder which, from its commencement to its end, is ready to come into possession the moment the particular estate determines. When this event happens, the estate is converted into possession. Thus, "to A for life, remainder to B and his heirs," creates a vested remainder in B. Wms. R. P. 227.

6. *Q.* What are contingent remainders?

*A.* Contingent remainders are those which are limited to an uncertain person or on an uncertain event. They are not ready to come into possession when the particular estate determines, as we have just seen is the case with regard to a vested remainder. Thus, if an estate is limited to A for life, remainder to the unborn son of B, this last limitation is contingent upon B having a son during A's lifetime. When B has a son the remainder is no longer contingent, but vested. Wms. R. P., 241.

7. *Q.* As the law now stands, are trustees to preserve contingent remainders necessary? Explain their use in settlements.

*A.* Since 8 & 9 Vic., c. 106, s. 8, they are no longer necessary in the event of the particular estate determining by forfeiture, surrender or merger. Should, however, the particular estate determine by any other means, trustees should be inserted if it be intended that the remainder should take effect in any event. Thus in the example put in the previous answer, if A dies before B has a son the remainder fails, but the interposition of trustees to support would, upon the happening of this event, prevent such a result. The use of the trustees is, therefore, to support the remainder.

8. *Q.* What are cross remainders? Can they be implied in a will or in a deed?

*A.* They are remainders which operate in transferring from one person deceased his share in property which he has in common with others to such other persons. Thus in a marriage settlement, on failure of sons, the estate is frequently limited to the daughters as tenants in common in tail, with a provision that on the death of any one of such daughters without issue her share shall go to the survivors. The object of such limitations is to keep the estate in the settlor's family if possible. They are never implied in deeds but may be in wills if the expressions used indicate such an intention. 1 Steph. Com., 358.

9. *Q.* What is the difference between a remainder and a reversion?

*A.* A remainder is created by express limitation, but a reversion arises by operation of law. Tenure exists between a reversioner and the particular tenant, but not between the particular tenant and-remainderman. A remainder requires a particular estate to support it, which, in the case of a contingent remainder, must be an estate of freehold, but a reversion requires no support. See authorities cited, *supra*.

10. *Q.* Will a chattel interest support a remainder?

*A.* It will support a vested, though not a contingent remainder of freehold.

11. *Q.* A, on his marriage, limited a freehold estate to the use of himself for life, with remainder to the use of his first and other sons successively in tail, with remainder to the use of B in fee; are either, and which, of the above remainders vested or contingent?

*A.* The remainder to the first and other sons of A is contingent upon his having children, but that to B is vested it being ready to come into possession when the particular estate determines.

12. *Q.* In limitations in strict settlement, is the estate limited to trustees to preserve contingent remainders, vested or contingent? State the reason for your answer.

*A.* The estate of the trustees is a vested remainder, as it is ready to come into possession the moment the particular estate of the tenant for life determines. Wms. R. P., 255.

13. *Q.* A testator devises real estate to A for life, with remainder over to A's first and other sons successively in tail male, with remainder to testator's own right heirs: under such a devise, when does the ultimate remainder become vested in the heir of the testator, viz., at his decease, or at the time of the failure of the prior limitations?

*A.* The remainder vests the moment the will operates, namely, at the death of the testator. The heir is then an ascertained person, and will take a vested remainder.

14. *Q.* An estate is limited to A for life, with the remainder to the first and other sons of B in tail, with remainder to C in fee. A dies, leaving B and C surviving, but B, being unmarried, to whom does the estate devolve?

*A.* The estate devolves upon C in fee. The limitation to the sons of B a bachelor is a contingent remainder which fails when the particular estate determines. Had trustees been interposed as mentioned *supra*, the result would have been otherwise.

15. *Q.* What is the difference between a contingent remainder and an executory devise?

*A.* A contingent remainder may be limited by deed or will; an executory devise by will only. The former relates to land only, the latter to realty and personalty. The former requires a particular estate to support it, the latter does not. A contingent remainder must vest at the latest when the particular estate determines. Also, contingent remainders may be barred, but executory devises cannot. Wharton's Law Lexicon, 348. See further as to executory devises *infra*. "Uses, Trusts and Powers."

16. *Q.* What is an estate in severalty?

*A.* It is an estate which an individual holds alone and individually. Thus, if land is conveyed to A and his heirs he has an estate in severalty. 1 Steph. Com., 343.

17. *Q.* What is an estate in joint-tenancy? and how may such estate be severed?

*A.* It is an estate held by two or more persons in the same land. They hold by unity of time, title, possession and interest, and an inseparable incident to the estate is a right of survivorship which exists between the tenants. The estate is created by express limitation. The joint tenancy may be severed by any of the joint tenants alienating his share *inter vivos*. Also by accession of interest, which takes place on the death of one joint tenant. Also by agreement to have a partition, or by decree of a Court of Equity. 1 Steph. Com., 349.

18. *Q.* What is the distinction between a joint tenancy and a tenancy by entireties?

*A.* They differ in that in joint tenancy either of the tenants may dispose of his share without the consent of the others, joint tenants being seised *per my et per tout*. Tenants by entireties, however, have no such power, being seised of the *whole* estate, and neither having a part. Thus, if the lands are given to A and B (husband and wife) and their heirs, they hold by entireties in consequence of their being considered as one person, and neither of them can dispose of part of the inheritance without the concurrence of the other. The husband is of course entitled to the rents and profits during coverture. Wms. R. P., 202.

19. *Q.* What is a tenancy in common? By what three means may there be tenants in common?

*A.* It is a tenancy which is enjoyed by two or more in lands, by several titles and conferred by limitation in a deed or will, or by the destruction of a joint tenancy or an estate in coparcenary. See the next answer. 1 Steph. Com., 356.

20. *Q.* State the difference between estates in joint tenancy and tenancy in common; and how may a joint tenancy be converted into a tenancy in common?

*A.* They chiefly differ in that amongst tenants in common there is not necessarily unity of time, title, or interest, as is the case between joint tenants. Nor is there any right of survivorship. A joint tenancy may be converted into a tenancy in common, by the alienation of one of the joint tenants, the alienee holding as tenant in common with the other tenant in common; and generally it may be said that any act which has the effect of dissolving a joint tenancy, without effecting an absolute partition, creates a tenancy in common. 1 Steph. Com., 357.

21. *Q.* If land be conveyed unto and to the use of A, B and C, and their heirs, what would be the nature of the estate which they would take, and how can they severally dispose thereof?

*A.* They would take an estate in joint tenancy in fee simple. Either of the tenants may dispose of his interest *inter vivos*, but not by will. The disposition would be by deed of grant, or if by one to the other, by release. They may also agree mutually to have a partition; also a partition may be effected by suit in equity. See *supra*.

22. *Q.* What is an estate in coparcenary? and what are its different kinds?

*A.* It is an estate which is created by the descent of lands to two or more persons, and is either by the common law or by custom. Thus, if A dies intestate seised of lands, and leaving two daughters, they will take as coparceners by the common law. If, however, the lands are of gavel kind tenure, and A dies, leaving two sons, they will take as coparceners by custom. 1 Steph. Com., 356.

23. *Q.* How does an estate in coparcenary differ from an estate in joint tenancy?

*A.* They differ in that the former arises by descent, the latter by express limitation. There is no entirety of interest amongst coparceners, and, consequently, no right of survivorship; also the interest of coparceners may accrue at different periods, which is not the case in joint tenancy, with one or two exceptions. Lastly, there is no equality of interest amongst coparceners. 1 Steph. Com., 352.

24. *Q.* A, B, and C are joint tenants at Blackacre, tenants in common of Whiteacre, and tenants in coparcenary of Greenacre; B dies, leaving A and C living: who, on B's death, will become entitled to his interest in the estates respectively, and in what proportions? If B had devised his interest, would the effect be different?

*A.* The interest of B in Blackacre will survive to A and C, but his share in Whiteacre and Greenacre will descend to his heir, or pass to his devisee. B cannot devise his interest in Blackacre. See *supra*.

25. *Q.* When two persons (not being partners) purchase an estate out of their own money in *equal* shares, and take a conveyance of the estate simply to themselves in fee, what is the effect of this conveyance at law and in equity?

*A.* The effect of the conveyance will be to make the purchasers joint tenants of the land, both at law and in equity, it being presumed that they intended to purchase jointly the right of survivorship. Per Sir J. Jekyll, M.R., in *Lake v. Gibson*. 1 L. C. Eq., 143.

26. *Q.* What difference would it make, either at law or in equity, if the purchase-money had been in *unequal* shares?

*A.* At law the fact of the money being paid in unequal shares makes no difference. In equity, however, this circumstance will be seized hold of as indicating an intention to create a tenancy in common, and though the legal estate survives upon the decease of one, yet equity will consider the survivor as a trustee for the representative of the deceased tenant in common. Ibid.

27. *Q.* If it be required to pass land by deed to A, B, and C, as tenants in common in fee, what words should be used in the operative part of the deed to vest such an interest in them?

*A.* "He the said X (vendor) doth hereby grant and confirm unto the said A, B, and C, and their heirs, all (the parcels), to have and to hold the hereditaments and premises unto and to the use of the said A, B, and C, and their heirs equally to be divided between them, as tenants in common, and not as joint tenants." 1 Prideaux's Precedents, 201.

28. Q. If there be three joint tenants in fee simple, and one of them releases his share to another of the three, what is the effect of such release, and what are the estates or interests of the various parties after such release?

A. The effect of the release is to sever the jointure as to the part released. The releasee will, therefore, hold one-third as joint tenant, with his co-tenant, and another third as tenant in common with himself and co-tenant. Litt., s. 304.

29. Q. A, B, and C, are brothers, A being the eldest; B and C become joint tenants of land in fee simple; B, without C's knowledge, conveys his undivided moiety in fee to D, by way of mortgage—B then dies: does C, on B's death, take the entirety, or does a moiety (subject to the mortgage) descend on A as B's heir-at-law?

A. The conveyance by way of mortgage will sever the tenancy, and constitutes the mortgagee a tenant in common with C. C cannot, therefore, take by survivorship, but the share of B will descend to his heir, subject to the incumbrance.

### VI.—*Tangible and Non-tangible Property.*

1. Q. What is the difference between corporeal and incorporeal hereditaments? and how were they respectively conveyed?

A. Corporeal hereditaments are those which may be seen and touched, and affect the senses, such as land and houses. Incorporeal, on the contrary, are invisible, and cannot be made the subject of sensation: such are rents, easements, commons, etc. They may be appendant or appurtenant to corporeal hereditaments, or they may exist separate and in gross as distinct subjects of property. Formerly incorporeal hereditaments were conveyed by deed of grant, and corporeal ones by feoffment, but by 8 & 9 Vic., c. 106, a grant is made appropriate to both classes. 1 Steph. Com., 75.

2. Q. State the sorts of incorporeal hereditaments.

A. They are—advowsons, tithes, commons, ways, water courses, lights, offices, dignities, franchises, corodies, pensions, annuities, and rents. 1 Steph. Com., 656.

3. Q. What is an advowson? How are its legal tenures denominated and distinguished?

A. It is the perpetual right of presentation to an ecclesiastical benefice, and being an incorporeal hereditament, it descends to the heir, upon the decease of the owner intestate. They are either—
1. Appendant to some manors, or, 2. In gross, *i.e.*, separate and distinct property. They are also *presentative*, which is the right of presenting a clerk by institution and induction. *Donative*, which is a right of nomination by the patron alone, without presentation,

institution, or induction. *Collative*, where the right of presentation is in the Bishop. L. C. Conv., 208.

4. *Q.* If two or more persons are seised of an advowson as joint tenants, how and by whom is the presentation to be made?

*A.* The joint tenants should concur, but if they present different clerks, the Bishop may admit either or refuse both. If he adopt the latter course the presentation will lapse. There may be a partition to present in turns. *Bishop of Salisbury* v. *Philips*. 1 Salk, 43.

5. *Q.* Is there any, and what, difference in the case of coparceners taking the advowson by descent?

*A.* There is this difference, viz., that if the coparceners do not agree to present, the law gives the first presentation to the eldest, and this privilege descends to her issue, and even passes to a purchaser from her. Co. Litt., 166 b.

6. *Q.* A is seised of an advowson, the incumbent dies, then A dies without having presented to the living. Who, on A's death, is entitled to present?

*A.* In this case the personal representatives of A are entitled to present, as the vacancy having occurred in the lifetime of the patron, a next presentation is carved out of the hereditament, which, being a chattel real, devolves upon the personal representative, and not the heir, excepting where the patron is also the incumbent. If the incumbent had died after the patron, or if the incumbent were the patron, the heir of the latter would have presented. Wms. R. P., 311.

7. *Q.* An advowson is mortgaged in fee; the incumbent dies: who has the right to present to the living,—the mortgagor or mortgagee? Give the reason why the right of presentation is in the one or the other.

*A.* The right to present is in the mortgagee, because he has the legal estate. Equity, however, considers him in the nature of a trustee for the mortgagor, and accordingly he will be compelled to present the nominee of the mortgagor. Notes to *Fox* v. *The Bishop of Chester*. 1 L. C. Conv., 218.

8. *Q.* What is a rent-charge; and how is it created?

*A.* It is a charge upon land in the nature of a yearly rent issuing out of it, granted by the owner of the land to another, with a power of distress to recover the rent. It is created by deed of grant operating by common law, or under the statutes of uses, which expressly provides for rent-charges. It may also be created by will. Wms. R. P., 297.

9. *Q.* In what cases is registration essential to the grant of an annuity, and in what cases not?

*A.* If an annuity is charged upon land, in order to make it affect such land in the hands of purchasers, mortgagees, and creditors, it is necessary to register it in the Court of Common Pleas. If the annuity is granted before the 26th April, 1855, or by marriage settlement, or will, for a life or lives, or for any estate determinable on a life or lives, registration is not necessary. 18 & 19 Vic., c. 15, ss. 12, 14.

10. *Q.* What is the difference between a rent-charge and a rent-seck?

*A.* They differ in that in a grant of the former a power of distress is expressly given, and it was the absence of such power that constituted a rent-seck. Now, however, this distinction is merely technical, as a rent-seck may be distrained for. 4 Geo. II., c. 28, s. 5.

11. *Q.* May not a rent-charge be granted in fee or limited by way of use in fee? Is it or not necessary or usual to give power of distress, and what, if any, other power for securing payment? Give briefly, but substantially, a form of such grant?

*A.* Yes; a rent-charge may be thus limited:—The term "rent-charge" implies a power of distress having been given, otherwise it would be a rent-seck. This latter may even now be distrained for by virtue of 4 Geo. II., c. 28. Power of entry on the lands to secure the rent is also generally inserted. In substance the grant would consist of:—Date. Parties. Recitals of seisin of land, and agreement. Testatum. Grant. Parcels. Power of distress and entry. Habendum. Uses. Covenant to pay the rents. Covenants for title.

12. *Q.* What is the effect of the release by an owner of a rent-charge or judgment of part of the land charged? Would the purchase of any part of the land, by the owner of the rent-charge, have the same effect?

*A.* The effect is now merely to release that part of the land intended to be released. Formerly the whole rent-charge was extinguished by the release, but this was remedied by 22 & 23 Vic., c. 35, s. 10. The purchase of part of the land by the owner of the rent-charge had formerly the effect of extinguishing the rent-charge. Such an act operated as a release, and there seems to be no sufficient reason for excluding the case from the operation of the clause just mentioned. Wms. R. P., 305.

13. *Q.* Of what do great and small tithes consist?

*A.* Tithes of corn, hay, and wood, are great tithes because, in general, they are of greater value than other tithes. The prœdial tithes of other less valuable vegetables, such as hops, potatoes, madder, woad, together with mixed and personal tithes, are small tithes. 2 Stephen's Clergy Law, 1296.

14. *Q.* What is a modus?

*A.* It is a peculiar method of paying tithes different from one-tenth of the annual increase, and is claimable by custom. Thus a custom that the person shall have only the twelfth cock of hay, and not the tenth, in consideration of the owner making it for him, is a modus. 3 Steph. Com., 86.

15. *Q.* What is a tithe rent-charge?

*A.* It is an annual payment which is substituted in lieu of tithes in kind, the amount of which is adjusted annually according to the average price of corn. 6 and 7 Wm. IV., c. 71.

16. *Q.* Is a rent-charge payable to the rector or vicar under the "Tithe Commutation Act" fixed, or does it vary? and if it vary, how is the amount to be ascertained?

*A.* As just mentioned, the rent-charge varies according to the average price of corn. Every January an advertisement is inserted in the *Gazette*, showing the average price of wheat, barley, and oats, for seven years past, ending on the Thursday before Christmas then next preceding. The rent-charge is deemed of the value of as many bushels of wheat, barley, and oats, in equal quantities, as it would have been competent to purchase according to the prices contained in the first published table. Each succeeding year the rent-charge will consist of the price of the same quantities, according to the average. It, therefore, varies in amount. 6 and 7 Wm. IV., c. 78, ss. 56, 57.

17. *Q.* Can a right of way be conveyed, and in what manner?

*A.* It may be conveyed by deed of grant, or in many instances, when appurtenant to an estate, it passes with such estate to the purchaser. 1 Steph. Com., 667.

18. *Q.* Define an easement.

*A.* It is a privilege without profit which the owner of one tenement has over a neighbouring one, by virtue of which the servient owner is obliged to suffer, or not to do, something on his own land, for the advantage of the dominant owner. Such are rights of way, water, light, etc. Gale on Easements, 5.

19. *Q.* How may easements, such as rights of way, or of drains, or of water, be created *de novo*, and how acquired by prescription?

*A.* They may be created *de novo* by grant under seal. Rights of way and water may be acquired by prescription after uninterrupted peaceable enjoyment for the period of twenty years, defeasible in certain cases, but indefeasible after forty years. 2 & 3 Wm. IV., c. 71. A right to the flow of water *from* drains cannot, however, be acquired by prescription, such channels being artificial and temporary in their nature. *Greatrex* v. *Hayward*, 8, Ex. 291.

20. *Q.* Give a succinct form in substance of a grant in fee *de novo* of an easement. For instance, a right of passage of water, or other easement, with the proper covenants on the part of the grantee in respect of the easement granted.

*A.* After the date and parties would come :—Recital of conveyance of servient tenement to A (grantor). Recital of title of B (grantee) to the dominant tenement. Recital of agreement for the easement of the water-course over A's land to that of B. Testatum. Consideration. Grant and covenant of the water-course with right to lay down and alter the pipe, for free flow of the water, with all necessary rights. Habendum. B would covenant to restore the surface and make compensation for surface damage. Then would follow the ordinary covenants for title by A. Lewis on Conveyancing, 364.

21. *Q.* State concisely the meaning of the terms :—Intercommon, and common of estovers.

*A.* Intercommon signifies a right of the occupants of two neighbouring manors to depasture their cattle promiscuously in each. Common of estovers is the right of taking wood for the use or furniture of a house or farm from the land of another person. It arises either by grant or prescription. 1 Steph. Com., 662.

## VII.—*Copyholds.*

1. *Q.* Explain, in a familiar manner, the origin of copyhold estates, the services rendered in respect of them, and to whom; and the reasons for the general discontinuance and commutation of such services into money payments.

*A.* Copyholds are supposed to have been created by lords of manors granting out to their slaves or villeins a portion of the lands of the manor, to be held at his will, and generally on the performance of certain base services, such as ploughing the land, carting manure, etc. These villeins must be distinguished from the freeholds tenants of the lord. By degrees the villeins, through the indulgence of the lord, have acquired vested and permanent rights, and can be no longer considered tenants at his will. Their estates and interests are recorded upon the rolls of the manor, and the transfer of their estates is effected in the customary court of the manor. In addition to the services above mentioned, fines, heriots, suit of court, fealty, and rent, may be mentioned. The reason for their discontinuance is their great uncertainty and multiplicity, and the various arbitrary payments, which cause serious mischief, and check agricultural improvements. Report of Real Prop. Commiss.; Wms. R. P., 315.

2. *Q.* What statute prohibited the further creation of manors?

*A.* The Act is that of 18 Edw. I., c. 1, by enacting that on all sales and feoffments of lauds the feoffee shall hold the same of the chieflord of the fee of whom the feoffer himself held. This prevents a perfect tenure being created between the feoffer and feoffee. 1 Scriv., 2.

3. *Q.* State the essentials of a copyhold estate.

*A.* They are:—1. A manor. 2. A court. 3. The land must be parcel of the manor. 4. It must have been demised or demisable by copy of court roll from time immemorial. Wharton's Articled Clerk's Manual, by Anderson, 101.

4. *Q.* What is a heriot? claimable by, and from whom, and when?

*A.* It is the best beast or other chattel of the tenant which the lord is entitled to seize on the death or alienation of the tenant, more frequently the former. The period for claiming the heriot is limited to twenty years from the accrual of the right to the same. 3 & 4 Wm. IV., c. 27, ss. 1, 2; Sugden's Real Prop. Stats., 17.

5. *Q.* What are the most common incidents of copyhold estate?

*A.* They are; that the copyholder cannot commit waste, except reasonable botes and estovers, or dig for minerals; the timber and minerals belong to the lord; the tenant is liable to quit rents, fines, and heriots; the conveyance is by surrender and admittance. They are also liable to escheat, and the copyholder cannot lease for more than a year without license. 1 Steph. Com., 631.

6. *Q.* Describe generally the nature of customary freeholds, and the mode of their transfer.

*A.* They are lands which are held by copy of court roll, and in many other respects resemble copyholds; but differ from them in that they are not at the will of the lord. The freehold is in the lord, and the mines and minerals also belong to him. The transfer is effected by surrender and admittance, or by deed of grant or bargain and sale according to custom, also by will. Scriven on Copyholds, 572 ; Wms. R. P., 321.

7. *Q.* What is a court-baron and a court-leet?

*A.* A court-baron is the court of the freeholders of the manor, in which they sit as judges. Its jurisdiction is to compel the performance of the various services, and for determining actions under forty shillings. It differs from the customary court which is for the copyholders, and in that the lord or his steward is the judge. A court leet is a court of criminal law for the purpose of punishing offenders within a manor or hundred. Its jurisdiction is confined to preservation of the peace, and the punishment of petty offences. The jurisdiction is entirely out of use. 4 Steph. Com., 401.

8. *Q.* Can copyhold estates be entailed; and by what means?

*A.* In certain manors a custom exists to entail lands, but in others a limitation to a tenant and the heirs of his body creates an estate analogous to a fee simple conditional at common law. Therefore, in the latter, no alienation can take place until issue is born. Copyholds are not within the statute *De donis.* Wms. R. P., 325.

9. *Q.* How are estates tail of copyholds barred; distinguishing between the modes of barring legal and equitable estates tail?

*A.* Legal estates tail may be barred by surrender, with the verbal concurrence of the protector, or given by deed. Equitable estates tail may be barred by deed or surrender. The deed must be enrolled on the court-roll of the manor within six months. *Honeywood* v. *Forster*; 30 Beav. 1; 3 & 4 Wm. IV. c. 74, s. 51.

10. *Q.* To whom, in the absence of any special custom to the contrary, belong the timber and minerals upon and under the waste lands of a copyhold manor? and to whom, the timber and minerals under copyhold lands?

*A.* In both cases the timber and minerals belong to the lord. 1 Watk. Cop., 332.

11. *Q.* Can a lord "approve" part of the waste lands of his manor; and if so, under what law and to what extent, and subject to what restrictions, if any?

*A.* The lord may, by the statute of Merton, 20 Hen. III. c. 4, approve, i.e. inclose, part of the waste as against common of pasture, though not generally against common of estovers or of turbary. The lord must, however, leave sufficient common for the commoners. 1 Steph. Com., 663.

12. *Q.* What is the meaning of "copyhold fine arbitrary," as descriptive of a tenure; and what is the practical effect of such a tenure?

*A.* This signifies that the lord may demand such a fine as he pleases. But this right is limited to two years' improved value of the land, beyond which the lord cannot claim. 1 Watk. Cop., 308.

13. *Q.* When copyholds are not subject to a fine certain, what fine is usually paid to the lord of the manor on death and alienation, and if the devisees be three trustees, how is the fine usually calculated?

*A.* The fine paid would be two years' improved value of the land. If the divisees were trustees they would pay two years' value on the first life, half that on the second, and half that on the third. 1 Steph. Com., 636.

14. *Q.* How should a copyholder seised in fee, whose estate is fine arbitrary, and who wishes to give it by his will to trustees for sale, make his will so as to prevent the necessity of the admission of the trustees, and thereby avoid the fine that would be payable on such admission?

*A.* The testator should direct the trustees to sell the lands without devising them. But the trustees must sell before the lord has had time to hold three customary courts in order to seize the lands. If this course is adopted, the purchaser is entitled to be admitted on payment of a single fine. A similar object may be attained by devising the property to such uses as the trustees shall appoint. 1 Prideaux's Precedents, 127; Wms. R. P., 347.

15. *Q.* A copyholder dies, having devised all his estates to B., with power to trustees to sell the copyholds. The trustees sell at once. By what instrument should they convey the copyholds, and what fine will be due to the lord, and by whom paid?

*A.* The trustees should convey by bargain and sale to the purchaser, reciting the will. See a form. Crabb's Precedents, by Christie, No. 221. One fine only will be payable. This the purchaser will pay. *Rex* v. *Lord of the Manor of Oundle.* 1 Ad. & E., 283.

16. *Q.* If copyholds were devised to trustees upon trust for A for life, and after his death to B absolutely, and B should sell his remainder, by what assurance should the property be conveyed to a purchaser, the trustee having been admitted?

*A.* The property would be conveyed by deed of assignment. B could not surrender, having only an equitable estate. Upon the death of A the purchaser should obtain a surrender from the trustees. 1 Scriven, 210, 4th ed.

17. *Q.* What is freebench? and how does it arise? State an example.

*A.* It is that allowance out of the copyhold lands of a deceased person to which his widow is entitled. It is usually in one-third of his lands, sometimes in the whole. It arises by special custom. The widows of copyholders of the manor of Cheltenham are entitled to freebench, and in this manor the right attaches on all the copyhold lands of which the husband was tenant at any time during the coverture. Wms. R. P., 349.

18. *Q.* Does the Dower Act apply to freebench?

*A.* The Dower Act, 3 & 4 Wm. IV. c. 105, does not apply to freebench, therefore it remains as before the Act. It is very analogous to dower at Common Law. 1 Scriv., 72, 4th ed.

19. *Q.* A person having no right in a copyhold, is admitted tenant by the lord; what, if any, act by the person having the right will perfect the title of the person admitted?

*A.* A surrender by the person entitled will not perfect the title; but a release by him will be effectual to vest the estate in the person admitted. *Stone* v. *Exton*, 2 Shaw., 83.

20. *Q.* How is copyhold property conveyed? Is there any difference in the form of assurance to a purchaser or mortgagee?

*A.* Copyholds are conveyed by surrender to the lord to the use of the surrenderee, and admittance of the surrenderee In the case of a surrender to a mortgagee, it is upon condition that the money remains unpaid at the time appointed. If the money is paid, the surrender becomes void. Even if the money is not paid the mortgagee seldom is admitted, unless he desires to enforce his security. 1 Steph. Com., 645.

21. *Q.* A being a surrenderee of copyhold estate, but not admitted, assigns his interest to B. Is the lord compellable to admit B on payment of a single fine? And how would the case stand, if instead of a surrender to A, there had been only a covenant to surrender?

*A.* A double fine would have to be paid in the first case, as, before the lord can be compelled to admit the purchaser, A must himself be admitted, upon which a fine is payable. Upon the admission of B another will be payable. If, however, there was merely a covenant to surrender to A, the lord could only insist on a single fine. B would take a surrender from the covenantor with A, and a private agreement between him and A, not followed by a surrender, does not give the lord a right to a fine. *Rex* v. *The Lord, etc., of Hendon*, 4 T. R., 484; Scriven, 211, 4th ed.

22. *Q.* A devisee of copyhold estate dies without having been admitted, will a devise by him operate to pass it, and under what authority?

*A.* A devise by him will now pass the estate, by virtue of 7 Wm. IV., and 1 Vic., c. 26, s. 3.

23. *Q.* Can a court of equity make the like decree for partition of copyhold estate as of freehold, and under what authority?

*A.* A court of equity has power to make such a decree by virtue of 4 & 5 Vic., c. 35.

24. *Q.* Can the lord of a copyhold manor be compelled to enfranchise? If so, in what cases, and by whom; and how are the expenses of enfranchisement to be borne?

*A.* The tenant may now, in almost all cases, compel the lord to enfranchise, and the lord has a similar power as against the tenant. The expenses of enfranchisement are borne by the party requiring it. 15 & 16 Vic., c. 51; 21 & 22 Vic., c. 94.

25. *Q.* How is enfranchisement effected at the suit of the tenant?

*A.* The tenant must first pay all fines due, and the fees consequent on any admittance. Notice requiring enfranchisement must be given to the lord, and a copy transmitted to the copyhold commissioners. A valuer is then appointed by the lord and tenant respectively, and if the lord make default in appointing his, the commissioners will, upon being called upon to do so, appoint one. The valuers then enquire into the rights of the parties, and make their award as to the amount to be paid. This award is confirmed by the commissioners, and is then sent to the steward of the manor. The compensation is a gross sum of money to be paid at the time of completion. 15 & 16 Vic., c. 51; 21 & 22 Vic., c. 94.

26. *Q.* How do the proceedings differ if the enfranchisement is at the suit of the lord?

*A.* The practical proceedings are very similar, but the payment of compensation is by way of an annual rent-charge issuing out of the lands enfranchised. But the parties may, with the sanction of the commissioners, agree that the compensation shall be either a gross sum, or a rent-charge, or a conveyance of land to be settled to the same uses as the manor is settled. 15 & 16 Vic., c. 51, s. 7; 21 & 22 Vic., c. 94, s. 21. It should be remembered that the above provisions as to an enfranchisement being effected through the medium of the commissioners, does not necessarily apply to cases where the parties agree upon an enfranchisement. In the latter case, it may be effected by a conveyance of the fee from the lord, or by a release of his manorial rights to the tenant; also by a surrender from the tenant to the lord, to the use of the lord, or by a release from the copyholder of all his rights to the lord. Wms. R. P., 336; Wharton's Law Lexicon, 224.

## VIII.—*Uses, Trusts, and Powers.*

1. *Q.* What is the principal enactment of the Statute of Uses, and its date?

*A.* The Statute of Uses enacted, that where any person or persons shall stand seised of any lands to the use, confidence, or trust of any other person or persons, the persons that have any such use, confidence, or trust, shall be deemed in lawful seisure and possession of the same lands and hereditaments, for such estates as they have in the use, trust, or confidence. This is its most important provision. 27 Hen. VIII., c. 10, A.D. 1535.

2. *Q.* State briefly what you consider to have been its intention and effect, and the causes that led to its enactment.

*A.* The causes for passing the statute were the inconveniences which arose from the greater part of the lands of the country being held by way of use. This led, as observed by Lord Bacon, to the wife being defrauded of her thirds, the husband of his curtesy, the lord of his wardship, relief, heriot, and escheat, the creditor of his extent, and the tenant of his lease. (Bac. Use of the Law, 153.). The intention of the legislature was to convert the use into an estate in possession, thereby making the *cestui que* use, the legal owner, and liable as such to all the incidents of legal estates, from most of which, as *cestui que* use, the use was free. The act effected this object, but as will be seen below, only temporarily.

3. *Q.* What is the difference between a use and a trust?

*A.* A use is that interest in lands which was introduced by the clergy to evade the statutes of Mortmain. Lands were conveyed to A to the use of the religious house, and such use was not at the time within the statutes of Mortmain. Subsequently this method of conveyance was generally adopted, and it became the practice to convey lands to A to the use of B, instead of to B direct. The estate of B was, therefore, termed a use. A trust is more in the nature of a confidence reposed in another person to deal with property in a particular manner. But the term is usually applied to a use upon a use which the statute of uses would not execute, but which the Court of Equity treated as a trust reposed in the owner of the legal estate. 1 Steph. Com., 360.

4. *Q.* Give the form of expression by which in one instrument a legal estate in fee simple, and an equitable estate in fee simple respectively, may be conferred in the same land.

*A.* If land is conveyed by deed of grant to A and his heirs, to the use of B and his heirs, to the use of C and his heirs, a legal estate in fee is conferred by the Statute of Uses on B, and in equity the fee is vested in C. C has, therefore, an equitable estate, and B the legal estate.

5. *Q.* What is a shifting use? Are such uses subject to restraint against perpetuities? Are they destructible, and by what means?

*A.* It is a use which shifts from one person to another, upon the happening of a given event, and operates in derogation of a preceding estate. For an example see the next answer. Such uses are within the rule against perpetuities, unless they are limited after an estate tail. If limited after estates tail shifting uses are destructible, but it is otherwise if limited after a fee simple. *Lloyd* v. *Carew*, Prec. Ch. 72; L. C. Conv., 286.

6. *Q.* Give a concise form of a springing *or* shifting, use, and state how each may be created.

*A.* A springing use would be, a grant to A and his heirs to the use of B and his heirs on the death of C. Here, on the death of C, the use springs up and is executed by the statute in B. A shifting use, unlike a springing use, has a preceding estate. Thus to A and his heirs, to the use of B and his heirs, and when C returns from Rome to the use of C and his heirs. In this case, it will be observed that the estate shifts from B to C on the latter returning from Rome, but in the springing use, no one under the deed has the estate until C dies, but it would revert to the grantor in the meantime. These limitations were introduced into deeds for the purpose of limiting an estate in fee simple in *futuro* and after a fee simple, which was not allowed at common law. Similar limitations in a will are termed executory devises. 1 Steph. Com., 553.

7. *Q.* What is an executory devise?

*A.* It is an executory limitation by will of an estate contrary to the strict rules of the common law in limitations *inter vivos*, and not operating as a remainder. The examples in the preceding answer omitting the conveyance to use, would be executory devises if in a will. Also, if lands are devised to A and his heirs; but, if he should die under twenty-one to B and his heirs,—the latter limitation is an executory devise. Wms. R. P., 284.

8. *Q.* What is the difference between an executory devise and a shifting use?

*A.* They differ in that the former is by will and the latter by deed. The latter operates by virtue of the statute of uses, the former does not. The latter is in derogation of a preceding estate, but an executory devise is not necessarily so. See previous answers.

9. *Q.* Give three instances of an executory devise.

*A.* See *supra*, Nos. 6, 7.

10. *Q.* How does an executory devise differ from a conditional limitation?

*A.* They differ in that the former is by will, but the latter by deed *inter vivos*. Conditional limitations also depend upon some condition, the performance of which defeats a preceding estate. This is not necessarily so with regard to executory devises. An example of a conditional limitation would be to A and the heirs of his body, until C returns from Rome then to C and his heirs. 1 Steph. Com., 305.

11. *Q.* In regard to what are called precatory or recommendatory words or expressions of belief or confidence in a devise, state, as far as you may have considered the subject, the rules for determining their import, that is, what class of words in a general sense create a trust, and what not?

*A.* The following words have been held to create a trust when addressed to a person to whom property is given absolutely in favour of another:—"Request," "wish and request," "recommend," "entreat," "not doubting," "under the firm conviction," "have fullest confidence," "heartily beseech," "full assurance and confident hope." If, however, the words merely give a discretion to the devisee, it will be otherwise. Notes to *Harding* v. *Glyn*. 2 L. C. Eq., 793.

12. *Q.* How far will the Court of Chancery construe words of recommendation, or request, as creating a trust by implication?

*A.* If it appears from the context of the instrument and other circumstances that the words were used imperatively, and if the subject and objects of the recommendation are certain, the Court will hold a trust to be created. *Harding* v. *Glyn*. 2 L. C. Eq., 791.

13. *Q.* A conveyed his estate to B, his heirs and assigns, to the use of C, his heirs and assigns. What estates do B and C respectively take?

*A.* Assuming the conveyance to have been made by deed of grant, B will take no estate, but C by force of the statute of uses will take the legal estate in fee. See *infra*.

14. *Q.* Where land is conveyed "unto and to the use of A and his heirs upon trust for B his heirs and assigns," is A in by the common law or by the statute; and does B take a legal or an equitable estate?

*A.* Upon this point great doubt has been felt, but it has been decided that A is in by the common law, and not by the statute. *Doe* v. *Passingham.* 6 B. & C., 305. This is upon the ground that the person seised to the use and the *cestui que* use should be distinct persons in order that the statute should operate. It has been said that A is in by the statute in order to prevent the execution of the use limited upon the use. But this reasoning does not appear to be satisfactory. See The Articled Clerk's Manual, by Anderson, 106.

15. *Q.* A, under a power, appoints an estate to B, his heirs and assigns, to the use of C, his heirs and assigns, in trust for D, and his heirs. What estates do B, C and D take under the appointment?

*A.* In this case B will take the legal estate in fee, C will take nothing and D will take the equitable estate in fee. B takes the legal estate by virtue of the statute, as a use is raised by the person creating the power. This use the statute executes in B. The use to C is a use upon a use which will not be executed, but equity will give the beneficial interest to D. The above answer assumes that A has a power of appointment over the fee. Wms. R. P., 268.

16. *Q.* A fee simple estate is conveyed to C to such uses as A shall appoint. A sells to B and exercises the power by conveying the estate to C (as trustee for B) and his heirs to the use of B and his heirs. In whom does the legal estate vest?

*A.* The legal estate in fee would vest in C. A has merely a power over the use, and the moment he appoints to any one (in this case to the feoffee to uses), the statute executes such use in the appointee (C). B will only have an equitable estate in fee. Ibid.

17. *Q.* A by bargain and sale enrolled conveys an estate to B and his heirs, to the use of C and his heirs, in trust for D and his heirs. What estates do B, C and D take?

*A.* As in the previous answer B will take the legal estate in fee, C nothing, and D the equitable estate in fee. The bargain and sale by A upon the maxim that that which is agreed to be done is looked upon as done, raises a use which the statute at once executes in the bargainee B. Wms. R. P., 163, 180.

18. *Q.* A feoffment to A and his heirs, to the use of B and his heirs, in trust for C and his heirs: explain the operation of the Statute of Uses in the above limitations?

*A.* The statute operates to convert the use into the possession of B, and vests in him the legal estate in fee. The trust to C it will not execute, but C takes the fee in equity. See *supra.*

19. *Q.* Suppose a feoffment to T. S. and his heirs, to the use of A for life, with remainder to the use of his first son (unborn) in tail, with remainder to the use of B in fee; does any and what estate remain to T. S. until the birth of a son to A.

*A.* No estate necessarily remains in T. S. until the birth of a son, to give effect to the use to the son, but such use takes effect by force of the seisin originally vested in T. S. 23 & 24 Vic., c. 38, s. 7. This statue has settled the much vexed question known as the doctrine of *Scintilla Juris.*

20. *Q.* Suppose T. S. makes a feoffment to the use of A for life, with remainder to the use of the heirs of his (T. S.'s) body: does any and what estate exist in T. S. ? and distinguish between the above case and that of a feoffment by T. S. to the use of A for the life of him T. S., with remainder to the use of the heirs of his (T. S.'s) body.

*A.* In the first case, T. S. by virtue of the rule in Shelley's Case takes an estate tail. The reason for this is that even if the use to A for life be well limited, the estate of A may determine before the remainder to the heirs of the body of T. S. comes into operation. Therefore, the intermediate use between the possible death of A and the death of T. S. results to the latter for his life, which estate coalescing with the limitation to the heirs of his body creates in him an estate tail. In the second case, however, the result will be otherwise, because an estate for the life of T. S. is given to A instead of an estate for the life of A. There can, therefore, be no resulting use to T. S., as he has disposed of the whole interest which can possibly exist until the contingent remainder to the heirs of his body vests. T. S., therefore, takes no estate, excepting a reversion in fee. 1 Fearne Cont. Rem., 48.

21. *Q.* A by statutory release conveys to B, his heirs and assigns, to the use of C, his heirs and assigns : what estates do B and C take?

*A.* By the statutory release B will take no estate, but C will take the legal estate, which is executed in him by the statute. But for the use to C, B would take the legal estate by the common law release. Watkins Conv., 299; Note 9th ed.

22. *Q.* Under a conveyance by statutory release to A and his heirs to hold to the use of A and his heirs, to the use of B and his heirs, who takes the legal estate ?

*A.* A will here take the legal estate, as the use to B is a use upon a use which the statute will not execute. As to whether A takes by common law or by statute see *supra,* No. 14.

23. *Q.* Settlement of fee simple estates to the use of A for life, with remainder to the use of B and his heirs, in trust for C and his heirs. Do B and C respectively take legal or equitable estates: and to whom must A surrender his life estate, in order to effect its merger ?

*A.* The settlement is presumed to be in the usual form, viz., a conveyance to trustees in the first instance, therefore, B will take the legal estate in remainder, and C an equitable estate. A would surrender his estate to the owner of the next estate, namely, to B, see *infra,* "Merger."

24. *Q.* Devise, since the "Wills Act," to A and his heirs in trust, to apply the rents for specified purposes for a limited time,

and then in trust for B and his heirs: in whom is the legal estate vested?

*A.* The legal estate would vest in A and his heirs. As to whether it would vest in B when A has applied the rents for the specified purposes depends upon circumstances. If A is to pay the rents to a person for life the legal estate will vest in B after such person's death. If, however, A is merely to pay an annuity to a person for life, A will take the whole legal fee, and not merely an estate during the life of the annuitant. This distinction is in consequence of the terms of s. 31 of 1 Vic., c. 26, which see, and the notes thereon by Eastwood, Hayes & Jarman, 71.

25. *Q.* A testator being owner of fee simple land, devises it to the use of A and his heirs in trust for B and his heirs; A, by deed disclaims the devise to him. By whom can the land be conveyed in fee simple to a purchaser?

*A.* The answer to this question depends upon a preliminary one, viz., in whom is the legal estate? This question is one of great difficulty, to be decided upon the context of the will. But the devise being to the use of A, I think the legal estate would be vested in him. Therefore the heir of the testator should be a party to the conveyance jointly with B, as upon the disclaimer, the legal estate will vest in the heir, subject to the trust for B. See the cases collected in the notes to *Tyrrel's case*, L. C. Conv., 292. 2 Jarm. Wills, 3rd. ed., 268.

26. *Q.* In a devise of real estate to A in fee in trust for B in fee, A by deed disclaims the estate, what is the effect of such disclaimer, viz., does it vest the estate in the testator's heirs or in B?

*A.* See the previous answer.

27. *Q.* Where an estate is devised to A and his heirs, in trust to *permit* B and his heirs to receive the rents and profits: what estate does B take?

*A.* Here B will take the legal estate in fee. There is no active duty imposed upon A which necessitates his having the legal estate, therefore, it will vest in B. 1 Steph. Com., 374.

28. *Q.* A devise to A for life, and in default of issue of his body to B for life, and after his death to the use of the heirs of his body; what estates do A and B respectively take?

*A.* Here A will take an estate for life, and B a contingent remainder in the event of A. dying without issue living at his decease. The words in default of issue indicate an intention that the estate should not go to B if A has issue, and since the "Wills Act" this means issue living at A's death. Therefore, A will not take an estate tail, but merely an estate for life. *Lethieullien* v. *Tracy*, 3 Atk., 774. As to what estate the issue (if any) of A would take seems doubtful. 1 Jarman on Wills, 524.

29. *Q.* A contracts to hold Blackacre to the use of B, to the use of C: what is its effect, and what are the respective interests of B and C resulting therefrom?

*A.* The contract has no effect, so far as the legal estate is concerned, but in equity A will be looked upon as a trustee for C, provided the contract is founded upon a valuable consideration. Otherwise it will not be enforced. Had the contract been by way of bargain and sale enrolled, B would have taken the fee by virtue of the statute and C the equitable estate. See *supra.*

30. *Q.* Within what period must an estate vest when limited by way of future use, or executory devise? From what time is such period reckoned?

*A.* The period referred to is that of the lives of any number of existing persons, and twenty-one years after their decease, with a further period of nine months for gestation, if any. This is termed the rule against perpetuities. The reason of the rule is to prevent property remaining perpetually in one family, and also to prevent its being rendered inalienable beyond a certain time, it being considered contrary to public policy that this should be permitted. *Cadell* v. *Palmer*, 1 Cl. & F., 372; L. C. Conv., 360. The period of limitation under deeds runs from the execution, and in the case of wills from the death of the testator. An exception to this occurs in the case of a special power. *Infra*, No. 34.

31. *Q.* What are powers appendant?

*A.* They are powers over land which may be exercised by a person having an interest in the land, to take effect out of that interest. Thus, if A is tenant for life of lands with a power to grant leases out of the land, this is a power appendant. Notes to *Edwards* v. *Slater.* L. C. Conv., 315.

32. *Q.* What are powers in gross?

*A.* They are powers possessed over an estate in which the owner of a power had an interest at the time of its creation or has one now, but which power is not to operate upon such interest. Such is a power given to a tenant for life to appoint the estate after his death among his children; also to jointure his wife after his death. Such powers cannot, like powers appendant, be suspended or extinguished by a partial or absolute conveyance of the estate. *Edwards* v. *Slater. Supra.*

33. *Q.* Where a power of appointment over real estate is executed, from whom does the appointee immediately take in point of estate, viz., the party creating, or the party executing the power? and state the reason.

*A.* The appointee takes in point of estate from the party creating the power. Thus, if A has a general power of appointment, and he appoints to B for life remainder to his children in strict settlement, these limitations will take effect as estates limited by the original deed. It is upon this ground that though a husband cannot convey to his wife, yet he may appoint to her, because her estate arises out of the original seisin. The reason for this rule is that the appointment is merely over the use, which the appointment puts in motion and transfers the estate to the appointee. As will be seen in the next answer, there is an exception with regard to the time from which the appointment operates. Sug. Powers, ch. 9, s. 3.

34. *Q.* What is the difference as regards the rule against perpetuities between a general and special power?

*A.* In the case of general powers, the period of limitation runs from the time of appointment; but, if the power is special, the limitations must be considered to have been inserted in the settlement creating the power. Thus, if A has a general power of appointment by will over a fund, and he appoints to an unborn child of his to be vested at twenty-three, the limit will be reckoned from the time the appointment operates, namely the death of A, when his child will be in *ventre sa mère*, or in being, and the appointment will be good. But, if the fund was settled on A for life, and afterwards to his children, by his marriage settlement, the above appointment could not be made, as the limit of perpetuities counting from the date of the settlement, A's is the life in being, and his child may not possibly obtain twenty-three within twenty-one years after A's death. Wms. Pers. Prop., 252.

35. *Q.* When a power is executed by will, at what point of time does it take effect? and would there be any difference in this respect if the power were executed by deed, with a power of revocation to the appointor?

*A.* As mentioned above, the power takes effect from the death of the testator when the will operates. The execution, however, by the deed will operate from its date subject to be rendered inoperative by a subsequent revocation. Sug. Powers, 457.

36. *Q.* How does an appointment under a power in a conveyance or settlement affect the estate, and the conveyance or settlement of it?

*A.* The appointment has the effect of vesting the estate in the appointee to the extent to which the power extends. But it will not disturb existing vested estates, unless indeed it amount to a power of revocation. Wms. R. P., 267.

37. *Q.* Can a person, having an absolute power of appointment over real estate, defeat judgments entered up against him, subsequently to the vesting of such power in him, in any and what way? State a reason for your answer.

*A.* The person having the power cannot now defeat the judgments, as they are made binding against an estate over which he has a power to dispose, which he may exercise for his own benefit without the assent of any other person. 1 & 2 Vic., c. 110, s. 13; Sug. Powers, 289.

38. *Q.* Is a purchaser under an appointment, as in the last question, affected, and how, by the statutes 1 & 2 Vic., c. 110, and 2 & 3 Vic., c. 11, or either of them?

*A.* The judgment, in order to be binding as against purchasers, must by virtue of these acts be registered in the Court of Common Pleas.

39. *Q.* When a man has a power of appointment and no estate in the lands, and makes a conveyance as if he was seised of the estate, does the grantee take any estate?

*A.* The grantee will take such an estate as the grantor has a power to dispose of, provided the circumstances necessary to the execution of the power are complied with. The instrument must be such a one as is required by the power. Sug. Powers, ch. 7, s. 7.

40. *Q.* Where a will contains a power to raise money out of an estate, not confined to raising it out of the rents, or a power to charge an estate generally,—would such power authorise a sale of the estate, and also a mortgage of it, both, or either, and which?

*A.* A power to raise a sum, or to charge an estate, generally enables a sale of the estate, and it seems also a mortgage. But the cases chiefly turn upon the particular wording of each devise, from which is ascertained the intention of the testator. Sug. Powers, ch. 8, s. 3.

41. *Q.* If in a strict settlement, a power of sale and exchange not expressly limited in its duration is given, is it valid? during what period or state of circumstances will it continue?

*A.* Such power is not limited by the rule against perpetuities, but continues and may be exercised so long as the trusts of the settlement are operative. That is until the fee vests in possession. Such a power has not a tendency to tie up property, but enables the alienation of it. *Lantsbery* v. *Collier*, 2; Kay & Joh., 709; Sug. Powers, 851.

42. *Q.* Where under a settlement or will a father has a power to appoint amongst all his children as he may think fit, will an appointment, which leaves out one or more of his children, be effectual, or is it necessary he should appoint a share to each; and, if so, must such share be a substantial, or may it be a merely nominal one?

*A.* An appointment leaving out one or more of the objects of the power will be bad, unless the power expressly authorise an exclusive appointment. But there is now no objection to appointing an illusory share since 11 Geo. IV., and 1 Wm. IV., c. 46.

43. *Q.* In case a father has the power of appointing a sum of money amongst his children, and in consideration of a sum paid to him by one of such children he makes an appointment in favour of such child, is the appointment good? Give a reason for your answer.

*A.* Such an appointment would be bad, as being a fraud upon the power, the objects being the children and not the father. The power must be executed for the end designed by the person creating it. This point was decided in *Aleyn* v. *Belchier*, 1 L. C. Eq., 304.

44. *Q.* A, by his will, gives to B a power to appoint a sum of money to all, or some, or one of his (B's) children, as B may think fit. B has several children; one of such children dies in B's lifetime, leaving children being B's grand-children. Is B authorised under such power to appoint any part of the money to such his grand-children, or any of them?

*A.* B cannot appoint to the grand-children or any of them, they not being objects of the power. *Alexander* v. *Alexander*, 2 Ves., 640; L. C. Conv., 330.

45. *Q.* Where an estate is limited to A for life, with power to grant leases for twenty-one years; and A conveys all his estate, right, and interest to B; can B execute the power, or grant a lease for any, and what, term of years?

*A.* The power being appendant is extinguished by the absolute assignment of the interest of A, therefore the power cannot be exercised. 1 L. C. Conv., 318.

46. *Q.* If a tenant for life, with power of leasing, mortgages his estate, how far is he thereby restrained from exercising his power? may or may not stipulations be made on the mortgage for the exercise of such power, and what would in ordinary cases be proper?

*A.* The tenant for life cannot exercise his power in derogation of the mortgage; but the power is not extinguished, the mortgage being looked upon merely as a security. Therefore, there might be a reservation of the power of leasing, and this reservation should be inserted. It should, however, also be provided that the leases should be granted with the concurrence of the mortgagee. *Ren* v. *Bulkeley.* Doug., 291; L. C. Conv., 321.

47. *Q.* State in general terms the rule for determining how far a power is suspended or extinguished by any act of the donee of the power having also an interest in the estate affecting that interest; could such a donee, after creating a charge on his estate, exercise a power in any way defeating such charge?

*A.* The rule will have been ascertained from the previous answers that a partial alienation of the interest out of which the power is to operate, will merely be a suspension of the power, not an extinguishment. But where the alienation is absolute, the power is gone. See *supra.*

## IX.—*Terms and their Merger.*

1. *Q.* What are terms in gross?

*A.* Terms which a purchaser of property had assigned to a trustee, without being made attendant upon the inheritance, were called terms in gross. The term was one which would have merged in the inheritance if united with it. See Sugden's Vendors, 625.

2. *Q.* What are outstanding terms? and for what purposes were they usually assigned?

*A.* They are those terms which, though the object for which they were created is accomplished, are, nevertheless, still in existence. They were usually assigned to a purchaser upon trust to attend the inheritance, and they were the means of protecting him from any incumbrances created subsequently to the creation of the term, and of which he had no notice. Wms. R. P., 376.

3. *Q.* What is the present law as to satisfied terms?

*A.* It is that all satisfied terms which on and after the 31st December, 1845, were attendant on the inheritance have ceased to exist. Satisfied terms, therefore, are no longer a protection to a purchaser since that date, by assignment to attend the inheritance. 8 & 9 Vic., c. 112; Sugden's Vendors, 622.

4. *Q.* Was there any, and what, advantage to a purchaser in taking an assignment of outstanding terms to trustees for the purchaser, in trust to attend the inheritance, over a general declaration

that all persons in whom outstanding terms were vested should stand possessed of them in trust for the purchaser?

*A.* The advantage in the former course was, that the assignment when effected formed a complete protection as against incumbrances and subsequent purchasers; whereas, if not assigned, and a declaration merely was given, it was in the power of a subsequent purchaser, without notice, by obtaining an assignment of the term, to get priority.

5. *Q.* In whom does a term vest upon the death of an assignee of a term?

*A.* It vests in his personal representatives, being personal property.

6. *Q.* What is meant by the merger of a term? and what are the requisites to effect it?

*A.* The merger of a term signifies its extinguishment, by being enveloped in some other estate. To effect a merger there must be— 1. Two estates in the same property; 2. the estates must be expectant upon each other, *i.e.*, there must be no intervening estate; 3. the estates must be held in the same rights. Thus, if A is the owner of the reversion, and he takes the term as executor of the lessee, there will be no merger. It would be otherwise if, having the term as executor, he were by his own act to purchase the reversion. Wharton's Law Lexicon, 589.

7. *Q.* Will a term of years under any circumstances merge in a term of shorter duration?

*A.* Yes, if the lessee in possession of the term surrender to a termor in reversion, the former will merge in the latter, even though it be of shorter duration. *Hughes* v. *Robotham*, Cro. Eliz., 302; Sugden's Vendors, 619.

8. *Q.* A person in whom a term of years is vested assigns it to the tenant for life; what is the effect upon the term?

*A.* The term will become merged in the freehold, provided there is no intervening estate. See *supra*.

9. *Q.* May a term created for raising portions, not assigned to attend, be at any time presumed to have become void, or to have been merged or surrendered? State instances.

*A.* The surrender of the term was presumed, though not assigned to attend the inheritance, in the cases of *Emery* v. *Grocock*, 2 B. & Ad., 573, and *ex parte Holman*, 1821, M. S., where there had been a considerable lapse of time.

10. *Q.* Where terms of years are created by settlements, what are the events usually expressed in the proviso for cessor of such terms?

*A.* It is usually provided that the terms shall cease—1. If the trusts never arise; 2. upon their becoming unnecessary or incapable of taking effect; 3. if they are performed. Sugden's Vendors, 621.

11. *Q.* An estate is granted to A for 1,000 years, subject thereto to B for life, remainder to C in tail, with reversion to D in fee. To whom should the term be surrendered for the purpose of merging the same?

*A.* The term should be surrendered to the tenant for life, and his estate being the next estate of freehold, it will swallow up the term. Ibid., 374.

12. *Q.* A demised land to B for twenty-one years, and afterwards demised the same land to C for ninety-nine years; D subsequently become seised in fee of the demised land: to whom should the term of twenty-one years be surrendered for the purpose of merger?

*A.* The term may be surrendered to D, as the term of C is merely an *interesse termini,* and it has been held that the intervention of such an interest will not prevent a merger taking place, the effect of which is to accelerate the possession under the *interesse termini.* 4 Petersdorff Abr., 275.

13. *Q.* Under what circumstances will a term of years merge in the freehold or inheritance?

*A.* See the previous answers.

14. *Q.* A seised in fee, demises to B for a term in mortgage; A then mortgages the equity of redemption to C in fee; A next pays off B's mortgage, and desires to merge B's term: how is this to be effected?

*A.* The term should be surrendered to the legal owner of the reversion, C. In practice, it is usual in such a case not to entail the expense of a surrender, but merely to endorse a receipt upon the mortgage deed, relying upon 8 & 9 Vic., c. 112, for a cessor of the term. This course is, however, not recommended, excepting where the saving of expense is a great object. Barry's Prin. Conv., 270.

15. *Q.* Settlement to the use of A for life, remainder to trustees for a term of 500 years, remainder to B for life, remainder to C in tail, all these estates being subsisting: how would you merge the term?

*A.* I should direct the trustees to surrender the term to B, the owner of the next succeeding estate of freehold. *Supra.*

16. *Q.* If a tenant for years die, having appointed the person seised of the freehold to be his executor, will the term merge or not? Give a reason why it would or would not.

*A.* The term will not merge. The reason is, that the term devolves upon the executor in another capacity to that in which he holds the reversion. If the executor was the legatee of the term the term would merge after all the creditors had been paid. Wms. R. P., 376.

### X.—*Choses in Action. Bonds. Simony.*

1. *Q.* What is a chose in action, and is it assignable at law or in equity?

*A.* A chose in action is the right to bring an action. It is a thing in action as distinguished from a chose in possession. Thus, a debt is a chose in action, but when the debt is paid, the money becomes a chose in possession. At law, with certain exceptions, choses in action are not assignable. Some of the exceptions are, bills and notes; covenants running with the land; bail bonds; book debts under the Bankruptcy Act, 1861. Equity, however, permits the assignment of equitable choses in action, both with and without consideration. *Kekewich* v. *Manning*, 1 D. G. M. & G., 176; Wms. Pers. Prop., 112.

2. *Q.* By what mode is the transfer of such property effected; and what precautions are to be taken by a purchaser to guard his title on the transfer being completed, as distinguished from a transfer of an estate in land?

*A.* Although technically a chose in action is not assignable so as to enable the assignee to sue in the assignor's name, yet practically an assignment is effected every day. This is done by the assignor giving the assignee a power of attorney to sue for the chose in his, the assignor's name, and also by signing a declaration of trust that the money recovered is for the benefit of the assignee. The purchaser of a debt should at once give notice of his purchase to the debtor, otherwise a subsequent purchaser, by giving such a notice, may gain priority over him. It is also important to give this notice in order to place the debt out of the order and disposition of the creditor within the bankrupt laws. Wms. Pers. Prop., 111.

3. *Q.* A and B (not partners) are to give their bond to C for the payment of a certain sum of money; how is the obligation to be framed, so that in case B should die and leave A surviving, C may have a legal claim upon B's personal representative?

*A.* The bond should be made several, or joint and several. The reason for this is that if the bond is merely joint the estate of a deceased obligor will be released both at law and in equity. *Other* v. *Ivison*, 3 Drew., 177; Wms. Pers. Prop., 283.

4. *Q.* Supposing one of the obligors to be merely a guarantee for the other, what would such guarantee require for his security from his co-obligor?

*A.* It is not necessary that such surety should require anything, as he may, if compelled to pay the debt, sue the debtor upon the original bond. 19 & 20 Vic., c. 97. If a counter bond were taken, the surety would be in hardly any better position, excepting that unless he appeared as a surety upon the face of the bond, he would not, at law, be entitled to the rights of a surety. This, however, would form a good ground of plea or replication on equitable grounds. *Pooley* v. *Haradine*, 26 L. J. Q. B., 156.

5. *Q.* Suppose there are two partners, and they give their joint bond for payment of money, and one of such partners dies, what extent of remedy has the obligee against the surviving partner, and against the representatives of the deceased partner?

*A.* The obligee may sue the surviving partner both at law and in equity. But at law he cannot sue the representatives of the deceased obligor, even for a partnership debt; but it is otherwise in equity, which latter court, in this case, disregards the rule of law as to the survivorship of a joint liability. Wms. Pers. Prop., 286.

6. *Q.* A and B partners in trade, and C as their surety, execute a bond, by which they bind themselves, their heirs, executors, and administrators, to pay the sum of £1000 to D. The £1000 is due to D from A and B on a partnership transaction. A and C die and B becomes insolvent. Has D any remedy; 1. at law; 2. in equity, against the estates of A and C?

*A.* At law, he will have no remedy against the estate of either, the bond being joint. Neither will he in equity against the estate of C; but he will against that of A, he being one of the partners. See previous answers.

7. *Q.* Can a person legally present himself to a living, the next presentation to which he has purchased either in his own name or in the name of a trustee? If not, why not?

*A.* A clerk cannot present himself to a next presentation he has purchased, either in his own name or that of a trustee. Such a transaction is prohibited by 12 Anne, stat. 2, c. 12; but the act is not supposed to prevent a clerk purchasing an advowson, and then presenting himself. Wms. R. P., 311.

8. *Q.* What is simony?

*A.* It is an offence which consists in buying or selling church preferment, when the living is vacant or when the incumbent is *in extremis*, if the purchase is made with a view of presenting a particular clerk. There is no objection to selling an advowson, or next presentation, if the living is full. *Fox* v. *Bishop of Chester*, 6 Bing. 1. L. C. Conv., 226.

9. *Q.* In what cases, and in favour of what persons, are bonds or covenants to resign a living legal?

*A.* Such bonds are valid in respect of an advowson the private property of the patron, and if made in favour of any *one* person named, or of *one of two*, each being by blood or marriage an uncle, son, grandson, nephew, or grand nephew, of the patron, or one of the patrons. One part of the bond must be deposited within two calendar months, in the office of the registrar of the diocese, and the resignation must refer to the engagement, and state the name of the person for whose benefit it is made. 9 Geo. IV., c. 94.

## XI.—*The Evidences of Ownership.*

1. *Q.* What constitutes a complete title to a freehold estate?

*A.* See *infra*, "vendor and purchaser."

2. *Q.* What are the ordinary modes of titles by which real estate is acquired?

*A.* They are: 1. Descent. 2. Purchase. The latter is subdivided into, 1. Escheat. 2. Occupancy. 3. Prescription. 4. Forfeiture. 5. Alienation. 2 Bl. Com., 197.

3. *Q.* What is the difference between taking an estate by descent and by purchase?

*A.* The former is where a man, on the death of his ancestor, inherits such ancestor's estate, which is vested in him by the act of the law. An estate by purchase is, however, acquired by a man's own act. The effects also are different, as a purchase breaks the descent, and the estate acquires a new inheritable quality. Also a purchaser is in a better position to the heir as to his liability on the obligations of former owners of the property. 2 Bl. Com., 198, 235.

4. *Q.* A devises land to B, his heir-at-law: does B take by descent or purchase? and has the law on that subject undergone any, and what, modern alteration?

*A.* Here B takes by purchase, and not by descent. This is provided by 3 & 4 Wm. IV., c. 106.

5. *Q.* Explain the nature of the title by escheat, and when it occurs.

*A.* Escheat is one of the consequences of feudal tenure, founded upon the principle that when the tenants of the land have become extinct, no one is left to perform the feudal services, therefore the tenure is determined, and the land reverts to the lord, the original grantor. It occurs upon failure of the heirs of the tenant, and also if the blood of the tenant is attainted. At the present day attainder only takes place in cases of treason and murder, in the former of which cases the land of the traitor is forfeited absolutely to the crown, if copyholds, to the lord. In murder, the crown takes them for a year and a day, and subject to this, they go to the lord. In other felonies there is no escheat. There is no escheat of gavelkind lands on conviction for murder, or of equitable estates on attainder for murder or failure of heirs. *Burgess* v. *Wheate*, 1 Eden., 177; Wms. R. P., 113. *Attorney-General* v. *Sir G. Sands*, L. C. Conv., 664—701.

6. *Q.* Is the tenant for life or the remainder-man, entitled to the custody of the title-deeds of the settled estates?

*A.* The tenant for life is entitled to the custody of the deeds, and if such deeds have been taken into court he can have them delivered to him. Sugden's Vendors, 445, n.

7. *Q.* What is the extreme period within which a person can bring an action to recover land or rent?

*A.* The extreme period is forty years from the time the right accrued. 3 & 4 Wm. IV., c. 27, s. 17.

## XII.—*Baron and Feme.*

1. *Q.* What interest in a wife's real property does a husband acquire on his marriage, irrespective of settlements?

*A.* He becomes entitled to an estate during the coverture in her freeholds and copyholds in possession. Thus, he may receive the rents and profits, and enjoy the estate, and even sell his interest in it. He may also grant leases without her concurrence, by virtue of 19 and 20 Vic., c. 120. Also, if he survive her, he is entitled to an estate by the curtesy. As to this, see *infra*, No. 36. Wms. R. P., 200.

2. *Q.* A similar question, with regard to the wife's personalty and chattels real?

*A.* The choses in possession of the wife vest absolutely in the husband upon the marriage, with the exception of her paraphernalia, which he cannot dispose of by his will, though he may do so during his lifetime. His interest in her choses in action does not become absolute until he has reduced them into possession by recovering them. Unless this is done, they will survive to her on his decease in her lifetime. If the wife dies first, they will go to the husband as her administrator.

The husband's right in his wife's chattels real is peculiar. He may dispose of them alone during coverture, but not by will. If he die first, without disposing of them, they will survive to her, free from the claims of his creditors, other than those having a mortgage upon them. If she die first, then he will become absolutely entitled in his marital right. Wms. Real Prop., 369; Wms. Pers. Prop., 344.

3. *Q.* If a married woman is entitled to money secured by bond, and the husband dies in her lifetime before the bond is paid off, who becomes entitled thereto?

*A.* See previous answer.

4. *Q.* State the nature and principal incidents of separate estate.

*A.* Separate estate is that property which a married woman is, in a Court of Equity, permitted to hold as if she were a *feme sole* and unmarried. Its incidents are that she has power to dispose of it, by deed or will, without her husband's concurrence. He cannot dispose of it without her concurrence, and not even then if a restraint against anticipation is also imposed. It is also liable to her debts. *Hulme* v. *Tenant*, 1 Bro. C. C., 16; 1 Tud. L. C. Eq., 394.

5. *Q.* If property be given to the separate use of an unmarried woman, will the restriction be valid on her subsequent marriage?

*A.* The restriction will operate upon her subsequent marriage, if apt words are used, unless it appear that it was not so intended. *Tullett* v. *Armstrong*, 1 Beav., 1.

6. *Q.* If property be given to a married woman for her separate use, with a proviso against anticipation, and her husband die, what will be her power over the property?

*A.* She may dispose of the property as if there were no restraint on anticipation. Such a clause is only effectual during coverture. *Woodmeston* v. *Walker*, 2 Russ. & M., 197; Hayne's Outlines, 212.

7. *Q.* A wife's reversionary interest in a leasehold estate, expectant on her mother's decease, is limited by a voluntary postnuptial settlement to the husband, during the joint lives of himself and his wife, and on the death of either, to the survivor absolutely. The mother dies during the joint lives of the husband and wife. Can the husband, after the mother's death, but during the wife's lifetime, and without her consent, make a good title to a purchaser?

*A.* The husband can make a good title without the wife's concurrence The settlement of the reversionary interest being voluntary is not binding against a purchaser of the leaseholds; and, independently of a settlement, the husband has a perfect right to dispose of his wife's terms of years as soon as they fall into possession. Leaseholds are within 27 Eliz., c. 4.

8. *Q.* What are a married woman's powers of disposition over

personal estate, settled to her separate use, either absolutely or for life?

*A.* She may dispose of her whole interest therein either by deed or will, without the concurrence of her husband; or she may bind it by incurring debts. Wms. Pers. Prop. 354.

9. *Q.* If land be limited to such uses as A, an unmarried woman, shall by deed appoint, without expressly providing that the power may be exercised during coverture, and she afterwards marries and appoints by deed, is the appointment valid?

*A.* The appointment is perfectly valid, as a married woman may exercise a power of appointment whether it be given to her when married or single. *Doe d. Blomfield* v. *Eyre,* 5 C. B., 713.

10. *Q.* Land is devised to such uses as A, who is a married woman, should appoint, and in default to her in fee. Can a good title be made without the concurrence of the husband, and what further is necessary to complete the conveyance?

*A.* As just mentioned A may alone appoint and vest a good title in a purchaser. Nothing further is necessary to vest the estate in him. Should not, however, the power be exercised, she can only convey the fee with the concurrence of her husband under 3 & 4 Wm. IV., c. 74.

11. *Q.* If a power be reserved to a feme sole, as such, to dispose of her estate by deed or will, can she exercise such a power during coverture? State the proper mode of framing a power enabling her to do so in either case.

*A.* If it appeared to be intended that the power was to be exercised only when sole, she could not exercise it during coverture. As where a power was given to a woman "being sole." *Lord Antrim* v. *Duke of Buckingham,* 1 Cha. Ca. 17. As to the frame of the power, it is usual and proper, to prevent doubt, to express that it may be exercised either before or after marriage; but this is not absolutely necessary, at least, as to cases coming within the previous answer. 2 Prideaux's Precedents, 202. Sug. Powers, 155.

12. *Q.* When, and of what property, may a married woman make a will?

*A.* A married woman may make a will with the concurrence of her husband, which, however, he may revoke at any time before probate. Also as to her separate estate, real or personal. Also in exercise of a power of appointment. Also if her husband has abjured the realm, or is an outlaw, or convicted felon. *In the goods of Coward,* 34 L. J. Prob., 120. She may also appoint an executor to continue the personal representation of a testator, of whose will she is sole or surviving executrix. Also when she is judicially separated. Hayes & Jarman, by Eastwood, 82, 6th ed.

13. *Q.* By what means can a married woman effectually convey her interest in fee simple lands?

*A.* If the lands are settled to her separate use and she is not restrained from alienating them, or if she have a power of appointment over them, she may dispose of them absolutely by deed or will as if she were a *feme sole; Taylor* v. *Meads,* 34 L. J. C., 203.

Under other circumstances she can only dispose of her lands by deed acknowledged in the presence of a judge of a superior Court at Westminster, or County Court, or two perpetual Commissioners, who must examine her separately and apart from her husband touching her free consent to the deed. Her husband must concur, and the certificate of the acknowledgement and an affidavit verifying it and of her identity must be filed in the Court of Common Pleas; 3 and 4 Wm. IV., c. 74, s. 80. Land acquired after a judicial separation may also be disposed of by the wife as if she were a *feme sole*; 20 & 21 Vic., c. 85, s. 25. She has a similar power if her husband is civilly dead. The foregoing applies to her lands whether in possession or reversion.

14. *Q.* Can a married woman dispose of a reversionary interest in a sum of money not settled to her separate use, and has the law as to this been changed, and in what respects?

*A.* She may now, by virtue of 20 & 21 Vic., c. 57, dispose of her reversionary interest in personal estate, taken under an instrument operating since 31st December, 1857. The husband must concur in the deed, and she must be examined as mentioned *supra* as to real estate. The act does not extend to interests created by her marriage settlement, or to cases where she is restrained from disposing of the property.

15. *Q.* Money in the funds and on mortgage is settled on A for life, remainder to B, a *feme covert* absolutely. Can B, with or without her husband, by any and what means, pass her reversionary interest to a purchaser?

*A.* See the previous answer.

16. *Q.* Does the 3 & 4 Wm. IV., c. 74, apply to the equitable as well as the legal estates of a married woman, or to leaseholds for years?

*A.* The act applies to both legal and equitable estates of freehold and copyhold, but not to leasehold, which, as above mentioned, the husband may dispose of without his wife's concurrence. Sugden's Real Prop. Stats., 187. *Supra*, No. 2.

17. *Q.* Where a husband and wife mortgage the leasehold estate of the wife, to whom will the equity of redemption belong, if the husband survive the wife?

*A.* The equity of redemption will belong to the husband in his marital right. *Supra.* 1 Roper, Husband and Wife, 173.

18. *Q.* In case the wife be the survivor, to whom will it belong?

*A.* If the wife survives, the equity of redemption will survive to her, provided it be reserved to the husband and wife. If, however, it be reserved to the husband alone, it seems that his administrator will be entitled in preference to the wife, though this is doubtful. 1 Wms. Exors., 614.

19. *Q.* Can a married woman by any, and what, means sever a joint-tenancy of real or personal estate?

*A.* She may do so by deed acknowledged under 3 & 4 Wm. IV., c. 74; or if the land is settled to her separate use, or the property is personal, she may sever the tenancy without these formalities.

20. *Q.* When a woman, seised of an estate of inheritance, marries, who can properly grant leases thereof, and to whom should the rent be reserved, and with whom should the covenants be entered into?

*A.* The husband may now grant leases alone in respect of his estate for a period of twenty-one years. 19 & 20 Vic., c. 120. The rent would be reserved to, and the covenants entered into with him. The leases must be conformable with the provisions of the act mentioned, *supra*, p. 145, No. 57, with regard to tenants for life. The above question was asked before this act, when it was the practice for such leases to be granted by both husband and wife, the rent being reserved to them both, and the heirs of the wife.

21. *Q.* In what cases must the husband take out letters of administration in order to obtain his wife's chattels personal?

*A.* He must take out administration when there are choses in action belonging to his deceased wife, which he has not reduced into possession during the coverture. 1 Rop., Husb. and Wife, 205.

22. *Q.* What are the rights of a husband with respect to his wife's reversionary property?

*A.* He has no power to dispose of such property, whether real or personal, or chattels real, without his wife's concurrence. The reason for this is that he cannot reduce the reversionary property into possession. It was once thought that he could pass a good title in such property for valuable consideration, but the contrary is now clearly settled. *Purdew* v. *Jackson*, 1 Russ. 1; 1 Wms. Exors. 764, m.

23. *Q.* A husband and wife execute a joint assignment of a legacy, which remains unpaid during the husband's life: will the purchaser have a good title if the wife survive her husband?

*A.* The purchaser will not have a good title as against the wife. The husband could only pass to a purchaser his own interest in the legacy, which was entirely dependent upon its being reduced into possession during the coverture. This was not done, and the concurrence of the wife could have no effect, her power to consent being taken away by marriage.

24. *Q.* What is common law dower, and who is entitled to it; and how does it differ from dower as regulated by the 3 & 4 Wm. IV., c. 105?

*A.* At common law, the widow's dower consisted of one-third of the freehold estates of inheritance of the husband, of which he was solely seized during the coverture, and to which issue which the wife might have had might by possibility have been heir. This right to dower, when it had once attached, could only have been barred by fine, the married woman being examined. To prevent it attaching lands were usually conveyed to dower uses. By the above act a simple disposition by the husband during the coverture, or by will, bars the right to dower. All partial alienations, such as incumbrances and debts, are good against the widow's claim. A simple declaration by deed or will is a sufficient bar, so is a devise to her of land out of which she is dowable. Another important alteration is that the widow can claim dower out of estates to which the husband has a right merely, without being seised; also out of equitable estates. 3 & 4 Wm. IV., c. 105 ; William's R. P. 211.

25. *Q.* Is the title to dower, since the act relating to dower, enlarged, and in what instances? Is the right circumscribed?

*A.* See the previous answer.

26. *Q.* State and explain the common uses to bar dower?

*A.* The uses were as follows :— A general power of appointment was given to the purchaser during his life; in default of appointment the estate was given to the purchaser for life; in the event of the determination of this estate in the purchaser's lifetime an estate was limited to a trustee and his heirs during the life of the purchaser; finally, there was a limitation to the heirs of the purchaser. The effect of the above was to give the husband a power of appointment, a life estate and a remainder in fee, out of none of which estates was the widow then dowable. Wms. R. P., 275.

27. *Q.* Is the widow of a tenant in tail, who died without issue, entitled to dower? Would the widow's right, if any, be affected, and how, if her deceased husband had been tenant in tail after possibility of issue extinct?

*A.* The widow would be entitled to dower if issue of hers might have inherited the estate. Birth of issue is immaterial. The tenancy in tail after possibility determines upon the husband's death, therefore, his widow (second wife) could not be entitled to dower. Notes, L. C. Conv., 57.

28. *Q.* What is the difference between a jointure and a dower; how is the former constituted, and how does the latter arise?

*A.* Jointure is a provision for the wife in lieu of dower, and consists of a rent charge upon the husband's lands. It accrues in consequence of express stipulation, whereas dower does not. So it is of uncertain amount, but dower, as above-mentioned, is out of one-third of the lands. Jointure is usually constituted by marriage settlement, a grant being made therein of a rent charge. As to dower see *supra*, No. 24.

29. *Q.* What is the effect of a jointure upon dower, when the instrument creating the jointure does not contain the common stipulation, that the jointure is to be in lieu of dower? Can a widow be entitled to both — if so, in what case?

*A.* In the absence of the common stipulation, dower would not be barred at law, but equity might imply an intention that it was intended as a bar. *Vizard* v. *Longdale*, 3 Atk., 8. A widow would be entitled to her dower and jointure if any of the following requisites were wanting.—1. The jointure must be for the widow's life, to take effect in possession after her husband's death. 2. It must be for her own life. 3. It must be to her and no other for her. 4. It must be in satisfaction of her whole dower. 5. It must (except as above-mentioned in equity) be expressed to be in satisfaction of her dower. Also, if made after marriage she may elect. 27 Hen. VIII., c. 10; Notes, L. C. Conv., 63.

30. *Q.* In what does dower consist, according to the custom of gavelkind?

*A.* It consists of a moiety of the husband's lands. But it continues only as long as the widow remains chaste and unmarried. Wms. R. P., 209.

31. *Q.* An estate is mortgaged to A in fee; he enters as mortgagee and then dies, leaving a widow. Is she dowable of this estate?

*A.* At law she would be dowable, but not so in equity, unless at her husband's death, in consequence of lapse of time or other circumstances, there be no one entitled to redeem. Notes, L. C. Conv., 59.

32. *Q.* A having married after the "Dower Act," purchased and was duly admitted to copyhold lands, and by a deed executed by him declared that his widow should not be entitled to dower out of such copyhold land. Will the widow be barred of her customary dower out of such copyhold land by such deed?

*A.* The customary dower of the widow will not be barred by the deed. The "Dower Act," 3 & 4 Wm. IV., c. 105, does not apply to Freebench. Sugden's Real Prop. Stats., 248, 2nd ed.

33. *Q.* What are the requisites necessary to be observed to bar the dower of a wife before marriage?

*A.* See *supra*, Nos. 24-29.

34. *Q.* How can the dower of a wife married before the "Dower Act," came into operation be defeated? and why do such limitations effectually bar dower? and how can the dower of a wife, married subsequently to that act be defeated?

*A. Supra*, No. 26.

35. *Q.* Can a husband act, to any, and what, extent, for his wife as executrix without her consent?

*A.* He may alone dispose of the personal estate vested in his wife as executrix. Also, he may release debts owing to the estate of the testator. Also, he may refer matters to arbitration. He may recover debts due to the testator, but in doing so he must join the wife. 2 Wms. Exors., 869, 5th ed.

36. *Q.* What is a tenant by the curtesy, and what is required to the creation of the estate?

*A.* He is one entitled on the death of his wife to the lands of inheritance of which she was seised during the coverture. The requisites are:—A legal marriage. Actual seisin. Issue born alive during the life of the mother, capable of inheriting. Lastly, the death of the wife. At common law, it extends to the whole of the lands, but in gavel-kind, only to half, and only on condition of the husband remaining unmarried, but it attaches whether there was issue born or not. Steph. Com., 1, 270.

37. *Q.* To entitle a husband to curtesy, is it necessary that the issue of the marriage should be the next heirs to the estate of the wife?

*A.* It is necessary that the issue take directly by descent from the wife. Notes, L. C. Conv., 52.

38. *Q.* How may curtesy be barred during the joint lives of husband and wife?

*A.* The birth and entry of a posthumous brother of the wife will bar the estate; also, a recovery of the wife's estate in an action? also, if the husband is attainted for treason or felony his curtesy cannot be claimed; also, the attainder of the wife before issue born will be a bar; so will a settlement before marriage giving a husband and wife a life estate in the wife's lands. Notes, L. C. Conv., 53.

## XIII.—*Infancy.*

1. *Q.* Can a father or mother appoint a guardian to his or her children? By what means may guardians of infants be appointed?

*A.* The father may by will, or deed in the nature of a will do so, but the mother has no such power. 32 Hen. VIII., c. 34. See further *infra*, Equity, "infants."

2. *Q.* Can the infant heir of an intestate mortgagee in fee convey the legal estate, and by what means?

*A.* The infant cannot himself convey, but an order may be obtained from the Court of Chancery vesting the estate in the person entitled, and such order has the same effect as if the infant had been of age and had conveyed. 13 & 14 Vic., c. 60, s. 7.

3. *Q.* Can infants make valid settlements of their real and personal estate upon their marriage? and state what infants can do so, and at what age.

*A.* Male infants at the age of twenty, and females at the age of seventeen may make binding settlements upon their marriage with the approbation of the Court of Chancery, obtained on petition. 18 & 19 Vic., c. 43. See next answer.

4. *Q.* Can an infant tenant in tail, or an infant having a power of appointment over property, make a valid settlement in all events? and if not, state the events upon the happening of which the settlement would be void.

*A.* The settlement would not be valid in the event of the death of the infant under age, so far as it operated as an exercise of a power of appointment, or a disentailing assurance. Ibid.

## XIV.—*Settlements.*

1. *Q.* State the usual heads of a marriage settlement of real estate.

*A.* They are—after the date and parties; the recital of the marriage, and agreement to settle; the testatum; declaration of the trusts of the property which has probably, by a separate instrument, being assigned to trustees; if real estate the limitations of it; provisions in the event of the limitations failing; provision for raising the pin money, jointure, and portions, by terms of years vested in trustees; hotchpot, maintenance, accumulation and advancement clauses; the various powers, such as those of leasing, sale, and exchange, and appointment of new trustees. Prideaux's Precedents, 16; *et seq.* and see *infra.*

2. *Q.* What words of limitation would you use in a settlement, by deed, of freehold estates for the purposes of creating estates tail in the sons of A, and B his wife, successively, according to seniority, with remainders to the daughters of A and B, as tenants in common in tail, with cross remainders between such daughters in tail?

*A.* They would be—"To the use of the first and every other son of the said A, by the said B successively in remainder, one after the other, according to their respective seniorities, and the heirs male of their respective bodies; and in default of such issue, to the use of the daughters of the said A by the said B, and the heirs of their respective bodies, in equal shares as tenants in common; and if and so often as any of the said daughters shall die without issue, then as well as to her original share, as also as to the share or shares which shall have survived or accrued to her, or to the heirs of her body, to the use of the others of the said daughters, and the heirs of their respective bodies, in equal shares as tenants in common. And if all the said daughters but one shall die without issue, or there shall be but one such daughter, then as to the entirety to the use of such one daughter, and the heirs of her body." 3 Davidson's Prec., 866—1117.

3. *Q.* In what manner would you by the same deed settle leasehold estates (held for a term of years) for the benefit of the same persons as are named in the previous question, and for the same estates (so far as the different nature and tenure of the property will allow), and with the same priority?

*A.* I should, after the previous life estates, give them to trustees, "upon trust to stand possessed of the premises, upon such trusts and with and subject to such powers, provisoes, agreements, and declarations as shall correspond with the uses, trusts, etc., hereinbefore declared of the said premises hereinbefore expressed to be granted, as near as the different nature and quality of the premises and the rules of law and equity will permit, and so that the same shall not vest absolutely in any person hereby made tenant in tail male, unless he shall attain the age of twenty-one years, but on his death under that age shall go as if they had been freeholds of inheritance, included in the grant and limitations hereinbefore contained." Ibid., 1012.

4. *Q.* On a proposed marriage, where the intended husband is seised in fee of real estate of the annual value of £1,000, and the intended wife's fortune is £10,000, what would be the usual and proper settlement of the wife's fortune, and settlement of the husband's real estate?

*A.* The wife's fortune would be assigned to trustees, upon trust to pay the income to her separate use during life, without power of anticipation. After her decease to the husband for life. After the decease of the survivor the fund to be in trust for the children, as the husband and wife, or the survivor, should appoint. In default of appointment for the children equally, sons at twenty-one, daughters at twenty-one, or marriage, with consent. In default of children, there would be an ultimate trust, as the wife should appoint; in default of appointment to the next-of-kin of the wife. The real estate would be settled in strict settlement, namely, to the first and other sons in tail (*supra*, No. 2). There would be no pin money or jointure terms, as the income of the £10,000 would be sufficient for the wife. The estate, moreover, is not large enough to be charged with portions, therefore the £10,000 must suffice for the younger children. The ultimate remainder of the estate would be to the husband and his heirs. Wms. Pers. Prop., Appendix B; 2 Prid. Prec., 237.

5. *Q.* On a settlement of personal estate only, where the whole or principal fund is derived from the wife, what is the usual and proper settlement of her property, and of that of her intended husband?

*A.* The wife's property would be settled as mentioned in the preceding answer. The husband's personalty would also be vested in trustees, upon trust for himself for life, then to the wife for life, the corpus to go to the children, as they jointly appoint; in default of appointment to them equally; in default of children as the husband should appoint; in default of appointment to his next-of-kin.

6. *Q.* A B, a barrister in considerable practice, on his marriage with C D, proposes to settle £10,000. The father of C D gives her £5,000 as a marriage portion. Upon what terms would you advise that these sums should be settled?

*A.* The husband should have a life interest in the £10,000, the income of it should then go to the wife for life. The £5,000 should be settled to the separate use of the wife, without power of anticipation; after her decease to the husband for life. Upon the death of the survivor, the two funds to be in trust for the issue of the marriage as the husband and wife, or in default, the survivor shall appoint; in default of appointment to the children equally, to vest at twenty-one, or marriage of females. In default of issue, the £10,000 to go to the husband absolutely, and the wife's £5,000 should be upon trust for her absolutely, if she survive her husband, if not, as she shall appoint: in default of appointment, then the fund to go to the persons who, under the Statute of Distributions, would have been entitled had she died intestate, and without leaving a husband surviving.

7. *Q.* You are instructed to prepare a settlement on the marriage of a client, and the property to be settled consists of money in the funds belonging to the wife. State the general provisions which should be made by the settlement in such a case.

*A.* See the previous answers, as to the limitations of the property. The other provisions would be—investment clause; hotchpot; maintenance and education and accumulation clauses; power of advancement; power to invest in the purchase of lands; trust for sale of the land to be purchased; power of leasing the purchased estate; power to appoint new trustees. Wms. Pers. Prop., App. B.

8. *Q.* Upon an intended marriage, it is proposed that the income of the personal property of the wife shall be settled upon the husband for his life, if it can be secured against being affected by any assignment or charge which he may make, and against his creditors. Can this risk be effectually guarded against, and how?

*A.* The income of the wife's property may be given upon trust for the husband for life, with a gift over to the wife, on any assignment, charge, or bankruptcy of the husband. See the next answer.

9. *Q.* If the personal property to be settled belong to the husband, and the first life interest be reserved to him, can that be secured against the assignment, charge, or incumbrance referred to in the preceding question?

*A.* No, it cannot, at least against his assignees in bankruptcy. The husband is not allowed to defeat the claims of his creditors by limiting his property in this way. As to such a settlement being good as against the alienees of the husband, depends upon whether they have notice of the settlement. An important exception to the above rule is where the husband has received a part of his wife's fortune, and his property is settled to go over on bankruptcy, etc. In such a case, the gift over to the extent of her property received by the husband will be valid, she being treated as a purchaser. 2 Prideaux's Precedents, 143.

10. *Q.* What provisions would you insert in a marriage settlement for the protection of a wife and children, where the intended husband is in a precarious trade?

*A.* See the previous answers.

11. *Q.* By a marriage settlement of personal estate, the fund was settled upon the wife for life, without power of anticipation, remainder to the husband for life; and after the death of the survivor it was to be divided amongst the children in equal shares, sons taking vested interests at twenty-one, and daughters at that age or date of marriage. The husband is dead, and all the children have attained twenty-one. The widow and children are desirous to have the fund transferred to them by the trustees: can this be done with safety to the trustees during the life of the widow? State a reason for your answer.

*A.* The trustees may safely transfer the fund if the widow and children concur. The coverture being over, the widow may dispose of her interest as she pleases; so can also the children, they being *sui juris*, therefore the trustees can obtain a valid discharge.

12. *Q.* Can trustees of a settlement under the ordinary powers of sale sell their trust estate, reserving the minerals?

*A.* Trustees have such a power, with or without the rights or powers of or incidental to the working, getting, or carrying away of such minerals, unless expressly forbidden to do so by the instrument creating the trust. They may also sell the minerals separately from the land. The sanction of the court must be first obtained on petition. 25 & 26 Vic., c. 108.

13. *Q.* By the act of the last session (24 & 25 Vic.), called the

Trustees and Mortgagees Act, passed 28th August, 1860, in all cases where, by deed, will, or other instrument of settlement, executed after the passing of the act, a power of sale is given,—there being given by the act authority to exercise such power of sale, in the way, under the restrictions, and with the powers therein mentioned,—describe in a general way the powers and authorities so given by the act.

*A.* They empower trustees to sell in lots, and either by public auction or private contract. The sale may be under special conditions, and the trustees may buy in. The trustees may convey, and the money to arise from the sale is to be laid out in other lands, or on the payment of incumbrances. The money not to be laid out, nor lands exchanged elsewhere than in the country in which the lands sold or exchanged are situate. Until the purchase of land, the money is to be invested at interest. No sale is to take place without the consent of the tenant for life. Sections 1—10.

14. *Q.* Considering that the Trustees and Mortgagees Act, 1860, gives to trustees who, under any instrument made after the act, have a power of sale, certain powers for facilitating that object, and that the provisions of the act may be negatived or adopted with variations; say, so far as you have considered the act, what in an ordinary case would, in your judgment, be the right course as to negativing or adopting these provisions?

*A.* I should negative these provisions, unless the land settled is inconsiderable, or where the settlor strongly objects to the increased expense. It is generally desirable that trustees should be able to ascertain what are their powers and duties with regard to a sale, without having to go beyond their deed. 2 Prideaux's Precedents, 149, 4th ed.

15. *Q.* Does or does not the proviso in the Trustees Act, 1860, making the receipt of the trustee for money payable to him in exercise of the trust or power, a discharge from liability to see to the application in practice supersede an express clause? Give reasons or remarks.

*A.* In consequence of the provision referred to, an express clause is now unnecessary, and should be omitted. The reason is, that its insertion would be surplusage, and an unnecessary expense. 2 Prideaux's Precedents, 149.

16. *Q.* In the case of a settlement or will, not negativing the powers or incidents of the Trustees Act of 1860, does or does not the act confer sufficient powers for the appointment of new trustees, so as in practice to supersede express powers, or what is necessary to be expressed to give the powers due effect?

*A.* To make the power conferred by the act effectual, it is necessary to name some person in the will or settlement as a donee of the power. The saving of length is therefore trifling, and it is advisable still to insert the express power as hitherto, more especially as it provides for a case not referred to in the act, viz., that of a trustee going to reside abroad. 2 Prideaux's Precedents, 149.

17. *Q.* What powers are usually inserted in marriage settlements where large estates are limited in strict settlement, and by whom, and under what authority, are they to be exercised?

*A.* The usual powers are—powers of distress and entry to the wife to recover her jointure; power to the trustees of the jointure term to raise the jointure by mortgage; powers to raise portions for younger children; power to the husband to jointure a future wife, and to charge with portions for children of a future marriage; power to the husband during life, and the trustees afterwards, to grant leases for various periods; powers to the trustees, at the request of the husband, to enfranchise the copyholds, to effect a partition, to sell and exchange, to revoke the uses, to purchase lands, excepting the minerals, and minerals excepting the surface; power to change trustees, and appoint new ones. 2 Prideaux's Precedents, 237.

18. *Q.* Suppose the case of a father, tenant for life, remainder to his eldest son in tail, remainders over, and that it is desired to disentail, and re-settle, the father joining as protector. Ought he to retain his life estate, or take a new one, and what ordinarily would be the uses of the re-settlement?

*A.* It is usual in practice to give the father the first life estate under the re-settlement. Subject to this an estate is given to the eldest son for life, remainder to the use of the first and other sons of the eldest son successively in tail male, remainder to the use of the second son of the father for life, remainder to his first and other sons successively in tail male, remainder to the use of the third son for life, and so on. There would be an ultimate remainder to the use of the father in fee. 3 Davidson's Prec., 907, 2nd ed.

19. *Q.* Suppose the last case to be on the son's marriage, what would ordinarily be the uses of the settlement with jointure, portions, and strict entail. Describe the uses briefly and generally.

*A.* The estate would be limited to the subsisting uses until the marriage; afterwards to the use that the intended husband may receive a rent charge during his life, and that the wife may receive a rent charge for jointure of a certain amount, during the life of the husband's father, and of larger amount after his death. Remainder to the rent charge trustees for 200 years; remainder to the father for life; remainder to the intended husband for life; remainder to the portions trustees for 600 years; remainder to the first and every other son of the husband in tail male; remainder to the husband's brothers for life, and to their first and other sons in tail male: remainder to the first and every other sons of the husband in tail; remainder to his first and every other daughter in tail; remainder to the brother's sons in tail and daughters in tail; ultimate remainder to the husband in fee. Ibid., 907.

20. *Q.* By a marriage settlement, a sum of money is to be raised for younger children of the marriage: what is the usual mode by which it is effected?

*A.* The portions are secured by limiting a term of years to trustees, whose duty it is to raise the portions of the younger children by mortgage or sale of the premises out of which the term is created. The aggregate amount of the sum for portions is fixed by the settlement, the actual share of each child being left to their father and mother's appointment. In default of appointment to them equally. The portion term is also used for the purpose of securing the jointure. 2 Prideaux's Precedents, 243.

21. *Q.* To what extent can real estate be settled without violating the rule against perpetuities?

*A.* See *supra*, "Uses and Trusts," p. 167, No. 30.

22. *Q.* State the principal provisions of the "Settled Estate Act," 19 & 20 Vic., c. 120.

*A.* See *infra* "Equity." "The Statutory Jurisdiction," and *supra*, p. 145, No. 57.

23. *Q.* What is a voluntary settlement? and can it be defeated in any, and what, manner?

*A.* It is a settlement which is made without a good or valuable consideration. That is, without any consideration whatever, as if in favour of a stranger; or upon what is termed a meritorious consideration, as in favour of a near relation. It may be revoked if a power of revocation is reserved; also by a sale to a *bond fide* purchaser. 27 Eliz., c. 4. Notes to *Twynne's Case*, 1 Sm. L. C., 1.

24. *Q.* Will a voluntary settlement bind a purchaser or mortgagee with notice of it?

*A.* A purchaser or mortgagee will not be bound by the settlement, even if they have notice of it. 27 Eliz., c. 4.

25. *Q.* Is a purchaser for a *good* consideration from a voluntary grantee in a better situation as to title than the voluntary grantee?

*A.* Assuming the word "good" to indicate "meritorious" or "voluntary," as distinguished from valuable, the sub-purchaser would be in no better position, as he would himself be merely a volunteer. If, however, the word "good" is intended to indicate "valuable," the sub-purchaser is in a much better position than his vendor, as he cannot be disturbed by a subsequent *bond fide* purchaser from the original settlor. *Prodgers* v. *Langham*, Keb., 486. (The word "good" is sometimes used by text writers to indicate two distinct kinds of consideration.)

26. *Q.* Against whom is a voluntary conveyance valid, and under what circumstance does it cease to be a flaw in a title?

*A.* It is valid against the settlor and all subsequent volunteers claiming under him, notwithstanding the want of consideration. It will cease to be a flaw in the title of a purchaser from the settlor so soon as it has been ascertained that the volunteer has not previously sold to a *bond fide* purchaser. The volunteer, on the other hand, will be safe as soon as the settlor dies without making a conveyance for value. *Doe* v. *Rusham*, 17 Q. B., 723. So, also, even before such death a purchaser from the volunteer will be safe if he purchased before the settlor has conveyed for value. See previous answer.

27. *Q.* So far as a voluntary settlement is void under the statute of Elizabeth (13 Eliz., c. 5), state under what circumstances of indebtedness and in respect of its existing at the time or arising subsequently, such a settlement is liable to be set aside? and does the law extend to a settlement of personal as well as real property?

*A.* It has been held that the settlor must be insolvent at the time of making the voluntary deed. The authorities are, however, conflicting. The result of them appears to be that there must be unpaid debts, which were existing at the time of making the settlement, and the settlor must have been at the time not necessarily insolvent, but so largely indebted as to induce the court to believe it was intended to defraud the creditors. *Holmes* v. *Penny*, 3 K. & J., 99. Notes to *Twynne's Case*, 1 Sm. L.C., 1. The act of 13 Eliz., c. 5, applies both to realty and personalty.

28. *Q.* A covenants by marriage settlement that he will, within three years from the marriage, settle real estates of the value of £10,000 upon certain trusts for the benefit of his intended wife, and the children of the marriage; no particular estates are specified in the covenant: at the time of the settlement A had two real estates only, each worth £5,000, which he afterwards conveyed to purchasers; to one within, and to the other after, the expiration of the three years: the wife and child of the marriage were living at the time of both the conveyances, and both the purchasers knew that fact, and were also aware of the covenant, and that A had no other real estates. Has the wife or child any, and what, claim on the two estates, or on either, and which of them?

*A.* In this case the wife or child have no remedy as to either of the estates against the purchasers, but they will be considered creditors by specialty of A. It has indeed been thought that if the covenant is limited as to time, as in the above case, a lien would be created upon lands then in the hands of the covenantor. *Randall* v. *Breary*, 2 Vern., 482. But this case has been impugned as being mis-reported. *Mornington* v. *Keane*, 2 De G. & J., 292. See 313.

29. *Q.* A, previously to marriage, covenants with trustees that he will lay out the sum of £10,000 in the purchase of freehold lands, to be settled to the use of himself for life, with remainder to his first and other sons, with remainder to his right heirs. He dies, leaving his wife surviving, and leaving issue a daughter only. No purchase having been effected, the daughter claims the £10,000. Is she entitled to it?

*A.* The daughter is not entitled; the reason being, that she does not come within the terms of the settlement, which is confined to "sons," and they only can enforce the covenant. If the covenant had been entered into by a stranger, or the money had been vested in trustees, it is presumed the daughter could have enforced the covenant, as the heir of the covenantee. But she, as heir under the circumstances mentioned in the question, has no equity against the personal representatives of A. *Pulteney* v. *Darlington*, 1 Bro. C. C.. 223; *Lechmere* v. *Lechmere*, Cases, *temp.* Talbot, 80.

## XV.—*Artificial Persons.*

1. *Q.* How can a corporation legally bind itself?

*A.* A corporation usually binds itself by its common seal. But in certain cases it is liable for acts not thus authorised. Thus, it is liable for acts of necessity, also for many acts done by its head, as the mayor or dean; also if something to be of avail must be done immediately, as to distrain cattle damage feasant. Chitty on Contracts, 250.

2. *Q.* How must freehold property be conveyed by a corporation?

*A.* Such property may be conveyed by feoffment, grant, or other common law conveyances, under their common seal, but not by those operating by virtue of the Statute of Uses, or by will. Watkins' Conv., 448.

3. *Q.* Can municipal corporations by their own, or what, authority, absolutely dispose of their lands?

*A.* They may absolutely dispose of their lands with the approbation of the Lords of the Treasury, or any three of them. They may, however, demise the lands for a period not exceeding thirty-one years, without such approbation. 5 & 6 Wm. IV., c. 76, s. 94; 6 & 7 Wm. IV., c. 104, s. 2.

## XVI.—*Bankrupt-Owner.*

1. *Q.* When does a bankrupt's real estate vest in his assignees?

*A.* The real estate, excepting copyholds, vests in them on their appointment, and their title relates back to the act of bankruptcy. Bankruptcy Act of 1849, s. 142.

2. *Q.* What is the effect of a bankruptcy on a general power to appoint real estate?

*A.* The power may be exercised by the assignees for the benefit of the creditors, unless it be the right of nomination to an ecclesiastical benefice. This the bankrupt may exercise. Ibid., s. 147.

## XVII.—*Landlord and Tenant, and the Law of Leases.*

1. *Q.* A, in writing, agrees to let land to B for a term of years, at a certain rent; B enters into possession, and pays the rent to A: what is B's tenancy, and what right has he against A?

*A.* B is a tenant for years, and he has the right to enjoy the land for the duration of the term, without interruption by A, so long as he (B) pays the rent, and in other respects conforms to his contract with A.

2. *Q.* What leases must be by deed?

*A.* All leases exceeding the term of three years from the making, or at a lower rent than two-thirds of the full improved value, must, by 29 Car. II., c. 3, be in writing. By 8 & 9 Vic., c. 106, all such leases must be by deed.

3. *Q.* For how long may an agreement for a tenancy be made by parol?

*A.* For the period of three years from the making of the lease, provided two-thirds of the full improved value is reserved. 29 Car. II., c. 3.

4. *Q.* What is a lease, whence is the word derived, what are the general provisions relating to it, and what is the lessee when he enters by force of the lease?

*A.* It is a conveyance of property for life, for years, or at will, by one who has a greater interest in the property. The person conveying is called the lessor, the person conveyed to, the lessee. The latter usually pays a certain rent for the privilege of enjoying the land. The word is derived either from *locatio*, the letting of property, or *laisser*, to let, or *leassum sax*, to enter lawfully. Upon entry, the lessee becomes the legal owner of the term, having the legal estate vested in him, as distinguished from an *interesse termini* above mentioned, p.148, No. 70. As to the provisions relating to a lease see *supra et infra*. Wharton's Law Lexicon, 518.

5. *Q.* What estate must a person have to enable him to make a lease, by which the lessee may derive a present tenancy and occupation?

*A.* He must have a present legal estate in possession in the land, otherwise he cannot grant an effectual lease. His estate must also be greater than that which he creates.

6. *Q.* If a remainder-man, not in possession, make a lease, what estate or interest would the lessee derive under it?

*A.* He would derive no present right to enter, but he would take an *interesse termini*, subject to the estate preceding that of the lessor. By virtue of this he would be entitled to enter upon the land when the lessor's estate came into possession. (It is difficult to see how a remainder-man could be in possession, at least if such possession was in respect of the remainder alluded to in the question.)

7. *Q.* Explain the provisions of the Acts 1849, 1850, for remedying defects in leases under powers. What provision is made for giving validity to leases invalid by reason of deviation from the terms of the power, and what provisions for the confirmation of such leases?

*A.* These acts were passed for the purpose of preventing leases under powers being set aside, owing to some informality. Now, leases under powers, if made *bond fide*, and the lessee has entered, are considered as contracts in equity for a valid lease, varied so as to conform to the terms of the power. If, however, the reversioner is able and willing to confirm the lease without variation, the lessee is bound to accept such confirmation. The confirmation may be by memorandum in writing, signed by the reversioner and lessee; also the simple acceptance of rent by the reversioner will be deemed a confirmation as against him, if he signs a receipt or memorandum confirming the lease. Wms. Real Prop., 277.

8. *Q.* If joint tenants make a demise, what tenancy has the lessee?

*A.* If the joint tenants concur, the lessee's interest continues, notwithstanding the decease of either of the lessors, and the whole rent is payable to the survivor. If one joint tenant makes a lease, it will be good as to his moiety during his life, and also that of the survivor. 1 Platt on L., 124—127.

9. *Q.* If tenants in common make a lease, what tenancy has the lessee?

*A.* The lease from a tenant in common will be good as to his landlord's undivided interest, and so long as his interest continues. If several tenants in common concur in leasing, the lease will operate as the distinct demise of each tenant of his part, and not as the joint demise of all. Ibid., 131.

10. *Q.* What leases can infants make, and what would be the tenancy of the lessee?

*A.* Infants cannot alone make leases binding upon themselves, unless by custom, at the age of fifteen; though they may enforce them against the lessee. The lease is voidable at the option of the infant, and he may confirm it on coming of age, as by the receipt of rent, etc. The Court of Chancery has, however, power to authorise binding leases of the estates of infants. 1 Wm. IV., c. 65, ss. 12, 16, and 17.

11. *Q.* Suppose the husband to demise the wife's lands, and she survive her husband, what positive or contingent tenancy has the lessee?

*A.* Until recently the tenant might have been ejected by the widow; his tenancy, therefore, was contingent upon this not being done. Now, however, as mentioned above, "Baron and Feme," No. 20, the husband may grant binding leases not exceeding twenty-one years of her land without her consent. 19 & 20 Vic., c. 120.

12. *Q.* What tenancy has a lessee by lease from an idiot or lunatic? and to have a secure tenancy for the term, what course should be adopted? and by what means can idiots and lunatics surrender and renew leases?

*A.* Such a lease is absolutely void. The committee should obtain an order from the Lord Chancellor to grant a lease. Upon their own responsibility they can only let the lands from year to year. Leases are to be surrendered and renewed by the same means. 16 & 17 Vic., c. 76, ss. 129—134; 1 Platt on L., 37.

13. *Q.* Mortgagor and mortgagee: what separate right has each to lease mortgaged premises? and what would be the lessee's tenancy holding a lease from the one without the concurrence of the other?

*A.* Leases by the mortgagor alone are not binding upon the mortgagee (unless he acknowledge their tenancy) who may eject the tenant, but they are binding as between the mortgagor and lessee. Leases by the mortgagee alone are valid as against him, but not against the mortgagor when the mortgage is paid off. The tenancy, therefore, of a lessee from the one without the concurrence of the other would be subject to be determined as above mentioned. It would be at the will of the mortgagee in one case and of the mortgagor in the other. *Keech v. Hall,* 1 Sm. L. C., 505.

14. *Q.* State the principal covenants, on the part of the lessee,

which should be contained in a building lease of land in a town, to be granted by a freeholder.

A. They would be by the lessee to pay rent and taxes; to build a dwelling house according to specification within a specified time; to insure; to keep the premises in repair; liberty to the lessor to enter and view the premises; the messuage only to be used as a dwelling house; proviso for re-entry on non-payment of rent or non-performance of the covenants. Covenant by lessor for quiet enjoyment. 2 Prideaux's Precedents, 43.

15. Q. Show the outline of an ordinary farming lease for seven years.

A. It consists of:—Date. Parties. Testatum. Demise of parcels reserving the minerals, underwood, game, etc. Habendum and reddendum. Covenants by lessee. To pay rent; to keep in repair; to deliver up the premises in good repair; liberty to the lessor to view the premises; the lessee to preserve the young trees, to cleanse the water courses, to protect the game, to cultivate the land in the best course of husbandry, not to take more than two crops of corn, beans, or pulse, successively, to summer fallow part of the land, to spread manure on the fallow, not to plough the meadows, to consume on the premises all the straw and fodder; in the last year the lessee to stack the hay, corn, and crops; the lessor to take the fallows at a valuation; the lessee not to underlet without license. Proviso for re-entry. Covenants by lessor to rebuild in case of accidental fire, for quiet enjoyment, and to pay for the fallows. Ibid, 62.

16. Q. Give the outline of an ordinary lease for twenty-one years of a private house in London.

A. In form the lease would be the same as in the preceding answer. The covenants by the lessee would be to pay rent and taxes; to keep in repair and deliver up in repair; to paint the outside every three years, and the inside every seven years; liberty to the lessor to enter and view the premises; to repair, to insure, to apply the insurance money in rebuilding; not to use the premises except as a dwelling-house, not to assign or underlet without license; proviso for re-entry. Covenant by the lessor for quiet enjoyment. Proviso for determining the term upon notice at the end of seven or fourteen years. Proviso enabling the lessee to purchase on notice. Ibid, 33.

17. Q. State generally the form of the *habendum* of a lease for lives and for years.

A. The *habendum* of the lease for lives would be:—"To have and to hold the said tenement or dwelling-house, hereditaments, and premises hereby granted and demised, or intended so to be, with the appurtenances, unto the said (lessee), his heirs, and assigns, for and during the natural lives of E P, of etc., now aged about   years, M D, of etc., now aged about   years, and R S, of etc., now aged about   years, and for and during the natural life of the longest liver of them." 2 Crabb's Precedents, 418, 3rd ed.

The *habendum* of the lease for years would be :—"To have and to hold the said messuages and premises hereby demised unto the said C D, his executors, administrators, and assigns, for the term of twenty-one years, from the      day of       ." 2 Prideaux's Precedents, 33.

18. *Q.* What is the best form of *reddendum* in a lease?

*A.* It should be :—" Yielding and paying therefore yearly and every year during the said term the rent of £      ." This form is a general reservation of the rent, so that there can be no difficulty in the reversioner, whoever he may be, taking advantage of it. The law carries the rent to the owner of the reversion after the lessor's death ; to his heirs if he be seised in fee; to his personal representatives if he have a chattel interest only. 2 Platt. on L., 88.

19. *Q.* Is a lessee under a covenant to repair liable to rebuild in case of fire?

*A.* The lessee is liable to rebuild under the covenant to repair, unless "damage by fire" is excepted from the covenant, a course which should always be adopted. A general covenant to repair is binding on the tenant, whatever may be the cause of the dilapidation. 2 Platt on L., 186.

20. *Q.* If in a lease the lessee covenant to keep the premises in repair, except damage by fire, or some particular repairs, can he compel the lessor to do the excepted repairs without an express covenant on his part for the purpose?

*A.* The landlord cannot be compelled to repair without an express covenant to do so. 2 Platt on L., 166.

21. *Q.* If a tenant in fee simple make a lease of lands to B, to have and to hold to B for term of life, without mentioning for whose life, what shall it be deemed, and why?

*A.* It will be deemed to be the life of the lessee, for this tenancy is more beneficial than for the life of the lessor. This is upon the maxim "*verba chartarum fortius accipiuntur contra proferentem.*" If, however, the lessor was merely a tenant for life, and the same demise was made, it would be taken to mean the lessor's life, this being the greatest estate he had power to grant. Broom's Maxim's, 572, 4th ed.

22. *Q.* Will a lease be forfeited if the covenant to insure be broken for one year, although performed in subsequent years?

*A.* The subsequent performance of the covenant will not prevent a forfeiture. Such forfeiture may, however, be waived by the landlord receiving rent due since the breach, with a knowledge of the breach. Relief against forfeiture may now be obtained from a court of equity, under 22 & 23 Vic., c. 35, and from a court of law under 23 & 24 Vic., c. 126. *Infra*, No. 30.

23. *Q.* Distinguish between privity of contract and privity of estate.

*A.* Privity of contract is that relationship which exists between two or more contracting parties, in respect of a contract entered into between them. As between vendor and vendee, lessor and lessee. Privity of estate exists in respect of an estate, in lands which has passed from one to another. As, between lessor and lessee (until assignment by the latter). Between lessor and assignee. *Spencer's Case*, 1 Sm. L. C., 43.

24. *Q.* Is a sub-lessee to any, and what, extent liable to the original lessor, under the covenants of the lessee in the original lease?

*A.* A sub-lessee cannot be sued by the lessor, upon the covenants in the lease, as there is neither privity of contract or of estate between them. The lessor must sue the lessee. *Spencer's Case*, 1 Sm. L. C., 43.

25. *Q.* What difference is there between the liability of the lessee and the lessee's assignee in regard to breaches of covenant?

*A.* The lessee is liable in respect of all covenants in the lease during the whole term; but the assignee only on those running with the land, as to pay rent, to repair, etc. The liability of the latter, moreover (excepting as to past breaches), ceases on an assignment by him. See *Spencer's Case*, 1 Sm. L. C., 43.

26. *Q.* How does such liability of the assignee of the lessee differ from the liability of the lessee's executor?

*A.* The assignee is only liable on covenants running with the land, and for breaches committed while he has the term. The lessee's executor is, however, like the lessee, liable on all the covenants. As to the rent, however, he is only liable to the extent of the annual yield of the property. 2 Platt on Leases, 372. If the lease is of no value, it is customary to assign it to a pauper, so as to discharge the executor. But now he should take advantage of 22 & 23 Vic., c. 35, s. 27, by virtue of which, after satisfying existing liabilities, and providing for future ones, and having sold the lease to a purchaser, he is protected from any subsequent claim, and may distribute the assets. Woodfall, 232, 8th ed.

27. *Q.* What is meant by the expression " a covenant running with the land"?

*A.* The expression is used to denote those covenants, which, as just mentioned, bind the assignee of the term. In order to bind him they must relate to the land, or be to do something to a thing *in esse* upon it. Thus, a covenant to repair an existing wall will run; not so, however, a covenant to build a wall. *Spencer's Case, supra,* first resolution. But in the latter case the assignee would be bound, if named in the covenant, as it is to do a thing upon the demised premises. Ibid., second resolution.

28. *Q.* What are the necessary incidents to make a covenant run with the land?

*A.* See the previous answers.

29. *Q.* A takes a beneficial lease, and afterwards assigns it to a purchaser. Do he and his executors remain liable to the rent and covenants? and if they do, how may they be most effectually protected against them?

*A.* As above shown, they remain liable to the rent and covenants. The practice is for the purchaser to covenant to indemnify the lessee against future breaches, and the non-payment of the rent. *Infra,*

No. 32. The liability of the executor is now limited to the time when he makes the sale, if before doing so he has satisfied all the liabilities under the lease which have accrued due, and shall have set apart a sufficient fund to answer any future claim in respect of any fixed or ascertained sum covenanted to be laid out. 22 & 23 Vic., c. 35, s. 27.

30. *Q.* What breaches of covenants in a lease will operate as a forfeiture? and has the lessee any, and what, relief in equity, on any, and what, terms, in regard to any, and which, of such breaches?

*A.* This will depend upon the terms of the lease, but usually the power of re-entry is given on breach of the covenant to pay rent, to repair, to insure, and, indeed, of all the covenants. Woodfall, 272, 8th ed. The courts of equity, and also of law, may relieve upon such terms as they think fit, against forfeiture for breach of covenant to insure where no loss or damage by fire has happened, and the breach has, in the opinion of the court, been committed through accident or mistake, or otherwise, without fraud or gross negligence, and there is an insurance on foot at the time of the application to the court, in conformity with the covenant. A record of the relief granted is to be made on the lease. The same person is not to be relieved more than once in respect of the same covenant or condition, and no relief is to be given where a forfeiture under the covenant has already been waived out of court. The lessor is to have the benefit of an informal insurance. Relief may also be obtained from a court of law and equity, for forfeiture for non-payment of rent. 22 & 23 Vic., c. 35, ss. 4—9; 23 & 24 Vic., c. 126, s. 2.

31. *Q.* Can the omission by a lessee to perform a covenant to insure, to repair, or to pay rent, be cured, and how?

*A.* As to insurance and payment of rent see the preceding answer. No relief can, however, be obtained for forfeiture for non-repair. *Gregory* v. *Wilson*, 9 Hare, 683.

32. *Q.* What are the usual covenants in an assignment of a lease?

*A.* They are, by the vendor; that the lease is valid and subsisting; and the rent and covenants paid and performed; that he has good right to assign, for peaceable enjoyment during the term, free from incumbrances and for further assurance. Covenants by the purchaser for payment of the rent and observance of the covenants, and for indemnifying the vendor therefrom. 1 Prideaux's Precedents, 164.

33. *Q.* In what position would a lessee, holding over after the expiration of his lease, stand with reference to his landlord?

*A.* He would be a tenant at sufferance and liable to be turned out at any moment. *Supra*, p. 148, Nos. 71, 72.

34. *Q.* Define and explain the nature and effect of attornment.

*A.* It is the acknowledgment by a tenant of a new landlord. In former times it was thought fair that a new landlord should not be forced upon a tenant without his consent, therefore, the tenant was allowed to exercise his will as to such change by attorning to the new landlord or not as he pleased. Now, however, the necessity of attornment is abolished, and upon a sale of lands a notice by the purchaser to the tenant to pay the rent to him is substituted. 4 Anne, c. 16, ss. 9, 10; 11 Geo. II., c. 19, s. 11. Nor by the latter act has an attornment any effect as to the possession of the lands, unless made with the consent of the landlord, or to a mortgagee after the mortgage is forfeited, or by direction of a court of justice.

35. *Q.* Does the surrender of an original lease affect an under-lease? and give a reason for your answer.

*A.* The under-lease is not affected, as the next vested estate is to be considered the reversion expectant upon the under-lease. That is, the estate in which the lease is merged supplies its place. Formerly the result was otherwise. 8 & 9 Vic., c. 106, s. 9.

36. *Q.* A holds a lease for several lives, and he makes under-leases; upon the death of one of the lives he wishes to surrender the existing lease, and to have a new lease for the existing lives, with the addition of one in the place of the deceased. Would it be necessary that the under-lessees concur in the surrender or not?

*A.* Their concurrence is not necessary. Formerly the effect of the surrender was to prevent the recovery of the rent from the under-lessee, but this was remedied by 4 Geo. II., c. 28. This enactment was extended to all cases by the act mentioned in the previous question. Wms. Real Prop., 224.

37. *Q.* A grants a lease to B of certain hereditaments for lives. B grants under-leases of those hereditaments, and afterwards is desirous to have a further or renewed lease of the premises from A. How is that to be effected?

*A.* It may be effected by a surrender to A of the lease for the remaining lives with an immediate renewal of the term by A. See the previous answers.

38. *Q.* In what way can a tenancy from year to year be created, and how can it be determined? Give a form of notice to a tenant from year to year, whose tenancy commenced from one of the usual quarter days? It is supposed to have commenced at Lady Day, but not certain.

*A.* It may be created by contract express or implied. The former is where an express agreement, either verbal or in writing, is entered into. The latter frequently arises where a tenant holds over after the expiration of his term. Also a tenancy at will is frequently converted into a yearly tenancy, a contract being implied from the fact of the yearly payment of rent. It may be determined:—1. By giving six months' notice to quit, to determine at the end of the current year of the tenancy. 2. By the determination of the interest of the lessor. 3. By surrender. 4. By effluxion of time. *Richardson* v. *Langridge*, L. C. Conv., 4, and the notes.

The following would be a good form of notice:—

"I hereby give you notice to quit and deliver up on the 25th day of March next, if the current year of your tenancy expires on that day, or otherwise on the day on which the current year of your tenancy will expire next after the end of half-a-year from the time of your being served with this notice, the possession of the messuage, No. 16, Belgrave Square, which you now hold of me as yearly tenant. Dated the 29th day of September, 1865.

"A. B. (Landlord.)
"To C. D. (Tenant)."

39. *Q.* May a tenancy from year to year, created by parol, be surrendered by parol?

*A.* It may be surrendered by note in writing, but not verbally, 29 Car. II., c. 3, s. 3, requiring all surrenders to be in writing. The writing, however, need not be a deed, as 8 & 9 Vic., c. 106, s. 4, excepts surrenders of interest which by law have been made without writing. The tenancy may, however, be surrendered by operation of law, as by granting to the tenant a lease. This puts an end to the existing tenancy. Woodfall, 253, 8th ed.

40. *Q.* Where a tenancy is for a term of years certain, is any, and what, notice to quit required?

*A.* No notice is necessary as the tenancy will determine by effluxion of time. See *supra*, Common Law, "Landlord and Tenant."

41. *Q.* If a tenancy continue after the expiration of a lease, without any new agreement, on what terms does the tenant hold?

*A.* If the tenant pays rent according to the terms of the old lease (until this is done he is merely tenant at sufferance), it will be presumed that he becomes tenant from year to year upon the terms of the lease, so far as such terms are not inconsistent with such a tenancy. *Doe v. Bell,* 2 Sm. L. C., 92, and notes.

42. *Q.* If a person seised in fee make a lease, reserving rent payable half-yearly, and die in the middle of a half-year, who is entitled to the half-year's rent when due?

*A.* His heir or devisee will be entitled to the whole of the rent. There will be no apportionment in this case with the personal representatives, because the interest of the landlord does not determine on his death. 4 & 5 Wm. IV., c. 22.

43. *Q.* Where a lessor brings an action of ejectment for non-payment of rent reserved by lease for want of sufficient distress on the premises, and obtains judgment and possession under an execution, can the lessee obtain relief at law or in equity?

*A.* He may obtain relief in equity on payment of the rent and costs, and this right to relief is also recognised in Courts of Common Law, C. L. P. Act, 1852, s. 211. *Peachey* v. *Duke of Somerset,* 2 L. C. Eq., 895, and Notes.

44. *Q.* What is the effect of a lease of two farms at an entire rent, one of which belongs to the lessor in fee, and the other is subject to his power of leasing?

*A.* During the lifetime of the lessor the lease would be good as to both farms, but after his death it would be bad against the remainder man as to the lands over which he has a power only. That is, assuming the power to be the ordinary one conferred on a tenant for life by a settlement. The rent should be reserved separately under the power. But even after the death of the lessor the rent will be apportioned as to the lands he held in fee, and the lease as to these will be valid. Platt on Leases, 1, 470.

45. *Q.* What is a disclaimer, and what are its consequences?

*A.* It is a renunciation or denial by a tenant of his landlord's title, either by refusing to pay rent, denying any obligation to pay, or by setting up a title in himself or a third person. The consequence of thus disclaiming is to cause a forfeiture of the lease. A devisee may also disclaim the devise to him, in which case he will take no interest. An heir cannot, however, disclaim as upon the death of his ancestor he becomes immediately seised. Trustees and executors may also disclaim the trust and executorship. Wharton's Lexicon, 283.

46. *Q.* What constitutes waste? State who may not commit waste, and the remedy to restrain it.

*A.* As to this subject see *infra,* "Equity."

## XVIII.—*Fructus Industriales.*

1. *Q.* What are emblements?

*A.* They are the produce of crops sown by a tenant of lands, but which do not come to maturity before the interest of the tenant determines. Under such circumstances, if the tenancy has not been determined by the act of the tenant, he or his personal representatives are deemed entitled to reap that which has been sown. The right to emblements extends to tenants for life, for years and at will. Emblements only include the produce of those crops which are raised by the yearly manual labour of the tenant. Thus fruit, grass, clover, are not emblements; but corn, turnips, potatoes, etc., are. Notes to *Richardson* v. *Langridge,* L. C. Conv. 86.

2. *Q.* When is the lessee of a tenant for life entitled to emblements, and when not? Give the legal rule or maxim as quoted by Blackstone.

*A.* He is entitled to them if the tenancy does not determine by his own act. To a certain extent such under-lessees are in a better position than their lessors, as they are entitled to emblements if the tenant for life determines his estate by his own act, but in such a case he would clearly not be entitled. 1 Steph. Com., 265. The maxim alluded to is "*actus Dei nemini facit injuriam,*" which signifies that the act of God is so treated by the law as to affect no one injuriously. Broom's Maxims, 227.

3. *Q.* What change has recently been made in the law with respect to claims for emblements, where tenancies determine by the death of the landlord, being tenant for life?

*A.* In such cases, the tenants, instead of claiming emblements, continue to hold until the expiration of the then current year of the tenancy, and may then quit, as if the tenancy had been determined by effluxion of time or other lawful means. 14 & 15 Vic., c. 25, s. 1.

4. *Q.* D is a rector, and has sown part of the glebe land with wheat, and dies before harvest time. To whom will this crop belong, and what is such crop denominated?

*A.* The crop is denominated "emblements," and belongs as such to the rector's personal representatives by virtue of 28 Hen. VIII. c. 11.

5. *Q.* Is a tenant at will entitled to emblements, and has he any time allowed him for taking them away?

*A.* A tenant at will is entitled to emblements if his landlord determines his tenancy before the crops are reaped, and to secure and carry them away he has free ingress, egress, and regress. Co. Litt. 56, a.

## XIX.—*Pledges securing Loans.*

1. *Q.* What is a mortgage?

*A.* It is the creation of an interest in property, defeasible upon performing the condition of paying a given sum of money with interest thereon. A day is usually named for the payment of the money, which if not done punctually the lender, called the mortgagee, becomes at law the absolute owner. Equity, however, treats the transaction in the light of a pledge, and allows the borrower, called the mortgagor, to redeem his property by paying off what is due to the mortgagee.

2. *Q.* What is the difference between the *vivum vadium*, or living pledge or vifgage, and the *mortuum vadium*, or dead pledge or mortgage?

*A.* The distinction is this: that in a *vivum vadium*, or living pledge, the property pledged is never lost to the borrower, but the lender enters into possession of the estate, and there remains until his debt and interest is repaid, after which the borrower re-enters. In a *mortuum vadium*, however, the security becomes at law dead or lost to the borrower, if he does not perform the condition of paying the money at the time appointed. A Welsh mortgage may be mentioned also as an instance of a *vivum vadium*, as such a pledge is always redeemable, but the interest is paid out of the profits. Wharton's Lexicon, 608; Wms. Real Prop., 382.

3. *Q.* What are the different kinds of mortgages?

*A.* Mortgages are either legal or equitable. See *supra et infra*.

4. *Q.* Explain what is meant by the term "Equitable Mortgage"?

*A.* The expression indicates a method of creating a charge upon land which has most of the advantages of a legal mortgage, but which is recognised in equity only. Where it appears that the owner of property intended to make it a security for money borrowed, equity considers it inequitable that the lender should not profit by such intention merely because he has not the legal estate. An example of such a security will be found in the next question.

5. *Q.* A deposit of deeds being made by way of mortgage, without a written memorandum: will this be a good security? If so, may or may not the object of the deposit be explained by parol evidence?

*A.* Such a deposit will be good even without a written memorandum for the purpose of creating an equitable mortgage. Formerly this point was much doubted as being an evasion of the statute of Frauds, which it certainly is. If the lands are registered under 25 & 26 Vic., c. 53, an equitable mortgage is created by a deposit of the land certificate. The object of the deposit may be explained by parol evidence, and if the circumstances were such as to raise an inference that a deposit was not intended, there will be no charge. *Lucas* v. *Dorrein*, 7 Taunt., 278; *Russel* v. *Russel*, 1 L. C. Eq., 541.

6. *Q.* Would such a deposit have preference over a subsequent purchaser or mortgagee of the legal estate, with or without notice of such equitable mortgage? Is a written memorandum of the deposit advantageous?

*A.* The deposit would be good against the purchaser or mortgagee with notice, but not in the absence of it, provided they have the legal estate. Notice would be imputed to such purchaser or mortgagee if he knew that the title deeds had been put by the owner into the possession of another. He will also be postponed if he have not inquired for the deeds. But it is otherwise if he has inquired, but a reasonable excuse has been given him. *Hewitt* v. *Loosemore*, 9 Hare, 458; 1 L. C. Eq., 553. A written memorandum is certainly advantageous, as it prevents any question being raised as to the nature of the deposit.

7. *Q.* What are the proper modes of mortgaging freehold, copyhold, and leasehold estates? State each severally.

*A.* Freeholds may be mortgaged by conveying the freehold to the mortgagee or by creating a term of years. The former is usually adopted, but the latter is convenient, as upon the decease of the mortgagee the security and the money vest in his personal representatives.

Copyholds are mortgaged by a conditional surrender, accompanied by a deed of covenant, containing the usual covenants by the mortgagor and mortgagee. See *supra* " Copyholds," p. 160, No. 20.

Leaseholds may be mortgaged either by assigning the whole term or by granting an underlease to the mortgagee. The latter is preferable, as he does not become liable to the covenants in the lease. Wms. Real Prop., 382, *et seq.*, *infra*, No. 17.

8. *Q.* A contracts to purchase a lease. B agrees to lend money on mortgage of another lease. What difference ought to be made in the instruments between the assignment to the purchaser and the mortgage to the lender.

*A.* The purchase would be effected by assignment, but the mortgage would be by underlease. See the previous answer.

9. *Q.* How should a mortgage of leaseholds be taken so as to protect the mortgagee from the covenants of the mortgagor's lease?

*A.* See the previous answers.

10. *Q.* What is the advantage of a mortgage in fee over a mortgage for a long term—say 1,000 years—and what are the disadvantages?

*A.* See *supra*, No. 6. Also if a mortgagee forecloses he is enabled to sell the fee instead of a term, which, however long, is not so valuable. Also a mortgagee by a demise, unless by special stipulation, is not entitled to the custody of the deeds, or to the other advantages incident to a freehold estate. Prideaux's Precedents, 308.

11. *Q.* Can an advowson and an ecclesiastical benefice be charged, and how?

*A.* An advowson, though not a good security on account of the mortgagor's right to nominate to a vacancy, may be mortgaged. The mortgage should be in fee. A direct charge on a benefice is however void, since 59 Geo. III., c. 99. But the incumbent may give a warrant of attorney, if it does not appear on the face of it that it was intended as a charge. Upon this, judgment may be entered up and a sequestration issued. Coote on Mortgages, 204.

12. *Q.* Is it legal to take procuration-money on a loan of money upon mortgage, and how much; and who is entitled to it, the solicitor for the mortgagee or the solicitor for the mortgagor?

*A.* Such a fee is quite legal, and it is not now limited in amount as formerly. 18 & 19 Vic., c. 90. The solicitor of the mortgagee is entitled to the fee, but in practice it is not unfrequent to divide it between the solicitor for the mortgagor and mortgagee.

13. *Q.* What covenants and powers are usually inserted in a mortgage deed? Is there any, and, if any, what recent legislation on the subject?

*A.* The covenants are by the mortgagor to pay the principal and interest, to insure, for good right to convey, for quiet enjoyment after default, free from incumbrances, and for further assurance. Powers of a sale and to appoint a receiver are inserted; but as to these there has been recent legislation, for which see the next answer. 1 Prideaux's Precedents, 359.

14. *Q.* State in substance the power of sale of the Trustee Act of 1860 incident to all mortgages, and say how far it is expedient in practice to rely on the statutory powers or to give express power. In whatever would you make it arise, and in what way make it unimpeachable in default of notice or other irregularity?

*A.* The power conferred is to sell the whole or any part of the property by public auction or private contract, subject to reasonable conditions, and to rescind or vary the contract, or buy in and re-sell the property. Six months' notice must be given of the sale, and the application of the purchase-money is provided for. The power given by the act is objectionable, inasmuch as it is inconvenient for a mortgagee not to know his powers without looking beyond his deed; that the power is not exercisable so soon as the ordinary power, as it cannot be exercised until twelve months from the time appointed for payment. The provisions as to notice are also inconvenient. In practice, therefore, it is desirable to insert the ordinary power, exercisable in default of payment after notice, or of the interest being in arrear. A proviso that the purchaser should not be bound to see or inquire whether there had been any irregularity would protect the purchaser. 1 Prideaux's Precedents, 362.

15. *Q.* In regard to the powers of sale and appointment of receiver given to mortgagees by the said Act of 1860 which, if not negatived would take effect, and might be adopted with variations, state so far as you have considered the act any reason for or against the adopting them or any of them?

*A.* I object to these provisions for the reason given in the previous answer; also because I prefer to have the limits of the powers mentioned, accurately defined in the mortgage deed, and not dependent on the construction of an Act of Parliament. I am nevertheless bound to say that the act is adopted by many who consider it a benefit as securing brevity in the deed.

16. *Q.* Can the mortgagee of real estate, without express power, sell the mortgaged property? Does the same rule prevail in the case of a mortgagee of personal chattels?

*A.* As to a mortgagee of realty see the previous answers. A mortgagee of personalty may sell without express power, or he may obtain a decree for foreclosure. Coote, 237, 3rd ed.

17. *Q.* Is a mortgagee with power of sale justified, as between himself and the mortgagor, in selling by auction, with a condition that he shall be at liberty to rescind the sale in case of any objection to the title, which he may be unable or unwilling to remove; and is a purchaser buying at a low price under such a condition, secure against future claims by the mortgagor?

*A.* It has been held that such a condition is justifiable, as against the mortgagor, it not being considered depreciatory. *Faulkner* v. *The Equitable Revers. Int. Soc.*, 28 L. J. Ch., 132. In that case, however, it should be borne in mind the mortgagees had power to sell, "subject to such special conditions as they should think proper." The second part of the question depends upon the first, as if the condition is not justifiable the mortgagor could recover the estate from the purchaser on payment of the debt, otherwise he would have no remedy. Ibid. Sugden's Vendors, 65.

18. *Q.* In what form should a mortgage of leasehold property be taken, and what provisions should be inserted in it?

*A.* It should be taken by way of under-lease, for the purpose of the mortgagee avoiding liability on the covenants. If it was taken by assignment there would be privity of estate between the lessor and mortgagee, which would make the latter liable on the covenants running with the land. *Spencer's Case*, 1 Sm. L. C., 43. The provisions of the mortgage would be—Demise to the mortgagee. Proviso for redemption. Covenants by mortgagor for payment of principal and interest, that the lease is valid, for right to demise, for quiet enjoyment, free from incumbrances, and for further assurance, for payment of rent and observance of the covenants. Power of sale. Trusts of purchase money. Power of sale to be exercised only in case of default. 1 Prideaux's Precedents, 375.

19. *Q.* What covenants should be included in a mortgage of leasehold houses?

*A.* In addition to the covenants to pay the debt, and for title as mentioned above, the mortgagor covenants for payment of the rents and observance of the covenants in the lease. After the power of sale, there is a declaration that the mortgagor shall stand possessed of the residue of the term in trust for the purchaser. 1 Prideaux's Precedents, 378.

20. *Q.* Write out the habendum in a mortgage of a house held on a lease for a term of eighty years, and enumerate shortly the usual covenants and provisoes in such a mortgage.

*A.* The habendum would be — "To have and to hold the said hereditaments and premises hereby assigned (or demised) unto the said C D, his executors, administrators, and assigns, for all the residue now to come of the said term of eighty years; (if by demise) 'except the last ten days of the said term,' subject to the proviso for redemption hereinafter contained." The covenants and provisoes would be—Proviso for redemption, covenants by mortgagor for payment of the money and interest, that the lease is valid, for right to demise, for quiet enjoyment, free from incumbrances and for further assurance, for payment of rent and observance of the covenants. Power of sale. 1 Prideaux's Precedents, 375, 378.

21. *Q.* A desires to mortgage his house in Belgrave Square, held on a lease for ninety years, to B, to secure to him the loan of £5,000. Write out verbatim the habendum in such mortgage-deed, and state the principle on which you would frame it, and enumerate shortly the covenants and provisoes that you would insert in such mortgage-deed.

*A.* See Nos. 17—19.

22. *Q.* In a mortgage in fee to three persons with a power of sale, state the proper words designating to whom such power should be reserved.

*A.* The power should be reserved to the mortgagees, "and the survivors and survivor of the them, and the executors and administrators of such survivor, their or his assigns." 1 Prideaux's Precedents, 319.

23. *Q.* Where trust money is lent on mortgage, is it expedient to keep the trust out of sight. If so, why? only declaring that the money belongs to a joint account, bearing in mind the provisions of the Law of Property Act, 1859, making effectual the receipt of a trustee for mortgage money. Give reasons?

*A.* The trust should be kept out of sight, in order that when the mortgage is paid off, the trust deed should not form a part of the mortgagor's title. It should be declared that the money is lent on a joint account, and that the receipt of the survivor, his executor, or administrator, shall be a good discharge. And this, notwithstanding the act of 1859. The provision there contained as to receipts applies only to the receipt of a trustee for mortgage money, but in the joint account clause the fact of the mortgagees being trustees is kept back and they are considered as joint lenders on their own account. 22 & 23 Vic., c. 35, s. 23, would therefore have no application.

24. *Q.* Mention the principal parts of a conveyance in fee by a mortgagor and mortgagee to a purchaser.

*A.* They are—Date, parties. Recitals of the mortgage and the contract for sale. Testatum, that in consideration of the debt being paid to the mortgagee by the purchaser at the direction of the mortgagor, and also of the residue of the price being paid to the mortgagor, the receipt for which being acknowledged, the mortgagee grants and the mortgagor grants and confirms the parcels to the purchaser in fee. The mortgagee covenants against incumbrances, and the mortgagor enters into the usual covenants for title. 1 Prideaux's Precedents, 181.

25. *Q.* Is it useful or necessary, and wherefore, to take a bond in addition to a mortgage deed and covenant?

*A.* It is now of no importance to take a bond in addition to the usual covenant in the mortgage deed, and in practice it is never done. Formerly there was an advantage in doing so, as if there was a bond the devisee of the mortgagor could be sued, but he could not be sued on the covenant. 1 Powell on Mortgages, 16 d. n., 6th ed. Now, however, the devisee may be sued in covenant upon the covenant. 11 Geo. IV., and 1 Wm. IV., c. 47, ss. 2, 3; 1 Selwyn's N. P., 538, 12th ed.

26. *Q.* What are the prominent disadvantages of a second mortgage, especially in the event of a foreclosure or sale, and considering the danger of tacking? Give your reasons.

*A.* They are that the claim on the estate is subject to that of the first mortgagee, that the second cannot bring ejectment; that a third incumbrancer advancing his money without notice *when he advanced*, of the second mortgage may pay off the first and thus tack his third mortgage to the first and keep out the second until both are paid; that he cannot redeem the first mortgage without bringing the mortgagor before the court to complete his foreclosure; that on foreclosure by the first mortgagee he must redeem him, the first mortgagee not being bound to pay him off, and that on a sale he will only have what is left after paying the first mortgagee and all the expenses.

27. *Q.* In the absence of an express bargain, can a mortgagor pay off at any time his mortgage debt, and can a mortgagee call in the mortgage money at any time?

*A.* In the absence of express contract there is an implied one by the mortgagor to give six months' notice before paying off the money. If he choses he may instead of notice, pay six months' interest in advance. The mortgagee may however after forfeiture enforce his security without any notice, and he may even file his bill for foreclosure though he has agreed not to call in the money before a later day, if the interest has not been punctually paid. Coote on Mortgages, 528; Seton on Decrees, 357.

28. *Q.* Is a mortgagor bound to give any, and what, notice of a prior mortgage to a second mortgagee; and what consequences, if any, result from the omission?

*A.* The mortgagor in effecting the second mortgage should disclose the first one, otherwise he forfeits his equity of redemption. Should however a third mortgage be effected the third mortgagee may redeem the two former. 4 & 5 Wm. & Mary, c. 16, ss. 3, 4.

29. *Q.* To whom should notice of a second mortgage of an equitable estate be given?

*A.* Notice should be given to the first mortgagee, in order to prevent his tacking further advances by him. An indorsement should be made upon the first mortgage deed and the conveyance to the mortgagor, of the second advance having been made, if the first mortgagee will allow this. Such an indorsement may effect with notice subsequent parties inspecting the deeds previous to advancing money to the mortgagor. The effect of such notice would be to prevent tacking.

30. *Q.* Can an advance of money on a mortgage or judgment subsequent to a second mortgage be tacked to a prior security, so as to have priority in payment to the second mortgage, and in what cases?

*A.* A third mortgagee may tack by buying up the first mortgage, thus obtaining the legal estate. But he can only thus gain priority over a second mortgagee, when he advanced his money without notice of such second mortgage. A judgment creditor cannot, however, by getting in the first mortgage obtain priority over a second mortgage, because he did not advance his money on the credit of the land, and it is doubtful if this rule is altered by 1 & 2 Vic., c. 110; *Marsh* v. *Lee*, 1 L. C. Eq., 494, *et seq.* But a first mortgagee may tack further advances made by him, whether on mortgage or judgment as against a *mesne* incumbrance of whom he had no notice when making the second advance. *Marsh* v. *Lee*, rr. 5 and 6.

31. *Q.* Estate is mortgaged first to A, then to B, then to C; B and C both having notice of A's mortgage, but neither B nor C having notice of each other's mortgage. Can C by any, and what, means acquire a priority over B?

*A.* C may buy up the mortgage of A, and thus obtain priority over B by tacking the two incumbrances. *Supra.*

32. *Q.* What is an equity of redemption, and who has it?

*A.* It is that estate which the mortgagor is in equity possessed of after the mortgage, by virtue of which he may redeem the mortgage by paying the mortgagee, and obtain from him a reconveyance of the legal estate. The owner may dispose of it as he pleases, and since 3 & 4 Wm. IV., c. 105, it is subject to dower. It is called an equity of redemption, because the right to redeem was acknowledged only by a Court of Equity. Wms. Real Prop., 386. As to the limit of time for redeeming, see *infra* "Equity."

33. *Q.* Mortgage to A for a £1000, then to B for £800. A

sells his charge to C, a stranger, for £700. Is C entitled as against B to the whole debt of £1000, or only to the £700 he paid?

*A.* The purchaser of the debt (C) is entitled to receive the whole sum of £1000, irrespective of what he actually gave for the debt. If, however, C were an executor or trustee for the mortgagor or his heir at law, he would not be entitled as against B to the whole. The difference will be deemed to be for the benefit of the estate, and he could merely claim the sum he actually paid, namely, £700. Notes to *Thornborough* v. *Baker,* 2 L. C. Eq., 881.

34. *Q.* If A mortgage Y estate to B for £1000, and Z estate to B for £2000, can A adversely to B redeem either estate, upon paying the money due upon it, or must he redeem both estates? and does the same rule apply to proceedings by B, for foreclosure?

*A.* He cannot redeem one estate without redeeming the other; but he must redeem both. At least, this is so if the security or title of the estate sought to be redeemed is inadequate or defective. Neither can B foreclose as to one estate, but he must foreclose both. Coote, 501, 3rd ed.

35. *Q.* A person makes a distinct mortgage for two different sums on two distinct estates to the same person (one of which is of insufficient value), can he redeem one of the mortgages without the other?

*A.* See the previous answer.

36. *Q.* Can a mortgagee grant a lease without the concurrence of a mortgagor, and suppose a mortgagee and mortgagor concur in granting a lease, to whom should the rent be reserved, and with whom should the covenants be entered into? State the reasons for your answer.

*A.* See *supra,* p. 192, No. 13. If the mortgagee and mortgagor concur the rent should be reserved to the mortgagee, his heirs and assigns, with a proviso that the rent may be paid to the mortgagor until notice by the mortgagee. A power is given to the mortgagor to distrain. The rent is reserved to the mortgagee because he has the legal estate. The covenants should be entered into with the mortgagee, and as separate covenants with the mortgagor. By this means when the mortgage is paid off the mortgagor may enforce the covenants, and during its continuance the mortgagee may do so. 2 Prideaux's Precedents, 38.

37. *Q.* A granted a mortgage of land in fee to B, and B died intestate. What instrument is necessary, and by whom to be signed, to restore the land to A discharged of the mortgage? Give the reasons.

*A.* A re-conveyance, by deed of grant, should be made of the estate by the heir of B to the mortgagor, the personal representatives joining to give a receipt for the mortgage money. The reason for this is that the legal estate descends to the heir of the mortgagee, whilst the administrator is entitled to the money; the land in equity being considered as a security for the debt. Upon payment, therefore, of the debt the land belongs to the mortgagor, and the money being the only thing left to the mortgagee, goes to his administrator. In such a case *"Equitas sequitur legem."* *Thornborough* v. *Baker*, 2 L. C. Eq., 857.

38. *Q.* A mortgagee in fee dies intestate. In whom do the estate and money vest? and how is the mortgagor to obtain an effectual re-conveyance of the premises?

*A.* See the previous answer.

39. *Q.* Lands are charged by way of mortgage in fee to A and B, their heirs and assigns. A dies, leaving B surviving, and afterwards the mortgage debt is proposed to be paid off. As a general rule, is the concurrence of the heir, or personal representative of A, or which of them, required in the re-conveyance or not? or upon what circumstances does the necessity for such concurrence depend? If the mortgage had been for a term of years, answer the same question under the same circumstances.

*A.* The concurrence of the heir of A would not be necessary as he is a joint tenant with B, and the legal estate survives. The personal representative, however, of A must concur. As in equity A and B are looked upon as tenants in common of the money, unless the usual survivorship clause is inserted, in which case his concurrence would be unnecessary. If the mortgage was by demise the concurrence of the heir of a deceased mortgagee is in no case necessary, as the security being a chattel real would devolve with the money upon the personal representative. But, in the above case the term would survive to B as a joint tenant.

40. *Q.* A mortgagee in fee dies without devising the security; the mortgagor is desirous to pay the money; the heir-at-law of the mortgagee is unwilling or incapable to re-convey; to whom may the mortgagor pay the money, and of whom obtain the re-conveyance?

*A.* The money should be paid to the personal representative of the mortgagee, and the conveyance must be effected by obtaining a vesting order from the Court of Chancery under 13 & 14 Vic., c. 60, s. 19.

41. *Q.* A mortgagee freehold estates to B, with powers of sale, and dies. B then exercises his powers of sale, and after retaining his principal, interest, and costs, there is a surplus. To whom will the surplus belong, viz., to the heir, or to the personal representative of the mortgagor?

*A.* The surplus will belong to the heir of the mortgagor, and not to the personal representatives. The reason of this is that the conversion merely takes place for the purposes of the mortgage; any balance that remains, although practically it is money, yet in reality it is still impressed with the character of real estate. The equity of redemption descended to the heir before a sale had taken place. If, however, the sale had occurred in the lifetime of the mortgagor his personal representatives would have been entitled. *Wright* v. *Rose*, 2 Sim. & Stu., 323.

42. *Q.* Mortgage money not being paid, what are the remedies to which a mortgagee may resort?

*A.* A legal mortgagee may file a bill of foreclosure, or he may bring ejectment, or he may sell under the power in the deed, or by statute. Also, he may bring an action for the money. See further *infra*; Equity; "Legal and Equitable Mortgages"; Wms. Real Prop., 385.

43. *Q.* When the land mortgaged is held either by tenancy created before the mortgage, or under a demise by the mortgagor after it, what are the distinct remedies in each case for the mortgagee's obtaining rent or possession?

*A.* In the first case the mortgagee may give the tenants notice to pay the rent to him, and after refusal distrain for arrears due both before and after the notice. But he cannot eject such tenants; though as he is placed in the position of the mortgagor it is presumed he may determine the tenancy by notice. *Moss* v. *Gallimore*, 1 Sm. L. C., 542. As to the demise by the mortgagor alone, the mortgagee may at once eject him. But he cannot on mere notice as in the first case distrain, though a new tenancy may be created between himself and the tenant by virtue of which he may distrain. *Brown* v. *Storey*, 1 M. & G., 117; *Keech* v. *Hall*, 1 Sm. L. C., 505, and the notes.

44. *Q.* Where land mortgaged is in the actual occupation of the mortgagor, what, if any, means can be taken in the mortgage deed for giving to the mortgagee power to obtain the interest out of the profits of the land?

*A.* It may be stipulated in the mortgage deed that the mortgagor shall be tenant to the mortgagee at a rent. This will confer on the mortgagee all the usual powers of recovery incident to rents. Also a power may be given enabling the mortgagee to distrain for interest. The former is preferable as it creates a tenancy, whereas the latter acts merely as a personal license from the mortgagor. Notes to *Keech* v. *Hall*, 1 Sm. L. C., 513.

45. *Q.* Can a mortgagee in possession, whose estate is absolute at law cut down timber?

*A.* He may do so if the estate is not sufficient security to pay his principal, interest and costs; otherwise he will be restrained. But even if the security is inadequate he must not commit wanton destruction. He may, also, work mines on the same terms, subject, however, to his having to bear the risk of any great loss incurred in working them. On the other hand the whole of the benefit derived from the working goes in liquidation of his security. *Mellitt* v. *Davey*, 32 L. J. Ch., 122.

46. *Q.* What is the highest rate of interest that can be reserved on a mortgage? Can a mortgagee stipulate that if the interest be not paid at the time provided it shall be converted into principal.

*A.* Since the repeal of the usury laws there is no limit as to the amount. 17 & 18 Vic., c. 90. Such a stipulation would be bad, as to convert the interest into principal, it must first become due and then it may be made a charge upon the estate by agreement. 2 Spence, 656.

47. *Q* A who is the owner and in the occupation of a manu-

factory makes a mortgage of it without mention of the machinery. Will fixed machinery pass; and is registration necessary under the "Bills of Sales Act?"

*A.* The fixed machinery will pass with the manufactory, unless a contrary intention appear, such machinery being considered as part of the freehold. (It must, however, be remembered that in the case of *Mather* v. *Fraser*, 25 L. J. Ch., 361, usually cited in support of this proposition, machinery was specially mentioned.) For the same reason registration is not necessary under 17 & 18 Vic., c. 31.

48. *Q.* A mortgages land to B to secure £1,000 advanced at the time, and also future advances, and subsequently mortgages the same land to C to secure a present advance, and C gives B notice of his mortgage. If B afterwards make A a further advance, will that advance rank in priority to C's mortgage?

*A.* The further advance will not have priority, even though the first mortgage extend to further advances. *Rolt* v. *Hopkinson*, 9 H. of L., 514.

49. *Q.* What is the effect of cancelling or destroying a mortgage deed on payment of principal and interest?

*A.* The mere cancelling of the deed has no effect if the debt is paid, as the mere payment extinguishes the debt in equity. The cancellation of the deed cannot re-vest the estate in the mortgagor, but the mortgagee must re-convey the legal estate to him. 2 Spence, 749.

## XX.—*Vendor and Vendee.*

1. *Q.* Describe the several conditions of sale to which sales by auction of freehold estates are usually made subject at the present day?

*A.* The chief conditions are :—That no bidder shall advance less than a certain sum. Also providing for the amount of deposit, and to whom payable. Also that the fixtures and trees are to be taken at a valuation. That the title is to commence with a certain deed or will, which is to be deemed a good root of title. That the vendors are to deliver the abstract at their expense, and the objections to the title to be delivered within a specified time. All attested copies, and other documents not in the possession of the vendor, to be furnished at the expense of the purchaser. The purchaser to admit the identity of the property with the description in the deeds. As to the date of completion, the preparation of the conveyance, the giving of possession, the payment of the purchase-money, and interest thereon—provision that if the above are not complied with by the purchaser, the vendor may rescind the contract. There may be also various other conditions, which see 1 Prideaux's Precedents, 14 *et seq.*

2. *Q.* What further conditions would it be advisable to insert if the property was leasehold?

*A.* It would be advisable to provide that a purchaser should not be entitled to the production of leases prior to the subsisting lease, the same having been surrendered for the purpose of renewal; that the lessor's title shall not be required, nor shall any objection be made in respect thereof; that the last receipt for the last payment of the rent shall be deemed evidence of the performance of the covenants; that no objection shall be taken to the lease because it is an underlease, or because it comprises property other than that which is sold. Ibid.

3. *Q.* Is it the duty of the vendor's solicitor to investigate the title of his client before he prepares the contract of sale? And if he does so, what advantages result to his client for so doing?

*A.* It is unquestionably the duty of the vendor's solicitor to investigate his client's title before preparing the contract. The advantages which ensue would be, that there would be no chance of the vendor selling that to which he had no title, a proceeding which would subject him to great expense and litigation. Also a good root of title would be ascertained, and the conditions could be so framed as to force the title on an unwilling purchaser, and also save the expense of producing documents and evidence to which the purchaser, in the absence of stipulation, might be entitled.

4. *Q.* A vendor wishes to sell by auction a small portion of his estate, and desires to retain the title-deeds which relate to the larger portion. Draw a proper condition of sale applicable to such a state of things.

*A.* "Inasmuch as the muniments of title in the possession of the vendor relate to other property as well as to the property now offered for sale, the same shall be retained by him, and he shall enter into the usual covenant with the purchaser for the production and furnishing copies to him of the same, the deed containing such covenant to be prepared by and at the expense of the purchaser," 1 Prideaux's Precedents, 33.

5. *Q.* Can a bidder at a public auction retract his bidding? and, if so, when?

*A.* It is generally stated that a bidding may be retracted at any time before the lot is knocked down, the retraction being sufficiently loud to be heard by the auctioneer. Sugden's Vendors, 13. The bidding, however, may be virtually retracted at any time before the purchaser, or his agent for him, has signed the contract, for until then he is not bound. The auctioneer may be his agent for this purpose. See *infra*, No. 12.

6. *Q.* Can the particulars and conditions of an estate be varied by parol at the sale?

*A.* Such parol variations would be inadmissible in evidence if contrary to the printed conditions, unless, perhaps, the purchaser has particular personal information given him of the mistake in the particulars. Such evidence may, however, be used in equity, as a defence against specific performance if the parol variation was in favour of the defendant. Sugden's Vendors, 15, 16, 158.

7. *Q.* It being a common practice to frame conditions of sale so stringently as to compel a purchaser buying subject to them to

accept an apparently, if not an absolutely, defective title, state your opinion whether trustees who invest of their own accord the moneys of their *cestuis que* trust in the purchase of lands, subject to such conditions, are personally liable in case of eviction, or whether the loss ought to fall upon the trust estate; and give your reasons.

*A.* I should say that if trustees having authority to invest on the purchase of land do so under conditions which, though stringent, are in everyday use, they would not be liable. If, however, the conditions were of such a character as to impart grave suspicion of there being a defective title, then I think the case would be otherwise. If they have no authority to invest in lands at all they will be personally liable in any event.

8. *Q.* Is it necessary to have an agreement in writing on the sale of an estate by auction?

*A.* Yes, a memorandum in writing is required by 29 Car. II., c. 3, s. 4.

9. *Q.* What are the requisites to make a contract for the sale of lands valid by the Statute of Frauds? and are there any, and what, exceptions recognised by the equity courts?

*A.* The contract must be in writing, signed by the party to be charged, or his authorised agent. Any memorandum will do, so as it contains, either expressly or by reference, the terms of the agreement. The consideration must appear upon the face of the agreement, or be capable of being drawn therefrom by necessary inference. Chitty on Contracts, 65. As to the exceptions referred to as recognised by courts of equity, see *infra* "Equity," "Specific Performance."

10. *Q.* State the date and some of the provisions of the act for the Prevention of Frauds and Perjuries, usually entitled the Statute of Frauds.

*A.* It was passed in the year 1677. 29 Car. II., c. 3. The unrepealed part provides that conveyances, leases, assignments, etc., of interests in land, should be in writing, excepting a lease not exceeding three years, and a feoffment by an infant. (For the fourth and seventeenth sections see *supra*, p. 9, Nos. 8, 9.) That declarations of trust of land, and all assignments of trusts, should be in writing. That the lands of a *cestui que trust* shall be liable to judgments entered up against him. That writs of execution shall bind the debtor's goods on delivery of the writ to the sheriff. That soldiers on actual service, or seamen at sea, might, notwithstanding other provisions in the act, now repealed by 1 Vic., c. 26, make nuncupative wills. That husbands may administer to their wives' estates. The Articled Clerk's Manual, 18, 9th ed., by Anderson.

11. *Q.* Is it necessary that a written agreement should be sealed, as well as signed, to satisfy the Statute of Frauds?

*A.* The statute merely requires that the agreement should be signed. 29 Car. II., c. 3, s. 4.

12. *Q.* How are the requisitions of the Statute of Frauds complied with at an auction as usually conducted?

*A.* The purchaser is bound at an auction by the auctioneer writing down the purchaser's name, and the amount of the bidding, opposite the lot in the particulars, as soon as the lot is knocked down. But it is usual, when the deposit is paid, for the purchaser or his agent to sign the conditions of sale, and for the vendor or his agent to sign a duplicate, and then exchange the parts. Sugden's Vendors, 42.

13. *Q.* When an owner has verbally agreed to sell land, and instructs his solicitor to prepare a written contract, what are the duties of the solicitor anterior to the signature of the contract by his client?

*A.* He should investigate the title, as mentioned *supra*, No. 3, and prepare a draft contract, in accordance with the state of the title, making the usual provisions to prevent delay or difficulty, and to avoid unnecessary expense. A plan should also be carefully prepared, the property if necessary being measured. The draft he should transmit to the purchaser's solicitor, who will return it approved as altered in red ink. The alterations must be considered, and if unobjectionable agreed to. The draft may be then engrossed in duplicate and signed. A solicitor is also frequently consulted as to the price being adequate. But though his opinion is often of great value upon this point, it is no part of his duty to give it.

14. *Q.* A man having contracted to purchase land, died intestate. Who is to pay the purchase-money and take the land? Give the reasons.

*A.* If the contract is a binding one the money will be considered as converted into land, from the time of the contract. The purchaser's heir will, therefore, be entitled to the land, and he may call upon the personal representatives to pay the price. See, as to conversion, *infra* "Equity."

15. *Q.* If a man seised in fee of land contract with another for the sale of it, and both parties die before the sale is completed, does the contract continue in force, and what is the consequence as regards the title to the land, and also as regards the title to the purchase-money?

*A.* The death of the parties has no effect upon the contract, but it may be enforced by their respective representatives. As to the consequences of the death of the purchaser, see the previous answer. On the other hand, the heir of the vendor will be bound to convey the estate; but his personal representatives will be entitled to the purchase-money.

16. *Q.* In preparing an abstract of title on a sale, is the vendor's solicitor personally liable for omitting to state all the incumbrances within his knowledge?

*A.* The vendor's solicitor is personally responsible for suppressing incumbrances. He, as well as his client, is also criminally responsible if he conceals any instrument material to the title, or any incumbrance, from a purchaser, in order to induce him to accept the title with intent to defraud. The offence is a misdemeanor punishable by fine or imprisonment, for a term not exceeding two years, with or without hard labour, or both. The sanction of the Attorney or Solicitor-General must be obtained before prosecuting. The purchaser or mortgagee who suffers from the fraud may also sue the solicitor. 22 & 23 Vic., c. 35, s. 24.

17   *Q.* In examining an abstract with the title-deeds on behalf of a purchaser, what would be the consequences to the solicitor personally of his overlooking notice of any incumbrance contained in any instrument abstracted and produced for examination, whether such notice were contained in the abstract or otherwise?

*A.* The solicitor who by his negligence overlooks incumbrances of which by ordinary care he might have obtained notice is personally responsible to his client. So also he is liable for any loss occasioned by his omission to make any of the usual searches, or when making them, if he does not detect an incumbrance. Dart's Vendors and Purchasers, 301.

18.   *Q.* An abstract of title has been delivered to the solicitor of a purchaser as an accurate and sufficient abstract of all the title-deeds. The solicitor has to compare the abstract with the deeds. The abstract of the first deed states fully the parcels contained in it, and the abstracts of all the other deeds refer to the parcels in the abstract of the first as the "premises comprised in the before abstracted indenture." The abstract of title also contains an abstract of a long and complex settlement with numerous special provisions, and clauses which have not been abstracted. What are the duties of the solicitor with respect to the parcels in the several deeds, and the provisions and clauses of the settlement, and generally with reference to the deeds and abstracts?

*A.* With regard to the parcels he should see, by inspecting them closely and comparing them, that those in the original deed are comprised in the subsequent ones. He should also carefully peruse the settlement and ascertain that the provisions not abstracted do not affect the title. Speaking generally the solicitor should see that the deeds correspond with the abstract, and that they have been correctly abstracted. That what is omitted is immaterial, that they are perfect, and that no indorsements appear upon them which might excite suspicion. Also, that they are duly stamped, properly executed, attested and registered. Dart's Vend. and Purch., cap. 9, s. 4.

19.   *Q.* A purchaser buys an estate free from incumbrances, and it turns out, on his investigating the title, that there is a rent-charge due to a jointress upon it. How is the defect to be remedied, so as to make a title to an unwilling purchaser?

*A.* The jointress must release her rent-charge, otherwise the purchaser cannot be compelled to take the estate. If such a question arose in a suit for specific performance, counsel should be instructed to appear for the jointress, and undertake that she will release. Properly she should be under a binding agreement to release. Sugden's Vendors, 350.

20.   *Q.* How far back has a purchaser of land a right to require the title thereto to commence? and on what principle is such period founded.

*A.* A purchaser in the absence of stipulation is entitled to a sixty years' title. The reason for this is, that inasmuch as vested remainders are allowed after estates for life, it is necessary to carry back the title to a point which will afford a reasonable presumption that the first person mentioned as having conveyed the property is not a tenant for life, but a tenant in fee. Thus suppose a settlement to be made on the settlor for life, with remainder to his first and other sons in tail, and that he has no son for a long period, and then suppressing the settlement he sells as owner in fee, and lives for forty or fifty years afterwards and leaves a son. Now time only runs against the son from the father's death, therefore for the purchaser's title remains in danger for a long time, possibly for much more than sixty years. The ordinary duration of life is sixty years, and assuming the conveyance to be made at twenty-one, and the death of the settlor to take place at sixty, the purchaser would not be safe for sixty years. Hence the necessity for this length of title. Wms. Real. Prop., 405. Sugden's Vendors, 515.

21. *Q.* A is possessed of a leasehold estate which he agrees to sell to B without any special conditions as to title; what title has B a right to require?

*A.* A sixty years' title must be shown. Thus, if the lease has not been granted for sixty years a portion of the landlord's title must be given to make up the sixty years. Wms. Real. Prop., 404.

22. *Q.* If A agrees to grant a lease of an estate to B for a term of years at an annual rent, without any premium and without any conditions as to title in the agreement, what if any title may the lessee require should be shewn by the lessor?

*A.* There has been considerable conflict of decisions upon this point; but the result of them is, that the lessee cannot enforce production of the lessor's title; but, on the other hand, the lessor cannot compel a specific performance without producing his title. 1 Platt on Leases, 618.

23. *Q.* What length of title should be shown to an advowson? and state the reason for your answer.

*A.* One hundred years' title should be shown to an advowson, the reason being that the presentations occur at such long intervals. Sugden's Vendors, 367.

24. *Q.* What is a guaranteed and what is an indefeasible title?

*A.* The word "guaranteed" was inserted in this question inadvertently, as there is no such thing as a guaranteed estate or title. An indefeasible *title* is one which is registered under the Land Transfer Act, 25 & 26 Vic., c. 53. When registered, it is considered for the purposes of any sale, mortgage, or contract for valuable consideration indefeasible against all persons and the crown, ss. 20—23. A similar object may be attained by petition to the Court of Chancery, under 25 & 26 Vic., c. 67. Lord St. Leonards observes "and singular as it may seem that two acts should be passed simultaneously for the same object, yet so it was." Sugden's Vendors, 511, 14th ed.

25. *Q.* So far as you are acquainted with the provisions of the Land Registry Act, 1862, state the purposes for which exclusively the title may be declared indefeasible.

*A.* See the previous answer. No title will be declared indefeasible under 25 & 26 Vic., c. 53, unless it is one which the Court of Chancery would hold to be a valid marketable title, s. 5. To obtain a declaration, under 26 & 27 Vic., c. 67, of the title being indefeasible, it must be found to be one which the court would force upon an unwilling purchaser, ss. 7—10.

26. *Q.* Can an agent authorised by parol to purchase an estate at a certain price, bind his principal by his written agreement to buy it for a larger sum? and if not, has the seller any, and what, remedy against the agent?

*A.* If the agent bids more than the price he is authorised to bid, the principal will not be liable. But the agent would be personally liable, and might be sued upon the contract by the vendor. Sugden's Vendors, 47.

27. *Q.* What principle should govern the practitioner in setting forth the title to land, after a contract for sale entered into? Should all deeds affecting the title be set out in the abstract? and what will be the consequence to the vendor and his solicitor if any be kept back?

*A.* The leading principle in preparing an abstract is to show upon the face of it that the vendor has a good title, and has the power of conveying the estate to the purchaser. With this view it is necessary to commence the abstract with a document of the requisite age, and such document should be one which deals with the entire legal and equitable estate. It should not depend on any previous instrument for its validity; thus a general devise would be a bad root of title, as it must be shown that the testator had the estate to devise. All subsequent documents dealing with the legal estate (except expired leases), should be abstracted in chief. Even if a mortgage has been paid off, the mortgage and reconveyance should appear. But it is otherwise if the mortgage is merely equitable. The abstract should also contain statements of deaths, marriages, &c., in their proper place. As to the consequence of keeping back material documents, see *supra*, No. 16. Dart's Vendors, cap. 8, s. 4.

28. *Q.* If you had to advise on the sale of building land, in fee lots, and were required to make the best provisions for the common use of streets, roads, drains, etc., or for the prevention of building, or securing easements, how would you proceed to carry out the object, either by vesting land for common use in trust, or by granting a rent-charge in favour of one lot over another, or by mutual covenants between the purchasers, framed in the best way the law would admit, so as to run with the land, or by what means?

*A.* In each conveyance the use of streets, roads, and drains, should be expressly given to the purchaser, his lot being at the same time expressly declared to be subject to a similar user on behalf of other purchasers. Each grant would probably include half of the road.

Thus, an easement is granted to the purchaser of each lot, and such purchaser takes subject to the easements of others. The prevention of building is secured by each purchaser covenanting with the vendor not to do so. Such a covenant will not run with the land at law, but equity will enforce it specifically, or, what amounts to the same thing, the owner of the land, whether the covenantor or an assignee from him, will be restrained from committing a breach of the covenant. Sugden's Vendors, 596, 14th ed.

29. *Q.* Where abstracted deeds are in the hands of persons living at a distance from the residence of the purchaser and his solicitor, is the vendor, in the absence of any special contract, bound to produce them to the purchaser or his solicitor at their place of residence or business for comparison with the abstract? and if not, is he bound to pay the expense of a journey by the purchaser's solicitor to the place where the deeds are, or of his employing an agent there? and may the vendor elect whether to pay for the journey, or the agent?

*A.* The vendor is bound to produce the deeds at one of three places, namely: in London, at his own residence, or on the property. He is not bound to produce them at the residence or place of business of the purchaser or his solicitor. But, if the deeds are not produced at any of the three places above mentioned, the purchaser must send and examine them where they are; but the vendor must bear the expense of the journey, but not of the examination. Therefore, if an agent was employed, it is presumed the vendor would not have to pay his charges. The purchaser, however, is not bound to employ an agent in a country town, but his solicitor may attend. It should, however, be borne in mind that if the deeds are produced in London, a country solicitor cannot come to town to examine them, but he must employ an agent. Sugden's Vendors, 430.

30. *Q.* State what title deeds must a vendor of an estate, agreed to be sold without special conditions, deliver to the purchaser on completion of the purchase. And what, if any, may he retain the possession of?

*A.* A purchaser is entitled to have delivered to him all the deeds in the hands of the vendor which relate exclusively to the property sold. If the deeds relate to other property of the vendor, the purchaser is only entitled to a covenant at the vendor's expense for their production, also to attested copies, at the vendor's expense, of such as are not enrolled in a court of record. And this is so even if the vendor retain the smaller portion of the property. If, however, the *whole* of the property to which the deeds relate is sold in lots, the purchaser of the largest lot is entitled to the deeds, the purchasers of the remaining lots being entitled, at the vendor's expense, to a covenant to produce and also to attested copies. Sugden's Vendors, 34; Wms. Real Prop., 412.

31. *Q.* In cases where the title-deeds cannot be delivered up to a purchaser, what is he entitled to require? In the absence of stipulation, who is entitled to the title-deeds of land contracted to be

sold which relate also to other lands of greater value? Upon a sale of part of an estate without any stipulation as to deeds, who is entitled to the custody of them? and if the purchaser, is he bound to furnish the seller (who retains the other part of the estate) with attested copies, and at whose expense? In the absence of special conditions of sale to the contrary, can a purchaser obtain copies of abstracted deeds, or instruments on record, at the vendor's expense?

*A.* See the previous answer.

32. *Q.* Where a purchaser has not obtained the title-deeds, or a covenant for the production of them, can he require such a covenant to be executed to him under the usual covenant for further assurances?

*A.* The covenant for further assurance does not appear to entitle the covenantee to a covenant to produce the title-deeds. Sugden's Vendors, 438.

33. *Q.* Where, under "The Tithe Commutation Act," tithes have been merged by an owner in fee-simple of both the tithes and the lands out of which they issue, and he afterwards sells the lands as tithe or rent-charge free, must he deduce his title to the tithes?

*A.* The title and the tithes must still be deduced commencing with the grant from the Crown. The reason for this is that no greater interest could merge than the party had. Sugden's Vendors, 431.

34. *Q.* If the grantee of an annuity employ the grantor's solicitor, is such solicitor bound to disclose any circumstances that may affect the title?

*A.* It has been decided that if the grantee merely employ the grantor's solicitor to prepare the deeds, their mere preparation does not make him bound to disclose circumstances affecting the title. *Adamson* v. *Evitt*, 2 Russ. & My., 661. But Lord St. Leonards says that the principle of this decision has not been followed. Sugden's Vendors, 6. If, however, the grantor's solicitor was employed more confidentially than to prepare the deeds, the solicitor would clearly be bound to disclose the circumstances.

35. *Q.* If the abstract shows a good title on the face of it, but the purchaser's solicitor on comparing it with the title-deeds discovers an incurable defect, is the purchaser entitled to recover from the vendor the expense of comparing the abstract with the deeds, and would he be so if the defect appeared on the face of the abstract?

*A.* The purchaser is entitled to recover the expense of the examination which the latent defect has rendered abortive. But it is otherwise if the defect appeared upon the face of the abstract, as the purchaser's solicitor ought to have discovered it by perusal. Had he done so the expense of the comparison with the deeds would have been saved.

36. *Q.* What is the usual mode of verifying an abstract and a pedigree?

*A.* An abstract is verified by the production of the abstracted deeds and by office copies of wills. Also the identity of parcels is proved by statutory declarations. A pedigree is verified by certificates of marriages, births, baptisms, and of burials to prove deaths. Entries also in family bibles are received as evidence of pedigree. Sugden's Vendors, 415.

37. *Q.* On a sale of lands what expenses are usually borne by the vendor, and what by the purchaser?

*A.* The vendor pays the expenses of preparing his abstract and answering the requisitions on title; also of the extra expense the purchaser may be put to in examining the deeds in the hands of third parties, and not produced in London, on the property, or at the vendor's residence. He also pays for attested copies of documents he does not hand over, and of a covenant to produce the originals, and he pays the expense of executing the conveyance. The purchaser bears the expenses of investigating the title, examining the deeds, the searches, preparing the conveyance, the stamp, and registering it where necessary. If the lands are copyholds the practice is similar, but the purchaser pays the steward's fees on surrender and admittance and the fine on surrender. See *infra*, No. 39.

38. *Q.* Is it customary for the vendor or the purchaser to bear the expense of preparing the abstract of the title to the estate to be conveyed? and which, according to custom, bears the expense of the conveyance?

*A.* In the absence of stipulation, the expense of the preparation and verification of the abstract is borne by the vendor. But the purchaser prepares and bears the expense of the conveyance and stamps, though the vendor bears the expense of his solicitor perusing it, and of obtaining the signature of the grantor. Sugden's Vendors, 261.

39. *Q.* At whose expense is the preparation and perusal, and obtaining of the execution of the conveyance of freeholds to a purchaser? and the surrender and admission to copyholds?

*A.* As to the freeholds, see the previous answer. In the case of copyholds, the purchaser must pay the fine on admittance and the steward's fees, both on the surrender and admittance. The vendor pays his private expenses of the surrender and those of the other necessary parties to it. Dart's Vendors, 464.

40. *Q.* If the vendor contract to surrender and assure a copyhold estate at his own expense, is he bound to pay the lord's fine?

*A.* In such a case the vendor is not bound to pay the lord's fine on the admittance of the vendee, because it is said the title is perfected on admittance and the fine is not due until after. Sugden's Vendors, 562.

41. *Q.* Ought the purchaser of an estate to ascertain the terms of the tenancy of the occupier of the estate, and why?

*A.* He should ascertain the terms of the tenancy, because if he has notice of the tenancy he is bound by the tenant's rights. Ibid., 548.

42. *Q.* If a contract for sale describe property as leasehold, can the purchaser successfully resist a bill for specific performance on the

ground that, after the contract, he discovered that the lease contained an unusual covenant?

*A.* The purchaser would have no defence to the bill, as notice of the lease is notice of all its contents. If there were misrepresentation on the part of the vendor, the case would be otherwise. Ibid, 6—7.

43. *Q.* Can a contract to purchase an estate at a price to be fixed by two valuers (one to be named by each party), or an umpire, to be named by the valuers, if they differ in opinion, be enforced against a party who refuses to appoint his valuer; and, if so, how?

*A.* Such a contract may be enforced if the price has been ascertained as directed. The agreement of the parties must be strictly followed, otherwise it will not be enforced. The court will not itself fix a price in such a case. But if the agreement was to sell at a fair valuation, the court will execute it though no price is fixed. Ibid, 287.

44. *Q.* If a man be outlawed in a civil action, is the outlawry any impediment to his making a good title and conveyance to a purchaser of his freehold estate?

*A.* I should certainly not advise a client of mine to purchase lands from an outlaw. The sale would probably be valid; but if judgment had been signed, that should be considered. Also after office found, the rents of the real estate belong to the Crown. 13 Petersd. Abr., 22.

45. *Q.* How does notice of a trust affect a purchaser for valuable consideration?

*A.* The purchaser will be bound by the trust if he had notice of it, and the estate may be recovered from him by the *cestui que trust* within twenty years from the conveyance to the purchaser. 3 & 4 Wm. IV., c. 27, s. 25. If, however, the case is one of concealed fraud the time will run from the time when it might with reasonable diligence have been known, s. 26. In reference to the above it should be remembered that if the trust is a voluntary one of land it may be defeated by the owner who has declared the trust selling it to a purchaser, even with notice. 27 Eliz., c. 4.

46. *Q.* In what case is a purchaser bound to see to the application of money paid to trustees? and who are the necessary parties to the conveyance? To what extent has the law in this respect been recently altered?

*A.* As to the application of the purchase money see *infra*; Equity; "Trusts." As to the parties to the conveyance, the trustees of course convey, and it is also usual to make any *cestui que trust* who receives a considerable portion of the purchase money join in the covenants for title according to his interest. This course, however, is not adopted on sales under an order of court. Sugden's Vendors, 574.

47. *Q.* How is a contract for sale affected by the bankruptcy of the vendor or purchaser? state the law in either case.

*A.* If a vendor becomes bankrupt, the purchaser, provided the contract was made before petition and without notice of an act of bankruptcy, can compel the assignees to convey the estate to him, and they can also compel him to pay the money. If, however, the purchaser becomes bankrupt it is optional with the assignees to be bound by the contract. The proper course for the vendor to adopt in such a case is to require the assignees to elect whether they will abide by the agreement or not, and if they do not elect, to apply to the court to order the delivery up of the agreement. 12 & 13 Vic., c. 106, s. 146.

48. *Q.* When will a purchaser or mortgagee be secure in paying the purchase or mortgage-money to a person subject to the Bankrupt laws?

*A.* The purchaser or mortgagee will be safe in paying the money, if the payment is made *bonâ fide* before petition and without notice of any act of bankruptcy having been committed. 12 & 13 Vict., c. 106, s. 133.

49. *Q.* A (a trustee of a real estate for B) purchases the estate from B soon after he attains twenty-one; can A make such a title as a purchaser from him is bound to accept, and if the purchaser does accept the title, does he incur any, and what liabilities to B?

*A.* This question involves the power of a trustee to purchase the trust estate from his *cestui que trust*. This he can do if, as here, the latter is *sui juris*. But the *cestui que trust* must have discharged the trustee from the trust, and it must appear that the trustee at the time had shaken off his confidential character, and that the price is adequate. Under these circumstances A can make a good title and the purchaser would be under no liability to B. If, however, the circumstances of the transaction were otherwise and the sale was one which the court would not enforce as between A and B, a purchaser, with notice that this was so, would be liable to the same equity as the trustee was subject to, and the sale could be upset by B, and he could recover the estate on paying the price, and for improvements. Sugden's Vendors, 693, 695.

50. *Q.* If a person contract for the sale of his estate, and afterwards becomes a lunatic, who can convey the estate to the purchaser? and what course should be pursued?

*A.* The committee of the lunatic may convey under an order of the Lord Chancellor authorising them to do so. To obtain such an order a petition must be presented by the purchaser. 16 & 17 Vic., c. 70, s. 122.

51. *Q.* Is a delay occasioned by defects of title which are ultimately removed a bar to a decree for specific performance at the suit of the vendor? and if not, what steps should a purchaser take to relieve himself from the contract, if the delay be injurious to him?

*A.* A decree for specific performance will be made notwithstanding objections which have caused a delay, if they are ultimately removed. The purchaser may give the vendor a written notice that he shall consider the contract at an end if it be not completed within a reasonable time. Sugden's Vendors, 268.

52. *Q.* An allotment of land is awarded to A in the inclosure of common field lands, in lieu of A's previously existing rights. Is the purchaser of the allotment from A entitled to any other evidence of A's title than the award of the commissioners, and proof of their authority to make it?

*A.* The purchaser in addition to the award would be entitled to evidence of A's title to the rights in respect of which the award was made. Also to evidence that the enclosure was authorised and the power to enclose pursued. Conditions should be inserted providing for such a case. 1 Prideaux's Precedents, 28.

53. *Q.* Will a person, buying an estate in a registry-county, with notice of a prior incumbrance not registered, be bound by such incumbrance?

*A.* Such a person will be bound although it is not registered, because he obtains notice, and to secure this is the object of the Registry Acts. Sugden's Vendors, 728.

54. *Q.* Before completing a purchase, either of freehold, copyhold or leasehold, what searches should be made; and what would be the consequence of not making them?

*A.* In the case of freeholds the search should be made in the Common Pleas Registry for the last preceding five years for judgments *lis pendens*, crown debts; and for annuities to the commencement of the registry (1855). 1 & 2 Vic., c. 110; 18 & 19 Vic., c. 15. If a judgment entered up since the 23rd July, 1860, and before the 29th July, 1864 is found registered, search must also be made for a writ of execution. 23 & 24 Vic., c. 38, ss. 1, 2. As to judgments entered up since the latter date, it is, probably, only necessary to search for writs of execution. 27 & 28 Vic., c. 112. If the lands are in a county palatine the common pleas registry of the county should be searched. If the land is situate in the register counties of Middlesex and Yorkshire, and the Bedford Level the registers must be searched, unless the lands have been registered under the "Land Registry Act," when the land registry supplies the place of the registries of Yorkshire and Middlesex. If the vendor is a tenant in tail or a married woman search should be made for disentailing deeds and acknowledgements, in the Courts of Chancery and Common Pleas respectively. The Bankruptcy Court should be searched. If the land is copyhold the courts roll of the manor should be also searched. If the property is leasehold the Common Pleas and local registries should be searched; also it is advisable to enquire at the under-sheriff's office if a writ of execution has been lodged with him. Dart's Vendors, cap. 11.

55. *Q.* What should be done to postpone searches for incumbrances until immediately before the completion of the purchase?

*A.* The vendor should be asked in the requisitions if there are any incumbrances. The effect of this request is that if the vendor answer in the negative, and upon search just before completion it appear there are incumbrances which prevent completion, the purchaser may recover all the expenses he has been put to from the vendor. Sugden's Vendors, 538.

56. *Q.* In what session of the present reign was the Succession Duty Act passed? how does this affect the title to be shown to real estate?

*A.* The act referred to is 16 & 17 Vic., c. 51. A vendor who is liable to the duty should show by production of the receipt that he has paid it, otherwise the purchaser will take subject to the duty, which is made a first charge upon the land. The production of the receipt exonerates the purchaser, ss. 42, 44, 52. Sugden's Vendors, 8.

57. *Q.* If A comes into possession of an estate as tenant in fee on the death of another who died since the Succession Duty Act of 1853, and sells it, what are the duties of the purchaser's solicitor with regard to any liabilities imposed by that statute?

*A.* See the previous answer.

58. *Q.* If a person who is tenant for life of property under a will die before all the instalments of succession-duty are paid, what is the effect with regard to the unpaid instalments, and what the effect where the person who is entitled to the fee-simple dies before all the instalments are paid?

*A.* In the case of the tenant for life the instalments cease to be payable, but it is otherwise as to the tenant in fee, he having power to dispose by will of a continuing interest in the property. Accordingly it will remain charged with the remaining instalments. 16 & 17 Vic., c. 51, s. 21.

59. *Q.* (1). State in general, but accurate terms, what is a succession, within the Succession Duty Act, 1853, and the description of property charged. (2). Say if leaseholds are treated as real or personal property. (3). Give an instance or instances of succession whereon the duty attaches. (4). Say how far the duty attaches on interests aliened before the succession takes effect. (5). By what rule is the value of the succession measured? (6). How does the charge affect alienees by titles arising after the duty attaches, and *that* in the cases of property, real and personal, respectively. (7). What power is there of making separate assessments so as to discharge portions of property from the liability? If you do not answer the whole, answer some parts of the question.

*A.* (1). A succession is where a beneficial interest is taken in real or personal property upon the death of any person dying after the 19th May, 1853. As to personalty, the interest must be one upon which legacy duty is not payable, s. 2.

(2). Leaseholds are considered real property, s. 1.

(3). If A seised in fee devises his land to B a stranger in fee, B must pay succession duty at the rate of £10 per cent. So if stock is settled by marriage settlement on the children of the settlor after his death, such children must pay succession duty at the rate of £1 per cent.

(4). The alienee of the property takes it, subject to the same duty as the alienor would have been subject to had he not sold, s. 15.

(5). The age of the successor is first ascertained. Let us suppose him to be fifty. Reference is then made to the tables annexed to the act, and it is found that an annuity of £100 a year for a life of this age is worth £1,242 19s. 6d. Assuming the yearly rental of the land, less deductions on account of repairs, &c., to be £100 a year, the duty will be charged upon the above sum at the rate to which the successor is liable. If the annual value of the property is more or less than £100, the amount upon which the duty is payable can be ascertained by a rule of three calculation. That is, if an annuity of £100 a year is worth £1,242 19s. 6d., how much is an annuity of £1,500 worth. With regard to money no difficulty arises, but the rate of duty is charged upon the amount of the corpus.

(6). As to the purchaser of real property, see *supra*, No. 56. The purchaser of personalty, however, does not take subject to any unpaid duty, as the act merely makes it a first charge upon such property while in the ownership or control of the successor, s. 42.

(7). The commissioners may make separate assessments on separate properties, or parts of property, to which the successor succeeds, if reasonably required so to do. The effect of this is to make each part liable only for its own share of duty, s. 43.

It will be seen that the above is treated as one question, whereas in truth it comprises seven distinct questions. For the benefit of students and practitioners I have answered them in detail; but candidates would, without much discredit, avail themselves of the permission given to answer some parts of the *question*.

60. *Q.* State shortly the course of proceeding in a sale and purchase of lands from date of contract to completion of purchase?

*A.* Upon the agreement being signed, the vendor must deliver a perfect abstract within the time specified, the purchaser will examine it with the deeds, and peruse it, he will then deliver his requisitions on title, which are often prepared by counsel. The vendor will then consider them, and comply or not as he thinks fit. Any disputes having been settled as to title, the conveyance will be prepared by the purchaser, and sent to the vendor for perusal. When approved, it is engrossed by the purchaser and stamped, an appointment to complete is made, the purchaser makes the searches mentioned *supra;* should no incumbrances be found the parties attend the completion, the vendor with the deeds, and conveyance duly executed, the purchaser with the money. This latter being paid, with interest, if any, the deeds are taken up, and the purchaser enters into possession, he having obtained an authority from the vendor to the tenants to pay the rent to him. Dart's Vendors and Purchasers, caps. 6—12.

61. *Q.* B purchases from A fifteen acres of land in a hamlet; A's title deeds disclose a clear sixty years' title to fifteen acres of land in that hamlet. Ought anything more to be done by B before he can safely take a conveyance from A and pay the purchase-money?

*A.* If the parcels as described in the deeds agree with the land bought there can be no difficulty. That this is so should be ascertained by B. He should also, if there is any doubt, obtain a statutory declaration from the vendor, or some one who knows the *locus in quo*, that the lands about to be conveyed have been occupied and known for a long time by the description contained in the title deeds.

62. *Q*. Who are the proper parties to assign a lease of a deceased testator who bequeathed it specifically, and why?

*A*. The executor may alone make a valid assignment. He has an absolute power of disposition over the whole personal effects, and after a sale they cannot be followed into the hands of the alienee. The concurrence of the legatee should be obtained for greater caution, but it is clearly unnecessary. 2 Wms. Exors., 838, 5th ed.

63. *Q*. A, possessed of leaseholds for years, appoints B and C his executors; B proves the will; C renounces; B's executor afterwards sells the leaseholds to D. Is any evidence of the title subsequent to A's death necessary, beyond the probates of the wills of A and B?

*A*. Evidence must be produced that C has renounced. An office copy of the renunciation will do. Since the Probate Act of 1857, the effect of C's renunciation is to operate as if he had never been named an executor, therefore B has ample power of transmission, s. 79. Formerly it was in C's power to retract his renunciation. Coote's Prob. Pract., 4th ed., 179.

64. *Q*. A devises land to B, and his trust estates to C, and afterwards contracts to sell his land to a purchaser, and dies before the conveyance is executed. Who is the person to convey?

*A*. The devisee B must convey the estate to the purchaser, and the personal representatives must concur for the purpose of giving a receipt for the money. In equity the devise is revoked by the contract—that is, the devisee will not take the purchase money, but at law the legal estate vests in him. The estate of A would not pass to C as a trust estate, the devise of the trust estates being considered as not embracing a constructive trust, which that of the vendor is after the contract. This, however, like almost all other questions of construction, turns upon the wording of the devise. 1 Jarm. Wills, 668, 3rd ed.

65. *Q*. Would a contract for the purchase of land be impeachable or not by a vendor on the ground of considerable inadequacy of consideration, but not of fraud?

*A*. A contract would not be impeachable on this ground alone. See *infra*, Equity. "Fraud."

66. *Q*. In conditions of sale of estates it is often provided that if, from any cause whatsoever, the completion should be delayed after the day named, the purchaser is to pay interest from that time until the day of completing the sale. Can this condition be enforced without qualification? and why not?

*A*. Such a condition will not hold good if the delay arise from the wilful default of the vendor, but it may be enforced in other events, even if the delay is owing to defects in the title. The reason for not enforcing the stipulation "from any cause whatever" in the above case is, that the words mean some cause not provided for by the contract and do not apply to the vendor committing a breach of contract, which he does by delaying the completion. *Vickers* v. *Hand*, 26 Beav., 630. Sugden's Vendors, 635.

67. *Q.* Give a sketch of the ordinary charges of a solicitor for a purchaser, on the purchase of a freehold estate, in respect of the conveyance, from the time of purchase to the completion of it.

*A.*

| | £ | s. | d. |
|---|---|---|---|
| Attending taking instructions | 0 | 6 | 8 |
| Copy draft contract | 1 | 1 | 0 |
| Perusing | 1 | 1 | 0 |
| Attending getting same signed | 0 | 6 | 8 |
| Attending exchanging | 0 | 6 | 8 |
| Perusing abstract, forty sheets (6s. 8d. every three sheets) | 4 | 13 | 4 |
| Attending examining same, with deeds, self and clerk, eight hours | 4 | 0 | 0 |
| Fee to counsel to advise on abstract (£1 1s. every six sheets) | 7 | 12 | 0 |
| Attending him | 0 | 6 | 8 |
| Instructions for requisitions | 0 | 6 | 8 |
| Drawing same and copy, six sheets | 3 | 0 | 0 |
| Perusing answers to requisitions | 2 | 2 | 0 |

| | £ | s. | d. |
|---|---|---|---|
| Instructions for conveyance | 0 | 6 | 8 |
| Drawing same, 90 folios | 4 | 10 | 0 |
| Fair copy | 1 | 10 | 0 |
| Fee to counsel to settle and Clerk | 3 | 5 | 6 |
| Attending him | 0 | 6 | 8 |
| Perusing alterations | 0 | 6 | 8 |
| Engrossing | 3 | 0 | 0 |
| Parchment, six skins | 1 | 10 | 0 |
| Paid stamps (*ad val.* on £5,000, £25 and five fol. £2 10s.) | 27 | 10 | 0 |
| Attending stamping | 0 | 13 | 4 |
| Attending searching for judgments, &c., Crown debts, and annuities, 13s. 4d. each | 2 | 0 | 0 |
| Paid search | 0 | 1 | 0 |
| Attending completion, taking up deeds, and paying money | 3 | 3 | 0 |
| Letters and messengers | 2 | 2 | 0 |

The above is merely an outline of the charges. Numerous letters and attendances occur for which the former are charged 5s., though on taxation only 3s. 6d. is allowed. Attendances are charged 6s. 8d. per hour. Counsel's fee for settling the draft is one guinea for every ten sheets, and there ought to be three folios in each sheet.

## XXI.—*Judgments as they affect Realty.*

1. *Q.* How do judgments affect real property? and how are such judgments to be enforced?

*A.* They are a charge upon all lands whether freehold, copyhold, or leasehold, which the defendant was seised of, possessed, or entitled to, at the time of entering up the judgments, or at any time afterwards. 1 & 2 Vic., c. 110, ss. 11, 13. As to registering and enforcing judgments, see *supra*, Common Law, p. 93, No. 23.

2. *Q.* A has a decree in Chancery against B for the payment of a sum of money: how is A to make that sum a charge upon B's estate, and under what authority?

*A.* The decree itself is a charge upon B's estate in the same manner that a judgment would be. As against purchasers, mortgagees, and creditors of B, registration is necessary, as is the case with regard to a judgment. *Supra.* Common Law.

3. *Q.* What is the effect of a judgment registered under 1 & 2 Vic., c. 110, upon the freehold, leasehold, and copyhold estates of the debtor at law, and in equity? and who are protected by that statute, and the 2 & 3 Vic., c. 11, against such a judgment in equity?

*A.* The effect of a registered judgment is to make it binding as against purchasers, mortgagees, and creditors of the judgment debtor. It is a charge upon the land as against the debtor himself when entered up, and without registration; but for the protection of purchasers and mortgagees the judgments were directed to be registered.

4. *Q.* A debtor sells his land charged with a judgment before the debt has been paid. Can the creditor in all cases recover the debt out of the land after it has been conveyed to the purchaser, or upon what does his right to recover it depend?

*A.* See the previous answer and *supra*, "Common Law."

5. *Q.* In what cases does a judgment against a tenant in tail bind his issue, and the remainder man?

*A.* It will bind them if the defendant could, without the assent of any other person, have barred their estates. 1 & 2 Vic., c. 110, ss. 13, 18.

6. *Q.* Do judgment against a mortgagee affect the mortgaged estate in the hands of a purchaser from the mortgagor, who pays off the mortgage out of the purchase-money; and does notice to the purchaser of the judgment prior to the completion of the purchase make any, and what, difference in such a case?

*A.* If the mortgage is paid off, the judgment will not affect the purchaser. 18 Vic., c. 15, s. 110. Before this provision it was necessary to search against the mortgagee. Notice to the purchaser is immaterial. As to the effect of this act, see *Greaves* v. *Wilson*, 28. L. J. Ch., 103.

7. *Q.* By the act of the last session (24 & 25 Vic.) to amend the law of property, what is necessary, after entering up a judgment, to be done, in order that the same may affect land as to a purchaser or mortgagee, and does it make any difference whether such purchaser or mortgagee have notice or not of the judgment?

*A.* See *supra*, "Common Law," p. 93, No. 23. Notice is immaterial.

8. *Q.* What is *lis pendens*, and where must a memorandum thereof be registered in order to affect a purchase of land?

*A.* It is a pending suit relating to lands, and to affect them in the hands of a purchaser must be registered in the Court of Common Pleas. As to what amounts to a *lis pendens*, see *infra*, "Equity."

9. *Q.* State the advantages of some of the principal clauses in 1 & 2 Vic., c. 110, with respect to judgments.

*A.* The act made judgments a charge as against all the debtor's lands, s. 13. It enabled the plaintiff to obtain a charging order upon the defendant's stock, shares, etc., ss. 14, 15. It provided registration, as against purchasers, mortgagees, and creditors, s. 19. Also that judgments of inferior courts might be removed and registered in a superior court, so as to affect the defendant's lands, s. 22.

10. *Q.* At what time does a judgment operate on land in a registered county; and is there any, and what, difference as to the period of its so doing in Middlesex and in Yorkshire?

*A.* As against the defendant himself, the judgment operates from the time of its being entered up in all cases. But, as against purchasers and mortgagees of lands in Middlesex, the judgment only operates from the date of registration. In the North Riding, the plaintiff has twenty days from entering it up to register it. 8 Geo. II., c. 6. In the East and West Ridings and Kingston-upon-Hull, he has thirty days. 5 Anne, c. 18, s. 11; 6 Anne, c. 35, s. 28; 9 Jarman by Sweet, 689.

## XXII.—*The Essentials of Deeds.*

1. *Q.* What is a deed and what are the chief requisites to a valid deed.

*A.* It is a writing sealed and delivered by the parties. Its requisites are:—1. Parties able to contract, and also a subject matter. 2. It must be written or printed upon parchment or paper. 3. The words must be sufficient to specify the agreement and bind the parties. 4. It should be read to a party desiring that it be read. 5. The instrument should be sealed and the universal practice is to sign it also, though the latter is thought unnecessary, except in certain cases. 6. It should be delivered by the party himself or his attorney. 7. For the better preservation of proof it should be signed, sealed, and delivered in the presence of witnesses who should attest the execution. 1 Steph. Com., 489.

2. *Q.* What are the formal parts of a deed?

*A.* They are:—1. The premises, setting forth the date, number, names, and additions of the parties. 2. The recitals of any facts necessary to explain the object of the deed. 3. The testatum, or witnessing part. 4. The parcels. 5, 6. The habendum and tenendum (to have and to hold). The former marking out the estate conveyed, the latter is now inoperative. 7. The reddendum, or reservation upon which the grant is made. 8. A condition, which is a clause upon which the grant may be defeated. 9. The covenants. 10. The conclusion. "In witness whereof, etc." Ibid, 491.

3. *Q.* Is it necessary to the validity of a deed that it should in any, and what, cases be read to the parties?

*A.* If a party desires that the deed be read, he should be allowed to read, or it should be read to him; otherwise it will be void as to him. 1 Steph. Com., 500.

4. *Q.* What mode of execution of deeds, in exercise of powers of appointment by deed or instrument in writing, not testamentary, is now in all cases sufficient, though not in all cases necessary?

*A.* It is now enacted that a deed executed after the 13th August 1859, in the presence of, and attested by two or more, witnesses, in the manner in which deeds are ordinarily executed and attested, shall so far as the execution and attestation thereof be a valid execution of a power of appointment by deed or instrument in writing not testamentary. But this provision does not do away with the necessity of obtaining any consent to the execution of the power. 22 & 23 Vic., c. 35, s. 12.

5. *Q.* Is a purchaser bound to take a conveyance executed by

the attorney of the vendor under a power of attorney, with any, and what, condition?

*A.* A purchaser is not bound to take a conveyance so executed, unless a necessity for it exists, as he is entitled to have the execution of the vendor. If, however, he does take under a power of attorney, the attorney should execute a declaration of trust of the purchase money in favour of the purchaser, until it either appear that the vendor was alive at the time of the execution of the deed, or if he be dead, until the estate is duly conveyed to the purchaser. Sugden's Vendors, 563.

6. *Q.* If a purchase deed be executed under a power of attorney from the vendor, in whose name should it be executed, and what is the form of attestation?

*A.* It is the practice for the deed to be executed in the name of the vendor. The attestation should be " signed, sealed, and delivered by the said E T as the attorney, and in the name and on behalf of the said A B (vendor), in the presence of, etc." 1 Prideaux's Precedents, 203.

7. *Q.* What is an escrow?

*A.* It is a term applied to a deed which is delivered conditionally on a certain thing being done. When the condition is performed, the deed operates from the date of sealing and delivery. 1 Steph. Com., 503.

8. *Q.* Can a deed be altered after it has been executed by all or any of the parties? and, if so, to what extent?

*A.* If the deed is altered by the grantee or obligee, or by a stranger, in a material part, the deed becomes void. The result is the same if the grantor or obligor alters the deed in a point not material. But if a stranger without his privity alters the deed in a point not material, the deed is not avoided. *Pigot's Case.* 11 Rep. 26, b. The effect of a deed becoming void in consequence of an alteration is not, however, to revest an estate conveyed by it in the grantor, but merely to prevent an action being brought upon a covenant contained in it. Broom's Maxims, 155; Wms. Real Prop., 135.

9. *Q.* Does a deed of grant of hereditaments in possession require more than one stamp?

*A.* Such a deed requires an *ad valorem* duty, upon the consideration as to which see the next answer. Also a progressive duty of ten shillings for every complete fifteen folios after the first fifteen. If, however, the *ad valorem* duty is less than 10*s.*, the progressive duty is equal in amount to the *ad valorem* duty. 13 & 14 Vic., c. 97.

10. *Q.* What is the *ad valorem* stamp on a conveyance, mortgage, and settlement?

*A.* Upon a conveyance the stamp is at the rate of 10*s.* for every £100 up to £600, when it is 10*s.* upon every fractional part of £100. Upon a mortgage the stamp is at the rate of 2*s.* 6*d.* upon every £100 up to £300, and after that it is 2*s.* 6*d.* upon every fractional part of £100. Upon a settlement of personal property it is 5*s.* per cent. upon every £100 or fractional part of £100 after the first

£100. 13 & 14 Vic., c. 97. There is no *ad valorem* duty upon settlements of real estate, such a settlement being liable to a deed stamp of £1 15s. 0d., and also the progressive duty with which also all the above are chargeable.

11. *Q.* Your client has purchased a freehold estate, with the timber upon it, and the furniture and fixtures of the mansion: and on the completion of the purchase, interest on the purchase-money is payable by him. Does the *ad valorem* duty on conveyances attach to the whole of the purchase-money and interest, or to what part of it?

*A.* The *ad valorem* duty will attach upon whatever is dealt with as property, therefore it would be payable upon the whole purchase money. It has, indeed, been decided, that the *ad valorem* duty attaches only on lands, rents, annuities, and other property, *ejusdem generis*. Warren v. Howe, 2 B. & C., 281. But this decision is not approved. Tilsley's Stamp Laws, 223, 2nd ed.

12. *Q.* What instruments can be stamped after they are executed, and on what terms?

*A.* Agreements may be stamped within fourteen days after execution, without penalty; afterwards, if the subject matter exceeds in value £20, on a penalty of £10, but if not exceeding that sum, £1. So also may attested copies, within sixty days after the date of attestation; afterwards on payment of £10. So may deeds within two months of date, or if executed abroad within two months of their arrival in England, afterwards on payment of £10, with interest, if the duties exceed £10. So may powers of attorney within three months. So may articles of clerkship, on payment of £5 within six calendar months. If the omission to stamp be unintentional and without fraud (forgetfulness and inadvertence are not sufficient grounds), the Commissioners of Inland Revenue have power to remit the penalty within twelve months from the date of the deed or instrument. For this purpose a memorial should be presented, setting forth the circumstances. 13 & 14 Vic., c. 97. The Lawyer's Companion, 198—201.

13. *Q.* In case of a doubt as to the proper stamp to be affixed to a deed, what course would you recommend to be adopted for your client's security?

*A.* I should recommend an application being made to the Commissioners of Inland Revenue to certify the proper amount of duty payable upon the deed; this they will do on payment of 10s. After the deed is stamped, as denoted by them, it cannot be objected to in any court, on account of the stamp being improper. 13 & 14 Vic., c. 97, s. 14.

14. *Q.* What do you understand by the doctrine of estoppel?

*A.* See *supra*, 10, No. 16.

15. *Q.* Can estoppel arise upon a deed-poll? Give a reason.

*A.* A deed-poll will not operate as an estoppel, for this reason, that estoppel must be reciprocal and binding on both parties; therefore, a stranger cannot be bound by or take advantage of an estoppel. A deed-poll is the deed merely of the party making it, but an indenture is the deed of both parties. Co. Litt., 47, a, b.; 1 Platt on Leases, 55.

16. *Q.* How may a deed be avoided?

*A.* As to avoiding a deed by alteration, see *supra*, No. 8. A voluntary deed may also be avoided by a subsequent conveyance of the land settled to a *bonâ fide* purchaser. Also by tearing off the the seal, or by cancellation. After breach a deed of covenant may also be avoided by accord and satisfaction. *Mayor, etc., of Berwick,* v. *Oswald,* 1 E. & B., 295. A deed may also be discharged by another deed, if such deed amounts to a release, or it may be merged by judgment being entered up upon it. So also a bond is avoided if the performance of the condition become impossible by the act of God. So a deed may be impeached, if founded upon an illegal or immoral consideration. *Collins* v. *Blantern,* 1 Sm. L. C., 310; 1 Steph. Com., 504, 5th ed.

XXIII.—*Alienation by act inter vivos.*

1. *Q.* What persons are incapable of alienating their lands? or of purchasing lands?

*A.* Infants, idiots, and lunatics, cannot alienate their lands, nor can married women, if not settled to their separate use, without the concurrence of their husbands. Municipal and ecclesiastical corporations are also under a partial incapacity to alien. Aliens and convicted felons can only alien subject to the rights of the Crown and lords. The parishioners, or inhabitants, or churchwardens of any place are absolutely incapable of purchasing lands by those names. Aliens may purchase, but they hold for the benefit of the Crown. This is also the case as to attainted felons and corporations, unless the latter are authorised by Act of Parliament, or license from the Crown. Infants, idiots, lunatics, and married women, are incapable of purchasing *sub modo.* Sugden's Vendors, 684.

2. *Q.* What conveyances take effect by force of the Statute of Uses, and what by the Common Law?

*A.* The following operate by virtue of the Statute of Uses:— 1. Appointment of uses. 2. Bargain and sale. 3. Covenant to stand seised. Common Law conveyances are—1. Feoffment. 2. Gift. 3. Grant. 4. Lease. 5. Exchange. 6. Partition. 7. Release. 8. Conformation. 9. Surrender. 10. Assignment. 11. Underlease. 12. Defeazance. The following operate partly by virtue of the common law, and partly by the statute:— 1. Feoffment to uses. 2. Grant to uses. 3. Statutory release. The Articled Clerk's Manual, 113, 9th ed., by Anderson; 1 Steph. Com., 511.

3. *Q.* In what respects do freeholds and copyholds principally differ as to alienation?

*A.* Freeholds are usually now conveyed by deed of grant, a form of conveyance which, before 8 & 9 Vic., c. 106, was only applicable to the transfer of incorporeal hereditaments. Many of those mentioned in the previous answer are also applicable to freeholds. Copyholds, on the other hand, are conveyed by surrender to the lord, and admittance by the lord of the surrenderee as tenant. See *supra* "Copyholds."

4. *Q.* Does the word "grant" in a conveyance imply in all, or in any, and what, cases, a warranty of title?

*A.* It only implies a covenant by force of some Act of Parliament. 8 & 9 Vic., c. 106, s. 4. Thus, by the Registry Acts of Yorkshire, the words *grant, bargain*, and *sell*, in a deed of bargain and sale duly registered, imply covenants for quiet enjoyment and further assurance. Also covenants for title are implied by the word grant, in conveyances by companies under the Lands Clauses Consolidation Act, 1845. 8 & 9 Vic., c. 18, s. 132. Also in conveyances to the Governors of Queen Anne's Bounty. 1 & 2 Vic., c. 20, s. 22. Wms. Real Prop., 402. The word *demise* in a lease operates as an absolute covenant for quiet enjoyment. *Spencer's Case*, 1 Sm. L. C., 43.

5. *Q.* What is a feoffment, and is there anything, and if so, what essential to perfect it?

*A.* It is a method of conveying corporeal hereditaments in possession, which was formerly much used in this country. It was accompanied by livery of seisin, signifying delivery of possession. This livery is either in deed, which was giving possession upon the premises, or in law which was effected in sight of the land. Wms. Real Prop., 129.

6. *Q.* What is the consequence of the omission of the indorsement of the livery of seisin on a feoffment?

*A.* The consequence of such omission is that the feoffment is not evidence of possession having been given. Still livery of seisin will be presumed after a lengthened possession of land. Smith's R. & P. Prop., 602.

7. *Q.* In what case prior to the Act 8 & 9 Vic., c. 106 (An Act to amend the Law of Real Property"), was feoffment a necessary form of conveyance, and why?

*A.* In conveyances by corporations a feoffment was necessary, because a corporation cannot be seised to a use, and, therefore, could not adopt any of the conveyances operating by virtue of the Statute of Uses. A lease with entry and a subsequent release would have effected the same purpose. Watkin's Conv., 283, 8th ed. Practically, also, a fee was conferred by a person having no right of property making a feoffment. This created an estate by wrong, but it could hardly be called a "conveyance." Ibid., 32.

8. *Q.* Why is a feoffment no longer a necessary form of assurance?

*A.* It is no longer necessary, because as before-mentioned corporeal hereditaments may be conveyed by grant. 8 & 9 Vic., c. 106. Indeed, long before this statute it was quite out of use owing to its inconvenience and publicity. The conveyances above-mentioned as operating under the statute of uses supplanted a feoffment. It is still, however, necessary in one or two cases. See the next answer.

9. *Q.* Is there any custom which enables an infant to convey by any, and what, form of assurance?

*A.* By the custom of gavelkind an infant may at the age of fifteen convey lands by feoffment and livery of seisin. This feoffment need not be by deed, and it is especially excepted from the operation of 8 & 9 Vic., c. 106. Wms. Real Prop., 133.

10. *Q.* How is the compensation for land taken from persons under disability under the provisions of 8 Vic., c. 18 ("The Lands Clauses Act") assessed, and how may the money be invested?

*A.* It is to be ascertained by the valuation of two able practical surveyors, one nominated by the promoters, the other by the other party. If they disagree, a third may be appointed by two justices. If the purchase-money amount to £200, it is to be paid into the Bank in the name of the Accountant-General, and is to be applied in the redemption or purchase of the land-tax or discharge of incumbrances. In the purchase of other lands. If money is paid in respect of injury to buildings, &c., in such way as the court may direct, or in payment to any person becoming absolutely entitled, ss. 9, 69. Sums exceeding £20 and not above £200 may either be disposed of as above-mentioned, or be paid to trustees nominated by the guardians, committee, &c. of the persons under disability to be by them applied as in the case of sums above £200. Sums not exceeding £20 are to be paid to the guardians, &c. of the persons under disability for their use. ss. 69, 71, 72.

11. *Q.* What parties are enabled to convey by the last-mentioned act?

*A.* The following persons may convey:—Corporations, tenants in tail or for life, married women, guardians, committees of lunatics and idiots, trustees, executors and administrators, and all parties for the time being entitled to the receipt of the rents and profits of the land in possession, or subject to any estate in dower, or lease for life, years, or any less interest, s. 7.

12. *Q.* Referring to the act to amend the law of real property, 1845, state the purport of its provisions, under these heads, or some of them:—1. The operation of a deed of grant, feoffment, exchange, and partition, respectively. 2. Allowing the giving of an immediate estate, or the benefit of a condition or covenant to a person, not a party. 3. The power of disposition by deed of contingent, executory and future interests. 4. The alteration of the law in regard to contingent remainders.

*A.* 1. By s. 4, the words give or grant are not to imply a covenant, a feoffment is not to have a tortious operation, and exchanges or partitions are not to imply any condition in law.

2. s. 5, permits this which was formerly only possible under a deed poll. Co. Litt., 26, a. 231.

3. By s. 6, such a power is conferred upon the owners of such

interests by deed. A married woman conveying must conform with the provisions of 3 & 4 Wm. IV., c. 74.

4. Contingent remainders are no longer destructable by the forfeiture, surrender or merger of the particular estate. s. 8.

13. *Q.* On an exchange of lands, where one party is ousted, what is his remedy?

*A.* His only remedy now is upon the covenants in the deed of exchange. Formerly he might re-enter upon the lands he has given in exchange by virtue of an implied warranty. This no longer exists, but of course a similar right may be stipulated for in the deed. 1 Steph. Com., 525.

14. *Q.* What are the objections to a deed of exchange as a mode of conveyance?

*A.* They are that a warranty was implied as just mentioned. Also entry is necessary to complete the conveyance, and there must be a mutuality of interest between the parties. In practice this method of conveyance is now never used, an exchange being effected by the execution of mutual releases. Watkins' Conv., 329.

15. *Q.* Describe the mode of effecting exchanges of real estate, where parties are under disability?

*A.* The exchanges may be effected as mentioned in the next answer, but first the parties under disability must have obtained leave to join in the application; if a lunatic, by order to the committee from the Lord Chancellor; if an infant, by order from the Court of Chancery to the guardian. The husband may concur on the part of his wife. Elmer on Lunacy, 152; 8 & 9 Vic., c. 118, s. 20.

16. *Q.* What is necessary to effect an exchange of lands under the "General Inclosure Act"?

*A.* The person interested in the lands proposed to be exchanged must make a written application to the Enclosure Commissioners. The latter will direct enquiries as to whether the exchange would be beneficial to the owners, and if so, they will make an order of exchange, with a plan of the lands to be given and taken in exchange. The order cannot be impeached by reason of any defect of title of the person on whose application it is made. The land taken in exchange enures to the same uses and trusts and is subject to the same charges as the land given in exchange. 8 & 9 Vic., c. 118, ss. 92, 147.

17. *Q.* What is a deed of partition, and by whom may it be made?

*A.* It is a deed made by joint tenants, co-parceners or tenants in common for the purpose of dividing the lands held by them. The effect of the partition is to make each a tenant in severalty of his allotted share. 1 Steph. Com., 526.

18. *Q.* What is the nature of a bargain and sale?

*A.* It is a conveyance of land operating without transmutation of possession. By means of this conveyance feoffment and livery seisin were rendered unnecessary. The bargainor to whom valuable consideration was paid by the bargainee was considered in equity as seised to the use of the latter, upon the principle that the bargain and sale was a contract to convey the lands, which ought to be performed. After 27 Hen. VIII., c. 10, this use was turned into possession, and the bargainee now has the legal estate. See *supra*: "Uses, Trusts and Powers," 164, No. 17.

19. *Q.* Is any, and what, formality necessary to the completion of a bargain and sale? and, if so, by what statute is it provided?

*A.* Enrolment of bargains and sales of estates of inheritance or freehold in one of the Courts of Record at Westminster is necessary by virtue of 27 Hen. VIII., c. 16.

20. *Q.* Explain how the conveyance by lease and release obviated the necessity of livery of seisin, or of giving corporal possession of the land conveyed.

*A.* When the statute just mentioned was passed bargains and sales of estates of freeholds were of course made public. To avoid this, a bargain and sale for a nominal consideration was made for a year, the effect of which was to vest in the bargainee the legal estate for this period without entry, and also without enrolment. 27 Hen. VIII., c. 16 not applying to terms of years. The bargainor then released to him the remainder of his interest and the lessee for a year became the owner of the freehold. The conveyance it will be seen operated under the Statute of Uses, in vesting the legal estate for a year in the bargainee. It also operated by common law, in that the release vested the freehold in the releasee. Thus, if A seised in fee bargained and sold to B for a year, he took the term by virtue of the statute. Upon the release being made the fee vests by the common law in B. If, however, the release was to B to the use of C the statute would have given the legal estate to the latter. Fearne, by Butler, 416.

21. *Q.* What was the advantage of taking a conveyance of a reversion by lease and release, instead of by grant?

*A.* The advantage was that in the case of a grant it was necessary in future dealings with the property to prove the existence of a particular estate. But in the case of the lease and release this was unnecessary. Watkins' Conv., 8th ed., 130.

22. *Q.* Where it is proposed to convey an estate by lease and release, can the lease be dispensed with under any, and what circumstances, and under what authority?

*A.* The lease is rendered unnecessary by 4 & 5 Vic., c. 21. A deed of grant has also supplanted a release. 8 & 9 Vic., c. 106.

23. *Q.* What are the technical names of each part of a conveyance in fee?

*A.* See *supra*, "The Essentials of Deeds," No. 2.

24. *Q.* What is a covenant?

*A.* It is an agreement, convention, or promise of two or more parties by deed in writing, signed, sealed and delivered, by which either of the parties pledges himself to the other that something is either done or shall be done, or stipulates for the truth of certain facts. The party promising is called the covenantor, the party to whom it is made, the covenantee. Wharton's Law Lexicon, 235.

25. *Q.* What are the ordinary covenants for title which a purchaser of an estate in fee can require from the vendor who is selling property belonging to himself for his own benefit?

*A.* They are:—1. That the vendor has good right to convey. 2. That the lands shall be quietly enjoyed. 3. That they are free from incumbrances. 4. That the vendor and his heirs will make further assurance if necessary. These covenants, if the vendor is a purchaser, only extend to his own acts, but if taken by descent, devise, or under a voluntary settlement, the covenants extend to the acts of the last purchaser, devisor, or donor, as the case may be. Wms. R. P., 402.

26. *Q.* In an ordinary conveyance in fee on a sale by a vendor, whose title is by purchase by himself, give a concise form substantially of the covenants for title binding the heirs of the covenantor and running with the land?

*A.* They would be as follows:— The said "A" (vendor) for himself and his *heirs* covenants with the said "B" (purchaser), that notwithstanding anything suffered by the said A, or through his default or to which he has been party or privy, he has good right to grant the premises in manner aforesaid. And that, notwithstanding, &c., the same may be peaceably enjoyed by B without disturbance, and that free from all incumbrances. And that, notwithstanding, &c., the said A will at the reasonable request and cost of the said B do all acts for further assuring the said premises to B. Lewis's Principles of Conveyancing, 81.

27. *Q.* What are the covenants from a vendor of leaseholds to a purchaser, and *vice versâ?*

*A.* See *supra*, p. 196, No. 32.

28. *Q.* When trustees sell land under a power or trust for sale, with the assent of the tenant for life of the property, what covenants are the trustees and tenant for life respectively bound to enter into with the purchaser?

*A.* The trustees can only be required to covenant that they have done no act to incumber. The tenant for life must enter into the ordinary covenants for title mentioned above. Sugden's Vendors, 575.

29. *Q.* Is there any, and what, difference between the covenants for title on a mortgage and on a sale?

*A.* They differ in that a mortgagor enters into absolute covenants, that is against the acts of the whole world. Those by a vendor, as above seen, are qualified. Wms. R. P., 403.

30. *Q.* What covenants is it usual for trustees or mortgagees to enter into?

*A.* Trustees covenant that they have done no act to incumber, and so also do mortgagees when they reconvey the land. They are not bound to enter into the usual covenants for title. Sugden's Vendors, 69, 14th ed.

31. *Q.* If A, on the sale of his estate, covenant for quiet enjoy-

ment against all persons claiming by, from, or under him, would a claim of dower, by his mother, come within the covenant?

*A.* The covenant would not include the claim for dower by A's mother, as the claim is not by, from, or under him, but under the father of A, for whose acts he does not covenant. The purchaser, therefore, would have no remedy against A upon the covenant. The purchaser, however, if not guilty of negligence, and if A had concealed the incumbrance, would probably be able to set the sale aside in equity, or bring an action on the case at law. Sugden's Vendors, 552, 14th ed.

32. *Q.* In the case of a purchase of lands by B, the conveyance being made to A and his heirs, to the ordinary uses to bar dower in favour of B (the purchaser), with a power of appointment given to B: with which of them should the covenants for title, &c., be entered into, and why?

*A.* They should be entered into with A. This is in order that they should run with the land in favour of a purchaser from B, as such purchaser would take in privity of estate from A out of whose seisin the estate of the purchaser is served. If entered into with B, the covenants would not run to a purchaser, because the estate of B would not pass, but would merely be divested by the conveyance to the purchaser. Sugden's Vendors, 578.

33. *Q.* Will a covenant for production of title-deeds run with the land in any, and what cases? and what ownership is necessary in the covenantor and covenantee?

*A.* Such a covenant will run with the lands purchased, so as to entitle any subsequent purchaser to enforce it against the covenantor, but it is doubtful if it will run with the lands retained by the covenantor so as to bind the alienee of them. *Onslow* v. *Lord Londesborough*, 10 Ha., 67. The better opinion is, that the covenant runs both ways. A privity of estate should exist between the covenantor and covenantee, and the former should have the custody of the deeds and be clothed with the legal estate in the land. Sugden's Vendors, 453, 14th ed.

34. *Q.* Where a covenantor to produce title-deeds sells the land and parts with the deeds, is his personal liability discharged, or how is the production secured to the covenantee?

*A.* The covenantor will still be liable upon the covenant. But as the better opinion is that the covenant binds the lands in the hands of the purchaser from the covenantor, he may be compelled to produce them by the covenantee. In such a case, it may be expedient for the covenantor to retain the deeds, giving a covenant to produce them to the second purchaser. Ibid.

35. *Q.* A has purchased a freehold estate, B and C, his wife's trustees, lending part of the money. It is desired to embrace in one deed the mortgage and conveyance. State shortly how the estate should be limited.

*A.* The estate should be conveyed by the vendor to A and his heirs to the use of B and C for 500 years, subject to a proviso for redemption and cesser of the term on payment to B and C of the money advanced by them, after the determination of the term, and, in the meantime, subject thereto to A to the usual dower uses. 1 Prideaux's Precedents, 419.

36. *Q.* Give a concise form in substance of an assignment of a life policy, on sale or mortgage, including the necessary power of attorney, and say if any further act is necessary to give it effect?

*A.* In substance the assignment on sale would be:—Parties. Recital of policy. Agreement for sale. Testatum. Consideration. Assignment. Power of attorney to sue in the name of the assignor, and a declaration of trust by him in favour of the assignee. Covenants by vendor that the policy is in full force, that he has right to assign, that he will not vitiate the policy and for further assurance. The mortgage, in addition, would contain a proviso for redemption. Covenant to pay principal and interest, to pay the premiums; in default, the mortgagor to pay them and add them to his debt. There would also be a power of sale and the usual trust of the purchase money. Notice in writing of the transfer should be given to the office. 2 Prideaux's Precedents, 401.

37. *Q.* A is to convey an estate to B for life: by what conveyance may this be effected?

*A.* This may be effected by deed of grant. It might also be conveyed by any of the conveyances above mentioned (No. 2), which are applicable to the transfer of freeholds.

38. *Q.* By what conveyance may land be limited to executory uses?

*A.* Land may be so limited by any of the conveyances above mentioned as operating by virtue of the Statute of Uses, and those operating partly by common law, and partly by the statute. *Supra*, No. 2.

39. *Q.* What is a defeazance, and in what cases is it usually required and executed?

*A.* It is a deed made contemporaneously with and for the purpose of defeating another deed. Defeazances of estate of freehold are now never used. But defeazances of chattel interests, bonds and warrants of attorney, are occasionally executed. As to defeazances of chattels real, see 22 & 23 Vic., c. 35, ss. 1, 2.

40. *Q.* What is a power of attorney, and how is it put an end to?

*A.* It is a writing authorising another person to be an attorney of the person appointing him to do any lawful act. It may be revoked by the person giving it, unless it be for valuable consideration, or it is coupled with an interest. Thus, if the attorney is authorised to collect debts, and out of the proceeds to pay a debt due to himself, this is irrevocable. Death of either party revokes the power. If the party appointing becomes a lunatic, or a bankrupt, or if a *feme sole*, she marries, the power is revoked. The power is also at an end if its object is completed by performance. Wharton's Law Lexicon, 525. As to the protection of the trustees and executors acting under powers, see 22 & 23 Vic., c. 35, s. 26.

41. *Q.* What are extraordinary conveyances, or those by matter of record?

*A.* They are—1. Private Acts of Parliament, which are found necessary where an estate is much entangled by various trusts and uses, also to confer powers on the tenants of family estates, which have been omitted in the settlement. 2. Royal grants, which are by letters patent under the great seal, which is impressed by virtue of a warrant under the royal sign manual, addressed to the Lord Chancellor. 14 & 15 Vic., c. 82; 1 Steph. Com., 622.

## XXIV.—*Registration and Enrolment of Deeds, etc.*

1. *Q.* What deeds require to be registered? and where should they be registered? and what may be the consequence from delay in doing so?

*A.* All conveyances by deed or will, of lands in the counties of Middlesex and York, and Kingston-upon-Hull, must be registered in the local registries. If not registered, they will be void as against subsequent purchasers of the lands without notice. 7 Anne, c. 20; 2 & 3 Anne, c. 4; 4 Anne, c. 18; 6 Anne, c. 35; 8 Geo. II., c. 6; Sugden's Vendors, 727. As to the memorial, and the exceptions to the operation of these acts, see *infra*.

2. *Q.* Show what memorial of a deed is required; and is it necessary that the memorial should be executed by a granting party, and attested by one of the witnesses to the execution of the deed by a granting party; or can the deed be duly registered without either, and which, of these formalities?

*A.* The memorial is engrossed on parchment, and contains the date of the deed, the names and descriptions of the parties as in the deed, a full description of the premises with the operative part of the deed. If there is a plan on the deed, it must be copied on the memorial, and also another copy left on paper. The christian and surnames of all the witnesses to the deed must be inserted in the memorial at length, also their places of residence and occupation. It must be under the hand and seal of a grantor *or* grantee, attested by two witnesses, one of whom must be a witness to the execution of the deed by a *grantor* (this is not now insisted on), and such witness shall, upon oath, before the registrar, prove the execution of both deed and memorial. Printed regulations at the Middlesex Registry.

3. *Q.* What lands and instruments are exempt from the Registry Acts?

*A.* The exceptions are—Copyhold estates; leases at rack rent; leases not exceeding twenty-one years, where the actual possession and occupation go along with the lease; chambers in Serjeant's Inn, and in the Inns of chancery and common law; lands in the City of London. As before mentioned, the registry acts of Yorkshire and Middlesex cease to apply to lands in those counties which have been and remain registered under the Land Transfer Act. 25 & 26 Vic., c, 53, s. 104; Sugden's Vendors, 731.

4. *Q.* What leases of property in Middlesex do not require to be registered?

*A.* See the previous answer.

5. *Q.* Is it necessary that a deed of appointment of a valuable leasehold interest under a power, should be registered or not?

*A.* Such an appointment requires registration, as a valuable leasehold would not be at rack rent, so as to bring it within the exception as to leases at such a rent. Sugden's Vendors, 727.

6. *Q.* Transcribe the form of attestation to a memorial for the Middlesex Registry.

*A.* "Signed and sealed by the said A B in the presence of William Yelverton, 16 Euston Road, in the county of Middlesex, grocer, and George Vincent, of 31 Chancery-lane, in the same county, lawyer's clerk."

7. *Q.* Is the non-registry of a lease cured by registering an assignment, in which the lease is recited, or not?

*A.* It is not. The lease must also be registered. Sugden's Vendors, 727.

8. *Q.* In a register-county, does registration of a second mortgage amount to notice thereof to a first mortgagee?

*A.* The mere registration does not amount to notice; therefore further advances by the first mortgagee would be good as against the second mortgagee, although the advances were made after registration by the latter. Sugden's Vendors, 728.

9. *Q.* In a register-county, where the vendor of a real estate is both heir at law and devisee, is it material that the will should be registered? and is it material if he should be devisee only?

*A.* In the first case registration is not material. But where the vendor is merely a devisee, the purchaser should not complete until the will is registered. Sugden's Vendors, 546.

10. *Q.* If a vendor claim leasehold estate in a register-county, as executor or legatee, can a purchaser from him insist upon the will being registered in either case? and state a reason.

*A.* A purchaser could not insist upon registration in either case. The reason is that after a sale by the executor or legatee no subsequent disposition by him would be good against the purchaser. Dart's Vendors, c. 13, s. 7.

11. *Q.* Is it necessary to register wills relating to property in a register-county? and state the reasons why it is, or is not, necessary?

*A.* Subject to the exceptions mentioned in the two preceding answers, registration of wills is necessary within the period fixed by the acts. In the absence of registration it is supposed that a devisee cannot make a good title, though considerable doubt rests upon the subject. The memorial is under the hand and seal of one of the devisee's attested by two witnesses. Ibid. Sugden's Vendors, 546.

12. *Q.* If, on a sale, the property be in a register-county, when should the conveyance of it be registered, and what may be the consequence from delay in doing so?

*A.* It should be registered forthwith. If delayed, the purchaser exposes himself to being defeated by a subsequent sale or mortgage by the vendor. Also by prior unregistered incumbrances, if they are registered between the execution and registration of the conveyance. It may here be mentioned that wills must be registered within six months after death within the Kingdom, or within three years after death beyond the seas. 7 Anne, c. 20, s. 8.

13. *Q.* What deeds should be enrolled, and when, and where?

*A.* Disentailing assurances must be enrolled within six months of execution in Chancery. 3 & 4 Wm. IV., c. 74, s. 41. So must conveyances to charities. 9 Geo. II., c. 36. Bargains and sales also must be enrolled within a similar time in one of the courts of record at Westminster (in practice the court of Chancery). 27 Hen. VIII., c. 16.

### XXV.—*Posthumous Destination of Property.*

1. *Q.* What is a will and testament? and what is the distinction if any, between them?

*A.* It is the declaration by a man of his intentions with regard to his property to be performed after his decease. This power of disposition of property is extremely ancient. It was in use amongst the ancient Hebrews. It was introduced amongst the Romans by the law of the Twelve Tables and has by degrees been adopted by almost all civilised nations. The term "will" is ascribed by ancient text writers to devises of land, "testament" being applied to dispositions of chattels. Practically, however, there is no distinction between the two terms. 1 Steph. Com., 596; Wharton's Law Lexicon, 950.

2. *Q.* Who may make, and who are disabled from making, a will?

*A.* All persons excepting the following may make a will:—
1. Minors. 2. Married women, with the exceptions mentioned *supra* "Baron & Feme," No. 12. 3. Persons of unsound mind, whether from idiocy, insanity, lunacy (unless in a lucid interval), drunkenness or any other cause. 4. Persons born deaf and blind (consequently dumb, as this follows from congenital deafness and want of sight). 5. Attained traitors or felons, and outlaws for treason or felony. 6. Outlaws in a civil action, and felons as to personal estate. 7. Aliens, except as to personalty. 8. Persons who have committed civil suicide, as monks. But this latter disqualification cannot now be considered to prevail in this country. Hayes & Jarman, by Eastwood, 82.

3. *Q.* At what age is a person capable of making a will?

*A.* Not until he has attained the age of twenty-one years. 1 Vic., c. 26, s. 7. It has, however, been considered that an infant soldier on active service may make a will of personalty, but this is doubted. Hayes and Jarm., by Eastwood, 9.

4. *Q.* If a man was born 11·30 P.M. on the 1st January, 1840, at what hour and on what day and year did he become capable of making a will?

*A.* When the clock struck 12 on the 30th December, 1860, he would be capable of making a will. He attains the age of twenty-one on this day (the 31st), being the one preceding the anniversary of his birth, and the day of course begins when the previous one (the 30th) ends, namely, at 12 o'clock. The law does not recognise fractions of a day. In the above case, therefore, majority is attained when the individual has only been 20 years 363 days and half-an-hour in the world. Ibid, 234.

5. *Q.* How must a will be executed to pass real and personal estates? and how attested? and from what period have such requisites been necessary? Does the Wills Act apply to the wills of all testators dying after that period?

*A.* Wills of real and personal estate must now be in writing, and signed at the foot or end thereof (as to this see 15 & 16 Vic., c. 24) by the testator, or by some other person in his presence, and by his direction; and such signature is to be made or acknowledged by the testator, in the presence of two or more witnesses present at the same time; and such witnesses must both sign in the presence of the testator. The above requisites have been necessary since 1st January, 1838. 7 Wm. IV., & 1 Vic., c. 26, ss. 9—38. The act applies only to *wills* made since the above date, and not to those made before.

6. *Q.* Must all the witnesses sign in the presence of each other?

*A.* The better opinion appears to be that this is unnecessary. *Re Webb*, D. & Sw., 1; *re Allen*, 2 Cur., 331.

7. *Q.* Is any particular form of attestation necessary, and what is the usual form?

*A.* No form of attestation is necessary. 1 Vic., c. 26, s. 9. But a form should always be used. The following is a very good one:—"Signed by the said testator 'A B,' as and for his last will and testament, in the presence of us, present at the same time, who, at his request, in his sight and presence, and in the presence of each other, have subscribed our names as attesting witnesses." Hayes & Jarm, by Eastwood, 121.

8. *Q.* Is a will unattested under any circumstances valid?

*A.* A soldier being in actual military service, or any mariner or seaman being at sea, may dispose of his personal estate by will unattested. 1 Vic., c. 26, s. 11.

9. *Q.* Is it requisite that the testator see the witnesses attest the will? and what are the proper solemnities to be observed on the execution of a will by a testator who is blind?

*A.* It need not appear that the testator actually saw the witnesses attest the will, but he must have been in such a position that he might have seen them subscribe if he had wished, and this is so even though the testator be blind. *Re Piercy*, 1 Rob., 278. The will should also be read over to a blind testator, though this is not essential. Hayes & Jarm., by Eastwood, 14—16.

10. *Q.* What is the consequence to an attesting witness of a will, so far as regards any, and what, legacies or devises given to him by that will? Can any objection be made to his attestation? What is the law as to the competency of executors and creditors being attesting witnesses?

*A.* The witness will lose his legacy or estate, but no objection can be taken to his being a witness. An executor or creditor may be a witness. 1 Vic., c. 26, ss. 15—17.

11. *Q.* Can the wife, or husband, or child, of any attesting witness, take a legacy or devise?

*A.* The wife or husband cannot, but there is no objection to the child doing so. Ibid.

12. *Q.* Does a will, executed in the presence of two witnesses, pass real estate in the British colonies, or any of them?

*A.* The Wills Act has been adopted by various colonial legislatures, so that as to them a will attested by two witnesses will suffice. Some of the colonies who have adopted the act are—India, New South Wales, the Australian colonies, Jamaica, Granada. Hayes & Jarm, by Eastwood, 76.

13. *Q.* Previous to the Wills Act, how many witnesses were required to a will devising real estate, and bequeathing personalty?

*A.* Three witnesses were required to a will of real estate. 29 Car. II., c. 3. But a will of personalty did not require any witnesses. Ibid.

14. *Q.* If alterations or erasures are made in a will previously to its signing, what precautions should you use with respect to them: and what is necessary if a testator make alterations after signing?

*A.* I should make a memorandum of the alterations I had made at the foot of the will, and declare the will as altered to be the testator's will. Then the testator and witnesses should sign. Alterations after the execution of the will must be executed in the same manner as the will. The names of the testator and the witnesses in the margin opposite the alteration, or at the foot or end of or opposite a memorandum referring to such alteration, and written at the end or some other part of the will, will suffice. 1 Vic., c. 26, s. 21. See a form of memorandum, Hayes & Jarm., by Eastwood, 559.

15. *Q.* What effect has a codicil properly executed under 1 Vic., c. 26, on a will made previously, which would have been good as the law then stood, but not so if made after the statute?

*A.* Such a codicil will operate as a revival of the will, if it appears to be intended that the codicil shall so operate. 1 Vic., c. 26, s. 34. The effect of such revival is to bring the date of the whole testamentary disposition, so far as the terms of the will permit, down to the date of the codicil. Hayes & Jarm. by Eastwood, 75.

16. *Q.* Can a testator, by a codicil duly executed, and referring to a prior will, give effect to such will though informally executed?

*A.* The testator may give effect to a prior will in this way:— There must be a sufficient reference in the codicil to make the prior will capable of identification. Ibid., 445.

17. *Q.* When a real estate is devised to a person without any words of limitation, what estate does the devisee take? Give the authority for your answer.

*A.* The devisee will take the fee simple, or other the whole estate or interest which the testator had power to dispose of by will in the real estate, unless a contrary intention appear. 1 Vic., c. 26, s. 28.

18. *Q.* In wills made previous to the 1st of January, 1838, what form of expression was necessary to confer on the devisee of freehold lands an estate in fee simple?

*A.* Before this act an estate in fee simple might have been disposed of by a devise to A in *fee simple*, or *for ever*, or to him *and 'his assigns for ever*, or by a devise of all the testator's *estate*, or *property*, or *inheritance*, also, of course, by the words "to A and his heirs." Wms. R. P., 195.

19. *Q.* Give in the most brief form of words a devise of freehold estate, say Blackacre, in fee by A to B.

*A.* "I devise Blackacre to B" would be sufficient, upon the authority mentioned *supra*, No. 17.

20. *Q.* A devises his farm at B to C, without any words of limitation: what estate would C take if the testator died in 1801; what if he died in 1857, and why?

*A.* If A died in 1801, a life estate only would pass to C. If the death was in 1857 and the will was made on or since the 1st January, 1838, C would take all the estate which A had to devise. If, however, the will was made before this date and had not been revived the old law would still apply. 1 Vic., c. 26, s. 34.

21. *Q.* When will a general devise of real estates pass estates held in trust or mortgage? and give the reason for your answer?

*A.* Such a devise will include trust or mortgaged estates, unless it is to be collected from expressions in the will or the purposes or objects of the testator that he did not mean they should pass. Such a contrary intention would be shewn if the general devise is to uses in strict settlement, with numerous limitations over. So, also, if the devise is to the separate use of a married woman. *Lindsell* v. *Thacker*, 12 Sims, 178. The reason for the above rule is that it is more convenient that such estates over which the testator has a clear right of disposition, should pass to the devisee. *Lord Braybrook* v. *Inskip*, 8 Ves., 417; L. C. Conv., 876, and the notes.

22. *Q.* A testator having borrowed money on his bond, and a mortgage on his estate, devises the latter without noticing the mortgage. Is the mortgage money to be paid out of the devised estate, or is any other or what fund liable thereto?

*A.* As between the devisee and the personal representatives of the testator the mortgage money will be paid out of the estate. That is, the devisee will take it *cum onere*, unless a contrary intention appear from the will. The remedy of the mortgagee is not affected. 17 & 18 Vic., c. 113. See *infra* "Equity."

23. *Q.* State fully the four periods during which the accumulation of the profits of real or personal property can be made, or any of them correctly? State the exceptions.

*A.* Income can now only be accumulated for the life of the

grantor or settlor, *or* twenty-one years from the death of any grantor, settlor, devisor, or testator, *or* during the minority of any person living or in *ventre sa mère* at the death of such persons, *or* during the minority of any person who under the settlement or will, would for the time being, if of full age, be entitled to the income directed to be accumulated. The exceptions to the application of the act are, provisions for the payment of debts, for the raising of portions for younger children, and directions as to the produce of timber. 39 & 40 Geo. III., c. 98. These latter are, however, within the rule against perpetuities.

24. *Q.* If the trust as created should exceed the period allowed by law, will it fail altogether, or how otherwise?

*A.* If the direction to accumulate does not exceed the rule against perpetuities it will not fail altogether, but be good *pro tanto*. Thus, in *Griffiths* v. *Vere*, 9 Ves., 127; L. C. Conv., 430, a trust for accumulation during a life, contrary to 39 & 40 Geo. III., c. 98, is good for twenty-one years. If, however, the accumulation would have been bad before the act, that is if it exceeds the rule against perpetuities, it will be bad now. Per Lord Eldon in *Griffiths* v. *Vere*. As to the time within which executory uses must vest see *supra*, "Uses, Trusts and Powers," No. 30.

25. *Q.* If Blackacre were wished to be devised to B in trust for two infant-children in moieties, but so that in case of the decease of one before the testator, the surviving child is to take the entirety, how is that to be accomplished?

*A.* This may be done by devising the estate to B upon trust for the children as tenants in common, but in the event of the decease of one in the lifetime of the other the share of the one so dying to go to the survivor. This is a cross remainder. 1 Steph. Com., 358.

26. *Q.* Is the devisee of an estate contracted for, but not conveyed to the testator, entitled to a conveyance from the vendor; and from what fund must the purchase-money be paid?

*A.* The devisee is entitled to a conveyance of the legal estate from the vendor, and he can have the purchase-money paid out of the personal estate of the purchaser. *Supra*, "Vendor and Vendee," Nos. 14, 15.

27. *Q.* A testator, seised in fee of lands, and also of the tithes of them; devises the lands without expressly including or showing his intention to include the tithes: will the latter pass to the devisee of the lands?

*A.* The tithes will not pass without being expressly mentioned, as they are distinct subjects of property. And this is so even though the word "appurtenances" is used. Wms. R. P., 312.

28. *Q.* Does the same rule apply to an advowson?

*A.* If an advowson is appendant to a manor, a conveyance of the manor, even without mentioning the appurtenances belonging to it, will be sufficient to comprise the advowson. If the advowson is severed the case would be otherwise. Ibid., 310.

29. *Q.* Will an appointment, attested by two witnesses, be good

in any, and what case, where the power requires more witnesses than two?

*A.* Now a power will be deemed well executed by will if the will is executed in conformity with the provisions of the "Wills Act," above-mentioned, notwithstanding that additional formalities may be required. 1 Vic., c. 26, s. 10.

30. *Q.* In any and what other cases of appointment, will strict compliance with the terms of the power be dispensed with?

*A.* As to the execution of a deed, *supra*, "The Essentials of Deeds," No. 4. As to when relief will be granted against the defective execution of a power, see *infra*, "Equity."

31. *Q.* What is the meaning of the word "mortmain?"

*A.* The term is derived from *mort*, dead, and *main*, hand (French) indicating that state of possession of land as makes it inalienable. Thus lands in the hands of religious and other corporations are said to be in *mortmain*, being free from feudal services and practically inalienable. Wharton's Law Lexicon, 611, 3rd ed.

32. *Q.* Can a valid conveyance be made of real property to charitable uses, and how?

*A.* Lands or money to be invested therein may be conveyed to a charity by deed executed in the presence of two witnesses twelve calendar months before the death of the grantor, and enrolled in the Court of Chancery within six calendar months next after the execution. Stock to be invested in land must be transferred six calendar months at least before the death. The estate must take effect in possession, and the conveyance be without power of revocation or any reservation, excepting of a nominal rent, or mines, or minerals, or covenants and provisions for the benefit of the estate. If the conveyance is for valuable consideration, the above provision as to the execution of the deed twelve months before the death of the grantor does not apply. Lands may also be devised to the two Universities, or their Colleges, and to the Schools of Eton, Winchester and Westminster, also to the British Museum; 9 Geo. II., c. 36; 24 & 25 Vic., c. 9. Conveyances as sites for schools have been excepted from the operation of these acts. Williams' R. P., 69.

33. *Q.* A testator possessed of:—1. Fee simple lands. 2. Stock in the Funds. 3. Mortgages of freehold interests in lands. 4. Mortgages of leasehold interests in lands. 5. Furniture. 6. Money at his bankers; and 7. Money owing to him in business; devises and bequeaths all his real and personal property to trustees to be divided amongst charitable institutions. As to what parts of the property will the will take effect, and as to what will it be inoperative?

*A.* The will operates as to Nos. 2, 5, 6, and 7; but will fail as to Nos. 1, 3, and 4, these being land or interests therein, within the mortmain act above cited.

34. *Q.* A contracts to sell his fee simple lands, but dies before completion, having made his will giving the purchase money to a charity. Is the gift good? Give a reason or authority for your answer.

*A.* The gift is invalid as savouring of realty, and consequently within the provisions of 9 Geo. II., c. 36; L. C. Conv., 487.

35. *Q.* A testator devises a farm at Tipperary to a charity in England, is such devise valid?

*A.* The devise is perfectly good, as the provisions of the "Mortmain Act" do not extend to lands in Ireland. *Campbell* v. *Lord Radnor*, 1 Bro. C. C., 272.

36. *Q.* Would lands already appropriated to charitable uses require the same formalities as above-mentioned if they were conveyed to trustees of another charity?

*A.* Such lands being already in *mortmain* a subsequent deed conveying them to another charity will not require enrolment. *In Re The London Dock Act*, 20 Beav., 490; Tudor's L. C. Conv., 482, 2nd ed.

37. *Q.* Give a form of bequest to a charity?

*A.* It should be as follows:—"I bequeath £1,000" to the rector for the time being of Bedale, Yorkshire, to be distributed at his discretion amongst the poor of the parish; and I direct that the aforesaid legacy shall be paid exclusively out of such part of my personal estate as may lawfully be appropriated to such purpose, and preferably to any other payment thereout." The effect of this will be to throw the debts, general legacies, &c., on some other fund (if any). This course should be adopted, if it is intended the charity legacy should not abate. It must be also borne in mind that there is no marshalling in favor of a charity. Hayes and Jarman by Eastwood, 170.

38. *Q.* To whom will estates purchased after the execution of a will pass?

*A.* They will pass to the residuary devisee under the will, if no contrary intention appears. As to a contrary intention see the next answer. If there is no residuary devisee the testator will die intestate as to the lands, and they will descend to his heir at law. 1 Vic., c. 26, s. 24.

39. *Q.* On what words or expressions in a will of real property, and on what other circumstances will depend the question whether or no real estate purchased after date of the will passes under the devises in it?

*A.* All the testator's lands otherwise undisposed of will pass under a general devise, unless a contrary intention appears by the will. Such a contrary intention would be where the testator specifies some particular property to which it is not to extend. *Circuitt* v. *Perry*, 23 Beav., 275. If the devise is of a specific estate, as of "the Quendon Hall Estates," subsequent additions by purchase to this estate will not pass. *Webb* v. *Byng*, 1 K. & J., 580. Also where the testator speaks of estates now vested in him and of others which may be at the time of his decease; under the former devise after purchased lands would not pass. *Cole* v. *Scott*, 16 Sim, 259. Also if the land purchased be again sold before the death, the will is revoked as to it. 1 Jarm. on Wills, 311.

40. *Q.* What is the effect of a purchase, by the testator, of a

freehold estate of inheritance upon a devise of "All my Real Estate" in a will made before the estate was contracted to be purchased?

*A.* The purchased estate will pass by the will under the general devise as the will speaks from the death and not, as formerly, from its date. *Supra.*

41. *Q.* If A by his will devises a farm to B, and sells it in his lifetime, but dies before the purchase is completed, who will be beneficially entitled to the proceeds of the sale?

*A.* It is assumed here that the contract is subsequent to the date of the will. The first question is whether the farm on A's death is land or money. If the contract is one which cannot be specifically performed, no conversion takes place and, therefore, the devisee takes the farm. If, however, it is a binding contract, A is merely a trustee for the purchaser, and it would seem to be the better opinion that the proceeds of the sale will go to his personal representatives. In *Lawes* v. *Bennett,* 7 Ves., 436, and *Townley* v. *Bedwell,* 14 Ves., 590, this was so decided. But in *Drant* v. *Vause,* 11 L. J. Ch., 170, and *Emuss* v. *Smith,* 2 De Gex. & Sm., 722, Knight Bruce, V. C., decided that a specific devise of property subject to an option to purchase carried to the devisee the purchase money. These cases have, however, not been followed in the most recent case on the subject of *Collingwood* v. *Row,* 26 L. J. Ch., 649, but there the devise was not specific and the law on the point can hardly be considered as settled. See the cases collected, Sugden's Vendors, 14th ed., 190.

42. *Q.* An estate, consisting partly of freehold and partly of leasehold, is devised to A for life, with remainder to B for life, with remainder to the heirs of the body of A. What interest does A take in the freehold and leasehold respectively?

*A.* A will take an estate tail in the freehold by virtue of the rule in Shelley's case, subject to the life estate of B. In the leasehold he will take an absolute interest, for words conferring an estate tail in real property confer an absolute interest in chattels. A will, however, only take subject to the life estate of B. *Leventhorpe* v. *Ashbie.* Tudor's L. C. Conv., 763, 2nd ed.

43. *Q.* Should the direction to sell an estate be absolute or discretionary, in order to constitute an equitable conversion of the freehold into personalty?

*A.* The direction should be imperative and express, for if the conversion be merely optional the property will be considered as real or personal, according to the actual condition in which it is found. A discretion, however, may be given as to the period when the sale is to take place. Hayes & Jarman by Eastwood, 265.

44. *Q.* Mention in what case "The Wills Act," 1 Vic., c. 26, prevents a devise or legacy from lapsing by the death of the devisee or legatee in the lifetime of the testator.

*A.* A devise or legacy will not lapse if made to a child or other issue of the testator, and such child or other issue dies in the lifetime of the testator leaving issue; the subject of devise or bequest not being determinable before or on the death of such child. Nor will an estate devised in tail lapse if the devisee dies in testator's lifetime, leaving issue living at the death of the testator, inheritable under the entail, ss. 32, 33.

45. *Q.* On a devise to A and the heirs of his body, A dies in the lifetime of his testator. Will the issue of A take, or will the devise lapse?

*A.* See the previous answer.

46. *Q.* Will a lapsed devise or real estate go to the residuary devisee, if any, or to the testator's heir?

*A.* It will fall into the residuary devise, if there be none it will go to the heir. 1 Vic., c. 26, s. 25.

47. *Q.* What is a vested, and what is a contingent, legacy?

*A.* A legacy is said to be vested when the legatee has a present interest which is transmissible to his executors or administrators upon his death, even though the legacy is not to be paid until a future period, as a legacy to A to be paid to him on his attaining twenty-one is vested and is not affected by the death of A under that age. If, however, it appears that the legatee attaining twenty-one is a condition precedent to the legacy vesting, it will be contingent and fail if he die before the happening of that event. Such are legacies to a person *at*, or *if*, or *when* he shall attain twenty-one. *Stapleton* v. *Cheales*. Tudor's L. C. Conv., 724, 748.

48. *Q.* A, by his will, gives a legacy of £200 to B (a stranger), and directs his executor to pay it on B's attaining twenty-one; B dies under twenty-one, after the death of A; who is entitled to the legacy, and why?

*A.* The personal representatives of B will be entitled, the legacy being a vested one. See the previous answer.

49. *Q.* A testator bequeaths the residue of his personal estate to several persons as tenants in common; two of the residuary legatees die in the lifetime of the testator, not being descendants of such testator: what becomes of their shares?

*A.* Their shares will lapse, but not into the residue, as there is no lapse of residue into residue. *Bagwell* v. *Dry*, 1 Peere Wms. 700; *Ackroyd* v. *Smithson*, 1 Bro. C. C., 503. The shares will, therefore, go to the next of kin of the testator. If the residue had been given to the legatees as joint tenants, or to them as a class, as to the children of A, there would have been no lapse, but the survivors would have taken. Wms. Pers. Prop., 323, 5th ed.

50. *Q.* What is a general legacy, what a specific legacy?

*A.* A general legacy is a gift by will of personalty payable out of the general assets of the testator, whereas a specific legacy is a bequest of a specific part of the testator's personalty. Thus a bequest of £100 is general. But a bequest of my china teapot is specific. Specific legacies in a deficiency of assets have priority over general legacies. Wms. Pers. Prop., 316, 5th ed.

51. *Q.* How should a legacy of stock in the funds be given so as to make it a specific and not a general legacy?

*A.* It should be given as follows:—"I bequeath £1000 consols now standing in my name at the Bank of England," or of "£100 consols, part of my stock." Ibid, 317.

52. *Q.* What are the advantages and disadvantages of a general over a specific legacy?

*A.* A general legacy is preferable to a specific one, in that it is not liable to ademption. But, on the other hand, the latter has priority of liquidation, and on a deficiency of assets is resorted to after a general legacy. A specific legacy may also be recovered at law if assented to by the executor. Ibid, 317.

53. *Q.* What is a demonstrative legacy?

*A.* It is a legacy which is to be paid out of a particular fund, but if that fund fail it is to be paid out of the general personalty. Thus a bequest "of £100 consols *to be paid* out of the £1,000 Consols now standing in my name" is demonstrative. If upon the testator's decease the £1,000 is sold out, the legatee will still get his legacy. It is not, therefore, liable to ademption, and is thus more advantageous than a specific legacy. Ibid., 317.

54. *Q.* A testator gives an annuity and directs a sufficient principal sum to be appropriated by his executors wherewith to purchase the annuity, but the intended annuitant demands the principal of the executors, claiming an option to do so. Can this demand be resisted? and if not, what precaution should be taken in the will to prevent the possibility of this occurring?

*A.* If the executors are directed to purchase the annuity, the annuitant is entitled to its value; and this is so even if the will says he shall not be entitled to have it. *Stokes* v. *Cheek*, 28 Beav., 620. To prevent the possibility of this occurring, the executors should be directed to invest an adequate sum in the purchase of stock yielding income until the decease of the annuitant. After this, the stock falls into the residue; or, in the case of the purchase, a proviso may be inserted that the annuity should cease on the annuitant assigning it. Hayes and Jarm. by Eastwood, 131.

55. *Q.* An annuity of £60 a-year was bequeathed by a testator to his son F, out of a certain stock, and the annuity was directed not to be sold until after F's and his wife's death, nor until F's son should attain twenty-one; was the annuity so given limited to F's life, or did he take a perpetual annuity by the bequest? Give the reason for your answer.

*A.* As a general rule where an annuity is given to a person, the annuitant takes for life only. But here there is an intention of appropriating certain stock for its payment, and this is considered as indicating an intention that it should be perpetual. Ibid., 141. The words, however, as to the sale of the annuity would seem to indicate an intention the other way; but this it is impossible to ascertain without looking at the whole will.

56. *Q.* By what acts may a will be revoked?

*A.* A will may be revoked—by marriage, unless the will is made in exercise of a power of appointment, and the estate would not have passed, in default of appointment, to the testator's representatives—by will or codicil, or some writing executed like a will showing an intention to revoke—by burning, tearing, or otherwise destroying (*animo revocandi*), by the testator or some one in his presence and by his direction—and it may be partially revoked by alienating the subject of devise or bequest prior to decease. 7 Wm. IV. & 1 Vic., c. 26, secs. 20—23.

57. *Q.* Will a mortgage in fee operate as a revocation of a will previously made, either at law or in equity?

*A.* The will, notwithstanding the mortgage, will operate upon the testator's equity of redemption. 1 Vic., c. 26, s. 23.

58. *Q.* State the effect of marriage upon the will of a man before and since the Wills Act.

*A.* Before the Wills Act marriage and the subsequent birth of a child revoked the will, but now marriage will alone do so, except as above mentioned, No. 56. 1 Vic., c. 26, s. 18.

59. *Q.* Is a will made before marriage and consequently thereby revoked, revived by a codicil made after marriage, giving legacies but not referring to the will otherwise than by the introductory words—"This is a codicil to my will?"

*A.* The expression given would hardly be sufficient to revive the former will, unless indeed the codicil were indorsed on it or written on the same paper. There should be a sufficient reference, so as to make the prior will capable of identification. Hayes and Jarm., by Eastwood, 445, *supra,* Nos. 15, 16.

60. *Q.* In what court or courts should a will of personalty be proved, where a testator has left *bona notabilia* in different dioceses?

*A.* The will may now be proved in the principal registry of the Court of Probate without regard to the abode of the testator, or if he had at the time of his death a fixed place of abode within any district, the will may be proved in the registry of the district. 20 & 21 Vic., c. 77, ss. 59, 46. Before this act, if the testator had goods of the value of £5, called *bona notabilia,* within two dioceses of the same province, either of Canterbury or York, the will had to be proved in the Prerogative Court of the Archbishop of the province. If there were effects in the two provinces, the will had to be proved in each. Wms. Pers. Prop., 306.

61. *Q.* Is anything, beyond probate of the will, necessary in order to perfect the title of a person to whom a leasehold estate for years has been given by will?

*A.* He should also obtain the assent of the executor.

62. *Q.* What is the difference of construction between a deed and a will; and why is the difference made?

*A.* See *infra,* "Equity." "The nature of Equity," No. 22.

63.* *Q.* A by will bequeaths £10,000 to "the heirs of the late B"; who will take under this bequest, assuming that there is nothing in the context of the will to explain the words.

*A.* In this case the word "heirs" would be taken to be used in its strict sense, and therefore the person who would be entitled to

---

* Nos. 63, 64, and 65 were asked under the Equity division, but are inserted here for conformity.

the real estate of B, at the death of B, will take the £10,000. *De Beauvoir* v. *De Beauvoir*, 3 Ho. of L. Cas., 524; *Danvers* v. *Earl of Clarendon*, 1 Vern., 35. Jarman on Wills, 2, 75.

64. *Q.* What construction does the Court of Chancery put upon the word "survivor" in a will? Is it ever construed to mean "other"; and if so, under what circumstances? Point out the distinctive force of the word "other" in the expression "survivor or other of them."

*A.* The term "survivor," when unexplained by other parts of the will, receives its literal meaning. It is construed "other" where the apparent intention of the testator seems to require such a construction. In the expression given, the word "other" indicates a person, though he may not be the actual survivor of the class referred to. This the following example will illustrate:—If A bequeaths £100 to each of his children, B, C and D, after their mother's life interest, but if any die in her lifetime leaving issue, the share of such one to go to such issue; but if any of them should die before twenty-one without issue, the share of such one to go to the *survivor* (or other) of them. B dies leaving children. C died under twenty-one and without issue. D therefore is the survivor, and, unless the words in brackets were inserted, would take C's share, and thus B's children would take no part of it. This was clearly not A's intention. See the cases collected. 2 Jarman on Wills, 648.

65. *Q.* What is the effect of a bequest of residuary or personal estate—1. "To my friends and relations"; 2. "To my near relations"; 3. "To my nearest relations"; 4. "To my poor relations"; and 5. "To the most necessitous of my relations"?

*A.* 1. and 2. These mean the next of kin, according to the statute, and their representatives. 3. The next of kin will take, to the exclusion of those, who, under the statute, would have been entitled by representation, thus, a living child would exclude the issue of a deceased child. 4. Same as No. 1., though authorities are conflicting. 5. Same as No. 1, the word "necessitous" like "poor," making no difference. Jarman on Wills, 2, 109, *et seq.*

66. *Q.* You are required to prepare the will of a client; his property consists of £5,000 in the funds, and a freehold estate of £5,000 a year. He wishes to leave a life interest in the whole to his wife, to secure £20,000 to his younger children, and to make a strict settlement of the freehold estate upon his eldest son and his issue. What would be the best mode of carrying the testator's intentions into effect?

*A.* The stock and the real estate should be bequeathed and devised to trustees, upon trust to pay the income and rents to the wife for life. Subject thereto the stock, and a further sum of £15,000, to be raised out of the real estate, as portions for the younger children. Subject thereto upon trust in strict settlement. See *supra*, "Settlements." Hayes & Jarman by Eastwood, 156.

67. *Q.* Give a sketch of a will of a gentleman having personal estate only, and desiring to leave it all to his wife for life, and after

her death to his children (some of whom are minors). Give the usual clauses.

*A.* He would bequeath the whole of his personal property to trustees, upon trust, to pay his debts, funeral, and testamentary expenses, and to invest the residue, and to vary the securities. Trusts of the residue, to pay the income to the wife for life, and after her death for the testator's children, and remoter issue, as the wife shall appoint; in default of appointment amongst the children equally, sons at twenty-one, daughters at twenty-one, or marriage. The issue of deceased children to take their parents' share. Hotchpot clause. Powers of maintenance, accumulation and advancement. Power to appoint new trustees. Appointment of executors and guardians. 2 Prideaux's Precedents, 337, 4th ed.

68. *Q.* What powers should be given to the trustees of a will of real estate directing sales and declaring trusts of the proceeds that may last many years?

*A.* They should be empowered to sell by public auction or private contract, to buy in or rescind, and to have special conditions of sale. Also to invest the money produced by the sales, either in the payment off of incumbrances, or on other lands to be settled to the same uses, or on other investments. They should also be empowered to appoint new trustees. 2 Prideaux's Precedents, 386.

69. *Q.* In regard to the Act of 1861, "to Amend the Law with respect to the Wills of Personal Estate," in case of a will by a British subject made *out* of the United Kingdom dying after the act, by the rule of what country must the will be executed, and in that respect is there any and what option, and is or not the will of a British subject made *in* the United Kingdom affected by his domicile?

*A.* The will of a British subject residing and dying abroad will be good in this country, as regards personal estate, if executed according to the law of the place where the same was made, or of the law then in force in that part of Her Majesty's dominions where the deceased has his domicile of origin, or of the law of the place where he was domiciled when the same was made. It is, therefore, optional to select any of these. The will of a British subject being made in the United Kingdom, is good if made according to the law existing in that part of the United Kingdom where it was made, regardless of his domicile. 24 & 25 Vic., c. 114.

70. *Q.* If a testator die leaving personal property in France, India, and Canada, and not transferable in England, are such assets liable to probate or legacy duty?

*A.* The property will not be liable to probate duty, as this is only payable upon assets within the jurisdiction of the Court of Probate. It is, however, liable to legacy duty, which is payable upon all the deceased's estate wherever it may be.

71. *Q.* State the principal points in which the law relating to wills was altered by 7 Wm. IV., and 1 Vic., c. 26.

*A.* See *supra.* Also as to the effect of the words "dying without issue" in a will, they do not now mean an indefinite failure of issue as formerly. Also provision is made as to the effect of devises to trustees. Sections 29—31.

## XXVI.—*Trustees.*

1. *Q.* Can a trustee delegate a power to give receipts?
*A.* A trustee cannot delegate his power to give receipts, or, indeed, transfer the duties and responsibilities of his trust to another; at least, if he do so, he will be liable for any loss. Lewin, 192, 4th ed.

2. *Q.* Can a trustee give a power of attorney to another person to act for him in the trust?
*A.* Though a trustee cannot delegate his trust, yet he may authorise another to do an act so long as he does not leave that other to exercise his discretion. Thus, a trustee having a power of presentation to a living, cannot delegate such power, but having fixed upon the person, there would be no objection to the presentation being signed by attorney. Ibid., 196.

3. *Q.* Can a trustee for sale become a purchaser of his trust estate?
*A.* He cannot do so while the trust continues, but he may purchase from the *cestui que* trust, if the relation of trustee and *cestui que* trust is previously dissolved, or if not dissolved, by the parties agreeing to stand with reference to each other in the characters of purchaser and vendor. *Fox v. Mackreth,* 1 L. C. Eq., 92; 1 Prid. Prec., 134.

4. *Q.* When an estate is offered to a trustee at a price below its actual value, upon condition that the title should not be investigated, is the trustee justified, under the usual indemnity clause inserted in settlements, in purchasing the estate out of the trust funds, at the request of his *cestui que* trust, upon those terms? and give a reason for your answer.
*A.* If a trustee was to purchase the estate under the above circumstances, and the title turned out to be defective, he would be responsible, even though it was at the request of the *cestui que* trust. The circumstances are open to the gravest suspicion that the title is a bad one, and it would be highly improper for the trustee to speculate thus with the trust funds. Lewin, 242.

5. *Q.* Upon the appointment of a new trustee, where the trust property consists of both realty and personalty, how is the legal ownership in each description of property to be conveyed so as to vest in the continuing and new trustee jointly?
*A.* The real estate should be conveyed by the surviving trustee to a stranger, to the use of the survivor, and the new trustee. This course was also formerly necessary with regard to personalty. But it is now provided that any person may assign personal property, including chattels real, directly to himself and another person, or other persons or corporation, by the like means, as he

might assign the same to another. 22 & 23 Vic., c. 35, s. 21. This act renders an assignment of personalty to a provisional trustee unnecessary.

6. *Q.* If a settlement by deed or will does not contain the usual powers of sale, and of appointing new trustees, how are these defects to be respectively remedied?

*A.* Application must be made to the Court of Chancery to supply the omission by authorising a sale. This it will do if it appears to be expedient. 19 & 20 Vic., c. 120. As to the powers conferred by Lord Cranworth's Act, 23 & 24 Vic., c. 145, where there is a power of sale given, see *supra,* "Settlements," 185, No. 13.

7. *Q.* Where lands are devised charged with the payment of debts alone, or charged with debts and legacies together, or charged with legacies only, can the devisee in either, and, if in either, which of these cases, make a good title to a purchaser or mortgagee, without his being obliged to look to the discharge of such debts and legacies?

*A.* The devisee can make a good title to a purchaser in the first two cases, as it would be practically impossible to oblige the purchaser to look to the payment of the debts. In the case of the legacies only being charged, the purchaser will be bound to see to the application of the purchase-money in their payment. Wms. Real Assets, 62. The above cases do not come within 22 & 23 Vic., c. 35, s. 23, as this act only applies to a *trust,* not to a *charge.* Ibid. See the next answer.

8. *Q.* In case of a charge by will of debts and legacies coming into operation since 22 & 23 Vic., c. 35, who is clothed with power to raise money necessary for the purpose, and by what means?

*A.* When the estate so charged is devised to trustees, for the whole of the testator's interest therein, and no express provision is made for raising the debts or legacies, the devisees in trust may raise the money by sale, by public auction or private contract, of the lands, or by mortgage, or partly in one mode and partly in the other. Where the fee is not so devised to trustees, the executors have a similar power. 22 & 23 Vic., c. 35, ss. 14—18. Perhaps in cases coming within these provisions a purchaser would not in any case be bound to see to the application of the purchase-money. Wms. Real Assets, 62, n. z. But such cases must not be confounded with those mentioned in the preceding question, the devisee there being assumed to take beneficially, and not as a trustee.

## XXVII.—*Executors and Administrators.*

1. *Q.* If no executor be named in a will, who can obtain probate?

*A.* In such a case administration with the will annexed will be granted to the residuary legatee. If there is no residuary legatee, it will be granted to the widow and next-of-kin. Coote's Practices, 43, 4th ed.

2. *Q.* What is an executor *de son tort;* and in what cases is a

discharge given by him available against a claim brought by the legal representative?

*A.* He is one who, without any lawful authority, takes upon himself to intermeddle with the goods and affairs of a deceased person, as by selling the goods. Mere acts of necessity or humanity will not, however, constitute the person doing them an executor *de son tort.* Such are—burying the deceased, locking up his goods, or milking his cows. See *supra,* 10, No. 17. Payments by him to creditors cannot be pleaded against the rightful executor, but they will be allowed him in mitigation of damages, unless, perhaps, upon a deficiency of assets, whereby the rightful executor may be prevented from satisfying his own debts. 2 Steph. Com., 214, 5th ed. If he is really acting as executor, and the party with whom he deals believes him to be an executor, receipts by him will be good against the rightful executor. *Thomson* v. *Harding,* 2 E. & B., 630.

3. *Q.* What is the order in which next of kin are entitled to letters of administration?

*A.* The husband or wife are entitled before the next of kin. The order, then, is—1. The children. 2. Grandchildren. 3. Great grandchildren. 4. Father. 5. Mother. 6. Brothers and sisters. 7. Grandfathers or grandmothers. 8. Nephews and nieces, uncles, aunts, great grandfathers, or great grandmothers. 9. Great nephews and nieces, cousins german, great uncles and aunts, and so on, according to proximity of relationship. Coote's Prob. Pr., 77, 4th ed.

4. *Q.* Can one of several executors, or one of several administrators, assign leaseholds of his respective testator or intestate, or must they all concur? State any distinction, if it exist, and the reason for it.

*A.* The assignment of one is good as against all, because they are all regarded as an individual person. The distinction referred to was at one time thought to exist with regard to administrators, but it is now clear that the acts of one administrator bind the others. *Willand* v. *Fenn,* 2 Ves. Sen., 267. *Jacomb* v. *Harwood.* Ibid., 2. Wms. Exors., 855.

5. *Q.* A, by will, appoints three executors who all die in his lifetime; who, at A's death, is entitled to administer to his will?

*A.* His residuary legatee will be entitled to take out administration *cum testamento annexo,* as mentioned *supra,* No. 1.

6. *Q.* What course should an executor adopt for his own safety, who has in his hands a legacy to which an infant is entitled, there being no trustee under the will?

*A.* He should pay it into the Bank of England, with the privity of the Accountant-General of the Court of Chancery, to be placed to the account of the person for whose benefit it is so paid. The legacy duty is to be first paid. 36 Geo. III., c. 52, s. 32. The county court has now power to make an order upon the executor to pay in, as above mentioned, a legacy found to be due to an infant or person beyond seas, in an administration suit in the county court.

The certificate of the Accountant-General is to be produced to the Registrar, and, if the legacy is not paid in, a warrant of execution is to issue to levy the amount. When levied with expenses, it is to be paid into the Court of Chancery. 28 & 29 Vic., c. 99, s. 5.

7. *Q.* A term of years is vested in B in trust; B, by his will, without reference to that trust, appointed C and D executors: D renounces probate, and by deed disclaims all trust and interest under the will; C alone proves the will, and dies, leaving D surviving. Who is the testator's personal representative, and how is the term to be assigned?

*A.* If C leave an executor he is the testator's personal representative. If not, administration *de bonis non* must be taken out by the next of kin of B. The term would be assigned by such representative by deed of assignment. D having renounced is considered as if he had never been mentioned in the will. 20 & 21 Vic., c. 77, s. 79.

8. *Q.* The assignee of a term appointed A executor, who died intestate; C took out administration to A, and died, appointing D executor. Who is the proper party to assign the term?

*A.* The next of kin of the assignee of the term must take out administration *de bonis non*. The executor of A would have represented the assignee, but A having died intestate his administrator does not. 2 Steph. Com., 211, 5th ed.

9. *Q.* If the executor of A die, who becomes A's personal representative?

*A.* If A's executor himself appoints an executor, the latter is A's personal representative, the office of executor being transmissible. If, however, A's executor do not appoint one, administration *de bonis non* must be taken out to A. See preceding answers.

10. *Q.* If the administrator of A die, who becomes A's personal representative?

*A.* See the preceding answers.

11. *Q.* If A die, leaving B, C, and D his executors, and B only proves his will and dies, leaving C and D him surviving, who will be the legal personal representative of A?

*A.* Assuming C and D not to have renounced probate, they will be the representatives of A. The practice is to reserve leave to them to come in and prove, or they should renounce. If they have renounced they will have no claim, but administration *de bonis non* must be taken out to A. Cootes' Prob. Pr., 31, 4th ed.

12. *Q.* What was the position, legal and equitable, of an executor in respect of residue undisposed of by the will previously to the statute 11 Geo. IV. and 1 Will. IV., c. 40; and what alteration did that statute make?

*A.* Before this act the executor was entitled to the residue undisposed of, unless the Court of Equity considered that a contrary intention appeared, as by leaving him a legacy, or by his being made a trustee. Now, however, he will not take it either at law or in equity, unless an intention appear that he shall do so, but is considered a trustee for those who would be entitled under the statute of distributions. If there are no next of kin the executor would still take. *Russell* v. *Clowes*, 2 Coll. C. C., 648.

## XXVIII.—*Intestacy and its Consequences.*

1. *Q.* What is the meaning of the phrase "dying intestate?"

*A.* It signifies that the individual alluded to has thought proper not to make a will indicating how his property is to be disposed of after his decease, but has preferred leaving such disposition to the existing laws. Upon his death his personal estate vests in the Judge for the time being of the Court of Probate, until letters of administration are granted. 21 & 22 Vic., c. 95, s. 19. The administrator is bound to dispose of the property as mentioned, *infra.* The real estate devolves upon the heir-at-law of the deceased.

2. *Q.* What is the difference between an heir-apparent and an heir-presumptive?

*A.* An heir-apparent is one who if he survives his ancestor must be his heir. Thus, an elder son is an heir-apparent. An heir-presumptive, however, is one who may be heir, but who may possibly be disinherited by the birth of another. Thus, a daughter is heiress-presumptive, but if a son is born she will be no longer so. Wms. R. P., 85, 6th ed.

3. *Q.* In case of persons dying intestate seised of real property, how does it descend according to the common law? and mention certain exceptional lines of descent allowed by custom.

*A.* It will devolve by the common law as altered by statute, according to the rules mentioned in the next answer. The exceptions are in the tenures of gavelkind, where all the sons take equally; and Borough English where the youngest son inherits.

4. *Q.* What are the general rules as to the descent of freeholds of inheritance?

*A.* They are—1. Descent shall be traced from the purchaser, excepting in cases coming under 22 & 23 Vic., c. 35, ss. 19, 20.

2. Male issue shall be admitted before the female.

3. Amongst males of equal degree the eldest shall inherit, but females all together.

4. All lineal descendants *in infinitum* of a deceased person shall represent their ancestor.

5. On failure of the lineal descendants of the purchaser, the ancestor shall inherit.

6. Amongst such ancestors the paternal line is preferred to the maternal; the male paternal to the female paternal; the male maternal to the female maternal.

7. The half blood shall inherit next after those in the same degree of the whole blood where the common ancestor is a male, and next after the common ancestor, when such ancestor is a female.

8. In the admission of female paternal ancestors, the mother of the more remote male paternal ancestor and her heirs is preferred to the mother of a less remote male paternal ancestor and her heirs; and in the admission of female maternal ancestors, the mother of

the more remote male maternal ancestor and her heirs is preferred to the mother of a less remote male maternal ancestor and her heirs.

9. When there is a total failure of the heirs of the purchaser, or where any land shall be descendible as if an ancestor had been the purchaser, and the heirs of such ancestor totally fail; descent is to be traced as if the person last entitled had been the purchaser. 3 & 4 Wm. IV., c. 106; 22 & 23 Vic., c. 35, ss. 19, 20; Wms. Real Prop., 89 — 99, 6th ed.

5. *Q.* State the law of primogeniture.

*A.* It is that the eldest male shall inherit in exclusion of the younger. This rule is of feudal origin, as it tends to keep a family inheritance whole and undivided through future generations. Wms. R. P., 91.

6. *Q.* If A claims to be heir-at-law, as the eldest son of B, what evidence is necessary to prove the heirship?

*A.* He should produce the marriage certificate of his father, and an extract from the registry of baptisms showing the date of his birth. He should also prove his identity with such certificate of baptism. The death of his father must also be proved by the certificate of his burial. Taylor on Ev., 558, 4th ed.

7. *Q.* Can a person of the half-blood, or semi-kindred, inherit real estates by descent in any, and what, cases, and under what authority?

*A.* He may inherit, see *supra*, No. 4, rule 7. Thus, if A buys land and dies intestate without issue leaving a sister by his, A's, mother, and a brother by his father's second wife, not A's mother; the sister being of the whole blood will take; but, on her death without issue the estate will devolve to A's brother by the half-blood. 3 & 4 Wm. IV., c. 106, s. 9.

8. *Q.* Explain the abrogated doctrine of *possessio fratris*.

*A.* It was a doctrine which had the effect of making a sister of the person last seised his heir in preference to a brother of the half-blood. Thus, if A bought lands and they descended to his son B, and B died without issue and intestate, having been seised of the lands; a sister of B by his mother was heir in preference to a son of A by a second wife, the latter being of the half-blood to B, the person from whom the descent had to be traced. In such a case the sister was heir by the possession of her brother. Now the descent would be traced from A, and the second son would take in preference to the daughter. 1 Steph. Com., 424, 5th ed.

9. *Q.* A dies intestate, seised of estates in fee simple, leaving a grandson (issue of a deceased daughter); a great-granddaughter (issue of a deceased son), and two daughters. Who will be entitled by descent to A's real estates?

*A.* If A is the purchaser the great-granddaughter will be his heir, as representing her grandfather under the fourth rule. See the next answer.

10. *Q.* A widow seised in fee dies intestate leaving a daughter, also a grandson being son of a deceased daughter, and a grand-

daughter being daughter of a deceased son; to whom will the fee simple estates of the widow descend?

*A.* It will descend to the daughter of the deceased son under the rule that the lineal descendants *in infinitum* of any person deceased, represent their ancestor, that is, stand in the same place that the person would have done had he been living. The son would have been entitled had he lived, therefore his daughter takes.

11. *Q.* A man dies unmarried, leaving his father and an elder brother surviving him. Which of these will be his heir at law? If he had left a widow, would it have altered the case?

*A.* His father will be his heir, according to the fifth rule. Leaving a widow would make no difference, the widow not being any blood relation.

12. *Q.* A dies seised of real estate without issue, and intestate, leaving his grandfather and his (A's) mother, and a brother and sister him surviving: which of these is his heir?

*A.* If A is the purchaser his brother will take as representing the nearest lineal ancestor of A, namely, his father. 1 Steph. Com., 419, 5th ed.

13. *Q.* A purchaser of real estate dies intestate after 31st December, 1833, when 3 & 4 Wm. IV., c. 106, came into operation. State in what order his father, mother, brother, and sister of the whole-blood, and brother and sister of the half-blood, on both the father's and mother's side, would take the estate.

*A.* 1. The father. 2. The brother of the whole-blood. 3. The sister of the whole-blood. 4. The brother of the half-blood. 5. The sister of the half-blood. 6. The mother. If she has married again, her children, a son and daughter, will be of the half-blood to the purchaser; therefore, she being the common ancestor, and a female, the son of the half-blood will take, 7, next after her; then the daughter will take. When the common ancestor is a male the half-blood take next after those in the same degree of the whole-blood (No. 4), but when a female next after the common ancestor (No. 7). 3 & 4 Wm. IV., c. 106, s. 9. (I have never seen the wording of this section explained; without explanation it is certainly ambiguous.)

14. *Q.* A man has one son B and two daughters. B purchases an estate in fee and dies intestate and without issue, leaving his two sisters and his father him surviving: what becomes of this estate?

*A.* The father will take in preference to the daughters. See *supra*.

15. *Q.* A dies, leaving two granddaughters, the issue of a deceased daughter; a grandson, the issue of another deceased daughter, and two daughters: to whom will his fee simple estate descend?

*A.* The estate will descend, one-fourth to the grandson, another to the two granddaughters, and the other half equally between the two daughters. The grandson and granddaughters take by representation of their ancestors. The daughters take *per capita* as coparceners. Wms. R. P., 101, 6th ed.

16. *Q.* A man dies intestate, leaving a wife, a daughter of an aunt on his mother's side, and the son of an aunt on his father's side his only relatives: to whom would his realty descend? Give the reasons for your answer.

*A.* If the deceased was the purchaser the son of the aunt on the father's side would inherit, subject to the widow's dower, as the male ancestors and their kindred derived from their blood, are admitted before the female ancestors and their kindred. If, however, the estate had descended to the deceased from his mother the cousin on her side would be preferred. Those of the blood of the mother only would be entitled, unless the descent is broken or there is a total failure of the heirs *ex parte materna*. 1 Steph. Com., 432, 5th ed. See the next answer.

17. *Q.* A seised *ex parte maternâ* makes a conveyance to the use of himself and heirs, what is the effect of this upon his estate?

*A.* The effect will be to make A a purchaser, and break the line of descent. The property will, therefore, devolve on the death of A without issue to his ancestors *ex parte paternâ*. Whereas, had the conveyance not taken place, the relations on the mother's side only could have taken. 1 Steph. Com., 432. 3 & 4 Wm. IV., c. 106, s. 3.

18. *Q.* A man, having had two sons, the elder of whom died before him, leaving two sons, dies intestate, seised in fee of gavelkind land, leaving issue two grandsons (sons of his elder son) and his second son; state the proper parties to convey the land to a purchaser?

*A.* The two grandsons and their uncle must convey. The estate being gavelkind descends to all the sons equally, and the grandsons take their parent's share. Wms. R. P., 116, 6th ed.

19. *Q.* One of two coparceners dies intestate, who will be entitled to her share?

*A.* If the deceased had a child her share would descend to such child. If no child her heir at law would take. The other coparcener might fill this capacity. There is no survivorship amongst coparceners. *Cooper v. France*, 19 L. J. Ch. 313.

20. *Q.* A dies intestate, seised in fee simple, leaving one daughter (B), a son by a deceased daughter (C), a son and a daughter by a deceased daughter (D), a daughter by a deceased son (E), and two daughters by a deceased daughter (F), to whom will A's real estate descend?

*A.* It will descend to the daughter of the deceased son (E), as representing her father. See *supra*.

21. *Q.* The owner in fee of freehold and copyhold estates dies intestate and without an heir. Who becomes entitled to the estates, and what is the technical term used to denote the transmission?

*A.* The estate will escheat to the Crown or the lord. See this subject discussed *supra*. "Evidences of Ownership," 175, No. 5.

22. *Q.* If a person who is illegitimate die intestate leaving no legitimate issue, who becomes entitled to any real or personal estate of which he may be possessed?

*A.* The land will escheat and the personalty will be forfeited to the Crown. See the next answer.

23. *Q.* If the bastard having purchased lands left a son, would the son inherit? If he did inherit and died intestate, and without issue, what would become of the lands?

*A.* The son would inherit, unless he also happened to be illegitimate; for a bastard may have heirs of his body. Co. Litt. 3 B. Upon the death of the son without issue and intestate, the descent would now be traced from him as the person last entitled, there being a total failure of the heirs of the purchaser (the bastard). The effect of this would be to let in the mother of the son and her heirs as his ancestor. This prevents an escheat taking place; that is, assuming the mother to be legitimate, as otherwise, if she were dead, she would have no heirs. 22 & 23 Vic., c. 35, ss. 19, 20.

24. *Q.* How is the personal property of intestates distributed under the statutes?

*A.* See the various answers, *infra.*

25. *Q.* A freeman of the City of London dies intestate, leaving a widow, two sons, and three children of a deceased son. How is the personal estate divided? and how would it be divided under similar circumstances if the deceased were not a freeman?

*A.* The widow will take one third; the remaining two thirds will be divided between the sons and grandsons, the latter taking their parent's share *per stirpes. Lloyd* v. *Tench*, 2 Ves. Sen., 215. All customary modes of administration are abolished by 19 & 20 Vic., c. 94, and, therefore, if the deceased be a freeman of London or York, it will make no difference.

26. *Q.* How is the disposition of the personal estate of an intestate Englishman domiciled in France regulated?

*A.* Upon the principle that the devolution of personal chattels (including leaseholds in England) is governed by the domicile of the testator, its disposition will be regulated by the law of France. Real estate on the contrary is governed by the law of the country where it is situate, *lex loci rei sitæ.* Hayes & Jarm. by Eastwood, 22.

27. *Q.* If a widower dies issueless, leaving a mother, mother-in-law, sister-in-law, two nephews, sons of a deceased brother, and a posthumous brother of the half-blood him surviving, who will be entitled to his personal estate as next of kin, and in what proportions?

*A.* The mother will take one-third; the nephews another third, and the posthumous brother the remaining third. 1 Jac. 2, c. 17. Before this Statute the mother took the whole. *Keilway* v. *Keilway*, 2 P. Wms., 344.

28. *Q.* State when the next of kin take *per stirpes* and when *per capita.*

*A.* They take *per stirpes* when they represent their ancestor, taking the share such ancestor would have had, if he had lived. Thus, if

A die leaving two sons and two grandsons, the children of a deceased son, the grandsons take *per stirpes* and, therefore, take less each than if they shared with their uncles. The latter take in their own right, *per capita*. 2 Steph. Com., 225, 5th ed.

29. Q. If a man die intestate leaving a widow and children, how is his personal estate to be distributed?

A. The widow will take one-third, and the residue will be equally divided between the children *per capita*. 22 & 23 Car. II., c. 10.

30. Q. If he leave no children, but a widow, a brother, and children by another brother or sister, how is his personal estate to be distributed?

A. The widow will take half, the brother one-fourth *per capita*, and the nephews one-fourth *per stirpes*. 22 & 23 Car. II., c. 10.

31. Q. If a person die intestate and possessed of real and personal estate, leaving a son, and two granddaughters the issue of an elder son, surviving, who becomes possessed of his real and personal estate?

A. The son will take half of the personalty. The remaining moiety will be divided between the two granddaughters. They will also take the realty as co-partners. See *supra*.

32. Q. If a man die intestate possessed after payment of his debts, funeral, and testamentary expenses, of (1) railway bonds, (2) railway shares, (3) a king's share in the New River Company, (4) leaseholds for lives, (5) leaseholds for years, (6) a policy for £5000 on the life of another person, (7) copyholds of inheritance, (8) and a freehold house, leaving a widow, five sons, and five daughters, him surviving, upon whom will each of these descriptions of property devolve, and in what proportions?

A. Numbers 1, 2, 5, 6, being personalty will devolve, one-third to the widow, the remaining two-thirds equally between the sons and daughters. Numbers 3, 4, 7, 8, descend to the eldest son as heir-at-law, subject to the widow's right of dower. The heir would take No. 4 as special occupant; but, if the estate was not limited to the intestate and his heirs, it would devolve upon the administrator to go with the rest of the personalty. 29 Car. II., c. 3, s. 12; Wms. R. P., 20, 6th ed.

33. Q. Is there any, and, if any, what, difference between the distributive share of an intestate's effects, taken by brothers and sisters of the intestate, of the whole and of the half-blood?

A. They are equally entitled. *Jessop* v. *Watson*. 1 M. & K., 665.

34. Q. An intestate dies without leaving a widow or any issue, leaving nephews, the children of a deceased brother or sister of the intestate, and great-nephews, the descendants of another deceased brother or sister of the intestate; who are entitled to share in the distribution of the personal estate?

A. The nephews will take the whole. The grandnephews will not take because they could only take *per stirpes*, and representation is not allowed beyond brothers' and sisters' children. 22 & 23 Car. II., c. 10. If there were no brother or nephews, but only grandnephews, the latter would be entitled because they would then take *per capita*. 2 Steph. Com., 225, 5th ed.

35. *Q.* A, seised and possessed of real and personal estate, dies intestate, leaving a widow, an eldest son, two daughters, and two grandchildren (the issue of a younger son), on whom do his real and personal estate devolve, and in what shares and proportions?

*A.* As to the real estate, it will devolve upon the eldest son subject to the widow's dower. The personalty will go one-third to the widow, the residue equally between the son, two daughters and the grandchildren, the latter taking their parent's share, *per stirpes*. See *supra*.

36. *Q.* A dies intestate, and without issue, leaving a widow, mother, and brother, what interest do they take in his personal estate?

*A.* The widow will take half, and the remaining moiety will be equally divided between the mother and the brother. 22 & 23 Car. II., c. 10; 1 Jac. II., c. 17.

37. *Q.* If A die intestate and unmarried, leaving a father, a mother, and a brother, who will take his personal estate?

*A.* The father will take the whole. Wms. Pers. Prop., 333.

38. *Q.* Would it make any difference if A left a widow?

*A.* In this case the widow would take half and the father half. Ibid.

## XXIX.—*Assets and debts.*

1. *Q.* What are assets; and how are they marshalled for payment of debts?

*A.* The term "assets" from *assez*, Fr. "sufficient," is applied to the property of a deceased person, which is chargeable with and applicable to the payment of his debts and legacies. They are of various kinds, namely, by descent or real, also personal. Another sub-division is into assets, legal and equitable. See this subject together with "marshalling" discussed, *infra*, "Equity," "Administration."

2. *Q.* The 3 & 4 Will. IV., c. 104, renders freehold and copyhold estates liable to the payment of specialty and simple contract debts. Under the statute are these estates legal or equitable assets; and is there any class of creditors entitled to be paid their debts before others?

*A.* It is considered that these assets are legal and not equitable. Specialty creditors, in which the heirs are bound, have priority under the statute, and it is in consequence of this preference and of the fact that the remedy is given by statute that the assets must be considered as legal. 2 Jarm. Wills, 587, 3rd ed.

3. *Q.* If a man die seised of lands, are they liable as against his devisee or heir-at-law for the payment of his debts of both kinds, or of either, and of which, kind? and if so, in what order of distribution?

*A.* A specialty creditor, in which the heir is bound, might at

Common Law sue the heir. Also by 3 & 4 Wm. & M., c. 14, he might sue the devisee. All creditors may proceed against the lands in equity, under the circumstances mentioned in the next answer. Also they may proceed under 3 & 4 Wm. IV., c. 104, preference being given to specialties in which the heir is bound. Wms. R. P., 74, 6th ed.

4. *Q.* A testator charges all his estate with payment of debts; are creditors by simple contract, by such a will on a level with specialty creditors who hold security where the heirs are bound?

*A.* All the creditors are put upon a level by reason of the charge. But this only applies to the land. For out of the personalty the creditors will be paid in their legal order of priority (see *infra*, "administration"), and it is not in the power of the testator to alter such order. The court will, however, prevent injustice being done to the simple contract creditors by the specialty creditors absorbing the personalty, and then coming upon the realty for any deficiency. In such a case if the specialty creditors have received 15s. in the pound out of the legal assets, they will not be allowed to participate in the equitable assets until the simple contract creditors have received 15s. in the pound also. For he who seeks equity must do equity. *Haslewood* v. *Pope*, 2 P. Wms., 323. Notes to *Silk* v. *Prime*, 2 L. C. Eq., 104, 2nd ed.

# A DIGEST

OF ALL THE

# EXAMINATION QUESTIONS AND ANSWERS

# IN EQUITY.

―――♦―――

### I.—*Nature and Object-matter of Equity Jurisprudence.*

1. *Q.* Give some account of the origin of the equitable jurisdiction of the Court of Chancery, and from whom was it borrowed?

*A.* Notwithstanding considerable controversy on the subject, it is generally admitted that the equitable jurisdiction of the Court of Chancery was called into existence for the purpose of remedying the defects of the courts of common law. These courts had a separate existence on being detached from the King's Council, and limited their powers of giving relief by adhering to certain forms of writs issued from the Court of Chancery, then a court of common law only. When the subject could not get relief from the common law courts, it was a frequent practice to petition the King. These petitions the King, during the reigns of the first two Edwards, frequently referred to his Chancellor, who was in those days his prime minister and secret adviser. He was, indeed, supposed to be the keeper of the King's conscience. By degrees all petitions to the King's equity were referred to his Chancellor's decision, and his jurisdiction in such matters was firmly established in the reign of Richard II. The Chancellor being the judge of the Court of Chancery, it followed, that the jurisdiction which was originally vested in him became vested in the court over which he presided. Hence it was, that the Court of Chancery is supposed to have acquired its equitable jurisdiction. Haynes' Outlines of Equity, Lect. 2; 3 Steph. Com., 420.

2. *Q.* Define "Equity."

*A.* Equity is that relief which, as is mentioned in the previous answer, was meted out by the Chancellor to remedy the harshness of the common law tribunals. The Chancellor, being universally an ecclesiastic, doubtless thoroughly believed in the justice of forcing a defendant to confess, and compelling him to do what, in conscience, he was bound to do. Thus, if B had given a bond to A, which the latter had lost, A could not recover upon the bond in the common law courts, in consequence of the rule requiring production of the bond itself in court. The Chancellor, however, disregarded a rule which worked such injustice, and by writ of subpœna compelled B to answer whether he had really given the bond or not. If it appeared that he had done so a decree was made that he should pay it, or the answer might be given in evidence in an action on the bond. Equity is, therefore, founded on the examination of the defendant, and compelling him to perform the dictates of conscience, in regard to the subject matter of the suit. The Court of Chancery also exercises jurisdiction in many cases where it has been specially empowered to do so by the Legislature; this latter is called its statutory jurisdiction.

3. *Q.* How far does the jurisdiction of the Court of Chancery extend? Can it make a decree relating to land out of the jurisdiction? State the rule.

*A.* The territorial jurisdiction of the court only extends to England and Wales, that is, it can only enforce its decrees within these limits. It can, however, entertain a suit relating to land, out of the jurisdiction, where the party against whom relief is sought is within the jurisdiction, and it is no objection to such a decree that, when made, it cannot be enforced. Thus, in *Penn* v. *Baltimore*, 2 Lead. Cases Eq., 767, specific performance was enforced of articles executed in England, concerning boundaries of two provinces in America. The reason for this is, that the Court acts *in personam* on the conscience of the defendant, and not necessarily *in rem*. The bill must not seek for the giving up of possession of land out of the jurisdiction, as if it does it will be demurrable, as the court cannot give possession. See the Notes to *Penn* v. *Baltimore*, *supra*.

4. *Q.* Define the technical meaning of Equity as contradistinguished from its general or ordinary meaning.

*A.* The equity administered by the Court of Chancery is unfortunately very different from equity in its ordinary sense. The latter consists in the golden rule of "do unto others as you would they should do unto you." In the administration of justice, however, where several conflicting rights are frequently involved, it is found impossible to apply this rule in its integrity. Hence it is that decrees are sometimes unavoidably inequitable to some of the litigants.

5. *Q.* The learned Selden has said, "For law we have a measure, and know what to trust to; equity is according to the conscience of him that is Chancellor, and as that is larger or narrower, so is equity." Is this an accurate description of equity as administered in our courts? State the grounds of your opinion.

*A.* At the time it was spoken, I think the opinion was tolerably correct, for then the jurisdiction of the court was being formed. There could be no precedents on many points, and the chancellor could, of course, decide as he chose. Now, however, lapse of centuries has established most of the principles and doctrines of the court upon a line of decisions, which precedents are as binding upon the Chancellor as much as if they were contained in statutory provisions. The conscience, therefore, of the chancellor has, at the present day, little or no control over equity.

6. *Q.* Before the jurisdiction of the court was settled, what

were the limits placed to its power? Mention some of the cases in the Year-books in which its interposition was applied for by way of illustration.

*A.* The court originally appears to have entertained petitions for redress in cases of personal torts or contracts, but its jurisdiction in this respect has been limited to interfering only in those cases where adequate redress cannot be obtained at law. In the calendars in chancery of Queen Elizabeth, the case of *Kymburley* v. *Goldsmith*, an action for the non-delivery of wood is mentioned. Also, in *Appilgarth, widow*, v. *Sergeantson*, the bill complained that defendant obtained money of the plaintiff, giving her to understand that he intended to marry her, but that he had married another woman, and refuses to return the money, pp. 20—41. Numerous other illustrations of the above cases may be found in the Year-books. Hayne's Outlines, Lect. 1, 2nd ed.

7. *Q.* What are the three principal cases in which the Court of Chancery grants relief, as stated by Lord Coke?

*A.* They are—fraud, accident, and trust. 4 Inst., 82.

8. *Q.* Name the distinguished Chancellors who reduced the system of equity to order, and to whom above all is the greatest share of merit ascribed in this respect.

*A.* Lord Bacon and Lord Nottingham were the most distinguished. The latter is the more celebrated, owing to the zeal with which he extended the jurisdiction of the court, by administering justice in its true spirit. The change wrought by Lord Nottingham, and the lethargy of his predecessors, is a good illustration of the soundness of Seldeu's opinion of equity above mentioned. 4 Steph. Com., 424.

9. *Q.* State the distinction between law and equity.

*A.* The leading distinction is the different method of procedure in the respective courts. Equity is not fettered by the strict rules of pleading, which are adhered to by courts of law. This enables equity to mould its decrees so as in many cases to meet the ends of justice more effectually than common law, and gives it jurisdiction in many cases of obvious right, where there is no remedy at law. Hence also it is, that the relief, when granted, is of a different character to that obtainable at law.

10. *Q.* Is there any, and what, difference between the general principles by which a Court of Equity is guided, and those of a Court of Law?

*A.* Both courts are guided by the leading principle of all administrative justice, namely—Equity.—It is not true, as is often alleged, that the common law tribunals have no equity. The judges at Westminster are as equitable as those at Lincoln's Inn, the only difference being that the latter deal equity out with a more liberal hand than the former are enabled to do, in consequence of their rules of procedure. Thus, in the administration of a deceased's estate, every creditor has a common law right to recover his debt by action against the executor, it would be inequitable were it otherwise. But equity is more equitable in preventing the assets being frittered away by separate actions. It makes a decree under which all the creditors must come in and make their claims, and it gives to each the share he may be by law entitled to.

11. *Q.* State generally the jurisdiction of Equity? In what cases has the Court of Chancery an equitable jurisdiction?

*A.* The jurisdiction of the Court, territorially, extends, as above mentioned, to England and Wales. It has jurisdiction in respect of :—

(Exclusive)—(a) Trusts. (b) Infants. (c) The equitable rights of wives. (d) Equitable mortgages. (e) The assignment of choses in action. (f) Partition. (g) The appointment of receivers. (h) Charities or public trusts.

(Concurrent)—(i) Fraud. (j) Accident. (k) Mistake. (l) Account. (m) Dower. (n) Interpleader. (o) The delivery up of documents and chattels. (p) The specific performance of agreements. (q) Set off. (r) Partnership.

(Auxiliary.)—(s) Discovery. (t) Perpetuation of testimony. (u) Bills of peace. (v) Bills to establish wills. Haynes's Outlines of Equity.; Wharton's Law Lexicon, 329.

12. *Q.* In what cases has Equity jurisdiction, exclusive of the Common Law?

*A.* See previous answer (a) to (h) inclusive.

13. *Q.* In what cases has it concurrent jurisdiction?

*A.* See previous answer, No. 11, (i) to (r) inclusive.

14. *Q.* In what cases is it auxiliary to the Common Law?

*A.* See previous answer, No. 11, (s) to (v) inclusive.

15. *Q.* What are the principal heads of remedial Equity?

*A.* They are cases coming under the heads of Accident, Mistake, and Fraud. Smith's Manual of Equity, 34—99.

16. *Q.* State some of the principal objects attainable by means of a Court of Equity.

*A.* They are :—The enforcement of trusts, the administration of estates, the protection of infants, relief in cases of fraud, accident, or mistake, specific performance of contracts, compelling discovery. See No. 11. *Supra.*

17. *Q.* In what cases have courts of equity either no jurisdiction, or decline to exercise it? give *exempli gratiâ* instances under each head, and explain shortly the meaning of each.

*A.* Equity has no jurisdiction to entertain matters where complete relief may be obtained at law. Thus, if a trespass has been committed, the court will leave the injured party to his remedy by recovering damages. There are numerous cases in which the court has jurisdiction, but in which, owing to some cause or other, it will not interfere. Thus, if the plaintiff has been guilty of laches, or of fraud, no relief will be given. So also if it is impossible to place the parties in *statu quo.*

18. *Q.* Will a court of equity interpose where one party has no more equity than the other, or will it leave the parties to their remedy at law?

*A.* If the equities between two parties are equal in every respect, the first in point of time will prevail. Thus, in *Stackhouse* v. *the Countess of Jersey*, 1 John's & H., the plaintiff was interested in a moiety of a fund invested on mortgage in the name of a trustee, who fraudulently deposited the mortgage deeds with the defendants to secure a debt of his own, the defendants having no notice of the plaintiff's interest, the court declared that the plaintiff was entitled in priority to the defendants even though purchasers for value without notice. But if one of the parties has obtained the legal title which will enable him to enforce his right at law, Equity will give such party the preference, under the maxim that where the equities are equal the law shall prevail. Thus, a third mortgagee advancing his money without notice of the second mortgage may get in the first mortgage as a *tabula in naufragio* and squeeze out the second mortgage. *Marsh* v. *Lee*, 1 L. C. Eq., 494, and notes.

19. *Q.* When two persons (plaintiff and defendant) have an equal equity, and have been equally innocent as well as diligent, what rule does the court apply in its judgment in a suit against a purchaser for valuable consideration, without notice of the adverse title of the plaintiff?

*A.* The court will, if the plaintiff is also a purchaser for value, decide in favor of him who has the legal estate, under the maxim that where equities are equal the law will prevail. If, however, neither party has the legal estate, it will decide in favor of he who is first in time, under the maxim *qui prior est tempore potior est jure*. Sugden's Vendors, 14th ed., 739.

20. *Q.* And when the parties are *in pari delicto*, what maxim will guide the court in such cases?

*A.* In such a case the court will not give relief, as he who comes into equity must come with clean hands. If, however, the fraud is so gross and notorious that it would infringe public policy to allow the transaction to stand, it will set it aside. Story's Eq., s. 695.

21. *Q.* What are the principal maxims or rules which govern Courts of Equity, and explain shortly the meaning of each?

*A.* The principal maxims are:—1. Equality is equity. This is illustrated by the equal distribution of assets amongst creditors when they can only enforce their rights through the medium of the court. *Silk* v. *Prime*, 2 L. C. Eq., 82. Also in the case of contribution between sureties. *Dering* v. *Earl of Winchilsea*, 1 L. C. Eq., 78. 2. He who seeks equity must do equity. This is exemplified by the case of a husband suing in equity for his wife's choses in action. The court, as a condition of their decree in his favour, will compel him to do equity, by settling on his wife a portion of the sum recovered. *Lady Elibank* v. *Montolieu*, 1 L. C. Eq., 341. 3. Where equities are equal the law shall prevail, and, as to which see the previous answer, No. 18. 4. Equity follows the law. This is illustrated by the manner in which the court, with regard to equitable estates, follows the same rules of descent as at common law. Also, equitable estates may be entailed in the same way as legal ones. 5. Equity considers that done which is agreed to be done. Upon this principle land agreed to be sold is looked upon in equity as money. *Fletcher* v. *Ashburner*, 1 L. C. Eq., 659. 6. Equity imputes an intention to fulfil an obligation. Thus, if a man covenants to buy and settle lands and subsequently buys lands without settling them, the lands bought will be taken in satisfaction of the covenant. *Wilcocks* v. *Wilcocks*, 2 L. C. Eq., 345. The following maxims are generally applied by courts of law and equity:— No right without a remedy, *Vigilantibus, non dormientibus æquitas subvenit*. *Qui prior est tempore potior est jure*. These were originally common law maxims, which Courts of Equity have adopted. See Broom's Legal Maxims.

22. *Q.* The modern system of Equity established, state in what respect, the maxim, "*Æquitas sequitur legem.*" Is the rule, with any and what exception?

*A.* In dealing with equitable estates and interests the Court is guided by the rules of law applicable to similar legal estates and interests. Thus in the descent of equitable estates, equity is guided by the common law rules of descent. The reason for this is that were it otherwise great uncertainty and confusion would ensue. Also in the payment of the debts of a deceased person out of assets which could be recovered at law, the legal order of payment is observed. But if the creditor would have no remedy at law, equity will not follow the law, deeming all creditors equal in conscience. This forms an exception to the application of the rule. *Cowper* v. *Cowper*, 2 Peere Wms., 720; Haynes' Outlines, 24, 2nd ed. Also *infra*, No. 25.

23. *Q.* What is the rule of equity in the construction of deeds and wills?

*A.* With regard to deeds the rule is that they should be construed liberally, so as to uphold them if possible, and carry into effect the intention of the parties. Also, that they should be taken most strongly against the grantor, and that a latent ambiguity may, but a patent ambiguity may not, be explained by parol evidence. In the construction of wills the polar star is that the intention of the testator should guide the court, provided such intention do not infringe any rule of law. If a rule of law is infringed the court will carry out the testator's general intention as nearly as possible, and *ut res magis valeat quam pereat*. A similar rule prevails as to wills with regard to parol evidence, as in the case of deeds. A will is, therefore, construed more liberally than a deed, the reason being that in a will only one person speaks, and his intention cannot conflict with that of others, as is the case in respect of contracts *inter vivos*. Broom's Legal Maxims, 521—659.

24. *Q.* When there are two clauses absolutely inconsistent with each other, which clause prevails, the first or the last; and is the rule the same in both deeds and wills, and if different in what particular?

*A.* It is a settled rule of construction that in a deed if two clauses are so inconsistent that they cannot both stand, the former will prevail, and the latter will be rejected. In a will, however, the rule is *cum duo inter se pugnantia reperiuntur in testamento, ultimum ratum est*. Therefore, if a testator in his will gives a person an estate in fee simple and in a subsequent part shows that he means the devisee to take for life only, the prior gift is restricted accordingly. In the application of this rule, however, the general intention must not be lost sight of as it appears from the context. Chitty on Contracts, 88; Broom's Maxims, 560.

25. *Q.* What is the rule of interpreting the Statute Law in Equity; and does it differ from that of common law?

*A.* With regard to the rules of construction of statutes, equity follows the law. The principal rules are to carry out the true intention of the legislature. A remedial statute (that is one passed to remedy a defect in the common law), must be liberally construed so as to include cases within the mischief the statute intended to remedy. *Twynne's Case*, 1 Sm. L. C., 1. But an act imposing a penalty must be construed strictly. The "golden rule" to be observed in construing the words used, is to look at the precise words of the statute and construe them in their ordinary sense only, if such construction would not lead to absurdity or manifest injustice; but, if it would, then the words ought to be so varied and modified as to avoid that which it could not be the intention of the legislature should be done. A statute shall not be retrospective unless a clear intention to the contrary is expressed. Broom's Maxims, 548—554, 34—43.

## II.—*The Equity Fora, their Judges and Officers.*

1. *Q.* Which are the courts of equity in England, and the several branches of such courts? distinguishing those in which the jurisdiction is limited and to what extent.

*A.* They are the Courts of Chancery, which have a general jurisdiction throughout England and Wales. The Courts of the counties Palatine of Durham and Lancaster, the courts of the Universities (Oxford and Cambridge), the Lord Mayor's Court of the City of London have a limited jurisdiction. The Superior Courts of Common Law and the County Courts have also equitable jurisdiction. 17 & 18 Vic., c. 125; 23 & 24 Vic., c. 126; 28 & 29 Vic., c. 99; 3 Steph. Com., 418.

2. *Q.* How many judges of the Court of Chancery are there, and how do they rank: and to what tribunals can their respective decisions be appealed against? Describe the mode of giving judgment in each.

*A.* There are seven judges who rank as follows:—1. The Lord Chancellor. 2. The Master of the Rolls. 3. The Lords Justices. 4. The three Vice Chancellors. An appeal lies from the Master of the Rolls and the Vice Chancellors to the Lord Chancellor sitting alone, or to the Lords Justices sitting together, or to the Lord Chancellor sitting with one Lord Justice. An ultimate appeal lies to the House of Lords. 14 & 15 Vic., c. 83. The judgments of the Courts are delivered orally by the judges. In the House of Lords, in addition to the judgments of the Law Lords, the judges of the superior courts deliver their opinions in writing upon certain points submitted to them. Their assistance, however, is not often sought on appeals from Equity. Ayck. C. Pr., 373, 7th ed.

3. *Q.* What is the distinction between the judicial and the administrative jurisdiction of the court? Name the officers who preside over each branch.

*A.* The judicial jurisdiction is that involving questions which are decided by the various judges of the court. Thus generally all questions of law and fact arising, forming the chief grounds of contention in a suit, are decided in open court by the judges. The administrative jurisdiction after the first decree is, however, usually disposed of in Chambers by the judge's deputy. Thus, in an administration suit, all the inquiries are conducted by the chief clerks. The officers presiding over the judicial branch of the court are those mentioned in the previous answer. They also have under their control the administrative jurisdiction. But the inferior officers chiefly conduct the latter. They are :—The accountant general. The registrars. The clerks of records and writs. The examiners, and the chief clerks. Hayne's Outlines, 51, 2nd ed.

4. *Q.* How and when did the House of Lords gain the power of sitting as the highest court of appeal?

*A.* The House of Lords gained the power of hearing appeals by virtue of a paramount judicial authority delegated to it by the Crown. The Barons being summoned by the King to the great council heard the appeals from the inferior courts of common law when those courts came into existence. This happened about the reign of Richard I., when the Court of Common Pleas is supposed to have been detached from the King's Court or *Aula Regis*. After this, the King sitting in his great council was in the habit of hearing appeals by writ of error from the courts of common law, and the Barons sitting with him acquired by delegation a similar power. The Lords acquired their jurisdiction as a Court of Appeal from the Court of Chancery at a later date. The first petition of appeal is said to have been presented in 18 Jac. I., Com. Jour., 13 Mar., 1704. Sir M. Hale says the earliest precedent is 3 Car. I. The Commons have disputed this latter jurisdiction, but it is now conceded that when the Court of Chancery acquired the power of deciding civil causes, an appeal became equally necessary as a writ of error from a judgment at common law. 3 Bl. Coms., 526; 3 Hal. Const. Hist., 18—27, 10th ed.

5. *Q.* What are the duties of the Registrars?

*A.* They are—To make out a list of causes, and for this purpose causes are set down with the Registrar. They have to be present in court and take down minutes of the decrees and orders made. These orders and decrees they afterwards prepare and settle in the presence of the parties. If any material difference exists between the Registrar's note of the proceedings and of that of Counsel, the former will direct the parties to set the cause down to be spoken to on the minutes.

6. *Q.* What are the duties of the Examiners?

*A.* Their duties are to take the examination and cross-examination of witnesses in Chambers, and to write down the evidence. They are also to administer the necessary oaths. See *infra*, "Evidence."

7. *Q.* What are the duties of the Record and Writ Clerks?

*A.* They are—To keep files for the filing of the various documents occurring in the course of proceedings in Chancery. Such are, *inter alia*, Bills, Answers, Interrogatories, Pleas, Demurrers, Replications, Special Cases, Affidavits.

### III.—*The Statutory Jurisdiction.*

1. *Q.* Name the statutes now in operation for regulating the courts in the various branches of their jurisdiction.

*A.* The following are amongst the most important:—36 Geo. III., c. 52, s. 32, Infants' Legacies; 3 & 4 Wm. IV., c. 104, Administration of Assets; 2 & 3 Vic., c. 54, Custody of Infants; 6 & 7 Vic., c. 73, Attornies and Solicitors; 8 Vic., c. 18, Lands Clauses; 10 & 11 Vic., c. 96, Trusts; 12 & 13 Vic., c. 74, Trusts; 13 & 14 Vic., c. 35, Procedure, c. 60, Trustees; 14 & 15 Vic., c. 83, Appeal; 15 & 16 Vic., c. 80, Masters' Abolition; 15 & 16 Vic., c. 86, Practice; 16 & 17 Vic., c. 78, Oaths; 18 & 19 Vic., c. 43, Infant Settlement; 19 & 20 Vic., c. 120, Leases and Sales; 21 & 22 Vic., c. 77, Leases and Sales Amendment; 21 & 22 Vic., c. 27, Procedure; 22 & 23 Vic., c. 35, Forfeiture, &c.; 23 & 24 Vic., c. 38; Investments-Trusts; c.145, Investments, etc., c.149, Prisoners in Contempt; 25 & 26 Vic., c. 42, Questions of Fact; 25 & 26 Vic., c. 89, Winding-up; Morgan's Chancery Acts, 1.

2. *Q.* To what extent are Courts of Equity enabled by recent acts of parliament, to exercise jurisdiction in matters which were formerly only cognisable at law?

*A.* The court is now empowered to award damages in addition to specific performance and an injunction. 21 & 22 Vic., c. 27. Also by 25 & 26 Vic., c. 42, further provision is made making it compulsory upon the court to try issues of fact without directing an issue to common law.

3. *Q.* Suppose a debtor dies seised of real estates, which he may have devised, but did not charge with the payment of his debts, the estates being assets in the hands of the heir for the payment of specialty debts, can simple contract creditors obtain any and what assistance from a Court of Equity in discharge of such simple contract debts; and how?

*A.* The simple contract creditors may by virtue of 3 & 4 Wm. IV., c. 104, administer the real estate in Equity, and have it applied in payment of their debts. Specialty creditors, in which the heirs are bound, will have priority over other creditors who share the surplus equally. The proceedings are taken by Bill. Haddan's Equity, 29, 30.

4. *Q.* If there be a decree for the sale of estates to pay debts, and such estates by descent or devise be vested in an infant, what authority has a Court of Equity in such cases to perfect such sale, and whence is that authority derived?

*A.* The court has power, under 13 & 14 Vic., c. 60, to make a vesting order perfecting the sale. The infant will be considered as holding upon a trust, so as to bring him within the powers conferred by the act. 13 & 14 Vic., c. 60, s. 29. Morgan's Chancery Acts, 85.

5. *Q.* If estates be liable to the payment of debts of a settlor or testator, and such estates be vested in a tenant for life, or other person having only a limited estate or interest, and the remainder or reversion in fee be vested in other persons, whether within or out of the jurisdiction of a Court of Equity, what assistance can such court give to perfect a sale of such estate?

*A.* The court may make an order vesting the estate in the purchaser, under 13 & 14 Vic., c. 60.

6. *Q.* To what extent can Equity relieve creditors, out of the copyhold property of persons dying seised of such property, and which persons shall not have charged such property with the payment of their debts?

*A.* Creditors may administer the copyhold property, under 3 & 4 Wm. IV., c. 104, to the same extent as freeholds, *supra*, No. 3.

7. *Q.* If a Court of Equity can relieve creditors out of such copyhold property, in what manner would such property be applied?

*A.* It would first be applied in payment of the specialty creditors, in which the heirs are bound. The residue would be equally divided between the other specialty creditors and the simple contract creditors. 3 & 4 Wm. IV., c. 104.

8. *Q.* In the case of money paid into court by a railway company for purchase of part of a settled estate, how may it be applied for the benefit of the owners of such estate?

*A.* The money is to be applied—1. In the purchase or redemption of the land tax or incumbrances. 2. The purchase of other land to be settled to the same uses. 3. In the removing, restoring, or replacing buildings taken or injured. 4. Payment to persons becoming absolutely entitled. 8 Vic., c. 18, s. 69.

9. *Q.* What are the principal alterations introduced by Mr. Headlam's Trustee Act (13 & 14 Vic., c. 60), in the principles and practice of the court?

*A.* This act enabled the court to direct what should be done with real and personal property vested in trustees upon trust, or mortgagees, in cases where the trustees or mortgagees are under any disability, such as infancy, lunacy, or absence beyond the seas, or on their death without personal representatives. These disabilities prevented the trust property being dealt with before the act, in accordance with the trust, or the mortgaged property being reconveyed. The act also conferred powers on the court to appoint by application on petition new trustees when required, owing to disabilities of the former trustees, and to make orders vesting the trust property in such new trustees. See the act fully discussed, Haddan's Chancery, cap. iii. As to the proceedings by petition to appoint a new trustee, see *infra*, "Petitions."

10. *Q.* Suppose a trust estate to devolve upon an infant or lunatic, how is such infant or lunatic to convey for the purposes of the trust?

*A.* A vesting order must be obtained from the Court of Chancery vesting the property in the parties entitled. If the trustee is a lunatic, a similar order should be obtained from the Lord Chancellor sitting in lunacy, or the Lords' justices. 13 & 14 Vic., c. 60, s. 3, and notes. Morgan's Chancery Statutes, 65—103.

11. *Q.* If a trustee refuse or neglect to convey real estate, what course should be adopted to compel or render unnecessary his concurrence?

*A.* Application should be made to the court for a vesting order, by virtue of which the concurrence of the trustee will be unnecessary. 13 & 14 Vic., c. 60. Haddan's Equity, 291.

12. *Q.* State the objects of the Trustee Relief Acts for better securing "Trust Funds and for the Relief of Trustees," and the course of proceeding under them on the part as well of trustees as of parties claiming the trust-funds.

*A.* The object of the acts referred to is to enable a trustee having money or stock in his hands, which he cannot safely administer without the direction of the court, to pay it into court without the preliminaries of a bill, answer, decree, petition, or evidence, excepting a short affidavit stating the amount of the fund, the nature of the trust, and the names of the persons he believes to be entitled. Upon this being done, the court will administer the fund as if a bill had been filed. The parties entitled to the fund paid in must petition to have the money paid to them. The trustee can only avail himself of these provisions where the trust estate is money or stock, and there is a *bonâ fide* doubt of fact or law. 10 & 11 Vic., c. 96; 12 & 13 Vic., c. 74. In re *Bloye's Trust*, 19 L. J. (N. S.), Eq., 89. As to the proceedings on a petition, see *infra*, "Petitions."

13. *Q.* Refer to any recent Act of Parliament under which the Court of Chancery (notwithstanding the absence of a power in the settlement) can authorise a sale or lease of settled estates without a special application to Parliament.

*A.* The act referred to is "The Leases and Sales of Settled Estates Act." 19 & 20 Vic., c. 120. Amended by 21 & 22 Vic., c. 77, and 27 & 28 Vic., c. 120.

14. *Q.* What powers are conferred upon the Court of Chancery by the Act commonly called "The Leases and Sales of Settled Estates Act?"

*A.* Under this act the Court is empowered to authorise leases of settled estates. Agricultural or occupation leases, twenty-one years; mining leases, or of water, water mills, way leaves, water leaves, or other easements, forty years. Repairing leases, sixty years. Building leases, ninety-nine years. Also for longer periods, if it is the custom of the country, and beneficial, excepting as to agricultural leases. The leases must take effect in possession at or within one year next after the making. The best rent must be reserved without fine. The felling of trees is not to be authorised, except for the purpose of clearing the ground for buildings. The leases must be by deed, and the lessee must execute a counterpart, and there must be a condition for re-entry on non-payment of the rent for not less than twenty-eight days, s. 2. The court may also authorise the sale of settled estates, if the sale is beneficial. The money to be so raised is to be paid to trustees or into court, and to be applied in redemption of the land tax, and payment of incumbrances, or in payment to the person beneficially entitled. Williams R. P., 31. Times of Equity, 3.

15. *Q.* A is entitled to the possession of a settled estate for a term of years determinable on his death. The settlement contains no power of leasing. Can the defect be supplied, and by what means? Will A have to obtain the concurrence of any other person interested under the settlement?

*A.* The court has power to supply the defect, under the before mentioned act, by authorising and approving of particular leases to be made for the periods above mentioned. It may also vest a general power of leasing in conformity with the act in trustees. 19 & 20 Vic., c. 120, s. 10; 27 & 28 Vic., c. 45. If there is a tenant in tail under the settlement in existence and of full age, he must consent; if several tenants in tail, then the first need only consent. Also all persons having any beneficial estate or interest under the settlement prior to the estate of the tenant in tail, and all trustees having any estate on behalf of any unborn child prior to the estate tail, must consent. In every other case the parties beneficially entitled must consent. 19 & 20 Vic., c. 120, s. 17.

16. *Q.* How is the consent of a married woman taken to an application for sale under the Settled Estates Act, and what persons are competent to take such consent?

*A.* The married woman must be examined apart from her husband, touching her knowledge of the nature and effect of the application, and it must be ascertained that she freely desires to make the application. The examination must be made whether the estate be settled to the separate use of the wife or not. Unless the married woman resides abroad, the examination must be either by the court or a solicitor appointed by the court. If she resides abroad any person, whether a solicitor or not, may be appointed. 19 & 20 Vic., c. 120, ss. 37, 38; 21 & 22 Vic., c. 77, s. 6.

17. *Q.* A freehold estate stands limited to A for life, remainder to his son B (an infant) for life, remainder to the first and other sons of B in tail, and the settlement contains no power of sale; can the estate be sold, and what proceedings are necessary for the purpose?

*A.* If the court thinks it proper and consistent with a due regard for the interests of all parties entitled under the settlement, a sale will be ordered on the petition of A. The consent of B is necessary, but he being an infant special application must be made to the court for a direction to the infant's guardian to consent. As to the proceedings on the petition, see *infra*, "Petitions." 19 & 20 Vic., c. 120, ss. 11, 36.

18. *Q.* Will a Court of Equity permit a tenant for life, whether impeachable for waste or not, to grant a lease for a longer period than twenty-one years, or the life of such tenant? if so, state under what circumstances, and by what authority it has such power.

*A.* The tenant for life may apply, under 19 & 20 Vic., c. 120, as above mentioned.

### IV.—*The Specially Delegated Jurisdiction.*

1. *Q.* What is the origin of the Lord Chancellor's jurisdiction in lunacy, and how derived? and to what other judges has it recently been extended?

*A.* The Chancellor's jurisdiction as to lunatics originated and is derived from the Crown, as the custodian of lunatics, by virtue of 17 Ed. II., c. 10. As keeper of the Queen's conscience, he also exercises the jurisdiction possessed by the Crown as *parens patriæ*. The Chancellor's jurisdiction has been recently extended to the Lords Justices by 14 & 15 Vic., c. 83. Smith's Manual of Equity, 415.

2. *Q.* What protection do lunatics receive from equity, and how is a lunacy to be established?

*A.* If lunatics have not been so found by inquisition, the Court of Equity will protect them in common with other persons under disability. It will, therefore, protect his person and property. Lunacy is established by a petition to the Lord Chancellor, or Lords Justices, generally presented by a member of the alleged lunatic's family, supported by affidavit. The Lord Chancellor or Lords Justices direct an inquiry before one of the Masters in lunacy. If the alleged lunatic require it, he is entitled to a jury. In making an order for a jury, an issue may be directed to be tried before one of the superior courts of common law. 25 & 26 Vic., c. 86, s. 4. The inquiry is conducted in a manner very similar to trials at nisi prius, each party supporting their case by evidence, which occasionally is very voluminous. If the lunacy is established, the inquisition is returned and filed by the Master's clerk in the Petty Bag Office. Elmer's Prac., 4, 4th ed.

3. *Q.* Has the Lord Chancellor power to appoint a guardian of the person of a lunatic, and a receiver to his estate, without a previous inquiry under a commission of lunacy?

*A.* The Lord Chancellor never interferes unless the lunacy has been first established under a commission. Ibid., 1.

4. *Q.* If a trustee, having stock or other property vested in him, become a lunatic, and a new trustee be appointed, how is a transfer of the stock, or a conveyance or assignment of the other trust property from the lunatic to the new trustee, to be made?

*A.* An order should be obtained from the Lord Chancellor or Lords Justices, vesting the right to transfer the stock in some person to the new trustee. The order is obtained on petition. 13 & 14 Vic., c. 60, s. 5.

5. *Q.* State shortly the mode by which a trustee may relieve himself from responsibility in respect of a fund held in trust for a person of unsound mind.

*A.* He should pay the money into court under the Trustee Relief Acts, 10 & 11 Vic., c. 96, though it has been doubted if this act applies to cases of lunacy; see the cases collected, Phillip's Lunacy, 25.

6. *Q.* If a person found lunatic by commission die before the costs of the proceedings are taxed and paid, what is the solicitor's remedy for his costs?

*A.* The solicitor may obtain an order from the Lord Chancellor or Lords Justices, directing the payment of the costs out of the lunatic's property, upon which the costs are made a charge. 23 & 24 Vic., c. 127, s. 29; 16 & 17 Vic., c. 70, s. 145.

## V.—*The Equity or Extraordinary Jurisdiction.*

### (1). *As it is Assistant or Auxiliary.*

#### (a) *Discovery.*

1. *Q.* What is the nature and object of a bill of discovery?

*A.* It is a bill filed for the discovery of facts in aid of proceedings at law. Until recently parties to suits could not give evidence at law, the consequence of which was, that the plaintiff at law might obtain a verdict to which he was not entitled, because the defence rested on the knowledge of the plaintiff and defendant only. To remedy this evil, equity allowed the defendant to file a bill for the purpose of interrogating the plaintiff on oath, as to the true state of the case. By this means the defendant at law was enabled to extract from the plaintiff (unless the latter committed perjury) an admission of the true facts of the case. This admission he could give in evidence at law, and so defeat the plaintiff's unjust claim. The filing of a bill of discovery is now seldom necessary, in consequence of the enactments of 14 & 15 Vic., c. 99; 17 & 18 Vic., c. 125, but the jurisdiction of equity to grant discovery in aid of proceedings at law still exists. *The British Empire Shipping Company v. Somes,* 26 L. J. Eq., 759; Outlines of Equity, 160.

2. *Q.* Of what matters will the court not compel a discovery?

*A.* Discovery will not be granted, amongst other cases, where such discovery would criminate the defendant, where the plaintiff has no interest in the suit, where the discovery relates to the defendant's case, and not to the plaintiff's, where the plaintiff is under some disability. Smith's Man., 450.

3. *Q.* When a bill of discovery has been filed, praying discovery only and no relief, can any, and if any, what further step be taken by the plaintiff or defendant in the suit after the answer has been filed, and the time for excepting to it has expired?

*A.* The defendant may, as soon as the time for excepting has elapsed, move for an order, as of course for his costs of suit. Ayck. Ch. Pr., 251.

4. *Q.* Is a defendant entitled to his costs of a bill filed against him for discovery and relief, or for discovery alone?

*A.* As above mentioned, the defendant is entitled to his costs in a bill of discovery, as of course, but if relief is also prayed, the costs will be in the discretion of the court.

5. *Q.* A brings an action against B, in which it is supposed that C, who has no interest in the matters in question between the two former parties, can give important evidence for A. Can A, on C refusing to disclose what the nature of his testimony will be, compel him to do so by a bill of discovery? and, in either way of answering this question, give the reason for your answer.

*A.* In this case there never was any objection to C being called as a witness in the action, therefore the chief ground for discovery fails. Discovery, consequently, will not lie against him. *Fenton v. Hughes,* 7 Ves.

6. *Q.* What is the distinction between a bill of discovery and relief, and a bill for discovery only? and in what respect do the proceedings under the two bills differ?

*A.* A bill of discovery merely prays the discovery of facts, but a bill of discovery and relief prays also for relief consequent upon the discovery. If discovery is sought as to destroyed, lost, or suppressed deeds, or even if relief *on equitable grounds* is also sought, no affidavit is necessary. But if relief could be had at law, and the plaintiff comes into equity for discovery in respect of the subject matter, and also for relief consequent upon such discovery, then an affidavit must accompany the bill, stating that the deeds are not in plaintiff's possession, and the fact of loss or suppression. The reason for requiring such affidavit is, that the plaintiff seeks to change the tribunal by substituting proceedings in equity for the less tedious and less expensive procedure of a court of law. A bill for discovery is never brought to a hearing, and cannot be dismissed for want of prosecution. Mitford's Pleadings, 65, 66; Smith's Manual of Equity, 37, 38.

7. *Q.* Can the defendant move to dismiss a bill filed for discovery?

*A.* No, he cannot, as mentioned in the previous answer.

8. *Q.* In order to sustain a bill of discovery, what must appear on the face of it?

*A.* It must state the matter touching which a discovery is sought, the interest of the plaintiff and defendant in the subject, and the right of the plaintiff to discovery. Ayck. Ch. Pr., 250.

9. *Q.* State the mode by which a defendant at law can now obtain discovery from the plaintiff at law; and how was such discovery obtained under the former practice of the court?

*A.* Discovery may be obtained at law by obtaining an order from a judge, for the inspection of documents in the control of the opposite party, by virtue of 14 & 15 Vic., c. 99. Also under 17 & 18 Vic., c. 125, s. 50, a party making an affidavit of belief that the other party has some document in respect of which a right of discovery exists, is entitled to a production and inspection of such document. Also under s. 51, interrogatories may be delivered to the opposite party, if such party might be examined at the trial as a witness. Under the old practice, it was usual to file a bill of discovery in equity, and thus obtain an answer from the defendant, and such a bill may now be filed in a proper case. *British Empire Shipping Company* v. *Somes*, 3 K. & J., 437.

#### (b) *Preservation of Testimony.*

1. *Q.* What is the nature and object of a bill to perpetuate testimony?

*A.* It is a bill filed by a person presumptively entitled to some future interest in property, who finds his title threatened by some other person interested in disputing it, but which title he cannot now assert, in consequence of the property being reversionary. The bill is filed against the parties interested in disputing the title, asking that witnesses may be examined as to the point in controversy, and that the testimony may be perpetuated. Haynes' Outlines of Equity, 172.

2. *Q.* A party entitled under a devise to real estate in remainder, after the death of another who is in possession, is apprehensive that the validity of the devise may be questioned at law, on the death of the party in possession, and that the witnesses to prove the validity of the devise may then be dead, will a court of equity give him any assistance, and in what manner?

*A.* He may file a bill to perpetuate the testimony (see preceding answer).

3. *Q.* Has any recent statute been passed on this subject? If so, state its general scope.

*A.* The act referred to is 5 & 6 Vic., c. 59, which was passed to extend the jurisdiction as to perpetuation of testimony, to cases where titles, dignities, or offices are claimed, also to a mere *spes successionis*. Before this act a bill could only be filed in respect of a claim to property in which the plaintiff had an interest. Thus, an heir at law could not file a bill, but a remainderman could. Per Lord Eldon, in *Dursley* v. *Fitzhardinge Berkeley*, 6 Ves., 251.

4. *Q.* By marriage settlement estates are limited to A for life, remainder to the eldest and other sons of the marriage successively in tail. The eldest son has attained twenty-one. The father and son concur in barring the entail, and they borrow money on the security of the estates. On the investigation of the title for that purpose, the certificate of the baptism or birth of the eldest son cannot be found, but an aged relative of the family, present at the birth of the son, can prove his birth and legitimacy: what proceedings should be adopted to make this evidence available in the event of litigation after the death of the witness, and state the general course of such proceedings?

*A.* The son should file a bill to perpetuate the testimony of the aged relative, making defendants his brothers (if any), and all persons *in esse* having estates in remainder. The bill being filed, an answer is put in, and replication filed, after which the evidence is taken, either *viva voce* before an examiner, under the old practice, or by affidavit, under the old practice. The bill does not come to a hearing, and the plaintiff pays the defendant's costs, unless the defendant, in addition to cross-examining the plaintiff's witnesses, examine witnesses of his own. In such a case defendant bears his own costs. Ayck. Ch. Pr., 248; Haynes' Outlines of Equity, 180.

5. *Q.* In what cases cannot the evidence taken under a bill to perpetuate testimony be afterwards used?

*A.* The evidence is not published, and cannot be used until the witness is dead. Haynes' Outlines of Equity, 179.

### (c) *Restraining Common Law Judgments.*

1. *Q.* Could a judgment obtained by fraud at common law, be set aside in equity? How was this settled in A.D. 1616, and by whom, and on what occasion?

*A.* Relief was given against such a judgment by King James the First before whom the question was brought in 1616, on a dispute between Lord Chancellor Ellesmere and Sir Edward Coke, Chief Justice of the King's Bench. Although the king decided the case by referring to his prerogative, it was then well settled that equity has the jurisdiction in dispute. 3 Steph. Com., 423.

### (II). *As it is Concurrent.*
### (a) *Fraud.*

1. *Q.* Are there any, and what, cases of fraud against which equity will not relieve?

*A.* Equity will not interfere where ample relief may be had at law, as in general, where goods have been sold under a fraudulent warranty, the party defrauded has an adequate remedy at law, by action for the deceit or recovery of the price he has paid for the goods. So the court will not set aside a will obtained by fraud, for the Court of Probate is the proper tribunal, (as to this see No. 3) nor in general will the court interfere where the fraud is of a criminal nature. No relief will be given where the plaintiff has himself been guilty of fraud, for then the parties are *in pari delicto*. Nor will the court interfere if it is impossible to put the parties *in statu quo*, as where an estate has been obtained by fraud and afterwards sold to a *bond fide* purchaser without notice. Nor will relief be given if on a sale there have been false statements, if the purchaser has not relied on them, but has taken due precautions to ascertain their truth. *Small* v. *Attwood*, Yo., 407; Sugden's Vendors, 736, 14th ed.; The Articled Clerk's Manual, 163, 9th ed., by Anderson.

2. *Q.* A testator, by his will, having given a pecuniary legacy

to A, is induced, when in a state of great mental and bodily weakness, and through the fraud, influence, and circumvention of B, to revoke the legacy, and by a codicil to his will to give it to B himself. Is, or is not, this a case in which, after the testator's death, and assuming that the facts above-stated could be clearly established, you would advise A to have recourse to a Court of Equity against B? If yea, state the relief that you would seek to obtain for A. If nay, give the reasons for you not recommending the suit?

*A.* I should advise A not to proceed against B in equity, as the court will not interfere to upset a will of personal estate on the ground of fraud, even though the fraud, as in this case, only goes to a particular bequest. The facts in this case are analogous to those in *Allen* v. *McPherson*, 1 H. L. Cas., 191, where upon demurrer to a bill filed by A it was so decided. Lords Cottenham and Langdale, however, dissented. The reason for the decision was that the Ecclesiastical Court is the proper tribunal. See the next answer.

3. *Q.* Explain the difference between the jurisdiction of the Court of Chancery and the Probate Court in the case of wills, and has the former lost any of its jurisdiction since the passing of the "Probate Act?

*A.* The Court of Chancery has jurisdiction to set aside a will of real estate on the ground of fraud at the suit of the heir, and also to establish the will at the suit of the devisee against the heir; but wills of personalty are entirely within the jurisdiction of the Probate Court. The Ecclesiastical Court, however, never had jurisdiction as to wills of real estate, though since 20 & 21 Vic., c. 77, s. 61, the Court of Probate has jurisdiction to a certain extent with regard to real estate. This section enacts that the heir or devisee shall be cited in suits to propound a will, after which the probate is to be conclusive against the heir or devisee. s. 62. These provisions will, probably, frequently render recourse to chancery unnecessary, but the court cannot be said to have lost any of its jurisdiction, as it can still set aside a will of real estate on the ground of fraud. 1 Wms. Exors., 341 ; *Boyse* v. *Rossborough*, 23 L. J. Ch., 305. See also the previous answer.

4. *Q.* Where a submission to reference has been made a rule of a Court of Common Law, has or has not a Court of Equity jurisdiction to afford relief against the award which has been made in pursuance of such submission?

*A.* The most recent decisions on this point show that equity has no jurisdiction in such a case, the jurisdiction being confined to the court of which the submission is made a rule. *Gwinnet* v. *Bannister*, 14 Ves., 530 ; Russell, 693, 3rd ed.

5. *Q.* What is the rule in equity as to time, barring or not barring relief against fraud?

*A.* The rule is that relief must be sought without unnecessary delay, otherwise the party injured will be deemed to have acquiesced in the fraud. *Vigilantibus non dormientibus equitas subvenit.*

With regard to suits against purchasers by *cestui que trusts* to whom a fraudulent conveyance has been made by the trustee, the time is limited to twenty years from the conveyance to the purchaser. In the event of concealed fraud, the time runs from the time at which it could with reasonable diligence have been first known. 3 & 4 Wm. IV., c. 27, ss. 25, 26.

6. *Q.* State some of the cases in which a Court of Equity will set aside a deed or contract.

*A.* Deeds and contracts will generally be set aside owing to the fraud of the parties, as where a vendor makes fraudulent representations as to the value of the property; also if the transaction is between trustee and *cestui que trust*, guardian and ward, solicitor and client, and other persons particularly liable to be imposed upon. So also, if the consideration is illegal, as contravening some statute or being against public policy. Such are, agreements in absolute restraint of trade. Mistake of fact is also a ground for setting aside instruments. Manual of Equity, 43, 53.

7. *Q.* A having sold his expectant interest in real estate, and received the purchase-money, afterwards files a bill to set aside the sale, on the ground of fraud which he succeeds in proving: on what terms will the court grant him relief?

*A.* Upon the maxim that he who seeks equity must do equity, the court will compel the plaintiff to repay the purchase-money with interest at £5 per cent. If the estate has fallen into possession the purchaser would probably be charged with an occupation rent, being at the same time allowed for lasting repairs and substantial improvements. Sugden's Vendors, 254, 14th ed.

8. *Q.* Define champerty and maintenance respectively, and state some of the cases in which exception is made to the general rule against them.

*A.* Champerty is a bargain between a plaintiff or defendant in a suit and a third person, to divide between them the land or other matter sued for, if recovered. It is also the purchasing a right of action. Choses in action are, however, assignable in some cases. Such are Bills of Exchange and others.

Maintenance is intermeddling in a suit which does not concern one, by assisting either party with money or otherwise to prosecute or defend it. But a master may maintain a suit for injury to his servant or for his near kinsman or poor neighbour out of charity and compassion. Steph. Com., 4, 316.

9. *Q.* Define constructive fraud?

*A.* It may be defined to be, any acts or contracts, which though not originating in any actual evil design, or contrivance to perpetrate a positive fraud or injury upon other persons, yet, by their tendency to deceive or mislead others, or to violate public or private confidence, or to impair or injure the public interests, are deemed equally reprehensible as actual fraud. 1 Story's Eq., 213.

10. *Q.* Is, or is not, inadequacy of price, or inequality of bargain, a sufficient ground of itself for avoiding a contract in a Court of Equity?

*A.* Inadequacy of price, alone, is not sufficient to avoid the contract, yet, if there is fraudulent concealment of the value of the estate by the purchaser it would be otherwise. Equity will not refuse to assist a vendor merely because the price is unreasonable, but, on the other hand, the contract will not be enforced if the purchaser was induced to give the unreasonable price by the fraud or gross mis-representation of the vendor; or by an industrious concealment of a defect in the estate. Sugden's Vendors, 272, 273, 14th ed.

11. *Q.* If A obtain the conveyance of an estate from B by fraud, and A sell the estate to a purchaser; will equity relieve B, and set aside such conveyance and annul the sale to the purchaser? state in what case the court would or would not do so.

*A.* B will have no remedy against the purchaser, unless he can show that he had notice of the fraud. B's remedy will be against A. The court shows great favour to a *bonâ fide* purchaser without notice. Ibid., 741.

12. *Q.* What will amount to fraud in a purchaser in not apprising the vendor of any advantage of which the latter is ignorant?

*A.* If the purchaser makes statements tending to mislead the vendor, the sale will not be enforced. He is not, however, bound to give the vendor information as to *latent* advantages of the estate, but he must not conceal the death of a person of which the vendor is ignorant and by which the value of the property is increased. Ibid., 5.

13. *Q.* When is a conveyance of property deemed fraudulent as against creditors or purchasers; and what is the effect of such a conveyance as respects the party making it?

*A.* All voluntary deeds made with the express intention of defrauding creditors are void against them. Insolvency of the debtor at the date of the deed, retaining possession of goods which are the subject of an immediate and absolute transfer, stating in the deed that it was made honestly, truly, and *bonâ fide*, have been considered evidence of fraud. 13 Eliz., c. 5. *Twyne's Case*, 1 Sm. L. C., 1. A conveyance is also void as against purchasers if made with the express intention of defrauding them, and even a voluntary conveyance is deemed fraudulent as against a subsequent purchaser with or without notice. Such conveyances are, however, good and may be enforced against the party making them. 27 Eliz., c. 4. Notes to *Twyne's Case*. 1 Sm. L. C., 23.

14. *Q.* What is the rule of Equity with respect to gift to persons in a confidential, fiduciary, or other relationship towards the donor?

*A.* The court will set such gifts aside if obtained by undue influence and owing to abused confidence. This is upon the principle of public policy and utility. In the leading case of *Huguenin* v. *Baseley* a voluntary settlement by a widow upon the defendant, a clergyman, was set aside. 2 L. C. Eq., 462.

15. *Q.* State some of the persons who are considered to fill the

confidential, fiduciary, or other relationship referred to in the last question.

*A.* They are :—Parent and child. Guardian and ward. Attorney and client. Counsel and client. Medical man and patient. Trustee and *cestui que trust.* Intended husband and wife. Principal and agent. See and read the Notes to *Huguenin* v. *Baseley.*

16. *Q.* How does the court look on a transaction between a father and son just of age, or just after he has come of age, on a consideration of love and affection?

*A.* If the transaction is one beneficial to the father, the court, even though there is no great evidence of undue influence, will look upon it with the most guarded jealousy and will set the transaction aside if any advantage has been taken of the son. 2 L. C., Eq., 489.

17. *Q.* Can persons placed in confidential positions become purchasers of property, the sale of which has been entrusted to them, or on which they have been consulted professionally? Instance persons who come within the scope of the rule.

*A.* As a general rule such persons cannot purchase the property unless it clearly appears that the connection between the parties has been dissolved, and unless all knowledge of the value of the property acquired by the party in the confidential position has been communicated to the owner of the property. Thus, in *Fox* v. *Mackreth,* 1 L. C. Eq., 92, a purchase by a trustee for sale was set aside. Other persons coming within the rule are :—Principal and agent, solicitor and client ; executors cannot purchase the deceased's estate, nor assignees in bankruptcy the bankrupt's property. Notes to *Fox* v. *Mackreth.*

18. *Q.* Explain and illustrate the general principles on which the Court of Chancery adjudicates on dealings and transactions between a solicitor and his client.

*A.* The court acts upon the rule that a solicitor cannot by act *inter vivos* take anything for his own benefit from his client, excepting his legal charges, unless the connection of solicitor and client be dissolved. Thus, in *Gresley* v. *Mousley,* 28 L. J. Ch., 620, a sale of real estate by a client to his solicitor at an undervalue, the client being in embarrassed circumstances and not having independent professional advice, was set aside, even after a lapse of twenty years. 2 L. C. Eq., 493.

19. *Q.* What right have remainder-men and reversioners to get the title deeds, being in the hands of the legal tenant for life, secured, and when will such right be enforced?

*A.* The tenant for life is entitled to the custody of the deeds, but if he threaten to destroy them or endanger their safety a remainder-man is entitled to have them secured by being brought into court. See *supra,* 175, No. 6.

20. *Q.* State what contracts and conditions in restraint of trade are void, and in what cases such contracts and conditions may be enforced.

*A.* Contracts or conditions in absolute restraint of trade are void as being against public policy. They will be enforced when the restraint is partial and founded upon consideration. They must be reasonable and the consideration, though it need not be adequate, must not be colorable. In the leading case of *Michel* v. *Reynolds*, 1 Sm. L. C., 340, a bond not to carry on the trade of a baker in Liquorpond-street, or the parish of St. Andrew's, Holborn, for five years, was held reasonable. This was a case at law, but Equity observes the same rules on the subject.

21. Q. Mention some cases in which Courts of Equity relieve against penalties.

A. The court will relieve where the penalty is inserted to obtain the payment of a sum of money, or the performance of some collateral act. Thus, the payment of the penalty to a bond will be relieved against. And now also at law, by virtue of 4 & 5 Anne, c. 16. Also where the penalty was to secure the enjoyment of a room in a coffee-house. *Sloman* v. *Walter*, 2 L. C. Eq., 907.

22. Q. What is waste by a lessee of a house and of a meadow; what is the effect on the lessee's title if he commits waste; and what is the effect of the reservation in the lease of a meadow of an additional rent of £20 per acre, if the grass is broken up and converted into tillage?

A. Such a tenant would commit waste by defacing the house or allowing it to go out of repair, or by ploughing up the meadow, or digging for mines. Such acts of waste would be a breach of the covenants in the lease, and the lease would be forfeited. The effect of the reservation would be that if the tenant was to break up the meadow, he would have to pay the additional rent of £20. It would not be treated as a penalty, but as liquidated damages. *Rolfe* v. *Peterson*, 2 Bro. C. C., 436; Notes to *Sloman* v. *Walter*, 2 L. C. Eq., 921.

23. Q. Does the court impose any, and what, terms upon a plaintiff seeking to set aside an usurious contract?

A. Upon the maxim that he who seeks equity must do equity, the court will not interfere, unless the party seeking relief pays that which is fairly due. The principle upon which the court acts in cases of fraud is not to punish by *mulcting* the defendant in damages, but to place the parties as nearly as possible in the same position as they were originally. Story, s. 301.

### (b) *Prevention of Fraud.*

1. Q. What is an injunction, and when is it to be applied for? how is the application to be supported, how is it put in force, and how dissolved?

A. An injunction is a writ issuing out of Chancery against a party to restrain proceedings in other courts, or the commission of unlawful or wrongful acts. It should be applied for promptly, and a bill must first be filed. The application should be supported by an affidavit of the facts in respect of which the writ is sought. When granted, the writ is enforced by motion that defendant stand committed. The order when obtained is handed to the messenger who obtains the Lord Chancellor's warrant and arrests the defendant. It is dissolved on motion by the defendant to dissolve, or at the hearing of the cause. Ayck. C. P., 260.

2. *Q.* State a few of the ordinary cases in which Courts of Equity grant injunctions.

*A.* They are:—To restrain the commission of waste; the infringement of patents, copyrights, and trade-marks; the breach of covenants; the sailing of ships; the commission of nuisances, such as blocking up ancient lights; to stay proceedings in other courts. *Earl of Oxford's Case*, 2 L. C. Eq., 304; Hayne's Outlines of Equity, Lect. IX.

3. *Q.* What are the different kinds of injunctions issued by a Court of Equity, and at what stages of a suit?

*A.* Injunctions are either, common, to restrain proceedings at law; or special, which are those issued in the other cases above mentioned. Both kinds may now be obtained at any stage of the suit. Ayck. C. P., 260.

4. *Q.* Is the filing of a bill, praying an injunction, necessary to the application for one? and is any notice of the application required?

*A.* A bill must in all cases be filed. Notice must be given, except in those cases where the grievance sought to be restrained is very pressing. Ibid, 263.

5. *Q.* When a party applies for an injunction, is the time when he first knew the circumstances, in regard to which the application is made, material? and give the reason.

*A.* Such time is very material. As, in granting the application, the court will consider whether the plaintiff has allowed any unnecessary time to elapse after knowledge of the circumstances. The right to relief will be forfeited by such delay, in accordance with the maxim, *vigilantibus non dormientibus equitas subvenit.*

6. *Q.* In what way is an injunction to be obtained, and in what case may it be obtained without notice?

*A.* An injunction is obtained on motion to one of the Vice-Chancellors, or the Master of the Rolls in court, after bill filed. No notice is necessary in cases of immediate urgency where the wrong complained of is being actually perpetrated, or appears to be imminent, unless instantly checked. In cases of less urgency notice must be served, and, after appearance to the bill, notice is in all cases necessary. Ayck, C. P., 263.

7. *Q.* What are the general principles which regulate the Court of Chancery in granting or refusing injunctions *ex parte?*

*A.* An injunction will only be granted *ex parte* when the court sees clearly that its interference will be of use, and where a case of extreme urgency is made out, as the staying of waste. Nor will it interfere where the plaintiff has been guilty of laches, or has acquiesced in the acts complained of. See the previous answer.

8. *Q.* The fifth volume of Macaulay's "History of England"

is published during the long vacation, after the courts have risen. A bookseller publishes a pirated edition, the owner of the copyright seeks your advice on his remedy. State the course which you would advise him to adopt, so far as the injury is remediable in equity; the proceeding, step by step, for obtaining such a remedy, and the time within which it can be obtained.

*A.* I should advise an immediate application to the vaction judge for an injunction to restrain the further publication of the edition. I should instruct counsel with all the facts to draw the bill. When settled, I should have it engrossed and filed together with the plaintiff's affidavit in support. Having obtained an appointment from the vacation judge, I should instruct counsel to attend him and make the motion. If granted, I should attend the Registrar with the brief and office copy, affidavit, certificate of the bill being filed, etc. He will draw up the order for the writ, upon which the writ itself may be issued and served. As soon as the order was made, I should have given the defendant notice of it. I should file a printed bill within fourteen days of filing the written one. If the vacation judge was in town I could obtain the order by the following day, but if he was away the time would be necessarily extended. Ayck, C. P., 264.

9. *Q.* Will a Court of Equity intefere to stay waste before the defendant's appearance?

*A.* If the defendant was pulling down the Mansion House, or doing any act which required the immediate intervention of the court, it would grant an injunction *ex parte* before appearance, *supra*, No. 7.

10. *Q.* In what respect does a tenancy for life " without impeachment of waste " differ from an estate for life, in the limitation of which those words are omitted?

*A.* The insertion of these words enable the tenant for life to commit all acts of waste with impunity, excepting those mentioned in the next answer.

11. *Q.* What is meant by equitable waste?

*A.* It is that waste which is punishable only in a Court of Equity. The common law courts consider a tenant freed from all liability, if the words "without impeachment of waste" are inserted in his limitation. Equity, however, under such circumstances, restrains him from exercising his legal power unconscientiously and to an unreasonable extent. Upon this principle it will not permit him to deface or pull down the family mansion. *Vane* v. *Lord Barnard*, 2 Vern., 738, where the defendant having taken displeasure against his son the plaintiff, collected suddenly two hundred workmen and cleared the family residence, Raby Castle, near Darlington, of all the lead, glass, doors, windows, &c., and was about to pull down the castle itself when he was restrained. The felling of timber, left standing for ornament or shelter, will also be restrained. *Garth* v. *Cotton*, 1 L. C. Eq., 559 and Notes. *Supra*, 145, Nos. 55, 56.

12. *Q.* Can a Court of Equity permit a tenant for life of an estate, who is impeachable for waste, to commit waste?

*A.* Yes, the court will occasionally order timber to be cut down if so near a house as to render it unhealthy, or when in a state of decay, or if it has arrived at maturity and will not improve by standing. This is on the ground of its being in the interest of the succession. The produce will be invested, and the interest paid to the tenant for life. The capital will be transferred to the first owner of the inheritance, or the first tenant for life, without impeachment of waste. 1 L. C. Eq., 623.

13. *Q.* Will a Court of Equity restrain a tenant for life without impeachment of waste from cutting down any, and what timber? and supposing such tenant for life to cut down such timber, and to sell the same, to whom will the money produced by such sale belong?

*A.* As to the first part of the question, see *supra*, No. 11. In addition to granting an injunction, the court will decree an account of the produce of the timber and direct it to be invested for the benefit of future owners of the estate having a limited interest. The fund will belong absolutely to the next owner in fee. Ibid.

14. *Q.* A client consults you on the means of putting an immediate stop to the felling of ornamental timber on his estate by his tenant under a color of right; state the proceedings, step by step, which should be taken by you for the purpose of obtaining an injunction *ex parte*, how soon it can be obtained, either whilst the court is sitting, or during the long vacation, and the course of proceeding after motion made and granted. State whether the defendant can be restrained by any, and what means, before the actual issue of the writ.

*A.* See *supra*, Nos. 1, 8, as to obtaining the injunction. The defendant may be restrained directly the order is pronounced by the judge, upon notice being given to him of the fact, and that the writ will be served as soon as it can be issued. Ayck., C. P., 267.

15. *Q.* If the defendant in the case supposed in the previous question is aware that an injunction is about to be applied for *ex parte*, and is advised that it would not be granted if the motion were opposed, what course should his solicitor adopt?

*A.* He should instruct counsel to show cause against the motion in the first instance. For this purpose, a brief should be prepared and a copy of the bill delivered to counsel.

16. *Q.* How does the owner of property acquire a right, as against an adjoining owner, to the enjoyment of light and air. Under what circumstances will the Court of Chancery interfere, by injunction, to restrain any interference with such right?

*A.* The right may be acquired either by grant, express or implied, or by prescription. The court will interfere where the right is clearly established, and the injury is of such a nature that no adequate compensation can be afforded by damages. Gale on Easements, 555.

17. *Q.* Has a party, by whom private letters have been written and sent to another person, any property absolute or qualified in

the letters so sent as regards the person receiving them? If so, under what circumstances, to what extent, and in what way, can he assert his title to this species of property in a Court of Equity?

*A.* A person writing a letter and sending it only parts with the property in it for the purposes for which it was sent. Therefore the party receiving it has no right to publish it without the permission of the author. The publication will, therefore, be restrained if carried further than is necessary to carry out the writer's wishes. An injunction is the proper remedy. *Pope* v. *Carl.* 2 Atkyns, 341. Where the defendant was restrained from publishing letters written by Pope, though the court would not prevent the publication of letters sent to Pope.

18. *Q.* A, in the course of a confidential employment by your client B, is entrusted by the latter with an important secret in connection with such employment, which he threatens to make public, is, or is not, this a case in which a Court of Equity has a jurisdiction to prevent the disclosure threatened? and if it have, state the remedy which you would advise B to adopt.

*A.* The court would have jurisdiction to restrain A. The proceeding would be by injunction, *supra.* Drewry, 229.

19. *Q.* What course would you advise a partner to take for his security, when his co-partner is likely to draw bills of exchange for his private use in the partnership name?

*A.* I should recommend him to apply for and obtain an injunction to restrain him from drawing the bills.

20. A lessee of a farm is under covenant not to plough up meadow land, or to remove hay or straw off the farm, the lessee takes steps which indicate the intention to plough up meadow, or to remove hay or straw; what remedy, if any, has the lessor in Equity?

*A.* He may obtain an injunction to restrain him from committing a breach of the covenant. See *supra.*

21. *Q.* Will the court interfere to protect the unauthorised use of trade-marks, and in what cases, and what must the plaintiff prove in order to succeed?

*A.* The court will interfere by way of injunction to protect the plaintiff from the injury arising from the use of his trade-mark by the defendant. The plaintiff must prove that he has the exclusive right to use the mark in connection with some manufacture or vendible commodity; also that the mark or symbol has been adopted or is used by the defendant, so as to prejudice the plaintiff's custom and injure him in his trade. Per Westbury C. in *The Leather Cloth Company* v. *The American Leather Company*, 33 L. J. C., 201.

22. *Q.* What relief will the court give in the cases referred to in the last question?

*A.* The court will grant an injunction restraining the unauthorised use of the trade-mark; but, in cases of doubt, it has occasionally directed an action to be brought first, the bill being retained. Since Mr. Rolt's Act (25 & 26 Vic., c. 42), it is presumed this course will be departed from.

23. *Q.* In what case does the Court of Chancery upon granting

an injunction sometimes direct an issue to be tried in a court of law ? and for what purpose is such issue generally directed ?

*A.* In cases of patents, copyrights, trade-marks, and other cases, the court before granting relief has frequently directed an issue to determine the legal title. This issue was for the purpose of informing the court as to the title of the plaintiff to relief. It is now made compulsory upon the court to determine this question itself, so that the former practice will be varied and the validity of the claim determined by the court itself with or without a jury. 25 & 26 Vic., c. 42, *Eaden* v. *Firth*, 1 Hem. & M., 573. The above act provides for the trial of questions of fact at the Assizes, or the sitting, in London or Middlesex, if more convenient.

24. *Q.* A patentee files his bill against one whom he charges with an infringement of his patent by the manufacture and sale of articles protected by the patent. What must he prove to support his case ? and to what relief will he be entitled if he succeed ?

*A.* He must prove the patent and the specification, by a certified copy under the seal of the Commissioners of Patents. 16 & 17 Vic., c. 115, s. 4. He must also show that the invention conforms with the specification, also that it is in reality a novelty. He must show that there has been an infringement by the defendant. Hayne's Outlines, 275, 2nd ed.

25. *Q.* What is the jurisdiction of a Court of Equity in patent cases ?

*A.* The jurisdiction of the court was originally founded in granting injunctions against the infringement of the patent, to which the plaintiff showed himself to be legally entitled. Now, however, as above mentioned, the court has also jurisdiction to try the validity of the plaintiff's right to the patent. 25 & 26 Vic., c. 42.

26. *Q.* Are other courts subject to restraint by the Court of Chancery; if so, under what circumstances ?

*A.* The court will restrain parties from proceeding in other courts where such proceedings are in contravention of some equitable right of the plaintiff, of which he cannot avail himself in the Court of Law. Thus, if a landlord enter into a contract with his tenant to sell him the property he occupies, and afterwards proceeds to bring ejectment (which he can do in respect of his legal title, the tenant having a mere equitable one, under the contract) the tenant may file a bill for specific performance and get an injunction to stay the ejectment. 2 L. C. Eq., 517.

27. *Q.* How is an injunction to stay proceedings at Law obtained ?

*A.* The proceedings are now analogous to those above mentioned with regard to other kinds of injunctions. They are granted either before or after the commencement of the action or to stay trial, or after verdict to stay judgment, and at any subsequent stage of the proceedings even to stay the money in the hands of the sheriff. Eden, 44.

28. *Q.* Will the court under any, and what, circumstances restrain a creditor from proceeding at law who is not a party to a suit ?

*A.* After a decree in an administration suit a creditor, though not a party, will be restrained by injunction; also a legatee suing for his legacy in the County Court. 2 L. C. Eq., 522, 523.

29. *Q.* What proceeding is to be taken to restrain such creditor from continuing his action?

*A.* A motion should be made to the court for an injunction in the usual way. Ayck. C. P., 530. In cases also within the jurisdiction of the County Court, application should be made to the County Court. 28 & 29 Vic., c. 99, s. 1, clause 8.

30. *Q.* Where an order for an injunction has been pronounced, what is the course to take to render it immediately effectual; and what is to be done if the defendant do not submit? State the steps therefore to be taken by the plaintiff. When and how can a defendant apply to dissolve an injunction?

*A. Supra*, Nos. 1 & 8.

31. *Q.* If a bill is filed to stay proceedings at law, and an injunction granted which is afterwards dissolved upon the defendant's answer, can a plaintiff amend his bill and again apply for an injunction?

*A.* The cause having been heard on replication filed, no amendment would be allowed. The rule as to amendments is that they shall not be allowed after the cause is at issue. Story on Pl., 886, 6th ed.

32. *Q.* May a plaintiff amend his bill without prejudice to his injunction?

*A.* The amendment will not prejudice the injunction, unless the record be changed as by the addition of a co-plaintiff. *Attorney General* v. *Marsh*, 13 Jur., 316; Morgan's Acts & Orders, 488.

33. *Q.* Is the jurisdiction of Courts of Equity in granting injunctions affected by "The Common Law Procedure Act, 1854," and what power in respect of injunctions is given by that act to any other, and what, courts?

*A.* The jurisdiction of Equity is not affected by the powers now conferred on Courts of Law with regard to injunctions. "The ancient jurisdiction of the court is never destroyed, because Courts of Law exercise jurisdiction which they did not exercise before." Per Lord Eldon in *Kemp* v. *Pryor*, 7 Ves., 273. Courts of Law have power to restrain after action brought, the repetition or continuance of any wrongful act, or breach of contract complained of. C. L. P. Act, 1854, s. 82. See further *supra*.

(c) *Accident and Mistake, with the doctrine of cy près or Approximation.*

1. *Q.* State some cases in which a Court of Equity will relieve against the defective execution of a deed or contract.

*A.* The court will relieve against the defective execution of powers as mentioned below; it will also supply the surrender of copyholds on the same grounds, namely, that of an intention being shown to execute the power in discharge of a natural or moral obligation.

1 L. C. Eq., 185. The court will also in certain cases mentioned below, 298, No. 3, enforce a contract specifically, though not reduced into writing.

2. *Q.* Will Equity relieve against acts performed under mistaken notions of law or of fact?

*A.* It is a general rule of Equity and also of the Common and Civil Law that mistake of fact is a ground of relief, but not mistake of law. Thus, if a man is ignorant of the death of a kinsman whose property is about to be dealt with, time shall not run against him; it is otherwise if he be aware of the death and his own relationship, but ignorant of his consequent rights. Hayne's Outlines, 132.

3. *Q.* What is the difference in equity and at law, as to the construction, and as to the performance of covenants?

*A.* With regard to the construction of covenants, the same rules prevail at law and in equity; but, in the performance they must, at law, be strictly and literally performed, but in equity a real and substantial performance according to the true intent and meaning of the parties, as far as circumstances will admit, is all that is required. *Eaton* v. *Lyon*, 3 Ves., 693.

4. *Q.* What is the general rule of equity in granting relief against breaches of covenants?

*A.* As a general rule the court will relieve against forfeiture, to carry out the intention of the parties where the court can replace the parties in their former position and give a fair recompense to the party against whom relief is sought. Upon this ground it looks upon the right of re-entry for non-payment of rent as a mere security for the rent and relieves against forfeiture upon the lessor being paid the rent due with interest and costs. 2 L. C. Eq., 909.

5. *Q.* Enumerate some of the principal cases in which equity will, and will not, relieve against the forfeiture of a lease by breach of covenant; and by what statute has the jurisdiction been enlarged?

*A.* Equity will relieve as just-mentioned in the event of forfeiture for non-payment of rent; also, generally, if by unavoidable accident, by fraud, by surprise, or ignorance, not wilful, parties may have been prevented from executing a covenant literally. No relief will be granted excepting, it is apprehended, under the peculiar circumstances just-mentioned; in cases where compensation cannot be made, as on the forfeiture for breach of covenant to repair. The jurisdiction has been extended to covenants to insure, by 22 & 23 Vic., c. 35, s. 4. (See *supra*, 196, No. 30). Notes to *Peachey* v. *Duke of Somerset*, 2 L. C. Eq., 908.

6. *Q.* A gives a bond to B, to secure the payment of a debt, the bond is lost, has B any, and what, means, to compel the payment of it?

*A.* He may bring an action for debt at law, and prove it by secondary evidence of the bond. Production of the original is not now absolutely necessary, *profert* and *oyer* being abolished by

15 & 16 Vic., c. 76, s. 55. Before this act it would have been necessary for B to have proceeded for the recovery of the debt in equity.

7. *Q.* On what general principle, and in favour of what persons does equity supply defects in the substance and execution of a deed or power?

*A.* The principle of interference is, that, whenever a man having power over an estate, whether ownership or not, in discharge of moral or natural obligations, shows an intention to execute such power, the court will operate upon the conscience of the heir, to make him perfect his intention. *Chapman* v. *Gilson*, 3 Bro. C. C., 229. The court will relieve in favour of purchasers, mortgagees, creditors, a wife, an intended husband, and a legitimate child of the person intending to exercise the power, and a charitable purpose. *Tollet* v. *Tollet*, 1 L. C. Eq., 184, and notes.

8. *Q.* Will equity relieve against the non-execution of a power?

*A.* As a general rule equity will not relieve against the non-execution. As where it arose from the sudden death of the donee or disability to sign from gout. But if the deed creating the power has been fraudulently detained by the person interested in its non-execution, equity will relieve. Also where the power is coupled with a trust, as where trustees are empowered to sell an estate and apply the produce in certain trusts. Ibid.

9. *Q.* Explain what is meant by the rule or doctrine administered by a court of equity, which is commonly termed *cy près*.

*A.* By the doctrine referred to is meant, that the court will, when the limits by law placed upon the limitation of property have been by will exceeded, carry out the testator's intention as nearly as the rules of law will permit. Thus, if a testator gives land to the unborn son of a living person for life, followed by a limitation after his decease to his sons in tail, an estate tail will be given to such unborn son in tail. This portion of the doctrine is adopted by the courts of common law and equity, but the latter apply it to charitable dispositions also, as mentioned in the next answer. Williams on Real Property, 248; L. C. Conv., 344.

10. *Q.* Where there is a bequest for charitable purposes, but the mode of application is impracticable, will the court carry the bequest into effect in any and what manner?

*A.* In such a case if a charitable intention is expressed the court will seize hold of such intention and execute it in favour of some other charity as nearly as possible in accordance with the testator's views. Thus, where there was a bequest to maintain a pest-house for patients from certain London parishes suffering under the Oriental plague, such disease not having appeared after the foundation of the charity, the money was applied in maintaining a hospital for persons who might be afflicted with the plague, if that event should arise; in the meantime for other sick persons. *Attorney-General* v. *Craven*, 21 Beav., 392. See also Notes to *Corbyn* v. *French*, L. C. Conv., 456.

### (d) Account.

1. *Q.* Is there any, and what, advantage in the proceedings of a court of equity over those of a court of common law in questions of account? and state some of the principal cases of account in which recourse is ordinarily had to a court of equity.

*A.* The chief advantage of equity with regard to account is its mode of procedure, which enables it to investigate in chambers intricate matters of account, and by its decree settle conflicting rights between various interests. The jurisdiction originated in the power to obtain discovery in equity, after which being obtained relief in the form of an account was granted. This cause is, however, now almost entirely removed, yet the court retains its jurisdiction. The principal cases where an account will be decreed are —in favour of a principal against his agent, though not in favour of the agent against the principal; between partners, and where there are mutual accounts; also where there are circumstances of special complication. Haynes' Outlines, 243.

2. *Q.* In what cases will a court of equity decree a dissolution of partnership? and what proceedings are necessary to be taken in order to secure the assets of the partnership?

*A.* A dissolution will be decreed when some circumstance renders the continuance of the partnership, or the attainment of the end which was in view morally impossible. Such would be the hopeless state of the business. The confirmed lunacy of one of the partners. Misconduct on the part of one or more of the members of the firm, and the destruction of mutual confidence. A bill should be filed praying for a dissolution, and an injunction against the defendant from interfering in the partnership affairs; also that a receiver may be appointed to get in the assets and wind up the concern. Lind. on Part., 180, 849.

3. *Q.* If a partner become a lunatic, does the lunacy occasion a dissolution of the partnership, or entitle the other partner to any, and what, relief from the contract of partnership?

*A.* The lunacy itself does not cause a dissolution, but the confirmed lunacy of an active partner is sufficient ground for a decree for a dissolution. *Jones* v. *Noy*, 2 M. & K., 125.

4. *Q.* In what form do accounting parties bring their accounts into the chief clerk's chambers, and is the oath of the accounting party sufficient evidence of the payments?

*A.* The accounts are to be written on foolscap paper book ways, Dr. and Cr. fashion. The items on each side are to be numbered consecutively, and the account is to be referred to by the affidavit verifying it, as an exhibit. If a party is dissatisfied with the account he may examine the accounting party *vivâ voce* in chambers. Independently of this the account must be vouched, by production of the receipts for all payments of forty shillings or upwards. Ayck. C. P., 482.

5. *Q.* If an account be settled between parties, and signed,

will a court of equity open the account generally or partially, and, if so, upon what principle?

A. An account stated will be opened if there be fraud, or any mistake which affects the whole account. If no fraud is proved an account will not be opened *in toto* after a lapse of considerable time, but the court will give leave to surcharge and falsify. This means that the account will only be opened as to particular items. The principle of the above is that the court considers fraud as such a grave offence, that no time should be allowed to protect the parties who have been guilty of it. Lind on Part., 825.

### (e) *Delivery of Specific Chattels.*

1. Q. In what cases can a bill be filed for the delivery up of specific chattels to the owner?

A. The court will decree the specific delivery up of heirlooms or chattels of peculiar value to the owner, upon the principle that the specific thing is the object, and that damages at law will not afford adequate compensation. Thus, in *Pusey* v. *Pusey*, 1 Vern., 273, land being held by the tenure of a horn, the heir was held entitled to recover it. So an altar-piece dedicated to Hercules was ordered to be delivered up. *Duke of Somerset* v. *Cookson*, L. C. Eq., 655.

2. Q. A being in possession of deeds belonging to B, will a court of equity compel A to deliver them, and what is the proper bill to be filed?

A. A bill may be filed founded on the same principle as mentioned in the previous answer, and a decree may be obtained for the specific delivery up of the deeds. Ibid., 658.

### (f) *Specific Performance of Contracts.*

1. Q. What is the original difference between the relief given at law and in equity upon a contract? and may a person take advantage of both?

A. The distinction between the remedies is, that at law damages only could be obtained for the breach of a contract, whereas, equity enforced the contract specifically, in cases where it appeared that damages at law did not give sufficient compensation. Equity also restrained the breach of certain contracts by injunction, the court considering that damages did not put the plaintiff in as beneficial a position as if the agreement were specifically performed. Now, however, courts of law can compel specific performance of contracts of a public or *quasi* public nature, and may also restrain by injunction the repetition or continuance of a breach of contract. 17 & 18 Vic., c. 125, ss. 68—79. At law, also, the specific delivery of goods sold may now be compelled, in an action for the breach of a contract, to deliver goods. 19 & 20 Vic., c. 97, s. 2. A party is not entitled to proceed both at law and in equity. *Prothero* v. *Phelps*, 25 L. J. Ch., 105.

2. *Q.* Under what circumstances will the specific performance of a contract or agreement be decreed?

*A.* 1. The agreement must be between parties competent to contract. 2. The subject matter must be defined and certain, and the whole contract must be capable of being executed on the terms specifically agreed upon. 3. It must be in its nature and circumstances unobjectionable, and the plaintiff must come with clean hands. 4. The agreement must be in writing (except in cases below). 5. Damages at law must be inadequate. 6. There must be a valuable consideration. 7. The enforcement in specie must be practicable, useful, and lawful.

3. *Q.* Are there any circumstances under which an agreement for a lease of twenty-one years, not made in writing, would be enforced by a court of equity? If so, state those circumstances, and on what grounds such an equity would prevail. In what cases will a court of equity decree a specific performance of a contract not reduced into writing?

*A.* Such a contract will be enforced if under a decree of the court, or where there has been part performance, or where the contract is set out in the bill admitted in the answer, and the Statute of Frauds not insisted on, or where it has been prevented being put into writing by the fraud of one of the parties. *Lyster* v. *Foxcroft*, 1 L. C. Eq., 625; Sugden's Vendors, 148.

4. *Q.* What acts are considered in the light of part performance, so as to take a case out of the Statute of Frauds, to enable a party to call for specific performance of an agreement, although there may be no memorandum in writing?

*A.* The acts must be such as could be done with no other design than to complete the contract. Delivery of possession, and the purchaser expending money in buildings or improvements, according to agreement, have been held sufficient. *Lyster* v. *Foxcroft, ubi sup.* Collateral acts, such as delivery of the abstract, valuing the stock, etc., are insufficient. Sugden's Vendors, 151.

5. *Q.* A person engages to perform an agreement under a penalty. Can he relieve himself by offering the penalty, or will a court of equity compel its performance?

*A.* If the agreement is one which the court would under ordinary circumstances enforce specifically, the party cannot relieve himself by paying the penalty. Sugden's Vendors, 220.

6. *Q.* If an estate be sold for a certain sum of money, and an annuity for the life of the vendor, and the vendor die before receipt of any of the annuity, will the court give his representatives any relief?

*A.* Upon the principle, that that which is agreed to be done is done, specific performance will be decreed against the vendor's representatives, even though he die before conveyance. Ibid., 294.

7. *Q.* After a contract for sale, who must bear any loss that may happen to the estate before the completion of the sale, and who will be entitled to any benefit that may accrue to the estate during the same time?

*A.* The purchaser must bear any loss, and is entitled to any benefit that may accrue. This is in accordance with the civil law; *nam et commodum ejus esse debet cujus periculum est.* Ibid., 294.

8. *Q.* An agreement has been entered into for the sale of a house, and before the sale is completed, or possession delivered to the purchaser, the house, which is not insured, is burned down; upon whom does the loss fall, and upon what principle is the law in this respect founded?

*A.* See previous answers, Nos. 6, 7.

9. *Q.* A writes a letter to B in these terms:—"I am willing to sell you my freehold house in Piccadilly for £5,000." B replies by letter to A in these terms:—"I accept the offer contained in your letter." Do these letters, taken by themselves, constitute an agreement, the specific performance of which can be enforced in equity by either party?

*A.* This is an agreement which will be enforced in equity, provided the acceptance was sent in a reasonable time, as damages would not be a sufficient compensation, and the letters form a complete contract. Of course there must be none of the objections mentioned, *supra,* No. 2.

10. *Q.* A writes to B, offering him £5,000 for the purchase of his (B's) freehold house in Berkeley Square. B writes to A, in answer, accepting the offer, and adding that he will instruct his solicitor to prepare an agreement. A and B differ afterwards upon the details provided for by the intended agreement, and none is signed. Can specific performance be enforced at the suit of A or B, or both?

*A.* In this case it is doubtful if the contract could be enforced against B or A, as it has been held that the sending the agreement to a solicitor, to reduce into form, is evidence that the parties do not intend to bind themselves until it is reduced into form. *Ridgway* v. *Wharton,* 27 L. J. Ch., 46. Before this case, which was decided in the House of Lords, it was the general opinion that, under such circumstances, it is merely intended to reduce the agreement into technical language. *Fowle* v. *Freeman,* 9 Ves., 351; Sugden's Vendors, 141.

11. *Q.* When will letters operate as a binding agreement for the sale and purchase of an estate?

*A.* Letters will constitute a binding agreement, if, taken together, they constitute a complete agreement between the parties. So, also, though not containing the whole terms, if they refer to a writing which does, though such writing be not signed. The contract must, of course, be free from objection on other grounds. Sugden's Vendors, 136, 141.

12. *Q.* A contracts with B for the sale of an estate, and C contracts with D for the sale of Government stock; B and D are desirous to enforce the completion of the contract made with each. State the remedy which is open to each.

*A.* B may file a bill for specific performance, or sue at law for damages. D has not the former remedy, but can only recover damages at law, as the Court of Equity considers such damages an adequate compensation. *Cuddee* v. *Rutter*, 1 L. C. Eq., 640.

13. *Q.* On the offer of the late East Indian loan, A tendered, in writing, to take £100,000, at 102 per cent., and the company, in writing, accepted the tender, but A refused to complete the bargain. Will a court of equity enforce the fulfilment of the contract? State the reason for your answer.

*A.* The agreement will not be enforced. See previous answer.

14. *Q.* What is a meritorious consideration, and will it support a contract in equity?

*A.* A meritorious consideration is one founded on natural love and affection, as a provision for a wife or children after marriage. In *Ellis* v. *Nimmo*, 1 L. & G. t. Sugd., Sir E. Sugden decided that a contract founded on such a consideration could be enforced, but this case is no longer law. *Jefferys* v. *Jefferys*, Cr. & Ph., 138; 1 L. C. Eq., 230.

15. *Q.* In what cases will courts of equity interfere to carry into effect the contracts of infants, married women, or lunatics?

*A.* A contract by an infant cannot be enforced in equity, either by (for the remedy is not mutual) or against him. The contracts of a married woman can only be enforced by and against her when they relate to her separate estate, which she is not prevented from alienating. Contracts by a lunatic cannot be enforced specifically, unless, indeed, he becomes lunatic subsequently to the contract, or if apparently sane at the time, he was subsequently found to be insane, the other contracting party being ignorant of such insanity. Sugden's Vendors, 206—209.

16. *Q.* In the case of a contract for the sale and purchase of a freehold estate, where the vendor dies before conveyance, who is entitled to the purchase-money, the heir or devisee, or the personal representative? and if the purchaser die before conveyance, to whom does the estate go, and by whom is the purchase-money to be paid?

*A.* In consequence of the equitable doctrine of constructive conversion, the land, from the time a binding contract is entered into, is looked upon as money in the vendor's hands. Therefore, it will go to his personal representatives, and the heir or devisee will be bound to convey the estate to the purchaser. So, on the other hand, the doctrine operates to give the estate to the heir or devisee of the purchaser, who is entitled to call upon the personal representatives to pay the money. Ibid., 187.

17. *Q.* State a case in which money is treated in equity as real estate, and a case in which land is regarded as personal estate.

*A.* See previous answer. And see *infra* "Trusts," No. .

18. *Q.* What is the meaning of the expression "a conversion out and out?"

*A.* The expression referred to signifies, that, owing to some express direction by the owner of property, that property is to be considered as converted, to all intents and purposes, into some other kind of property. Thus, land directed to be sold by will for purposes which have not failed, is, even before any sale has actually taken place, looked upon as money. It will be treated as such in every respect. Haynes' Outlines, 373, 2nd ed.

19. *Q.* He who seeks equity, must do equity—and equity considers as done that which ought to be done. Explain the meaning of these maxims, and particularly a consequence of the latter one, as regards conversion of realty into personalty, and *vice versâ*, when directed.

*A.* The first maxim may be explained by a reference to the husband's taking proceedings in equity to recover his wife's property. In such a case the court, acting upon the maxim, will compel him to do equity by settling upon his wife a portion of the property sought to be recovered. *Murray* v. *Lord Elibank*, 1 L. C. Eq., 349. The latter maxim signifies that when a person is under an obligation to do a thing, that thing must be considered, to all intents and purposes, as performed. Thus, if land is by will directed to be sold, and the produce divided equally between A, B, and C, they will take their shares as personalty. Consequently, if A dies after the testator, his personal representatives will take his share, regardless of the actual state of the property. Also, if a similar bequest was made of money to be invested in land, the heir of A would take his share. *Fletcher* v. *Ashburner*, 1 L. C. Eq., 659; *Ackroyd* v. *Smithson*, ibid, 690.

20. *Q.* If land is held in trust for sale and conversion into money, and distribution of the proceeds amongst A, B, and C, can they, or any one of them, elect to take the land, or their shares of it, as realty?

*A.* If they all concur, they may elect to effect a reconversion; but one cannot elect to take his share as land, as such a proceeding would probably affect the sale of the whole. *Holloway* v. *Radcliffe*, 23 Beav., 163. It should be borne in mind that the same rule would not apply if the direction was to convert money into land. *Seeley* v. *Jago*, 1 P. Wms., 389.

21. *Q.* An agreement for the sale of a reversion provides that the purchaser shall take the vendor's title as it stands—that the purchase shall be completed on a fixed day, and that time shall be the essence of the contract. What is the effect of this last provision?

*A.* The effect of this provision is to enable the vendor to rescind the contract, if the purchase is not completed at the time fixed, and specific performance cannot be enforced. But in the absence of such a provision, the property being reversionary, the court considers it of the essence of justice that the contract be performed without delay. The utmost diligence must be shown by both parties. Sugden's Vendors, 260.

22. *Q.* Will a Court of Equity in any, and what, cases compel a purchaser to accept an equitable title without a conveyance of the legal estate?

*A.* A purchaser of an estate under a decree of the court, where the legal estate is outstanding and cannot be got in, will be compelled to accept an equitable title; as if the legal estate is vested in an infant. But this exception to the general rule is only allowed where there are no claims upon, or interests in such legal estate. Now, however, the court has power to vest the legal estate in the purchaser. 13 & 14 Vic., c. 60. Under certain circumstances, also, where the legal estate is outstanding and a re-conveyance would from lapse of time be presumed at law, an equitable title has, though the sale did not take place under a decree, been forced on a purchaser. Sugden's Vendors, 387, 399.

23. *Q.* A makes a voluntary settlement of his estate, and then enters into an agreement, for valuable consideration, to sell the estate; will a Court of Equity compel a specific performance of the agreement?

*A.* Specific performance will be enforced at the suit of the purchaser, even if he have notice of the settlement; but the vendor A cannot enforce it against the purchaser. Ibid, 720.

24. *Q.* When will the court not enforce a contract for specific performance?

*A.* Performance will not be enforced when the contract was entered into under a mistake of facts, surprise or misrepresentation; where the vendor has no title, or merely an equitable one (excepting as above mentioned); where the parties are under disability; where the agreement is in contravention of public policy; where the consideration is voluntary; and, generally, where any of the requisites before mentioned (No. 2), are wanting. Sugden's Vendors, 213, *et seq.*

25. *Q.* Will or will not a Court of Equity decree a specific performance of an agreement for reference to arbitration? and give the reason for your answer.

*A.* Such an agreement will not be enforced in equity unless the parties have already agreed upon the questions to be referred, upon the power to be given to the arbitrators and upon the arbitrators themselves. The reason is, that if either of the parties objected to the person nominated by the other it would be unjust to compel him to submit to the decision of the person so objected to as a judge chosen by himself. Mitf. Pl., 308; Russell, 65.

26. *Q.* In what cases will the court decree a specific performance of the sale or purchase of an estate when the price is agreed to be fixed by the arbitration of third persons?

*A.* Specific performance of such an agreement will only be enforced where the price has been actually fixed by such third persons. If, however, the agreement was to sell at a fair valuation, the court will execute it, though no value is fixed; that is, it will itself ascertain the fair value. Sugden's Vendors, 287.

27. *Q.* What covenants would be inserted by a Court of Equity in a lease of a dwelling-house in pursuance of a contract for a lease subject to " usual covenants?"

*A.* The court would insert such covenants as are necessary for the enjoyment of the property by the lessee, thus it would make the lessor covenant for quiet enjoyment. The covenants by the lessee would depend, to a certain extent, on the custom of the country and the circumstances of the case. Thus he would have to covenant to pay rent and to repair and to permit the lessor to enter and view the premises, also to give up the premises at the end of the term. But covenants not to assign or underlet; or not to carry on a particular trade; or, perhaps, a covenant to insure; or, probably, a covenant to pay land tax or sewers' rate, are not "usual." 2 Platt on L., 260.

28. *Q.* Will a Court of Equity decree the specific performance of a covenant to invest money in lands, and to settle them in a particular manner?

*A.* Such a covenant, if for valuable consideration, will be enforced in equity at the suit of persons within the consideration of the settlement. Thus, if A on his marriage was to covenant to invest £5,000 in land and settle it on himself for life, remainder to his wife for life, remainder to his first and other sons, remainder to himself and his heirs, and then his wife died, after which he died, leaving a son, such son could insist on the money being laid out in land. But a daughter would have no such right. So if A left no children, his nephew, as his heir, could not claim the land against A's personal representatives, as the money would be "at home" in A's pocket, and a reconversion would take place. It would be otherwise if A's wife survived him, as she would be entitled to call for a conversion in respect of her life interest in the land. *Lechmere* v. *Earl of Carlisle,* 3 P. Wms., 211. *Chichester* v. *Bickerstaff,* 2 Vern., 295, 1 L. C. Eq., 669. It should be remembered that such a covenant will be considered to be performed wholly or *pro tanto* by the purchase of lands subsequently to the covenant, which he has not settled. *Lechmere* v. *Lechmere,* Ca-temp. Talbot, 8. *Wilcocks* v. *Wilcocks, Blandy* v. *Widmore,* 2 L. C. Eq., 345.

29. *Q.* A being an attorney agrees to sell his business to B. Is or is not this such an agreement as a Court of Equity will enforce? and give the reason for your answer.

*A.* As a general rule the court would not enforce such an agreement, owing to the uncertainty of the subject matter and the incapacity of the court to give directions as to what is to be done to transfer it. But if the sale is of the business connected with the business premises, and of liberty to continue the name of the seller, and he agrees to give his recommendation to the purchaser, it will be specifically executed. Fry., 17.

30. *Q.* If A, supposing he has the right, enter into a written agreement for sale of an estate to B, which estate belongs to C, will B, in a bill for specific performance filed against A and C, be entitled to a decree?

*A.* B, in this case, has no remedy in equity, there being no privity between himself and C, neither could the contract be enforced by A and C against B, even if C were to offer to make a good title, for there is no mutuality of remedy. Sugden's Vendors, 217.

31. *Q.* If a bill be filed for a specific performance of an agreement, and the only question in dispute relates to the title, is it

necessary to set down the cause to be heard, or can any, and what, shorter course be adopted?

*A.* Under the circumstances stated in the question, either party, certainly the plaintiff, may on interlocutory motion obtain a reference to one of the counsel of the court as to the title. If, however, there are other grounds of defence, such an application will be refused. As, where the defence was that no good title was made; secondly, that if it had, it was not made in due time. *Reed* v. *The Don Pedro Mining Company,* 32 L. J. C., 773. Sugden's Vendors, 351.

32. *Q.* If the only question in a suit is the title to land, can the court dispose of it by any, and what, interlocutory proceeding before answer?

*A.* See the preceding answer.

33. *Q.* State the proceedings that the plaintiff's solicitor must in such case take to prosecute his client's case to a final result?

*A.* He must obtain the order on motion, and leave a copy of it and the abstract of title together with written objections to the title at Judges Chambers. It is then referred to one of the conveyancing counsel of the court, and the certificate is made upon his report. If the chief clerk's certificate is objected to, it should be appealed against. If the title is approved, an order may be obtained on motion for the purchaser to pay his purchase money. If he does not comply with this order, he may be proceeded against for contempt. Ayck., C. Pr., 236.

34. *Q.* Your client buys an estate; on the investigation of the title it appears that the vendor cannot make a good title to a small field detached from the rest of the property, and not of any material consequence to your client, who, however, wishes to be off his bargain; will a Court of Equity compel him to fulfil his contract, and upon what terms?

*A.* The contract may be enforced against him as to the portion to which a title is made out, a proportionate reduction of the price being made, the amount of which must be ascertained in Chambers. If the portion to which a title was not made was large or of material consequence to my client, I could resist the bill with success. Sugden's Vendors, 315.

35. *Q.* A purchaser of an estate under a sale by the Court of Chancery dies before the certificate becomes absolute, without having signed an agreement. What effect has such death upon the sale? and is, or is not, a sale by the court within the Statute of Frauds?

*A.* If the purchaser dies before the certificate is absolute, the contract will be considered at an end; but if the death is after its confirmation, it will be enforced against his representatives, although he signed no contract. This is because sales by the court are not within 29 Car. II., c. 3, s. 4. Sugden's Vendors, 109.

36. *Q.* In a suit for specific performance of an agreement, is the plaintiff bound by the title, as shown by him at the time of filing his bill?

*A.* If the vendor shows a good title at the date of the certificate this will suffice ; and even after the certificate, if he can satisfy the court that he can remove the objection, a decree will be made in his favour. Ayck., C. Pr., 237.

37.  Q. What lien has a vendor on the estate after conveyance for unpaid purchase-money; and how is such lien affected if the vendor take a separate security for such unpaid purchase-money ?

A. If the vendor gives the purchaser possession of the estate without being paid the purchase-money, the vendor has a lien on the land for the money. This lien can be enforced against all persons deriving title from the purchaser, with the exception of a *bond fide* purchaser, for value without notice having the legal estate. (As to how the right may be lost, see next answer). *Mackreth* v. *Symmons*, 1 L. C. Eq., 235. Sugden's Vendors, 671.

38.  Q. When will a vendor lose his lien on the estate for his unpaid purchase-money ? If a vendor die before payment of the purchase-money, to whom is it payable ?

A. The lien will be lost if the vendor take an independent security for the purchase-money ; as, where he accepted some stock for the money, or accepted a mortgage on another estate, or on part of the estate sold. A bond or note alone will not affect the lien. In the case put, the vendor's personal representatives are entitled to the money. Sugden's Vendors, 675.

39.  Q. How far is the maxim "*caveat emptor*" carried by the courts in suits for specific performance ; does it warrant misrepresentation or artifice in a vendor to procure a contract ? State the principle upon which the courts proceed.

A. The maxim, "Let the purchaser beware," is only applied in those cases, where the defects in the estate, set up as a defence, are apparent to ordinary observation. As, if there is a footpath over the property depreciating its value, it is no defence to say that the purchaser was not aware of it. Every prudent purchaser should go to see the property, and if this had been done the footpath would have been observed. If, however, the vendor was to make a positive representation on the subject matter of the sale, which is false, the maxim will not apply; as, if he stated in his conditions that there was no footpath, and the purchaser did not know of it. So, also, if the defect could not possibly be discovered by the purchaser, and the vendor, being aware of it, does not inform him on the subject, the maxim will not apply. As, where a hole in a wall is papered over to keep the defect from the purchaser's knowledge. And the maxim, it is considered, would be equally inapplicable in such a case, even if the house was sold " with all faults." Sugden's Vendors, 328—335.

40.  Q. In case of a voluntary settlement, does a Court of Equity require that a perfect trust shall have been created before it will enforce the settlement?

A. It is not absolutely necessary that a trust should be created at all. A complete assignment to the volunteer is effectual, though it is highly expedient to declare a trust in his favour. This is because the court will not assist a volunteer to perfect an assignment in his favour which is incomplete. Thus in *Antrobus* v. *Smith*, 12 Ves., 39, an endorsement on one of the receipts for one of the subscriptions in the Forth and Clyde Navigation, purporting to assign the owner's interest to Anna Crawford, could not be enforced because a legal assignment was attempted, which was incomplete. A trust, therefore, should always be created, and such trust must be perfect and clearly intended to be compulsory. A declaration of trust by the owner, or an assignment of the property to trustees upon trust, will suffice. *Ellison* v. *Ellison*, 1 L. C. Eq., 199.

41. *Q.* Can an alien enforce in a Court of Equity a trust in his favour relating to real estates or chattels real in England, or to personal estate?

*A.* An alien cannot enforce a trust of land bought for him by a natural born subject, nor of chattels real, except, perhaps, a lease for twenty-one years for the purpose of his trade or residence. The Crown, it seems, can claim the land. *Barrow* v. *Wadkin*, 27 L. J. C., 129. But if lands are directed to be sold and the produce given to an alien, he may enforce the conversion and the Crown has no claim. *Du Hourmelin* v. *Sheldon*, 1 Beav., 79; 8 L. J. Ch., 133. There is no objection to trusts of personalty in his favour, which he can enforce.

42. *Q.* What proofs are required by Courts of Equity from a party who seeks the specific performance of a contract which is disputed?

*A.* The plaintiff will be required to prove a contract in writing, excepting in those cases above mentioned (No. 3), where writing will be dispensed with. He must also show that he has done every thing on his part to be performed, and that the defendant has refused to perform the contract. If the plaintiff is vendor, he must show a good marketable title. Sugden's Vendors, 218.

43. *Q.* What does the court usually require to establish the validity of a purchase from an expectant heir?

*A.* It must be shown either that an adequate consideration was given and that no advantage was taken of the position of the expectant, or that the intended sale was made known to and approved by the person whose estate was to be inherited, and that such person was in a position to relieve him. It will also be set aside if fraud or imposition is proved. Sugden's Vendors, 275; St., ss. 334, 340.

44. *Q.* What is the rule of Courts of Equity with regard to decreeing specific performance where inadequacy of consideration is shown?

*A.* The rule is, that the court will not refuse its aid to a purchaser owing to inadequacy of price, unless indeed the inequality of bargain is so startling that it would be impossible to state it to a man of common sense without his exclaiming as to its inequality. If the property purchased be reversionary, the objection as to inadequacy will derive greater weight. Sugden's Vendors, 275.

(III.) *As it is Exclusive.*
(a) *Trusts and the Administration of Assets.*

1. *Q.* Define a trust; and in what respect does the legal differ from the equitable interest in the subject-matter of a trust?

*A.* A trust is a confidence reposed either expressly or impliedly in a person (called the trustee) for the benefit of another (called the cestui que trust). The legal interest is vested in the trustee, and the beneficial ownership in the cestui que trust. The latter has his remedy in Equity only, but the trustee may proceed for injuries to the trust property at law. He is also protected and assisted in the performance of his trust in Equity. Another important distinction is that a trust estate in land does not escheat on the attainder of the cestui que trust for felony. *Burgess* v. *Wheate,* 1 Wm. Black, 133.

2. *Q.* What are the different kinds of trusts recognised in our courts of equity?

*A.* Trusts are either express or by operation of law. The former class include trusts executed or complete, and trusts executory or incomplete. Those by operation of law include constructive, resulting, and implied trusts. Wharton's Lexicon, 915.

3. *Q.* Define trusts executed and trusts executory, and state if there is any, and what, difference in their construction?

*A.* A trust is executed when no act remains to be done to perfect it, as if stock is assigned to A in trust for B. But if the stock was assigned to A upon trusts, to be thereafter declared as for such person as the owner shall appoint, the trust would obviously be incomplete and executory. When an appointment was made, the trust would be executed. The construction put upon executed trusts is strictly in accordance with that put upon limitations of legal estates. But executory trusts are moulded more according to the intention of those who create them. *Lord Glenorchy* v. *Bosville,* 1 L. C. Eq. 1.

4. *Q.* What is an implied trust, a resulting trust, and a constructive trust?

*A.* An implied trust is one which though not expressed is implied from circumstances, as where a purchase of property is made in the name of a stranger (see *infra,* No. 5). A resulting trust is also implied from the acts of the parties, as where the owner of land conveys it to another *upon trust,* but does not declare any trusts, there is a resulting trust for the grantor. A constructive trust is one not arising from the presumable intention of the parties, but from construction of the Court of Equity. A familiar instance is the lien which the court gives to a vendor for his unpaid purchase money. Here the purchaser is by construction of Equity considered a trustee for the vendor to the extent of the money unpaid. *Harding* v. *Glyn,* 2 L. C. Eq., 789; *Mackreth* v. *Symmons,* 1 L. C. Eq., 235.

5. *Q.* A purchases and pays for a freehold estate, which is conveyed by the vendor to B, a stranger. C purchases and pays for government stock, which is transferred to the name of D, a stranger. Is there a resulting trust in both or either of these cases in favor of A or C, upon simple proof of payment of the purchase money by him?

*A.* There will be an implied resulting trust of the freehold estate for A by B, and of the stock in favour of C by D, B and D being strangers to A and C. Parol evidence may be given to prove the payment of the purchase money both by A and C, trusts of land by implication of law (which they both are) being specially excepted from the operation of the Statute of Frauds. Moreover, trusts of personalty are not within the Act. 29 Car. II., c. 3, ss. 7, 8. Sugden's Vendors, 701.

6. *Q.* A purchases a freehold estate, and by his direction it is conveyed unto and to the use of himself, his wife and son, and their heirs. A died intestate. Who is entitled to the estate?

*A.* At law the wife and son are joint tenants in fee of the estate. They will also be considered joint tenants in fee in Equity, there being no resulting trust in this case to A. The purchase will be presumed to be an advancement and provision for the wife and child. A resulting trust may, however, be raised as to the child's share by showing that he was already sufficiently provided for, and as to the whole by parol declaration of A that he did not intend an advancement. The declaration must be contemporaneous with the purchase, unless upon the oath of the father. *Devoy* v. *Devoy*, 26 L. J. C., 290. The objection which has been urged against admitting parol evidence in such a case, is that it is attempted to raise a trust of land without writing. This objection is met by saying that as the relationship of the wife and child (but for which a resulting trust by operation of law would arise) is proved by parol evidence, it is only fair to explain this away by the same means. The facts above stated are very similar to those in *Dyer* v. *Dyer*, 1 L. C. Eq., 165.

7. *Q.* When is a purchaser of land, sold by trustees for sale under a will not containing an express power to the trustees to give receipts for the purchase money, not bound to see to the application of the purchase money?

*A.* The purchaser will not be bound to see the purchase money applied in any case, unless a contrary intention is declared in the will. 22 & 23 Vic., c. 35, s. 23 ; 23 & 24 Vic., c. 145, s. 29. Before this Act the purchaser was generally bound to see to the application of the trust money, unless his doing so would have involved him in a trust of long continuance, or it was expressly declared he should not be liable to do so. *Elliott* v. *Merryman*, 1 L. C. Eq., 45. See *supra*, 255, Nos. 7, 8.

8. *Q.* An estate being conveyed to trustees to sell and pay debts, will the court compel the performance of the trust at the suit of a creditor?

*A.* Under the above circumstances it is considered that the creditors are not constituted cestuis que trust, a direction merely being given to the trustee to hold the property for the benefit of the owner. He may, therefore, revoke the trusts, and they cannot be enforced against him, unless the trust has been communicated to the creditors or creditor, in which case it is irrevocable and may be enforced at the suit of the creditors. 1 L. C. Eq., 209.

9. *Q.* If real estate be devised upon trust for sale for a particular purpose, and that purpose either wholly fail or does not exhaust the proceeds of the sale, will the whole or the part that remains unapplied (whether the estate has been actually sold, or not), result to the heir-at-law, or go to the next of kin of the testator?

*A.* If the whole purposes of conversion fail before the will operates there will be no conversion, and the estate will result to heir-at-law. As if A devises an estate to be sold, and the produce divided equally between C and D, who both predecease him. But should one of them (D) survive him, conversion will take place as to his share; but B's share will result to the heir-at-law of A. And as a sale is necessary for the purpose of giving B his moiety as money, the remainder will result to the heir of A, not as realty, but as personalty. Consequently, if A's heir is dead, it will go to his personal representatives, according to the Statutes of Distribution. *Smith* v. *Claxton*, 4 Maddock, 484; *Ackroyd* v. *Smithson*, 1 L. C. Eq., 690; Hayne's Outlines, 376.

10. *Q.* If money is directed by a testator to be laid out in land for particular purposes, and those purposes should fail of taking effect, does it belong to the heir or to the next of kin?

*A.* This is the reverse of the case put in the preceding question, but it has been decided that the same principle applies to the case of money directed to be laid out in land, as to land directed to be converted into money. Therefore, there will be a resulting trust in favour of the next of kin to the extent of the objects of conversion. *Cogan* v. *Stevens*, 1 Beav., 482, n.; 1 L. C. Eq., 709.

11. *Q.* When property is given upon trusts which fail either in the whole, or partially, by deaths, or by illegality, or indefiniteness of the trusts themselves, or when they are finally fulfilled without exhausting the property, to whom does the resulting trust of such remaining property belong?

*A.* If the property given is land and the trusts wholly fail, it will belong to the heir or residuary devisee of the person declaring the trust. If it is personalty it will go to the residuary legatee or next of kin. If, however, there is a direction by will to convert land into money for certain purposes, and those purposes partially fail, the undisposed of portion will result to the heir or devisee not as land, but as money. Therefore, if he be dead, his personal representatives will take and not his heir. *Ackroyd* v. *Smithson*, *supra*. If, however, the conversion is directed by deed and the trust partially fail, the heir will have no claim to such residue, as the conversion takes place from the date of the deed, and the property is from that moment personalty. It would be otherwise if from the date of the deed the objects of conversion had totally failed, as in such a case there would be no conversion. *Smith* v. *Claxton*, 4 Mad., 492; *Clark* v. *Franklin*, 27 L. J. Ch. 567.

12. *Q.* Where a conveyance or transfer of property, real or personal, is made without consideration, but upon trust, of which no distinct use or trust is declared, to whom then will the implied trust devolve?

*A.* The real estate will devolve to the party declaring the trust, or, if dead, on his heir or devisee. The personalty will result to him or his residuary legatee or next of kin. If there is no heir the trustee will take the land beneficially in preference to the crown. *Burgess* v. *Wheate*, 1 Eden, 177. But if there were no next of kin the personalty would be forfeited to the crown. *Taylor* v. *Haygarth*, 14 Sim., 8.

13. *Q.* A by deed conveys lands to trustees upon trust to sell the same, and out of the proceeds to pay certain debts due from A. A dies intestate before any sale has taken place. The trustees sell enough of the land to pay the debts, but a portion remains unsold. To whom does it belong?

*A.* The residue will be looked upon as personal property, and go to the personal representatives of A. If the direction had been by will, it would, as mentioned above, have gone to the heir. But the deed operates from its date, and the land is converted from that moment, unless the objects wholly fail from the date of the deed. The conversion, moreover, is quite irrespective of the time at which the sale takes place. *Clarke* v. *Franklin*, 27 L. J. C., 567; Haynes' Outlines, 377. See further as to conversion, *supra*, 300, 301.

14. *Q.* How can trustees and executors obtain protection in the execution of their trusts and duties? and what is the consequence as to their right to deal with the assets in the payment of debts?

*A.* They may pay the money into court under the provisions of 10 & 11 Vic., c. 96, mentioned below. Executors may also file a bill for the administration of the deceased's estate. The effect of a decree is that no step can be taken in disposing of the estate without the sanction of the court. Executors also after inserting the same advertisements for creditors as would be given in an administration suit, may distribute the assets without liability as to claims not sent in. 22 & 23 Vic., c. 35, s. 29. Also, by the subsequent section of the same act, trustees and executors are empowered to apply by petition or summons to a judge in chancery for his opinion, advice or direction respecting the management or administration of the trust property. Haddan's Equity, 33.

15. *Q.* In the case of a will of doubtful construction, how are the executors to proceed so as to avoid personal responsibility?

*A.* They should proceed by Bill to administer the deceased's estate. Also, if the parties interested consent, a special case may be agreed upon for the opinion of the court. 13 & 14 Vic., c. 35.

16. *Q.* A trustee has money in his hands for the benefit of a widow for life, and afterwards for her children. By what summary proceedings may he effectually relieve himself of the trust?

*A.* The trustee may pay the money into the Bank of England with the privity of the Accountant-General in the matter of the trust. 10 & 11 Vic., c. 96. The trustee must file an affidavit, intituled in the matter of the act and of the trust, and setting forth :— 1. His name and address. 2. The place where he may be served with any petition or notices. 3. The amount proposed to be paid in. 4. A short description of the trust. 5. The names of the persons interested. 6. The submission of the trustee to answer such enquiries as the court may direct. If it is deemed unnecessary to have the money invested in the mean time, the affidavit must contain a statement to that effect. The affidavit being filed, and an office copy obtained and produced to the Accountant-General, a direction to pay in the money will be prepared. Consol. Ord., 41, r. 3; Ayck. Pr., 430. The County Court has now jurisdiction under this act as to sums not exceeding £500. 28 & 29 Vic., c. 99, s. 1, cl. 5.

17. *Q.* What is the course of proceeding on the part of persons beneficially entitled to the funds referred to in the last question, to enable them to get out the funds, and on whom must notice be served?

*A.* They should apply by petition, or if the trust fund does not exceed £300, by summons, for payment out of the fund. Notice of the application must be served upon the trustee. As to the proceedings on a petition or summons, see *infra.* Ayck. C. Pr., 432.

18. *Q.* If a testator devises real estate to A, and by an unattested writing communicated to A after testator's death, informs A that the testator had made the devise in full confidence that A would devote the real estate to charitable uses, will a court of equity permit A to retain the property for his own use?

*A.* If it does not appear on the face of the will that the devise was upon trust, A will be entitled to the estate, because the unattested writing can have no effect in altering the will. The result will, as to the charity, be the same if it were devised upon trust, and no trust were declared. In such a case A would be trustee for the heir or devisee of the testator. Independently of the declaration of trust being informal, the charity are prevented from taking the lands by virtue of 9 Geo. II., c. 36. Lewin on Trusts, 48.

19. *Q.* Trustees of a settlement, made previous to the marriage of John and Sarah, have power to sell real estate with the consent of John and Sarah during their joint lives, or with the consent of John during his life if he should survive Sarah. John dies in the life-time of Sarah. Can the trustees exercise the power?

*A.* In this case the power contemplates John's consent; the consent of Sarah alone would be insufficient. Therefore, the trustees cannot exercise the power.

20. *Q.* If one trustee receive trust-money, and hand it over to his co-trustee, are both, or which of them, liable?

*A.* If a loss occurs to the trust-fund, both will be liable to make it good. It is the duty of a trustee not to allow the fund to be under the entire control of his co-trustee, unless in cases of necessity, as where he transmits him money in the ordinary course of business. Money paid into a bank should be to their joint account. *Townley* v. *Sherborne; Brice* v. *Stokes,* 2 L. C. Eq., 718 —766.

21. *Q.* Where a trustee has accepted the trust, but refuses to act, what assistance will the court grant?

*A.* The court may compel him to perform the duties of the trust, at the suit of the *cestui que trust,* or it will remove him and appoint another in his place. Lewin on Trusts, 547, 553.

22. *Q.* Where a trustee has been appointed, but has not accepted the trust or acted, and refuses to act, what relief will be given?

*A.* In this case the only course to pursue is to obtain the appointment of another in his stead. Ibid.

23. *Q.* If a trustee be dead or incapable, or cannot be found, will a Court of Equity appoint a new one?

*A.* A new trustee will be appointed in these and other cases such as gross misconduct, conviction for felony, becoming bankrupt. Lewin on Trusts, 548.

24. *Q.* Where a party, sole or surviving executor, dies intestate, how is a legal personal representative of the original testator constituted?

*A.* Administration *de bonis non*, must be taken out to the original deceased. His residuary legatee is entitled to the grant in precedence to the next of kin. Williams on Executors, pt. 1, bk. 5, c. 3.

25. *Q.* Are executors or trustees liable for losses arising from acts not authorised by the will or deed? A trustee having power to advance the trust-fund upon mortgage of real estate, can he advance the same upon leaseholds for lives renewable for ever?

*A.* They are liable to make good losses incurred in consequence of departing from the terms of their trust, especially with regard to improper investments. There appears to be no objection in trustees having power to advance upon mortgage of real estates, investing on long terms of years at a peppercorn rent, which practically are as good as freeholds. It has, however, not been decided that long terms answer the description of real estate. Lewin on Trusts, 243.

26. *Q.* If a loss to an estate occur by a breach of trust on the part of an executor or trustee, and a profit arise to the same estate by any other act on the part of the executor or trustee contrary to the trusts of the will or deed, is the executor or trustee in the first instance liable; and in the latter case, can he set off any gains to the estate from any losses that have occurred by his breach of trust?

*A.* The executor or trustee is liable to make good the loss incurred owing to the breach of trust, and he will not be entitled to set off against such loss any profit that may have accrued to the trust from other transactions. *Robinson* v. *Robinson*, 11 Beav., 375.

27. *Q.* Are executors or trustees allowed their expenses?

*A.* Executors or trustees are allowed all reasonable and necessary expenses incurred in carrying out the trust, but can have no allowance for their care or trouble. *Robinson* v. *Pett*, 2 L. C. Eq., 206.

28. *Q.* One of a firm of solicitors is appointed with others trustee under an instrument which contains no power enabling him to charge for his services as solicitor. Will a court of equity allow him or his firm in any, and what, cases to make any, and what, professional charges? Refer to any recent decisions on this subject.

*A.* As a general rule the solicitor cannot charge, nor can a firm of which the trustee is a partner, even though the business is done by the partner who is not trustee. But in *Cradock* v. *Piper*, 1 M. N. & S., 664, where several co-trustees were made defendants, one of them, being a solicitor, was held entitled to his full costs for the defence of himself and co-trustees, upon the ground that their defence was forced upon them. See also *Broughton* v. *Broughton*, 5 De G. M. & G., 160 ; Lewin on Trusts, 216.

29. *Q.* Are trustees under any, and if any, what, circumstances entitled to remuneration for the performance of their duties as trustees ?

*A.* They are not entitled to remuneration unless it be specially stipulated by the instrument creating the trust that they shall be. *Robinson* v. *Pett*, 2 L. C. Eq., 206.

30. *Q.* A settlement dated in 1861 authorises the trustees to invest the trust funds in Government or real securities in England; may the trustees invest such trust funds in any other, and what, countries, and by virtue of what authority ? Is there any difference if the settlement is dated in 1840 ?

*A.* In addition to the Government or real securities in England, the trustees may invest in real securities in Scotland and Ireland, or in the stock of the Bank of England or Ireland, or East India stock, unless expressly forbidden to do so. 22 & 23 Vic., c. 35, s. 32. This power extends to all settlements, the enactment referred to being made retrospective by 23 & 24 Vic., c. 38.

31. *Q.* Upon what securities may cash under the control of the Court of Chancery be invested ?

*A.* Such cash may be invested in Bank stock, East India stock, Exchequer Bills, £2 10s. per cent. annuities, and upon mortgage of freehold and copyhold estates in England and Wales, Consols, reduced £3 per cent. annuities, and new £3 per cent annuities. 23 & 24 Vic., c. 38, ss. 10, 11; Ord. 1 Feb. 1861. Trustees and executors, having power to invest their trust funds upon Government securities, or upon Parliamentary stocks, funds, and securities, may also invest in the above. 23 & 24 Vic., c. 38, s. 11.

32. *Q.* If a trustee pays money under a power of attorney from a person who, at the time of payment, was dead or had revoked the power, will the trustee under any, and if any, what, circumstances be liable to repay the money ?

*A.* Formerly a trustee was placed in a position of great hardship under the above circumstances, as the payment by him was invalid and he could be proceeded against, unless indeed the power was expressed to be valid notwithstanding death. *Kiddill* v. *Farnell*, 3 Sm. & G., 428. Now, however, the trustee is not liable, provided he made the payment in ignorance of the death or revocation and *bonâ fide.* Of course, the power is still determined by the death or revocation. 22 & 23 Vic., c. 35, s. 26.

33. *Q.* Under what circumstances other than an express trust or power for that purpose can a devisee in trust now raise money for the payment of a testator's debts or legacies ?

*A.* If the testator has charged his real estate or a portion thereof with the payment of his debts, and has devised the whole of his interests therein to trustees, they may, if the testator died since the 13th August, 1859, raise the money by sale or mortgage. If there is a charge of debts, but no devise to trustees, the executors have a similar power. 22 & 23 Vic., c. 35, ss. 14—16.

34.  *Q.* In the absence of the usual receipt clause, when can a purchaser now pay his purchase-money without being bound to see to its application?

*A.* In buying from trustees a purchaser is now in all cases exonerated from seeing to the application of his purchase-money. If, however, there is a charge of a sum of money upon land, and the owner sells in his capacity as owner, the purchaser having notice of the charge will be bound to see to its application. He does not sell as a trustee, but as a beneficial owner. If, in such a case, debts generally are charged, the purchaser is not bound to see the money applied in their payment. 22 & 23 Vic., c. 35, s. 23; 23 & 24 Vic., c. 145, s. 29; Williams on Real Assets, 49—61.

35.  *Q.* An estate is devised to trustees in trust for sale. Certain pecuniary legacies are to be paid by the trustees out of the proceeds. The will does not contain any trustee's receipt. The estate is sold to A B, who pays the purchase-money to the trustees. The trustees neglect to pay the legatees. Have the legatees any claim upon A B, or on the estate? State the reasons for your answer.

*A.* See previous answer, and see *supra*, No. 7, & p. 255, Nos. 7, 8.

36.  *Q.* The Court of Chancery prohibiting persons filling certain characters from becoming purchasers, name the principal of such characters, and upon what grounds the prohibition is founded.

*A.* The following persons are prohibited from purchasing the property with which their duties are connected, except under certain circumstances:—Trustees having accepted the trust, unless mere nominal trustees, agents, commissioners of bankrupts, and assignees or their partners in business, solicitors, auctioneers and creditors who have been consulted as to the mode of sale, counsel, and indeed any persons who have in consequence of their employment acquired a special knowledge of the property of their employer. The reason for the above rule is that such persons, were they free from restriction, would turn their own knowledge to their own benefit, regardless of that of their employer. Sugden's Vendors, 687.

37.  *Q.* If a trustee or agent purchase an estate which he is employed to sell, will a Court of Equity protect the sale? and give a reason for your answer. What course would you advise on behalf of a trustee-purchaser, in order to assure his title and prevent any after-impeachment of it?

*A.* Such a purchase could be set aside, unless indeed the relationship of trustee or agent has determined previously to the sale. The property would have to be reconveyed, an allowance being made for substantial improvements, and the plaintiff paying back the purchase-money with interest at £4 per cent. The defendant would also have to account for the rents. As to the principle in such cases see the previous answer. Also *Ex parte Lacey*, 16 Ves., 625; *Ex parte James*, 8 Ves., 348. I should advise my client to determine his relationship of trustee before he purchased, or, if the sale was by the Court, obtain leave to buy the estate. If he gave double the value of the property, I should also advise him that he was safe, but, at the same time, most improvident. Sugden's Vendors, 693; 1 Prideaux's Precedents, 93.

38. Q. State the principle upon which the Statute of Limitations cannot be pleaded by a trustee in bar to the claim of his *cestui que trust*?

A. The reason for the rule is that during the continuance of the trust there can be no adverse title. The possession of the trustee is the possession of the *cestui que* trust. The rule, however, only applies to *direct* trusts and not to those which are *constructive*, with regard to which latter long acquiescence by the *cestui que* trust will be a bar to his claim. Lewin on Trusts, 560.

39. Q. Is there any limitation in point of time to relief against a trustee for alleged fraud in the execution of his trust?

A. There is no limit in the case of trustee and *cestui que* trust; but in other cases, if the fraud is concealed, time will run from the time within which it might have been discovered with ordinary diligence. After discovery the Statute runs. Lewin on Trusts, 560, 566.

40. Q. If a person appoint a creditor his executor, who proves the will; will such executor stand in any, and what, better circumstances than the other creditors?

A. Such creditor has a right to retain his own debt out of the assets in preference to those of equal degree with himself; but this privilege does not extend to executors *de son tort*. An administrator has a similar right. The right to retain extends to debts barred by the Statute of Limitations. *Hill* v. *Walker*, 4 K. & J., 166. Williams on Personal Property, 305.

41. Q. Is an executor chargeable with profits made by him from the employment of his testator's estate in trade, or is he chargeable with interest only?

A. The *cestui que* trust has the option of taking the actual profits, or of charging the executor with interest at £4 per cent. on the estate employed. In all cases, however, he is charged with the actual profits if they exceed this rate of interest. Lewin on Trusts, 253, 254.

42. Q. Is an executor justified in paying a simple contract debt before a specialty debt, *or* one simple contract or specialty debt before another simple contract or specialty debt?

A. An executor has no right to pay a debt of lower degree before one of a higher degree of which he has notice. If he make the payment he becomes personally responsible both at law and in equity to the prejudiced creditor. He may, however, give a preference to one of creditors of equal rank without incurring liability. Thus he may pay one simple contract creditor before another. He should not, however, make a voluntary payment to one, after a declaration has been delivered in an action by another. Williams' Executors, 931.

43. *Q.* Can an executor by any, and what, means give priority to one creditor of his testator over others, after a bill has been filed to administer the estate?

*A.* The executor may, by payment, or by confessing judgment, give priority to one creditor over others, provided preference be given before decree. But after the ordinary decree on behalf of *all* the creditors, he cannot give preference. It is otherwise if the suit is for his own debt alone. Wms. Exors., 934, 935.

44. *Q.* An executor having paid his testator's debts so far as known, and divided the estate among the legatees, is called upon to pay another debt. Will the same fall on the executor, or will equity afford him any, and what, relief against the legatees?

*A.* In such a case the executor will be liable to pay the debt of which he had no notice, unless he have protected himself by an administration suit, or under 22 & 23 Vic., c. 35, s. 29. But he may compel the legatees by bill to refund rateably, for the purpose of reimbursing himself. The creditor also has a right to sue the legatees. Wms. Exors., 1308.

45. *Q.* Is an executor justified in paying a debt of his testator which is barred by the Statute of Limitations?

*A.* He may pay the debt, as he is not bound to plead the statute. In an administration suit, however, any party to the suit may take the objection, though the executor may not do so. His right of retainer also extends to debts barred by the statute. Wms. Pers. Prop., 374.

46. *Q.* A testator has by will given his real and personal estate to trustees, upon trusts for sale and conversion, to pay certain life annuities, and subject thereto, has given the residue to your client, who doubts the responsibility of the trustees, and is desirous to take the most effectual measures for securing the trust funds. State the advice which you would give in these circumstances, and the general course of the proceedings which should be instituted.

*A.* I should advise my client to file a bill against the trustees for the administration of the estate of the deceased. As to the proceedings in the suit, see *infra*.

47. *Q.* An executor has advertised for creditors of his testator; has paid all debts of which he had notice, but which were by simple contract; and he has distributed the residue amongst the legatees without any decree having been made for the administration of the estate. Afterwards, a specialty creditor, of whose debt he had not any knowledge, files a bill for an administration of the estate. In taking the accounts, is the executor entitled, as against such specialty creditor, to take credit for the payments made to the simple contract creditors, and to the legatees, or to either, and which of them?

*A.* If the advertisements given by the executor are such as the court would approve of in an administration suit, all the payments by him would be good as regards his own liability. He could, therefore, take credit for all the payments. 22 & 23 Vic., c. 35, s. 29. See *supra*, and the next answer.

48. *Q.* State in what respect recent legislation has affected the previous liability of an executor to the creditors of his testator, in respect of debts of which he had no notice, before he had paid all the debts of which he had had notice, and had distributed the residue of the estate among the residuary legatees.

*A.* The recent legislation referred to, is the act mentioned in the previous answer. Before this act, an executor, whatever precaution he took short of an administration suit, was never safe from the claims of creditors of which he had no notice, as regarded assets distributed among legatees. Payments to creditors of whatever degree were a complete answer to other creditors, but the executor could not set up a payment to legatees. Now, if he takes the precaution to insert advertisements he will be safe from future claims, but the remedy of the creditors against the legatees to make them refund is expressly reserved. 22 & 23 Vic., c. 35, s. 29.

49. *Q.* Define a general legacy and a specific legacy; and state whether, in case of a deficiency of assets, specific legacies can be required to abate.

*A.* See *supra*, 249, No. 50, *et seq.* Specific legacies must abate, but not until the general assets are exhausted, and then only in favour of creditors. They are also liable to ademption, by the testator having disposed of the subject matter in his lifetime. Wms. Pers. Prop., 316.

50. *Q.* What is a demonstrative legacy, and is it preferable to other legacies ?

*A.* See *supra*, 250, No. 53.

51. *Q.* What is the meaning of a *donatio mortis causâ*? and how does it differ from a legacy and a gift *inter vivos*?

*A.* The term is applied to a gift of personal property, in prospect of approaching death. To be valid, it must be made—1. In contemplation of the conceived approach of death. 2. The gift must be intended to take complete effect only after the donor's decease. 3. There must be a delivery or *traditio* of the subject of the gift to the donee for his use, or upon trust for another, or for a particular purpose. It differs from a legacy in that—1. It is not liable to probate duty. 2. It does not require the executor's assent. It differs from a gift *inter vivos*, in that—1. It may be revoked by the donor during his life. 2. It may be made to the wife of the donor. 3. It is liable to the debts of the donor. 4. It is liable to legacy duty. 5. Mortgage deeds, bonds, etc., are good *donationes mortis causa*, by simple delivery of the security, but to constitute a valid gift of such property, there must be a legal transfer to, or a trust created, for the donee. *Ward* v. *Turner*, 1 L. C. Eq., 721, and Notes.

52. *Q.* What is the course to be pursued by a legatee, to compel payment of his legacy, whether charged on realty or otherwise? and upon what equitable principle is such procedure founded?

*A.* The legatee should file a bill in equity against the personal representatives of the deceased for the payment of the legacy. The courts of common law never had any jurisdiction to compel payment of a legacy, but the jurisdiction was originally vested in the Ecclesiastical courts. These courts, however, did not administer due relief, having no means, where the assets were deficient, of making provision for the payment of debts. Executors, therefore, for their own protection, when sued for legacies, went to equity to administer the estate, and the legatee was restrained from suing in the Ecclesiastical Court. After this, legatees were practically compelled to resort to the Court of Equity, who assumed jurisdiction in consequence of the inadequate remedy in other courts. Haynes' Outlines, 109.

53. *Q.* Where a legacy is charged on real and personal estates, and the legatee dies before the day of payment, how is the legacy treated?

*A.* With regard to the personal estate, out of which the legacy will have to be satisfied, in the first instance, it will be looked upon as vested, if the period at which the legacy is to be enjoyed refers to the time of payment. Thus, a legacy to A, *to be paid to him at* twenty-one, is vested. But to A, *if* or *when* he attains twenty-one is contingent on his attaining that age, and if he die before, his representatives cannot claim it. Should there be a deficiency of the personal estate resort must be had to the real; and, so far as this is necessary, the legacy will be looked upon as contingent in both the cases above mentioned, and the legacy will fail for the benefit of the land. If, however, the legacy appears to be postponed for the convenience of the estate, as, when there is a devise to one for life, and after his decease the land is charged with a legacy, it will vest on the legatee at once. *Stapleton* v. *Cheales,* L. C. Conv., 724 and notes. *Supra,* 249, No. 47.

54. *Q.* A having a judgment against B issues an *elegit,* under which he gets possession of B's estate; B afterwards charges his estate with the payment of an annuity to C, and subsequently to this A takes a conveyance of the estate from B, in consideration of his judgment debt; has this conveyance any, and what, effect upon C's annuity?

*A.* If B takes the conveyance with notice of the annuity, the effect will be to let in the annuity before the judgment, though posterior to it in date. Therefore the property not being sufficient to pay both, the annuity must be first satisfied. Sugden's Vendors, 747, 14th ed.

55. *Q.* If a legacy or annuity be given on condition that the legatee or annuitant shall not dispute the will, what will a Court of Equity decree?

*A.* The decree will be, that he must elect either to take the legacy or not. If he take the legacy, he will not be allowed to dispute the will. See the next answer.

56. *Q.* A testator gives a specific bequest to A, and directs that, in consideration of such bequest, A shall pay his testator's debts, and makes A his residuary legatee and executor. The debts far exceed the value of the bequest. Is A bound to pay them in full or not? Give the reason for your answer.

*A.* A is bound to pay the debts if he accepts the bequest, as it is the condition upon which he is to take it. But he is not bound to take the legacy, and in such case he need not pay the debts, except in his capacity as executor to the extent the assets extend. The principle is, that he who takes the benefit must also take the burden. Also, a man must not blow hot and cold at the same time.

57. *Q.* Is a pecuniary legatee entitled to interest; and if so, from what time, and what rate of interest, where no time or rate of interest is mentioned in the will?

*A.* A general pecuniary legacy carries interest from one year after the decease of the testator. If the legacy is specific, interest runs from the death. So, also, if the legacy is to a child of the testator. So, also, where the legacy is in satisfaction of a debt. So, also, if the legacy is charged on land. Interest at 4 per cent. per annum is allowed. 2 L. C. Eq., 256.

58. *Q.* From what time does the interest of a legacy, given by a parent to his child, commence?

*A.* Interest runs from the death. But the child must be an infant, not otherwise provided for, and legitimate. Ibid., 258.

59. *Q.* If an annuitant under a will die before the day of payment, is any portion of the annuity payable in such case; and under what authority?

*A.* The authority referred to is doubtless the Apportionment Act, 4 & 5 Wm. IV., c. 22, by virtue of which the personal representatives of a person entitled to a life interest in income coming due at fixed periods are entitled to recover from the remainderman an apportioned part of such income up to the time of the death. Where the annuity is given to several persons in succession, and continues as a subsisting payment, the act applies; but it appears inapplicable to a mere life annuity. See *Reg. v. The Lords of the Treasury*, 16 Q. B., 357; Hayes and Jarman, 146.

60. *Q.* What is the effect of the Statute of Limitations on a legacy or annuity?

*A.* The legatee or annuitant, if the annuity is charged on land, is barred from recovering the legacy or annuity, after the lapse of twenty years after a present right to receive the same has accrued to some one capable of giving a discharge for it, unless there has been part payment of principal or interest, or an acknowledgement in writing. If there have been any of these, the twenty years runs from such time. The disabilities of infancy, coverture, and absence beyond seas, apply to suits for legacies. 3 & 4 Wm. IV., c. 27, s. 40. Mere personal annuities do not appear to be within the above enactments. Only six years' arrears of an annuity, or of interest on a legacy, are recoverable. 3 & 4 Wm. IV., c. 27, s. 42. Shelford's Real Property Statutes.

61. *Q.* Where a legacy has been given to a child, and the testator afterwards makes advances for the child's benefit, are these advances deemed part payment of the legacy?

*A.* In the absence of a contrary intention, the legacy will be considered as adeemed by the advances, either totally, if of larger or the same amount, or *pro tanto*, if of less amount. They must be substantially the same, and as equally beneficial as the legacy. The reason is, that the court looks upon the legacy as intended to be a portion, and it leans against double portions. This rule has no application with regard to legacies to strangers. *Ex parte Pye*, 2 L. C. Eq., 303, and Notes.

62. *Q.* Explain the doctrine of "Ademption," with reference to specific legacies, and as to legacies given as portions. Illustrate your answer by examples.

*A.* The doctrine of ademption is, that a specific legatee will be disappointed if the particular thing bequeathed to him does not exist at the testator's decease, or if the testator has otherwise disposed of it during his life. With regard to the ademption of legacies given as portions, see the previous answer. *Ashburner* v. *Macguire*, 2 L. C. Eq., 229; *Lady Thynne* v. *Earl of Glengall*, 2 H. of L. C., 131.

63. *Q.* In what case is a legacy in money to a creditor of the testator considered in equity to be an extinguishment of the debt?

*A.* Upon the maxim *Debitor non presumitur donare*, the legacy, unless it is equal to or greater than the debt, will not extinguish it. No satisfaction will take place where the legacy is of less amount than the debt, or payable at a different time, so as not to be equally advantageous to the legatee as the payment of the debt, or where the legacy is of a different nature; thus land is not a satisfaction of money. 2 L. C. Eq., 337.

64. *Q.* Is there any, and if any, what, difference between the rule of law and the rule of equity, with respect to a debt due from an executor to a testator, whose will appoints him executor?

*A.* At law the debt is considered extinguished, the debt being regarded as a mere right to bring an action, and the executor cannot sue himself. Equity, on the contrary, considers the debt to have been paid by the executor to himself, and on this supposition he is accountable for the amount as assets. Williams on Executors, 1128.

65. *Q.* Explain the doctrine of election. Take a case where it arises under a will.

*A.* The doctrine of election applies where a person claims two interests under an instrument, under circumstances from which the court implies a condition that he is not to enjoy both. Thus, if A seised of two acres, one in fee simple and the other in tail, and having two sons, by his will devises the fee simple acre to his eldest son and issue in tail, and the entailed acre to his youngest son, the eldest son cannot take both acres, but the devise to him of the fee simple acre is considered to be upon the condition that he should suffer the younger one to enjoy the tail acre, or that the younger one should have an equivalent out of the fee. *Noys* v. *Mordaunt*, 1 L. C. Eq., 271, and Notes.

66. *Q.* A, by his will, bequeaths B's property to C, and gives a legacy to B. Can B insist on being paid the legacy, and retain his property bequeathed by A?

*A.* See previous answer.

67. *Q.* An estate is absolutely limited by settlement to a married woman, in the event of her surviving her husband. The husband, misconceiving his rights, devises the estate to a third party, and also bequeaths a legacy to his wife. On his death, can his widow claim both her estate and the legacy? Or what are the respective rights of the widow and the devisee?

*A.* The widow cannot take both, she must elect. See *supra*.

68. *Q.* In the distribution of assets, where there is not sufficient for the payment of all the legacies and annuities, how is an annuity in this respect treated?

*A.* The annuity should be valued by an actuary, after which such value must abate proportionably with the other legacies. That is, if the legacy be only charged on the personal estate (see the following answer). Wms. Exors., 1231.

69. *Q.* A testator, by his will, charges his real estate with payment of an annuity and the legacies given by his will. The personal estate is absorbed, and the real estate is insufficient to keep down the payments of the annuity. What is the effect upon the annuity and legacies under these circumstances?

*A.* The annuity being charged upon lands, would, no doubt, be upon certain specific lands, with a power of distress. This was the case in *Creed* v. *Creed*, 11 Cl. & F., 49 b., where the annuities were held entitled to priority over legacies charged generally on the real estate. In the administration of the estate, therefore, the real estate would have to be sold, and a fund set apart to pay the annuity, or its value paid to the annuitant. The legatees would be entitled to the surplus. Wms. Exors., 1231.

70. *Q.* Describe the doctrine of marshalling assets amongst creditors and legatees.

*A.* Assets are said to be marshalled when a creditor or legatee having a claim on two funds of a deceased proceeds against them in a different order to that intended by the testator, or proceeds against some fund which is the only resource of some other creditor or legatee. Thus, if a mortgagee should exhaust the personal estate, equity allows the other creditors to stand in his place, as against the mortgaged lands. *Aldrich* v. *Cooper*, 8 Ves., 381. So, if the creditors exhaust the personal estate, the legatees will be entitled to be paid out of lands devised in trust to sell, or lands descended, or lands charged with the payment of debts. So, if legatees charged on land exhaust the personalty, legacies not so charged are entitled to proceed against the land. But there is no marshalling in favour of a charity. Williams on Real Assets, 108.

71. *Q.* A testator gives a legacy of £500 to A, and the residue of his personal estate to B. He dies intestate as to his real estate. His personal estate is worth £1,600, and his real estate £10,000. His debts amount to £1,500. What will the legatee receive? What would he have received if the testator had himself paid his debts shortly before his decease, thereby reducing his personal estate to £100?

*A.* In this case, if the creditors exhaust the personalty, except

£100, the legatee will be entitled to this £100, and also to go against the land descended for the residue. The assets will be marshalled in the legatee's favour, as against the heir, the legatee being a more favoured individual than the heir. If there were no debts, the legatee would only take £100, as there being no creditors the doctrine of marshalling cannot arise.

72. *Q.* State the course of distribution of an intestate's personal estate in the following cases:—1, where there is a widow and children; 2, where there is a widow and collaterals only; 3, where there is neither widow nor children, but a father, brothers, and sisters; 4, where there is not a father, but a mother, brother, sisters, and children of a deceased brother or sister.

*A.* 1. One-third to the widow, two-thirds to the children. 2. Half to the widow, the other half amongst the collaterals according to degree. 3. All to the father. 4. Equally between the mother, brothers and sisters and nephews, the latter taking their parent's share. 22 & 23 Car. II., c. 10; 1 Jac. II., c. 17.

73. *Q.* An intestate, married since 1834, dies, possessed of real as well as personal estate, leaving a widow, a son, and several other children; what are their respective rights and interests in the intestate's property?

*A.* The real estate will go to the eldest son, subject to the widow's dower, unless barred. The personalty will go two-thirds to the children equally, the other third to the widow. See, as to this, *supra,* 258, *et seq.*

74. *Q.* If A dies intestate, leaving a mother, wife, two sons, and three daughters, him surviving; how will his property be divided, consisting of (*a*) freehold farm in Kent; (*b*) freeholds intermixed with leaseholds in Sussex; (*c*) freehold farm in Surrey, contracted to be sold; (*d*) railway bonds; (*e*) government stock; (*f*) New River share?

*A.* (*a*) The farm in Kent will go to the two sons, subject to the widow's right to a moiety for dower, so long as she remains unmarried and chaste. (*b*) The freeholds will go to the eldest son, subject to the widow's dower. The leaseholds will be divided in the same way as the personalty (*c*), (*d*), and (*e*) mentioned below. (*c*), (*d*), and (*e*), Two-thirds to the brothers and sisters equally, one-third to the widow. (*f*) The New River share, being realty, goes to the eldest son. (*c*) Is considered as personalty, under the doctrine of constructive conversion, under which, that which is agreed to be done is considered as done; the farm in Surrey is therefore personalty. *Fletcher* v. *Ashburner,* 1 L. C. Eq., 659. *Supra,* 263, No. 32.

75. *Q.* State the cases in which it is peculiarly advisable to administer the estate of a deceased person under a decree of a Court of Equity.

*A.* Proceedings should be taken to administer an estate in Chancery in those cases where difficulty is apprehended in disposing of the assets of the deceased, owing to there being a deficiency of assets to meet his liabilities. Where questions, as to priorities of claims, are likely to arise, or where the executor owing to the peculiar terms of the will would not be safe in acting upon it without the advice of the court. Wms. Exors., 1819.

76. *Q*. An executor desires to be protected under a decree of the court, in administering his testator's personal estate; what steps should he take, and how soon may they be taken, after the testator's decease?

*A*. He may apply to the court by motion or petition of course, or to a judge at Chambers by summons, for an order to take an account of the debts and liabilities affecting the personal estate of the deceased and for the application of the personal estate in payment of such debts and liabilities. The application may be made immediately after probate is granted. 13 & 14 Vic., c. 35, s. 19; 23 & 24 Vic., c. 38, s. 14.

77. *Q*. How does a Court of Equity assist the creditors of persons deceased? and what takes place if the executor do not admit assets?

*A*. The court will entertain a suit by a creditor for the payment of his debt against the representatives of the deceased. If the executor admits assets, the court will simply decree payment of the debt; but if he do not admit assets, a decree will be made for the administration of the estate under the direction of the court. Williams Exors., 1859.

78. *Q*. In administering an estate where the deceased was possessed of land, subject to a mortgage, secured also by the bond of the deceased, as between his real and personal estate, which is to pay the debt?

*A*. The debt would be payable out of the estate, by virtue of 17 & 18 Vic., c. 113, unless a contrary intention appeared. The act only applies to cases of persons dying intestate after 31st December, 1854, or having devised the mortgaged estate after that date. Leaseholds are not within the act. *Solomon* v. *Solomon*, 12 W. R., 540. In cases not coming within this enactment, the personal estate is the primary fund. Williams' Real Assets, 95.

79. *Q*. Is a devisee of a mortgaged estate entitled to have the mortgage paid off out of the personal estate, or is he to take it subject to the mortgage?

*A*. See previous answer. *Supra*, 244, No. 22.

80. *Q*. Define the terms legal and equitable assets.

*A*. Legal assets are those which may be recovered in a Court of Law, or which come to an executor by virtue of his office. Such are, debts due to the deceased on judgments, specialties and simple contract, leaseholds, stocks, shares, ready money, &c. Equitable assets are those which the creditors can only make available in a Court of Equity. Thus, lands devised for the payment of debts, and the separate estate of a married woman, are equitable assets. As to the order of payment of debts out of them, see next answer. *Silk* v. *Prime*, 2 L. C. Eq., 82. *Supra*, 265, No. 4.

81. *Q*. What distinction prevails in Courts of Equity in the mode of paying debts out of legal and out of equitable assets?

*A.* If the assets which the court is administering are legal, it will observe in their distribution the common law order. This is— 1. Reasonable funeral and testamentary expenses. 2. Probate and administration and costs of administration suit. 3. Debts due to the Crown by record or specialty. 4. Debts by certain statutes to be preferred to others. Such are, money due for poor rates from overseers, to the post office for postage of letters up to £5, debts due to friendly societies from their officers, regimental debts due from soldiers dying on service. 5. Registered judgment debts of a Court of Record. 23 & 24 Vic., c. 38, ss. 3, 4. 6. Statutes and recognisances. 7. Specialty debts, including rent of lands in England and Wales. 8. Simple contract debts, amongst which those due to the Crown, and servants' wages, are preferred. 9. Dilapidations. 10. Voluntary bonds.* Where, however, the assets are equitable, the above priorities will not be observed; but all the creditors will participate equally in such assets, unless any creditor have a charge upon any particular property. Wms. Real Assets, 7, *et seq.*

82. *Q.* How does the court administer assets as between judgment, bond, and simple contract creditors, and as between judgment creditors themselves, though of different priorities of date?

*A.* See the previous answer. With regard to the priorities of judgment creditors, *inter se,* the court administers the assets amongst them according to their priorities in date. 1 L. C. Eq., 92.

83. *Q.* What is the order in which assets are under a decree administered amongst creditors?

*A.* The assets of a deceased are distributed in the following order:—1. The general personal estate. 2. Estates devised upon trust for the payment of debts. 3. Estates descended. 4. Estates devised, but charged with the payment of debts. 5. General legacies. 6. Lands comprised in a residuary devise. 7. Estates specifically devised and specific legacies. 8. Real or personal estate appointed under a general power of appointment vested in the testator. Wms. Real Assets, cap. 7. *Ancaster* v. *Mayer,* 1 L. C. Eq., 505. *Silk* v. *Prime,* 2 L. C. Eq., 82, and Notes.

84. *Q.* What is the distinction between a legal and an equitable debt?

*A.* A legal debt is one which is recoverable in a Court of Law, such as debts due on bonds, specialties, and simple contract. Equitable debts are those which can only be recovered in equity. Thus, an unpaid legacy is an equitable debt. So, also, debts of married women binding on their separate estate.

85. *Q.* State the order and distribution of the assets when there is real as well as personal estate, the former being charged with mortgages, and there being bond and other specialties of the deceased.

*A.* See *supra,* Nos. 66, 83.

---

* Equity does not follow the law as to deeds without consideration. At law such deeds rank with other specialties, as they import a consideration.

86. *Q.* Where the personal estate of the testator has been exhausted in paying mortgages and specialty debts, have the simple contract creditors any claim against the real estate?

*A.* In such a case the court will marshall the assets in favour of the simple contract creditors. But now, independently of the doctrine of marshalling, the simple contract creditors may proceed against the lands in equity. 3 & 4 Wm. IV., c. 104.

87. *Q.* A dies, leaving real and personal estate. By his will he gives specific and pecuniary legacies, charges all his property with his debts and legacies, and appoints his son residuary legatee. His property is more than enough to pay his debts, but not sufficient to satisfy all the legacies. How are his assets to be administered?

*A.* The debts will be first paid in full. The specific legatees will then be satisfied, after which the general legacies must abate rateably. The residuary legatee will get nothing. See authorities cited, *supra*.

88. *Q.* How is an Irish judgment regarded in the administration of assets in England?

*A.* It will be considered as a simple contract debt upon the ground that it is a "foreign judgment," even since the union. Wms. Exors., 900.

89. *Q.* If a testator by his will charge his real estates with the payment of his debts, will or will not such a devise have any, and if any, what, effect on a debt which had been previously barred by the Statute of Limitations?

*A.* The charge will not revive the debt which is statute barred. *Burke* v. *Jones*, 2 Ves. & Bea., 275; Wms. R. Assets, 42.

90. *Q.* A person conveys his estates to trustees, upon trust to sell, and apply the proceeds of the sale in discharge of all his bond debts, and the interest then due, and to grow due thereon up to the day of payment. Upon taking the accounts, it is found that the principal and interest upon some of them exceed the penalty of the bonds. In such case, are the obligees entitled to the excess?

*A.* As a general rule interest will not be allowed beyond the penalty. *Tew* v. *Winterton*, 3 Bro. C. C., 489. It would be otherwise, however, if the obligee had a mortgage for the debt. *Clarke* v. *Lord Abingdon*, 17 Ves., 106. Other special circumstances would also form an exception to the rule, but no case appears to have been decided giving to the obligee additional interest, under a will worded like the question.

91. *Q.* Under the usual decree for the administration of an estate, is an executor or administrator entitled to retain a debt due to himself in preference to other creditors of equal degree?

*A.* He may retain his debt, even though it be barred by the Statute of Limitations. *Sharman* v. *Rudd*, 27 L. J. C., 844.

92. *Q.* What is the effect of a decree in a creditor's suit upon the common law remedies of creditors?

*A.* After the decree is made all proceedings at common law will be stayed by injunction. The decree is viewed as a judgment in favour of all the creditors, to be paid according to their priorities. This would be disturbed if any creditor was allowed to proceed at law. Wms. Exors., 1731.

93. *Q.* Is the claim of a *cestui que trust* against a trustee for a breach of trust, a simple contract or specialty debt? State the reasons for your answer.

*A.* Such a claim is considered as in the nature of a simple contract debt, unless, indeed, the trustee have signed a deed by which he expressly or implicitly acknowledge his liability as a trustee. Thus a declaration by a trustee that he will stand possessed in certain trusts, &c. is sufficient. *Richardson* v. *Jenkins*, 1 Drew., 477. The reason is that until the trustee does sign some deed his liability is by simple contract liability and nothing more. Lewin on Trusts, 158.

### (*b*) *Infancy.*

1. *Q.* What jurisdiction does the Court of Chancery exercise as regards the persons and property of infants?

*A.* With regard to the infant's person and property, the court will appoint a guardian, to act under the directions of the court. The infant will not be permitted to leave the country or marry without permission from the court. The court will also deprive the parent of the custody of his infant children if he ill-treats them or leads a grossly immoral life. Also, it will give the custody of infants, under seven years of age, to their mothers, and make an order for the access of the mother to them above that age. 2 & 3 Vic., c. 54. It has also jurisdiction to authorise infants to make binding settlements on their marriage. 17 & 18 Vic., c. 43, see also *Eyre* v. *Countess of Shaftsbury*, 2 L. C. Eq., 538.

2. *Q.* Will equity enforce the contracts of an infant for and against him?

*A.* The court will not enforce contracts against an infant, unless, perhaps, where he has been guilty of fraud, as where he held himself out to be of full age. Neither will they enforce a contract at his suit, as the remedy is not mutual. Sugden's Vendors, 209.

3. *Q.* What is necessary to be done to make an infant a ward of court; and in what cases will the court allow maintenance for an infant?

*A.* A summons should be taken out at chambers by the next friend of the infant. Upon the return of the summons evidence must be given as to —1. The infant's age. 2. The nature and amount of the infant's fortune. 3. What relations the infant has. The fitness of the proposed guardian must also be proved by affidavit. A written consent of the proposed guardian to act must also be produced, and his signature thereto must be verified by affidavit. Maintenance will in general be ordered out of the infant's property, unless, indeed, he has a father living who is capable of supporting him in a manner suitable to his station and the fortune he will have. 2 L. C. Eq., 598; Ayck, C. P., 571; Sm. Ch. Pr., 967.

4. *Q.* Will a court of equity interfere as to the guardianship of an infant, where there is no property within the jurisdiction?

*A.* The court will not interfere in such a case. There must be some means to enable the court to exercise jurisdiction, otherwise the court would have to look after all the pauper children in the country. *Wellesley* v. *the Duke of Beaufort*, 2 Russ. 21.

5. *Q.* In what cases will courts of equity interfere to deprive a father of the custody of his children, being minors; and mention some cases in which such power has been exercised and on what ground.

*A.* The father will be deprived of the custody of his children when his character is bad, or he has deserted his children, or is endangering their property, and neglecting their education. Also, the custody of the children will be given to the mother if under seven years of age on her petition, if she is ill-treated by the husband and compelled to cease living with him. 2 & 3 Vic., c. 54. *Warde* v. *Warde*, 2 Ph., 786. In *Shelley* v. *Westbrooke*, Jac., 266, where the father had been living in adultery, and was an atheist, the jurisdiction was exercised. So also in *Creuze* v. *Hunter*, 2 Cox, 242, where the father was an outlaw and lived abroad, he was restrained from taking his son there, or improperly interfering with his education. So, also, in *Wellesley* v. *The Duke of Beaufort*, (sup.) where the habits of the father were profligate, his language profane, and he was living in adultery with the wife of another man, he was not allowed the custody of his children. The grounds of the jurisdiction are public policy and conscientious feeling for the benefit of the children. 2 L. C. Eq., 575.

6. *Q.* By what instruments can a father appoint guardians to his children.

*A.* A guardian may be appointed by the will of the father or by a deed in the nature of a will by virtue of 12 Car. II., c. 24. The mother has no such power. 2 L. C. Eq., 565.

7. *Q.* In the absence of a guardian so appointed, what is the summary course of proceeding after the father's death for the appointment of a guardian, and procuring an allowance for an infant's maintenance?

*A.* See answer No. 3.

8. *Q.* If a father have a power of appointing a trust fund among any one or more of his children, and if he make an appointment with a condition annexed that the son shall join him in raising money upon the fund in question, is or is not the appointment valid, and give a reason for your answer?

*A.* The appointment will be set aside as being a fraud upon the power, and the arrangement would be for the benefit of the father which is not the end designed by the person creating the power. *Aleyn* v. *Belchier*, 1 L. C. Eq., 304, & Notes.

9. *Q.* If a parent be of ability to maintain his children, can he have an allowance out of the interest of such children's fortunes?

*A.* He will not be entitled to any allowance out of their property for maintenance if he is able to maintain the child and to give it an education suitable to the fortune which the child expects. But the rule in question has no application to a mother who is therefore entitled to maintenance, whether of ability to maintain a child or not. 2 L. C. Eq., 598. As to trustees allowing maintenance, see *infra*, No. 11.

10. *Q.* In the case of a suit for the administration of the estate of a deceased person who has left children entitled to legacies, or to the surplus of the estate, at what stage of the suit, and in what state of the proceedings, can an order be obtained for the allowance of maintenance to the children?

*A.* As soon as it is ascertained in the suit that the estate will be sufficient to meet all the claims upon it, the court will allow maintenance to the children. 15 & 16 Vic., c. 86, s. 57. This could not be ascertained until the claims had been entered and the amount of the estate ascertained in Chambers.

11. *Q.* When may trustees apply the income of their infant *cestui que* trust's property for the maintenance of such infants in the absence of any express power?

*A.* They may without any express power apply to the maintenance or education of the infant the income of his property, whether there be any other fund applicable to the same purpose, or any other person bound by law to provide for such maintenance or not. 23 & 24 Vic., c. 145, s. 25.

12. *Q.* If access to her infant children be refused to a mother by the father or guardian, will the court interfere to any, and what, extent, and, if so, under what authority?

*A.* Yes, the mother may by petition obtain an order for access to her children at such times and places as may seem convenient and just to the court. The petition may be to the Lord Chancellor, the Master of the Rolls, or Vice-Chancellors. 2 & 3 Vic., c. 54, *re Taylor*, 10 Sim., 291.

13. *Q.* In what cases, and how will the court interfere relating to the marriage of an infant?

*A.* The court will not allow its ward to contract an improvident marriage. If, therefore, it appears that the ward is about to marry a person much beneath his station in life, or of improper religious tenets, or of bad character, it will prevent the marriage taking place. If any one marries a ward without leave, or assists, or connives at the marriage they will be arrested and put in prison for contempt of court. Lady Shaftesbury being a peeress a sequestration was issued. *Eyre* v. *Countess of Shaftesbury*, 2 L. C. Eq., 538.

14. *Q.* A desires to marry a female ward of court, what steps must be taken to obtain the sanction of the court, and on what terms will it be granted?

*A.* After having obtained the lady's consent A must present a petition to the court, asking its consent to the marriage and stating all circumstances, such as his property, religion, etc., necessary for the court to form an opinion, also offering to make a proper settlement. If the chief clerk certifies that A appears to be an eligible husband, the court will sanction the marriage upon the condition of a settlement being made of her property on the terms mentioned in the next answer. The settlement will be approved by one of the conveyancing counsel of the court. Davidson's Conveyancing, 734.

15. *Q.* Supposing A, a ward of court, about to marry B, each entitled to £10,000. State the terms of the settlement which the court would sanction on behalf of the ward.

*A.* The settlement would be an assignment of the funds to trustees upon trust to pay the interest of the lady's £10,000 during the lives of both, to the wife for her separate use, without power of anticipation. The income of the husband's money to him. The income of the whole to the survivor. Both funds, subject to a provision for children by a future marriage of the ward, to be on trust for the children of the marriage as the husband and wife, or survivor, shall appoint. In default of appointment to the child or children of the marriage equally at 21 or marriage. In default of children the wife's money as she should appoint; in default, to her relations. The husband's to his relations, or as he should appoint. Peachey on Settlements, 792.

16. *Q.* What are the usual trusts of a settlement of the property of a ward of court on her marriage with a gentleman who brings little or no property into settlement?

*A.* They would be similar to those mentioned in the previous answer as to the wife's property.

17. *Q.* Will the court compel the husband of a female minor, marrying without its consent, to make a settlement of her property? and will it allow him to derive any benefit from such settlement, and under what circumstances?

*A.* The court will compel the husband to make a proper settlement of her property. Such settlement will in general be exclusively for her benefit, especially if he be a beggar who has married her for her fortune. But if the husband was not aware that his wife was a ward of court, and there are " alleviating circumstances " attending the contempt, the settlement will be more favourable to the husband. 2 L. C. Eq., 596.

18. *Q.* When an infant is made a ward of court what is the effect as regards his person and property?

*A.* His person and property are placed entirely under the control of the court. Thus, he cannot leave the country or marry without the court's concurrence, and his property must be disposed of according the directions of the court in every minute particular. See further *supra*, No. 1. *Eyre* v. *Countess of Shaftesbury*. *Supra.*

(c) *The Equitable Rights of Wives.*

1. *Q.* State the difference (if any) in which the Court of Chancery and a court of common law would deal with an interest to which a married woman might become entitled.

*A.* The Court of Equity would compel the husband to make a settlement on his wife out of the interest in question, if he was compelled to resort to that court for its recovery. But a court of law would not recognise such a claim on her behalf, but would let him receive her interest if he could recover it in the courts of law. Thus, he may recover debts due to her before marriage, and put the money in his pocket. But if the *chose in action* was a legacy which he can only recover in equity, the wife's equity to a settlement will attach. *Lady Elibank* v. *Montolieu*, 1 L. C. Eq., 341.

2. *Q.* How are *femmes covert* favoured by equity courts? Can a married woman sue there, and how?

*A.* See previous answer. A married woman may sue in equity jointly with her husband. But where she claims in opposition to her husband, she may sue by her next friend. Thus, in suits as to her separate estate, and for her equity of settlement, she must sue by next friend. Mitf. Pl., 30.

3. *Q.* Out of what property, and to what extent, is a "wife's equity to a settlement" enforced by courts of equity against the husband, or those claiming under him?

*A.* Her right to a settlement attaches upon property of hers which can only be recovered in equity, or which incidentally becomes the subject of a suit in equity. *Sturgis* v. *Champneys*, 5 My. & Cr., 97. The right extends to a fair portion of the fund, occasionally, if of small amount, to the whole. It will be enforced, not only against the husband, but also against his creditors and purchasers from him. 1 L. C. Eq., 362.

4. *Q.* How may a wife lose her right to a settlement?

*A.* She may formally waive it, by consent in open court, or before commissioners appointed for the purpose. Also by deed acknowledged pursuant to 3 & 4 Wm. IV., c. 74; 20 & 21 Vic., c. 57. If the husband get the fund into his possession her right will also be gone. So, also, she will have no right to a settlement, if an adequate one has already been made upon her. So, also, if she is living in adultery. 1 L. C. Eq., 384.

5. *Q.* What is the meaning of a "fraud upon marital rights?"

*A.* It means a disposition by an intended wife, pending the treaty of marriage, of her property, the effect of which disposition is to defeat the intended husband's rights therein. Thus, if she holds herself out to be possessed of certain property, which will be his on the marriage, and then settles it without his knowledge or concurrence, it will be a fraud upon him. If, however, the intended wife sells her property, or incurs liabilities founded on valuable consideration, without the intended husband's knowledge, it will not be a fraud upon him, against which relief will be given. *Countess of Strathmore* v. *Bowes*, 1 L. C. Eq., 325, and Notes.

6. *Q.* If a *feme covert* have rights opposed to those claimed by her husband, and which she wishes to enforce, how must she proceed to do so?

*A.* She must do so by bill filed by her next friend. See *supra*,

No. 2. If her husband is an exile, or has abjured the realm, she may sue alone. Mitf. Pl., 25.

7. *Q.* How is the consent of a married woman taken to an application for sale under the Settled Estates Act? and what persons are incompetent to take such consent?

*A.* She must be examined apart from her husband, touching her knowledge of the nature and effect of the application, and it must be ascertained that she freely consents. The examination, if she does not reside abroad, must be before the court, or a solicitor actually practising. All other persons are incompetent. But if she reside abroad, any person, whether a solicitor or not, may be appointed. 19 & 20 Vic., c. 120, s. 37; 21 & 22 Vic., c. 77, s. 6.

8. *Q.* If a legacy be given to a married woman, and her husband sue for it in another court, will equity interfere to prevent the payment to him? and, if so, upon what principle is such interference founded?

*A.* The legacy can only be recovered in equity, unless, indeed, it is specific, and the executor has assented to it, or where the executor has admitted it in an account stated with the legatee, or where it does not exceed £50, when it may be recovered in the County Court. The court will, however, as a general rule, not interfere in any of these cases, but will give the wife a settlement only where the husband comes to the court to recover the legacy. The interference is upon the principle that "he who seeks equity must do equity." It is probable, however, that in proceedings under 28 & 29 Vic., c. 99, to recover a legacy up to £500, relief could be obtained either from the County Court or the Court of Equity.

9. *Q.* Are there any circumstances under which the rule referred to in the last question will be relaxed in favour of the husband? If so, give an instance or instances in which such rule will be relaxed.

*A.* See *supra*, No. 4.

10. *Q.* To what amount of principal money, or of an annual income, will the Court of Chancery pay to a married woman or her husband, without order? and if the sum in court exceed that amount, what is necessary to be done in order to obtain its payment?

*A.* Sums on the whole not exceeding £200 of principal, or £10 in annual payments, will be paid to her, upon an affidavit of the husband and wife that no settlement has been made, or if there has been a settlement, then they must identify it. Their solicitor must also swear that the settlement does not affect the fund. Consol. Ord. 1, r. 1. The wife may insist on her right to a settlement, though the fund is under £200. *Re Kincaid's Trust*, 1 Drew., 326. If the sum exceed the above amounts, the husband and wife must present a petition for payment out of court, supported by affidavit as above. Proof by affidavit, identifying the marriage certificate, must also be given, and the Accountant-General's certificate of the fund in court produced. When the petition is called on, the wife must appear to be examined by the court as to her consent. If she resides twenty miles from London, her consent may be obtained by commission. On the return to the commission being produced the order will be made. The wife's examination is not necessary if the fund is settled absolutely to the wife's separate use. Ayck. C. P., 447.

11. *Q.* A married woman is entitled to a sum of money standing in the name of the Accountant-General of the Court of Chancery. It is not subject to any settlement or trust. To whom is the money payable, and how is it to be obtained?

*A.* See previous answer. The money is paid to the husband. Ib.

12. *Q.* Suppose the husband to be insolvent, and the wife wishes to have the fund appropriated to her own benefit, as far as may be; to what extent will the court give effect to her wish?

*A.* She may file a bill by her next friend to have the fund settled upon her and her children. Where the husband is insolvent, the whole amount has frequently been settled. In other cases of insolvency, half has been given to the wife, and the other half to the creditors. There is no established rule, but it is in the discretion of the judge, after considering the particular circumstances of each case. Per. Kindersley, V. C., *In re Kincaid's Trust*, 22 L. J. Ch., 395.

13. *Q.* At the time of marriage a wife is entitled to a beneficial lease for years, and she outlives her husband, can the husband sell the lease during the coverture without her consent, and if it is not sold, to whom will it belong on the death of the wife?

*A.* The husband may, during the coverture, sell the lease without the concurrence of the wife. If not sold it will, upon the wife's death, in the husband's lifetime, belong to him in his marital right. If, however, she survives him, it will belong to her free from her husband's debts, and on her death will go to her personal representatives. The husband has no power over the lease by will during his wife's life. Wms. Real Prop., 369.

14. *Q.* Can a married woman or her husband assign or give any security upon any property to which she is entitled on the happening of a future event?

*A.* The wife can, with the concurrence of her husband, make an effectual conveyance or assignment of such an interest in both real and personal estate, by deed acknowledged. 3 & 4 Wm. IV., c. 74. This power, with regard to personalty, she did not possess until recently, and it extends only to interests taken under instruments made after 31st December, 1857. She has no power to dispose of interests taken under her marriage settlement, or which she is restrained from alienating. 20 & 21 Vic., c. 57.

15. *Q.* Can a married woman dispose of her choses in action?

*A.* She may do so if they are settled to her separate use. As to her reversionary choses in action, see the previous answer.

16. *Q.* What operation has a clause against anticipation upon a gift of the income of real or personal estate to a woman, who, being unmarried at the time of the gift, afterwards marries, and then becomes a widow?

*A.* The clause in question has no operation whatever in such a case. The restraint is only effectual during coverture, as the court makes this exception to the general rule, which forbids restraint on alienation, only in favour of a married woman. Haynes' Outlines, Lect. 7.

17. *Q.* Is the separate property of a married woman liable for the payment of her simple contract debts? and, if so, under what circumstances?

*A.* In equity the wife is looked upon as a *feme sole*, with regard to her separate estate, and all contracts entered into by her, whether simple or otherwise, will be considered as binding on such estate, unless it appears that she intended not to bind it. *Hulme* v. *Tenant*, 1 L. C. Eq., 394, which was a case of a bond debt jointly with the husband. The separate estate was held liable, and the principle of the case has been extended to all other contracts, whether in writing or not. See the notes to this case.

18. *Q.* What is necessary to give validity to the will of a married woman?

*A.* It is necessary that it should be made with the consent of her husband, if desired to defeat his right to survivorship in her personalty. Such consent may be revoked any time before probate. She may also make a will without his consent as to her separate estate, both real and personal. *Taylor* v. *Meads*, 34 L. J. Ch., 203. Also, by virtue of a power of appointment vested in her. Also, as executrix for another. Also, if her husband has abjured the realm, or is an outlaw, or convicted felon. Also when she is judicially separated. *Supra*, 177, No. 12. Rop. Husb., & W., 169. The requirements of 1 Vic., c. 26, must of course be complied with.

19. *Q.* What power has a married woman of dealing with property settled to her separate use? Is there any and what distinction as regards her "pin money" and other property?

*A.* If there is not the usual restraint on alienation, she may dispose of the property, whether real or personal, by deed or will, as if she were a feme sole. With regard to pin money, she has no such power.

20. *Q.* If a married woman entitled to pin money permit her husband to receive it, can any, and if any, what arrears be recovered against the husband or his representatives?

*A.* It was decided in the case of *Howard* v. *Digby*, 2 Cl. & F., 634, by the House of Lords, that no arrears were recoverable. The law of this case has been doubted, but its authority of course cannot be questioned, except by Act of Parliament, as the House of Lords cannot reverse its own decisions. The better opinion appears to be that one year's arrears can be recovered against the husband or his representatives. Lewin on Trusts, 643.

21. *Q.* If property be given to the separate use of a woman unmarried at the time of the gift, will the separate use be enforced on her subsequent marriage? and what will be the effect of the death of her subsequent husband, and what the effect in case of her contracting a second marriage?

*A.* Upon her marriage, the separate use clause will attach, unless she have previously disposed of the property. *Tullett* v. *Armstrong*, 1 Beav. 1. It will also attach upon a second marriage, if apt words are used, and unless restrained to a particular marriage. Ibid., Hayne's Outlines, Lect. vii.

22. *Q.* When do the *choses en action* of the wife, who survives her husband, pass to the husband's executors?

*A.* They will only do so when they have ceased to be such, by his having reduced them into possession before death, or where he has recovered judgment upon them in his own name. This he may do as to *choses en action* accrued to the wife *after* marriage. Wms. Pers. Prop., 346.

23. *Q.* If a marriage settlement be lost or destroyed, how is it possible to carry out the trusts?

*A.* Notwithstanding the destruction or loss of the instrument, the trusts will be carried out, if clearly shown by secondary evidence, such as a draft, what those trusts were. The fact of the loss or destruction must be clearly proved. Taylor on Ev., 414.

*(d) Legal and Equitable Mortgages.**

1. *Q.* What is the difference between the way in which the Courts of Chancery and the Courts of Common Law regard a mortgage?

*A.* Equity considers the property mortgaged merely as a pledge for the security of the money, to be returned to the borrower on payment. The common law courts, on the other hand, view the transaction as an absolute forfeiture to the mortgagee of the security, if the money is not repaid on the day agreed upon. Now, however, the legislature has empowered Courts of Law to recognise the mortgagor's right of redemption, possessed by him in equity; but the jurisdiction and remedy in equity being more complete and satisfactory, the common law remedy is seldom exercised. 15 & 16 Vic., c. 76, s. 219.

2. *Q.* A, being tenant for life of an estate, pays off a mortgage thereon. Can the benefit of the charge be secured to him, and how would you do it?

*A.* If A pays off the mortgage, it will be considered that he paid it off for his own benefit, and therefore the transfer might safely be made to himself. If, however, he were a tenant in tail in possession, the presumption is the other way, and he should take the assignment to a trustee if he means to keep the debt for the benefit of his personal representatives. It would be more prudent for the tenant for life also to adopt this course.

3. *Q.* What is the remedy in case a mortgagor is desirous to redeem his estate after the mortgage has become forfeited? Is there any, and what, limit to the period within which such proceedings must be commenced?

---

* Upon this subject, see also *supra*, 200—210.

*A.* He should file a bill in equity, to redeem the mortgage. He must take this proceeding within twenty years of the time when the mortgagee obtains possession, or from an acknowledgment of the mortgagor's title. 3 & 4 Wm. IV., c. 27, s. 28.

4. *Q.* What is the mode of proceeding in case a mortgagee is desirous to foreclose or to prevent the mortgagor's right of redemption?

*A.* A bill should be filed to foreclose the right to redeem, the proceedings in which are conducted in the usual manner. See *infra*.

5. *Q.* Under the usual decree for a foreclosure, is any time of payment allowed?

*A.* The mortgagor or second incumbrancer is allowed six calendar months after the chief clerk's certificate to redeem. If there is a third incumbrancer a further period of three months is given to him to redeem, and so on throughout the other subsequent incumbrancers. Ayck., C. P., 240. *Infra*, No. 48.

6. *Q.* When a second mortgagee files a bill of foreclosure, how is the first mortgagee to be dealt with?

*A.* If the bill is merely for foreclosure, the first mortgagee need not be a party, and the decree will be made subject to his charge. If the plaintiff make the first mortgagee a party, the bill as to him is one for redemption, and he will have to be paid his debt, interest and costs by the plaintiff. Seton on Decrees.

7. *Q.* Is it competent for the court, in a foreclosure suit, to direct a sale of the mortgaged estate, instead of a foreclosure; and *e converso?*

*A.* The court in a foreclosure suit may at the request of a mortgagee or mortgagor direct a sale of the estate instead of a foreclosure. If, however, the sale is at the request of the mortgagor or a subsequent mortgagee, and the consent of the first mortgagee cannot be obtained, a reasonable sum of money must be deposited by the party making the request. 15 & 16 Vic., c. 86. The court has no power to decree a foreclosure in a suit for a sale merely, but the bill should be filed for a foreclosure or sale.

8. *Q.* A mortgagee has called in the mortgage-money, which the mortgagor is unable to pay, but a third party is willing to advance it upon a transfer of the mortgage. Is the mortgagee bound to transfer the mortgage, and what course must be pursued if he refuse?

*A.* The mortgagee is not bound to transfer the mortgage; but he must reconvey the estate, if his money is paid. The proper course therefore to pursue, if he refuses, is for the mortgagor to pay him off out of borrowed money, and then make a fresh security to the lender. Coote, 347, 3rd ed.

9. *Q.* What is the meaning of the maxim, once a mortgage always a mortgage?" and by what tests is a proviso for repurchase by a vendor distinguished from a mortgage?

*A.* The maxim signifies that when a mortgage transaction is effected the parties cannot disannex from it the ordinary incidents of a mortgage, such as the right to redeem and foreclose. If the purchase is *bonâ fide* of an interest out and out, it will not be considered as a loan on account of a power to repurchase having been given to the seller, although at an advanced price. But if there are peculiar circumstances, such as gross inadequacy of price, retention of possession by the grantor, or if a security be taken by the purchaser for the repayment of the principal, the transaction will be vitiated as a sale, and be considered only as a mortgage. Sugden's Vendors, 199.

10. *Q.* What is the meaning of "tacking?"

*A.* It is a proceeding by which a subsequent incumbrancer obtains priority over a previous charge of which he had no notice when he advanced his money. See examples given, *supra*, 206, No. 29.

11. *Q.* A lends money to B on a deposit of title deeds, and an agreement to execute a mortgage with power of sale; B fails to pay the money or to execute the mortgage, and A wishes to sell the property: can he sell under the power before the mortgage has been executed?

*A.* He cannot sell, as no power to sell has been conferred but merely an agreement for one. He may, however, file a bill for a sale, or for a conveyance and foreclosure, by virtue of the agreement to execute a legal mortgage. 1 Prideaux's Precedents, 318.

12. *Q.* A mortgages to B without delivery of the title deeds, and executes a subsequent mortgage of the same property to C (who has the title deeds) without notice of the first mortgage: will B be postponed to C?

*A.* In this case B will, probably, be postponed to C, for though C has priority in date, yet, if he has by his carelessness or negligence allowed A to retain the deeds he has put it in his power to appear as absolute owner, and assisted A to commit a fraud on C. 1 Prid.'s Prec., 339.

13. *Q.* Can a mortgagee proceed against a mortgagor both at law and in equity at the same time, and how? or will he be compelled to elect?

*A.* A mortgagee may exercise all his remedies concurrently. Thus he may sue on his covenant and bring ejectment at law. In equity he may file a bill of foreclosure or for sale. He may, also, proceed to enforce his power of sale. 1 Prideaux's Precedents, 317.

14. *Q.* What responsibility does a mortgagee incur by entering into the possession of lands mortgaged to him?

*A.* He is bound to account to the mortgagor for the rents received by him, and is also liable for gross and wilful negligence or injury, such as pulling down buildings, losing the title deeds, &c. He is allowed for necessary repairs. He cannot grant leases, which will be binding on the mortgagor, nor open mines, nor speculate in any way with the security, and generally he is bound to deal with it as any prudent man would with his property. Ibid., 324. But he may work mines and cut timber if the security is insufficient. *Millett* v. *Davey*, 32 L. J. Ch., 122.

15. *Q.* State the general purposes for which a mortgagee in

possession may expend money upon the mortgaged estate, which will be allowed to him by a court of equity in taking the account between the mortgagor and mortgagee.

*A.* He will be allowed for necessary repairs to support the property, and doing what is essential to protect the title of the mortgagor. But he is not allowed to "improve the mortgagor out of his estate" by laying out money he may suppose will increase the value of the property, so as to prevent the mortgagor with his means from redeeming. Nor, without authority, can he charge the mortgagor with insurance. 2 L. C. Eq., 893.

16. *Q.* What is an equitable mortgage, and how is it made available by the mortgagee? and in what respect was the equitable relief more extensive and beneficial than in the case of a legal mortgage?

*A.* An equitable mortgage is a method of effecting a security upon lands, unaccompanied by a transfer of the legal estate, and, consequently, recognised in equity only. A simple deposit of deeds, either accompanied or not by a memorandum as a security for the re-payment of money advanced, is sufficient to create an equitable mortgage. An equitable mortgagee by deposit may file a bill for sale, and in this respect the security was more beneficial than a legal mortgage, the holder of which, before 15 & 16 Vic., c. 86, and in the absence of an express power, was compelled to resort to the dilatory proceeding of foreclosure. If the mortgage is accompanied by an agreement to execute a mortgage, the mortgagee is entitled to a conveyance and foreclosure. If such agreement also charges the property, it is optional with the mortgagee to have a sale or foreclosure and conveyance. 1 Prideaux's Precedents, 318.

17. *Q.* What relief should be prayed in a bill filed against the mortgagor by an equitable mortgagee desirous of obtaining the benefit of his security?

*A.* (See previous answer.)

18. *Q.* In what respects is an equitable mortgage objectionable as a security?

*A.* It is objectionable in that the mortgagee, not having the legal estate, cannot recover possession of the land by ejectment, nor can he compel the tenants to pay the rent to him. Also, unless he has the deeds, he may be defeated by a subsequent mortgagee who obtains them without notice. Also, he may be postponed by a subsequent legal mortgagee without notice. *Russell* v. *Russell*, 1 L. C. Eq., 541, and Notes.

19. *Q.* Can title deeds in the hands of an equitable mortgagee by deposit be made a security (subject to the lien of the depositary) to another person making a subsequent advance of money to the owner of the estate?

*A.* Yes, a security may be effected on the property for money subsequently advanced. The security may be either by a mere memorandum of charge, or by a formal legal mortgage. The subsequent advance will, of course, rank after the equitable mortgage. See *supra*, No. 12.

20. *Q.* By the power of sale in a mortgage of real estate, the mortgagee is to hold the surplus produce of the sale for the mortgagor, his executors, administrators and assigns. The mortgagor dies. Is such surplus the mortgagor's real or personal estate?

*A.* If the sale has been effected in the lifetime of the mortgagor the surplus will have been appropriated by him as money, and go to his personal representatives. If, however, the sale takes place after his death the surplus will belong to the heir of the mortgagor. The effect of reserving it to the personal representatives will not defeat the heir's title, the whole mortgage transaction being only looked upon as effected for the purpose of the loan, and not in any way altering the devolution of the property. Haynes' Outlines, 389, 2nd ed.

21. *Q.* A mortgagee, after foreclosure, sold the mortgaged estate, but it did not produce enough to pay the principal, interest, and costs due, and he sued at law for the residue upon the mortgage bond: will a court of equity interfere to stop him? What would have been the case if the mortgagee had not sold the estate after foreclosure, but had sued for an alleged deficiency on the bond? Would the foreclosure be opened or not in equity?

*A.* In the first case an injunction could be obtained to stay the legal proceedings, as after a foreclosure and sale the other remedies of the mortgagee are at an end, as by selling the property he has put it out of his power to return the property to the mortgagor. *Palmer* v. *Hendrie*, 27 Beav., 349. If no sale had taken place, and the estate remained in his power the court would not restrain the action, but the mortgagor would have a right to redeem if he choose, the foreclosure being opened. Hence it is advisable to exhaust the collateral remedies first. 1 Prideaux's Precedents, 323.

22. *Q.* In a devise in the form following:—"I devise my estate at Blackacre to my son A, and as to all my personal estate, I give the same to my son B." Suppose Blackacre to be subject to a mortgage for £5,000, which son has to bear the mortgage-debt? and has any change been recently made in the law on this subject? State any special circumstances which may govern the answer.

*A.* The son A will have to pay the debt, and is not as formerly entitled to have it paid out of the personalty, unless a contrary intention appear. A bequest of personalty "subject to the payment thereout of all the testator's debts," following a devise of land in mortgage has been decided to indicate a contrary intention. *Mellish* v. *Vallens*, 2 Joh. & H., 194; *Eno* v. *Tatham*, 32 L. J. Ch. 159, 211; 17 & 18 Vic., c. 113. Before this act the devisee was entitled to have the mortgage paid out of the personalty, unless the testator expressed a contrary intention.

23. *Q.* What amounts to an equitable assignment?

*A.* It is not necessary in equity that there should be an actual formal legal transfer of property, nor are any particular words necessary; any will do, so long as it clearly appears that an assignment was intended. But for an incomplete assignment there must be a valuable consideration, otherwise it will not be enforced. Thus, an order given by a debtor to his creditor upon a third person, having funds of the debtor, to pay the creditor out of such funds, is a binding equitable assignment of so much money. *Burn* v. *Carvalho*, 4 My. & C., 702 ; *Row* v. *Dawson*, 2 L. C. Eq., 612, and Notes to *Ryall* v. *Rowles*, Ibid.

24. *Q.* If two persons advance a sum of money by way of mortgage, and take a mortgage to themselves as joint-tenants, and one of them dies, what are the rights of the survivor as to the mortgage debt and the securities?

*A.* In equity the survivor will be considered a trustee for the personal representatives of the deceased as to his share of the money. The securities will vest absolutely in the survivor, but unless there is a joint account clause, the personal representatives will have to join in the re-conveyance, to give a valid receipt to the mortgagor. In the above case the answer would be the same whether the money was advanced equally or unequally. *Rigden* v. *Vallier*, 2 Ves., 258; *Lake* v. *Craddock*, 1 L. C. Eq. and the Notes.

### (*e*) *Partition.*

1. *Q.* How may a partition be obtained of lands or houses held in joint-tenancy, co-parcenary, or common ?

*A.* It may be effected by the party seeking partition filing a bill making defendants the owners of the other undivided shares. The suit is brought to a hearing, as in ordinary cases (*infra*), when a decree is made declaring the right to partition, and directing that proposals for a partition be laid before a judge for approval. This direction is proceeded on in chambers; valuations and affidavits are brought in and the scheme of partition is approved by the judge without a commission, as was formerly the practice. *Clarke* v. *Clayton*, 2 Giff., 333 ; *Agar* v. *Fairfax*, 2 L. C. Eq., 374; Haynes' Outlines, 154.

2. *Q.* Has the court exclusive jurisdiction to decree partition, and does it extend to copyholds?

*A.* The jurisdiction of equity as to partition is now practically exclusive, the right of partition at common law having been abolished by 3 & 4 Wm. IV., c. 27, s. 36. The jurisdiction was extended to copyholds by 4 & 5 Vic., c. 35, s. 85.

### (*f*) *Charities or Public Trusts.*

1. *Q.* A testatrix bequeaths a charitable legacy of £900, and charges it on all her property, which consists of £6,000 realty, £4,000 mixed, and £2,000 pure personalty, what amount will the charity be entitled to receive, and on what principle?

*A.* The charge so far as it extends to the £6,000 realty and £4,000 mixed, will fail, as being within "The Mortmain Act,"

9 Geo. II., c. 36. Nor will the court assist the charity by marshalling the assets in its favour so as to enable the £900 to be taken exclusively out of the £2,000 pure personalty, throwing the other claimants on the personalty upon the realty and mixed funds. The court would appropriate the various funds as if no legal objection existed, to applying any part of it to the charity, and allow the charity to take that only which on such principle would be payable out of the £2,000. Thus, if the £900 is divided into as many shares as there are thousands of pounds, viz., twelfths, ten twelfths will fail and two will not. Now a twelfth of £900 will be found to be £75. Therefore the charity will get double this, £150. *Robinson* v. *Governors of London Hospital*, 10 Hare, 19; 2 L. C. Eq., 78.

2. *Q.* Will a Court of Equity sustain a bequest of money to executors to build almshouses or an hospital, in case any person should, within a limited time, purchase or give land as a site? What law was supposed to stand in the way of such a bequest, and what is now the established doctrine as to this?

*A.* Such a bequest with an accompanying direction that no part of the bequest should be applied in the purchase of land has been held to be valid. It was supposed to be otherwise as infringing "The Mortmain Act," having a tendency to bring lands into mortmain. The case is very similar to that of *The Attorney-General* v. *Philpott*, 27 L. J. Ch., 70; but the will there expressly excluded the purchase of land, and the bequest was held to be valid by the House of Lords overruling the decision of the Master of the Rolls.

3. *Q.* A by his will gives to charitable uses the residue of his property, consisting of consols, railway shares, a share in the New River Company, shares in various insurance and dock companies, long leaseholds for years, and leaseholds for lives, a common money bond, and arrears of unreceived rents. Are any, and which, of these gifts void, and why? and who is entitled to the benefit of such portions of the said property as do not pass to the charitable uses?

*A.* The consols, railway shares, shares in various insurances and dock companies, the common money bond and the arrears of rent are valid; but the share in the New River Company, the leaseholds for years and lives, are void as being realty within 9 Geo. II., c. 36. The share in the New River Company will go to the heir or residuary devisee, the leaseholds for lives will devolve on the heir if there is a special occupant, if not, they will go to the personal representatives together with the leaseholds for years. L. C. Conv., 486, *et seq.*, and *supra*, 246. Nos. 31—37.

## VI. *Notices.*

1. *Q.* What precaution is necessary, on the part of a purchaser of a bond-debt, or other *chose en action*, as a protection against subsequent purchasers?

*A.* The purchaser should at once give notice of the assignment to the debtor, in order to prevent him paying the debt to the creditor and also for the purpose of completing his title to the debt, and taking it out of the order and disposition of the assignor within the meaning of the Bankrupt laws. *Ryall* v. *Rowles*, 2 L. C. Eq., 615; Wms. Pers. Prop., 112.

2. *Q.* In the construction of the Registry-Act, by which a registered deed takes priority of one unregistered, what relief will the court afford if the party knew of the unregistered deed?

*A.* In such a case the court will consider that the object of the Act, viz., to give notice, has been carried out, and will accordingly allow the unregistered deed to prevail against the person claiming under a subsequently registered instrument. But it must be clearly proved that the person who registers the subsequent deed had notice; mere suspicion is not sufficient to justify the court in breaking in upon the Registry-Act. *Le Neve* v. *Le Neve*, 2 L. C. Eq., 23; Sugden's Vendors, 728.

3. *Q.* A party entitled to a fund in the hands of trustees, executes an assignment of it by way of security for money borrowed. Is anything, and what, besides the assignment, necessary for the effectual security of the lender?

*A.* The lender should give notice of the charge to the trustees. See *supra*, No. 1.

4. *Q.* Will notice of the contents of a deed be presumed against a party from his having attested its execution, and why?

*A.* The better opinion is that being a witness to the execution of a deed will not of itself be notice, the reason being that in practice a witness is not privy to the contents of a deed. Sugden's Vendors, 780, 14th ed.

5. *Q.* Where a purchaser would be affected by notice of an incumbrance, must such notice be actual, or would a court of equity hold any circumstances equivalent to actual notice?

*A.* The notice need not be actual, but will be of equal consequence if constructive. Thus, notice to the purchaser's counsel, or solicitor, although himself the vendor, or although he be concerned for both vendor and purchaser, is considered notice to the purchaser, and he is as much bound as if notice had been given to him personally. Also notice that land purchased is in possession of a tenant is notice of the lease. Sugden's Vendors, 756.

6. *Q.* What is the rule with respect to notice to the counsel, attorney, or agent, being notice to the client or principal?

*A.* See the previous answer. The notice to the counsel to be effectual against the principal must be in the same transaction, unless where one transaction is closely followed by and connected with another, or where it is clear that a previous transaction was present to the mind of the counsel when engaged in another transaction. 2 L. C. Eq., 49; Sugden's Vendors, 757.

7. *Q.* Are there any, and what, cases in which evidence of constructive notice of an incumbrance will be deemed sufficient?

*A.* See *supra*, No. 5. Public Acts of Parliament and *lis pendens* are also binding, though no actual notice is given of them. Also if a man knows that the legal estate is in a third person at the time he purchases, he is bound by the trusts. Also notice that title deeds are in another man's possession may be held to be notice of any equitable claim which he has on the estate, and as a security for which he holds the deed. Sugden's Vendors, 762.

### VII.—*Retainer and Commencement of Litigation.*

1. *Q.* What authority should a solicitor take from his client for the prosecution or defence of a suit in Equity?

*A.* He should take from him an authority in writing to file the bill. This special authority is not necessary to defend a suit. The authority need not be in writing, but it is prudent to have it so. An authority will be implied where the client acquiesces in and adopts the proceedings. Sm. Ch. Pr., 279.

2. *Q.* If a solicitor files a bill without authority of the client, what step should the latter take upon discovery of the fact; and if he fail to apply, what would be the consequence to him? On the other hand, if the party aggrieved should satisfy the court of the fact, what would be the result to the solicitor?

*A.* The client should serve a notice of motion that his name may be struck out of the record. If he do not apply with due diligence after having made the discovery, the court will presume acquiescence and refuse the application. If the application is successful, the solicitor will have to pay the costs of it. Smith's Ch. Pr., 280. *The Legal Examiner,* 62.

3. *Q.* Who are incapacitated from suing in Equity themselves, and how do parties under such disability sue? State the two distinguishing characters of the disabilities.

*A.* The Crown must sue by its Attorney or Solicitor-General. Infants by their next friend. Married women sue jointly with their husbands or by next friend. Idiots and lunatics by their committees or by the Attorney-General. Persons incapable of acting for themselves, not being idiots or lunatics, sue by next friend. Mitford. Pl., 25. The distinguishing characters are that the disability of the Crown arises from a privilege; but that of other persons, such as infants, from disability. Sm. Ch. Pr., 268.

4. *Q.* By whom does the Sovereign sue, and how, and who is the *dominus litis* of such a suit or information, and who is responsible for its conduct? Must a Queen Consort sue in a like manner?

*A.* The Sovereign sues by the Attorney or Solicitor-General, who is the *dominus litis.* If the suit is one concerning also the rights of others, a relator must be named in addition who is responsible for the conduct of the suit. Still, the Attorney or Solicitor-General possesses entire dominion over every information filed in his name either *ex officio* or in the name of a relator. Where the Crown alone is interested, the proceeding is by information. But where the relator has an interest, the proceeding is termed an information and bill. The Queen Consort partaking of the prerogative of the Crown may also inform by her attorney. Ibid, 24; Sm. Ch. Pr., 268.

5. *Q.* What preliminary step is necessary where an infant, or a

married woman, or other party under disability, is plaintiff in a suit, and what authority should the solicitor obtain?

*A.* A next friend should be appointed. The solicitor should obtain an authority in writing to himself from the next friend to sue in the name of such person, and the authority must be filed with the bill. 15 & 16 Vic., c. 86, s. 11.

6. *Q.* What are the modes of instituting proceedings in the Court of Chancery at the present time? and to what class of cases is each mode more particularly applicable. Mention the first step in each proceeding.

*A.* Proceedings in chancery may be commenced:—1. By bill in the nature of a petition to the Lord Chancellor for relief in some matter within the extraordinary jurisdiction of the court. 2. By information. 3. By information and bill (as to these see *supra,* Nos. 3, 4). 4. By petition, which is a summary proceeding adopted generally under the direction of some act of parliament, where a detailed statement of facts is required, as to obtain the payment of money out of court. Morgan's Orders, 521. 5. By special case, where it is desired to obtain by consent the opinion of the court as to the construction of documents or the title to property. 13 & 14 Vic., c. 35. 6. By summons, which is a summary proceeding, by which certain matters not involving difficulty are settled in chambers, such as the administration of a deceased's estate where no complications are anticipated. See *infra.*

7. *Q.* Explain the difference in form between an information and bill, and the general objects to which each is applicable?

*A.* The difference in form between an information and bill consists in offering the subject matter as the information of the attorney or solicitor-general, and in stating the acts of the defendant as injurious to the Crown, or to those whose rights the Crown endeavours to protect; whereas a bill is at the suit of a subject, and is in the nature of a petition praying relief. As to the latter part of the question see *supra*, No. 4.

8. *Q.* How are proceedings commenced when any other party besides the crown has an interest in the subject-matter of the intended suit, and what steps must be taken to obtain the Attorney-General's sanction to the suit?

*A.* They are commenced by information and bill filed by the Attorney or Solicitor-General at the relation of the party interested. To obtain the concurrence of the Attorney-General, get counsel's certificate that the information and bill is proper for his sanction. Leave a copy of it with his clerk with a certificate thereon by the solicitor, that the relator is competent to pay costs, and that the copy is a true one of that prepared by counsel. The Attorney-General will then sign it. Ayck. C. P., 258.

9. *Q.* Can a foreign sovereign sue in the Court of Chancery in respect of a supposed injury to property belonging to him or his subjects in his dominions, and intended to be committed out of the jurisdiction, and give your authority?

*A.* The actual reigning sovereign of a foreign state in amity with Great Britain may sue in chancery, in respect of a substantial injury to the property of such foreign state situate there, and of the plaintiff's subjects, whom he has a right to represent. To support the jurisdiction the damage must be done or threatened by persons resident within the jurisdiction of the court. Thus, documents proporting to be notes of the Kingdom of Hungary manufactured here were ordered to be delivered up and destroyed, and the further publication restrained at the suit of the Emperor of Austria on the allegation that the introduction of such notes into his kingdom would cause great detriment to his subjects. *Emperor of Austria* v. *Day*, 30 L. J. Ch. 690.

10. *Q.* The necessity of a suit by bill being assumed, set forth the mechanical steps of instituting one; by whom drawn, settled, and signed; how engrossed, printed, or written; where filed, and how endorsed; the service and notice required.

*A.* The solicitor having received instructions, prepares instruction for counsel to draw the bill. It is drawn, settled and signed by counsel. It is then printed. As to when a written bill may be filed see *infra*, No. 36. It is endorsed with a command to the defendant to appear within eight days after service; and that if he fail to do so an appearance may be entered for him, and he will be liable to be arrested and imprisoned, and have a decree made against him in his absence. It is also stated that appearances are to be entered at the Record and Writ Clerks' Office. 15 & 16 Vic., c. 86. Schedule. The bill is filed at this office. As to the subsequent proceedings in the suit see *infra*. "Miscellaneous," No. 1.

11. *Q.* What are the usual parts of a bill in equity?

*A.* They are:—1. The title of the court and cause. 2. The address to the Lord Chancellor. 3. The names, descriptions, and residences of the plaintiffs. 4. The statement of facts in respect of which relief is sought. 5. The prayer for relief and counsel's signature. 6. The names of the defendants. Mitf. Pl., 49.

12. *Q.* What is the strict rule in equity as to the necessary parties to a suit, and how does it differ from the rule at law?

*A.* The strict rule is that all parties interested in the subject matter of litigation should be parties either as plaintiffs or defendants; but at law the necessary parties are those between whom a privity exists, and these latter courts do not entertain in one suit the claims of other interested parties, unless they claim in the same right, and against the same defendants. C. L. P. Act, 1852, s. 41.

13. *Q.* Has any recent alteration been made as to parties to a suit in equity? If so, state the authority, and give one or two examples.

*A.* The strict rule above-mentioned has been relaxed by 15 & 16 Vic., c. 86, by virtue of which *inter alia*, any one person interested in property to be administered under a will, or intestacy, may obtain a decree for administration without making the other persons interested parties. Also in suits for the protection of property one person may sue on behalf of himself and all others interested. Even before this act one creditor could obtain a decree for administration on behalf of himself and all other creditors. Ayck. C. P., 3.

14. *Q.* State some of the principal cases in which it is no longer competent for a defendant to take any objection for want of parties to a suit.

*A.* See previous answer.

15. *Q.* Is it necessary that all parties having an interest in real estates should be made parties to a bill against trustees, in order to carry the trusts into execution, or will it be sufficient to make the trustees only parties to the bill?

*A.* The trustees represent the persons beneficially interested, and the parties interested need not be made parties unless the court direct them to be parties. 15 & 16 Vic., c. 86, s. 42, r. 9.

16. *Q.* To a bill filed by a *cestui que trust*, is the trustee a necessary party.

*A.* The trustee should be a party to the suit, unless in a suit for breach of trust where he has never acted in the trust, though he may have signed the deed appointing him new trustee. *Wilkinson* v. *Parry*, 4 Russ., 274. In suits for breach of trust it is not necessary to make all the trustees parties. Consol. Ord., vii., r. 2.

17. *Q.* In a suit to execute the trusts of a will, is it necessary in all cases, or when, to make the heir-at-law a party?

*A.* It is only necessary to make the heir a party when it is desired to establish the will against him. Consol. Ord., vii., r. 1.

18. *Q.* May an executor file a bill before he has obtained probate; and if so, in what stage of the suit must he obtain it?

*A.* An executor or administrator may institute a suit before probate or administration, but he must obtain the grant before the hearing. Ayck. C. Pr., 597.

19. *Q.* Can or cannot a bill be filed on behalf of an infant, without his consent?

*A.* There is nothing to prevent any one instituting a suit for an infant without authority, and his consent is not necessary. Mitf. Pl., 31.

20. *Q.* If a suit be instituted on behalf of an infant, which is considered to be injurious to his interest, in what way will the court, on a representation to that effect being made, proceed in order to ascertain whether it be well or ill founded, and if the latter, what course will it adopt.

*A.* In such a case the court will as a check upon the general license to institute a suit on behalf of an infant, above-mentioned, direct an inquiry to be made into the fact by the chief clerk, and the proceedings will be stayed if the certificate is to the effect that the suit is ill founded. Mitf. Pl., 29.

21. *Q.* Can the *prochein ami* of an infant sue *in formâ pauperis*, or can any objection be sustained to such *prochein ami* on the ground of his poverty?

*A.* The next friend of an infant is allowed to sue *in formâ pauperis*, no objection can be taken to him on the ground of poverty, but the next friend of a married woman may be compelled to give security for costs. Sm. Ch. Pr., 863 — 870, 7th ed.

22. *Q.* When the next friend of an infant plaintiff dies, and there is delay in appointing another, what is the proper course of proceeding by the defendant?

*A.* The defendant should obtain an order for the court to approve of a new next friend, four days' notice of which should be given to the plaintiff's solicitor. *Glover* v. *Webber*, 12 Sim, 351.

23. *Q.* Can admissions be made on behalf of an infant who is a party to a suit?

*A.* No admissions can be made by an infant, but strict proof will be required against him. *Holdern* v. *Hearn*, 1 Beav., 445; Ayck. C. Pr., 138.

24. *Q.* Can a married woman in any, and what, case institute a suit as a *feme sole*?

*A.* She may institute a suit alone where she has obtained a judicial separation or a protection order under 20 & 21 Vic., c. 85, s..21. Also where her husband is civilly dead or has abjured the realm. *Pannell* v. *Taylor*, 1 Turn. & R., 96; *Bathe* v. *The Bank of England*, 27 L. J. C., 630.

25. *Q.* Is the wife a necessary party to a suit in equity for recovery of property accruing to her after her marriage; and is there any difference in the rules of Law and Equity in this respect?

*A.* Suits respecting the wife's property are usually instituted by the husband and wife jointly, but if the property in question is her separate estate, she should sue by next friend. At law, the wife's property accrued since the coverture may be sued for by the husband alone. Mitf. Pl., 29.

26. *Q.* If a bill be filed on behalf of a married woman against her husband, without her consent, will this circumstance, on its being made out to the satisfaction of the court, involve any, and, if any, what, consequences?

*A.* Such a bill cannot be instituted without her consent, and on it appearing that her consent has not been obtained the bill will be ordered to be taken off the file. Mitf. Pl., 31.

27. *Q.* If some of the parties, defendants, are out of the jurisdiction, what is the plaintiff's course of proceeding? Will the court make a decree in the absence of such parties?

*A.* The plaintiff should apply to the court for an order for leave to serve the bill and interrogatories out of the jurisdiction. This may be obtained on satisfying the court in what place or country the defendant is or may be found. The order limits a time for appearance and answer. A copy of the order for service must also be served. If the defendant do not appear the court may order an appearance to be entered for the defendant, and a decree may be obtained in his absence. Consol. Ord., x., r. 7.

28. *Q.* Is the Attorney-General a necessary party to a suit, the subject-matter of which is a legacy given to a charity already established?

*A.* The Attorney or Solicitor-General is a necessary party. *Corporation of the Sons of the Clergy* v. *Mose.* 9 Sim., 610; Mitf. Pl., 195.

29. *Q.* May an alien sue for any, and what, demands in the Court of Chancery? and if so, is his right to sue dependent upon any, and what, circumstances?

*A.* Alien friends may sue in the Court of Chancery as regards personal property, but if they sue to recover land which they are incapacitated from holding, their alienage would be a good defence. An alien enemy might sue if he came here under a safe conduct from the Crown. Mitf. Pl., 268; *supra*, No. 11.

30. *Q.* Can an arbitrator under any, and what, circumstances be made a party to a suit for the purpose of impeaching his award?

*A.* As a general rule an arbitrator, if made defendant, may demur owing to want of interest; but if the award is impeached on the ground of gross misconduct in the arbitrators they may be made parties, and if the award is set aside will probably be ordered to pay the costs. Mitf. Pl., 187.

31. *Q.* Can a solicitor of a defendant be made a party to a suit for the purpose of compelling a discovery from him?

*A.* As a general rule such solicitor could not be made a party, he being a mere witness. *Queen of Portugal* v. *Glyn,* 7 Cl. & Fin., 466. But it would be otherwise if he had assisted a client in obtaining a fraudulent deed. St., § 1,500. In any case, the solicitor cannot be compelled to disclose his client's secrets.

32. *Q.* Is a bankrupt a necessary party to a bill filed against his assignees?

*A.* He should not be made a party, all his interest having passed to his assignees. If, however, discovery is sought as to acts before his bankruptcy, he would be a proper party and must answer. So also if fraud is charged against him and costs are prayed for. Mitf. Pl., 187.

33. *Q.* What is the distinction between multifariousness and misjoinder, as applied to bills in Chancery? and is there any, and what, difference in their consequence?

*A.* Multifariousness is the improperly joining in one bill distinct and independent matters. Thus, on a sale in lots, the purchasers cannot file one bill against the vendor, or *vice versa.* Misjoinder is the introducing parties to the suit who have no interest. The latter objection will usually be amended, but multifariousness is in general fatal to the bill. Mitf. Pl., 208.

34. *Q.* What is the advantage of the prayer for general relief in a bill in chancery?

*A.* The advantage of such a prayer is that if the plaintiff mistakes the relief to which he is entitled, the court may yet afford him that relief to which he has a right. Mitf. Pl., 40.

35. *Q.* By whom are bills signed?

*A.* By counsel. Informations and informations and bills are signed also by the Attorney or Solicitor-General. Ibid., 57.

36. *Q.* In what cases and upon what terms may a written copy

of a bill in Chancery be filed and served, instead of a printed copy (15 & 16 Vic., c. 86)?

*A.* A written bill may be filed if it prays a writ of injunction, or a writ of *ne exeat regno,* or if filed for the purpose of making an infant a ward of court. An undertaking of the plaintiff or his solicitor to file a printed bill within fourteen days must be given. 15 & 16 Vic., c. 86, s. 6.

37. *Q.* Can a suit be maintained by a plaintiff residing out of the jurisdiction of the court?

*A.* A party may sue although he be residing out of the jurisdiction, but he will have to give security for costs. Ayck. C. Pr., 407.

38. *Q.* Within what period after the filing of a bill must it be served on a defendant within the jurisdiction, and what is sufficient service?

*A.* It must be served within twelve weeks from its being sealed. A copy of the bill should be delivered to the defendant personally, or left at his dwelling-house with one of his family or a servant, unless the court direct some other mode of service. Consol. Ord., x. r. 1.

39. *Q.* In what cases may the bill be served upon the solicitor of the party?

*A.* Substituted service of the bill will be ordered where it is difficult to serve the defendant. As where he is secreting himself or is out of the jurisdiction. It must clearly appear that the party on whom it is proposed to effect service is the solicitor of defendant. 15 & 16 Vic., c. 86, s. 5.

40. *Q.* What is the practice with respect to the mode of serving a bill and citation in any part of the United Kingdom or abroad?

*A.* As to service within the jurisdiction see *supra.* The court may order service out of the jurisdiction on it appearing in what country the defendant is. Consol. Ord., x. r. 7, art. 1. The service is effected in a similar manner to service within the jurisdiction. *Supra,* No. 38. The order usually directs certain limits within which service may be effected, as anywhere in Scotland. *Blenkinsopp* v. *Blenkinsopp,* 8 Beav., 612.

41. *Q.* Suppose A and B both file bills to have the estate of C administered by the Court of Chancery; which is entitled to priority, and how and upon what terms is A or B entitled to stay proceedings in the other suit?

*A.* As a general rule, the suit first instituted will be entitled to priority; but the second suit will not be stayed if it seeks anything more than can be obtained in the former. The proceedings would be stayed on the terms of the costs up to notice of decree being allowed to the party whose suit is stayed. The proceedings will not be stayed until a decree has been obtained in the most beneficial suit. Ayck. C. Pr., 320.

42. *Q.* Has the Court of Chancery any jurisdiction in any, and what form of proceeding to declare its opinion upon any, and what, questions, without proceeding to administer any relief consequent upon such declaration?

*A.* The court may upon a special case being stated, as mentioned above, No. 6, declare its opinion upon the construction of any will, deed, Act of Parliament, or other instrument in writing, or as to the title or evidence of title to any real or personal estate, contracted to be sold or otherwise dealt with, and generally upon any question of law coming within the jurisdiction of the court, without proceeding to administer consequent relief. 13 & 14 Vic., c. 35.

43. *Q.* In cases of doubtful construction of deeds or instruments referring to matters falling within the jurisdiction of equity, is there any mode of obtaining the opinion of the court judicially by persons interested without filing a bill?

*A.* The parties may by consent submit the question for the decision of the court in the form of a special case by virtue of 13 & 14 Vic., c. 35.

44. *Q.* When lunatics, married women, or infants, are concerned, how are their respective interests to be represented so as to show their concurrence in the necessary application to the court?

*A.* Lunatics, if found so by inquisition, are represented by their committee, if not so found the court will appoint a guardian. Married women concur with their husbands where the interests of the wife are not distinct from those of her husband. If they are distinct, the wife concurs in her own right, provided the husband also concurs in the case. Infants concur by guardian. 13 & 14 Vic., c. 35, ss. 3—6.

45. *Q.* How are executors, administrators, or trustees, protected and indemnified in respect of matters comprised in a special case, and on the declaration of the court to be made thereon, are the rights of others not comprised in such declaration affected thereby?

*A.* They are protected in the same manner as if there had been a decree in an ordinary suit, provided they act in conformity with the declaration of the court. The rights of others are not affected. 13 & 14 Vic., c. 35, s. 15.

46. *Q.* Can a special case be registered? Where? And under what title?

*A.* After the filing of a case and the entering of an appearance thereto, it may be registered in the Court of Common Pleas, as a *lis pendens*, in the names of the plaintiffs and defendants. 13 & 14 Vic., c. 35, s. 17.

47. *Q.* What are the several kinds of bills?

*A.* Bills are divided into three classes:—1. Original bills. 2. Bills not original. 3. Bills in the nature of original bills. Original bills are such as commence litigation in the court, and are subdivided into:—1. Bills for relief. 2. Bills not praying relief. Bills for relief are those praying for a decree as to some right claimed by the plaintiff in opposition to a right claimed by the defendant. 3. Bills of interpleader. 4. Certiorari bills. Those not praying relief are: —1. Bills to perpetuate testimony. 2. Bills of discovery.

Bills not original are:—1. Bills of supplement. 2. Revivor. 3. Revivor and supplement.

Bills in the nature of original bills are:—1. Cross bills. 2. Bills of review and to set aside a decree on the ground of fraud. Mitf. Pl., c. 1, s. 3.

48. *Q.* What is the nature and effect of a bill of foreclosure, and within what time must it be brought?

*A.* It is an original bill filed by a mortgagee for the purpose of obtaining absolute possession of the mortgaged estate, and foreclosing the equity of redemption. The court will decree an account to be taken of the amount due and will name a time at the end of which, if the money be not paid, the mortgage will be foreclosed. It cannot be filed after the expiration of twenty years from the last payment of principal or interest. 7 Wm. IV., & 1 Vic., c. 28; *infra* 402 "Miscellaneous," No. 4.

49. *Q.* What is the nature and effect of a bill of interpleader? and what must the plaintiff show by his bill to enable him to maintain it?

*A.* It is in the nature of an original bill, and is filed where two or more persons claim the same right in separate interests; and the plaintiff, ignorant as to the rightful claimant and to protect himself, files a bill stating the facts and praying that the defendants may interplead, and that the court may decide to whom the thing belongs, and that he may be indemnified. The bill must show that each of the defendants claims a right, and must contain an offer to bring the money into court. Mitf. Pl., 58.

50. *Q.* What affidavit must a plaintiff make on filing a bill of interpleader?

*A.* He must file an affidavit stating that there is no collusion between himself and any of the parties. The reason for this is, that the court will not permit the proceedings to be used collusively so as to give advantage to either party. Ibid., 59.

51. *Q.* Has there been any, and what, recent change in the form of affidavits in chancery? and what is the consequences if such form be not observed?

*A.* The change referred to is, that all affidavits must be expressed in the first person of the deponent, otherwise the costs of preparing and filing the affidavit will not be allowed. Consol Ord., xviii., r. 1, 2.

52. *Q.* Before whom must an affidavit be sworn by a person resident in Scotland?

*A.* It may be sworn before any judge, court, notary public, or person lawfully authorised to administer oaths in Scotland. 15 & 16 Vic., c. 86, s. 22.

53. *Q.* What is the rule with respect to facts deposed to in an affidavit when the facts are within the deponent's own knowledge of them, and when the knowledge of them is derived from information obtained from others, is it necessary to show upon the affidavit what are the deponent's means of knowing, or sources of information?

*A.* The deponent's means of knowledge must appear. Ord. 5th Feb., 1861, r. 23.

54. *Q.* What formalities should be observed in drawing affidavits?

*A.* In addition to those mentioned in the preceding answers, Nos.

51—53, the affidavit should set forth the title of the cause, the name, residence, and description of the party making it; that the deponent made oath; it must be divided into paragraphs, numbered consecutively, and each paragraph must be confined as nearly as may be to a distinct portion of the subject; it must be engrossed on foolscap paper bookways in words at length; it should be read over to the deponent and signed by him or his mark placed to it A jurat should be added at the foot on the right hand side. It is then sworn. A memorandum is written at the foot of it stating by whom it is filed. Ayck., C. Pr., 295.

55. *Q.* Mention the principal cases in which a bill must be accompanied by an affidavit; and how is the omission of such affidavit taken advantage of?

*A.* An affidavit must accompany the bill in suits for an injunction, or for a writ *ne exeat regno*, or for interpleader, or to perpetuate testimony, or for discovery where relief is also prayed consequent upon the discovery, which relief might have been obtained at law. The objection may be taken in the last three cases mentioned by demurrer. In the two former the court would not grant the application without some evidence on oath, and this objection could be taken on the motion for the writ of injunction or *ne exeat regno*. Mitf. Pl., 65; 166.

56. *Q.* What is a supplemental bill?

*A.* It is a bill filed for the purpose of supplying some defect in an original bill, the original parties and interests not being altered. If new parties with new interests are added, arising from events which have happened since the institution of the suit, the bill is termed "A bill in the nature of a supplemental bill." Story's Eq. Pl., 265. Such facts may now be added by supplemental statement, but this proceeding is seldom resorted to. 15 & 16 Vic., c. 86 s. 53. Ayck., C. Pr. 388.

57. *Q.* What is a bill of revivor? and how has it been superseded?

*A.* It is a bill to revive a suit when an abatement has taken place owing to the death, marriage, or bankruptcy of the parties. It is now virtually abolished by 15 & 16 Vic., c. 86, s. 52, substituting in such cases a simple order of revivor.

58. *Q.* State the nature and objects of a bill of review? Is leave of the court necessary before filing it?

*A.* It is in the nature of an original bill, and is filed for the purpose of obtaining the reversal of a decree which has been signed and enrolled. It lies for error in law apparent on the face of the decree or in respect of new matter which could not have been adduced at the original hearing, and in the latter case leave must be obtained to file the bill. Mitf. Pl., 101.

59. *Q.* What is a cross-bill, and for what purpose is it adopted?

*A.* It is a bill filed by a defendant against a plaintiff or other defendant in the suit, either to obtain a discovery in aid of his defence, or to obtain relief touching the matters in the original bill, which relief he could not otherwise obtain. Mitf. Pl., 97. A cross-bill for discovery alone is now rendered unnecessary, the defendant being allowed to file interrogatories. 15 & 16 Vic., c. 86, s. 19.

60. *Q.* What is the effect of a plaintiff amending the original bill before answering a cross-bill?

*A.* By so doing he loses the right he possessed of insisting upon an answer to the original bill before answering the cross-bill. In such a case the plaintiff in the cross-bill should obtain an order that the proceedings in the original bill be stayed until the plaintiff shall have fully answered the cross-bill. Ayck., C. Pr., 254.

61. *Q.* What is the practice with respect to reading the answer to a cross-bill for discovery?

*A.* The answer may be read and used by the party filing the cross-bill in the same manner, and under the same restrictions, as the answer to a bill praying relief may be read and used. 19 Consol. Ord., r. 6, *infra*, "Evidence."

62. *Q.* How and at what stage of a suit may a defendant obtain discovery from a plaintiff without filing a cross-bill? (15 & 16 Vic., c. 86)?

*A.* The defendant may by filing interrogatories for the examination of the plaintiff obtain discovery. They cannot be filed before a sufficient answer has been put in, in cases where an answer is required. It is optional to the defendant to adopt this course or file a cross-bill. 15 & 16 Vic., c. 86, s. 19.

63. *Q.* When is a bill taken *pro confesso?* What is the consequence of a bill being so taken?

*A.* A bill may be taken *pro confesso* in two cases. 1. Where defendant absconds to avoid answering. 2. Where he is taken on process of contempt for want of answer. The effect of the bill being so taken is, that all the statements in it are taken as confessed by the defendant. Ayck., C. Pr., 63.

64. *Q.* How is a bill taken *pro confesso?*

*A.* 1. Where defendant absconds to avoid answer, an attachment must first be issued and returned *non est inventus*. If defendant has appeared in person, or by his solicitor, the plaintiff may serve a notice on the defendant or his solicitor that he intends on a certain day (not less than fourteen days after the notice) to move the court for an order to take the bill *pro confesso*. If the court is satisfied that the defendant has absconded to avoid answering, and no answer has been put in, the order will be made. If an appearance has been entered for the defendant, instead of by him, the notice must be advertised in the "London Gazette," the time of motion being not less than four weeks from the first insertion. The notice must be repeated every week until the motion. The motion is made in court by counsel. After the order is made, the cause must be set down as mentioned in the next answer. 2. When defendant is taken on process of contempt, the modern practice is to serve a notice of motion within three weeks after arrest, the motion to be not less than three weeks after the service. This course is much more simple than the old procedure under 1 Wm. IV., c. 36. An affidavit of service of the notice of motion must be filed, and the attachment and return produced with a certificate of the record and writ clerks that no answer is filed. Upon this, the order will be made and must be served. Ayck., C. Pr., 63.

65. *Q.* Where a defendant is not in custody, can a bill be taken *pro confesso* on motion, without setting down the cause?

*A.* No, it cannot be so taken. After the order is obtained to take the bill *pro confesso*, the cause must be set down to be heard on a subsequent day. Consol. Ord., xvii., r. 6.

66. *Q.* How does the practice differ when the defendant is in custody?

*A.* There is now no distinction in this case. *Brown* v. *Home*, 16 L. J. Ch., 177.

67. *Q.* Exceptions being filed to an answer of a defendant, against whom process of contempt had issued, what may a plaintiff do on the exceptions being submitted to, and the answer ordered insufficient, with a view to get the bill taken *pro confesso?*

*A.* He may, as soon as the exceptions are submitted to, take up the process of contempt at the stage at which it was stopped by the defendant putting in his answer and obtaining the common order to clear his contempt. Consol. Ord., xii., r. 7. *Taylor* v. *Salmon*, 3 M. & Cr., 109.

68. *Q.* If a defendant be in prison under an attachment for not answering, is it incumbent on the plaintiff to take any, and if any, what step? If he do not take such step, what is the consequence?

*A.* The plaintiff should proceed to take the bill *pro confesso*, as above mentioned, No. 61. If this step is not taken within fourteen days after the arrest, the defendant will be entitled to be discharged. 1 Wm. IV., c. 36, s. 15, r. 13. See also 23 & 24 Vic., c. 149.

69. *Q.* If a defendant have absconded, or refused to obey the process of the court, and an appearance have been entered for him, and he do not afterward appear in person or by solicitor, what course should the plaintiff pursue to get on with his suit?

*A.* See *supra*, No. 63.

70. *Q.* Describe a traversing note and the effect of it; and state how issue is joined. Can a defendant, after such note has been filed, put in an answer as of course? or, if desirous to answer, what steps must he take?

*A.* It is a note filed by a plaintiff in cases where the defendant, being required to answer, has not done so. It has the effect of traversing the case made by the bill. Issue is joined upon it by the plaintiff filing a replication. After the note has been filed, an answer cannot be put in without leave of the court. To obtain leave the defendant should move on notice to take the traversing note off the file, and for liberty to answer. *Towne* v. *Bonnin*, 1 De G. & Sm., 128; Consol. Ord. xiii.

71. *Q.* What is the difference in effect between taking a bill *pro confesso* and filing a traversing note? and to what proceedings at law may they be compared respectively?

*A.* Upon a bill being taken *pro confesso* the statements contained in it are admitted to be true, but a traversing note has the effect of denying them. The taking a bill *pro confesso* may be compared to signing judgment by default of plea, the cause of action, as stated in the declaration, being confessed by the defendant's not pleading. The filing of a traversing note, on the other hand, has the effect of traversing the bill, and, therefore, in its effect it is similar to the defendant having pleaded the general issue, or some plea traversing the declaration. The comparison here alluded to is the respective *effect* of the two proceedings. Taken in any other sense, the latter part of the question would be meaningless.

72. *Q.* State the course to be adopted under the recent act in cases where a suit becomes abated by death or marriage of parties, or defective by reason of any change or transmission of interest or liability.

*A.* An order to revive the suit may be obtained as of course, on motion upon allegation of the abatement, or transmission of interest. When drawn up, the order is served, and has the same operation as the former proceeding by bill of revivor. 15 & 16 Vic., c. 86, s. 52.

73. *Q.* Does the marriage of a female plaintiff abate a suit?

*A.* Upon the marriage of a female plaintiff the suit abates. Ayck. C. Pr., 383.

74. *Q.* Does the marriage of a female defendant abate a suit?

*A.* No; revival, therefore, is not necessary, but the husband should be named in the subsequent proceedings. Ibid.

75. *Q.* Does a suit abate upon the death of a person having joint interests with co-plaintiffs or co-defendants?

*A.* If the whole interest of the party dying survives to the other parties, so that no claim can be made, by or against the representatives of the party dying, the suit will not abate. Thus, if the suit is by joint tenants, and one die. Mitf. Pl., 70.

76. *Q.* If a bill be filed by a man and his wife touching the personal property of the wife, and the husband die pending the suit, does or does not that circumstance cause an abatement of the suit?

*A.* If the widow do not proceed with the suit it is considered as abated, but if she chooses she may proceed in the cause without revivor, as she has the whole interest, the husband being a party in her right. Mitf. Pl., 71.

77. *Q.* Where husband and wife are defendants to a suit, how does the death of the husband affect the suit?

*A.* The suit does not abate, but if the wife were to die it would be otherwise. Mitf. Pl., 71.

78. *Q.* If a sole plaintiff become a bankrupt, what proceeding is it necessary a defendant should take to free himself from the suit, if the assignees neglect to proceed?

*A.* The defendant should apply to the court, on notice, that the assignees may make themselves parties within a given time, or in default that the bill be dismissed. Ayck., C. Pr., 311.

79. *Q.* In a suit for the administration of an estate, one of two

executors (defendants) dies pending the suit: is the suit thereby abated? and is it necessary to bring the representative of the deceased executor before the court, and for what purpose?

*A.* The suit, as a general rule, will not abate, as the interest survives to the co-executor. It would, however, be otherwise, if the deceased executor had possessed himself of any of the property in question, or done any act which may be questioned in the suit. In such case the representatives would have to be made defendants. Mitf. Pl., 70.

80. *Q.* Will a suit by a corporate body abate by the death of some of the members of the corporation, who are in that character parties to the suit by name? and will there be a defect of parties if others who become members after the commencement of the suit be not joined?

*A.* If the suit is by a corporation aggregate suing in their corporate capacity only, the suit will not abate, even though the members of the corporation are parties to the suit by name. It is otherwise if the members named have an individual interest in the suit, and subsequent members having a like interest must be joined. *Blackburn* v. *Jepson*, 3 Swanst., 138. If the bill is by a corporation sole, having a personal interest, the suit will also abate. Mitf. Pl., 72, n. d.

## VIII.—*Appearance.*

1. *Q.* Why was the writ of *subpœna* to appear and answer in chancery at variance with the first principles of the common law? In whose reign was it invented, and when was the writ abolished?

*A.* The reason was, that it compelled the defendant to answer questions; whereas, at common law, the parties were never allowed to be examined. It also had a tendency to subvert the jurisdiction of the common law courts. The suit is supposed to have been invented, or rather adopted by John Waltham, Bishop of Salisbury, who was Keeper of the Rolls about the 5th of Richard II. 3 Reeves, 192. The writ was abolished 1st November, 1852. Consol. Ord., xxviii., r. 10 ; 15 & 16 Vic., c. 86.

2. *Q.* Can a plaintiff under any, and what, circumstances, make a motion in a suit before the defendant has appeared?

*A.* The plaintiff may apply *ex parte* for a writ of injunction, or *ne exeat regno*, before appearance, or even before the bill is served. The application will only be granted where injury is likely to arise from delay. See *supra*, 288.

3. *Q.* By what means is a defendant called upon to meet the plaintiff's demand?

*A.* By being served with a bill, endorsed with a notice, calling upon him to appear and observe what the court directs. A note is also added that, on non-compliance, the defendant will be liable to be arrested and imprisoned. Haynes' Outlines, 69. *Supra*, 344, No. 10.

4. *Q.* If the defendant be a peer, having privilege of parliament, or be a member of the House of Commons, what is the mode of citation?

*A.* If the defendant is a peer, a letter missive must be obtained, on petition to the Lord Chancellor, who will grant the letter without order. The letter, a copy of the petition, and a copy of the bill, without indorsement, is then served on the defendant, or left at his house. A member of the House of Commons is proceeded against as in ordinary cases. Mitf. Pl., 40.

5. *Q.* How may a member of Parliament be compelled to appear?

*A.* After service of the bill in the usual way, an appearance may be entered for him; or the plaintiff may proceed by sequestration under the old practice. Sm. Ch. Pr., 382, 7th ed.

6. *Q.* Under Consolidated Order x., rule 11, in what cases may a defendant be bound upon the service of a copy of the bill by all the proceedings in the cause?

*A.* A defendant may be bound by the proceedings where no account, payment, conveyance, or direct relief is sought against him. But the order does not prevent the plaintiff prosecuting the suit against the defendant in the ordinary way if he chooses.

7. *Q.* Can a defendant so served be admitted to defend the suit in the ordinary mode, or by what other form of proceeding? and what is the rule regarding his costs?

*A.* The defendant, if he desires it, may have the suit prosecuted against him in the ordinary way, and enter a common appearance. Or he may enter a special appearance, and be served with notice of all the proceedings. The time for appearance is within twelve days after service of the bill. If he take either of these courses he will have to pay the costs caused thereby, unless the court order to the contrary. Consol. Ord. x., rr. 11—16.

8. *Q.* In cases where the practice renders it necessary for the plaintiff to serve the defendant with a copy of the bill, and the service is not effected within due time, what step should the plaintiff take to cure the omission?

*A.* He should apply on motion to the court for leave to serve the bill, notwithstanding the time for service has expired. Consol. Ord. x., r. 18.

9. *Q.* What time is allowed to a defendant to appear after he has been served with a copy of the bill and citation?

*A.* He must appear within eight days upon service of a copy of the bill. A common or special appearance may be entered by a formal party within twelve days of service. Consol. Ord. x., r. 2.

10. *Q.* If a defendant refuse or neglect to enter an appearance, how and when are you to proceed? and how is he to be served with any notice of motion or petition in the cause?

*A.* The plaintiff may enter an appearance for the defendant, as of course, within the jurisdiction, not being an infant or person of unsound mind. The time for taking this step is after eight days and within three weeks from service. After this period, a special order must be obtained. An affidavit of service must be produced to the record and writ clerk. So also if a defendant absconds, the court may order an appearance to be entered for him on it appearing that the defendant has been within the jurisdiction at some time, not more than two years, before the bill was filed, and that he is beyond seas, and cannot be met with. A copy of the order with a notice to appear must be inserted in the "London Gazette." Consol. Ord., x., rr. 4, 5. Notices of motion or petitions must be served as the court directs.

11. *Q.* How is an appearance to a bill enforced?

*A.* An appearance may be enforced by attachment, the bill being first served with the proper indorsement. The attachment is obtained on special application to the court by motion. When obtained, the writ is handed to the sheriff, who executes it. Consol. Ord., x., r. 10. Ayck., C. Pr., 52.

12. *Q.* How can you enforce an appearance by an infant or married woman or a person of weak or unsound mind, not so found by inquisition?

*A.* Process of contempt cannot be issued against infant defendants, or those of unsound mind; but if it is made to appear to the court that the defendant is an infant or person of unsound mind, the court will order one of the solicitors of the court to be assigned as a guardian of such defendant to appear for him. A copy of the bill must be previously served, and notice of the application served six days before, upon or at the dwelling-house of the person with whom the infant or person of unsound mind is residing. With regard to the married woman an attachment may be issued against the husband, unless he obtains an order that the wife may appear and answer separately. If such an order is obtained, an attachment may issue against her. Morgan's Orders, 415. Consol. Ord., vii., r. 3.

13. *Q.* Has a plaintiff any means of enforcing the appearance of a defendant who resides abroad; and in what cases, and how far, is such appearance conclusive in case of the return of such person to England?

*A.* The bill may be served, as mentioned *supra*, 346, No. 27, and an appearance entered for the defendant. If the defendant returns, no attachment can issue against him for non-appearance. The defendant may afterwards enter an appearance, but such appearance is not to affect proceedings already duly taken or rights acquired by the plaintiff, or prejudice the plaintiff's right to be allowed the costs of the first appearance. Consol. Ord., x., r. 9.

14. *Q.* What is the mode of proceeding against a corporation failing to enter an appearance?

*A.* An appearance should be entered by the plaintiff. Ayck., C. Pr., 601.

15. *Q.* How do infants defend?

*A.* They may appear in person, but they cannot plead, answer, or demur, excepting by guardian *ad litem*. The order is obtained on motion or petition, of course, presented at the Rolls, supported by an affidavit. Ayck., C. Pr., 569.

## IX.—*The Defence.*

1. *Q.* What are the several modes by which a defence may be made to a suit in equity? and explain the nature of each.

*A.* They are : — 1. Answer. 2. Demurrer. 3. Plea. 4. Disclaimer. As to their nature, see *infra*.

2. *Q.* How long has a defendant to a bill to plead, answer, and demur, respectively; and would you calculate from the same and what periods?

*A.* The defendant must plead, answer or demur, within twenty-eight days after service of interrogatories If no interrogatories are served, the time is limited to fourteen days from the expiration of the time within which they might have been served. A demurrer alone must be filed within twelve days from appearance. Times of Equity, 1.

### § 1. *Answer.*

1. *Q.* If an answer be required from a defendant, by what proceeding, and to be taken within what period, is such answer to be obtained?

*A.* Interrogatories for the examination of the defendant must be filed and delivered within eight days after the time limited for appearance. Times of Equity, 3.

2. *Q.* What time is given to a defendant to answer the interrogatories to a bill? and if more time be required, what proceeding is necessary to obtain it; and upon what condition is it usually allowed? and how often can it be done?

*A.* He must answer within twenty-eight days from service of the interrogatories. If further time is required, an application should be made at chambers by summons. If the defendant can show that he is unable to prepare his answer in due time an order may be obtained, also further orders if necessary. Under the old practice a third order for time was made upon certain conditions, which it is unnecessary now to mention. The only condition now is, that after the first order the defendant often has to pay the costs of the application. The application is seldom successful oftener than twice or three times. Consol. Ord., xxxvii., r. 8. Sm. Ch. Pr., 424.

3. *Q.* If the plaintiff should amend his bill, what time has the defendant to put in his answer to such amended bill?

*A.* He must answer within twenty-eight days from the service of the interrogatories to the amended bill. Times of Equity, 1.

4. *Q.* What is the last day which the defendant has for putting in an answer to the amendments of a bill, before a replication can be filed, where the plaintiff has amended on terms of not requiring a further answer?

*A.* The time for putting in a voluntary answer to an amended bill is within fourteen days from the expiration of the time within which interrogatories might have been served to such amended bill. Ibid., 1 ; Consol. Ord., xxxvii., r. 7.

5. *Q.* An answer serves two distinct purposes ; what are they?

*A.* Firstly, the answer is a pleading in that it sets forth the case upon which the defendant relies. Secondly, it furnishes the discovery sought by the plaintiff in aid of his suit. Mitf. Pl., 51. The Articled Clerk's Manual, by Anderson, 178.

6. *Q.* What is the practice as to a defendant answering interrogatories?

*A.* The defendant must answer fully those statements in the bill to which he is interrogated. A defendant should not answer any statement to which he is not interrogated by stating his ignorance of the matter, but he may answer to such statements any matter tending to strengthen his case. He may also insert in his answer such statements material to his case as he may think advisable. The answer must not be evasive, and the substance of each charge must be confessed or traversed. The answer must not be impertinent; as, by inserting immaterial or scandalous matter. It must be divided into paragraphs, numbered consecutively, each containing a separate and distinct statement. No interrogatory need be answered to which defendant might have protected himself by demurrer. Mitf. Pl., 365. Consol. Ord., xv.

7. *Q.* In answering a bill, can a defendant introduce into his answer any other matter than that inquired of by the interrogatories? State the authority for your answer.

*A.* Yes, he may, under 15 & 16 Vic., c. 86, s. 14. See previous answer.

8. *Q.* Where a defendant is not required to answer interrogatories, what is considered to be the effect of putting in a voluntary answer?

*A.* He is deemed to have traversed the bill, and issue may be joined by filing a replication. Consol. Ord., xvii., r. 1; 15 & 16 Vic., c. 86, s. 26.

9. *Q.* When a husband and wife are defendants in a suit, in what cases is the wife entitled to an order to answer separately?

*A.* She is entitled to an order to answer separately if she claims in opposition to any claims of her husband, or if she lives separate from him, or disapproves the defence he wishes her to make. Mitf. Pl., 125.

10. *Q.* In what cases can a married woman be compelled to appear and defend a suit separately from her husband?

*A.* In cases where she obstinately refuses to join in defence with her husband, an order may be obtained to proceed against her alone. Ibid., 126.

11. *Q.* What is the course to be pursued to obtain the answer of an infant-defendant? and what notice is necessary to be given?

*A.* The procedure is similar to that above-mentioned with regard to appearance. *Supra*, "Appearance," No. 12.

12. *Q.* What is the mode of putting in an answer; and may the oath or signature be dispensed with, and how?

*A.* An answer is put in upon oath of the defendant. It is in writing upon paper, then filed and afterwards printed. It is signed by counsel. The oath may be dispensed with if the plaintiff consent, and an order must be obtained in motion or petition of course. This is occasionally done in amicab  suits, and where the oath cannot be obtained without expens  and delay. Wharton's Law Lexicon, "Answer."

13. *Q.* Within what time after the filing of his answer must a defendant leave a printed copy of such answer with the clerks of the records, and to what liabilities is a defendant subject if he fails to do so?

*A.* The printed copy must be left before the expiration of four days from the filing of the answer with the solicitor's certificate that the print is a true copy. If this is not done the defendant will be liable to be proceeded against for want of answer by attachment as mentioned, *infra*. Ord. March 6, 1860, r. 3.

14. *Q.* What is a commission to take pleas, answers, disclaimers or examinations; and in what cases is it necessary?

*A.* It is a commission issued to certain commissioners authorising them to take the answer of a defendant. It is now never resorted to, having been entirely abolished as to defendants within the jurisdiction, and superseded as to other places by provisions as to the swearing of answers before persons resident out of the country. 15 & 16 Vic., c. 86, ss. 21, 22; 18 & 19 Vic., c. 42.

15. *Q.* What are the proper steps to compel an answer?

*A.* The plaintiff should proceed against the defendant by attachment, as mentioned above with regard to default of appearance, 357, No. 11. Also upon a return of *non est inventus* to an attachment, an order may be obtained on motion, as of course for the Serjeant-at-Arms, who will, upon receiving the order, obtain the warrant and execute it. If *non est inventus* is returned to this writ or to the attachment, a sequestration may be obtained directed to commissioners to enter upon defendant's real estates, and sequester the rents and goods and chattels. Ayck. C. Pr., 51.

16. *Q.* What is the process to compel the answer of a peer or peeress?

*A.* An order for sequestration must be obtained on motion, as of course supported by affidavit of delivery of the interrogatories, with a certificate of no answer being filed. A copy of the order is then personally served on the defendant. If no cause is shown within seven days after service of the order, the plaintiff may on motion as of course make the sequestration absolute. Upon this order the sequestration may issue. Ibid., 61.

17. *Q.* What is the process to compel a corporation to answer a bill?

*A.* The proceeding is by writ of distringas. The writ issues without order. Ibid., 601.

18. *Q.* When will an answer be deemed sufficient?

*A.* It will be deemed sufficient, if not excepted to within six weeks, or if the exceptions are not set down after eight days and within fourteen days, or where within fourteen days after filing a further answer plaintiff does not set down the old exceptions; also, if plaintiff obtains and serves an order to amend his bill, files a replication, sets down the cause on bill and answer, or gives notice of motion for decree. Times of Equity, 1.

19. *Q.* When is a voluntary answer deemed sufficient?

*A.* It is deemed sufficient as soon as filed. Ibid.

20. *Q.* What is the difference between an evasive and an insufficient answer; and how are they respectively treated?

*A.* An answer is said to be evasive when it avoids the interrogatory, as where a defendant answers conjunctively that he is unable to answer several things; his answer is evasive unless he adds that he cannot answer any of them. *Tipping* v. *Clarke,* 2 Hare, 390. Such an answer may be taken off the file. An answer is insufficient when it omits to answer the interrogatories, or the answer is not precise or full to the interrogatory. Exceptions should be filed to an insufficient answer to compel a further answer. Mitf. Pl., 366; Ayck. C. Pr., 118.

21. *Q.* Within what time must a plaintiff except to an answer for insufficiency?

*A.* He must except within six weeks after the filing of the answer. Times of Equity, 3.

22. *Q.* If the plaintiff do not pursue that remedy, what is the consequence?

*A.* The answer will be deemed sufficient and he will be precluded from objecting to its insufficiency.

23. *Q.* Exceptions being taken to an answer for insufficiency, what time has the defendant to determine whether he will submit to them, before the same can be set down?

*A.* He has eight days to submit after they are filed. Times of Equity, 1.

24. *Q.* When can a plaintiff, who has excepted to a defendant's answer for insufficiency, set down such exceptions?

*A.* He may set them down at the expiration of eight days from filing, unless in a case of election he shall be required by notice to set them down in four days. Consol. Ord., xvi., r. 11.

25. *Q.* May the plaintiff except to an answer for any other cause than insufficiency, and for what?

*A.* Yes, he may except to it for containing scandalous matter. Mitf. Pl., 373. Formerly also for impertinence, but exceptions on this ground are now abolished, the party introducing such matter being now saddled with the costs occasioned by it. 15 & 16 Vic., c. 86, s. 17.

26. *Q.* When a defendant is required to put in a further answer, in consequence of exceptions to his first answer having been allowed or submitted to, what time has he to put in such further answer?

*A.* If the exceptions are allowed after argument, or the defendant submits to them after they are set down, the defendant can only take such time to put in a further answer as the court allows him. Consol. Ord. xvi., r. 14. If, however, the plaintiff submits to the exceptions before they are set down for hearing he has fourteen days from the submission to answer. Ibid., r. 9.

27. *Q.* State the different ways in which a plaintiff tacitly waives his right to except to an answer for insufficiency?

*A.* He waives his right to except by taking any of the steps above-mentioned, No. 18, as rendering the answer sufficient.

28. *Q.* An attachment having issued against a defendant for not putting in his answer, and the defendant not having been taken, what must be done before granting an order for the serjeant-at-arms?

*A.* The sheriff must return *non est inventus* to the writ of attachment. *Supra*, No. 15.

29. *Q.* If defendant swears, on his being brought up in custody, that he is unable from poverty to put in his answer, what will the court thereupon do?

*A.* The court will, if not satisfied with the truth of the allegation, direct an inquiry as to its truth. If found to be true, the court will assign a solicitor and counsel for such defendant. Consol. Ord. xii., r. 4.

30. *Q.* What is the meaning of an answer being impertinent? and when considered to be so by the plaintiff, what course should he adopt?

*A.* An answer is said to be impertinent when it is stuffed with long recitals, or with long digression of matters of fact, which are unnecessary and immaterial, as if a long deed is stated, which is not prayed to be set forth *in hæc verba*. The plaintiff should apply to the court when the costs are disposed of, that the defendant be not allowed the costs of the impertinent matter. Sm. Ch. Pr., 878.

31. *Q.* When it is apprehended a defendant is likely to abscond without answering, what mode of proceeding is to be adopted in such a case?

*A.* The plaintiff should apply *ex parte* to the court on motion for an order for an attachment against the defendant, for want of answer, supported by an affidavit as to the fact of the defendant going to abscond, and of service of the interrogatories. Consol. Ord. xii., r. 1.

§ 2. *Demurrer.*

1. *Q.* Explain the nature and effect of a demurrer.

*A.* A demurrer is in the nature of a defence to the bill, founded upon some matter apparent upon the face of the bill. The grounds of demurrer are on account of matter contained in the bill, or defect in its frame, or in the case made by it. Its effect is to admit the statements in the bill to be true; by means of it the defendant asks the judgment of the court as to whether he ought to answer or not. Mitf. Pl., 128.

2. *Q.* In what case would you demur to a bill instead of answering?

*A.* I should demur when my ground of defence appeared upon the face of the bill, and when I conceived that such defence would effectually protect me from answering, and the bill would be dismissed. Ibid., 130.

3. *Q.* State how a demurrer differs from an answer in regard to the facts alleged in the bill.

*A.* As above mentioned, a demurrer necessarily admits the bill to be true. This admission is, however, only for the purposes of argument, as if the demurrer is overruled the court will permit an answer to be filed. An answer is taken as a denial of those facts which it does not expressly admit. Ibid., 129.

4. *Q.* An appearance being entered on the 2nd of November, what is the last day for demurring?

*A.* The defendant should file his demurrer on the 14th of November, the time allowed for demurring alone being within twelve days from appearance. If an answer is put in with the demurrer, the time is regulated by the time to answer. See *supra*, Consol. Ord. xxxvii. r. 3.

5. *Q.* Can a demurrer be set down for hearing by the plaintiff, or by the defendant, or by both? and within what time?

*A.* Either party may set it down immediately it is filed. If to the whole bill, it should be set down within twelve days of filing; if to part, within three weeks from filing, otherwise it will be deemed sufficient. Consol. Ord. xiv., rr. 11, 14, 15.

6. *Q.* What effect has the overruling of a demurrer on the future defence of the party filing it?

*A.* Its effect is, that defendant cannot demur again, except to an amended bill. He should obtain leave of the Court to answer or plead. Morgan's Orders, 423.

7. *Q.* What is the difference in effect of the allowance of a partial demurrer, and that of a general demurrer?

*A.* Frequently the court will allow the plaintiff to amend his bill, if a partial demurrer is allowed, but if it is to the whole bill there will be an end of the proceedings. In the former case, the defendant will have to pay the costs of the demurrer and amendment, in the latter, the costs of the suit also. Ayck. C. Pr., 104.

8. *Q.* What are the requisites of a demurrer, and must it be put in upon oath?

*A.* The demurrer must be engrossed on paper, signed by counsel, and filed within twelve days of appearance. Notice of filing must be served on the plaintiff. It must state the grounds of demurrer, and if to part only of a bill, it should state correctly to what part it applies. It must state no facts, if so it will be bad as a speaking demurrer. It is not put in upon oath. Mitf. Pl., 127.

## § 3. *Plea.*

1. *Q.* Explain the nature and effect of a plea.

*A.* A plea is a method of defence to a bill upon some ground forming a single point of defence, not apparent upon the face of the bill, which shows that the plaintiff is not entitled to relief. Thus, a release, or the Statute of Limitations would be subjects for a plea. The effect of it is to demand the judgment of the court as to whether the defendant, taking into consideration the matter adduced in his plea, is bound to answer. Mitf. Pl., 15.

2. *Q.* Is the objection for want of parties to a bill taken in the same manner where such objection appears on the face of the bill

itself, as where it does not so appear? If different, then state what are the proper modes of objection applicable to each of these two cases.

*A.* In the former case a demurrer, in the latter a plea, should be resorted to. See No. 1. Mitf. Pl., 190.

3. *Q.* Must a plea be put in upon oath or not?

*A.* A plea should be put in upon the oath of the defendant, unless the matter alleged in it already appears by matter of record. Thus, a plea of outlawry, or of conviction for felony, need not be upon oath. ———— v. *Davies*, 19 Ves., 81. Consol. Ord. xiv., r. 2.

4. *Q.* When must a plea be accompanied by an answer?

*A.* If fraud or notice of title is charged in the bill against the defendant, the court will not allow him to evade answering by putting in a plea, as these allegations are strong equitable grounds in favour of the plaintiff which should be answered on oath. Mitf. Pl., 350.

5. *Q.* Distinguish a plea from an answer.

*A.* A plea differs from an answer in that the former is a short statement of facts forming one point of defence only, whereas, an answer may contain several separate grounds of defence. If a plea was to contain several points of defence it would be a bad plea. An answer contains a discovery of facts upon the oath of the defendant, but a plea avoids discovery. Ibid.

6. *Q.* What is a double plea, what objection is there to it, and is a double plea ever allowed?

*A.* It is a plea which sets up two points of defence to the bill, or some particular part of it, either of which if taken alone would be a complete defence. Thus, the statute of limitations, and that defendant was a *bona fide* purchaser for value without notice of plaintiff's claim, would be double. The objection to such a plea is, that, if allowed, the court would be compelled to give judgment on various points of defence depending on numerous facts unsupported by proof; whereas, the object of a plea is to reduce the defence to a single point and save the expense of going into evidence, or to protect the defendant from discovery. A double plea will occasionally be allowed for convenience by the court on special application. Thus, to a bill filed by an heir to recover land, the statute of limitations and a plea that the plaintiff is not the heir, has been allowed. Mitf. Pl., 343.

7. *Q.* A plaintiff having replied to a plea before it was set down for argument, can he dispute its validity?

*A.* The effect of replying to the plea is to admit its validity in point of law, therefore no objection can be taken to it, but it may be disproved. Thus, in the above mentioned case (No. 4), if the defendant pleaded a purchase for value, but omitted to deny notice of the plaintiff's title, no objection could be taken to the plea if issue was joined on it. The question of notice would not be in issue. Mitf. Pl., 354.

8. *Q.* What is the course of proceeding on a plea?

*A.* The plaintiff should set the plea down to be argued on its merits. If it is not true in fact, he may take issue on it; but, by so doing, he admits its validity. As a matter of practice a plea is universally true, therefore I should advise its being set down for argument. Ibid.

### § 4. *Disclaimer.*

1. *Q.* If a defendant have no right or interest in the property or thing claimed by the plaintiff, how should the defendant proceed, and within what time should he take the necessary step?

*A.* He should file a disclaimer accompanied by a short answer showing the grounds upon which the disclaimer is founded. Occasionally, a disclaimer may be put in alone. The time for filing it in the latter case is within six weeks of appearance. If with an answer, the period is the same as an answer. Mitf. Pl., 379; Times of Equity, 2.

2. *Q.* If a person have been appointed a trustee without his consent, and have not acted, and be not desirous to act, and a bill is filed against him, what defence should he make?

*A.* He should answer and disclaim. See No. 1.

### X.—*Amendment of Bills.*

1. *Q.* Can a bill in equity be amended? and, if so, in what manner?

*A.* The bill may be amended at various stages of the suit up to and at the hearing, by the introduction of new matter rendered necessary from the nature of the defence set up. Leave to amend must be obtained by order obtained on motion, petition, or summons, or at the hearing. See *infra*, No. 5, as to the limit of the amendments.

2. *Q.* In a suit where an injunction has been obtained, is the plaintiff entitled to an order to amend his bill without prejudice to such injunction?

*A.* He is entitled to such an order; but even though it be not granted "without prejudice," it will not affect the injunction unless the record be changed by the amendment; as, where an information and bill was amended by adding a co-plaintiff, the injunction was held to be gone. *Att. Gen.* v. *Marsh*, 13 Jur., 316.

3. *Q.* When a plaintiff has sued out an attachment against a defendant for want of answer, can he amend his bill without waiver of the pending proceedings of contempt?

*A.* The attachment will be gone. If, however, the defendant is in custody, and, on being brought to the bar of the court, refuses to answer, an order to amend may be obtained on special application, without prejudice to the proceedings already taken for contempt. Ayck. C. Pr., 35. 1 Wm. IV., c. 36, r. 10.

4. *Q.* If from the answer, or otherwise, matter should arise not comprised in the plaintiff's bill, and of service to his suit, what step must he take?

*A.* The bill should be amended. See *supra et infra.*

5. *Q.* State what matters arising after filing a bill can be now introduced on the record by means of an amended bill.

*A.* Generally matters may be introduced which are material to the questions in controversy in the suit as originally framed. Thus, ordinary mistakes as to facts already wrongly stated may be amended, and additional parties and material facts may be introduced, so that the amendment does not change the character of the suit. For example, a bill for specific performance cannot be turned into a bill of interpleader. Nor can a bill for discovery alone be turned into one for relief. Ayck. C. Pr., 26.

6. *Q.* What are the restrictions imposed upon a plaintiff with regard to amending his bill?

*A.* See previous answer.

7. *Q.* Within what time, from the filing of a defendant's answer, must a plaintiff obtain an order to amend his bill?

*A.* One order of course may be obtained within four weeks of the answer being deemed sufficient, and before replication and undertaking to reply where one answer only; where there are several answers, within the same time of the last answer. After this period, a special order must be obtained. Times of Equity, 1; Consol. Ord., ix., rr. 10—13.

8. *Q.* To whom must a plaintiff apply for an order to amend?

*A.* The order, if of course, is obtained on motion of course in court, or petition of course left with the secretary of the rolls. Special orders are obtained on summons before a Judge at Chambers. Amendments at the hearing are made by the court. Ayck. C. Pr., 29.

9. *Q.* If a plaintiff obtain an order to amend his bill without prejudice to an injunction, within what time from the date of the order must he amend his bill?

*A.* He should in this and in all cases, amend his bill within fourteen days* from the date of the order, unless the order limits the time. Consol. Ord., ix., rr. 17, 24.

10. *Q.* If a defendant file an answer to the plaintiff's bill, without being required to do so, what time has the plaintiff to amend his bill "as of course?"

*A.* The time limited is within four weeks after the answer is sufficient; therefore the time in this case will be reckoned from the time the answer is put in, a voluntary answer being at once sufficient. If the amendment, however, is merely required as to clerical errors, an order of course may be obtained at any time. Consol. Ord., ix., rr. 9—13. Ayck. C. Pr., 29.

11. *Q.* What will be the consequence to the plaintiff if he neglect to amend within the time allowed?

*A.* He will be compelled to obtain a special order. See next answer. The amendment should be made within fourteen days after the date of the order. Consol. Ord., ix., r. 17.

---

* Formerly the time was within seven days.

12. *Q.* Under what circumstances can a plaintiff, desirous to amend his bill, obtain an order of course for leave to amend; and if he apply for a special order, what is the effect of the affidavit he must make?

*A.* An order of course may be obtained before answer, or for clerical errors, at any time. After answer, see *supra*, Nos. 7, 10. In order to obtain leave to amend a second time after answer (except as to clerical errors), the affidavit must state:—1. That the draft of the proposed amendment has been settled, signed, and approved by counsel. 2. That the amendments are not for the purposes of delay or vexation, but because they are material to the plaintiff's case. A further affidavit showing that the matter of the proposed amendments is material, and could not, with reasonable diligence, have been sooner introduced is required after the plaintiff has filed or undertaken to file a replication, or after the expiration of the four weeks from the answer being sufficient. Consol. Ord., ix., rr. 14, 15.

13. *Q.* If a plaintiff change his residence after the filing of the bill and then amend, what is his duty with respect to such change, and what is the consequence of neglecting it?

*A.* He should describe himself as of his new residence, otherwise he may be compelled to give security for costs. Daniel's Pr., 250.

14. *Q.* State in short detail the steps to be taken for the first amendment of a plaintiff's bill in chancery after answer?

*A.* If the order is obtained on motion, instruct counsel with a hand brief to move for an order as of course to amend. Supply him with the dates of the proceedings, and state if a further answer is required. Hand the brief to counsel, who will get the registrar to mark it, after which an order is drawn up. If by petition, engross a form from a precedent and leave it at the office of the secretary of the rolls, who will draw up the order. Ayck. C. Pr., 30.

15. *Q.* In what cases are the vacations not reckoned in the computation of times of procedure?

*A.* Vacations are excluded in amending or obtaining orders to amend, Consol. Ord., xxxvii., r. 13. In filing or setting down exceptions for scandal or insufficiency, where in the former case the time is not limited by notice under Ord. xlii., r. 6. In setting down pleas and demurrers. In filing replications or setting down causes under Consol. Ord., xxxiii., r. 12, where a defendant puts in an answer to amendments to which the plaintiff has not required an answer. As to drawing up decrees. Manual of Times, 37.

XI.—*Equitable Bail in aid of the concurrent Jurisdiction of Equity.*

1. *Q.* Where a debtor or an accounting party is about to quit the country, will a court of equity interfere to prevent him; what is the proceeding to be taken; and what is the writ called?

*A.* If the debt is one recoverable in equity, or in case an account is required, the court will prevent the defendant leaving the kingdom by process called a writ *ne exeat regno*. A bill must be filed—

which may be a written one—and the writ prayed for by it. The writ is obtained on *ex parte* motion to the court, supported by an affidavit verifying the allegations in the bill. If the case is clearly made out, an order will be made, upon which the writ will issue, and is delivered to the sheriff to make the arrest. Ayck. C. Pr., 269.

### XII.—*Nemo debet bis vexari pro eâdem causâ.*

1. *Q.* A plaintiff proceeds both at law and in equity. What proceedings can be adopted to protect the defendant, and when?

*A.* The defendant should allege in his answer that the plaintiff is prosecuting him also at law for the same matter. If this answer is not excepted to by the plaintiff, or set down on former exceptions, defendant may, after the expiration of eight days from filing the answer, obtain as of course on motion or petition an order for plaintiff to elect where he will proceed. This order cannot be obtained by a mortgagor, unless indeed the mortgagee has so dealt with the property as to render it impossible for him to restore it on full payment. *Palmer* v. *Hendrie*, 27 Beav., 349; Consol. Ord., xlii., r. 5.

### XIII.—*Receivers.*

1. *Q.* What are some of the ordinary cases in which a receiver is appointed *pendente lite?* and state any special cases?

*A.* Receivers are frequently appointed *pendente lite* in disputes between partners, also in an administration suit, and in cases where there are disputes as to property, the produce of which the court considers should not be received by any of the parties. Thus, a receiver will be appointed in a suit for partition. Receivers will also be appointed to protect the property of infants and lunatics, even though there is no cause pending. Ayck. C. Pr., 626.

2. *Q.* What are the duties of a receiver?

*A.* It is his duty to take the necessary steps to protect and collect the property intrusted to his care. He should collect the rents, and for this purpose he may distrain within the year, afterwards an order is necessary. He must under the authority of the court take and defend any necessary proceedings. He should let the estate to tenants and make allowance for repairs. He should also deliver his accounts into the Chambers of the Judge, and pay in the balance to the accountant-general. Sm. Ch. Pr., 1025.

3. *Q.* Give instances of persons who, in a suit in equity, praying for a receiver, are disqualified from being appointed such receiver.

*A.* Parties to the suit cannot act as receivers unless by special leave, and then without salary. A solicitor in the cause cannot, nor the solicitor under a commission of lunacy, nor the next friend of an infant plaintiff, nor a trustee, at least not with a salary, nor generally a peer. Morgan's Orders, 481.

4. *Q.* What course does the court usually take to protect property pending litigation, either in the case of rents, or in the case of money in the defendant's hands?

*A.* The court will appoint a receiver, see *supra et infra.* Also it will frequently direct money in the defendant's hands to be paid into court to await the result of the suit.

5. *Q.* In the case of a receiver being appointed of a real estate, to what amount is he required to give sureties for the due performance of his duty?

*A.* He will be required to give his own security together with two sureties for double the amount of the annual income. Seton on Decrees, 533.

6. *Q.* Is a receiver liable under any, and what, circumstances for moneys belonging to the estate deposited by him with a banker who afterwards fails?

*A.* The receiver being in the position of a trustee will be liable for the loss of moneys deposited in the name of another, or to his own credit at the bank, if the banker fails. He is not liable if he keeps a separate account for the estate, or transmit money in the ordinary course of business. Morgan's Orders, 483.

7. *Q.* After such receiver has received the rents, and paid all out-goings, what is his duty with respect to the balance in his hands?

*A.* He should pay the balances appearing to be due upon the accounts or such parts thereof as the chief clerk certifies into court. If this is not done, he will be disallowed his salary and charged with interest at £5 per cent. per annum on the balance. Consol. Ord., xxiv. r. 2.

8. *Q.* If previously to a decree a receiver is appointed, and the decree does not in any way notice the appointment, does the omission affect the continuance of the receiver?

*A.* If the decree do not notice the receiver, he will be superseded by it. Seton on Decrees, 1003, 3rd ed.

9. *Q.* On an original application for the appointment of a receiver, to whom should the application be made? and is there or not any difference in the practice where it is sought to supply a vacancy in the office?

*A.* If the appointment is made for the first time it ought to be made in court, unless by consent. When the application is to supply a vacancy, the application should be at Chambers. Seton on Decrees, 532. *Blackborough v. Ravenhill,* 16 Jur., 1085.

## XIV.—*Replication.*

1. *Q.* What is a replication? Can it be dispensed with when an adverse decree is sought by evidence to contradict the defence; and, if so, what is the plaintiff's course to obtain a decree?

*A.* It is a proceeding taken by a plaintiff for the purpose of joining issue upon the defendant's case as put forward by his answer or plea. It may be dispensed with by giving notice of motion for decree, the effect of which is, as in the case of issue joined, to put the parties to strict proof of their respective cases. Mitf. Pl., 382; 15 & 16 Vic., c. 86, s. 15. *Infra,* "Motion for decree," 383, No. 4.

2. *Q.* What must be done, on the part of a plaintiff, to put a cause at issue against defendants?

*A.* He should file a replication engrossed on paper at the Record and Writ Clerks' Office, and give notice to the opposite party of the filing on the day of filing. Ayck. C. Pr., 134.

3. *Q.* What is the effect of not replying to a defendant's answer?

*A.* By not replying to the answer it will be admitted to be true, and may be read by the defendant as evidence for himself. The defendant may also, in certain cases, move to dismiss the bill if no replication is filed. See *infra*, "Dismissing suits," No. 1.

4. *Q.* What effect has the filing of a replication on the answer of a defendant?

*A.* The truth of the answer is denied, and the defendant cannot read it as evidence in support of his case; but the plaintiff may read the answer against the defendant. Filing a replication also prevents the cause being brought to a hearing on bill and answer or motion for decree. Ayck. C. Pr., 132.

5. *Q.* When the defendant has filed an answer, which does not admit the allegations of the plaintiff's bill, what is the effect as respects the answer of filing a replication?

*A.* See previous answer.

6. *Q.* Can a plaintiff file a replication to the answer of a deceased defendant?

*A.* No, he cannot. The suit should be revived against the deceased's representatives. *Deeks* v. *Stanhope*, 2 W. R., 651.

## XV.—*Dismissing Suits.*

1. *Q.* What course must be adopted by a defendant in the event of the plaintiff not proceeding in the suit with due diligence, and how does the practice vary at different stages?

*A.* The defendant should give notice of motion to dismiss the bill for want of prosecution. Where the defendant is required to answer the bill or has answered he may give notice of motion. 1. Where having obtained no order to enlarge time, plaintiff do not within four weeks of answer being deemed sufficient, or after filing a traversing note, file replication, set down the cause to be heard on bill and answer, or set down cause on motion for decree or obtain and serve an order to amend the bill. 2. If plaintiff undertakes to reply to plea to whole bill, but does not file same within four weeks after date of undertaking. 3. If plaintiff, having obtained no order to enlarge time, does not set down cause to be heard, and obtain and serve subpœna to hear judgment within four weeks after the evidence is closed. Also where the plaintiff, after answer, amends his bill without requiring an answer to the amendments, and having no order to enlarge the time does not file replication, set down cause on bill and answer, or on motion for decree. 1. Within one week after expiration of time to answer, if answer to amendments had been required, where defendant does not require to answer the amendments. 2. Within fourteen days after refusal to allow further time where defendant desiring to answer has not put in his answer in time, and Judge has refused further time. 3. Within fourteen days after filing answer to amendments, unless special order obtained within such fourteen days to except to such answer, or to re-amend bill. Where defendant is not required to answer and has not answered. After expiration of three months of appearance, unless in meantime motion for decree or cause set down to be heard. Ayck. C. Pr., 302.*

2. *Q.* State what bills it would be irregular for a defendant to move to dismiss for want of prosecution.

*A.* A defendant cannot move to dismiss a bill for discovery only; to perpetuate testimony, or to appoint a receiver *pendente lite*, as these suits never come to a hearing. Ayck. C. Pr., 304.

3. *Q.* How soon after filing his answer is a defendant at liberty to move that the plaintiff's bill may be dismissed for want of prosecution?

*A.* See *supra*, No. 1.

4. *Q.* When a plaintiff is served with a notice of motion to dismiss his bill for want of prosecution, what step must be taken by him to prevent dismissal?

*A.* See *supra*, No. 1.

5. *Q.* Under what circumstances, and upon what terms, may a plaintiff and defendant respectively dismiss a bill before a decree?

*A.* A plaintiff may move to dismiss any time before decree. If before appearance it is without costs, but after the plaintiff must pay the defendant's costs. After decree the plaintiff cannot move to dismiss. The defendant may move to dismiss for want of prosecution, as to which see No. 1. Also if the suit has abated. The suit will be dismissed on payment of the defendant's costs, unless the court order to the contrary, which it will sometimes do, as where the bill was filed on the authority of a reported case, which was afterwards reversed. Ayck., C. Pr., 310.

6. *Q.* May a bill be dismissed after decree?

*A.* Technically, a bill cannot be dismissed after decree, but proceedings having the same effect may be taken by obtaining a rehearing or by appeal. But these proceedings are to reverse the decree, not to dismiss the bill.

7. *Q.* Can a defendant in any, and what, cases set down a cause to be heard instead of moving to dismiss the bill for want of prosecution?

*A.* The defendant may set the cause down if the plaintiff does not within four weeks after the evidence is closed set it down and obtain and serve a *subpœna* to hear judgment. Consol. Ord., xxi., r. 1.

---

* The answer to this question will, doubtless, alarm the student, but I recommend him not to occupy valuable time in working up the subject, one of the most intricate in chancery practice. It is absurd to expect candidates to answer such a question correctly, and I trust no examiner will ask it again.

## XVI.—*Evidence.*

1. *Q.* How must the parties to a suit in equity proceed for the purpose of proving such facts of the case as are not admitted?

*A.* This will vary according to the manner in which the cause is brought to a hearing. If issue is joined the facts may be proved either wholly or partially by the evidence of witnesses taken on affidavits, or *vivâ voce*, before an examiner. Also an order may be obtained to take the evidence orally at the hearing. If the cause comes to a hearing on motion for decree the evidence is taken by affidavit, or the witnesses are examined and cross-examined before an examiner. (*Infra,* "Motion for Decree," Nos. 4—6.) The attendance of the witnesses is secured by *subpœna*. See this answer more in detail, *infra*.

2. *Q.* Is it necessary to give any notice with respect to whether the evidence in a suit is to be taken orally or by affidavits?

*A.* This proceeding was formerly necessary, but now either party in a cause in which issue is joined, may at their option support their case, either wholly or partially by affidavits, or wholly or partially by the oral examination of witnesses *ex parte* before an examiner. The above does not apply as to facts in respect of which an order to take the evidence *vivâ voce* at the hearing has been obtained. Ord. Feb., 1861, rr. 3, 4. As to such facts the evidence is wholly oral at the hearing.

3. *Q.* By what mode of taking evidence do you consider the truth is arrived at the nearest?

*A.* I am much in favour of the oral examination of a witness in open court upon oath. If the evidence of a witness is given by affidavit it is difficult to know whether he is deposing to the truth or not; but, if the examination is in open court a lie may be easily detected from the manner in which the testimony is given, and the general demeanour of the witness. Moreover, in an oral examination fresh questions are constantly suggested by the previous answers. This method of examination has long been one of the distinguishing features of the procedure in the common law courts. Equity also is now introducing the system. There can be no doubt as to its being the best way of eliciting the truth, but grave doubts are entertained of its being well adapted to chancery tribunals as at present constituted.

4. *Q.* Who are the officers appointed to take evidence, and where is it filed?

*A.* The officers referred to are called examiners. The evidence when taken is filed at the office of the Record and Writ Clerks in Chancery Lane. Ayck. C. P., 152.

5. *Q.* How do you proceed to examine a witness *vivâ voce*, and at what period of the suit can this be done?

*A.* Having procured the attendance of the witness (*infra,* No. 6.) at the time appointed by the examiner, I should examine him in the presence of the examiner, who would write down the examination in the form of a narrative. The witness would sign his depositions, or if he refused the examiner would sign it. This examination takes place in the presence of both parties, excepting where the evidence is to be used at the hearing of a cause in which issue is joined. In such cases it is taken *ex parte*, excepting in suits to perpetuate testimony, or where the witness is old or infirm, or where there is an agreement to take the evidence under the old practice. The old practice is to examine the witness in the presence of both parties, and the cross-examination follows upon the examination. As to examining a witness *vivâ voce* at the hearing, see *infra*, No. 8. If the evidence is required in support of an interlocutory motion, as for an injunction, the witness may be examined any time before the motion. If issue is joined he must be examined before the closing of the evidence, *i.e.*, within eight weeks after issue joined. Orders, 5th February, 1861.

6. *Q.* How is the attendance of a witness to be enforced for the purpose of examining him before the examiner?

*A.* His attendance is enforced by *subpœna ad testificandum*, which writ may contain the names of three witnesses. Consol. Ord., xxviii., r. 3.

7. *Q.* Must a *subpœna ad testificandum* be served personally on a witness, or will merely leaving it at his house be sufficient?

*A.* Personal service upon the witness is necessary. A copy of the writ and its endorsements must be delivered to him; the original writ being at the same time produced. Consol. Ord., xxviii., r. 6.

8. *Q.* Can evidence be now taken *vivâ voce*, at the hearing of a cause; if so, state in what cases, the proceedings to be taken for the purpose, and the time for taking them?

*A.* In causes in which issue is joined, either party may now apply by summons for an order to take the evidence-in-chief as to certain facts and issues, which are to be stated in the summons, *vivâ voce*, at the hearing. If an order is made no other evidence will be admitted at the hearing, as to such facts. The application must be made within fourteen days after issue joined. Also independently of the above, the cross-examination of a deponent or witness is to take place, *vivâ voce*, at the hearing of a cause after issue joined, excepting in cases where the parties agree to take the evidence under the old practice, or the witnesses are old and infirm, or the suit is to perpetuate testimony. Orders, 5th February, 1861, rr. 3—7.

9. *Q.* Are there any cases in which one party cannot examine another party to a suit as a witness?

*A.* As a general rule, parties to suits, including husband and wife, are now competent and compellable to give evidence on behalf of one another. They are, however, not bound to answer any question which would criminate them. Nor are husband and wife bound to divulge any communication made to one another during the marriage. 14 & 15 Vic., c. 99; 16 & 17 Vic., c. 83.

10. *Q.* For what period of time after notice of a witness being under examination before the examiner, must the party examining

such witness keep him in town for the purpose of being cross-examined?

*A.* This question applies to cases coming under the old practice, when the cross-examination before an examiner followed the examination-in-chief, and the party examining the witness was bound to keep him in town forty-eight hours after the notice. Under the rules of February, 1861, the party wishing to cross-examine a witness who has made an affidavit, or been examined *ex parte*, must give a notice to the opposite party to produce the witness; therefore, the above rule will not now apply. Nor can it apply to cases where the evidence is taken orally at the hearing, as the cross-examination is to follow the examination-in-chief, and the whole evidence must be taken during the hearing. Ord. 5th Feb., 1861, r. 3; *infra*, No. 12.

11. *Q.* If a party omit to avail himself of the time allowed him for cross-examination referred to in the last question, is he thereby precluded from such cross-examination altogether, or can he on any, and what, terms still procure a cross-examination?

*A.* In such a case he could obtain the attendance of a witness for cross-examination, but he would have to bear the costs. See the previous answer.

12. *Q.* How and by whom is the attendance of a witness for cross-examination obtained, and has the practice in this respect been altered, stating authority?

*A.* If one party to any cause or matter in which issue is joined or not, has filed an affidavit, or examined a witness *ex parte* before an examiner, the opposite party is entitled to cross-examine such deponent or witness. The witness is to be produced by the party who has filed the affidavit, or examined the witness, upon notice from the party desiring the cross-examination. The notice, if issue is joined, is to be given within fourteen days after the closing of the evidence. If notice of motion for decree has been given, the time for giving notice is within fourteen days after the end of the time allowed for the plaintiff to file affidavits in reply. In all other cases the notice must be given within fourteen days after the filing of the affidavit or examination upon which a cross-examination is desired. Ord. Feb., 1861, r. 19. Before this order, the party desiring to cross-examine had to produce the witness. The attendance of the witness is compelled by *subpœna*.

13. *Q.* What is a commission to examine witnesses, and in what cases is it necessary?

*A.* It is an authority to certain persons to take the evidence of witnesses residing abroad, in answer to certain specified questions. It is now almost wholly superseded, as the court has power to order a special examiner, to take evidence of witnesses, both within and without the jurisdiction, a much more preferable method to adopt. Ord. Feb., 1861, r. 11.

14. *Q.* In what cases is it advisable to file a bill to perpetuate testimony, or to obtain an order to examine witnesses *de bene esse*, and what is the nature of the proceedings under it?

# EVIDENCE.

*A.* As to perpetuating testimony see *supra*, "Preservation of Testimony," 281. An order to examine witnesses *de bene esse* (*i.e.*, conditionally on their not being able to attend and give evidence in person) may be obtained when an important witness is of great age, or exceedingly ill, or is going abroad, and there is reason to fear that his personal attendance cannot be obtained. The order for an examiner to take the examination is obtained on motion, or by summons. The evidence being taken, it is filed, and office copies may at once be obtained of it. The nature of the proceeding is very distinguishable from perpetuating testimony, as a bill for the latter purpose cannot be filed if the subject matter of dispute may be at once litigated; whereas, evidence *de bene esse* is taken in aid of proceedings already commenced. *Ellice* v. *Roupell*, 32 L. J. Ch., 563, 624.

15. *Q.* What are the modes by which the execution of deeds, or the handwriting of letters may, according to the ordinary rule of courts of equity, be proved for the purpose of being given in evidence on the hearing of a cause?

*A.* The execution or handwriting may be proved by witnesses *viva voce* at the hearing, or by making the instruments exhibits to affidavits. But for this an order is necessary to be obtained on motion or petition of course, for properly the proof ought to have been made before the closing of the evidence orally or by affidavit. Ayck., C. Pr., 142.

16. *Q.* Where, by the answer of a defendant, the validity of a deed relied on by the plaintiff is impeached on the ground of fraud; does, or does not, that circumstance form any, and, if so, what exception to the general rule referred to in the last question? If so, how must such a deed be proved by the plaintiff? And give the reason why.

*A.* In such a case the deed cannot be proved at the hearing, as mentioned in the previous answer, unless, indeed, an order has been obtained to take the evidence as to it *vivâ voce* at the hearing, under the rules of February, 1861. The deed must be proved orally before an examiner (or the court, if an order is obtained under the new orders), the reason being that, in proving an instrument alleged to be fraudulent, the opposite party should have an opportunity to cross-examine the witness. *Hitchcock* v. *Carew*, 23 L. J. Ch., 166.

17. *Q.* Can a plaintiff read the answer of one defendant against another defendant?

*A.* On motion for decree he may adopt this course, but he must first give notice that he intends to do so. *Stephens* v. *Heathcote*, 29 L. J. Ch., 529. If issue, however, is joined, the practice is otherwise, excepting in an interpleader suit, when the plaintiff may read the answer of one defendant against a co-defendant. Ayck., C. Pr., 138.

18. *Q.* Can a defendant, and in any, and what, circumstances, read his co-defendant's answer against the plaintiff?

*A.* As a general rule, he cannot do so, but there is an important exception in cases where notice of motion for decree has been given. In such cases the answer may be read, notice being previously given. *Stephens* v. *Heathcote, supra.*

19. *Q.* If a defendant desires to read his own answer as evidence against the plaintiff, what course must he pursue to entitle him to do so?

*A.* If issue has been joined in the cause the defendant may make his answer evidence, by making it an exhibit to an affidavit, verifying it, or by filing an affidavit as follows:—"The contents of my answer, sworn and filed in this cause on the    day of    are true as therein set forth, and are within my personal knowledge, except, etc., and I am desirous to read the same as evidence on my behalf at the hearing of this cause." If the cause comes on on motion for decree, notice must be given to the plaintiff of the defendant's intention to read it. If the cause is set down on bill and answer, the defendant, unless a corporation, can read his answer as a matter of course. *Stephens* v. *Heathcote; supra;* Smith's Ch. Pr., 399.

20. *Q.* What advantage, if any, in respect of evidence, has a plaintiff in equity, compared with one at common law?

*A.* This question was probably asked before the recent changes, giving courts of law power to compel discovery and enabling parties to deliver interrogatories. C. L. P. Acts, 1852, 1854. The balance is now the other way, as the plaintiff at common law having obtained the advantages formerly enjoyed exclusively in equity, has also the privilege of examining his witnesses *vivâ voce* in open court; a course which is seldom pursued in equity. See *supra,* No. 3.

21. *Q.* In what manner, when, by whom, and against whom is the production of documents in a suit, according to the modern practice, obtained?

*A.* The application is made by summons at chambers, proceeded on in the ordinary way. The production may be applied for either by the plaintiff or defendant against one another. It is now not material, as formerly, to consider whether an answer has been put in or not. The order is usually applied for after an answer, but may even be made after the hearing. A defendant, however, if he has been required to answer, cannot apply for production until he has put in a sufficient answer to the bill. 15 & 16 Vic., c. 86, ss. 18, 19.

22. *Q.* What is the practice with regard to the production of books, accounts, and documents, the possession of which is admitted by the defendant? If they relate to other matters besides those which are the subject of the suit, how is the defendant protected from such other matters being disclosed to the plaintiff?

*A.* If the defendant has admitted the possession of the documents in his answer, an order will be made for their production by him, unless, indeed, the documents are privileged. *Infra,* No. 25. That portion of the books which relate to other matters will, on affidavit of the fact, be ordered to be sealed up. If, however, the various matters are so intermingled that they cannot be separated, the plaintiff is entitled to see the whole. Ayck., C. Pr., 329.

23. *Q.* Can a defendant obtain an order for production of documents by a co-defendant; and, if so, how can he obtain such production?

*A.* He cannot obtain the ordinary order for production, excepting after decree in an administration suit. *Hart* v. *Montefiore,* 31; L. J. Ch., 333. He must file a cross-bill. *Attorney-General* v. *Clapham,* 10; Hare, App. lxviii.

24. *Q.* In a suit for an account, is it competent for the court to direct that the books in which the accounts required to be taken have been kept should, to any and what extent, be deemed evidence of the truth of the matters therein contained?

*A.* The court has power to direct that such books shall be taken as *primâ facie* evidence of the truth of the matters therein contained. 15 & 16 Vic., c. 86, s. 54. This provision is to save expense in proof.

25. *Q.* Are there any and what documents stated in an answer which are privileged from production?

*A.* The production of documents cannot be compelled if they relate exclusively to the title of either party; nor can confidential letters which have passed between a solicitor and his client; nor, upon grounds of public policy, can state papers which have passed between a Government and its agents. *The Rajah of Coorg* v. *The East India Company,* 25; L. J. Ch., 345.

26. *Q.* Under what circumstances will the courts of equity relax the ordinary rule as to the place where and the person with whom documents scheduled to an answer are to be lodged for production?

*A.* The ordinary rule for their production at the office of the clerks of records and writs will be departed from when the books are in the constant use of the party producing them. In such a case they will be ordered to be produced at the office of such party or of his solicitor. It is also not unfrequent in amicable suits to adopt this course. Ayck., C. Pr., 329.

27. *Q.* State what evidence can be read on the hearing of a cause on bill and answer.

*A.* The parties are restricted to the statements contained in the bill which the answer admits, and the whole of the statements in the answer; also, documents which are not disputed by the answer, and yet are not admitted by it, may be proved *vivâ voce,* or by affidavit, at the hearing. From these facts the court makes its decree. Hence it is only in amicable suits that a cause is set down for hearing on bill and answer. Ayck., C. Pr., 136.

28. *Q.* If either party in a cause in which issue is not joined is desirous of cross-examining on affidavits filed by the opposite party, before whom is it done, and what notice must be given?

*A.* The cross-examination takes place before an examiner, before whom the witness is to be produced on notice by the party desiring to cross-examine, as mentioned *supra,* No. 12. Forty-eight hours' notice must be given of the intention to cross-examine, and the notice may be given within fourteen days after the filing of the affidavit. As to cases where notice of motion for decree is given, see *supra*, No. 12. The notice must contain the name and description of the witness, and the time and place of the cross-examination, unless dispensed with by the court. Ord. Feb., 1861, rr. 19, 22.

29. *Q.* Does the court, under any and what circumstances, permit either a plaintiff or defendant, or both, to go into parol evidence to explain or vary a written agreement?

*A.* As a general rule, either party is allowed to explain any latent ambiguity in a written agreement, but not to explain a patent ambiguity. *Supra*, 271, No. 23. Thus evidence may be given to show what is parcel or not of the thing sold, this being an ambiguity which is only ascertained by parol evidence, and, therefore, it is but fair to explain it away through the same medium. Also, such evidence will be admitted to vary an agreement, if such variance is rendered necessary in consequence of mistake in fact or fraud; so, also, a defendant is permitted to resist a specific performance, unless upon the terms of introducing into the agreement parol variations which it is clearly proved were made. Subject to the above exceptions, the rule is, that parol evidence is not allowed to vary a written agreement. It may, however, be adduced to show that the agreement has been totally waived or discharged. Taylor on Ev., 968; *Wollam* v. *Hearn*, 2 L. C. Eq., 404 and notes.

30. *Q.* In a suit in equity by an incumbrancer against a purchaser for valuable consideration, in which such purchaser is sought to be affected with notice of the incumbrance, and in which such notice is proved by one witness only, but is positively and expressly denied by the answer, in whose favour will the court decree?

*A.* The court would decide in favour of the defendant, and dismiss the bill. This is upon the principle that it is fair to attach equal weight to the testimony of the defendant as to that of the plaintiff's witness. The corroborating evidence of an additional witness, or of a letter of the defendant, or of other circumstances, will turn the balance in favour of the plaintiff. 2 Taylor on Ev., 832, 4th ed.

31. *Q.* In what case is the answer of a defendant evidence for himself?

*A.* See *supra*, No. 19.

32. *Q.* Can a plaintiff at law select parts of an answer to read as evidence at law, or can the defendant at law insist that the whole shall be read?

*A.* The whole of the answer must be read, but the jury need not give equal credit to the whole of it. The defendant at law can also insist upon the whole of the bill being read in addition, a suit in equity being looked upon as a conversation between the parties, one portion of which is not intelligible without the other. Taylor on Ev., 627.

33. *Q.* To whom must a party apply for an order to enlarge the time for closing evidence?

*A.* He should apply by summons to a judge at chambers. Judges' Regulations, 10th Nov., 1852.

34. *Q.* What is the effect of closing the evidence? when does it

close? and within what time after closing is the cause to be set down for hearing?

*A.* Closing the evidence has the effect of bringing to a conclusion the examinations in chief by either party, unless, indeed, the evidence is to be taken at the hearing. It is closed within eight weeks after issue joined. Ord. 5th Feb., 1861, r. 5. As to setting the cause down, see *infra.*

35. *Q.* Can or cannot witnesses be examined or re-examined after evidence closed? Give your reason if they cannot; and if they can, state instances in which it is done.

*A.* A witness cannot be examined or re-examined after the evidence is closed, excepting by special leave. The reason is, that a sufficient time is allowed by the rules of the court for the purpose, and if a party is diligent, he ought to complete his case in due time. If, however, one of the parties is taken by surprise by evidence filed by the opposite party at the last moment, the court will frequently allow him further time to rebut such evidence. Also, the court has power to order the examination of a witness at the hearing, if special grounds for so doing appear. As to cross-examination, see *supra*, No. 12. 15 & 16 Vic., c. 86, ss. 38, 39, and Notes by Morgan.

36. *Q.* Can infants, married women, or lunatics consent to any order, as to evidence or otherwise?

*A.* Such consent is binding and valid if made with the sanction of the court or of the judge in chambers by the next friend, guardian, or committee. The consent of the committee must, however, be with the sanction of the Lord Chancellor or Lords Justices sitting in Lunacy. Ord., Feb. 1861, r. 25.

37. *Q.* For and against whom is a decree in a cause evidence, and how are its contents proved?

*A.* Being a decree *in personam*, it is evidence only for and against the parties to it and their privies, not against strangers. Mere production of the record is sufficient evidence of the decree having been made; but if it is sought to show that the decree adjudicated upon certain matters, the bill and answer must also be proved by production from the record and writ clerks' office of the documents as filed. Taylor on Ev., 1324.

38. *Q.* At what distance of time do deeds, bonds, and other writings prove themselves, and thereby render their proof unnecessary?

*A.* They are said to prove themselves when they are thirty years old, and are unblemished by alterations. After this lapse of time, the witnesses are presumed to be dead. They must, however, come from custody, which, though perhaps not strictly legal, affords a reasonable presumption of their genuineness. Taylor on Ev., 101.

## XVII.—*Setting down Causes.*

1. *Q.* When a cause is at issue in Chancery, before whom must it be set down for hearing? and within what time?

*A.* The cause must be set down for hearing before the judge to whose court the cause is attached, unless otherwise ordered by the Lord Chancellor or Lords Justices. As to the time for setting it down, see *supra*, "Dismissing Suits," No. 1. Consol. Ord., vi., rr. 2—4.

2. *Q.* Are there any cases in which a plaintiff may set down a cause upon bill and answer? if so, state under what circumstances, and with what proceeding at law, does it correspond?

*A.* See *supra*, "Evidence," No. 27. The proceeding corresponds with a judgment by default at law upon a writ not specially indorsed, as the defendant then admits the cause of action as stated in the declaration filed by the plaintiff. The plaintiff then has merely to get the damages assessed.

3. *Q.* May a plaintiff set down his cause for hearing without examining witnesses; and, if so, can he rely upon any facts not admitted by the answer, or deny any facts that are stated therein?

*A.* He may set the cause down upon bill and answer; but, as already mentioned, he must rely for a decree upon the admissions of the defendant, and cannot rebut the facts stated in the answer.

4. *Q.* Can a defendant set down a cause for hearing?

*A.* See *supra*, "Dismissing Suits," 371, No. 7.

5. *Q.* How is a cause set down on notice of motion for decree?

*A.* It is set down with the Registrar within seven days after the notice is served. The record and writ clerk's certificate, that the cause is in a fit state to be heard on motion for decree, must be produced, endorsed by the plaintiff's solicitor with a memorandum, when the notice was served and when it will expire, and if there is an infant defendant stating that a guardian *ad litem* is appointed, or that there is no infant defendant. After the seven days, the defendant's consent to the cause being set down must be produced. Ayck., C. Pr., 127.

6. *Q.* What is a *subpœna* to hear judgment, and upon whom should it be served?

*A.* It is a writ which is issued to the opposite party, calling upon him to appear to hear judgment in the cause. It should be issued by the plaintiff within four weeks after the evidence is closed; after this time the defendant may obtain the writ. Service should be effected on all the defendants. The service may be effected by delivering a copy of the writ and endorsements to the defendant's solicitor. Consol. Ord., xxviii., r. 7.

## XVIII.—*The Hearing.*

1. *Q.* State the progressive steps of a Chancery suit up to the hearing.

*A.* See *infra*, "Miscellaneous and General," No. 1.

2. *Q.* When a suit is commenced by bill it may be conducted to a hearing, amongst other ways, on bill and answer, and replication filed, or on bill and answer only, or on motion for decree. State shortly the difference between those various steps.

*A.* The cause is set down on bill and answer in those cases only where the statements in the plaintiff's bill are sufficiently admitted by the answer to enable him to obtain a decree. The cause is heard on issue joined where the suit is contested, and the facts and issues to be decided are numerous and complicated. Hearing on motion for decree is also adopted in contentious suits, but usually where the points at issue are in a small compass. The latter course has the advantage of being more expeditious. Also the defendant has the opportunity of considering the plaintiff's evidence before he prepares his affidavits; whereas if issue is joined, both parties have, until the expiration of the eight weeks for filing their evidence. With regard to cross-examination, there is no material distinction between the two latter modes of hearing, excepting that if issue is joined the cross-examination can only be at the hearing; and also an order may be obtained to take the evidence-in-chief *vivâ voce* at the hearing. See *supra,* "Evidence."

3. *Q.* If the plaintiff does not require an answer, what steps must he take to bring his cause to a hearing?

*A.* See *infra,* "Motion for Decree."

4. *Q.* Where a cause has proceeded to a hearing, and is then ascertained to be defective for want of parties, does or does not that circumstance form a ground for a dismissal of the bill, or will the court adopt any other; and, if so, what course in consequence of such defect?

*A.* If the want of parties appears for the first time at the hearing; that is, no objection having been taken by the defendant by plea or answer, the bill will not be dismissed; but the court may, if it thinks fit, make a decree saving the rights of the absent parties. Consol. Ord., xxiii., r. 11. Or it may give leave to amend and order the cause to stand over for the purpose. If when brought on a second time a similar defect appears, the bill will be dismissed. *Williams* v. *Page,* 28 Beav., 148. *Leyland* v. *Leyland,* 10 W. R., 149.

5. *Q.* Explain the mode of preparing the brief for counsel on the hearing, and what is necessary to be done on the part of the plaintiff before the hearing, and after the decree made to its completion, step by step.

*A.* The brief should consist of a copy of the bill, interrogatories and answer, accompanied by observations upon the case. The depositions of the witnesses should be copied on brief paper; also complete copies of the affidavits should be made for each counsel. Before the hearing, the plaintiff's solicitor should issue and serve a *subpœna* to hear judgment, set down the cause, retain and deliver briefs to counsel, obtain office copies of the evidence filed, serve notices to produce documents; issue and serve *subpœnas* for the witnesses to attend at the hearing; appoint and hold a consultation with counsel, and also watch the list of causes, so as to be in court and fully prepared when the cause is reached. As to the proceedings after the decree is pronounced, see *infra,* 385, No. 11.

6. *Q.* What are the inquiries usually inserted in a decree made on the hearing of an ordinary administration suit?

*A.* If the decree is in a creditors' suit, it will direct—1. An account of what is due to the plaintiff and all other creditors. 2. An account of the funeral expenses. 3. An account of the personal estate come to the hands of the defendants, the administrators or executors. 4. An inquiry of what parts of the personal property is outstanding or undisposed of, and a direction that the personal estate be applied in payment of the debts and funeral expenses, in a due course of administration. If the personalty will be clearly insufficient, and there is real estate, the decree proceeds. 5. An inquiry as to what real estate the deceased was seised of or entitled to. 6. An inquiry what incumbrances there are upon it. 7. (If sale directed) An account of what is due to such of the incumbrancers as consent to the sale. 8. An inquiry as to their priorities. 9. Direction to sell real estate, and apply it in due course of administration. A legatee's suit is very similar, excepting that an inquiry is introduced as to what legacies and annuities are given by the will, and such legacies and annuities are directed to be paid after the debts. If the deceased is intestate, the inquiry will be for the next of kin. Haddan's Equity. Appendix.

7. *Q.* If a cause have been heard and a decree made, before whom must that cause be heard on further consideration?

*A.* It should be heard before the judge before whom the cause was originally heard, unless the contrary is ordered by the Lord Chancellor or Lords Justices. Consol. Ord., xxi.

8. *Q.* Can a cause be set down for hearing on further consideration by a defendant?

*A.* The defendant, or any other party, may set the cause down on further consideration, if the plaintiff have not done so within fourteen days from the filing of the certificate of the chief clerk. Consol. Ord., xxi. r. 10.

### XIX.—*Legal Rights, Doubtful Facts, and Damages.*

1. *Q.* If a Court of Equity doubt the law of a case, what is now the course taken to determine it?

*A.* By 25 & 26 Vic., c. 42, the court is in future to determine questions of law itself, but it may call to its assistance a common law judge, by virtue of 14 & 15 Vic., c. 83, s. 8. See *supra*, 291, 292, Nos. 22, 23.

2. *Q.* In what cause does a Court of Equity direct an action to be tried?

*A.* See *supra*, 291, 292, Nos. 22, 23.

3. *Q.* In case the facts are doubtful upon the depositions in equity, how does the court proceed?

*A.* In such a case the court would direct a trial in equity, with or without a jury, or it might, if more convenient, direct a trial at *nisi prius*, or at the assizes. 25 & 26 Vic., c. 42.

4. *Q.* In case an heir-at-law dispute a will, what proceeding will the court direct to decide the question?

*A.* This question was asked before the recent alteration in the law above mentioned. The heir was formerly entitled to an issue, but now it is presumed that this course will not be adopted. See *supra*.

5. *Q.* In case of motion for a new trial of an issue, to what court must it be made—to the court directing the issue, or to the court where it was tried?

*A.* The application should be made to the judge who directed the issue. Consol. Ord., vi., r. 13.

6. *Q.* In what cases can a Court of Equity award damages?

*A.* The court has power to award damages in cases where it has jurisdiction to entertain an application for an injunction against the breach of any covenant, contract or agreement, or against the commission or continuance of any wrongful act, or for the specific performance of any covenant, contract or agreement. The damages may be in addition or in substitution for the injunction or specific performance. The damages may be assessed before the court alone, or with a jury, or before a common law judge and jury. 21 & 22 Vic., c. 27.

## XX.—*Motion for Decree. Decrees and their Enforcement.*

1. *Q.* By what process does a Court of Equity execute its decrees?

*A.* The performance of a decree will be enforced by attachment or sergeant-at-arms against the person of the defendant, or by sequestration issued against his lands and goods. If the decree is for the giving up possession of land, a writ of assistance will issue. If a conveyance is decreed, a party will be appointed to convey. If payment of money or costs is ordered, execution may issue, as mentioned *infra*, No. 13. Ayck., C. Pr., 220.

2. *Q.* Is the decree of a Court of Equity binding in any, and, if any, in what cases on a party to the suit who is a minor?

*A.* As a general rule the court has no power to make a decree binding upon an infant, and he may repudiate the whole proceedings on coming of age. An exception, however, exists in selling lands under a decree for the payment of the debts of the infant's predecessor under 1 Wm. IV., c. 47, s. 11; also under 13 & 14 Vic., c. 60, s. 29. Seton on Decrees, 689.

3. *Q.* How would you proceed to render a decree binding upon an infant?

*A.* I should wait until he came of age, and then issue a *subpœna* against him to show cause why the decree should not be absolute against him. He has six months to show cause; in some cases a further time is allowed. This period having expired, I should make an affidavit of service, and move the court to make the decree absolute, at the same time producing a certificate of baptism and the registrar's certificate of no cause being shown. Ayck., C. Pr., 571. Seton on Decrees, 686, 3rd ed.

4. *Q.* Has any practice been recently adopted for shortening the mode of taking evidence and proceeding to a decree? If so, state the steps.

*A.* The practice referred to is that of bringing a cause to a hearing on motion for decree. This may be done as soon as the time for answering has expired, but before replication is filed. One month's notice of motion must be given, and at the foot of the notice a list is appended of the evidence filed by the plaintiff in support of the motion. The evidence may, it seems, be taken orally if the names of the witnesses be added to the notice. *Pellatt* v. *Nichols*, 26 Beav., 298. The defendant has fourteen days to file affidavits in answer to this evidence, and the plaintiff has seven days to file affidavits in reply. The cause is set down and a *subpœna* to hear judgment issued and served. Ayck., C. Pr., 124.

5. *Q.* Where a plaintiff has given notice of motion for decree, and afterwards desires to adduce further evidence for the hearing, in what way can that object be accomplished?

*A.* He must make special application to the court on notice to the defendant for leave to adduce further evidence. Thus in one case, seven months after the notice of motion had been given, the defendant having given material evidence in another cause, the plaintiff was allowed to use the additional evidence, though the cause was in the paper. *Watson* v. *Cleaver*, 20 Beav., 137; Consol. Ord., xxxiii., r. 8.

6. *Q.* When is the proper time, in a suit commenced by bill, for a motion for a decree? what notice of it must be given? to whom is it to be given? and what parties does it bind?

*A.* See previous answers. The decree when made is binding upon the parties to the suit. The hearing on the motion is equivalent to the hearing of a cause. *Norton* v. *Steinkopf*, 1 Kay, 45.

7. *Q.* How far is a decree made on the hearing of a cause binding, or how can it be made binding against a defendant who is abroad and does not appear?

*A.* The decree will be binding upon parties abroad if they have been duly proceeded against as mentioned *supra*. 346. An affidavit of service of the *subpœna* to hear judgment, and of the order for service of it (if any) must be produced. The decree is absolute in the first instance. Consol. Ord., xxiii. r. 12. If the bill has been taken *pro confesso* against a defendant abroad, notice of the decree must be served. After this it will be absolute on the expiration of the time limited by the notice of the decree. Consol. Ord., xxiii., r. 11. It is absolute after three years from its date, where it has not been served at all. Ibid. r. 15.

8. *Q.* If a party to a suit, who is ordered by the court to execute a deed, obstinately refuse to do so, is there any, and if any, what, mode of giving effect to the order without the signature of the party?

*A.* The court may direct another person to execute the deed, or in certain cases it may make a vesting order. 13 & 14 Vic., c. 60. See *supra*, 275.

9. *Q.* If a party, who is by order or decree of the court directed to pay money or to do any other act within a limited time, and after due service of the order or decree neglect to obey the same, what is

the nature of the order which may, under these circumstances, be obtained against such party?

*A.* Under such circumstances, a writ of attachment may be issued against the defendant, but for this no order is necessary. The writ is obtained on filing an affidavit of service of the decree. If, however, a sequestration is decided upon after the attachment, an order is necessary. Ayck., C. Pr., 222.

10. *Q.* Can persons, not parties to a suit, enforce obedience to an order? Can such obedience be enforced against them?

*A.* Persons, though not parties to suits, may now enforce obedience to orders obtained by them, or to orders made in their favour. Similar orders may also be enforced against persons not parties to the cause. Consol. Ord., xxix., r. 2.

11. *Q.* After a decree has been pronounced in court, how is it drawn up?

*A.* The decree is prepared by the Registrar, who was in court at the time of its being pronounced. The draft is drawn from the minutes of the decree taken down by the Registrar and by counsel on their briefs. (The briefs and other documents are to be left with the Registrar within seven days after the decree is pronounced.) The solicitor having the carriage of the decree obtains a copy of the draft, of which he serves copies on the other solicitors. An appointment is made to settle the decree in the presence of the Registrar. If a party is dissatisfied with the form of the decree, he must obtain leave from the Court to have the cause put in the paper to be spoken to on the minutes, or he may give notice of motion to vary the draft. When the draft decree is finally settled, it is passed by the Registrar and entered in books kept in the Report Office. Barber's Statement, Ir. Ch. Rep., 1863; Haynes' Outlines, App., 2nd ed.; Ayck., C. Pr., 201.

12. *Q.* If a party having the conduct of a suit do not proceed with due diligence in the prosecution of a decree or order before the chief clerk, what remedy has any other party interested to prevent further delay?

*A.* If the decree is not drawn up, he should apply to the Registrar to draw up the decree. This the Registrar will do. The party having thus obtained the carriage of the decree, he may take out a summons to proceed upon it, when the chief clerk will prosecute the enquiries directed. Ayck., C. Pr., 200. If the decree has been already drawn up, this course may also be adopted.

13. *Q.* How is a decree to be enforced where money or costs is ordered to be paid to a person?

*A.* Such an order may after one month from the time when the order for payment was passed and entered, be enforced by *fieri facias* against the goods, or by *elegit* against the lands and goods of the defaulter. 1 & 2 Vic., c. 110, s. 20. The order may, if desired, be enforced by attachment, *infra*, 401.

14. *Q.* What is the nature of a writ of assistance, and when is it issued?

*A.* It is a writ directing the sheriff of the county in which lands are situate to enter the premises and eject the defendant. It is therefore issued when it is desired to obtain possession of lands under a decree. Ayck., C. Pr., 224.

15. *Q.* By what authority is a retired Chancellor enabled to deliver judgment in cases which have been heard before him? To whom is such judgment to be delivered, and what are the necessary requisites in order to render a decree or order drawn up in pursuance of such judgment of the same force and effect as if it had been given before the retirement of the Chancellor?

*A.* The authority referred to is 15 & 16 Vic., c. 80, s. 60. The judgment must be delivered to the Registrar within six weeks of the great seal having been delivered up. The judgment must be signed by the late Chancellor.

## XXI.—*Appeals.*

1. *Q.* To what courts or tribunals do appeals lie against the decrees of the Master of the Rolls, the Vice-Chancellors, and the Lord Chancellor respectively?

*A.* An appeal lies from the Master of the Rolls and Vice-Chancellors to the Lord Chancellor, or Lords' Justices sitting together or separately. From this court an appeal lies to the House of Lords. 14 & 15 Vic., c. 83.

2. *Q.* Does, or does not, an appeal to a superior court necessarily stay the proceedings under the decree or order appealed from?

*A.* The proceedings are not necessarily stayed by the appeal, but an order to stay should be applied for pending the appeal. The application should be made promptly. Consol. Ord., xxxi., r. 2.

3. *Q.* What is the effect of enrolling a decree of a Vice-Chancellor or the Master of the Rolls, and within what time should it be enrolled? Are decrees generally enrolled?

*A.* The effect is to prevent a re-hearing, or an appeal to the Lord Chancellor or Lords' Justices, and compels the party who is dissatisfied with the decree to appeal to the House of Lords. The decree should be enrolled before a caveat has been entered against its enrolment, and within five years from its being made. Decrees are only enrolled where it is desirable to prevent an appeal to the Court of Appeal. By adopting this course, a dissatisfied party will often shrink from the expense of an appeal to the House of Lords. Also where the point in dispute is of great importance, and it is probable the parties will not be satisfied with the opinion of the Court of Appeal, it may be desirable to proceed at once to the ultimate tribunal. Ayck., C. Pr., 215.

4. *Q.* Within what time must a decree be enrolled, without special leave of court?

*A.* It should be enrolled within six calendar months after its being pronounced. Consol. Ord., xxiii., r. 25.

5. *Q.* Is there any means of preventing the enrolment of a decree?

*A.* A party desiring to have a re-hearing, or to appeal to the

Court of Appeal in Chancery, should at once enter a caveat against the enrolment. The caveat must be prosecuted; that is, the petition of appeal or re-hearing must be presented, and the appeal set down, within twenty-eight days of the docket being left for the signature of the Lord Chancellor with the Clerks of Records and Writs. Ayck. C. Pr., 219.

6. *Q.* Suppose a plaintiff appeals to the Lords' Justices from a judgment of one of the Vice-Chancellors, and their Lordships differ in their opinion, what is the effect on the judgment below?

*A.* The judgment of the court below will be affirmed. 14 & 15 Vic., c. 80, s. 9.

7. *Q.* If a plaintiff's bill is dismissed with costs, and he appeal to the Lords' Justices, and the appeal is dismissed with costs, and the costs are not paid, can he appeal to the House of Lords before he has paid the costs incurred in the courts below?

*A.* He may appeal without paying the costs, but pending the appeal the proceedings will not be stayed if the costs are unpaid. Therefore the defendant will be compelled to pay the costs before his appeal can be heard. Ayck., C. Pr., 315; Morgan's Acts and Orders, 504.

8. *Q.* What is the nature and extent of the security required by the House of Lords before their Lordships give leave to appeal?

*A.* An appellant must give security to the Clerk of the Parliaments, by recognizance in the penalty of four hundred pounds, conditioned to pay such costs as the House orders. Stand. Ord. 61, June 22, 1829. An officer of the Crown appealing is not within this order. *Lord Advocate* v. *Douglas*, 9 Cl. & F., 174.

9. *Q.* What is the nature of a Bill of Review, and is leave ever necessary before filing it?

*A.* It is a bill in the nature of an original bill, filed for the purpose of reversing a decree which has been signed and enrolled. It may be filed on two grounds: 1. For error apparent upon the face of the decree; 2. In consequence of the discovery of new matter, which could not have been adduced at the original hearing, and in the latter case it cannot be filed without leave. Mitf. Pl., 78.

10. *Q.* When is it proper after decree to present a petition of re-hearing? When to proceed by supplemental bill in the nature of a Bill of Review?

*A.* A petition for a re-hearing should be presented for the purpose of reversing a decree not enrolled, upon error in law apparent upon the face of it. As the case is re-heard before the same judge who made the decree, it is obvious that such a course should only be pursued when a change in the law has taken place. Few judges are disposed to reverse their own decisions. A supplemental bill, in the nature of a Bill of Review, should be filed when new matter has been discovered since the decree, and where the decree has not been enrolled. Mitf. Pl., 108.

11. *Q.* What are the several steps which are necessary to be taken by the solicitor of a party complaining of the decree of the

Master of the Rolls, or a Vice-Chancellor, in order to obtain a rehearing, by way of appeal, before the Lord Chancellor?

*A.* He should, after the decree is passed and entered, present a petition of appeal to the Lord Chancellor, with a certificate at the foot by two counsel that the appeal is proper. A deposit of twenty pounds is to be made with the Registrar. The petition is allowed on the terms of the petitioner, or his solicitor, consenting to pay such costs as may be awarded. An order is drawn up and served, and the appeal set down with the Registrar's clerk. It then comes on in its turn, and is disposed of by the Court. Ayck., C. Pr., 367.

12. *Q.* Set forth the various steps from the first decree of a Vice-Chancellor, to the highest court of appeal in the realm.

*A.* If the decree has not been enrolled proceed as in the previous answer. If the decree of the Lord Chancellor or Lord Justices is unsatisfactory, or if the decree has been enrolled give notice of appeal to the opposite party. Instruct counsel to prepare a petition of appeal, and obtain the certificate of two counsel that there is reasonable cause of appeal. The petition and certificate must be signed by two counsel, who must be either engaged in the court below or on the appeal. Have the petition engrossed on parchment, and endorse upon it the day upon which notice of appeal was given, and lodge it with the clerk of appeals. It is presented to the House by a peer who obtains an order allowing the appeal. Security for costs is given (see *supra*). The respondent after order obtained and served on him, answers, after which the appeal may be set down by either party. Each party then prepares his case, which is a narrative of the proceedings below, and the appendix, which contains copies of the documents referred to. The case is signed by one or more counsel engaged in the court below, or who are engaged in the appeal. The case and appendix should be printed, counsel instructed, and the appeal, when reached, argued. Judgment is given and the order of the House obtained. Ayck., C. Pr., 373.

13. *Q.* What is the time limited for appealing to the House of Lords from a decree which has been enrolled?

*A.* The appeal must be made within two years of the enrolment, and the petition presented within the first fourteen days of the session ensuing the end of the two years. If, however, the party desiring to appeal is under disability a similar period is allowed after the disability ceases. The disabilities are, infancy, coverture, imprisonment, being *non compos mentis*, or absence beyond seas. Stand. Ord., 118, 24th March, 1725.

### XXII.—*Funds in Court, Stock, &c.*

1. *Q.* Where a person is entitled in expectancy or otherwise to a share of funds in court, and assigns his interest therein, what remedy has the assignee to protect himself against the transfer or payment out of court to the assignor of the share so assigned to him?

*A.* The assignee should obtain a stop order upon the fund as mentioned in the next answer. Such an order has the effect of preventing a transfer or payment out of the fund without notice to the assignee. It also has the effect of giving priority over any previous assignee of the fund who has not obtained such an order. Ayck., C. Pr., 456.

2. *Q.* How is a stop order obtained?

*A.* If the assignor consents, the order may be obtained at Chambers by summons. In other cases a petition must be presented setting out the title of the assignor to the fund, and shewing the assignment. The statements in the petition must be proved by affidavit, unless already proved in a cause. The order being granted it is drawn up, passed, entered, and a copy served on the solicitor of the person in whose name the fund is standing, and also a copy is left at the Accountant-General's Office. Ayck., C. Pr., 456.

3. *Q.* Upon whom ought a petition or summons for a stop order to be served?

*A.* They should be served upon the assignor and all parties interested in the fund sought to be affected by the stop order. Consol. Ord., xxvi., r. 2; Morgan's Acts and Orders, 489.

4. *Q.* What is a *distringas*? in what cases is it resorted to, and what is the course of proceeding for obtaining it?

*A.* It is a writ which issues to prevent the transfer of stock in the books of the Bank of England. The writ is issued where a person takes such stock as a security for money lent, and where it is not desired to make a transfer of the stock. It issues without order, but an affidavit by the party entitled or his solicitor must be filed, stating that he or his client is entitled to the stock, and describing it. A notice of the writ and the writ itself is then taken to Messrs. Freshfields & Newman, 5, Bank Buildings, the Bank solicitors, who will examine and mark the writ. The writ and notice are then taken to the Bank and served on the Chief-Accountant. Ayck., C. Pr., 272.

5. *Q.* What is a restraining order?

*A.* It is an order which is obtained for the purpose of restraining the Bank of England or any other public company from transferring stock in their books or paying the dividends thereon. The order is obtained on motion or petition in a summary way supported by affidavit. It differs from a distringas in that it applies to stock in all companies, and is of a more permanent nature. Still, after obtaining a restraining order a bill should be filed within a reasonable time. 5 Vic., c. 5, s. 4.

6. *Q.* By what means can the party in whose name the stock is standing proceed to remove the restraint?

*A.* If he has obtained the writ he may obtain an order to discharge it, on petition, of course, to the Master of the Rolls. If any other person, other than the party who has obtained it, is desirous of discharging the writ, notice of motion must be given. A request to the Bank to transfer the stock will also enable the person in whose name it is standing to transfer it after eight days from the request. Consol. Ord., xxvii., r. 3.

7. *Q.* What are the duties of the Accountant-General? Is it his duty to manage the investment of funds under the control of the court, and is he a judicial officer in any respect?

*A.* His duties are to receive all money lodged in the court, and place the same in the Bank of England for security. He is also to see that the orders of the court, with regard to these funds, are carried out by investing the funds or paying them out of court upon proper authority. His functions are purely administrative.

8. *Q.* What are the investments authorised by the court for cash under the control of the court?

*A.* The investments are, Bank Stock, East India Stock, Exchequer Bills, and £2 10s. per Cent. Annuities, and upon mortgage of freehold and copyhold estates respectively in England and Wales, as well as in Consolidated £3 per Cent. Annuities, Reduced £3 per Cent. Annuities, and New £3 per Cent. Annuities. Order, 1st February, 1861.

9. *Q.* It is admitted by the answer of a defendant trustee, that there is a large sum of money belonging to the trust fund in his hands; what course would you advise to be adopted by the plaintiff who is interested in the fund?

*A.* I should advise a motion being made to the court for an order that the money should be paid to the Accountant-General to the credit of the cause. The admission in the defendant's answer would be sufficient to support the motion, and the order will be made for the purpose of protecting the fund. Ayck., C. Pr., 420.

10. *Q.* An order is made for payment of money by the Accountant-General to a party who dies without having received it. By whom and by what means can the money be received?

*A.* If the order authorises the payment to the deceased or his personal representatives, the money may be paid to them on production of the probate or letters of administration. If no mention is made of the representatives, the Accountant-General will not act upon the order, but an application to the court will be necessary for a further order. Daniel's Practice, 1324; *The Legal Examiner*, 256.

11. *Q.* What does the Accountant-General require to authorise him to pay money out of court?

*A.* He will not pay out the money without an order authorising him to do so. The order must be left at his office, and a cheque upon the bank will be prepared. The solicitor usually attends with the party to receive the cheque, to identify him. The cheque will be cashed at the bank. Ayck. C. Pr., 439.

12. *Q.* What does the Accountant-General require to authorise him to transfer stock?

*A.* He will require the Registrar's certificate for the transfer, also the order directing the transfer, to be left at his office, with a note signed by the solicitor at the foot of the certificate, containing the name, address, and quality of the transferee, and into what stock. Upon this the transfer will be made, and an office copy certificate of its having been effected may be obtained at the Accountant-General's office. Ayck., C. Pr., 442.

13. *Q.* Your client has brought an action to recover a debt due to him, and has obtained a judgment, but the debtor refuses to pay. The debtor has a life interest in funded property, standing in the names of trustees. Can the judgment creditor take any and what proceedings, and when, to render his life interest available for the payment of his debt?

*A.* The creditor may obtain an order from a common law judge, charging the property with the judgment. Such an order entitles him to the same remedies as if he had had a charge made in his favour by the debtor. No proceedings to enforce the order are to be taken for six months from its date. The Court of Chancery will, however, prevent the trustees paying the dividends to the debtor which accrue due between the interval of the date of the charging order and the expiration of the six months limited by 1 & 2 Vic., c. 110, s. 14. *Watts* v. *Jeffryes,* 20; L. J. Ch., 659. Also, as to real estate, see *Yescomb* v. *Landor,* 28; L. J. Ch., 876; 1 & 2 Vic., c. 110, s. 13, providing that no proceedings to enforce a judgment in equity as to real estate can be taken for a year.

## XXIII.—*Costs.*

1. *Q.* In what cases will a plaintiff be ordered to give security for costs, and at what stage of the proceedings? How must the application be made?

*A.* Security for costs will be ordered if the plaintiff resides permanently out of the jurisdiction of the court; also where he has no fixed residence; also where the plaintiff has left his residence soon after bill filed, and no information can be obtained from his solicitors as to his abode. The application should be made directly the defendant ascertains that he is entitled to security, and before he takes any fresh step in the cause. If it appears by the bill that the plaintiff is abroad, the application may be by motion or petition as of course. In other cases, it must be made by summons or motion, supported by affidavit. The bond is given to the record and writ clerk in whose division the suit is, and is in the penal sum of £100. Ayck., C. Pr., 407.

2. *Q.* When is a defendant to a suit entitled to an order as of course for the plaintiff to give security for costs, and to what amount?

*A.* He is entitled to an order as of course, on motion or petition, when it appears by the bill that the plaintiff is abroad. The amount of security is a bond in the penalty of £100. Ayck., C. Pr., 409.

3. *Q.* A person having become security for costs, dies pending the suit. Can the defendant oblige the plaintiff to give further security for costs?

*A.* Further security will be ordered in the event of the surety's death, or even his bankruptcy; and the proceedings will be stayed until a new security is given. Smith's Pr., 866.

4. *Q.* How are the costs of a suit to be obtained? State the steps *seriatim*.

*A.* The decree directing the taxation of the costs is taken to the taxing master's office, with a copy of it, also the bill of costs. Indorse on the decree a reference to the sitting master. Hand it to his clerk, who will get marked the name of the master in rotation. The decree is then taken to the master in rotation, whose clerk will examine it with the copy, and file it. The bill is left with him, and a warrant on leaving taken out. A warrant to tax, prepared by the solicitor, is then taken out, and served on the opposite parties. The papers in the cause must be left with the master, together with vouchers for fees and disbursements. Upon the return of the warrant to tax, the parties attend the master, and the taxation is gone into. The master's certificate is obtained, and filed at the report office, after which payment may be enforced by *subpœna* for costs, or execution may be issued under 1 & 2 Vic., c. 110. Ayck., C. Pr., 400.

5. *Q.* Who is liable for costs incurred by an infant plaintiff?

*A.* His next friend is liable for the costs. But the infant may make himself liable to the costs if, after attaining twenty-one, he proceeds in the cause. Mitf. Pl., 27.

6. *Q.* Is there any and what recent alteration made with regard to the allowance of costs between party and party?

*A.* The alteration referred to is, that the taxing master is to allow all costs which are just and reasonable in the conduct of the cause, and which appear to have been necessarily incurred for the attainment of justice, and not through over caution, negligence, or mistake. This rule is no longer a recent one, having been made in 1845. Consol. Ord. xl., r. 32.

7. *Q.* How many distinct modes or principles of taxation are acknowledged by the court?

*A.* They are either between party and party, or solicitor and client. As to the former, see the previous answer. The latter are more liberal than the former. If the subject matter of the suit be under the amount or value of £1,000, a lower scale of charges is provided. Above that sum, a higher scale is allowed. Regul. 2 to Consol. Ord.

8. *Q.* What parties are usually allowed to attend the taxation of costs?

*A.* The solicitors of the parties to the suits, and their clerks are usually allowed to attend, but it is in the discretion of the taxing master to determine the proper parties to attend. *Stahlschmidt* v. *Lett*, 9 W. R., 830; Ayck., C. Pr., 403.

9. *Q.* When a party is dissatisfied with the certificate of the taxing master, what course can he take to have the taxation reviewed?

*A.* He must object in writing to the allowance or disallowance of certain items, and carry in his objection to the master, and apply to him for a warrant to review the taxation. He may then apply by summons to the judge who made the order for taxation, to review the same. Order xl., r. 33; Order of 2nd of Aug., 1864, r. 3.

10. *Q.* In what manner are applications for taxation of a bill, or for delivery up of deeds and papers, now to be made?

*A.* Both applications may be made to a judge by summons instead of by petition as formerly, except applications for orders of course, which are made on motion or petition as of course. Order, 2nd Aug., 1864, r. 1.

11. *Q.* What is the proper form in which a bill of costs must be delivered by a solicitor?

*A.* In delivering a bill to his client it should be signed by the solicitor, or be accompanied by a letter, so as to enable him to sue for it. The form of the bill is an arrangement of the items, in chronological order, with the dates and details sufficient to show the extent and purpose of the business charged for. It is usually copied on foolscap paper, bookways. If the bill is for taxation, the dates must be within the body of the bill, so as to leave the left-hand margin for deductions. Ayck., C. Pr., 402.

12. *Q.* How soon after its due delivery may a solicitor commence proceedings for the recovery of his bill of costs? And within what times can the party chargeable obtain a reference for taxation under general and special circumstances respectively?

*A.* He may sue on the expiration of one calendar month from the delivery. 6 & 7 Vic., c. 73, s. 37. An order for taxation may be obtained *ex parte* by motion or petition, by the party chargeable, within a month after the delivery, or after that period, and within one year from delivery, provided the solicitor has not in the meantime obtained a verdict for such costs. After the expiration of the year, or if a verdict has been obtained, or the costs have been paid, provided the application is within twelve months of payment, an order to tax can only be obtained under special circumstances. Such are—gross overcharges, extreme pressure having been exercised by the solicitor in obtaining payment. The solicitor cannot obtain an order for taxation until the expiration of a month from delivery. Ayck., C. Pr., 656.

13. *Q.* Define the nature and extent of a solicitor's lien on papers in his hands belonging to his client, and also of his lien on a fund in court recovered in a suit.

*A.* The lien of a solicitor is in its nature general. That is, he may retain any deeds or papers of his client come to his hands in respect of his professional employment, for his general account against such client. He also has a lien on a fund in court recovered by his exertions, and is entitled to priority out of such fund against a judgment creditor, who has obtained a charging order before the solicitor. This right is quite independent of 23 & 24 Vic., c. 127, s. 28, which see and consider. *Haymes* v. *Cooper*; *Cooper* v. *Jenkins*, 10 Jur., N. S., 303.

14. *Q.* Have the town-agents of a country solicitor any, and what, lien upon the papers in their hands belonging to the clients of the country solicitor?

*A.* See *supra*, "Common Law," "Attorney and Client," No. 3.

15. *Q.* If a person, not a party to a cause, take proceedings in

a cause, and be ordered to pay or to receive from a party in a cause costs in respect to such proceedings, how are the costs recovered by or from such persons?

*A.* They are recovered as mentioned *supra*, 385, No. 13. Consol. Ord. xxix., r. 2.

16. *Q.* Has the court any power to order the payment of interest on costs, or to charge the property recovered with the payment of costs?

*A.* Any court of justice may now order interest to be paid on costs at the rate of £4 per cent., from the date of the certificate. It may also order the costs of the plaintiff or defendant to be a charge upon property recovered or preserved in the court. Such charge is to be valid against all persons, excepting a *bona fide* purchaser, for value without notice. Such an order, however, cannot be made if the right to recover the costs is barred by the Statute of Limitations. 27 & 28 Vic., c. 127, ss. 27, 28.

17. *Q.* When two or more trustees appear in a suit by one solicitor, can they afterwards sever their defence and have separate bills of costs? State the rule in this respect that now prevails.

*A.* The rule is, that trustees should not sever their defence unless there is some good reason for doing so, such as fraud by one in which the other has not participated; or if one has a personal interest which conflicts with his duty as trustee. If they sever their defences improperly, only one set of costs will be allowed. Lewin on Trusts, 650.

## XXIV.—*Business at Chambers.*

1. *Q.* State some of the usual proceedings before a judge at chambers under the recent statutes and orders of the court.

*A.* The following are some of the proceedings:—Applications for time to plead, answer, or demur; for leave to amend bills; for enlarging time for closing evidence, and for production of documents; applications relating to the conduct of suits or matters, or to the guardianship, maintenance, or advancement of infants; applications for the payment of dividends to a person to whose separate account funds are standing; application under 10 & 11 Vic., c. 96, where the trust fund does not exceed £300; for payment into court of purchase-moneys under sales, by order of the court, and investing the same. The various accounts and enquiries frequently directed by decrees are made in chambers, and the chief clerk's certificate made thereon. 15 & 16 Vic., c. 86, s. 27; Consol. Ord. xxxv., r. 1.

2. *Q.* Specify the various matters which *must* be commenced before a judge at chambers.

*A.* They are:—Applications as to the payment of dividends, and applications under 10 & 11 Vic., c. 96, just mentioned; applications under 36 Geo. III., c. 52, s. 32 (the Legacy Duty Act); where the sum paid in or transferred does not exceed £300; applications on behalf of infants, under 1 Wm. IV., c. 65. Also proceedings to administer the estate of a deceased person's estate *may* be commenced at chambers. See previous answer.

3. *Q.* State the mode of proceeding by which executors or administrators of deceased persons are enabled to ascertain whether there are any outstanding debts or liabilities affecting the estates of such persons without an administration suit.

*A.* They may obtain an order on motion or petition of course for an account to be taken in chambers, of the debts and liabilities affecting the personal estate of the deceased. The order may now be obtained immediately upon probate and letters of administration are granted. 13 & 14 Vic., c. 35, s. 19; 23 & 24 Vic., c. 38, s. 14. The order is proceeded on as mentioned below, No. 5.

4. *Q.* By what summary process can a creditor of a deceased person procure the administration of his real and personal estate?

*A.* The proceeding referred to is by summons at Chambers. This course is, however, inapplicable for the purposes of administering real estate, unless the *whole* of it is by devise vested in trustees who are by the will empowered to sell it and authorized to give receipts for the produce. 15 & 16 Vic., c. 86, s. 47.

5. *Q.* Set out the various steps to be taken in such a suit.

*A.* A summons must be taken out and a duplicate filed at the Record and Writ Clerk's Office. It is served and an appearance is entered. The summons is returnable in seven days. Upon the hearing, the judge makes the ordinary decree for administration. *Supra*, 381, "The Hearing," No. 6. The enquiries are prosecuted, advertisements for creditors are inserted and the claims entered in the claim book, the chief clerk, from time to time satisfying himself upon the correctness of the accounts brought in. If any question of difficulty arises the judge is consulted. When the enquiries are completed the chief clerk prepares his certificate, which is settled in the presence of the various solicitors. It is then signed by the chief clerk. Unless appealed against, the further consideration of the cause comes on by summons and a final order is made.

6. *Q.* Who are the parties who can obtain an order before a judge at chambers for the administration of a deceased person's personal estate?

*A.* The following persons may take proceedings:—1. Creditors, whether by simple contract or specialty. 2. Beneficiaries, such as legatees and next of kin. 15 & 16 Vic., c. 86, s. 45. As to executors and administrators, see *supra*, No. 3.

7. *Q.* In what case may a person interested under a will apply for an administration (real estate) summons?

*A.* See *supra*, No. 4.

8. *Q.* Give a brief outline of the proceedings in equity to administer an intestate's personal estate, when there are no next of kin, *ab ovo usque ad mala*.

*A.* In such a case a creditor should obtain administration to the intestate, but he must first issue a citation to the Crown's representative. If the Crown appears, the administration would be granted to the Solicitor of the Treasury under 15 & 16 Vic., c. 3,

If not, the creditor will be entitled to the grant. Upon this he would file a bill, or proceed by summons, against the other creditors, making the Attorney-General a party; a short answer would be filed and the cause set down on Bill and answer. A decree would be made directing enquiries at Chambers as to the property and creditors, and the chief clerk would make his certificate for payment of the debts, the residue to be paid to the Crown. If the Crown solicitor took out administration, a creditor should proceed against him for administration. This proceeding it would seem should be by petition of right under 23 and 24 Vic., c. 34, which Act makes the proceedings in such a cause analogous to those in ordinary suits. As to proceedings by summons, see *supra.*

9. *Q.* What is the first usual proceeding in the chief clerk's Chambers after the copy decree or order has been left; and what is done thereupon?

*A.* A summons is issued returnable in two days to proceed with the decree. Upon its return, the judge must be satisfied that all the persons who under the old practice were necessary parties, have been served with notice of the decree. Directions will then be given as to the prosecution of the accounts and enquiries. A time is fixed for the accounting party (if any) to bring in his accounts. The accounts are brought in and verified by affidavit, and the items of discharge over 40s. vouched. The accounting party may be examined in Chambers. The certificate is then prepared as mentioned *supra*, No. 5. Consol. Ord., xxxv. r. 66.

10. *Q.* In what form do accounting parties bring their accounts into the chief clerk's Chambers, and is the oath of the accounting party sufficient evidence of the payments?

*A.* The account is prepared "ledger fashion," that is with a Debtor and Creditor side. The items are numbered consecutively. In addition to the oath of the accounting party, items of discharge over 40s. must be vouched. Consol. Ord., xxxv., r. 33.

11. *Q.* Do the certificates of the chief clerks, upon inquiries prosecuted before them, correspond with the reports of the late masters in Chancery? Must such inquiries be prosecuted with or without the direct intervention of the judge, and has the suitor the right of appealing to the judge before or after the certificate is signed by the latter, and can exception be taken to the certificate?

*A.* The certificate does not correspond with the report of the masters, inasmuch as it is more brief than the report. It does not, unless rendered specially necessary by circumstances, set out the decree or order, or any documents, or evidence, or reasons. Nor does it set out in a schedule the accounts taken. The above were set out in the report, but need now only be referred to. Consol. Ord., xxxv, r. 47. Most of the inquiries are prosecuted without the intervention of the judge, though any suitor has a right, whenever he chooses, to take the opinion of the judge personally, and for this purpose the chief clerk is bound to refer the matter to the judge. *Wadham* v. *Rigg*, 10 W.R., 365. As to appealing from the certificate see answer No. 13. Exceptions cannot be filed to the certificate. 15 & 16 Vic., c. 86, s. 33.

12. *Q.* Where the chief clerk has under a decree settled interrogatories for examining one of the defendants who refuses or neglects to put in his examination, by what steps can the plaintiff compel him to answer the interrogatories?

*A.* Upon the refusal of the defendant to answer, application should be made to the judge to examine him himself. If he then refuse, the witness may be at once committed for contempt. The chief clerk cannot examine on interrogatories, unless specially empowered to do so by the judge. 15 & 16 Vic., c. 80, s. 30; Morgan's Acts & Ord., 104.

13. *Q.* What steps should be taken to appeal from the certificate of a Judge's chief clerk made under a decree?

*A.* A summons should be taken out within four days after the signature of the certificate by the chief clerk, to discharge or vary it. If the Judge has signed the certificate, it may be appealed against by summons at chambers or motion to the court within eight days after such signature. After the expiration of the eight days, the certificate is binding on all parties, and can only be varied on very special grounds. 15 & 16 Vic., c. 80, s. 34. Consol. Ord., xxxv. r. 52.

14. *Q.* Are creditors who have come in and established their debts before the chief clerk under a decree or order in a suit entitled to any, and if so, what, benefits under the orders of the 26th August, 1841 (Consol. Ord. xlii., r. 10), to which they were not previously entitled?

*A.* Such creditors are entitled to interest at the rate of £4 per cent. per annum upon their debts, from the date of the decree, to be paid out of any surplus there may be after satisfying the debts, costs of suit and interest upon debts by law carrying interest.

15. *Q.* Can, or cannot, a creditor prove his debt in a creditor's suit, after the chief clerk has made his certificate? If he cannot, say why; and if he can, explain how, and under what circumstances.

*A.* He cannot do so without special leave obtained from the Judge on summons. The Consolidated Orders provide that all claims shall be excluded, unless entered before the time limited by the advertisement, excepting in the case of claims entered before any adjournment day. Consol. Ord., xxxv. rr. 41—43. The order will only be made before the creditors have been paid, or where there are assets still undisposed of. It will be on such terms as to costs as the Judge thinks fit. Ibid., see *Halliley* v. *Henderson*, 4 Jur., N. S., 202.

16. *Q.* State the steps in the proceeding for appointment of a guardian without suit.

*A.* A summons should be taken out returnable in seven days. The application should be supported by evidence showing the proposed guardian is a proper person and has no interests opposed to those of the infant. If a cause is pending, the application is by an ordinary summons entituled in the cause. A guardian *ad litem* is appointed on motion or petition of course. As to applications for maintenance, *supra*, 327, No. 9. Ayck., C. Pr., 571.

17. *Q.* A dies intestate, leaving three infant children entitled to property. B, his brother, is desirous to be appointed guardian of the infants, and to have an allowance out of their property; what proceedings are to be adopted for this purpose?

*A.* See previous answer.

18. *Q.* Can an executor be charged with wilful default upon an administration summons?

*A.* He cannot, proceedings by summons being merely applicable to simple cases. A bill should be filed. *Portington* v. *Reynolds*, 4 Drew., 253.

19. *Q.* Trace the course of proceeding on a sale of an estate under the direction of the Court, from the order directing the sale, to the confirmation of the certificate of the result of the sale.

*A.* When the order is drawn up it is left at the chief clerk's chambers, and a summons taken out to proceed upon it. This is served by the plaintiff, who usually has the conduct of the sale upon the defendants. The summons is attended and directions made for advertising, also as to reserved biddings, and generally as to the conduct of the sale. The advertisement is prepared by the solicitor, and submitted to the chief clerk for approval. It is then inserted in the "London Gazette." Particulars and conditions of sale are prepared, and a copy, marked by the chief clerk, laid with the abstract before one of the conveyancing counsel of the court, who settles them (practically, he draws them also). A surveyor's valuation having been obtained, the reserved biddings will be fixed by the chief clerk. These he encloses under a sealed cover and hands to the plaintiff's solicitor. The auctioneer and day of sale are appointed by the chief clerk, and the sale conducted as in ordinary cases. The biddings and signatures of purchasers are afterwards verified by affidavit, which is filed and an office copy taken with the conditions and bidding paper to the chief clerk. The subsequent proceedings are carried on as in an ordinary case, excepting that the various steps with regard to requisitions on title, &c. are taken with the sanction of the chief clerk and conveyancing counsel. The purchaser must obtain an order to pay his purchase-money to the Accountant-General, upon which being paid, he is entitled to possession. The chief clerk embodies the result of the sale in his certificate. If no objection is taken to it, the judge signs it four clear days after it is signed by the chief clerk. It is then filed with the clerk of records and writs. If no proceedings are taken to discharge or vary it within eight clear days from the filing, it is confirmed. Ayck., C. Pr., 489, 509.

20. *Q.* What time is allowed for opening biddings? under what circumstances will an application for that purpose be entertained? and what steps must be taken by a person who is desirous of having the biddings opened.

*A.* The application should be made before the certificate is confirmed; but in some cases of fraud the court has opened them after this time. The application must be made by summons served on the purchaser's solicitor and on the solicitor to the parties. The application will not be successful unless the biddings are considerably increased, say an advance of from eight or ten per cent. on the purchase-money. The deposit offered must amount to £40 at least. The costs of the first purchaser must be paid. Ibid., 501.

21. *Q.* If a person purchase an estate sold under the direction of the Court of Chancery, to whom does he pay the purchase-money, when is he entitled to a conveyance, and who bears the expense of obtaining its execution?

*A.* The purchase-money he pays into court, having previously obtained an order for that purpose. He is entitled to a conveyance at his own expense as soon as the certificate is confirmed, and he has paid the purchase-money into Court. The expense of execution is borne by the vendor. Sugden's Vendors, 102.

## XXV.—*Motions and Petitions.*

1. *Q.* State generally the practice in presenting, serving, and bringing to a hearing a petition.

*A.* The petition is addressed to the Lord Chancellor if intended to be heard before a Vice-Chancellor, but if to be heard before the Master of the Rolls, it is to be addressed to him. After engrossment it is left with the secretary of the Lord Chancellor, or the secretary to the Rolls. The secretary will write the answer in the margin, and a copy is left with him, upon which he will set it down. Copies are then served on the parties two days before the day of hearing. The petition is supported by affidavit, which may be filed at any time before the hearing. The consequence of this is, that the petition is often adjourned, to enable the opposite parties to answer the affidavit. Counsel are instructed, and the petition comes on in its order in the list. The order being made, it is drawn up by the Registrar in the presence of the parties. Ayck., C. Pr., 287.

2. *Q.* State in detail the steps to be taken to get money out of court by petition, when the money has been paid in by a Railway Company as the price of land taken by the Company?

*A.* The proceedings will be taken as mentioned in the preceding answer. The costs are borne by the Company. See *supra*, 275, No. 8.

3. *Q.* What is the distinction between applications to the court on motion and petition?

*A.* Proceedings by motion are usually adopted in interlocutory applications which do not depend upon numerous facts, but which are necessary in the course of a suit. Thus applications for writs *ne exeat regno* and injunction may be by motion. Petitions are usually adopted in cases where it is necessary to state various facts or set out documents showing the title of the applicant. Thus to obtain money paid into court by trustees or Railway Companies, is by petition. Both motions and petitions are divided into those "special" and "as of course." Special motions are made in open court by counsel, and special petitions are also heard in court, but motions as of course are by what is termed a hand brief, signed by counsel; and petitions "as of course" are simply presented to the secretary at the rolls. A vast number of interlocutory proceedings may be taken by motion or petition as of course. Ayck., C. Pr., 287.

4. *Q.* Who draws up the orders made thereon? and describe what is done by the solicitor before they are completed and to be acted on?

*A.* The orders made upon special motions and petitions are drawn up by the Registrars in the presence of the parties. Orders on motions as of course are usually drawn up by their clerks. Orders on petition as of course are drawn up by the secretary of the rolls. The solicitor should get the order settled by the registrar, according to the terms indorsed upon counsel's briefs. It should be engrossed, passed by the registrar, and marked with his initials. After this, it is left for entry by the clerk of entries. Ayck., C. Pr., 200.

5. *Q.* What time must elapse between the service of a notice of motion and the day named in the notice for the hearing of the motion?

*A.* In the case of a motion for decree the notice is one month; ordinary special motions two clear days; motions to appoint a guardian to a defendant six days. Consol. Ord., xxxiii., r. 2.

6. *Q.* How would you proceed practically to appoint a new trustee in a case where the deed creating the trust contains no power for that purpose? State shortly the course of proceeding from the beginning to the end.

*A.* The proceeding would be by petition, as mentioned *supra*, No. 1. 13 & 14 Vic., c. 60, s. 32. This proceeding will, however, now be seldom necessary, in consequence of the provisions of 23 & 24 Vic., c. 145, s. 27. This section, however, does not provide for the cases of a trustee being abroad, nor of all the trustees retiring simultaneously, nor for there being two sets of trustees of the same instrument, nor for an augmentation or reduction of the number of trustees. Morgan's Acts and Orders, 319, 3rd ed.

7. *Q.* What is the necessary evidence to support a petition for leave to sue in *formâ pauperis?*

*A.* The petition should be supported by an affidavit showing that the plaintiff is not worth £5, excepting his wearing-apparel and the subject matter of the suit. There must also be at the foot of the petition a certificate of counsel that he conceives the case to be proper for relief in equity. Ayck., C. Pr., 619.

8. *Q.* What is the necessary statement which must now be made at the foot of every petition?

*A.* If it is intended to serve the petition on any person, it must be stated upon whom it is to be served. If no one is intended to be served, it must be so stated. The above only applies to special petitions. Consol. Ord., 34, r. 1.

## XXVI.—*Contumacy.*

1. *Q.* What is the meaning of being in contempt?
*A.* It signifies that a party has done some act which is inconsistent with the deference which ought to be shown by suitors and others to so high a tribunal. Thus if the defendant refuses to answer or to perform a decree, he is in contempt. If one marries a ward of court without permission he is in contempt.

2. *Q.* How is a party proceeded against in the case of a contempt of court?
*A.* He may be proceeded against by writ of attachment, serjeant-at-arms, and sequestration. See further, *supra*, titles, "appearance," and "answer."

3. *Q.* What is the first thing to be done by a party in contempt, and who wishes to apply to the court on any other subject?
*A.* He should clear his contempt; that is, he should conform to the rules of the court by performing that which he has hitherto treated with contempt.

4. *Q.* Describe the proceedings against a defendant who has committed a breach of an injunction?
*A.* A motion must be made to the court supported by affidavit stating the service of the writ and the circumstances of the breach, and an order obtained that the defendant stand committed. The order when obtained is handed to the messenger who obtains the Lord Chancellor's warrant and arrests the defendant. Ayck., C. Pr., 260.

## XXVII.—*Miscellaneous and General.*

1. *Q.* State what are the principal proceedings which occur in the usual course of a chancery suit commenced by bill.
*A.* The bill being filed, it is served upon the defendant who appears and gives notice of his appearance to the plaintiff. If he does not appear, an appearance may be entered for him, or process of contempt issued. After appearance, interrogatories are filed and delivered.* These the defendant answers. If no interrogatories are filed, a voluntary answer may be put in. Instead of, or in addition to, an answer, the defendant may plead, or demur. The plaintiff, after answer, files replication or sets down the cause on bill and answer, or gives notice of motion for decree, or if there is a demurrer or plea sets them down for argument, or he may amend his bill, or he may except to the answer, or he may move to dismiss. If he proceeds by replication or motion for decree, evidence is gone into, the cause set down, and a *subpœna* to hear judgment issued and served. If the evidence is intended to be taken at the hearing, an order for that purpose is obtained and witnesses are subpœnaed to attend. Briefs are prepared and counsel instructed.

---

* Interrogatories are to be filed within eight days from appearance. They must be delivered, where defendant appears in proper time, within eight days after time for appearance; where defendant does not so appear, within eight days after appearance.—Consol. Ord. xi.

The cause is heard and the decree made. If not satisfactory to all parties, it may be appealed against. The decree when drawn up, passed, and entered, is then enforced by the process of the court. If the decree directs inquiries at Chambers, these are carried out and the cause set down on a future occasion for the final decree. See *supra* the various titles.

2. *Q.* What are the principal innovations in chancery practice made by the Act 15 & 16 Vic., c. 86.

*A.* They are:—As to the printing, endorsement, service, and frame of bills; as to the abolition of the *subpœna* to appear; as to the delivery of interrogatories, the introduction of motion for decree; as to the production of documents; the filing of interrogatories by the defendant; as to the taking of evidence; as to the necessary parties to suits in various cases; as to proceedings by summons for administration; as to sale in a foreclosure suit; as to making declaratory orders without giving relief; as to the revival of a suit by order to revive; as to the proceedings on a sale; as to injunction to stay proceedings at law; as to sending cases to be tried at law, see the above provisions considered in detail, *supra*.

3. *Q.* Describe some of the proceedings in a suit which are termed "interlocutory."

*A.* They are those proceedings in the cause at which a decision of the court is arrived at, but which decision does not operate as a final termination of the suit. Thus, motions for injunction and orders thereon, are interlocutory. So also are petitions and orders made thereon. The term is sometimes applied to the ordinary proceedings in the cause, but it seems to be more properly applicable to those which obtain directly something material in the suit, though not final. Wharton's Law Lexicon, 472.

4. *Q.* State the steps of a suit to foreclose a mortgage of real estate from first to last.

*A.* Proceed as mentioned, *supra*, No. 1, up to decree, which directs an account to be taken of what is due upon the mortgagee, and that it be paid with the costs within six months after the certificate. The chief clerk having made his certificate the mortgagee should attend at the time and place appointed for payment, and receive the money. If the money is not paid, an affidavit of attendance and non-payment is made, and an order obtained on motion or petition for the defendant to be absolutely foreclosed. This order is drawn up, passed and entered. The time of payment will be enlarged upon application in certain cases. See *supra*, 350, No. 48; Ayck., C. Pr., 240.

5. *Q.* How many writs of *subpœna* are used, and for what purposes, in courts of equity?

*A.* They are:—1. *Subpœna* to hear judgment, issued before a cause comes on to be heard. 2. *Subpœna ad test.*, for the attendance of a witness. 3. *Subpœna duces tecum*, for the attendance of a witness with a document. 4. *Subpœna* for costs, to compel their payment. Consol. Ord., 28.

6. *Q.* Name and give a short description of the several writs usually issued in the course of a suit.

*A.* See the previous answer. Also may be mentioned writs of injunction, writs of attachment, serjeant-at-arms, sequestration, writs of assistance, writs of *fi. fa.*, *fi. fa de bonis ecclesiasticis*, *ca. sa.*, and *elegit*, writs of *ne exeat regno* and *distringas*. See more fully as to their objects, *supra*, "enforcement of decrees," "contumacy."

7. *Q.* Does an order take effect from the time it is pronounced or from the time it is served?

*A.* As a judicial decision the order of the court operates the moment it is pronounced. But the parties against whom the order is made are not bound by it until it is served. That is process of contempt cannot issue against them before this is done. The rights of the parties are, however, settled (subject to appeal) when the decree is made, the service being merely a necessary formality enjoined by the procedure of the court. Consol. Ord., xxx., r. 4.

8. *Q.* What proceedings in the Court of Chancery operate as a *lis pendens*, and how do you avail yourself of them?

*A.* Suits instituted in the court, whether by bill, special case, or summons originating proceedings at chambers, operate as *lites pendentes*. Also a petition to wind up a company under 25 & 26 Vic., c. 89, is a *lis pendens*. To make them available against purchasers or mortgagees without express notice of them, the name, place of abode, and title of trade of the person whose estate is intended to be affected, together with the title of the court and cause must be registered in the Court of Common Pleas, and re-registered every five years. 2 Vic., c. 11, s. 7.

9. *Q.* What is a condition precedent? Give an example.

*A.* It is a condition upon the happening of which an estate is to vest in a person named. If the condition is not fulfilled the estate never vests. Thus, conveyance to A for one year, and on B's return from Rome in six months then to A in fee. Here the return of B is a condition precedent to A taking the fee. Steph. Com., 305.

10. *Q.* If a donee of a general power of appointment over a fund exercises the power, can his creditors claim the fund against the appointee and purchasers from him?

*A.* Yes, they may in equity claim the fund, if the power is properly exercised, against the appointee, if he is a volunteer. But against a *bonâ fide* purchaser either directly from the appointee or from the volunteer, they would have no claim, such purchaser having a better equity. 2 L. C. Eq., 103 — 4.

11. *Q.* What are uses in strict settlement?

*A.* They are the ordinary uses upon which a family estate is limited on the marriage of the owner. They are to the owner for life, and after his death to his first and other sons in tail. As to the details of the uses see *supra*, 183, No. 2 *et seq.*; 1 Steph. Com., 337, 5th ed.

# APPENDIX.

*The following directions to be observed before and at the examination are extracted from "The Articled Clerk's Manual," 9th ed., by Anderson. Appendix, which also see for Forms of Articles of Clerkship, Notices, Affidavits, etc.*

XI. About a fortnight or three weeks before the examination takes place, the candidate will receive at the address, stated in his notice for examination, the following intimation, with a copy (31) of the questions to be answered by himself and principal:—

Sir, ——, 186—.
    I am directed by the examiners appointed for the examination of persons applying to be admitted attornies, to inform you that you are required to attend on —— the ——, and —— the —— next, at half-past nine in the forenoon, at the Hall of the Incorporated Law Society, in Chancery Lane, in order to be examined. The examination will commence at ten o'clock precisely, and close at four o'clock each day.
    I have to remind you that your articles of clerkship and assignment, if any, with answers (33) to the questions as to due service, according to the regulations approved by the judges, must be left with me on or before —— the —— (35).
    Where the articles have not expired, but will expire during the term, or in the vacation following such term, the candidate may be examined conditionally (36); but the articles must be left within the first seven days of term, and answers up to that time. If part of the term has been served with a *barrister, special pleader,* or *London*

---

(31) Where there is an assignment, or the articled clerk has passed some of the term in town, with a barrister or agent, another copy of these questions must be obtained from the Incorporated Law Society, for the answers of the gentleman to whom the articled clerk was signed, or the barrister or agent with whom he passed such time. Where a principal improperly refuses to answer these questions, the court will grant a rule *nisi* calling upon him to show cause.

(33) Where it is manifest to the court that the attorney improperly refuses to answer the questions as to the service of his articled clerk, or to certify that he has duly served and is a fit person to be admitted as an attorney, the court will grant a rule calling upon the attorney to show cause why he should not return answers to the questions and sign the certificate.

(35) Candidates under the 4th section of the Attorneys' Act, 1860, may, on application, obtain copies of the further questions relating to the ten years' service antecedent to the articles of clerkship.

(36) And where the candidate is under age, but will attain it during the term, he may be examined *de bene esse* during such term.

*agent*, answers to the questions must be obtained from them, as to the time served with each respectively.

On the first day of examination, papers will be delivered to each candidate, containing questions to be answered in writing, classed under the several heads of—1. Preliminary; 2. *Common and Statute Law*, and Practice of the Courts; 3. *Conveyancing*.

On the second day further papers will be delivered to each candidate, containing questions to be answered in — 4. *Equity*, and Practice of the Courts; 5. *Bankruptcy*, and Practice of the Courts; 6. *Criminal Law*, and Proceedings before Justices of the Peace.

Each candidate is required to answer *all* the preliminary questions (No. I.); and also to answer in *three* of the other heads of inquiry, viz.:—*Common Law, Conveyancing*, and *Equity*.

The examiners will continue the practice of proposing questions in *Bankruptcy* and in *Criminal Law* and *Proceedings before Justices of the Peace*, in order that candidates, who have given their attention to these subjects, may have the advantage of answering such questions, and having the correctness of their answers in those departments taken into consideration in summing up the merits of their general examination.

In case your testimonials were deposited in a former term, they should be re-entered, the fee paid, and the answers completed to the time appointed.

I am, Sir,
Your very obedient servant,
A. B.,
*Secretary.*

The articles, assignment (if any), and questions, duly answered by the articled clerk and his principal, must be lodged at the Law Institution, and the fee of fifteen shillings paid, on or before the day named in the above circular; a receipt for the articles and assignment is given.

The candidate, upon entering the Hall of the Law Institution on the morning of the examination, will have a numbered ticket given to him; he will then take his seat at the end of the table on which the corresponding number is placed.

The following is the mode of proceeding at the examination, as laid down by the examiners in their printed instructions to the candidates, a copy of which is laid before each person on commencing his examination.

"The candidates for examination are requested to attend to the following directions:—

Each candidate (37) will (as I have already stated) have a number given to him, and will take his seat at the end of the table on which such number is placed.

---

(37) The chairman, who is invariably one of the masters of the common law courts, addresses the candidates, and calls their attention to the rules, especially that against assisting, or copying from, one another.

A paper of questions (38) will be delivered to him, with his name and number upon it, containing questions to be answered in writing, classed under the several heads of—

1. Preliminary.
2. Common and Statute Law, and Practice of the Courts.
3. Conveyancing.
4. Equity, and Practice of the Courts.
5. Bankruptcy, and Practice of the Courts.
6. Criminal Law, and Proceedings before Justices of the Peace.

Each candidate is required to answer *all* the preliminary questions (No. I.); and also to answer in *three* of the other heads of inquiry—*Common Law, Conveyancing,* and *Equity*.

The answers under the *six above-mentioned* heads are to be written on one side only, on *separate* papers for each head, prefixing to each answer the number of the question; and each paper should be written in a plain and legible manner, and *signed*.

The candidates are expected to finish their papers by four o'clock, but no answers will be received from any candidate before one o'clock.

The following are the preliminary questions :—

1. *Preliminary.*

1. What is *now* your age?
2. Where, and with whom, did you serve your clerkship?
3. State the particular branch or branches of the law to which you have principally applied yourself during your clerkship.
4. Mention some of the principal law books which you have read and studied.
5. Have you attended any, and what, law lectures?

The answers to the questions are to be written on the papers (foolscap) which are prepared for them. These papers have a margin ruled off for the number of examiner's marks; and there are two numbers on every sheet for the answers.

After the examination has begun, no candidate is to leave the hall (without permission obtained from the examiners) until he shall have delivered in his answers, and any candidate who leaves the hall without permission will not be allowed to return.

No candidate will be allowed to communicate with, receive assistance from, or copy from the paper of, another: and in case this rule be discovered to be infringed, such person will be considered *not to have passed his examination*.

At the top of the red-ink ruled sheets for the answers is printed this recommendation :—" You are requested to attend carefully to the wording of the question, and answer every part of it concisely.

---

(38) Fifteen independent questions are proposed in each branch.

Each answer should, if possible, be comprised within the limits allowed to it in this paper."

When the candidate has finished his answers, he will call an attendant in the room, who will tie them together, with the printed copy of the questions; the candidate will then deliver them, and the ticket given on his entrance, to the secretary, at the examiners' table; whereupon he will receive another ticket, which he is to give to the person at the door when he goes away.

The result of the examination is not made known to the candidate till the second or third day following, when, if he be successful, he will receive a printed letter intimating that he can obtain the examiner's certificate on a named day, and also the articles and assignments (if any) upon producing the receipt for them. If unsuccessful, a lithographed letter, regretfully communicating the result, will be addressed to him.

The list of honours conferred is not generally known until a week after the examination. The successful candidate will then receive a letter from the Secretary of the Incorporated Law Society, informing him that the examiners have certified his having passed his examination with distinction, and the Council thereupon have awarded a Prize or Certificate of Merit, as the case may be. The Honourable Societies of Clifford's Inn and Clement's Inn respectively, usually give one prize; and the Incorporated Law Society present four or five. The candidate is allowed to select his own books, the value not to exceed five guineas. Macaulay's History of England, Campbell's Lives of the Chancellors, and Hallam's works, are amongst the most popular, though some prefer Williams on Executors, and other law books. The number of Certificates of Merit varies from four to ten. The books will be forwarded to the Prizeman as he may request.

# INDEX.

## A.

**ABATEMENT:**
plea in . . . . 59, 61
of an action . . . 69, 92
of a suit . . . 354, 355

**ABSTRACT** (*see* "Vendor and Purchaser.")

**ACCIDENT** (*see* "Forfeiture") . 293
where relieved against . . 293

**ACCOUNT:**
advantage of proceedings in equity for . . . . 296
form of . . . . . 296
settled, when opened . . 297

**ACCOUNTANT-GENERAL:**
duties of . . . . 390

**ACCUMULATION** (*see* "Perpetuities.")
time limited for . . 244, 245
effect of periods being exceeded 245

**ACTION:**
what it is . . . . . 3
real, personal, and mixed . . 3
causes of . . . . . 4
*ex contractu* . . . . 4
of covenant . . . . 4
of *assumpsit* . . . . 4
of debt . . . . . 4
of trover . . . . . 6
of detinue . . . . . 6
on lost bond . . . . 6
and indictment for some offence 6
for libel and slander . . . 6
for a nuisance . . . . 6
on a bill or note . . . 6
of ejectment . . . . 6
of tort . . . . . 7
of trespass . . . . 7
of trespass on the case . . 7
of trover . . . . . 7
of replevin . . . . 7
actions which die with the person 32
parties to . . . . 39
consolidating . . . . 58
local and transitory . . . 56
how commenced . . 45, 46
joining causes of . . 7, 58
various steps in . . . 109

**ADEMPTION:**
of portions and legacies . 319, 320

**ADMINISTRATORS:**
do not represent executors 42, 257
power of one of several . . 256

**ADMINISTRATION:**
with the will annexed . . 256
what next of kin entitled to . 256
*de bonis non* . . . 42, 257
suit for . . . . . 322
effect of decree for . . . 325
enquiries in decree for . . 382
proceedings for, in chambers 395, 396
who may institute suit for . 395
*ab ovo usque ad mala* . . 395

**ADMIT NOTICE TO**
object of . . . . . 73
time for . . . . . 73
consequences of not giving . 74

**AD VALOREM STAMP** . . 229
(*see* "Stamp Duty.")

**ADVOWSON:**
what it is . . . . . 153
joint tenants of . . . . 154
coparceners of . . . . 154
who presents on death of patron 154
if mortgaged . . . . 154
mortgage of . . . . 202
when it passes with land . . 245

**AFFIDAVIT:**
how entitled . . . . 51
refusal to make . . . 51
form of . . . . 52, 350
description of deponent . . 52
jurat . . . . . . 52
before whom sworn . 52, 55, 350
of merits . . . . . 52
of increase . . . . 52
to hold to bail . . . . 52
must state means of knowledge . 350

**AGENT:**
*del credere* . . . . . 13
when to be authorised by deed . 13
acts of sub-agent . . . 13
clerk of, making a valuation . 14
liability of, when principal abroad 14
when he may sue . . . 43

## INDEX.

**AGENT**—*continued.*
set off against principal . . 65
authorised by parol . . . 216
purchase of estate by . . 314
lien of town . . . . 36

**AGREEMENT** (*see* "Contracts.")

**ALIENS:**
cannot hold lands . , . 231
what trusts they may enforce . 306
suits by . . . . 347

**AMENDMENT:**
of writ after plea in abatement . 61
of the record . . . 85, 91
of bills, effect on injunction 293, 365
effect of, on attachment . . 365
time for . . . . 366
how order for, obtained . 366, 367
at the hearing . . . . 381

**ANNUITY:**
bequest of . . . . 250
how dealt with on administration 321

**ANSWER:**
nature of . . . . 358
distinguished from demurrer and plea . . . 362, 364
to interrogatories . . . 358
time to . . . . 358
voluntary . . . 358, 359
requisites of . . . . 359
by married woman . . . 359
by infant . . . . 359
printed . . . . 360
how compelled . . . . 360
evasive . . . . 361
insufficient . . . . 361
exceptions to . . . . 361
when sufficient . . . . 360
further . . . . 361
impertinent . . . . 362
and disclaimer . . . . 365
when evidence . . . 375, 376
when against co-defendant . 375
evidence at law . . . . 378
effect on, of filing replication . 370
deed impeached by . . . 375

**APPEAL:**
to what courts . . . 88, 273
on motion for new trial . . 88
from County Courts . . . 130
to the House of Lords . 273, 386
from Chancery Courts . . 386
to the Lord Chancellor . . 387
time . . . . 388

**APPEARANCE:**
to writ of summons . . . 50
time for, in various cases . . 50
undertaking to enter . . 51
by infant . . . . 40

**APPEARANCE**—*continued.*
by *feme covert* . . . 51
in person . . . . 51
giving false address . . 51, 57
in ejectment . . . . 111
to bill in Chancery . . . 355
how compelled . . 355, 356, 357
formal . . . . 356
time for . . . . 356
by infant . . . . 357
by idiot . . . . 357
by married woman . . . 357
if defendant abroad . . . 357

**APPOINTMENT** (*see* "Powers.")
exclusive, when good . . 169
fraudulent . . . . 169
to children, does not include grand-children . . . 169
consent of Sarah to . . . 311

**APPORTIONMENT:**
of rents . . . 146, 198
of annuity . . . . 319

**APPROVEMENT:**
by lord . . . . 158

**APPROPRIATION OF PAYMENTS** . 38

**ARBITRATION:**
how matters submitted to . . 123
in what cases . . . . 123
how attendance of witness enforced . . . . 123
setting aside award . . 123, 124
time for . . . . 123
power of arbitrator over costs . 124
award how enforced . . . 125
relief against in equity . . 283
agreement to refer to, not enforced . . . . 302
suit to impeach award . . 347

**ARREST** (*see* "Bail.")
on mesne process abolished . 53
privilege from . . . 53
of absconding debtors . . 55
of judgment . . . . 88

**ASSAULT** . . . . 32

**ASSETS:**
what they are . . . 264
when legal . . . 264, 323
when equitable . . 265, 323
marshalling . . . 321, 322
order of administration of . . 324

**ASSIGNMENT:**
equitable . . . . 338

**ASSISTANCE:**
writ of . . . . 385

**ASSUMPSIT:**
action of . . . . 4

INDEX. 411

| | PAGE |
|---|---|
| ATTACHMENT (*see* "Contempt of Court.") | |
| of debts . . . . | 89, 108 |
| ATTESTATION: | |
| form of, to a will . . | 242 |
| to warrant of attorney . | 121 |
| ATTORNEY (*see* "Solicitor and Client.") | |
| power of . . . . | 338 |
| lien of . . . . | 36, 393 |
| negligence of . . . | 36 |
| change of . . . . | 37 |
| ATTORNMENT . . . | 196 |
| AUCTION: | |
| sale by . . . . | 212 |
| AVERAGE: | |
| general . . . . | 20 |
| particular . . . . | 20 |
| AVOWRY (*see* "Replevin") . | 119 |
| AWARD (*see* "Arbitration.") | |
| AWAY GOING CROP . . | 18 |

B.

| | |
|---|---|
| BAIL (*see* "Arrest.") | |
| proceedings to hold to . | 53 |
| below and above , . | 54 |
| who may be . . . | 54 |
| objections to sufficiency of | 54 |
| bond . . . . | 55 |
| discharge of . . . | 55 |
| BANKRUPT: | |
| actions by assignees of . | 42 |
| when his estate vests in the assignees . . . | 190 |
| what payments to, valid . | 221 |
| party to suit by assignees . | 347 |
| BANKRUPTCY: | |
| plea of . . . . | 64 |
| effect of on contract of sale | 220 |
| effect of on power to appoint | 190 |
| BARGAIN AND SALE . | 164, 234, 235 |
| BASE FEE: | |
| how created . . . | 142 |
| definition of . . . | 143 |
| how it differs from a fee simple | 143 |
| BEQUEST: | |
| to a charity . . . | 247 |
| "to the heirs of B" . . | 251 |
| to various poor relations . | 252 |
| upon condition not to dispute the will . . . . | 318 |
| BIDDING: | |
| retraction of . . . | 211 |

| | PAGE |
|---|---|
| BIDDINGS: | |
| opening the . . . | 398 |
| BILL AND ANSWER: | |
| hearing on . . . | 381 |
| evidence . . . . | 377 |
| BILL OF EXCEPTIONS . | 78 |
| BILL OF LADING . . | 20 |
| BILL OF SALE . . . | 19 |
| requisites of a valid . . | 122 |
| what affidavit must state . | 122 |
| BILLS AND NOTES: | |
| definition of bill of exchange | 21 |
| definition of promissory note | 21, 26 |
| how they differ from other contracts . . . . | 22 |
| liability of parties to . . | 22 |
| how to be sued on . . | 22 |
| who may accept . . | 23 |
| notice of dishonour . . | 23, 24 |
| acceptance *per pro* . . | 23 |
| summary procedure on . | 24 |
| acceptor staying proceedings | 25 |
| evidence in actions on . | 25 |
| effect of the payee of a note appointing the maker his executor . . . . | 26 |
| BILL IN CHANCERY: | |
| difference between and information . . . . | 343 |
| who may file . . . | 342 |
| how prepared . . . | 344 |
| parts of . . . . | 344 |
| parties to . . . | 344, 345 |
| prayer . . . . | 347 |
| by whom signed . . | 347 |
| written copy . . . | 347 |
| service of . . . | 348, 356 |
| service of, abroad . . | 348 |
| two, filed for same purpose | 348 |
| several kinds of . . | 349 |
| when affidavit to accompany | 351 |
| supplemental . . . | 351 |
| of revivor . . . . | 351 |
| of review . . . . | 351 |
| cross . . . . | 351, 352 |
| reading answer to cross . | 352 |
| of foreclosure . . . | 350 |
| of interpleader . . . | 350 |
| BOND: | |
| what it is . . . . | 11 |
| lost . . . . . | 6 |
| effect of death of joint obligor | 173 |
| assignment of, to surety . | 173 |
| joint, or joint and several . | 173, 174 |
| judgment by default on . | 91 |
| of resignation . . . | 174 |
| interest on . . . . | 325 |

## INDEX.

BOROUGH, ENGLISH:
  tenure of . . . . 135
BRIEF:
  mode of preparing . . . 381
BUILDING LAND:
  sale of . . . . . 216

### C.

CAPIAS (see "Bail").
CAPIAS AD SATISFACIENDUM . 104
  (see "Execution").
CARRIER:
  who to sue . . . 15, 43
  liability of . . . 15, 34
CAUSES, SETTING DOWN:
  before whom . . . . 379
  by whom . . . . 380
  in various cases . . . 380
  demurrer . . . . . 363
CAVEAT EMPTOR . . . . 305
CESTUI QUE TRUST (see "Trustees.")
  time does not run between, and
    trustee . . . . 315
  is a simple contract creditor . 326
CHAMBERS (see "Summons"):
  matters conducted in . 394, 395
  appointment of receiver . 369
  proceedings in on decree . 396
CHAMPERTY . . . . 284
CHANCELLORS:
  distinguished . . . . 268
CHARITY:
  how lands conveyed to . 246
  what bequests to void 246, 247, 340
  what devises to valid . 247
  form of bequest to . 247, 340
  no marshalling in favour of . 339
  suits in respect of, parties to . 346
CHARTER-PARTY . . . . 20
CHATTELS:
  real and personal . . 133
  real, defined . . . 147
  specific delivery up of . 297
CHEQUE:
  definition of . . . 26
  when to be presented . 26
  crossing . . . . 26
CHIEF CLERK:
  certificate of . . . 396
  interrogatories by . . 397
  appeal from . . . 397
CHOSE IN ACTION:
  nature of . . . . 18
  who to sue on . . . 41

CHOSE IN ACTION—continued.
  assignment of, in equity . 172
  when and how assigned at law 172, 173
  form of assignment of a policy 238
  notice on assignment of . 340
CLAIMS:
  when to be entered . . 397
CLERGYMAN:
  arrest of . . . . 53
CLIENT (see "Attorney," "Solicitor and Client.")
  who to sue, for bill . . 41
CODICIL (see "Will.")
  effect of, on will . . 243
COGNOVIT:
  difference between, and Warrant of Attorney . . 120
  when to be stamped . . 120
  infant cannot give . . 120
  how executed . . . 121
  advantage of filing it . 121
COMMISSION:
  del credere . . . . 13
  to examine witnesses . 76, 374
  to take answer . . . 360
  costs of . . . . 76
COMMON, tenancy in . . . 151
  difference between, and joint tenancy . . . . 151
  the tenant's power of disposition 151
COMMON OF ESTOVERS . . 156
COMMON LAW:
  what it is . . . . 1
  acts relating to . . . 1
  superior courts of . . 2
  transfer of equity to . . 2
COMPELLING plaintiff to proceed 67, 81
COMPENSATION:
  under Lands Clauses Act, how assessed . . . 233
  how money invested . . 233
  who may convey . . 233
  how applied when paid into court by a railway company . 275
CONDITION:
  estate upon . . . 136
  precedent . . . . 403
CONDITIONS OF SALE:
  the ordinary . . . 210
  on selling leaseholds . . 210
  as to retaining the deeds . 211
  cannot be varied by parol . 211
  on sales by trustees . . 212
  as to payment of interest . 225
CONDITIONAL LIMITATION . 163

INDEX. 413

CONFESSION AND AVOIDANCE (*see* "Pleas.")
CONSIDERATION . . . 8, 43
   inadequacy of . . 225, 285, 306
   meritorious . . . . 300
CONSOLIDATING ACTIONS . . 58
CONSTABLE:
   action against . . . . 44
CONTEMPT OF COURT:
   punishment for . . . 126, 401
   in what cases . . . 127, 401
CONTRACTS (*see* "Specific Performance.")
   of record . . . . . 7
   specialty . . . . . 7
   simple . . . . . 7
   maxims relating to . . . 8
   essentials of . . . . 8
   consideration . . . . 8
   moral obligation . . . 8
   *nudum pactum* . . . . 8
   when to be in writing . . 9
   for the sale of goods . . 17, 18
   not to be performed within a year 18
   for the sale of lands . . . 212
   effect of lunacy on . . . 221
   when set aside in equity . . 284
   on what terms . . 284, 287
   relief on, at law and in equity . 297
   privity of . . . . 18, 194
   of infants . . . . . 10
   of married women . . . 11
CONVERSION . . . . 132, 248
   out and out . . . . 300
   consequences of doctrine of 300, 301
   failure of objects of . 309, 310
   if directed by deed . . . 309
CONVEYANCING:
   origin of . . . . . 132
CONVEYANCES:
   by statute . . . . . 231
   by common law . . . 231
   of freeholds . . . . 231
   of copyholds . . . . 231
   persons incapable of making . 231
   extraordinary . . . . 238
   by mortgagor and mortgagee . 205
COPARCENARY:
   estate in . . . . . 152
   how it differs from a joint tenancy 152
COPYHOLDS:
   origin of . . . . . 157
   essentials of . . . . 157
   heriots . . . . . 157
   incidents of . . . . 157
   how entailed . . . . 158
   mines under and timber upon . 158

COPYHOLDS—*continued*.
   fine arbitrary and certain . . 158
   amount of fine . . . . 159
   trustees for sale of . . . 159
   effect of wrongful admission to . 160
   how conveyed . . . . 160
   devise of . . . . . 160
   when lord compellable to admit
      to . . . . . . 160
   enfranchisement of . 160, 161
   mortgage of . . . . 201
   who bears expense of surrender 219
   liable to debts . . . . 275
   partition of . . . . 339
CORPORATION:
   sue and defend, how . . . 42
   service of writ on . . . 48
   its common seal . . . . 190
   how it conveys . . . . 190
   how compelled to appear . . 360
   suit by, when it abates . . 355
COSTS (Common Law):
   double costs . . . . 94
   security for . . . 95, 367
   security for, in ejectment . 113, 114
   executors when liable to pay . 95
   on cross issues . . . . 96
   in trespass . . . 97, 98
   in case . . . . . 97
   in ejectment . . . . 113
   can married woman recover . 97
   in slander and libel . . . 97
   of one of several defendants . 98
   how plaintiff is deprived of . 98
   when a juror withdrawn . . 99
   on judgment *non obstante veredicto* . . . . . 99
   of new trial . . . . 99
   higher scale of . . . . 99
   lower scale . . . . 100
   on judgment by default . . 100
   when no certificate required under
      £20 . . . . . 100
   where there is concurrent jurisdiction with the County
      Court . . . 129, 130
   in case of set off . . . 100
   of proceedings after summons to
      stay . . . . . 101
   when plaintiff not entitled to . 101
   when certificate for required . 101
   of the day . . . . 102
   in *scire facias* . . . . 103
   bill of . . . . . 103
   taxation of . . . 35, 36
   of taxation to be paid by
      Attorney, when . . . 50
   how recovered . . . . 105
   of arbitration . . . . 124
   conveyancing, bill of . . . 226
   of commission in lunacy . . 279

COSTS (Equity):
 security for . . . 391
 death of the surety . . 391
 how obtained . . . 392
 next friend liable for . . 392
 between party and party . 392
 principles of taxation of . 392
 who may attend taxation of 392
 reviewing taxation of . 392
 applications for taxation of 393
 delivery of bill of . . 393
 recovery of . . . 393
 solicitor's lien for . . 393
 interest on . . . 394
 of trustees . . . 394

COUNTERMAND:
 notice of trial . . . 82

COUNTS . . . . 60
 (*see* "Declaration.")

COUNTY COURTS:
 origin of . . . . 128
 jurisdiction of . . 128, 129
 concurrent . . . 129
 how causes removed from . 129
 how suits commenced . 129
 judge of exceeding jurisdiction 130
 appeal from . . . 130
 equitable jurisdiction of . 131

COURT ROLLS:
 tenant's right to inspect . 76

COURTS OF EQUITY (*see* "Equity").

COURTS OF COMMON LAW . 2

COUNTY . . . . 128
 (*see* "County Courts.")

COURT BARON . . . 2, 158

COURT LEET . . . 2, 158

COVENANT TO SETTLE LANDS . 189

COVENANT TO STAND SEISED . 231

COVENANTS (*see* "Leases."):
 what are . . . . 235
 in leases . . . . 193
 to repair . . . . 194
 to insure . . . . 194
 running with the land . 195, 237
 in assignments of leases . 196
 for title . . . . 236
 when limited . . . 236
 by trustees . . . 236
 by mortgagees . . . 236
 for quiet enjoyment, what they
  include . . . 237
 construction of, in equity . 294
 what are "usual" . . 302

COVERTURE:
 how pleaded . . . 64

CREDITORS:
 how assisted in equity . . 323
 order of satisfaction of . . 324
 effect of decree on remedies of . 327
 proof of debts by . . 397
 claim against fund appointed . 403

CROSS REMAINDERS: . . 149, 245

CURTESY:
 tenancy by the . . . 181
 requisites of . . . 181
 how barred . . . 182

CUSTOMARY FREEHOLDS . . 157

CY PRÈS:
 doctrine of . . . 295
 is adopted at common law, when 295

## D.

DAMAGES:
 distinction between liquidated
  and unliquidated . . 35
 power of equity to award . . 383

DEATH:
 of plaintiff, effect of . . 69
 of defendant . . . 93
 in prison . . . . 107
 from negligence . . . 33

DEBTS (*see* "Contracts."):
 administration of real estate, to
  pay . . . 274, 275
 order of payment of . . 324
 distinction between legal and
  equitable . . . 324

DECLARATION:
 what it is . . . . 57
 when to be filed . . . 57
 time to declare . . . 57
 several counts . . . 58
 setting aside . . . 58
 common counts . . . 60

DECREES (*see* "Motion for Decree"):
 how pronounced . . 272
 how drawn up . . . 385
 default in drawing up . 385
 how enforced . . 383, 385
 by whom enforced . . 385
 on whom binding . . 383, 384
 enrolment of . . . 386

DE DONIS (*see* "Tail."):
 Statute of . . . . 138

DEEDS:
 only the parties to, may sue on
     5, 42, 233
 how enforced . . . 7
 proof of . . . . 7

INDEX. 415

| | PAGE |
|---|---|
| DEEDS—*continued*. | |
| consideration | 10 |
| prove themselves, when | 77, 379 |
| where to be produced for examination | 217 |
| covenant to produce | 218 |
| requisites of | 228 |
| formal parts of | 228 |
| reading | 228 |
| in execution of powers, how executed | 228 |
| alteration of | 229 |
| stamps on (*see* " stamp duty ") | 229 |
| estoppel under | 230 |
| how avoided | 231 |
| covenant to produce | 237 |
| how construed in equity | 271 |
| inconsistent clauses in | 272 |
| when set aside in equity | 284 |
| DEFEASANCE | 238 |
| DEFENCE: | |
| modes of | 357 |
| DEMURRER AT LAW: | |
| example of | 63 |
| difference between, and plea | 63 |
| joinder in | 63 |
| books, how made up, and delivered | 63 |
| special, abolished | 63 |
| DEMURRER IN EQUITY: | |
| nature and effect of | 362 |
| requisites of | 363 |
| how it differs from an answer | 362 |
| time | 363 |
| who may set it down | 363 |
| overruling | 363 |
| partial | 363 |
| setting down | 363 |
| DENOTING STAMP | 230 |
| DESCENT: | |
| title by | 174, 175 |
| by common law | 258 |
| by custom | 258 |
| rules of | 258, 259 |
| primogeniture | 259 |
| illustrations of the rules of | 259—262 |
| breaking the | 261 |
| of lands of a bastard | 262 |
| DETINUE: | |
| action of | 6 |
| DEVISE (*see* " Wills."). | |
| general | 244 |
| of lands, whether tithes pass | 245 |
| of lands, whether advowson passes | 245 |
| lapse of a | 248 |
| executory | 161 |
| effect of, to heir at law | 175 |

| | PAGE |
|---|---|
| DISCLAIMER: | |
| of landlord's title | 199 |
| defence to suit, by | 365 |
| DISCOVERY: | |
| nature of bill of | 279 |
| when not compelled | 279, 280 |
| affidavit to accompany bill of | 280 |
| cannot dismiss bill of | 280 |
| at law | 280, 281 |
| bill for, cannot be filed against a witness | 347 |
| how obtained without cross bill | 352 |
| DISENTAILING DEED | 139 |
| DISHONOUR: | |
| notice of, time for | 23, 24 |
| DISMISSING SUITS: | |
| time for | 371, 372 |
| suits which cannot be | 371 |
| by plaintiff and defendant | 371 |
| after decree | 371 |
| DISTRESS: | |
| what it is | 114 |
| who may distrain | 117 |
| what may be distrained | 114 |
| what things privileged | 115, 116 |
| time to make | 115 |
| how made | 115 |
| breaking open doors | 115 |
| course to be pursued in making a | 115, 116 |
| sale of | 116 |
| authority to make a | 116 |
| damage feasant | 116 |
| impounding | 117 |
| remedy by, when suspended | 117 |
| for tithe rent charge | 118 |
| unlawful, remedy for | 118 |
| DISTRIBUTION, STATUTES OF | 262 |
| (*see* "Next of Kin.") | |
| DISTRINGAS: | |
| to compel appearance | 360 |
| writ of | 389 |
| DOCUMENTS: | |
| notice to produce | 74 |
| notice to admit | 73 |
| production of, in a suit | 376, 377 |
| DOMICILE: | |
| devolution of personalty governed by | 262 |
| will executed according to law of | 253 |
| DONATIO MORTIS CAUSA: | |
| definition of | 317 |
| how it differs from a legacy | 317 |
| how from a gift *inter vivos* | 317 |
| DOWER: | |
| what it is | 179 |
| where recovered | 3 |

## INDEX

DOWER—*continued.*
 uses, how they operate . . 180
 distinction between, and jointure 180
 effect of jointure upon . . 180
 in gavelkind lands . . . 181
 out of mortgaged estate . . 181
 how barred . . . 179, 180

### E.

EASEMENT:
 definition of . . . . 156
 how acquired . . . . 290
 injunction against interference
  with an . . . . 290

ECCLESIASTICAL BENEFICE:
 mortgage of . . . . 202

EJECTMENT:
 when it lies . . . . 110
 not by equitable owner . . 110
 time of limitation . . . 110
 writ in, how served . . . 111
 time to appear . . . . 111
 limitation of defence in . . 111
 leave to appear in . . . 112
 tenant bound to inform landlord 112
 venue in . . . . . 112
 issue in . . . . . 112
 costs in . . . . . 113
 security for costs in . . 113, 114
 action for mesne profits . . 114

ELECTION:
 doctrine of . . . 320, 321
 order for . . . . . 368

ELEGIT:
 writ of . . . . 109, 318

EMBLEMENTS . . . 199, 200

ENFRANCHISEMENT:
 of copyholds, how effected . 160
 at the suit of the lord and tenant
  respectively . . . 160, 161

ENROLMENT (*see* "Registration.") 241

ENTIRETIES:
 tenancy by . . . . 151

EQUITY:
 origin of . . . . . 266
 definition of . . . . 266
 territorial jurisdiction of . . 267
 technical meaning of . . 267
 Selden's opinion of . . . 267
 distinction between law and . 268
 subjects of its jurisdiction . . 269
 exclusive . . . . . 269
 concurrent . . . . 269
 auxiliary . . . . . 269
 cases where it will not interfere 269
 when equal . . . 269, 270

EQUITY—*continued.*
 clean hands in . . . . 270
 maxims of . . . 270, 271
 follows the law . . . . 271
 how it construes deeds and wills 271
 courts of, in England . . 272
 Judges of . . . . . 272
 judicial and administrative jurisdiction of . . . 273
 acts regulating the court of . 274
 jurisdiction of as to fraud in a
  will . . . . . 283
 he who seeks, must do . 270, 301
 to a settlement . . . . 330

EQUITY OF REDEMPTION:
 what it is . . . . . 206
 when mortgagor cannot recover 335

ERROR (*see* "Appeal") . . 81

ESCAPE:
 effect of . . . . . 107

ESCHEAT:
 nature of, and when it occurs . 175

ESCROW:
 what it is . . . . . 229

ESTATES:
 division of . . . . . 135
 by operation of law . . . 135
 by acts of the parties . . . 135
 words necessary to create . . 135
 in tail (*see* "Tail") . . . 137
 for life . . . . . 145
 on condition . . . . 136
 less than freehold . . . 147
 how destroyed . . . . 147
 distinction between estate for life
  and for years . . . 147
 legal and equitable . . . 162
 in possession, reversion, and remainder . . . . 148
 privity . . . . . 194

ESTOPPEL . . . . . 10
 not under a deed poll . . 230

EVIDENCE:
 classes of . . . . . 72
 alterations in the law of . . 72
 of a deed . . . . . 74
 of a will . . . . . 74
 of parties to suits . . . 74
 of parties abroad, how obtained 76
 in action for goods sold and delivered . . . . 76
 parol, to explain or alter . 77, 378
 under plea of *non est factum* . 78
 in action for libel . . . 78
 in action of Bill of Exchange . 25
 in action of trover . . . 78
 in action on attorney's bill . 78

# INDEX. 417

EVIDENCE—continued.
| | PAGE |
|---|---|
| answer in Chancery is | 79 |
| of record | 79 |
| of letters patent | 79 |
| of a will | 112 |
| not upon oath, when admitted | 80 |
| of heirship | 259 |

EVIDENCE (Equity):
| | |
|---|---|
| preservation of | 281 |
| what may be adduced in various cases | 372 |
| notice as to | 372 |
| how truth best ascertained | 372 |
| who takes | 372 |
| vivâ voce at the hearing | 373 |
| de bene esse | 375 |
| of deeds and letters at the hearing | 375 |
| answer, when | 375, 376 |
| on hearing on bill and answer | 377 |
| of notice of incumbrance | 378 |
| closing the | 378, 379 |
| of decree | 379 |
| who may consent to order as to | 379 |
| on motion for decree | 383, 384 |

EXAMINERS:
| | |
|---|---|
| their duties | 274, 372 |

EXCHANGE:
| | |
|---|---|
| mode of effecting an | 234 |
| objections to deed of | 234 |

EXCEPTIONS:
| | |
|---|---|
| bill of | 78 |
| to answer | 361 |

EXECUTION:
| | |
|---|---|
| different kinds of | 163 |
| what property can be taken in | 104 |
| what cannot be taken | 104, 108 |
| by fi. fa. | 104 |
| by ca. sa. | 104 |
| fi. fa. after a ca. sa. | 105 |
| ca. sa. when it may issue | 107 |
| what writs of, after a fi. fa. | 105 |
| time to be issued | 105 |
| how costs recovered by | 105 |
| may issue into any county | 106 |
| against one of two defendants | 106 |
| alteration by 1 & 2 Vic. c. 110 | 106 |
| writs of, how endorsed | 107 |
| escape from custody | 107 |
| death in prison | 107 |
| release on promise to return | 108 |
| sheriff to deduct the rent due | 108 |
| by eligit | 109 |
| by sequestration | 109 |
| in ejectment | 113 |

EXECUTORS:
| | |
|---|---|
| actions against and by | 42 |
| de son tort, what constitutes | 10, 255 |
| effect of discharges by | 255 |

EXECUTORS—continued.
| | PAGE |
|---|---|
| power of one of several | 256 |
| paying legacy into court | 256 |
| effect of one renouncing | 257 |
| when entitled to residue | 257 |
| how they may protect themselves | 310, 323 |
| for what losses liable | 312 |
| are allowed their expenses | 312 |
| cannot make a profit | 312, 315 |
| appointment of creditors | 315 |
| order of payment of debts by | 315 |
| their powers of giving preference | 316 |
| paying debts barred | 316 |
| advertisements by | 316, 317 |
| creditor appointing debtor | 320 |
| may retain debts due to them though barred | 325 |
| when they may file bill | 345 |

EXECUTORY DEVISE:
| | |
|---|---|
| what it is | 161, 162 |
| distinction between, and contingent remainder | 150 |
| distinction between, and shifting use | 163 |
| instances of an | 163 |
| how it differs from a conditional limitation | 163 |

EXPECTANCY:
| | |
|---|---|
| estates in | 148 |

EXTRAORDINARY CONVEYANCES | 238 |

## F.

FEE SIMPLE:
| | |
|---|---|
| what it is | 136 |
| what words will create | 136, 137 |
| inter vivos, and by will | 137 |

FEIGNED ISSUE | 68
proceedings after verdict on | 91

FEME COVERT (see "Husband" and "Married Woman.")

FEOFFMENT:
| | |
|---|---|
| what it is | 232 |
| omission of indorsement | 232 |
| when a necessary conveyance | 232 |
| why no longer so | 232 |
| by an infant | 233 |

FIERI FACIAS | 104
(see "Execution.")

FINE (see "Copyholds.")

FIXTURES:
| | |
|---|---|
| what tenant may remove | 28 |

FORECLOSURE:
| | |
|---|---|
| time of payment under decree for | 335 |

E E

## INDEX.

FORECLOSURE—*continued.*     PAGE
  sale instead of . . . 335
  opening . . . . 338
  nature of bill for . . 350
  proceedings in suit for . 402
FORFEITURE:
  for breach of covenant . 194
  relief against in equity . 196, 294
  at law . . . . 196
FORMÂ PAUPERIS (*see* "Pauper.")
  suing in . . . . 45
FRAUD:
  jurisdiction of equity as to, concurrent . . . . 269
  when equity will relieve against 282
  will obtained by . . 282, 283
  will time bar relief against 282, 315
  constructive . . . 284
  on sale of estate . . 285
  against purchasers and creditors 285
  gifts to what persons fraudulent 285
  purchases by persons in confidential positions . . 286, 314
  on a power . . . 327
  on marital rights . . 330
FRAUDS, STATUTE OF . 9, 10, 17, 212
FREEBENCH . . . . 159
FREEHOLD:
  what it means . . . 135
  of inheritance . . . 136
  not of inheritance . . 136

### G.

GAME:
  pursuit of . . . . 33
GARNISHEE (*see* "Attachment.")
GAVELKIND:
  tenure of . . . . 134
  peculiarities of . . . 135
  dower in . . . . 181
GRANT:
  deed of . . . . 232
  when the word implies a covenant . . . 232, 233
GUARANTEE:
  nature of . . . . 13
  liability on a . . . 13
  discharge of a guarantor . 13
GUARDIAN:
  father may appoint . . 182, 327
  how appointed . . 326, 397

### H.

HABEAS CORPUS, ACT: . . 3
  ad testificandum . . 75

HABENDUM:     PAGE
  in fee simple . . . 136
  in leases, form of . . 193
  in a mortgage . . . 204
HEARING:
  various ways of bringing a suit to a . . . . 381
  on further consideration . 382
HEIR:
  apparent . . . . 258
  presumptive . . . 258
  bargains with, expectant . 306
  liability of for debts of his ancestor . . . . 264
HEREDITAMENTS:
  most comprehensive word . 132
  distinction between corporeal and incorporeal . . . 153
  different kinds of . . 153
HERIOT . . . . 157
HIGHWAYS:
  how stopped up, diverted, or turned . . . . 131
HUNDREDORS:
  liability of . . . 31
HUSBAND (*see* "Married Woman.")
  liability of, on contracts of his wife . . . . 11
  liability after coverture . 11
  deserting his wife . . 12
  marrying his creditor, effect of . 12
  interest of, in wife's lands . 175
  in her personalty and chattels real . . . 175, 176
  may grant leases of her estate 179, 192
  his interest in her reversionary property . . . 179
  may act for his wife as executrix 181
  fraud on marital rights of . 330

### I.

IMPERTINENCE, exceptions for . 361
IMPOUNDING Cattle . . 117
INCREASE:
  affidavit of . . . 95
INCUMBRANCES:
  search for . . . . 222
INFANTS:
  can enforce a contract . 10
  ratification of debt . . 10
  liability of father of . . 10
  contracts of . . . 10, 326
  liable for tort . . . 30
  torts to . . . . 30
  how they may sue . . 40

## INDEX.

INFANTS—*continued.*
  how defend . . . . 40
  cannot convey . . . . 182
  settlements of . . . . 182
  leases by . . . . . 192
  sale of lands of, to pay debts . 275
  jurisdiction of equity as to . 326
  how made wards of court . . 326
  guardianship of . . . 327
  how guardian appointed . . 327
  maintenance of . . . . 328
  access to, by mother . . . 328
  marriage of . . . . 328
  custody of . . . . . 327
  next friend to . . . . 346
  bill filed on behalf of, without consent . . . . . 345
  suing *in formâ pauperis* . . 345
  cannot make admissions . . 346
  decrees against . . , . 383

INFORMATION:
  by whom filed . . . . 342
  distinguished from a bill . . 343
  and bill . . . . . 34

INHERITANCE:
  estates of . . . . . 136

INJUNCTION, AT LAW . . . 68
  to stay proceedings at law 282, 292
  what it is . . . . . 287
  how enforced . . . . 287
  in what cases granted . 288–293
  different kinds of . . . 288
  notice of motion for . . . 288
  when obtained *ex parte* . 288, 289
  should apply for, without delay 288
  against publication of letters . 290
  notice of . . . . . 293
  effect of amendment of bill as to 293
  jurisdiction of equity as to, not taken away . . . . 293
  how enforced . . . . 401

INJURIES (*see* "Torts.")

INNKEEPER:
  liability of, for goods of guest . 16
  cannot detain his guest . . 16
  is bound to receive a traveller . 16

INQUIRY:
  writ of . . . . . 90

INSURANCE:
  relief against forfeiture for non . 30

INSPECTION:
  of documents . . . . 73
  of the rolls of a manor . . 76

INTERCOMMON . . . . 156

INTERESSE TERMINI . . . 148

INTEREST:
  when payable at common law . 20
  how debts made to carry . . 20
  rate of . . . . 20, 209
  on a legacy . . . . 319
  on a bond . . . . . 325
  on costs . . . . . 394
  after a decree . . . . 397

INTERLOCUTORY PROCEEDINGS . 69

INTERPLEADER:
  what it is . . . . . 125
  proceedings on an . . . 126
  by sheriff . . . . . 126
  nature of bill of . . . 350
  affidavit to accompany . . 350

INTERROGATORIES:
  Common Law . . . . 72
  Equity—by plaintiff . . . 401
    " time for . . . 401
    " by defendant . . 352

INTESTACY (*see* "Descent.")
  meaning of "dying intestate" . 258
  effect of, as to realty . . . 258
  as to personalty . . . 262

INVESTMENTS:
  by trustees . . . . 313
  of funds in court . . 313, 390

IRREGULARITY:
  in declaration . . . . 58
  in other cases . . . . 69
  summons to set aside proceedings for . . . . . 70
  time to apply to set aside . . 70
  distinction between, and a nullity 70

ISSUABLE PLEADING . . 65, 66

ISSUABLE AND NON-ISSUABLE TERMS . . . . . 81

ISSUE AT LAW:
  how joined . . . . 67
  what it is . . . . . 68
  in fact and of law . . . 68
  feigned . . . . . 68
  when directed out of Chancery . . . . 292, 382

ISSUE IN EQUITY:
  how joined . . . . 369

## J.

JOINDER OF ACTIONS . . . 7

JOINTURE (*see* "Dower") . . 180

JOINT TENANCY:
  estate in . . . . . 151
  how severed . . . 151, 153

## INDEX.

JOINT TENANCY—continued.
  distinction between, and tenancy
    by entireties . . . 151
  where purchase-money advanced
    equally . . . . 152
  not, in equity, where unequally . 152
  release by one tenant . . 153
  leases by joint tenants . . 191

JUDGE:
  functions of . . . 84

JUDGMENT:
  distinction between, and verdict. 89
  different kinds of . . . 89
  interlocutory and final . . 89
  of *non pros.* . . . . 89
  by default . . . . 90
  by default on bond . . . 91
  time for signing . . . 91
  after nonsuit . . . . 91
  revival of a . . . 92, 93
  how enforced against the representatives . . . . 92
  registration of a . . 93, 227
  how made a charge on stock . 93
  how enforced . . . 103
  against public officer of a company . . . . 107
  in ejectment . . . 113
  how they affect realty . . 226
  decree has effect of a . . 226
  no charge on estate of mortgagee 227
  effect of, on land in a register
    county . . . . 227
  Irish, how regarded . . . 325

JURISDICTION:
  of common law courts . . 2
  of Chancery courts . 266, 267
  defendant out of . . . 346
  plaintiff out of . . . 348

JUROR:
  withdrawing a . . . 85

JURY:
  functions of . . . 84
  special, costs of . . . 84
  discharging . . . . 85

## L.

LAND:
  what it includes . . 133

LANDLORD:
  obtaining possession of premises 29
  his liability to repair . . 29

LAND REGISTRY . . . 215, 216

LANDS CLAUSES ACT (*see* "Compensation.")

LAPSE (*see* "Wills") . . . 248
  none of residue, into residue . 248

LEASE AND RELEASE . . . 235
  lease abolished . . . 235

LEASES (*see* "Terms of Years.")
  what they are . . . 191
  when to be in writing . 28, 190
  when to be by deed . . . 190
  by tenants for life . . . 145
  by remaindermen . . . 191
  defects in, under powers . 191
  by joint tenants . . . 191
  by tenants in common . . 192
  by infants . . . . 192
  by husband of wife's lands 179, 192
  by idiots and lunatics . 192
  by mortgagor alone . . . 192
  by mortgagee alone . . . 192
  covenants in building . . 193
  form of farming . . . 193
  London, outline of . . . 193
  habendum in . . . . 198
  for lives . . . . 194
  liability of under-lessee . 195
  liability of assignee . . . 195
  covenants in, running with the
    land . . . . 195
  assignments of, covenants in . 196
  holding over, after determination
    of . . . . . 198
  lease of two farms at an entire
    rent . . . . 198
  proper parties to assign, on the
    death of the lessee . . 225

LEET:
  court . . . . 2, 158

LEGACY (*see* "Lapse")
  vested . . . 249, 318
  contingent . . . 249, 318
  of residue to tenants in common 249
  general . . . . 249
  specific . . . . 249
  specific, of stock . . 249, 250
  demonstrative . . . 250
  of annuity . . . . 250
  duty . . . . 253
  payment of into court . . 256
  how payment compelled . 317
  on condition of paying debts . 318
  interest on . . . . 319
  ademption of . . 319, 320
  to creditor . . . . 320
  abatement of . . 321, 325

LETTERS:
  restraining publication of . 290, 291

LETTER-MISSIVE . . . 355

LEX LOCI . . . 4, 262

LEX FORI . . . 4

## INDEX. 421

**LIBEL:**
what is a . . . . 31
action for . . . . . 6
what communications not libellous . . . . . 31

**LIEN** . . . . . . 19
of vendor for unpaid purchase money . . . . 305
how lost . . . . 305

**LIFE ESTATES:**
what are . . . 144, 145
how destroyed . . . 145

**LIMITATION:**
Statutes of . . . . 37
disabilities . . . . 37
when the statutes run . 38
effect of acknowledgment . 38
how time prevented from running . . . . 38
effect of on lien . . . 39
executor paying debts barred by 316
effect of on legacies and annuities 319

**LIS PENDENS:**
what is a . . . 272, 403
special case is a . . 349

**LIVERY OF SEISIN** . . . 232

**LORDS, HOUSE OF:**
appeal to . . . . 273

**LUNATICS:**
origin of jurisdiction of Chancellor as to . . . 278
how found . . . . 278
guardians of . . . . 278
trustees . . . . 278
death of before costs are taxed . 279

### M.

**MAINTENANCE** . . . 284
of infants . . . . 328
power of trustees to allow . 328

**MANDAMUS:**
writ of . . . . . 68
to examine witnesses . 76

**MANOR** (see "Copyholds.")

**MARRIED WOMAN** (see "Husband," "Separate Estate.")
when she may sue . . 40
when to be joined with her husband . . . . 40, 346
separate estate of . . 176
appointment by . . . 177
will of . . . 177, 333
how she may convey her lands . . . 177, 178
her reversionary interests 178, 332

**MARRIED WOMAN**—*continued.*
mortgage of her estate, the husband joining . . . 178
may sever a joint tenancy . 178
consent under Settled Estates' Act, how taken . 277, 331
how she may sue in equity 330, 331
her equity to a settlement 330, 331
payment out of court to . 331
settlement on if husband insolvent . . . . 332
sale of her chattels real by husband . . . . 332
may bind her estate . . 333
her pin money . . . 333
bill filed without consent of . 346

**MARSHALLING** (see "Assets") . 321

**MASTER:**
liability of for contracts of servant . . . . 18, 19
when he may discharge the servant . . . . 18
liability of for damage by servant . . . . 33, 34

**MASTERS:**
matters referred to . . 71, 90

**MEMORIAL:**
of deeds . . . 239, 240

**MERCANTILE LAW AMENDMENT ACT** . . . . . 2

**MERGER** (see "Terms of Years") 170

**MESNE PROFITS:**
action for . . . . 114
what may be recovered . 114

**MINES AND MINERALS:**
under copyhold . . 158

**MISJOINDER:**
effect of . . . . 62
distinguished from multifariousness . . . . 347

**MISTAKE:**
when relieved against . 294
when not . . . . 294

**MODUS** . . . . . 155

**MORAL OBLIGATION** (see "Consideration.")

**MORTGAGE:**
what it is . . . 200, 334
distinction between *vivum vadium* and *mortuum vadium* . 200
equitable, how created 200, 201, 337
objections to . . . 337
of freeholds . . . 201
of leaseholds . . 201, 203
of copyholds . . . 201
of ecclesiastical benefice . 202

## INDEX.

MORTGAGE—*continued.*      PAGE
  covenants inserted in . 202, 204
  power of sale . . . . 202
  to whom power reserved . . 204
  habendum in . . . . 204
  by trustees . . . . 204
  disadvantage of a second . . 205
  subsequent advance on . 206, 210
  by tenants in common . . 208
  rate of interest on . . . 209
  whether machinery passes by . 210
  cancelling . . . . . 210
  stamp duty on a . . . 229
  and conveyance in one deed 237, 238
  money, payable out of the land . . . . 244, 323, 338
  what is a contrary intention . 338
  once a, always a . . . 335
  agreement to execute . . 336
  joint advance on . . . 339

MORTGAGEE:
  remedies of . 208, 335, 336, 337
  statutable power of sale . . 203
  under what conditions he may sell . . . . . 203
  may call in money without notice 205
  effect of leases by . . 192, 207
  death of, who to reconvey . . 207
  death of one of two . . . 208
  how to obtain possession . . 209
  cutting down timber . . . 209
  covenants for title by . . 236
  is not bound to transfer . . 335
  taking possession . . . 336
  what he may expend . 336, 337
  after sale, to whom surplus to be paid . . . . 208, 338
  cannot sue after foreclosure and sale . . . . . 338

MORTGAGOR:
  must give notice before paying off 205
  must give notice of prior mortgage . . . . . 206
  purchaser of the debt at a discount, what entitled to against 207
  when he must redeem two estates 207
  effect of leases by . . 192, 207
  what representatives of, entitled to surplus . . . 208, 338
  remaining in possession . . 209
  time to redeem . . . . 335

MORTMAIN:
  meaning of word . . . 246
  Statute of . . . . . 246

MOTION:
  distinguished from petition . 399
  notice of . . . . . 400

MOTION FOR DECREE . . 383, 384
  evidence on . . . . 384

MULTIFARIOUSNESS . . . 347

## N.

NE EXEAT REGNO:          PAGE
  writ of . . . . . 367

NEGLIGENCE:
  death from . . . . 33
  contributory . . . 34, 35

NEW ASSIGNMENT . . . 62

NEW TRIAL:
  application for . . . . 86
  time to move for . . . 86
  grounds for . . . . 87
  when on payment of costs . . 87
  appeal . . . . . 88
  on issue directed . . . 383

NEXT FRIEND . . . . 346

NEXT-OF-KIN:
  order in which they are entitled to administration . . . 256
  now take the undisposed of residue . . . . . 257
  examples of distribution amongst . . 262—264, 322
  when they take *per stirpes* 262, 263
  when *per capita* . . 262, 263

NEXT PRESENTATION:
  clerk cannot present himself to . 174
  when it can be sold . . . 174

NISI PRIUS:
  derivation and meaning of . 83

NONJOINDER:
  plea in abatement of . . . 62
  notice objecting to . . . 62

NON OBSTANTE VEREDICTO:
  motion . . . . . 87
  time for . . . . . 87
  costs . . . . . . 99

NONSUIT:
  what it is . . . . . 84
  effect of . . . . . 84
  against consent . . . . 84
  voluntary . . . . . 85

NOTICE:
  to quit . . . . . 27
  to quit, when to be in writing . 27
  to quit part . . . . 27
  before action . . . . 44
  of proceeding after a year's delay 82
  to produce . . . . 74
  to admit . . . . . 73
  of a deed, attesting witness . 341
  to counsel and attornies . . 341
  actual . . . . . 341
  constructive . . . . 341
  of motion . . . . . 400

NOTICE OF TRIAL . . . 82

NUISANCES:
  what are . . . . . 35

INDEX. 423

## O.

ORDER, JUDGE'S:
  neglect to obey . . . 71
  how served . . . . 71
  making it a rule of court . 71
  how enforced . . . 106
  when to be filed . . . 122
  from what time order takes effect 403

OUTLAWRY . . . . . 127
  effect of or power to . . 127
  contract . . . . 220

## P.

PARTICULAR ESTATE (*see* "Reversion.") . . . . 148

PARTICULARS OF DEMAND, ORDER FOR . . . 65, 70
  when obtainable. . . . 70

PARTIES TO ACTIONS . . . 39
  who cannot sue . . . 39
  to action on bond . . 41

PARTIES TO SUITS . . 344—347

PARTITION . . . . 234
  how effected in equity . 339
  of copyholds . . . 339

PARTNERS:
  liability of *inter se* . . 14
  can sue one another . . 14
  representatives of deceased, liable in equity . . 174
  restrained from drawing bills . 291
  lunacy of . . . . 296

PARTNERSHIP (*see* "Partners"):
  what constitutes a . . 14, 15
  real estate purchased out of partnership funds . . 133
  when dissolution of decreed . 296

PATENTS:
  infringement of, restrained 291, 292
  jurisdiction of equity, as to . 292

PAUPER:
  suing *in formâ pauperis* . 45
  rules affecting actions by . 46
  infant suing as . . . 345
  petition to sue as a . . 400

PAYMENT INTO COURT:
  in what cases . . . 65
  effect of . . . . 64, 65
  when leave necessary . 65
  by trustees . . . . 390

PAYMENT OUT OF COURT:
  authority for . . . 390
  to personal representatives . 390
  proceedings to obtain . . 399

PENALTY:
  relief against a . . . 287
  additional rent is not a . 287
  payment of does not relieve from performing agreement . 298

PERPETUATION OF TESTIMONY:
  nature of bill for . . 281
  in what cases . . . 281
  how jurisdiction recently extended . . . . 281
  evidence, when to be used . 282

PER PROCURATION:
  acceptance . . . 23

PERPETUITIES (*see* "Accumulation"):
  rule against . . . 167
  effect of, under appointments . 167

PERSONAL CHATTELS (*see* "Chattels")

PETITION:
  proceedings by . . . 399
  how distinguished from motion . 399
  orders on . . . . 400
  statement at foot of . . 400

PLEAS AT LAW. (*see* "Pleadings.")
  in bar . . . . 59
  in abatement, their requisites 59, 61
  time to plead . . . 59
  how computed . . . 70
  further time . . . 70
  the like after order for particulars of demand . . 65
  in traverse . . . 59
  in confession and avoidance . 59
  *non assumpsit* . . . 60
  payment . . . . 61
  the general issue . . 60, 61
  never indebted . . . 60
  *non est factum* . . . 59, 78
  not guilty . . . . 60
  non-joinder . . . 62
  *plene administravit* . . 64
  *plene administravit præter* . 64
  *puis darrein continuance* . 66
  what may be pleaded without leave . . . . 61
  what must be specially pleaded . 61
  by statute . . . . 61
  difference between, and demurrers . . . . 63
  when false and tricky . 64
  issuable . . . 65, 66

PLEA IN EQUITY:
  nature and effect of a . 363
  when on oath . . . 364
  when accompanied by answer . 364
  distinguished from answer . 364
  double . . . . 364
  how to be treated . . 364

PLEADINGS. (see "Pleas.")
  the various . . . . 56
  service of . . . . 67
  in replevin . . . . 119
  issuable . . . . 65, 66
POLICY:
  assignment of a. . . . 238
  *Possessio Fratris*, doctrine of . 259
POOL:
  what passes by grant of . . 134
POSSESSION:
  meaning of the term . . . 138
POSTEA:
  origin of the word . . . 85
POWER OF ATTORNEY:
  deed executed under, purchaser
    not bound to take . . 228, 229
  in whose name deed executed . 229
  form of . . . . 238
  how put an end to . . . 238
  payments by trustees under . 313
POWERS. (see "Appointment.")
  appendant and in gross . . 167
  appointments of uses under . 167
  effect of appointments under on
    judgments . . . . 168
  extinguishment of . . 169, 170
  suspension of . . . . 170
  leases under . . . . 191
  deeds and wills in execution of,
    how executed . . . 228
  defective execution of, relieved
    against . . . . 294, 295
  non-execution of . . . 295
  frauds on . . . . 327
PRÆCIPE, tenant to the . . 139
PRINCIPAL AND AGENT. (see "Agent.")
PRIVILEGED COMMUNICATIONS . 31
PRIVITY:
  of estate and contract 18, 194, 303
PROBATE:
  when evidence . . . . 74
  duty, when payable . . . 253
PROBATE COURT:
  jurisdiction of, as to fraud . . 283
PRO CONFESSO:
  when bill taken . . . 352
  how taken . . . 352, 353
PROCURATION MONEY:
  who entitled to . . . . 202
PRODUCE, NOTICE TO
  when to be given . . . 74
  extends to subsequent trials . 74

PROHIBITION:
  writ of . . . . . 130
PROMISSORY NOTES. (see "Bills and Notes.")
PROPERTY:
  different kinds of . . . 132
  distinction between real and personal . . . . 133
PROTECTOR:
  of the settlement. (see "tail."). 139
  lunatic . . . . . 140
  married woman . . . 140
  who was before 3 & 4 Wm. IV., c. 74 . . . . . 140
  who is in various cases . . 140
  consent of, how given . 140, 141
  must be appointed by same deed 141
PROVISO:
  trial by . . . . 81, 82
PUIS DARREIN CONTINUANCE, PLEA . . . . . 66
PUR AUTRE VIE. ESTATE . 144
PURCHASE. (see "Vendor and Purchaser.")
  title by . . . . . 174
  in another's name . . . 307
  in the name of a wife or child . 308
  money, how paid, on sale by court 399

## Q.

QUARE IMPEDIT:
  action of . . . . . 3
QUARTER DAYS . . . . 27

## R.

RAILWAY. (see "Compensation.")
RECAPTION:
  of a stolen horse . . . 35
RECEIVER:
  when appointed . . 368, 369
  duties of . . . . 368, 369
  who cannot be . . . 368
  security by . . . . 369
  liability of . . . . 369
  effect of decree on . . . 369
  how appointed . . . 369
RECORDS, how enforced . . 6
  how proved . . . . 79
RECORD AND WRIT CLERKS':
  their duties . . . . 274
RECOVERY, COMMON . . 139
REDDENDUM . . . . 194

## INDEX. 425

REDEEM (see "Mortgagor.")
REDEMPTION (see "Mortgagor.")
REGISTRARS:
   their duties . . . . 273
REGISTRATION AND ENROLMENT:
   of deeds and wills . . . 239
   requisites of memorial . 239, 240
   the exceptions . . . 239, 240
   whether notice . . . . 240
   when a vendor is heir and devisee 240
   time for . . . . 240
   effect of notice of unregistered deed . . . . . 341
   of a special case . . . 349
RE-HEARING (see "Appeal.") . 387
REJOINDER . . . . . 67
REJOINING GRATIS . . . 65
RELATOR . . . . . 342
RELEASE:
   by a joint debtor . . . 20
   after action, how pleaded . . 67
REMAINDERS:
   vested . . . . . 149
   contingent . . . . 149
   cross . . . . 149, 245
   trustees to preserve . . 149, 234
   distinction between and reversions . . . . . 149
   examples of estates in . . 150
   distinction between contingent, and executory devises . . 150
REMOVAL OF CAUSES:
   from inferior courts . . . 129
RENT. (see "Distress.")
   effect of receipt for . . . 27
   distress for . . . 28, 114
   of premises destroyed . . 28
   forfeiture for non-payment of . 30
RENT-CHARGE:
   what is a . . . . 154
   how created . . . . 154
   when grant of to be registered . 154
   distinction between and a rent seek . . . . . 155
   may be limited in fee by way of use . . . . . 155
   release of . . . . 155
RENT. SECK:
   what it is . . . . 155
REPLEVIN:
   what it is, and when brought . 118
   writ in . . . . . 119
   removal of . . . . 119
   the pleadings in . . . 119
   the avowry . . . . 119
   position of defendant in . . 120

REPLICATION:
   at law . . . . . 67
   in equity . . . . . 369
   effect of, on answer . . . 370
   to answer of a deceased defendant 370
RESIGNATION:
   bonds of . . . . 174
RESTRAINING ORDER . . . 389
REVERSION:
   estate in . . . . . 148
   distinction between and remainder . . . . . 149
REVIEW:
   bill of . . . . 351, 387
   supplemental bill in nature of . 387
REVIVOR:
   writ of . . . . 69, 92
   bill of . . . . . 351
   order of . . . . . 354
RULE OF COURT:
   how order made . . . 71

### S.

SALE (see "Vendor and Purchaser").
   course of proceeding on . . 224
   by the court . . . 398, 399
SCIRE FACIAS . . . . 93
SCINTILLA JURIS:
   doctrine of . . . . 165
SEARCHES FOR INCUMBRANCES . 222
SEA-SHORE:
   ownership of . . . . 134
SEDUCTION:
   action for . . . . . 6
   who to sue . . . . 40
SEPARATE ESTATE:
   nature and incidents of . . 176
   given to unmarried women, 176, 334
   restraint on its alienation . . 176
   its liability to debts . . . 333
SEQUESTRATION . . . . 109
SERVANT (see "Master.")
SET-OFF:
   when it may be pleaded . . 66
   when a mis-joinder of plaintiffs . 62
   against agent . . . . 66
SETTING-DOWN CAUSES (see "Causes.")
SETTLED ESTATES ACTS:
   leases under . 145, 276, 277, 278
   sales under . . . . 277
   who to consent . . . . 277
   how consent of married woman taken . . . . . 277

|                                          | PAGE |
|---|---|
| **SETTLEMENTS:**                         |      |
| heads of on marriage                     | 182  |
| words of limitation in strict        183,| 403  |
| of leaseholds                            | 183  |
| of personalty                       183, | 184  |
| providing against insolvency of husband  | 185  |
| trustees of, may sell, reserving the minerals | 185 |
| usual powers inserted in                 | 187  |
| re-settlement, provisions of             | 187  |
| portions under, how raised               | 188  |
| voluntary, what are                      | 188  |
| how revoked                              | 302  |
| against whom valid                       | 188  |
| covenant to settle lands                 | 189  |
| stamp duty upon                          | 229  |
| of wards of court                        | 329  |
| destruction of                           | 334  |
| **SEVERALTY:**                           |      |
| estate in                                | 151  |
| **SHERIFF:**                             |      |
| trial by                                 | 86   |
| attachment against              107,     | 108  |
| action against                           | 108  |
| **SHELLEY'S CASE:**                      |      |
| rule in                                  | 137  |
| **SIMONY**                               | 174  |
| **SHIP:**                                |      |
| transfer of                              | 21   |
| **SLANDER:**                             |      |
| what is                                  | 31   |
| **SOLICITOR AND CLIENT:** (see "Attorney.") |   |
| transactions between                     | 286  |
| authority to to file bill                | 342  |
| lien of former                           | 393  |
| his bill of costs                        | 393  |
| **SPECIAL CASE:**                        |      |
| when to be filed                    348, | 349  |
| how persons under disability consent     | 349  |
| how trustees indemnified                 | 349  |
| is a *lis pendens*                       | 349  |
| **SPECIAL INDORSEMENT:** (see "Writ of Summons.") |  |
| **SPECIAL JURY:**                        |      |
| costs of                                 | 84   |
| **SPECIAL OCCUPANCY**                    | 144  |
| **SPECIFIC DELIVERY UP OF CHATTELS**     | 297  |
| **SPECIFIC PERFORMANCE OF A CONTRACT:**  |      |
| to sell a lease                          | 220  |
| if price to be fixed by valuers          | 220  |
| after delay in completion                | 221  |

|                                          | PAGE |
|---|---|
| **SPECIFIC PERFORMANCE OF A CONTRACT**—*continued.* | |
| requisites to enforce                    | 298  |
| when not in writing                      | 298  |
| entered into by letter                   | 299  |
| to sell stock, not enforced    299,      | 300  |
| of an infant, not enforced               | 300  |
| of a married woman, when                 | 300  |
| of a lunatic                             | 300  |
| when not enforced                        | 302  |
| where price to be fixed by arbitration   | 302  |
| to grant a lease with "usual" covenants  | 302  |
| of covenant to invest money in land      | 303  |
| to sell an attorney's business           | 303  |
| to sell another estate                   | 303  |
| reference of title to chambers           | 304  |
| compelled through no title to part       | 304  |
| where sale is by the court               | 304  |
| time for making a title        304,      | 305  |
| "*caveat emptor*" in suits for           | 305  |
| of a voluntary settlement     305,       | 306  |
| **STAMP DUTY:**                          |      |
| payment of at the trial                  | 73   |
| upon conveyance                          | 229  |
| upon mortgages and settlements           | 229  |
| progressive                              | 229  |
| what *ad valorem* includes               | 230  |
| what instruments may be stamped after execution | 230 |
| denoting                                 | 230  |
| **STATUTES:**                            |      |
| what they are                            | 1    |
| repealing former acts                    | 1    |
| **STATUTES OF ELIZABETH,    9, 188,**    | 189  |
| **STATUTES OF DISTRIBUTION**             | 262  |
| (see "Distribution.")                    |      |
| **STET PROCESSUS**                       | 69   |
| **STOCK:**                               |      |
| charging                                 | 391  |
| transfer of                              | 390  |
| **STOP ORDER**                           | 389  |
| **STOPPAGE IN TRANSITU**                 | 21   |
| **SUBPŒNA:**                             |      |
| *ad testificandum*             75,       | 373  |
| *duces tecum*                            | 75   |
| refusal of witness to obey               | 75   |
| to hear judgment                         | 388  |
| writs of                                 | 402  |
| **SUCCESSION DUTY:**                     |      |
| when act passed                          | 223  |
| is a charge upon land                    | 223  |
| payable by instalments                   | 223  |
| upon real and personal property          | 223  |
| how assessed                    223,     | 224  |

INDEX. 427

SUFFERANCE:
   estate at . . . . . 148
SUGGESTION:
   entry of, of death . . . 69
SUIT IN EQUITY:
   authority before commencing . 342
   consequence of not obtaining . 342
   who may institute . . . 342
   by the Crown . . . . 342
   by a Queen Consort . . . 342
   by infant . . . 342, 343
   by married woman . . 342
   how instituted . . 343, 344
   by foreign sovereign . . 343
   principal proceedings in . . 401
   interlocutory proceedings in . 402
SUMMONS (Common Law):
   when order may be obtained on 70
   for time to plead, when to be
     served . . . . . 70
   is not a "proceeding" . . 82
SUMMONS (Equity)
   proceedings by . . . 394
   wilful default cannot be charged
     on . . . . . 398
SUPPLEMENTAL BILL . . .
SURETY:
   discharge of . . . . 13
SURRENDER OF COPYHOLDS:
     (see "Copyholds.")
   of leases . . . 170, 197

T.
TACKING . . . 206, 336
   (see "Mortgage.")
TAIL:
   estate . . . . . 137
   what it is . . . . . 137
   how it differs from a fee simple . 143
   general and special . . 138
   cannot exist in personalty . 138
   in remainder . . . 138
   how now barred . . 139, 143
   how before barred . . 139
   consent of protector . . 140
   disentailing deed, when enrolled 142
   in copyholds, how barred . 158
TENANT IN TAIL:
   power to grant leases . . 143
   after possibility . . 143, 144
   paying off incumbrances . 144
TENANT FROM YEAR TO YEAR:
   notice to quit . . 27, 30, 197
   his liability for repairs . . 29
   how tenancy created . . 197

TENANT FROM YEAR TO YEAR—continued.
   how determined . . . 197
   how tenancy surrendered . . 198
TENANT FOR LIFE:
   his powers over the estate . . 145
   when he may cut timber . . 145
   what leases he may make . . 145
   effect of his leases on incumbrances . . . . . 146
   paying off incumbrances . 146, 334
   how he may create a permanent
     charge . . . . 146
TENANCY IN COMMON:
     (see "Common, Tenancy in.")
TENDER:
   requisites of . . . . 44
   refusal of . . . . . 45
   effect of . . . . . 45
TENURES:
   what exist . . . . . 134
   allotment under Inclosure Act . 134
   gavelkind . . . . 134
   Borough English . . . 135
   of lands less than freehold . 135
TERMS:
   issuable and non-issuable . . 81
TERMS OF YEARS (see "Leases"):
   in gross . . . . 170
   outstanding . . . . 170
   satisfied . . . . 170
   merger of . . . 170, 171
   proviso for cessor of . . . 170
   surrender of . . . . 171
TIME:
   to plead (see "Pleas").
   when essence of a contract . 301
   computation of . . . . 83
TITHES:
   great and small . . 155, 245
TITHE RENT CHARGE:
   how recovered . . . . 118
   what it is . . . . 155
   how amount of ascertained 155, 156
TITLE :
   the different kinds of . . . 174
   by descent . . . . 174
   by purchase . . . . 174
   by escheat . . . . 175
   length of . . . . . 215
   on sale of leaseholds . . . 215
   in granting a lease . . . 215
   to an advowson . . . . 215
   indefeasable . . . . 215
   root of . . . . . 216
   covenants for . . . . 236

## INDEX.

**TITLE**—*continued.*
deeds, custody of . . 175, 286
equitable, when forced on a purchaser . . . . 301, 302
reference of to chambers . . 304
in suit for specific performance . 304

**TITLE DEEDS** (*see* "Vendor and Purchaser"):
who entitled to . . . . 175

**TORTS**. (see various titles) . . 30, 35
liability of infants for . . 30

**TRADE:**
covenants in restraint of . . 286

**TRADE MARK:**
restraining use of . . . 291

**TRAVERSING NOTE** . . . 35
distinguished from *pro confesso* . 353

**TRESPASS:**
action of . . . . . 7
damages for wilful . . . 35

**TRIAL:**
notice of . . . . . 82
short notice of . . . 65, 82
countermand . . . . 82
when fresh notice necessary . 83
writ of . . . . . 86
new . . . . . . 86
compelling plaintiff to proceed to 81

**TROVER:**
action of . . . . . 6

**TRUSTS:**
definition of . . . . 306
different kinds of . . . 307
how they differ from uses . . 162
what words will create . . 163
when enforced . . . 305, 306
in favour of an alien . . . 306
executed and executory . . 307
implied, resulting and constructive . . . . 307, 309
purchase in name of a stranger . . . . 307, 308
to pay debts may be revoked, when . . . . . 308
failure of objects of . . 308, 309

**TRUSTEES:**
powers conferred on by 23 & 24 Vic., c. 145 . . . 186
cannot delegate . . . 254
purchase by of trust estate 254, 314
appointment, of new . 254, 255, 400
application of moneys received by . . 220, 235, 308, 314

**TRUSTEES**—*continued.*
alterations in law, as to, by 13 & 14 Vic., c. 60 . . . 275
infant and lunatic . . . 276
payment into court by . 276, 310
how they may protect themselves 310
how money paid into court by, obtained . . . . 311
liability of, for each others' acts 311
refusal of, to act . . 311, 312
for what losses liable . . . 312
are allowed their expenses . . 312
cannot make a profit . 312, 313
investments by . . . . 313
payments by, under power of attorney . . . . 313
their power to raise money by sale . . . . . 314
when they may sever defence . 394

## U.

**USES:**
statute of . . . . . 161
intention and effect of statute . 161
distinction between, and trusts . 162
shifting and springing . . 162
examples of the operation of the Statute of Uses . . 162—166
appointments of . . . . 167
dower . . . . . 180

## V.

**VENDOR AND PURCHASER** . . 210
duty of vendor's solicitor before contract . . . 211, 213
effect of death of vendor . . 300
effect of death of purchaser 213, 300
effect of death of both parties . 213
liability of vendor's solicitor for omissions . . . . 213
overlooking incumbrances in abstract . . . . 214
duties of the solicitors, of . . 214
release of rent-charge . . 214
what title to be shown . . 216
sale of building land in lots . 216
where deeds to be produced for examination . . . . 217
what deeds purchaser entitled to 217
covenant to produce the deeds 217, 218
abstract good on face, but title defective . . . . 218
verification of abstract . . 218
what expenses borne by . . 219
on sale of copyholds . . . 219
purchaser bound by the tenancies 219
notice of a trust . . . 220
application of purchase-money . . . 220, 255

## INDEX. 429

**VENDOR AND PURCHASER**—*continued.*
purchase from *cestui que trust* . 221
purchase of enclosed land, title . 222
searches to be made . . . 222
postponement of . . . 222
course of proceedings on a sale . 224
proper parties to convey and
   assign . . . . . 225
bill of costs . . . . 226
purchase by persons in fiduciary
   position . . . . . 286
which bears loss happening after
   the contract . . . 298, 299

**VENUE:**
meaning of word . . . 56
local and transitory . . . 56
in action against justice . . 55
change of . . . . 56
in ejectment . . . . 112

**VERDICT** (*see* "Non-suit"):
distinction between, and judgment . . . . . 89

**VOLUNTARY CONVEYANCE** . . 188

### W.

**WARD OF COURT** (*see* "Infants."):
marriage of . . . . 328
how infant made a . . . 326
effect of making . . . 329
settlement on marriage of . . 329

**WAIVER** . . . . 29

**WARRANT OF ATTORNEY:**
difference between, and cognovit 120
how executed . . . . 121
infant cannot give a . . . 120
judgment on . . . 121, 122
effect of filing . . . . 121

**WARRANTY:**
of a horse . . . . 17
need not be in writing . . 17
remedies on breach of . . 17

**WASTE:**
by tenant for life . . . 145
equitable . . . . 289
how restrained . . . 289
nature of relief against . . 290

**WATER:**
right of . . . . 156

**WAY:**
right of . . . . 156
how conveyed . . . 156
form of grant of . . . 159

**WILL:**
distinction between and testament 241
who may make and who not . 241
at what age . . . . 241
how to be executed . . . 242
form of attestation . . . 242
when valid, if unattested . . 242
legacies or devise to witness
   of a . . . . 242, 243
of property in colonies . . 243
alterations and erasures in a . 243
how revived . . . . 243
words by to pass the fee . 243, 244
effect of general devise . . 244
form of bequest to charity . 247
after purchased lands pass by,
   when . . . . . 247
speaks from death of testator . 248
devise by, when revoked . . 248
directions to sell by, should be
   imperative . . . . 248
when devise or bequest
   lapses . . . . 248, 249
on whom a lapsed devise devolves . . . . . 249
how revoked . . . 250, 251
in what court to be proved . 251
"survivor" meaning of in a . 252
of personal estate, form of . 253
powers of trustees of a . . 253
of British subject out of the
   kingdom . . . . 253
domicile . . . . 253
alterations made by Wills Act . 253
how construed in equity . . 271
fraud as to . . . 282, 283
effect of unattested writing on . 311

**WILL, ESTATE AT:**
distinction between and yearly
   tenancy . . . . 147

**WITHDRAWING A JUROR:**
effect of on costs . . . 99

**WITNESS** (*see* "Evidence."):
attesting, when to be called . 77
death of . . . . 77
party to suit . . . . 373
how examined in equity . . 372
how cross-examined . . 374, 377
notice to keep in town . . 374
examination of after evidence
   closed . . . . . 379
distinction between admissibility and credibility of . . 79
how compelled to attend . . 75
how compelled to attend on a
   commission . . . . 80
the like before arbitrator . . 123
arrest of . . . . 80

WRIT OF SUMMONS:
  against peers . . . . 46
  against British subjects abroad
                46, 49, 50
  against foreigners abroad . . 50
  may include any number of defendants . . . . 46
  description of defendant . . 49
  each defendant must be served . 47
  how tested, and when dated . 47
  service of . . . . . 47
  substituted service . . . 47
  memorandum of service . . 49
  how long in force . . . 46
  how renewed . . . . 50

WRIT OF SUMMONS—*continued.*
  indorsements on . . . 48
  special endorsement . . . 48
  concurrent . . . . 49

WRIT:
  of summons . . . 45, 46
  of inquiry . . . . 90
  of trial . . . . . 86
  the various kinds of, in a suit . 402

Y.

YEARS:
  terms of . . . . . 170

www.ingramcontent.com/pod-product-compliance
Lightning Source LLC
Chambersburg PA
CBHW022114300426
44117CB00007B/703